The Principles of Manufactu

H. R. Procter

Alpha Editions

This edition published in 2024

ISBN 9789362518699

Design and Setting By
Alpha Editions
www.alphaedis.com
Email - info@alphaedis.com

As per information held with us this book is in Public Domain.
This book is a reproduction of an important historical work.
Alpha Editions uses the best technology to reproduce historical work
in the same manner it was first published to preserve its original nature.
Any marks or number seen are left intentionally to preserve.

Contents

CHAPTER I. INTRODUCTORY AND HISTORICAL.	- 1 -
CHAPTER II. INTRODUCTORY SKETCH OF LEATHER MANUFACTURE.	- 6 -
CHAPTER III. THE LIVING CELL.	- 9 -
CHAPTER IV. PUTREFACTION AND FERMENTATION.	- 15 -
CHAPTER V. ANTISEPTICS AND DISINFECTANTS.	- 21 -
CHAPTER VI. THE ORIGIN AND CURING OF HIDES AND SKINS.	- 31 -
CHAPTER VII. STRUCTURE AND GROWTH OF SKIN.	- 42 -
CHAPTER VIII. THE CHEMICAL CONSTITUENTS OF SKIN.	- 55 -
CHAPTER IX. THE PHYSICAL CHEMISTRY OF THE HIDE-FIBRE.	- 71 -
CHAPTER X. WATER AS USED IN THE TANNERY.	- 87 -
CHAPTER XI. SOAKING AND SOFTENING OF HIDES AND SKINS.	- 100 -
CHAPTER XII. DEPILATION.	- 110 -
CHAPTER XIII. DELIMING, BATING, PUERING AND DRENCHING.	- 141 -
CHAPTER XIV. ALUM TANNAGE OR TAWING.	- 169 -
CHAPTER XV. IRON AND CHROME TANNAGES.	- 181 -
CHAPTER XVI. PRINCIPLES OF THE VEGETABLE TANNING PROCESSES.	- 199 -
CHAPTER XVII. COMBINATION OF VEGETABLE AND MINERAL TANNAGE.	- 213 -
CHAPTER XVIII. VEGETABLE TANNING MATERIALS.	- 218 -
BOTANICAL LIST OF TANNING MATERIALS.	- 222 -

CHAPTER XIX. THE CHEMISTRY OF THE TANNINS.	- 275 -
CHAPTER XX. THE SAMPLING AND ANALYSIS OF TANNING MATERIALS.	- 280 -
CHAPTER XXI. GRINDING OF TANNING MATERIALS.	- 297 -
CHAPTER XXII. THE EXTRACTION OF TANNING MATERIALS, AND THE MAKING OF EXTRACTS.	- 309 -
CHAPTER XXIII. FATS, SOAPS, OILS AND WAXES.	- 335 -
NON-DRYING FATS AND OILS.	- 340 -
VOLATILE OR ESSENTIAL OILS.	- 354 -
MINERAL OILS AND WAXES.	- 355 -
CHAPTER XXIV. OIL TANNAGES, AND THE USE OF OILS AND FATS IN CURRYING.	- 359 -
CHAPTER XXV. DYES AND DYEING.	- 373 -
CHAPTER XXVI. EVAPORATION, HEATING AND DRYING.	- 395 -
CHAPTER XXVII. CONSTRUCTION AND MAINTENANCE OF TANNERIES.	- 415 -
CHAPTER XXVIII. WASTE PRODUCTS AND THEIR DISPOSAL.	- 429 -

CHAPTER I.
INTRODUCTORY AND HISTORICAL.

The origin of leather manufacture dates far back in the prehistoric ages, and was probably one of the earliest arts practised by mankind. The relics which have come down to us from palæolithic times, and the experience of the modern explorer, alike tell us that agriculture is a later and a higher stage of development than the life of the hunter; and since, in the colder regions, clothing of some kind must always have been a necessity, we may conclude that it was first furnished by the skins of animals.

See also Gen. iii. 21.

While wet skins putrefy and decay, dry ones are hard and horny; and nothing could be more natural to the hunter than to try to remedy this by rubbing the drying skin with the fat of the animal, of which he must have noticed the softening effect on his own skin. By this means a soft and durable leather may be produced, and this process of rubbing and kneading with greasy and albuminous matters, such as fat, brains, milk, butter and egg-yolks, is in use to this day, alike by the Tartars on Asiatic steppes and the Indians on American prairies; and not only so, but we ourselves still use the same principle in the dressing of our finest furs, and in the manufacture of chamois, and many sorts of lace- and belt-leathers.

Such a process is described in the *Iliad* (xvii. 389-393) in the account of the struggle over the body of Patroclus:

"As when a manA huge ox-hide drunken with slippery lardGives to be stretched, his servants all aroundDisposed, just intervals between, the taskPly strenuous, and while many straining hardExtend it equal on all sides, it sweatsThe moisture out and drinks the unction in."

It must also have been early noticed that wood smoke, which in those days was inseparable from the use of fire, had an antiseptic and preservative effect on skins which were dried in it, and smoked leathers are still made in America, both by the Indians and by more civilised leather manufacturers. To this method the Psalmist refers when he says, "I am become like a bottle in the smoke;" and such bottles, made of the entire skin of the goat, are still familiar to travellers in the East.

Ps. cxix. 83.

The use of vegetable tanning materials, though prehistoric, is probably less ancient than the methods I have described, and may possibly have been discovered in early attempts at dyeing; an art which perhaps had its origin even before the use of clothing! The tannins are very widely distributed in the vegetable kingdom, and most barks, and many fruits, are capable of making leather.

The employment of alum and salt in tanning was probably of still later introduction, and must have originated in countries where alum is found as a natural product. The art was lost or unknown in Europe till introduced into Spain by the Moors.

Leather manufacture reached considerable perfection in ancient Egypt. A granite carving, probably at least 4000 years old, is preserved in the Berlin Museum, in which leather-dressers are represented. One is taking a tiger-skin from a tub or pit, a second is employed at another tub, while a third is working a skin upon a table. Embossed and gilt leather straps have been found on a mummy of the ninth century B.C., and an Egyptian boat-cover of embossed goat leather, as well as shoes of dyed and painted morocco, are still in comparatively good preservation. The art is of very early date in China, and was well understood by the Greeks and Romans. In the Grosvenor Museum at Chester is the sole of a Roman *caliga*, studded with bronze nails, which is yet pretty flexible. After the fall of the Roman empire many arts were lost to Europe, and it was not until the Moorish invasion of Spain that the art of dyeing and finishing the finer kinds of leather was reintroduced.

England was very backward in this manufacture up to the end of the last century, owing to the fossilising influence of much paternal legislation, and of certain excise-duties, which were only repealed in 1830. Since this time the art has made rapid strides, especially in the use of labour-saving machinery, and England may at the present moment be considered fairly abreast of any other country as a whole; though in some special manufactures we are surpassed by the Continent and by America. In making comparisons of this kind, it must, however, be remembered that, especially in sole-leather tannage, the most rapid progress has been made during the last few years in those countries which were more backward, and that therefore our superiority is much less pronounced than formerly, and in a few years will probably cease to exist unless marked improvements are introduced in the methods of production.

In the sketch of the development of leather manufacture which has just been given, it has been implied that its object is to convert the putrescible animal skin into a material which is permanent, and not readily subject to decay, while retaining sufficient softness or flexibility for the purposes for which it is intended. As these range from boot-soles to kid-gloves, there are wide divergences, not only in the processes employed, but also in the materials used and in the principles of their application.

The most important method of producing leather is by the use of vegetable tanning materials, and this is perhaps the only one which is really entitled to be called "tanning," though the distinction is not very strictly adhered to. It includes the whole range—from sole leather, through strap, harness and dressing leather, to calf and goat skins, and the various sumach tannages which yield morocco and its imitations. All of these products but the first and the last undergo, after tanning, the further processes of "currying," of which the most important operation consists in "stuffing" with oily and fatty matters, both to increase the flexibility and to confer a certain amount of resistance to water. Sumach-tanned skins are not strictly "curried" but usually receive a certain amount of oil in the process of "finishing."

Next in importance to the vegetable tannages are the "tawed" leathers produced by the agency of alum and salt, including the "white leathers" for belt laces and aprons, and calf- and glove-kid. A connecting link between tanning and tawing is found in the "green leather," "Dongola," and "combination" tannages, in which alum and salt are employed in conjunction with vegetable tanning materials, and especially with gambier.

Salts of several of the metals, and particularly those of aluminium, iron, and chromium, have the power of converting skin into leather; and processes in which salts of chromium are used have recently attained very considerable commercial importance.

In the production of calf- and glove-kid, in addition to alum and salt, albuminous and fatty matters, such as egg-yolk, olive oil and the gluten of flour, play a considerable part, and are thus linked both to the primitive methods in use by the Indians and Kalmucks, and to those by which "crown" and "Helvetia" leather, and many other forms of belt- and lace-leathers are now produced by treatment with fats and albumens.

From these again the step is a short one to the "chamois" and "buff" leathers, and the German *"fettgar"* leathers, in which oils and fats only are used; and these are probably again related chemically to leather produced by the aid of formaldehyde and other aldehydes.

In an attempt to view all these complex processes from the scientific standpoint, the reader should constantly realise that the present methods of leather manufacture are the results of tens of centuries of experience, and of innumerable forgotten failures, and must not therefore expect that they can be easily superseded. Science must follow before it can lead, and its first duty is to try to understand the reasons and principles of our present practice, for we can only build the new on the foundation of what has been already learned. Another fact, which is scarcely understood by the practical man in his demands on science, is that in leather manufacture every question which is raised seems to rest on the most recondite problems of chemistry and physics; the chemistry of some of the most complex of organic compounds, and the physics of solution, of osmose, and of the structure of colloid bodies—problems which are yet far from completely conquered by the highest science of the day.

It may seem bold to attempt the scientific treatment of such a subject at all; and, indeed, it must be admitted that our knowledge is still far from adequate for its complete accomplishment, but enough has been done to lay a foundation for future work, and this can at least be summarised and arranged in an available form. The subject falls naturally into two sections, in the first of which the processes of manufacture would only be described in general terms, and with sufficient fulness to enable the reader to understand the scientific considerations on which they are based, and the methods of investigation which can be applied to them; while in the second an effort should be made to give working details of the various processes sufficient to enable those with a general knowledge of the trade to experiment successfully in its various branches. It was at first intended that these two sections should be published in one book as a second edition to the Author's 'Text-book of Tanning,' but owing to the long delay in its publication, it was decided to publish the first section under the present title 'Principles of Leather Manufacture,' leaving the latter section 'Processes of Leather Manufacture' to a later, and I fear, somewhat uncertain date; while the strictly chemical portion has already appeared in the 'Leather Industries Laboratory Book,' frequently referred to in the following pages under the abbreviation "L.I.L.B." Where quantities and details are given, they must not be taken as recipes to be blindly followed; or even, in every case, as the best known methods; but rather as mere guides to experiment, which must be modified to suit varying conditions and requirements. It is the special virtue of the scientific, as opposed to the merely traditional way of looking at such questions, that knowing the cause and effect of each part of the process, it can so adjust them as to get over difficulties, and to suit novel conditions. It is needless to add that many methods are jealously preserved as trade secrets, and full details are frequently unattainable.

After what has just been said, it may be well to emphasise the great importance of practical knowledge and experience to the leather manufacturer. Even in trades which have reached the highest scientific development, such, for instance, as the manufacture of the coal-tar colours, the small experiments of the laboratory are not transformed into manufacturing operations without experience and sometimes even failure; and this must still more often be the case in a trade like that of leather-making, where our knowledge of the actual changes involved is still so incomplete. On the other hand, the cost of experiments on a manufacturing scale is usually so heavy that the least scientific must admit the advantage of learning all which the laboratory can teach before venturing on anything more; while even our present imperfect knowledge of the chemical changes involved will often warn us off hopeless experiments, and give us hints of the directions in which success may be attained. A knowledge of chemistry will probably prove at least as important to the future of our trade as that of mechanics has been in the past.

CHAPTER II.
INTRODUCTORY SKETCH OF LEATHER MANUFACTURE.

The object of tanning has been stated to be the rendering of animal skin imputrescible and pliable, but as we now rarely require leather with the hair on, preliminary processes are needed to remove it, and to fit the skin for tanning, and the nature of these processes has great influence on the subsequent character of the leather produced.

The first step is usually a washing of the skin to remove blood and dirt; while, where it has been salted or dried, a more thorough soaking is needed to remove the salt, and to restore the skin to its original soft and permeable condition.

The hair is then loosened by softening and partial solution of the epidermis structures (see p. 47) in which it is rooted. This is most generally accomplished by soaking for some days in milk of lime, which is occasionally assisted by the addition of caustic alkalies or of sulphides. When the latter are used in concentrated solution, the hair itself, as well as the epidermis tissues, is softened and destroyed in the course of a few hours. The lime not only serves to loosen the hair, but swells and splits up the fibre-bundles of which the hide tissue is composed, and so fits it to receive the tannage (cp. p. 125).

For some purposes a regulated putrefactive process is substituted for the liming; the hides or skins being hung in a moist and warm chamber (see p. 119), when the soft mucous layer which forms the inner part of the epidermis is disintegrated, partly by direct putrefaction, partly by the action of the ammonia evolved, so that the hair can be scraped off. In this case the hide-fibre is not swollen, and the necessary swelling has to be obtained by subsequent processes.

In whatever way the hair has been loosened, it is scraped off with a blunt and somewhat curved two-handled knife on a sloping rounded "beam" of wood or metal; this operation being termed "unhairing" (see p. 144).

This is generally followed by "fleshing," which is performed on the same beam with a somewhat similar knife, which, however, is two-edged and sharp. In this operation, portions of flesh, and the fat and loose tissue which underlie the true skin (see p. 147) are removed by scraping and cutting. Machines for fleshing are also largely in use for certain purposes (see p. 148).

For sole leather, the hide, after some washing in soft water to cleanse from lime, is then ready for the actual tanning process; but for the softer leathers more thorough treatment is needed to remove the lime, and to still further soften the skin by solution and removal of a portion of the cementing substance of the fibres.

This treatment is generally of a fermentive or putrefactive nature, and the most common form is that known as "bating," which consists in steeping in a fermenting infusion of pigeon- or hen-dung. The theory of its action is not yet thoroughly understood, but the effect is largely due to the unorganised hydrolysing ferments produced by the *bacteria* present; while at the same time the lime is neutralised and removed by the weak organic acids and salts of ammonia which are produced; and the fibre which had been plump and swollen with lime, becomes extremely relaxed and flaccid.

In the lightest leathers, such as kid- and lamb-skins for gloves, and goat and sheep for moroccos and the like, dog-dung is substituted for that of fowls, and the process is then called "puering" (see p. 170).

These processes are often followed by "drenching," which sometimes indeed takes their place, the skins being soaked in a fermenting bran infusion. In this, the small quantities of acetic and lactic acid formed by fermentation are the active agents, neutralising and dissolving the lime, and cleansing and slightly plumping the pelt (see p. 166).

The tanning process which follows consists in soaking the pelt in infusions of various vegetable products containing bodies of the class known as "tannins," which have the power of combining with skin-fibre and converting it into leather.

If at first strong infusions were used, they would act too violently on the surface of the skin, hardening and contracting it so that the subsequent tannage of the interior would be impeded, and the "grain" or outer surface would be "drawn" and wrinkled. This is avoided by the use at first of very weak infusions which have already been used on goods in a more advanced stage. In the later part of the process much stronger solutions are employed, and the hides are frequently "dusted" in them with ground tanning material.

In the case of sole leather, these processes may require from two to twelve months for completion; after which the leather is dried, smoothed, and compressed by mechanical means, and is then ready for use.

Dressing-leathers, ranging from calf-skins to harness-hides, receive a much shorter tannage, and the subsequent treatment with fats and oils, which, together with mechanical manipulations, constitute "currying." The thin film of grease distributed over the surface of the fibres renders them supple, and to some extent waterproof.

The lighter fancy leathers, such as morocco, are dyed, and undergo many complex processes to fit them for their required purposes and improve their appearance.

Many skins such as calf, glove, and glacé kid, are not tanned, but "tawed" by a solution of alum and salt, which is often supplemented with mixtures of flour and egg-yolk to fill and soften the leather.

Salts of chromium are also employed in place of alum and salt, and produce an equally soft, but more permanent and enduring leather.

Lastly, wash-leather, or so-called "chamois," and buff-leather are produced by fulling the prepared pelt with fish or whale oil, which converts the skin into leather by subsequent oxidation, during which aldehydes are evolved.

CHAPTER III.
THE LIVING CELL.

The larger part of the materials employed in leather manufacture are organic in their origin, and the skin itself is an organised structure, while the life-processes of putrefaction and fermentation play a large part in the tannery. Some knowledge, therefore, of biological structures and processes is necessary to a full understanding of much which follows, and a few words are not out of place with regard to the foundations of life itself.

The bricks of which all living structures are built are the living "cells" and their products, and these first elements differ little, if at all, whether the life is animal or vegetable, the distinction being produced rather by the way in which they are put together, than by differences in the cells themselves. This is so much the case that it is often difficult to decide in which of the two classes to place the simplest organisms, since most of these forms are capable of active movement, and their modes of nutrition and reproduction are common to both kingdoms.

In its simplest form, the cell, whether animal or vegetable, is strictly speaking not a cell at all, but consists merely of a minute mass of living jelly or protoplasm. Such is the amœba found in water and damp soil, such are the lymph-cells and white blood-corpuscles of our bodies, and such also some stages at least of the lowest forms of fungi, like the *Æthalium septicum* which is sometimes found on old tan-heaps as a crawling mass of yellow slime. If a drop of saliva be examined with the microscope under a cover-glass, with one-sixth objective and small opening of diaphragm, a few scattered semi-transparent objects will be found, of the apparent size of a lentil or small pea, and of rounded form. These are lymph-corpuscles (Fig. 1). Their contents are full of small granules, and if they be observed quickly, or if the slide be kept at about the warmth of the body, it will be noticed that these are in constant streaming motion. If the warmth can be kept constant, which is difficult without special apparatus, and the cells can be observed from time to time, it may be seen that they lose their circular form, and put out protuberances (pseudopodia, "false feet") one of which will gradually increase in bulk, till it absorbs the whole cell, which thus crawls about. It will now readily be understood how these cells wander through all the tissues of the body, passing through the smallest pores like the fairy who put her finger through a keyhole, and grew on the other side till she was all through! This independent vitality, in a warm and suitable nutrient liquid, may continue for more than a week, and, in the case of amœba, quite indefinitely.

For details of microscopic manipulation in this and the following chapter see L.I.L.B., p. 234 *et seq.*

FIG. 1.—Lymph-corpuscle of frog, showing gradual change of form. (Ranvier.)

It is possible that by close attention, a rounded or elongated body, somewhat like an oil-globule, may be seen within the cell, though it is generally more obvious when the latter has been killed and stained with a weak solution of iodine. This is the nucleus, and within it is a still smaller speck called the nucleolus, which bears an important, and as yet little understood, part in the life-history of the cell. After a period, it undergoes certain somewhat complicated changes, and divides into two, the nucleus elongates, and also divides, each half carrying with it a portion of the living protoplasmic jelly, and thus forming two complete and independent cells. This is the life-history, not only of the lymph-cell, but with more or less modification, of every living cell or tissue.

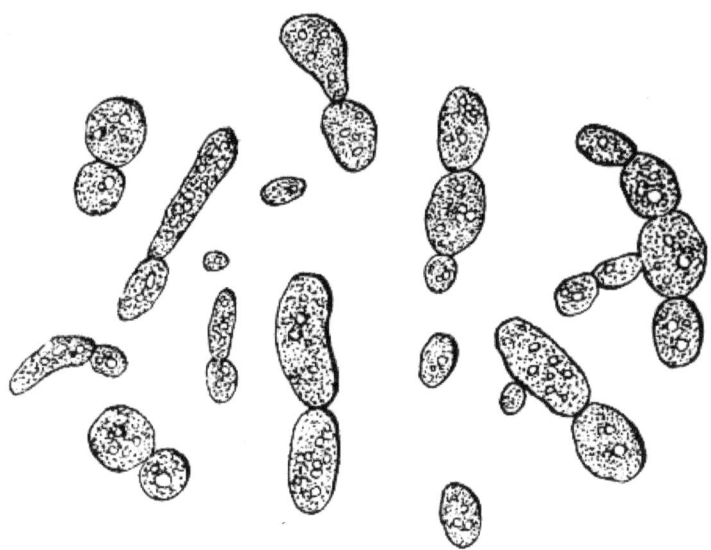

FIG. 2.—Yeast-cells, much magnified.

These cells, like all living things, feed on the nutriment which surrounds them, and even enclose small particles of solid food, which are gradually dissolved and disappear. In this way the white blood-corpuscles are said to feed upon and destroy the still smaller organisms which gain access to the blood, and which might otherwise cause disease. The matter which cells consume is not, of course, destroyed, but simply converted into other forms, some of which are useless, or even poisonous to the cells, and which, like the secretions of higher animals, are discharged into the surrounding fluids; while others are retained, and contribute to the growth of the cell. Thus most vegetable cells secrete cellulose, or plant-tissue, which forms a wall enclosing the protoplasm, and so justifies the name of cell. If to warm water and a little sugar we add enough yeast to render it slightly milky, and examine it like the saliva, we shall have before us typical vegetable cells of the simplest form (Fig. 2). There is the same granular protoplasm, and there is the nucleus, though it cannot be seen without special preparation, the rounded spaces which look like one, being simply filled with transparent fluid, and called vacuoles. There is, however, no motion, as in the case of amœba, for the cells are enclosed in a tough skin of cellulose, which will be evident if they are crushed by putting some folds of blotting paper on the cover-glass, and pressing it with the handle of a needle or a rounded glass rod, when the protoplasm will be forced out and the skin remain like a burst bladder. This will be more obvious if the cells are previously stained with iodine or magenta, which will stain the protoplasm, but not the membrane. It is easy to observe the multiplication of the yeast-cells, which is somewhat different to that of the corpuscles. Instead of enlarging as a whole, and dividing into two equal cells, a small bud appears on the side of the parent-cell, and enlarges till it becomes itself a parent-cell with buds of its own. These do not break away at once, and hence chains and groups of attached cells are formed which are easily noticed in growing yeast if a microscope be employed. The principal nutriment of yeast is grape-sugar or glucose; and much more of this is consumed than is needed to produce the cellulose wall and the substance of new cells; just as in the animal, sugar, starch and fat are consumed to give heat and energy. In the yeast, this extra sugar is split up into carbon dioxide, which escapes as gas, and to which yeast owes its power of raising bread; and into alcohol, which in too large proportion is poisonous to the yeast itself.

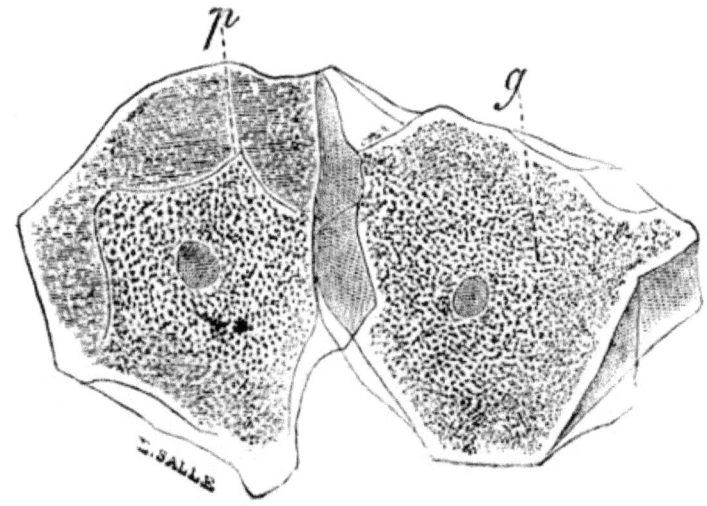

FIG. 3.—Epithelium-cells. Ranvier.
p, pressure-marks; *g*, granular protoplasm.

In examining the saliva for lymph-cells, it is probable that some much larger objects may have been noticed of irregular polygonal outline and with a well-marked nucleus. These are cells from the lining *epithelium* of the mouth, and only differ from those of the *epidermis* of skin in their form and size (Fig. 3). Note the markings caused by the pressure of overlapping cells. In these cells the wall is formed of keratin or horny tissue, which takes the place of the cellulose of the yeast.

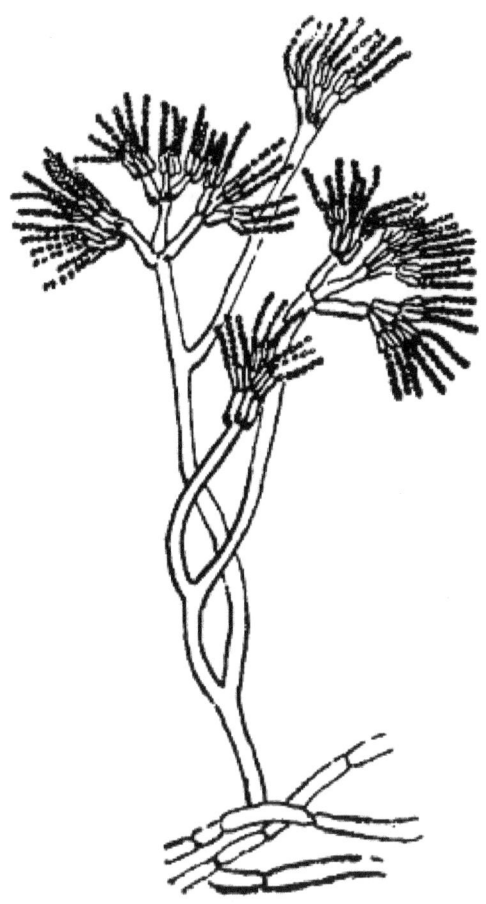

FIG. 4.—*Penicillium glaucum*, a common green mould.

Other simple forms of cell are those of *Saccharomyces mycoderma* or *torula* which forms a skin on the surface of old liquors, and which much resembles a small yeast; and of the various ferments which are found in liquors, bates and drenches, which will be more fully described in the chapter following.

Many of these, such as the acetic and lactic ferments, which, like all other *bacteria*, multiply by division, do not separate, but remain connected in chains or chaplets, like a string of beads. From these, the step is not a long one to the *hyphæ* or stems of the higher moulds, which are too frequently found on leather which has been slowly dried, and which consist simply of tubular cells which elongate and divide by the formation of *septa* or cross-partitions, and thus build up a complicated plant-structure (Fig. 4). As we proceed higher in the scale of plant and animal life, the forms and products of the cells become more varied, and instead of one single cell, fulfilling all the functions of the plant or animal, each class of cell has its own peculiar duties and properties, while all work together for the maintenance of the complex structure of which they form a part.

CHAPTER IV.
PUTREFACTION AND FERMENTATION.

The chemical changes produced by the unicellular plants, such as yeasts and bacteria, to which allusion has been made in the last chapter, are known as fermentation and putrefaction, and are of such importance to the tanner, both for good and evil, that the subject must be treated in some detail. No scientific distinction exists between fermentation and putrefaction, though it is customary to restrict the latter term to those decompositions of nitrogenous animal matter which yield products of disagreeable smell and taste.

The organisms which are the cause of both fermentation and putrefaction are known by the general term of "ferments." This term has also been extended in recent years so as to include the so-called "unorganised ferments" (enzymes, zymases) which are active products secreted by the "organised ferments" or living organisms.

These latter are again divided into three classes:—

- 1. Moulds.
- 2. Yeasts (Saccharomycetes).
- 3. Bacteria.

The members of one class are distinguished from those of another by their form, and, more especially, by the substances they produce during their life-history. All three classes are now considered to be fungi.

All ferments possess the following three properties:—

1. They are nitrogenous bodies.

2. They are unstable, i.e. they are destroyed by heat, chemicals, etc.

3. A relatively small quantity of the ferment is capable of producing great changes in the substances upon which it acts, especially if the products of the change can be removed as they are formed.

The general character of fermentation will be best understood by a closer study of the yeast cell, which has already been described (p. 12), and its life-history briefly sketched. It has been shown that it is a growing plant of a very simple type, belonging to the fungi. These are devoid of the green colouring matter which enables the higher plants to utilise the energy of sunlight to assimilate the carbonic acid of the atmosphere, exhaling its oxygen, and employing its carbon for the building up of tissue; and they must therefore, like animals, have their nutriment ready formed, and capable of supplying energy by its oxidation. For yeast, as has been stated, the appropriate nourishment is glucose, or "grape-sugar." This is broken down, in the main, into the simpler compounds, alcohol and carbonic acid, while a small portion is utilised for the building up of the cell and the formation of secondary products. The main reaction is represented by the following equation:

$$C_6H_{12}O_6 \quad = \quad 2C_2H_6O \quad + \quad 2CO_2$$

Glucose *Alcohol* *Carbon dioxide*

Yeast cannot directly ferment ordinary cane-sugar ($C_{12}H_{22}O_{11}$), but secretes a substance called invertase, which so acts on the sugar as to break it up, with absorption of one molecule of water, into two molecules of fermentable glucose (dextrose and levulose) which serve as nourishment for the yeast. This invertase is the type of the series of bodies which are known as "unorganised ferments," enzymes, or zymases, differing from the organised ferments in being simply chemical products without life or power of reproduction, but capable of breaking up an unlimited quantity of the bodies on which they act, without themselves suffering change. The way in which this is done is not clearly understood, but some parallel may be found to it in the action of sulphuric acid on alcohol, of which it will convert an unlimited quantity into ether, without itself suffering any permanent change. The action of enzymes is limited to breaking down complex bodies into simpler forms, often with absorption of water, as in the case of sugar, while some of the products of living ferments are often complex, a part of their nutriment being broken down into simple products such as carbonic acid, marsh gas and ammonia, to supply the necessary energy to elaborate the remainder.

Compare O'Sullivan and Thompson, Jour. Chem. Soc., 1890, p. 834; 1891, p. 46.

Very many different unorganised ferments are known to exist, as they are not only produced by yeasts and bacteria, but are formed by the cells of higher plants and animals; thus the digestive principles, pepsin, trypsin, ptyalin, are of this character—ptyalin, like diastase, converting starch into sugar; and such bodies fulfil many functions both in animal and vegetable economy. In fermentation, as in disease, it is often difficult to distinguish what is due to the direct action of bacteria, and what to the unorganised ferments which they produce, and the question is further complicated by the fact that in most natural fermentations more than one ferment-organism is present. Sometimes the action of the unorganised ferments may be distinguished by the fact that the addition of chloroform has little effect on their activity while it paralyses that of the living organism. By exposure to high temperature both are destroyed, the bacteria, yeasts and moulds being killed and the unorganised ferments coagulated like white of egg, and so rendered inoperative. Many antiseptics also destroy the activity of both organisms and enzymes; but others, like chloroform, have no action on the latter. In some cases, as in that of invertase, the actual zymase can be precipitated by alcohol from its aqueous solution, filtered off, and restored to activity by transference into water. Since both classes of ferments are destroyed by high temperatures, all fermentation-processes are completely and permanently arrested by exposure to sufficient heat, and subsequent preservation in vessels so closed that no new ferment-germs can gain access. A familiar instance is that of tinned meats. All fully developed bacteria are destroyed by a very short exposure to a boiling temperature, and most by 60° to 70° C., but many species produce spores which are extremely difficult to destroy. The thermophilic bacteria discovered by Globig and further investigated by Rabinowitsch, thrive at a temperature of 60° C. About eight species are known, and they take part in the heating of hay and similar fermentations where high temperatures are involved, and are therefore presumably present in spent tan.

Centr. Blatt für Bakt., II. Abth. vol. i. p. 585.

For absolute sterilisation it is therefore necessary either to boil under pressure so as to raise the temperature to, say 110° C., or to heat repeatedly for a short time to temperatures of 80°-100° C. at successive intervals of 24 hours, in order to allow the spores to develop. This process is frequently performed for bacteriological observation in flasks or test-tubes merely stopped with a plug of sterilised cotton-wool, which has been found to efficiently filter the germs from the air which enters through it (see L.I.L.B., p. 270).

The ferment-organisms cannot thrive and multiply unless they have proper nourishment and conditions of growth, the amount of moisture and the temperature being two of the most important of the latter. Use is made of this in the preservation of many articles of food, etc., since by ensuring that at least one of the conditions necessary for growth shall be absent, these substances are prevented from decomposing. For instance, hides are preserved by drying them; the absence of sufficient moisture hindering the growth of any organisms in them so long as they are dry, but as soon as they become somewhat damp, putrefaction commences at once.

The waste products of organisms are often poisonous to themselves, and for this reason fermentations frequently come to an end before the whole of the substance is fermented. Thus neither beer nor vinegar can be obtained of more than a certain strength by direct fermentation, the alcohol or acetic acid checking the growth of their respective ferments. A solution of glucose "set" with the lactic ferment of sour milk will only produce lactic acid to the extent of about half a per cent.; but if chalk be added, the lactic acid will be neutralised as produced, and the fermentation will go on till the whole of the glucose is converted into insoluble calcium lactate. When this is accomplished the lactic ferment dies from want of nutriment, and its place is taken by another organism, of which some germs are sure to be present, which ferments the calcium lactate into calcium butyrate. If the nourishment fails, or the conditions become less favourable for one ferment than for some other which exists even in small quantity in a liquid, the former is quickly overgrown and killed, and the latter takes its place. Thus the ordinary ferment of the bran drench will die out rapidly unless constantly transferred to fresh bran infusions.

For the practical preparation of lactic acid, the solution may contain $7\frac{1}{2}$-11 per cent. of glucose, and some nitrogenous nourishment. The solution should be slightly acid. See Journ. Soc. Ch. Ind., 1897, p. 516.

Many of the products of bacteria (like those of some of the higher plants) are intensely poisonous both to animals and man. Many of the severe symptoms of disease are caused by these poisons produced in the body. Thus the tetanus-bacteria produce a poison similar in its effects to strychnine, and quite as virulent. Not only are such poisons produced by disease-bacteria in the body, but frequently also in the earlier stages of putrefactive fermentation. The latter are known as *ptomaines*, and when present in cheese and preserved foods are liable to cause poisoning. Such putrefactions are often unaccompanied by any disagreeable odour or flavour.

The fermentations which are most important in the tannery are, firstly, the ordinary putrefaction which attacks hides as well as other animal matter, and which is usually a complicated process carried on by many sorts of bacteria and other micro-organisms. This may be regarded as generally injurious to the tanner; but it is utilised in the "sweating" process for depilation and in the "staling" of sheepskins, in both of which advantage is taken of the fact that the soft mucous layer of the epidermis, which contains the hair-roots, putrefies more rapidly than the fibrous structure of the hide itself. In soaking also, use is made of the power of putrefactive ferments to dissolve the cementing substance of the hide, though in this case with doubtful advantage to the tanner. In the liming process putrefaction makes itself felt when the limes are allowed to become stale and charged with animal matter, softening the hide and finally rendering the leather loose, empty and inclined to "pipe." Here the effect is in many cases useful if not carried too far.

In bating and puering, the action is almost entirely due to the enzymes and other products of bacterial activity, the original chemical constituents of the dung being apparently of minor importance. Naturally the liquid is adapted to the growth of many other organisms beside those acting most advantageously on the hide, and injury in the bates from wrong forms of putrefaction is very common, if indeed it is not always present in greater or less degree.

In drenching, the effect is, at first, entirely due to the weak acids produced by bacterial fermentation of the bran, but becomes complicated in its later stages by putrefactive and other fermentations which may be desirable or otherwise.

In the tanning liquors, fermentation is not so marked, but is of great importance owing to the production of acids by bacterial action from the sugars present in the material. The acids themselves are apt to be fermented and destroyed, principally by the oxidising action of *Saccharomyces mycoderma* and the higher moulds (see p. 14), which also act destructively on the tannins.

The effect of these acids on the hides is to swell them and to neutralise any lime they may contain. They also give to the liquors a characteristic sour taste, as a consequence of which, liquors containing acetic and lactic acids are usually known in the tannery as "sour liquors."

It is doubtful whether the action of fungi is completely stayed even by the drying process. The heating of leather in the sheds is due to bacteria and the higher moulds, and Eitner considers their growth one of the causes of the "spueing" or "gumming" of curried leathers.

From what has been said, it is obvious that, with regard to fermentations, a double problem is presented to the leather manufacturer, since he desires to utilise those which make for his advantage, while controlling or destroying those which are injurious. The first step to a solution of these problems is a more complete knowledge of the organisms which serve or injure us, that we may, as it were, discriminate friends and enemies. We may then approach the question in two ways. Taking the drenching process as an example, we may on the one hand introduce a "pure cultivation" of the right ferment into a sterilised bran infusion, and so induce only the one fermentation which we require; or, on the other hand, as different ferments are affected in varying degrees by antiseptics, we may perhaps choose such as permit the growth of the organism we want, while killing or discouraging the rest. We may also arrange the nutriment, temperature, degree of acidity and other conditions, so as to favour one organism rather than another. All three methods have been applied in brewing with good results.

CHAPTER V.
ANTISEPTICS AND DISINFECTANTS.

"Antiseptics" are often defined as substances which check putrefaction without necessarily destroying bacteria and their spores, while "disinfectants" are poisonous to ferment-organisms, and actually destroy them; great differences exist in the extent of their sterilising power, and the whole distinction is one rather of degree than of kind, and has little practical value. Thus common salt is incapable of *killing* most bacteria, even in concentrated solution, though it holds putrefaction in check both by withdrawing water from the hide and by directly preventing the multiplication of bacteria. If the salt be washed out of the hide, putrefaction is at once resumed by the organisms present. Hides, on the other hand, which have once been sterilised by powerful disinfectants, such as phenol ("carbolic acid") or mercuric chloride, do not again putrefy till the organisms which are killed are replaced by fresh ones from outside. The action of sodium sulphate, and many other salts, is similar to common salt in this respect, while a large proportion of the aromatic compounds are permanently disinfectant, though their efficiency varies with the species of bacteria involved.

Biernacki and others have shown that some disinfectants when extremely diluted actually stimulate alcoholic fermentation, and probably the growth of other ferments, e.g. mercuric chloride 1 in 300,000, salicylic acid 1 in 6000, and boric acid 1 in 8000, and in many cases organisms become habituated to antiseptics in doses which would at first have proved fatal.

The number of antiseptics available is now so great that it is impossible to give a detailed account of all, but the following are among those which are best known and have been practically employed.

Lime possesses some antiseptic properties, and is largely used in the preservation of fleshings before they are sent off to the glue factory. They are most conveniently stored in a large vat filled with a strong milk of lime. Dilute solutions of caustic alkalies have an effect similar to that of lime.

Common salt, sodium chloride, NaCl, acts to a certain extent by its solubility and a dehydrating effect on animal tissues common to chlorides, which removes water from hides and other materials which it is used to preserve. Probably the latter characteristic has a good deal to do with its effect in checking the development of bacteria, since many species thrive quite well in weak salt solutions, and some even in brine, and the dehydrating effect of the salt enables it to harden many animal tissues if used in sufficient quantity, the water they contain running away in the form of brine.

Ordinary rock salt frequently contains ferric chloride, and this, either originally present in the salt, or in some cases derived from the action of the latter upon the iron contained in the blood, is the cause of what is known as "salt-stains." These show but little during the liming of the hides, unless sulphides are used, when stains appear of a greenish black, from the formation of sulphide of iron; when, however, the hides come into the tanning liquors, black or blue stains are produced by the action of the tannin, which are partially removed by the acids of the liquors during the tanning process, but generally show to some extent in the finished hide. There is another species of salt-stain, not apparently due to iron, but to the colouring matter produced by some fungoid or bacterial growth, which it is practically impossible to remove, and which is stated to be sometimes caused by the use of old salt with which hides have been previously salted. Iron stains are most readily recognised by the use of a solution of potassium ferrocyanide or thiocyanate slightly acidified by hydrochloric acid. If this be applied to the leather, the stains will be changed from a blackish to a blue, if the former, or a red colour if the latter salt has been used. A more absolutely conclusive proof is to lay a piece of filter paper soaked in dilute hydrochloric acid upon the stain, and then to test for iron upon the paper with ferrocyanide or thiocyanate. The freedom of the paper itself from iron must be ascertained before use. Iron-stains produced in the salted state are more difficult to discharge than those which are caused later in the tanning process, since iron salts have distinct tanning power, and attach themselves firmly to the untanned fibre. On the Continent, where common salt is heavily taxed, alum, carbolic acid, naphthalene and other materials are frequently added to it to "denaturise," or render it incapable of being used as food, and these additions are often the cause of trouble to the tanner.

Sodium sulphate, Na_2SO_4, has little if any disinfectant power in dilute solution, but if used in the calcined form (anhydrous sodium sulphate) as proposed by Eitner as a substitute for common salt in preserving hides, it withdraws water from the hide and crystallises with 10 Aq (about 56 per cent.). This does not run away like brine, but remains in the hide, which retains its weight, and remains plump and swells well in the limes and liquors, which chlorides have a great tendency to prevent; 10-15 per cent. on the weight of the hide is sufficient, while salt must be used in nearly double this quantity. Care must be taken that the sulphate used is free from bisulphate, $NaHSO_4$, which has a powerful swelling effect upon the hide-fibre, like sulphuric acid. The neutral sulphate does not redden methyl orange or litmus. Pickled skivers may be in part preserved by the sodium sulphate formed by the action of sulphuric acid upon the salt employed in the pickling bath (see p. 90).

Gerber, 1880, p. 185.

The stronger mineral acids have considerable antiseptic power, and are of course especially fatal to such ferments as thrive best in alkaline solutions. The use of sulphuric acid in pickling skivers has already been alluded to, and a very dilute solution applied without salt to raw hides prevents putrefaction, though the principal object in using it is to plump the hides and produce a fictitious weight and substance which disappear on tanning. Such hides of course have a powerful acid reaction to litmus. Sulphuric acid in small quantities has been used with advantage in soaking E.I. kips. A very small excess of hydrochloric acid will sterilise putrid effluents, and no doubt nitric or sulphuric acid would have the same effect. The powerful effect of mineral acids on animal fibre, and their solvent action on cements and iron, preclude however, their general use as antiseptics.

More important is the use of sulphurous acid and sulphur dioxide, which, from their mild acidity and great antiseptic powers, are capable of a variety of useful applications. Considerable doubt has been raised as to the germicide power of sulphur dioxide, and it is certain that the dry gas is less effective on dry objects than when applied in solution, or to moist materials, as is almost invariably the case in the tannery. It may possibly be more efficient in its action on some moulds and putrefaction-ferments than on the pathogenic bacteria which have been most frequently used to test the power of disinfectants; but in practice it is found extremely useful in the brewery and in gelatine manufacture, and there is no reason that it should be less so in the tannery.

The gas is most conveniently produced by burning sulphur, which produces double its weight of sulphur dioxide. If used for "stoving" drying rooms and other places infested with moulds, care must be taken to avoid risk of fire. A shallow cast-iron pot set on bricks or sand is generally the most suitable vessel, and the sulphur may be ignited by a piece of red-hot iron or a rag which has been previously dipped in melted sulphur. It is corrosive to metalwork, and bleaches many colours, but does not produce any marked injurious effect on leather, though the sulphuric acid formed by oxidation may, if not removed, ultimately make it tender.

For many purposes a solution of the gas is required, and this is most easily made by burning the sulphur in a small metal or firebrick stove from which the fumes are sucked through a "scrubber," which, on a small scale, is conveniently made of large glazed sanitary pipes, packed with coke or broken earthenware, over which water is allowed to trickle. The lowest pipe has an opening for a branch pipe, which is connected with the stove and rests on three bricks in a tub, which collects the acid solution and forms a water-seal to prevent the escape of gas. Above the inlet for the gases is fixed a wooden grating on which the coke rests. The scrubber may be 10-15 feet in height and connected at the top with a chimney or steam ejector to produce the draught. The arrangement is illustrated in Fig. 5. Another method is to burn the sulphur in a closed cylinder and to force the products through water with an air-compressor or steam-jet injector.

In place of using a scrubber, the fumes may be blown by a steam ejector direct into a tank. This is a very good arrangement for washing and bleaching hair, etc., but where large quantities of solution are required is inferior to the scrubber. Ejectors of hard lead or regulus metal should be used, and are less acted on by the dry gases than by the very dilute moist exhaust from the scrubber (see p. 335).

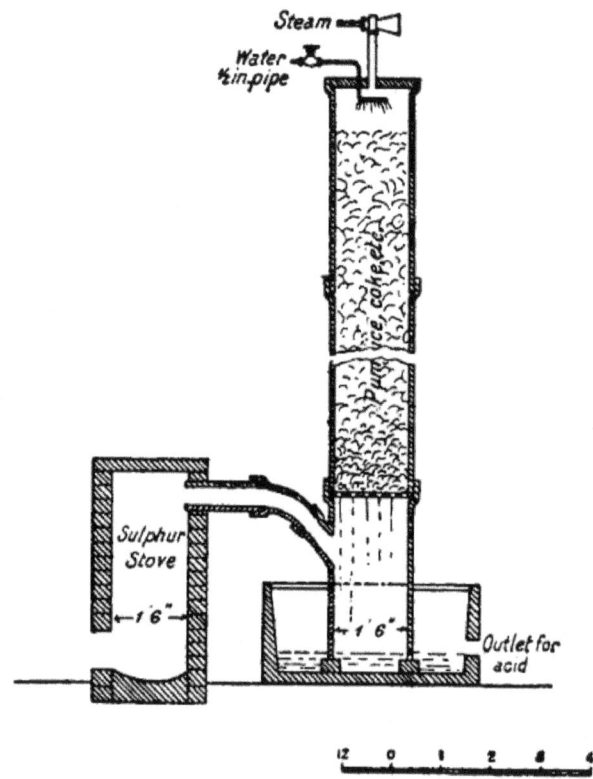

FIG. 5—Sulphurous acid apparatus.

Bisulphites have also strong antiseptic properties. "Bisulphite of soda" (hydric sodic sulphite) solution may be made by supplying the scrubber with solution of soda-ash or washing soda; bisulphite of lime, by using milk of lime or packing the scrubber with chalk or limestone (free from much iron) in place of the coke. In either case a much stronger solution is obtained than with water alone.

Boakes' "metabisulphite of soda" is a very convenient source of sulphurous acid when the latter is wanted in small quantities. It is an anhydrosulphite, $Na_2O.2(SO_2)$, and contains 67·4 per cent. of its weight of SO_2. One molecule of the salt (= 190) requires one molecule of H_2SO_4 (= 98) to set free the whole of the sulphurous acid. For many purposes the sulphate of soda formed may be neglected and the acidified solution used direct.

Patented by Boakes, Ltd., Stratford, London, E.

For analysis of sulphites and sulphurous acid solution, see L.I.L.B., pp. 16 and 37.

Boric acid, *borax* and other *borates* are not very powerful disinfectants. They have no injurious action upon the skin, but to be effective require to be employed in pretty strong solutions, say 1 per cent., and their comparatively high cost unfits them for general use as antiseptics in the tannery, though boric (boracic) acid is very useful as a drenching and deliming agent (see pp. 156, 229, and L.I.L.B., p. 37).

Mercuric chloride, corrosive sublimate, $HgCl_2$, is an extremely powerful antiseptic, preventing the growth of some species of bacteria in solutions so dilute as 1 in 300,000 (Koch). 1 in 14,000 is disinfectant (Miquel), but its power varies very much upon different organisms (Jörgensen states that 1 in 400 is required to kill *Penicillium glaucum*), and it is unsuited for most purposes in leather manufacture, both from its extremely poisonous character, and because it is rendered inactive by various substances present in the materials used.

Mercuric iodide dissolved in iodide of potassium solution was patented by Messrs. Collin and Benoist as an antiseptic in tanning, but it is ineffective for the same reasons as mercuric chloride; although under favourable circumstances it is even more powerful than the latter.

Copper sulphate, *zinc chloride* and *sulphate*, and many other metallic salts are powerful antiseptics, but have only a limited application in leather industries, and do not usually actually sterilise. *Arsenic* (arsenious acid), which has been used in curing hides, is an excellent insecticide, but not particularly effective as an antiseptic; and sulphide of arsenic (realgar) when used in limes (see p. 139) seems to have but little antiseptic effect. Arsenious acid is easily soluble in alkaline solutions.

Fluorides have been suggested as antiseptics in the tannery, but do not seem of much practical value.

The most important antiseptics at present are those derived from coal tar, and belonging to the aromatic series. Of these, the phenols (carbolic acid, cresol, etc.) are the most used.

Pure phenol, "pure crystallised carbolic acid," is hydroxybenzene $C_6H_5(OH)$, but the crude forms which are generally employed contain cresols and higher members of the series in which one or more of the atoms of hydrogen are substituted by CH_3 groups. These are oily bodies scarcely soluble in water, and even pure phenol is only soluble in cold water to the extent of some 7 per cent. Crude carbolic acid should not be employed in the tannery, since the insoluble oily particles stain the hide, and render it unsusceptible of tanning. Suitable carbolic acid should be of a pale yellow colour when fresh (though it will darken on exposure to air and light), and it should be wholly soluble in a sufficient quantity of water. Its specific gravity should be 1·050 to 1·065. For methods of chemical examination, see L.I.L.B., p. 40. A saturated solution of carbolic acid sterilises hide completely against most putrefactive organisms, but has a sort of tanning effect, adhering obstinately to the fibre so that it cannot be removed by washing; and hides which have been cured with it cannot be unhaired by sweating, though they may be limed in the usual manner, if somewhat more slowly. Care should be taken in mixing with water or liquor, as undissolved drops will produce the same effects as those of the crude acid. Hides are occasionally stained, as has just been described, by salt which has been denaturised with common sorts of carbolic acid. Eitner recommends the use of a solution of carbolic acid in an equal weight of crude glycerine, which readily dissolves in water, and seems to prevent any injurious effect on the hide.

An aqueous solution containing 1 per cent. of carbolic acid is sufficient for mere sterilising of hides, but if it be desired to preserve them for a long period, stronger solutions (up to 4 per cent.) may be employed.

Gerber, 1889, p. 98.

Quantities so small as 1 part per 1000 control the fermentation of liquors, and prevent the formation of moulds on the surface, economising tannin, and preserving vegetable acids already present, but at the same time lessening their production by fermentation, and therefore sometimes leading to difficulties in the early stages of tanning. Carbolic acid is not, strictly speaking, an acid, but rather of the nature of an alcohol, although it forms weak combinations with bases. It is a powerful narcotic poison, and if dropped on the skin in a concentrated form it produces severe burns; these are best treated with oil, while in cases of poisoning, oil and chalk must be administered internally, but if the quantity of carbolic acid taken has been large, are not likely to be effective. From its cheapness and efficiency, carbolic acid is likely to be increasingly used, although for special uses some of the newer antiseptics have great advantages.

Eudermin is a tar-oil manufactured by Speyer and Grund, of Frankfort-on-Main, which is intended as an antiseptic addition to stuffing greases to prevent mould and spueing. It is recommended for the purpose by Eitner and can be used in proportions such as 10 per cent. of the grease. Creasotes and cresols can be dissolved in oils and stuffing greases, and act as antiseptics, though less powerfully than in aqueous solution. Rosin oils and turpentine have also antiseptic properties.

Gerber, 1893, p. 41.

Creasote, "heavy coal oil," or "dead oil," is a complex mixture of hydrocarbons, phenols and cresols, obtained by distillation of coal tar, heavier than water, and almost insoluble in it. It is largely used as a preservative for timber. Carbolineum is an oil of this class, boiling at over 300° C., and intended for application to wood. One or more coats are applied to the dry wood at a temperature of 80° C. The workman's hands must be protected by gloves, as the hot creasote raises painful blisters. Eitner recommends its use for preserving pits, posts and other woodwork in tanneries. Wood-creasote is a somewhat similar product obtained from wood-tar.

Gerber, 1889, p. 183.

The heavier cresols are so little soluble in water as to be valueless in their ordinary form as antiseptics, but several preparations are made under the names of "Creolin," "Jeye's fluid," "Lysol," "Izal," "Soluble phenyl," etc., in which they are treated with additions of soap or alkalies, which cause them to emulsify or dissolve in water, generally as milky liquids. These are powerful germicides and have the advantage over phenol of being non-poisonous. 0·1 to 0·5 per cent. solution of creolin will sterilise hides after bating so that no putrefaction takes place in the liquors. Mr. J. T. Wood specially recommends creolin for the general purposes of the tannery, disinfecting pits and tubs, and for checking the action of puers and drenches on goods which have gone a little too far, by throwing them into a 0·2 per cent. solution.

Salicylic acid, orthohydroxybenzoic acid, $C_6H_4OH(COOH)$, is now artificially prepared from phenol. It is much less poisonous than the latter and has no smell, which makes it valuable for certain purposes, but is too dear for most technical applications. Many bacteria appear to become gradually habituated to its action, and the same is true of phenol to a less degree.

Salicylic acid is closely related to protocatechuic and gallic acids, and, like these, gives a blackish colour with iron salts. It is freely soluble in hot water, but very sparingly in cold. The addition of 1-2½ parts of sodium phosphate, sulphate, or potassium nitrate to each part of salicylic acid greatly increases its solubility. It seems much more powerful in preventing the development of bacteria than carbolic acid; a solution of 1 part of salicylic acid in 666 of water is said to be equal in this respect to 1 part of carbolic in 200.

Benzoic acid, C_6H_5COOH, though not much employed, except in medicine, is a still more powerful disinfectant, and has the advantage of being non-poisonous to human beings.

"*Cresotinic acid*," which is derived from the cresols as salicylic acid is derived from phenol, is more soluble than salicylic acid. It is not very poisonous, and a powerful disinfectant. In a crude form it has been introduced by Hauff, of Feuerbach, for bating or removing lime from hides. This it does very well, though without the softening action of a true bate. It has a tendency to produce a pinkish stain, and in some degree a sort of tanning of the fibre. Its price, moreover, is rather high for extensive technical use. (See also p. 162.)

"*Anticalcium*" is a more recent preparation introduced as a bate by the same firm. It is a solution of mixed sulphonic acids derived from cresols, and has considerable disinfectant powers. It removes lime very effectively, but from its acid character somewhat swells the skin. It is used very successfully as a drench for thin skins (p. 163).

Gerber, 1895, p. 133.

"C.T." (coal-tar) bate is a grey crystalline pasty mass, with a tarry smell, and is chemically very similar to anticalcium if not identical with it.

Naphthalene sulphonic acid has strong antiseptic properties. Its use in bating has been patented by Burns and Cross. (See p. 163.)

Naphthols, $C_{10}H_7(OH)$.—These bodies, which have the same relation to naphthalene as the phenols to benzene, are powerful antiseptics; and naphthalene itself appears to have antiseptic power, and is occasionally used for denaturising salt. There are two naphthols, varying in the position of the OH group in the molecule, and denominated α and β, of which α naphthol is the more powerful antiseptic and the less poisonous, though β, being cheaper, is the common commercial article. It is said that quantities so small as 0·1-0·4 grams of α naphthol per liter are sufficient to prevent the development of microbes, while of β naphthol about ten times that quantity is required.

Naphthols are not very expensive, but their value is diminished by the fact that they are insoluble in water. They are soluble in alkaline solutions, but their compounds with bases are of much lower antiseptic value, and the same is true of their alcoholic solutions; when an alcoholic solution is added to water the naphthol is precipitated, but if an addition of soap or camphor be made to the alcoholic solution, the naphthol remains in a very finely divided condition, if not dissolved.

Adopting Eitner's suggestion with regard to oxynaphthoic acid (see below), hides may no doubt be sterilised by treatment first with an alkaline naphthol solution, and then with a very dilute acid to set the naphthol free.

"*Hydronaphthol*," β tetra-hydro-naphthol, $C_{10}H_{12}O$, is obtained by the reduction of β naphthol by sodium (Rideal). It seems to be an excellent disinfectant.

Oxynaphthoic acid, α hydroxynaphthoic acid, $C_{10}H_6(OH)COOH$, which bears the same relation to naphthol as salicylic acid does to phenol, is cheaper than salicylic acid, and said to be a more powerful antiseptic. Its salts have no antiseptic power. In its commercial form it is a reddish crystalline powder, inodorous, but with a burning taste, and its dust causes violent sneezing. It is scarcely soluble in water, and is said to undergo some change on keeping which lessens its germicide power; it is readily soluble in alcohol, and the solution produces a milky fluid on mixture with water. Such a solution containing 15 grams of the acid in 4 liters of water, will sterilise a hide. Eitner recommends that it should be dissolved in dilute soda solution, and the hides, after soaking in it, passed through water slightly acidified with hydrochloric acid, as has been suggested in the case of naphthol; the method is also applicable to creosotinic acid, the hides being permanently sterilised so that they cannot be unhaired by sweating, though they will lime in the usual manner.

Gerber, 1888, p. 101; 1889, pp. 99 *et seq*. See also p. 163.

Carbon disulphide.—Moret has suggested an aqueous solution of this compound as an antiseptic, and it seems to have considerable sterilising powers, but from its inflammability, poisonous character, and unpleasant smell, it is not likely to come largely into use.

Formaldehyde, COH_2, has recently been introduced as an antiseptic in aqueous solution containing 40 per cent. of formaldehyde together with a little formic acid, under the names of "formalin," "formol," etc. It seems to have great disinfectant powers, and may possibly be valuable in various processes of leather manufacture as it becomes cheaper, but has a curious hardening tanning effect on hide fibre and gelatinous matters, so that in very dilute solution it will produce leather. The vapour of formaldehyde, or of its condensation-product paraform, may be employed to harden microscopic preparations. 1 part of formaldehyde, and consequently 2½ parts of "formalin" in 12,000 parts of water, is said to sterilise, and this proportion would form a good disinfectant solution. Even in considerably larger proportion than the above, it does not appear to be poisonous, and thus possesses the bactericidal power of sublimate without the latter's poisonous properties. Formaldehyde has another advantage over most, if not all other antiseptics, in that it may be used as well in the gaseous as in the liquid state, and on that account it is largely employed in the disinfection of rooms or of articles which would be spoiled if they were to be wetted, as the gaseous formaldehyde, though thoroughly disinfecting them, will not injure the colours of materials of the most delicate fabrics.

Gerber, 1897, p. 67; ibid., 1899, pp. 101, 205, 218.

On account of its capability of rendering gelatinous matters hard and insoluble in water, formaldehyde requires to be employed with great care, but 0·2-0·3 per cent. may be successfully used in admixture with egg-albumen in the preparation of "seasoning" in the finishing of morocco leather. It is also used commercially to produce different varieties of white leather for soldiers' accoutrements and similar purposes (p. 380).

Triformol (tri-oxymethylene, "paraform") is a product of the polymerisation of formaldehyde, and is prepared by evaporating a solution of the latter to dryness on the water-bath. It is said to be more powerful than formalin in its antiseptic properties, but has not entered very largely into use as a disinfectant, though considerable use is made of it to "fix" bacteria in gelatin for bacteriological purposes.

Camphor and essential oils, as well as oil of turpentine, have considerable antiseptic powers, and the cheaper essential oils such as those of wintergreen, black birch, sassafras and aniseed are frequently employed, especially in America, in preserving pastes, finishes and seasonings, and at the same time covering offensive odours. The odour of essential oils becomes much more powerful as they are diluted, and very small quantities suffice for the purposes mentioned. Birch-tar oil, such as is used to give the scent to Russian leather (p. 372), has considerable antiseptic effect.

CHAPTER VI.
THE ORIGIN AND CURING OF HIDES AND SKINS.

A considerable proportion of the hides and skins used in leather manufacture are those of animals killed by the butcher for food, and these are frequently employed by the tanner without any preliminary curing. Domestic hides and skins are now generally sold by auction in weekly markets in the principal towns, after sorting and classification in weight and quality. This is in many respects an improvement on the old method of purchase direct from the butcher, but it often leads to delay in delivery, and in hot weather hides suffer from putrefaction. In most cases, the damage is not sufficient seriously to affect the durability of the leather, but the delicate membrane of the "grain" is injured, and the hide or skin unfitted for coloured leather, or any purpose where small damages to appearance are important. Butchers are adverse to the use of salt, because it withdraws water from the hide in the form of brine, and so causes it to lose weight; but much injury would be saved by a light salting, and all hides or skins on which the hair is "slipping" should be regarded as damaged for fine leather manufacture.

The weight of English market-hides as credited to the butcher is usually marked on the edge of the butt near the tail, by cuts with a knife, the mode of numeration being sufficiently explained by Fig. 6, in which cuts crossing the horizontal line each represent 20 lb., that above it 10 lb., while less amounts are expressed in Roman figures.

On the Continent weights are usually given in pounds of half a kilogramme (50 kilos = 110 lb. English). In Paris the marking is on the tail, and is also shown on Fig. 6.

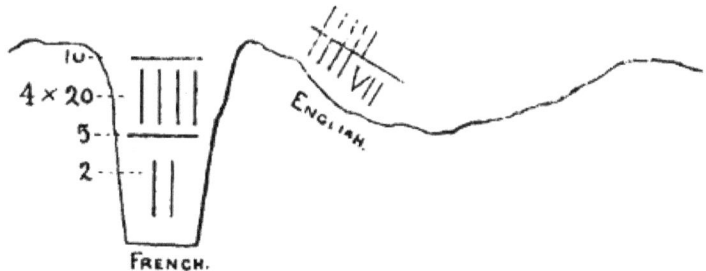

FIG. 6.—Method of marking weight on hides; 97 lb.

Sheep-skins are not usually bought direct by the tanner, but by the fellmonger, who removes the wool; and as this is usually of much greater value than the skin, the latter is frequently handled very carelessly, and its quality sacrificed for the sake of real or fancied improvement to the wool. In very many cases the skin is "sweated" or "staled" by hanging in a warm and moist chamber, heavily charged with ammonia derived from the putrefaction of the skin, until the wool is sufficiently loosened to be "pulled." If this treatment is conducted with extreme care the skin may escape serious injury, but in most cases the grain is weakened, and the foundation is laid of damage, which makes itself felt throughout the tanning process. For the purposes of the tanner, a much better way is to lime the skins by painting with thick limewash on the flesh-side, and after folding the skins down the back, flesh-side in, to prevent as much as possible the access of the lime to the wool, to place them in a pit, and cover them with water, till the wool is loosened by the penetration of the lime through the skin. A still more satisfactory method, and one which is in general use in the American stockyards, and to some extent also in Europe, is to wash the skins in water to free them from blood and dirt, and then, laying them in a wet condition, flesh side up, to paint them with a solution containing about 25 per cent. of sulphide of sodium, thickened with lime. The skins, as they are painted, are doubled down the back, flesh-side in, and laid on a floor, overlapping each other like tiles on a roof, for some hours, or overnight, till the wool is sufficiently loosened to pull, after which the pelts are limed and treated in the ordinary way. As a general rule the English fellmonger keeps his skins in lime till they are sold to the tanner, and as in small yards some time is taken to accumulate a parcel, the earlier skins may suffer great injury from overliming. Even sweet fresh limes dissolve the cementing substance of the fibre, and increase the naturally loose texture of the sheep-skin, but the injury is much more considerable when old and stale limes, charged with ammonia and bacterial products, are employed, as is frequently the case. In the American stockyards the skins are generally limed only for the necessary time to act upon the grease, and to swell and differentiate the fibres, and are then at once puered, drenched and preserved by "pickling." For details of "pickling" see p. 89. It is very probable that the Pullman process of liming (p. 137) would answer well for fellmongered skins, as goods will keep for a considerable length of time uninjured after treatment with calcium chloride.

Where hides or skins cannot be used at once in the fresh state, there is probably no better method of preserving them than the use of salt. Although salt is not fatal to bacteria, it so slows bacterial growth, partly by its direct antiseptic effect on many organisms, and partly by withdrawing water from the skin, that well-salted skins can be kept in good condition for almost an unlimited time. Where it is only required to preserve goods for a week or two, a moderate sprinkling on the flesh side is efficient, but if they are to be preserved for any length of time, more thorough treatment is necessary. It is said that however carefully hides are salted they deteriorate if kept in this condition above twelve months.

The method of salting employed in the Chicago stockyards for "packer" hides may be taken as a good type of a thorough salting. The hides are first trimmed from useless "switches," and any large portions of adhering fat are removed. The curing takes place in large and cool cellars, with concrete floors. The detail is well given in the following extract from the 'Shoe and Leather Reporter':—

"Great care is taken to make the sides of a pack higher than the middle, so that the brine which is made by the juices of the hide coming in contact with the salt will be retained. The brine can only escape by percolation and hence the fibre of the hides is thoroughly cured. The floor of a hide cellar is usually of concrete, and a pack is from 15 to 20 feet long and as wide as the space between the posts which support the floor above. The sides of a pack are built first to a height of from 4 to 6 inches; the cross layers are then put on, generally three on each side, two being inside and one having the butts drawn out to the edge. In a pack 20 feet long, the side layers will contain about 25 medium-sized hides each, and a cross-layer 12 or 14. To begin a pack a truck-load of hides is run along to the front of the place selected, one spreader grasps the butt and his partner the head of a hide, and together they carry it to what is to be the rear of the bed. The hide is then dropped, so that the folded back is parallel to and from 15 to 20 inches from the inside line of the posts, the head a trifle closer than the butt. The front man takes the dewlap and front shank in his left hand, and extends his right along the belly of the hide as far as is necessary to raise the edge, the rear man holding the flank with one hand and the hind shank with the other. They keep their legs well out of the way of the salt thrower, who with a single throw covers the whole hide, being particular that enough salt strikes against the edges held by the men to make a pronounced ridge when they are lapped down. A little salt is thrown on the hair surface and the butt folded over about a foot. The folded edge is then drawn out even with the outer line of the pack. More hides are placed the same way until the corner is high enough. After this, each hide is put further forward to make a level surface from rear to front, the heads at the front corner being folded back as the butts were at the starting place. The other side is built the same way, and then the cross layers are put on alternately until the pack is level, when sides are again built as before. In putting on the first hides of the cross layers, they are thrown over the edge, to lap back again when the salt is thrown on; the layer is then continued on to the front. The spreader who holds the butt does the guiding in every case. He drops the butt down at exactly the proper place, takes the upper flank and shank in each hand, sets one foot on the lower shank to keep it firm, and throws the one in his hands from him with considerable force. The man at the head watches his partner, keeps the folded hide taut, and drops it at the same time as the latter. He takes the fore-shank at the knee in the one hand and the upper head-piece in the other, and setting his foot on the lower side, throws the upper side forward simultaneously with the rear man. Two expert spreaders, accustomed to working together, spread a hide at a single throw, but some little straightening has to be done by hand before the hide is ready for the salt. A gang composed of two spreaders, one salt thrower and a salt trucker put down forty hides an hour. When gangs are doubled, two men do all the spreading; the other two place the hides where they can be got at conveniently. A double gang put down eighty hides an hour. The salt trucker brings the salt to the pack in box-trucks open at one end to permit the entrance of a shovel. The salt thrower keeps the edges and corners of the pack full of salt. He must see that every part of the flesh-side is well covered. Each hide takes two scoop shovelfuls of ground rock or coarse white salt, mixed with an equal quantity of old or second salt. The salt thrower throws the shovel forward and to one side and back again with a peculiar swinging jerk, causing the salt to fall regularly over the entire surface of the hide. The ease and rapidity with which a gang operates depends greatly upon the efficiency of the salt thrower. When the pack gets too high to be comfortable for the men, it is brought to a dead level and covered over with clean salt. It then presents a very neat and workmanlike appearance. Spreaders and salt throwers receive 20 cents an hour, and truckers get 17½ cents. When the temperature is kept at an even average, two weeks is ample time to cure the hides.

"In 'taking up,' two men strip the hides from the pack. As they were put down from the rear to the front, they are taken up in the reverse direction. No matter how much loose salt is lying on the top, the man knows exactly where to place his hand on a shank; as the hides are moved forward, the loose salt is thrown off toward the front. One man takes away the salt as it accumulates and trucks it to the salt bins, where it is mixed with new, to be used again. A 'horse' made of a network of scantling about 3½ feet wide by 6 feet long, and standing 2½ feet from the floor, is placed in front of the pack, on this the hides, flesh side down, are shaken to remove the salt that is clinging to them. This process requires four men, one at each corner. The hide is brought down heavily on the horse twice, and then spread on the floor flesh side up for examination by the inspectors, of which there are two, one representing the house and the other the buyer of the hides. They sweep off any salt that may be left, and examine for cuts, sores, brands, manure and grubs. They also see that the hide is properly weighed and classified. If the contract calls for a special trim it is now done. Two men then roll the hide, beginning by lapping over the shanks, head and neck. Then the sides are folded over and lapped again, leaving the roll 15 to 18 inches wide. The ends are thrown inward, slightly overlapping each other; a final fold is then given, and the hide is ready to be tied. Rope the size of clothesline is used for tying, and is cut into lengths of about seven feet. It takes three men to tie for a gang such as we have described. After tying, the neat bundles are weighed and loaded on the cars for shipment. A small tare is allowed the buyer. Ordinary workmen in hide cellars get $17\frac{1}{2}$ cents an hour, and inspectors 25 cents an hour."

About 25 per cent. of salt on the green weight of the hide is required for thorough curing. Rock salt merely crushed is frequently employed, but this is very liable to contain iron in the form of oxide and chloride, which causes the peculiar marbled markings known as "salt-stains." It is therefore much better to use a white crystallised salt, though it is possible even in this case that stains may arise from the iron present in the blood. Some salt-stains appear also to be due to the action of pigment-bacteria, and not to contain iron. A reddening of the flesh side is often noticed in hides which have been kept in salt long or under unsatisfactory conditions, and is very frequent in wet-salted South American hides. Such hides are said never to produce so firm a leather as those which are sound.

Hides are not unfrequently cured by steeping in salt brine, instead of strewing with dry salt. This method is principally resorted to in order to give fictitious weight. Brined hides do not plump well in tanning, the leather is not so good in quality as from those salted with dry salt, and the cure is much less efficient.

Many hides are not only salted but also dried in order to preserve them. Not much detail has been published with regard to the methods used, which no doubt vary much in different places, but probably in some cases the hides are salted in pile and in others by brining, and then hung up to dry. The principal object of this drying is to economise weight and cost of transport, but it makes the hides much more difficult to wash and soften for tanning, and probably the crystallisation of the salt has a weakening effect on the fibre. Hides cured in this way are styled "dry salted."

A large number of the hides of the small native cattle of India are imported into this country in a dry-salted condition. The following particulars of their cure are taken from a paper by the Author and Mr. W. Towse.

Journ. Soc. Ch. Ind., 1895, p. 1025.

Dry-salted, or, as they are commonly called "plaster cures," such as those of Dacca and Mehapore, are thickly coated with a white material, which in the first instance is merely the insoluble portion of a saline earth used in the cure; though in many cases it is applied in larger quantities than necessary, with the simple object of giving weight. The salting is thus described by Mr. W. G. Evans, who some years since had considerable experience as a tanner at Cawnpore:—

"The salt used by the natives is a salt-earth; and is so called by them. It is found extensively in the districts of Cawnpore, Agra, Delhi, Lucknow, Patna, etc., and has no doubt something to do with the localisation of the hide-curing and kindred industries in these places. The mode of procedure used is pretty much as follows:—the salt-earth is mixed into a very thin paste, and this is lightly brushed on to the flesh side one day, and the hide allowed to remain over night under cover. Next day, for best hides, the same solution is again spread on the flesh side of the outstretched hide and rubbed into it with a porous brick, and then for legitimate salting, the hide is allowed to dry under cover. If for export, the saltings may be three or four, and the hides are treated out in the open, subject to the intense heat of the sun; which accounts for the number of hides which go back in the soaks in England and elsewhere."

"We had a clause in our agreement with hide-factors, that any hides which did not come down to natural suppleness in two days in clean water were to be returned. Of arsenic curing I know nothing, and it is not so much in vogue as formerly. There is quite a trade in Cawnpore, Lucknow, Allahabad, etc., in treating old and inferior hides with new for export, and great efforts are made by native holders to get their stocks down before the rains commence, as they say, and rightly I think, that hides are not worth so much after the rains by 30 per cent. The peculiar latent moisture of the rains affects them very detrimentally."

Under certain circumstances this mode of cure gives rise to extensive iron-staining of the skins, and analyses of the material scraped off Dacca and Mehapore kips were undertaken with a view to elucidating the causes of this injury. The following are the results of the analyses referred to, which were made upon the residue after the rather considerable quantity of fibrous organic matter, which had been scraped off with the cure, had been destroyed by ignition, together no doubt with traces of ammoniacal salts:—

—	Dacca. Entire Cure.	Mehapore. Entire Cure.
Sand and silica	20·55	27·38
Fe_2O_3	2·77	1·86
Al_2O_3	2·48	2·74

Mn₃O₄	0·60	0·40
CaO	2·60	3·70
MgO	3·38	3·69
Na₂O	28·97	26·80
SO₃	38·90	33·75
Cl	0·22	0·18
H₃PO₄ and CO₂	Traces	Traces
	100·47	100·50

The soluble salts of the Dacca cure were also analysed separately with the following result:—

CaO	0·70
MgO	0·60
Na₂O	29·00
SO₃	37·90
Cl	·22
Insoluble	32·12
	100·54

It thus consisted exclusively of sulphates, with the exception of a trace of chloride. The cures, after ignition, were both neutral to phenolphthalein, but before ignition the Dacca was distinctly alkaline, in consequence probably of the presence of ammonium salts, and both showed considerably larger traces of carbonates before than after.

The most striking feature of these analyses is the absence of more than the smallest traces of chlorides. The cures are thus practically free from common salt, and owe their antiseptic power to the sodium sulphate which they contain, and which indeed forms their principal constituent. Nitrates appear to be entirely absent. Sodium sulphate sometimes forms large crystals in pits used for soaking these kips.

The iron-staining of hides which has been mentioned appears to result only when the hides after cure are exposed for a lengthened period to a moist atmosphere, in which the carbonic acid present probably also plays its part, the iron passing into solution as hydric carbonate.

The analyses show a striking resemblance to those of the soda deposits of Wyoming, given by Dr. Attfield, except that their percentage of sodium carbonate is smaller, which is quite intelligible in the light of Mr. Brunner's abstract on the 'Probable origin of natural deposits of sodium carbonate,' which supports the view that the sodium carbonate is derived from sodium sulphate by the reducing and carbonating action of low organisms.

Journ. Soc. Ch. Ind., 1895, p. 4.

Ibid., 1893, p. 116.

It may be noted here that the preservative properties of sodium sulphate are well known, and the anhydrous sulphate has been recommended as a substitute for common salt (see p. 23).

Drying is a very common method of preserving hides as well as other putrescible matters. It has no effect in killing bacteria, but putrefaction can only go on in presence of a considerable amount of moisture. As applied to hides, it is, to the tanner, one of the least satisfactory modes of cure, involving very considerable difficulties in bringing hides back to the moist and swollen condition which is necessary at the outset of his operations, but it is the only practical method in districts far from the coast and with primitive modes of transit, both on account of the cost of salt, and the lessened weight of the dried hide. Great differences are found in the ease with which dried hides soften, according to the way in which the drying has been accomplished, the difficulty being greater the higher the temperature which has been used (see p. 111). The best mode of drying is to hang in the shade in a good draught of cool air, with the flesh side out. Hides or skins dried in a tropical sun are not only difficult to soften, but are liable to damaged portions, which either refuse to soften, or blister and go to pieces in liming, owing to the structure of the hide being destroyed by heat, the outer surface drying first and forming an impervious layer which hinders evaporation from the inside, so that the moist interior becomes melted, while the outside appears quite sound. Such injuries are often only to be discovered by soaking and liming. Very similar damage may occur from putrefaction of the interior after the outside has become dry, and to get good results, the drying must be gradual, but rapid, especially in hot climates. South American hides are mostly dried in the sun, suspended by head and tail from stakes, with the hair side out.

The risk of injury by putrefaction during drying is diminished by the use of antiseptics. Solutions of arsenic have been frequently used for this purpose, and many of the dried Indian kips are of what are known as "arsenic cures," although the writer has never been able to detect arsenic in any which he has examined, and its use seems by no means general. The arsenious acid is usually dissolved in soda solutions. Unless used pretty freely it has little antiseptic effect, but is useful in preventing the attacks of insects, which are often very destructive. The larva of a small beetle, *Dermestes vulpinus*, frequently devours the whole tissue of patches of the hide, leaving only the epidermis.

It may be well here to say a few words about the injuries and defects to which hides and skins are liable, although some of them are not strictly due to the cure. The most serious, and yet preventable injury is that due to butchers' cuts. As the value of the hide bears only a small proportion to that of the meat, many butchers do their work extremely carelessly, and this is encouraged by the loose classification of "damaged hides" in some markets. There is also an idea that the appearance of the meat is improved by a thin layer of the white skin-tissue being left on it, and for this reason as well as mere carelessness, butchers frequently score the flanks of the hide with shallow cuts which greatly diminish its value. The "packer hides" of the United States, and the products of the large saladeros or slaughtering ("salting") establishments of South America, such as Liebig's, show what can be done by skilled work in this respect. In the United States, much of the flaying is done by means of a wooden cleaver, instead of a sharp knife. Another method to some extent in use, and which may be recommended for calf and sheep skins, is to inflate the carcase before skinning, with air from a compressing syringe, which tears the connecting tissue between the skin and the body, and renders flaying much easier.

Brands are a great source of damage to hides, but where cattle roam at large on unfenced plains, as on the prairies of Texas and the Pampas of South America, it seems indispensable for the recognition of ownership; no other mode of marking being sufficiently permanent and conspicuous. It is unfortunate, that as the animals crowd together, and cannot be closely approached, it is necessary that the brands should not only be large, but placed on the most valuable part of the hide. Generally on the Pampas an effort is made to keep them on one side only, so that in South American hides it is possible to select clear and branded sides. In the United States much land is now fenced with barbed wire, which while it obviates the necessity of branding, introduces another evil in the form of "barbed wire scratches," which are frequently troublesome in "packer hides."

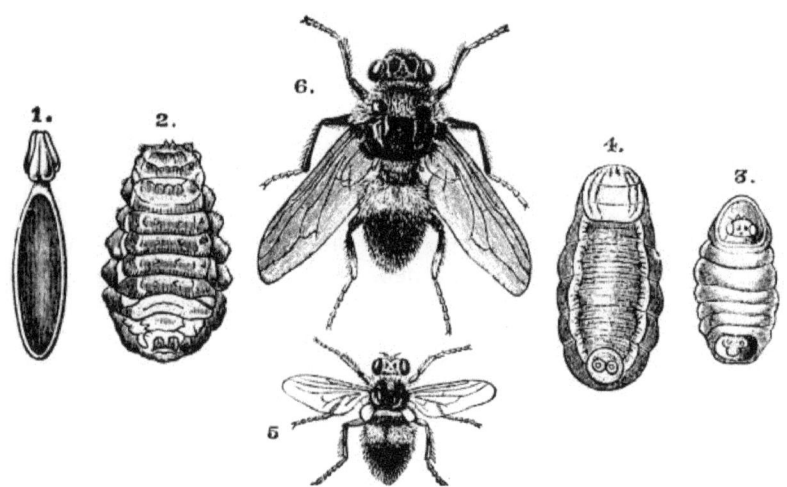

FIG. 7.—*Hypoderma bovis.* 1, egg; 2, maggot; 4, chrysalis case; 6, fly, magnified (Brauer); 3, 5, chrysalis and fly, natural size (B. Clark).

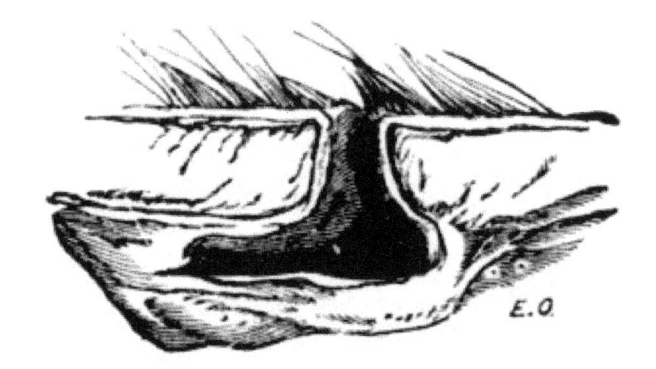

FIG. 8.—Sac of warble, showing growth of epidermis round aperture.

In countries where cattle are used for draught purposes, goadmarks are a frequent source of injury, and some of the large cattle-ticks do considerable damage to the hides of Spain and South America. From the tanners' point of view, however, the most injurious insects are the "bot-flies" or "warble-flies" (*Hypoderma bovis* and allied species, Fig. 7). There is still some controversy as to how the eggs of these insects are deposited. In the horse-bot fly it is known that the eggs, first deposited on the skin, are licked off and swallowed by the animal, and develop in the stomach, where they pass their larval and pupal life hanging on to its interior coats, and only drop off and are passed out with the dung before their final change to the complete fly. Fortified by this, and by some direct observation, some American naturalists are of opinion that the American species at least, hatches in the stomach, and as a minute larva wanders through all the intervening tissues till it reaches the skin, where it undergoes its further development. The late Miss Ormerod, who has made a careful study of the English species, states that the egg hatches on the hair, and that the *larva* simply eats its way below the skin, leaving a minute red puncture which it subsequently enlarges to obtain air for its spiracles, which are in the tail. As it grows it continues to irritate the lower part of the cavity with hooked mandibles, and lives on the pus and matter so produced. It grows to a length of fully ¾ inch, and the cavity, Fig. 8, situated between the skin and the subcutaneous tissue is often as large as half a walnut. It remains in the sac not only during its larval, but its pupal stage, which do not differ much in appearance, and falls out on the ground before complete development. In small numbers, the warble seems to do little injury to the general health of the animal, but cases have been known where animals have actually died of the inflammation produced. Some idea of the extent of the plague may be realised from the statement that an Indian kip in the possession of the writer has not less than 680 warble holes, and that almost equal numbers have been counted in English hides. Preventive measures are the sheltering of the cattle during the summer months when the fly is most prevalent; the application of mixtures of oil or grease with tar-oil and sulphur to the hair, to prevent egg-laying; and the destruction of the *larva* in its early stages, in autumn and winter by smearing the breathing aperture with grease, or better, with mercurial ointment. When this is done sufficiently early, the hole heals up without permanent injury, but when it is allowed to remain open during the period of growth, its sides become partially coated by the growth of epidermis, and this permanently prevents their proper union by skin-tissue. It is believed that if the *larvæ* were systematically destroyed in a district, they would soon become extinct, as they are not supposed to travel far.

'Some Observations on the Œstridæ,' E. A. Ormerod, Simpkin and Marshall, London, 1884, price 4*d*.

A very troublesome injury to the skins of lambs and sheep is the disease known as "cockle," in which the skin becomes thickly dotted with spots of thickened tissue, which bear some fanciful resemblance in form to a cockleshell. The affection is prevalent during the spring while the wool is thick, and disappears almost immediately on shearing, but little is known of its causes or mode of prevention.

Climate and breed have a considerable effect on the quality of hides and skins. As a rule the less highly bred races, and those which are most exposed to the extremes of weather, have the thickest hides, and in most cases highly bred animals have had their meat-producing, or in the case of sheep, their wool-bearing qualities developed at the expense of the characteristics most valued by the tanner.

CHAPTER VII.
STRUCTURE AND GROWTH OF SKIN.

Although, at first sight, the skins of different animals appear to have little in common, a closer examination shows that all the Mammalia possess skins which have the same general structure, and thus an anatomical description of the skin of an ox applies almost equally to that of a sheep, goat, or calf, though on account of the difference in texture and thickness the practical uses of these various materials may differ widely. The skins of lizards, alligators, fishes and serpents differ from those of the higher animals, chiefly in having considerable modifications in the epidermis, so that it becomes harder and forms "scales," and the arrangement of the fibres presents considerable difference. In many fish-skins for instance, the fibres are in successive layers, at right angles to each other and diagonal to the skin, but not interlaced.

In its natural condition, the skin is not merely a covering for the animal, but at the same time an organ of sense and of secretion, and hence its structure is somewhat complicated. It consists of two principal layers, the *epidermis* (*epithelium*, cuticle) and the *corium* (*derma*, *cutis* or true skin). These are totally distinct, not only in structure and functions, but in their origin. In the egg of a bird and the *ovum* of a higher animal, the living germ consists of a single cell, which, as soon as fertilised, begins to multiply by repeated division. The mass of cells thus formed early differentiates into three distinct layers, from the upper of which the epithelium arises, while the true skin, together with the bones and cartilages, is derived from the middle one.

This distinction of origin corresponds with a wide difference of both anatomical and chemical characteristics. A diagrammatic section of calf-skin is shown in Fig. 9, and a more correct representation of its actual appearance is given in Plate I. (Frontispiece). The *epidermis* is very thin as compared with the true skin which it covers, and is entirely removed preparatory to tanning; it nevertheless possesses important functions. It is shown in Fig. 10 at *a* and *b*, more highly magnified. Its inner mucous layer *b*, the *rete malpighi*, which rests upon the true skin *c*, is soft, and composed of living nucleated cells, which multiply by division and form cell-walls of keratin. These are elongated in the deeper layers, and gradually become flattened as they approach the surface, where they dry up, and form the horny layer *a*. This last is being constantly worn away, thrown off as dead scales of skin, and as constantly renewed from below, by the multiplication of the cells. It is from the epithelial layer that the hair, as well as the sweat and fat-glands, are developed.

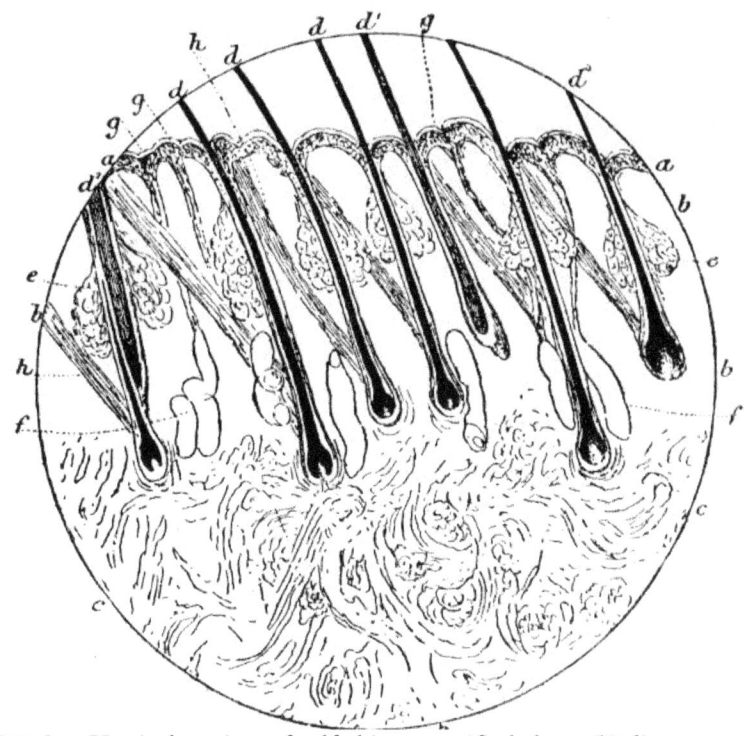

FIG. 9.—Vertical section of calf-skin, magnified about 50 diameters. *a*, epidermis; *b*, grain or papillary layer; *c*, fibrous layer of skin; *d*, hairs; *e*, fat-glands; *f*, sweat-glands; *g*, opening of ducts of sweat-glands; *h*, hair-muscles.

Each hair is surrounded by a sheath which is continuous with the epidermis, and into which the young hair usually grows as the old one falls out. The hair itself is covered with a layer of overlapping scales, like the slates on a roof, but of irregular form. These give it a serrated outline at the sides, and when strongly developed as in wool and some furs, confer the property of felting. Within these scales, which are called the "hair cuticle," is a fibrous substance which forms the body of the hair; and sometimes but not always, there is also a central and cellular pith, which under the microscope frequently appears black and opaque, from the optical effect of imprisoned air. On boiling or long soaking in water, alcohol, or turpentine, the air-spaces become saturated with the liquid, and then appear transparent.

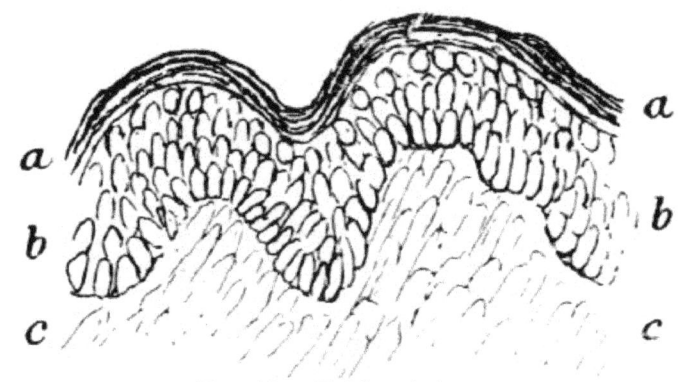

FIG. 10.—Epidermis layer.

The fibrous part of the hair is made up of long spindle-shaped cells, and contains the pigment which gives the hair its colour. The hair of the deer differs from that of most other animals in being almost wholly formed of polygonal cells, which, in white hairs, are usually filled with air. In dark hairs, both the hair and sheath are strongly pigmented, but the hair is much the most so, and hence the bulb has usually a distinct dark form. The dark-haired portions of a hide from which the hair has been removed by liming still remain coloured by the pigmented cells of the hair-sheaths, which can only be completely removed by "bating and scudding."

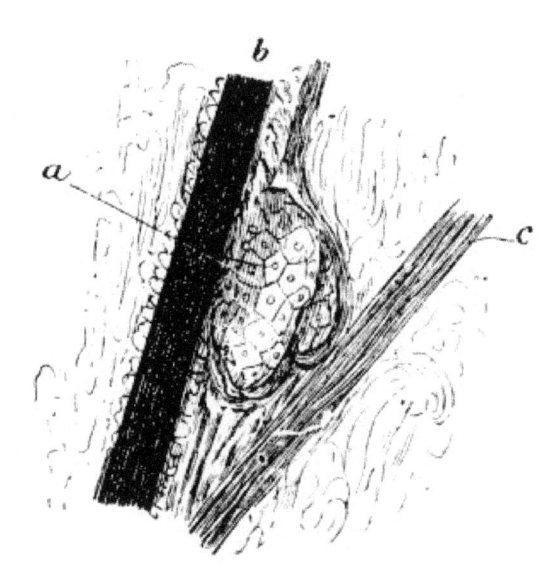

FIG. 11.—*a*, sebaceous gland; *b*, hair; *c*, erector muscle. Mag. 200.

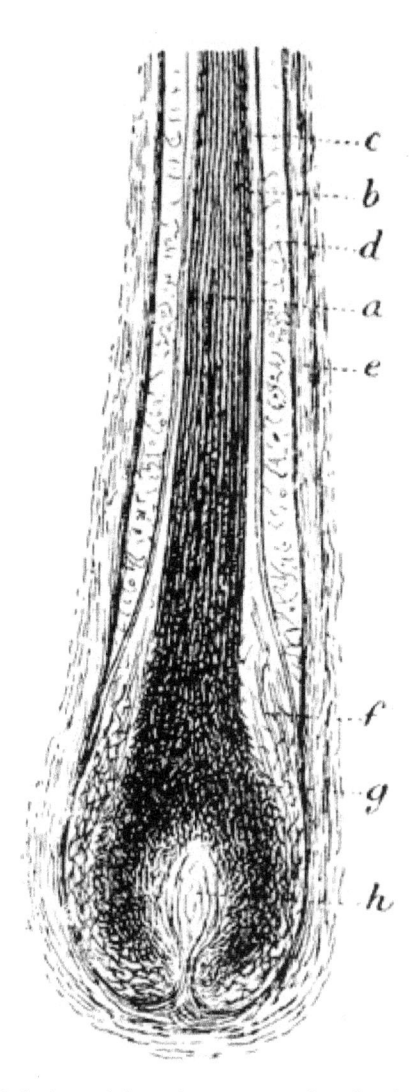

FIG. 12.—*a*, hair; *b*, hair cuticle; *c*, inner root-sheath; *d*, outer root-sheath; *e*, dermic coat of hair-sheath; *f*, origin of inner sheath; *g*, bulb; *h*, hair-papilla.

Near the opening of the hair-sheath to the surface of the skin the ducts of the sebaceous or fat-glands pass into the sheath and secrete a sort of oil to lubricate the hair. The glands themselves are formed of large nucleated cells arranged somewhat like a bunch of grapes; the upper and more central ones being highly charged with fatty matter. Their appearance is shown in Fig. 11. The base of the hair is a bulb, enclosing the hair papilla *h* (Fig. 12), which is a projecting knob of the true skin and which by means of the blood-vessels contained in it supplies nourishment to the hair. The hair-bulb is composed of round soft cells, which multiply rapidly, and pressing upwards through the hair-sheath, become hardened, thus increasing the length of the hair.

The cells outside the bulb, shown at *f* in Fig. 12, pass upwards as they grow, and form a coating around the hair, known as the "inner root-sheath."

In embryonic development, a small knob of cells forms on the under side of the *epidermis*, over a knot of capillary blood-vessels in the *corium*, and enlarges and sinks deeper into the latter, while the root-bulb of the young hair is formed within it, surrounding the capillaries from which it derives nourishment, and which form the hair-papilla, Fig. 13. In the renewal of hair in the adult animal the process is very similar. The bulb of the old hair withers, and the hair falls out, and in the meantime a thickening takes place in the epidermal coating of the bottom of the sheath, and the young hair is formed below, and usually to one side of the old one, growing into the sheath, and taking the place of the old hair. This is one cause of the difficulty of removing ground-hairs in the process of unhairing, since they are not only short, but deeper seated than the old ones.

The process of development of the sudoriferous or sweat-glands is very similar to that of the hairs. They consist of more or less convoluted tubes with walls formed of longitudinal fibres of connective tissue of the *corium*, lined with a single layer of large nucleated cells, which secrete the perspiration. The ducts, which are exceedingly narrow, and with walls of nucleated cells like those of the outer hair-sheaths, sometimes open directly through the epidermis, but more frequently into the orifice of a hair-sheath, just at the surface of the skin. Each hair is provided with a slanting muscle called the *arrector* or *erector pili* (see Fig. 11), which is contracted by cold or fear, and causes the hair to "bristle," or stand on end; by forcing up the attached skin, it produces the effect known as "goose-skin." The muscle, which is of the unstriped or involuntary kind, passes from near the hair-bulb to the epidermis, and just under the sebaceous glands, which it compresses when it contracts.

Beside the hair, and hair-sheaths, and the sebaceous and sudoriferous glands, the *epidermis* layer produces other structures of a horny character, including horns, hoofs, claws and finger-nails; which both chemically and anatomically are analogous to exaggerated hairs, such as the quills of the porcupine.

The whole of the epidermis, together with the hairs, is separated from the *corium* by an exceedingly fine membrane, called the hyaline or glassy layer. This forms the very thin buff-coloured "grain-" surface of tanned leather, which is evidently of different structure from the rest of the *corium*, since, if it gets scraped off before tanning, the exposed portion of the underlying skin remains nearly white, instead of colouring. The whole of the hair-sheath is enclosed in a coating of elastic and connective-tissue fibres, which are supplied with nerves and blood-vessels, and form part of the *corium*.

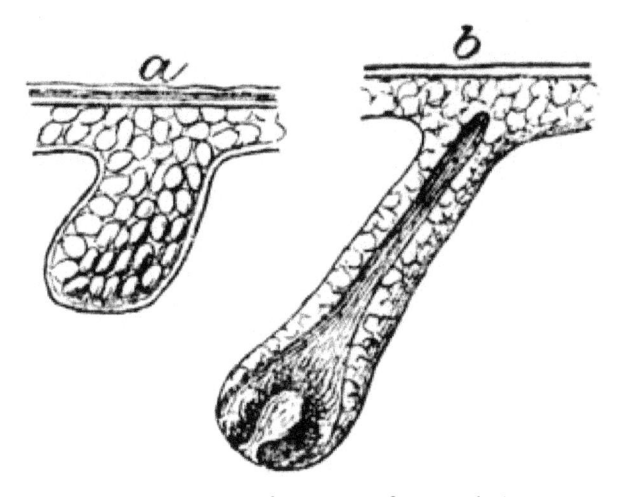

FIG. 13.—Development of young hair.

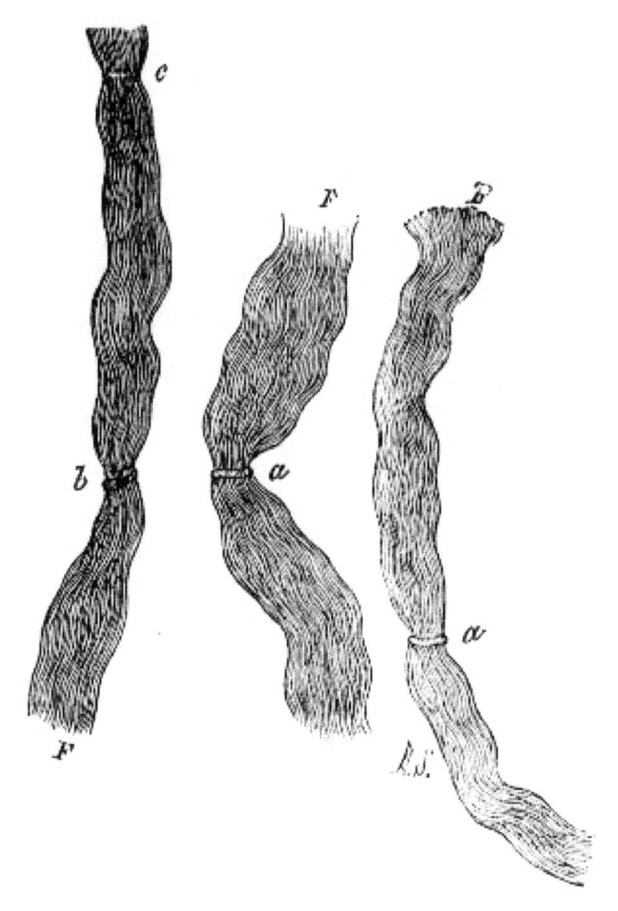

FIG. 14.—Connective-tissue fibres. (Ranvier.)

The structure of the corium or true skin is quite different from that of the epidermis which has just been described, as it is principally composed of interlacing bundles of white fibres, of the kind known as "connective tissue" (see Fig. 14); these are composed of fibrils of extreme fineness, cemented together by a substance somewhat more soluble than the fibres themselves. The fibres are not themselves living cells, but are apparently produced by narrow spindle-shaped cells lying against them. The felted fibre-bundles are more loosely interwoven in the middle portion of the skin, but become compacter again near the flesh. In the case of sheep-skins this is especially marked, the middle part being full of fat-cells and very loose. Any ill treatment of the pelt during the wet-work is liable to still further loosen this middle layer so that grain and flesh may sometimes be torn apart. The flesh-splits of sheep-skins must have this loose fatty layer frized off before chamoising, and American "waxed fleshes" from ox-hides are levelled by splitting away this portion, and finished on the flesh. The outermost layer, just beneath the epidermis, is exceedingly close and compact, the fibre-bundles that run into it being separated into their elementary fibrils, which are so interlaced that they can scarcely be recognised. This is the *pars papillaris*, and forms the lighter-coloured layer, called (together with its very fine outer coating) the "grain" of leather. It is in this part that the fat-glands are embedded, while the hair-roots and sweat-glands pass through it into the looser tissue beneath. It receives its name from the small projections or *papillæ*, with which its outer surface is studded, and which form the characteristic grain of the various kinds of skin. (See Fig. 9 and Plate I.)

It will be noted that the word "grain" is used by the tanner in at least three different senses, which are productive of much confusion. The extremely thin hyaline layer forms a natural glaze to the skin, and might well be spoken of as such; the form and arrangement of the *papillæ* and hair-pores might be called the "pattern" of the grain, leaving the use of the word "grain" itself restricted to the *pars papillaris*.

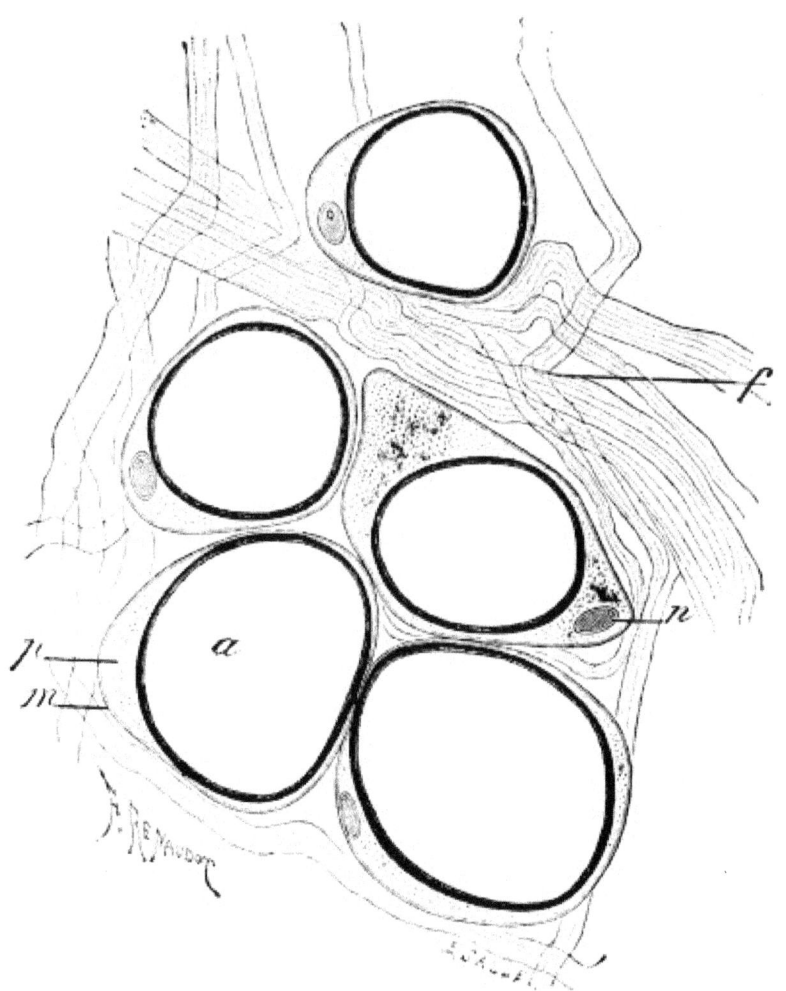

FIG. 15.—Fat-cells in connective tissue. *a*, fat-globule; *p*, protoplasm; *n*, nucleus; *m*, cell-wall. (Ranvier.)

The study of the structure of the grain, and especially of the arrangement of the hair-pores is very important, as it is usually the readiest means of identifying the kind of skin of which a leather is made, which in finished skins with artificially printed grain is often very difficult. (Plate II.) The examination is facilitated by wetting and stretching the skin, and by the use of a good lens, or a low power of the microscope.

Under the microscope, the skin is of course lighted from above by direct light from a window, or by that of a lamp concentrated by a "bullseye" condenser. The reversal of the image in the microscope often causes a pseudoscopic effect very puzzling to the beginner, prominences appearing as hollows, and *vice versa* till the real direction of the lighting is considered.

PLATE II.

PHOTO-MICROGRAPHS OF GRAIN OF VARIOUS SKINS (*A. Seymour-Jones*).

1. Cow-hide; 2. Calf-skin; 3. East India Goat; 4. Pig-skin; 5. East India Sheep; 6. Welsh Sheep.

[*Face p.* 52.

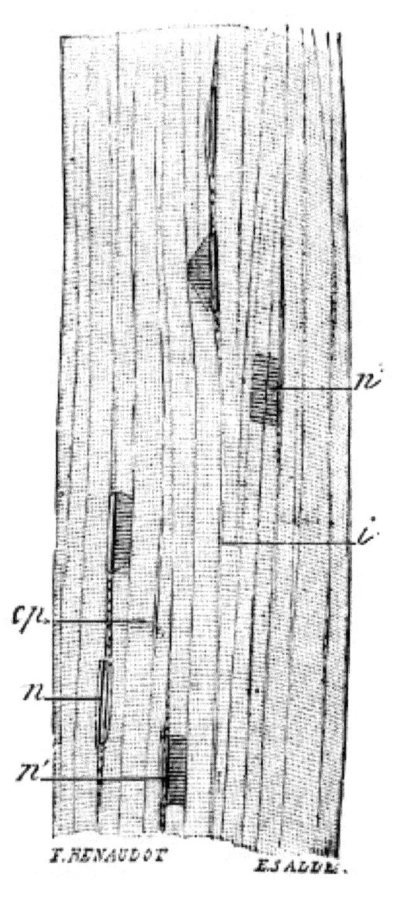

FIG. 16.—Striped, or voluntary muscular fibre. (Ranvier.)

As stated above, the surface of skin which is next to the flesh is firmer than that in the centre, and as the fibres run nearly parallel with the surface it has a more or less membranous character. The skin is united to the body of the animal by a network of connective tissue (*panniculus adiposus*), which is frequently full of fat-cells and is then called adipose tissue. This constitutes the whitish layer which is removed, together with portions of actual flesh, in the operation of "fleshing." If a minute portion of adipose tissue be examined microscopically, it will appear to consist of a mere mass of fat-globules entangled in connective tissue. If, however, it be stained with carmine or logwood it may be at once observed that each globule is contained in a cell, of which the nucleated protoplasm, by which the fat was secreted, is pressed closely against the wall (Fig. 15). Similar cells are contained in considerable quantities throughout the hide, and especially in the loose tissue of the central part; hence in leather manufacture it is impossible to expel or wash out the fat until the cells have been broken down by "liming" or in some other way.

Many animals (ox, horse, etc.) possess a thin layer of voluntary muscle (red flesh) spread over the inner side of the skin, and used for twitching to drive off flies. In rough fleshing this is sometimes left on and may be a cause of dark flesh in sole leather. Even in the finished leather its striped structure may be detected microscopically (Fig. 16).

Besides the connective-tissue fibres, the skin contains a small proportion of fine yellow "elastic" fibres. If a thin section of hide be soaked for a few minutes in a mixture of equal parts of water, glycerine, and strong acetic acid, and then examined under the microscope, the white connective-tissue fibres become swollen and transparent, and the yellow "elastic" fibres may be seen, as they are scarcely affected by the acid. The hair-bulbs and sweat- and fat-glands are also rendered distinctly visible by this treatment. On the other hand, the white gelatinous fibres are most easily seen by examining the section in a strong solution of common salt, or in one of ammonium sulphate; or by staining with some aniline dyes such as safranine. Sections are most readily cut for these purposes by the use of the freezing microtome, or after previous hardening in alcohol. For further details see L.I.L.B., p. 254.

Ordinarily in the production of leather only the corium, or true skin is used, and in order to obtain it in a suitable condition for the various tanning processes, the hair or wool, together with the epithelium, must be completely removed without damaging the skin itself; and especial care must be taken that the grain, or portion next to the epidermis, does not suffer any injury during the treatment. All the methods employed depend upon the fact that the epidermis cells, especially the soft growing ones next to the corium, and those of the epidermis layer which surround the hair-roots, are more easily destroyed than the corium itself owing to their different chemical character. The "unhairing" process consists essentially in breaking down these cells by chemical or putrefactive agents, and removing the hair together with the rest of the epidermis by mechanical means. Of the various substances which may be used for this purpose, lime is one of the most convenient, as its solubility in water is so slight, that a solution of such a strength as to injure the hide cannot be easily made. Caustic alkalies, on the other hand, are much more soluble, and unless care be taken to use only the proper quantity, a dangerously strong solution may be made with consequent damage to the skin. The addition of small amounts of sulphides to the lime-solution accelerates the unhairing owing to their special solvent action on the epidermis-structures, and also in the case of alkaline sulphides, by the caustic alkali which is produced by their reaction with the lime. Even if used alone, strong solutions of alkaline sulphides rapidly destroy both hair and epidermis, converting them into a mass which may be swept off the skin like wet pulp, and yet they have practically no injurious action on the true skin.

In the "sweating" process the epidermic cells are broken down by putrefactive organisms and their products, so that the hair becomes loose and may then be either rubbed or scraped off. Ammonia, which is produced during the putrefaction, has also an important solvent action, and its presence doubtless tends to quicken the processes both of unhairing and of destruction.

To obtain useful knowledge of the structure of any particular skin, it is not necessary to have a very elaborate or expensive microscope, and it is quite possible to obtain useful information merely by the use of a good pocket lens, as for instance, in the examination of various forms of "grain," and the embossing of one skin to imitate another.

For further details of the manipulation and selection of the microscope, the reader must consult L.I.L.B., pp. 234 *et seq*.

CHAPTER VIII.
THE CHEMICAL CONSTITUENTS OF SKIN.

The chemistry of the various constituents of skin is still very imperfectly understood, but Beilstein, in his great handbook of organic chemistry, places gelatin, albumens and keratins in the "aromatic" series, and implies therefore that they contain the "benzene" ring. It is at least certain that all are very complex.

The epidermis structures belong to the class of keratins, which are closely related to coagulated albumin; while the white fibres of the corium (or true skin) are either identical with gelatin, or only differ from it in their molecular condition or degree of hydration. This gelatinous tissue constitutes the bulk of the corium, but it also contains albumen as a constituent of the lymph and blood which supply its nourishment, keratins in the epithelial structures of the blood and lymph vessels, and "yellow fibres," which are perhaps allied to the keratins, but which cannot well be isolated for analysis.

The white connective tissue of the corium is converted into gelatin (glutin) by boiling with water. Owing to the impossibility of obtaining unaltered hide-fibre free from the other constituents, and still more to that of deciding to what point it should be dried to remove uncombined water, it is impossible to prove by analysis whether its composition is identical with that of glutin; but as the white fibre constitutes by far the largest part of the corium, and the other constituents do not differ largely from it in their percentage composition, an analysis of carefully purified corium is practically identical with that of the actual fibre. The following analyses of hide and gelatin are therefore of interest.

The analyses of Von Schroeder and Paessler are of special importance as being the average of a large number of separate determinations. Their nitrogen determinations are by Kjeldahl's method. Small amounts of ash and traces of sulphur are neglected, and probably included in the O, which is obtained by difference.

Ding. Polyt. Journ., 1893, cclxxxvii. pp. 258, 283, 300.

ANALYSES OF PURIFIED CORIUM.

Analyst.	Material.	C	H	N	O	S
Stohmann and Langbein	..	49·9	5·8	18·0	26·0	0·3

Analyst	Source	C	H	N	O	
Müntz	Ox-hide	51·8	6·7	18·3	23·2	..
Von Schroeder and Paessler	Ox, calf, horse, camel, pig, rhinoceros	50·2	6·4	17·8	25·4	..
,,	Goat and deer	50·3	6·4	17·4	25·9	..
,,	Sheep and dog	50·2	6·5	17·0	26·3	..
,,	Cat	51·1	6·5	17·1	25·3	..

ANALYSES OF GELATIN (free from Ash).

Analyst.	C	H	N	O
Von Schroeder and Paessler	51·2	6·5	18·1	24·2
Mulder	50·1	6·6	18·3	25·0
Fremy	50·0	6·5	17·5	26·0
Schützenberger	50·0	6·7	18·3	25·0
Chittenden and Solly	49·4	6·8	18·0	25·1

Contained also 0·7 sulphur. Journ. Physiol., xii. p. 23.

It will be noted that the above analyses of skin differ more widely among themselves than their average does from that of the gelatin analyses, though on the whole the nitrogen is somewhat higher in the latter. The molecular weight of gelatin must be very high, and any empirical formula founded on ultimate analysis therefore quite hypothetical. Bleunard, Schützenberger and Bourgois, and Hofmeister agree on the formula $C_{76}H_{124}N_{24}O_{29}$, which leads to the following percentage composition:—

per cent.

C_{76} = 912 = 49·7

H_{124} = 124 = 6·8

N_{24} = 336 = 18·3

O_{29} = 464 = 25·2

1836   100·0

Paal (Berichte D. Ch. Ges., xxv. (1892) pp. 1202-36, and Ch. Soc. Abst., 1892, pp. 895-7) calculates a molecular weight of about 900 from physical (freezing, boiling point) methods.

Annales de Chimie xxvi. p. 18.

Compt. Rend., lxxxii. pp. 262-4.

The addition of a molecule of water would make a difference in the percentage composition indicated by these formulæ which would be less than their probable experimental error, and the change may therefore be one of hydration.

Gelatin certainly contains both carboxyl and amido-groups, and is capable of combining with both acids and alkalies (see p. 84).

Reimer obtained what he supposed to be pure unaltered fibre-substance by digestion of purified hide with ½ per cent. acetic acid for many days and subsequent neutralisation. His analysis showed C = 48·45 per cent., H = 6·66 per cent., N = 18·45 per cent., O = 26·44 per cent., thus deviating considerably from direct analysis of unaltered skin. It is obvious that little weight can be placed on this result, Reimer's precipitate being probably a mere decomposition product.

Ding. Polyt., ccv. p. 164.

Hofmeister notes that on heating gelatin it loses water and forms an anhydride which he considers identical with collagen or hide-fibre. When gelatin is dried at a temperature of 130° C. it becomes incapable of solution in water, even at boiling temperature, and can only be dissolved by heating under pressure. It is certain that collagen (hide-fibre, ossein) is less easily soluble in hot water than ordinary gelatin.

Bied. Centr., 1880, p. 772.

So far as our present knowledge goes, we may regard hide-fibre as merely an organised and perhaps dehydrated gelatin.

Gelatin or *glutin* (not to be confounded with the gluten of cereals), when pure and dry is a colourless, transparent solid of horny toughness and of sp. gr. 1·3. It begins to melt about 140° C., at the same time undergoing decomposition. It is insoluble in hydrocarbons, in ether, or in strong alcohol. In cold water it swells to a transparent jelly, absorbing several times its weight of water, but does not dissolve. In hot water it is soluble, but a solution containing even 1 per cent. of good gelatin sets to a weak jelly on cooling. Gelatin jellies melt at temperatures which vary considerably with the quality or freedom from degradation products, but which within pretty wide limits (5-10 per cent.) are little affected by the concentration. A 10 per cent. solution of best hard gelatin melts about 38° C., while low glue may fail to set at 15° C. A useful technical test for the setting power of gelatin, based on this fact, consists in placing an angular fragment of the jelly in a small tube attached to a thermometer, and stirring in a beaker of water, which is slowly heated till the jelly melts, when the temperature is noted. The exact point is perhaps more easily seen if the tube is drawn to a conical point. The jelly may also be allowed to set in capillary tubes open at the bottom, and the moment noted when water rises into the tube. The temperature of fusion is raised by the addition of formaldehyde, salts of chromium, alumina and ferric salts, which produce a tanning effect, and in a less degree by sulphates, tartrates, acetates, some other salts, and diminished by iodides, bromides, chlorides and nitrates. Solutions of gelatin too weak or too warm to gelatinise possess considerable viscosity. Gelatin may therefore be estimated, in the absence of other viscous matters, by the viscosimeter, an instrument which measures the time taken by a liquid in flowing through a capillary tube. The firmness of a jelly, which is often important for commercial purposes, is frequently measured by Lipowitz's method, in which a slightly convex disc, conveniently of exactly 1 cm. diameter, and cemented to the bottom of a thistle-head funnel tube, is loaded gradually with mercury till it sinks in the jelly. The jelly (5 or 10 per cent.) should be allowed to set some hours before the test is made.

See Pascheles, 'Versuche über Quellung,' Archiv für ges. Path., Bd. 71.

See Prollius, Ding. Polyt. Journ., ccxlix. p. 425, who employs a 1 per cent. solution; also Stützer, Zeit. Ann. Ch., xxxi. pp. 501-15.

Solutions of gelatin from skin and bone are powerfully lævorotatory to polarised light. At 30° C. $(A)_D = -130°$, but temperature and the reaction of the solution have much influence on the value found.

Gelatin is precipitated from aqueous solution by the addition of strong alcohol and concentrated solutions of ammonium sulphate and some other salts. Many other colloid bodies such as dextrin and gums behave similarly. In the absence of these substances, precipitation by alcohol may be utilised for the technical analysis of gelatins and glues, printers' roller compositions and gelatin confectionery. 25 c.c. of the gelatinous solution, which is preferably of about 10 per cent., is placed in a small beaker tared together with a glass stirring rod, and thrice its volume of absolute alcohol added. On stirring, the gelatin sets firmly on the rod and sides of the beaker, and may be washed with dilute alcohol or even with cold water, dried and weighed. A very pure French gelatin gave 98·6 per cent., while a common bone-glue only yielded about 60 per cent. precipitate. Absolute alcohol withdraws water from gelatin-jelly, leaving a horny mass. Gelatin may also be precipitated completely by saturating its solution with sodium chloride, and then acidifying slightly with sulphuric or hydrochloric acid; and masses of jelly become hardened in acidified salt solution as in alcohol, though a neutral solution has little effect. The cause of this is difficult of explanation, but its bearing on the pickling of sheep-skins (p. 89) and the production of white leather (p. 186) is obvious.

Decompositions.—When aqueous solutions of gelatin are heated under pressure, or in presence of glycerin and other bodies which raise the boiling-point, or more slowly at lower temperatures, they gradually lose the power of gelatinising on cooling, the gelatin being converted into modifications soluble in cold water, but still capable of being precipitated by tannin. Hofmeister states that the gelatin takes up 3 molecules water and is split up into *hemicollin*, soluble in alcohol and not precipitated by platinic chloride solution; and *semiglutin*, insoluble in alcohol and precipitated by platinic chloride solution. Both are precipitated by mercuric chloride. Dry gelatin is soluble in glycerin at high temperatures, but probably suffers a similar change. Hence high temperatures and long-continued heating must be avoided in gelatin manufacture; and in making printers' roller compositions, which are mixtures of gelatin and glycerin, the gelatin must be swollen with water and melted at a low temperature with the glycerin.

Bied. Centr., 1880, p. 772, and Ch. Soc. Abs., 1881, p. 294.

Gelatin is also converted into soluble forms (peptones), perhaps identical with the above, by the action of heat in presence of dilute acids and alkalies. These, like gelatin, are precipitated by tannin and by metaphosphoric acid. Heated for longer periods or to higher temperatures with aqueous solutions of the caustic alkalies, baryta, or lime, gelatin is gradually broken down into simpler and simpler products, ending in nitrogen or ammonia, water and carbonic acid. Among the intermediate products may be mentioned various acids of the amido-acetic series, as amido-acetic (glycocine, glycocoll), amido-propionic (alanine), and amido-caproic (leucine); and of the amido-succinic series (amido-succinic = aspartic acid).

Lorenz, Pflüger's Arch., xlvii. pp. 189-95; Journ. Chem. Soc., 1891, A. p. 477.

Compare Schützenberger, Comptes Rend., cii. pp. 1296-9; Journ. Chem. Soc., 1886, A. p. 818.

Treatment with acids produces very similar effects. The first products are soluble peptones. Paal on treating 100 parts of gelatin on the water-bath with 160 parts water and 40 parts concentrated HCl till the product was soluble in absolute alcohol, obtained, on purification, a white hygroscopic mass of peptone salts containing 10-12 per cent. of hydrochloric acid.

Berichte, xxv. pp. 1202-36; Journ. Chem. Soc., 1892, A. p. 895.

See also Buchner and Curtius, Ber., xix. pp. 850-9; Journ. Chem. Soc., 1886, A. p. 635.

The products of digestion of gelatin with gastric and pancreatic juice are peptones which do not differ materially from gelatin in ultimate composition, and the action is probably mainly hydrolytic.

Chittenden and Solly, Journ. Chem. Soc., 1891, A. p. 849.

The earlier products of putrefaction are very similar. Many bacteria have the power of liquefying gelatin-jelly. This has been shown by Brunton and McFadyen to be due not to the direct action of the bacteria, but to a soluble zymase secreted by them which peptonises the gelatin. Its action is favoured by an alkaline condition, and destroyed by a temperature of 100° C. As putrefaction progresses, the solution becomes very acid from the formation of butyric acid, and later on ammonia and amido-acids are formed.

R. S. Proc., xlvi. pp. 542-53.

Compare pp. 17, 171; also Ch. Zeit., 1895, p. 1487.

Fahrion, starting with the idea that albuminoids and gelatin were condensation products of a lactone character (L.I.L.B. p. 185), and that they might, like lactones, be depolymerised by saponification, digested these bodies with alcoholic soda till they were dissolved, and on neutralising the solution with hydrochloric acid, of which the excess was driven off by repeated evaporation, and removing the sodium chloride by treatment with alcohol, obtained in each case bodies of acid reaction, which from their composition he supposed to be identical with Schützenberger's proteic acid, $C_8H_{14}N_2O_4$, which is soluble in water and alcohol, insoluble in ether and petroleum, uncrystallisable, and forming uncrystallisable salts. Fahrion suggested that the nitrogenous character which Eitner attributed to his "dégras-former" (p. 370) was probably due to contamination by this body; and that its formation might be utilised in the analysis of leather and other proteid bodies. These products have since been further investigated by Prof. Paal and Dr. Schilling, who show that they contain hydrochloric acid, to which their acid reaction is due, and that they are identical with the peptone salts previously obtained by Prof. Paal (v. s.) by digestion of proteids with hydrochloric acid. The free peptones are strongly basic.

Ch. Zeit., 1895, p. 1000.

Ch. Zeit., 1895, p. 1487.

By dry distillation of gelatin a mixture of pyrrol and pyridin bases are produced. This is commercially obtained by the distillation of bones, and is known as "bone oil," or "Dippel's animal oil." Pyrrol, C_4H_5N, resembles phloroglucol in giving a purple-red colour to fir wood moistened with hydrochloric acid (p. 299).

Reactions of Gelatin.—Gelatin is precipitated by mercuric chloride, in this respect resembling peptones, but not by potassium ferrocyanide, by which it is distinguished from albuminoids, and it differs from albumin in not being coagulated by heat. Solution of gelatin dissolves considerable quantities of calcium phosphate; hence this is always present in bone-glues. Gelatin and some of its decomposition products are precipitated by metaphosphoric acid. The precipitate contains about 7 per cent. P_2O_5, but gradually loses it on washing. Various salts diminish the solubility of gelatin in hot water, and especially those of the alum type. Chrome alum and basic chrome salts are especially powerful, rendering it practically insoluble. The addition of about 3 per cent. ammonium or potassium dichromate causes glue or gelatin to become insoluble by the action of light with the formation of basic salts of chromium, and has been utilised in photography and as a waterproof cement. Other colloids besides gelatin are similarly affected.

Lorenz, Pflüger's Archiv, xlvii. pp. 189-195.

Gelatin is precipitated by all tannins, even from very dilute solutions; one containing only 0·2 grm. per liter is rendered distinctly turbid by gallotannic acid or infusion of gall-nuts; but some other tannins give a less sensitive reaction. The precipitate is soluble to a considerable extent in excess of gelatin, so that in using the latter as a test for traces of tannin care must be taken to add a very small quantity only. The addition of a little alum renders the reaction more delicate. Whether the precipitate is a definite chemical compound has been disputed, as its composition varies according to whether gelatin or tannin is in excess. Böttinger states that the precipitate produced by adding gelatin to excess of gallotannic acid contains 10·7 per cent. of nitrogen, indicating the presence of 66 per cent. of gelatin on the assumption that gelatin contains 16·5 per cent. N (see p. 57). Digested with water at 130° C., the precipitate is decomposed, yielding a solution which precipitates tannin, and probably indicating the formation of a more acid compound. Gelatin with excess of oak-bark tannin gives a precipitate containing 9·5 per cent. of nitrogen, corresponding to 57·5 per cent. of gelatin. Treated with water at 150° C., this precipitate yielded three products: one soluble in cold water, another in hot only and one insoluble. On addition of a solution of formaldehyde (formalin) to one of gelatin no visible action takes place in the cold, unless the solution of gelatin be very concentrated and alkaline, but on heating, the gelatin is rendered insoluble owing to the formation of a compound with the formaldehyde. From the very small amount of formalin which is required to produce formo-gelatin it is very doubtful if this is a definite compound.

Liebig's Ann. der Ch., ccxliv. pp. 227-32.

Weiske states that bone-gelatin, carefully freed from all mineral matter, is not precipitated by tannin till a trace of a salt (e. g. sodium chloride) is added. So far as is known, bone-gelatin is identical with that of skin.

Bied. Centr., 1883, p. 673.

Chondrin is the gelatinous body produced by the digestion of cartilage with water at 120° C. for three hours. In most of its physical properties it is identical with gelatin, but differs from the latter in being precipitated from its solution in water by acetic acid, lead acetate, alum, and the mineral acids when the latter are not present in excess. Chondrin also differs from gelatin in producing a substance capable of easily reducing cupric oxide when it is boiled for some time with dilute mineral acids. It is extremely probable that chondrin is merely an impure gelatine.

Cp. Petri, Berichte, xii. p. 267; Mörner, Skand. Archiv f. Physiol., i. pp. 210-243; and Journ. Chem. Soc., 1889, A. p. 736 and Zeit. Physiol. Chem., 1895, xx. pp. 357-364; and Journ. Chem. Soc., 1895, A. i. p. 254. See also Richter, Org. Chem., i. p. 559.

Coriin.—Rollet has shown that when hide and other forms of connective tissue are soaked in lime- or baryta-water, the fibres become split up into finer fibrils, and as the action proceeds, these again separate into still finer ones, till the ultimate fibrils are so fine as to be only distinguished under a powerful microscope. At the same time, the alkaline solution dissolves the substance which cemented the fibres together, and this may be recovered by neutralising the solution with acetic acid, when the substance is thrown down as a flocculent precipitate. This was considered by Rollet to be an albuminoid substance; but Reimer has shown that it is much more closely allied to the gelatinous fibres, and, indeed, is probably produced from them by the action of the alkaline solution. Reimer used limed calf-skin for his experiments, and subjected it to prolonged cleansing with distilled water, so that all soluble parts must have been pretty thoroughly removed beforehand. He then digested it in closed glasses with lime-water for 7-8 days, and precipitated the clear solution with dilute acetic acid. He found that the same portion of hide might be used again and again, without becoming exhausted, which strongly supports the supposition that the substance is merely a product of a partial decomposition of the hide-fibre, and indeed that there is no distinct "cementing substance," but merely a difference in the hydration or physical condition of the fibre substance which causes it to split more readily in certain directions. The dissolved substance, which he called "coriin," was purified by repeated solution in lime-water and reprecipitation by acetic acid. It was readily soluble in alkaline solutions but not in dilute acids, though in some cases it became so swollen and finely divided as to appear almost as if dissolved. It was, however, very soluble in common salt solution of about 10 per cent., from which it was precipitated both by the addition of much water and by saturating the solution with salt. Reimer found that a 10 per cent. salt solution was equally effective with lime-water in extracting coriin from the hide, and that it was partially precipitated on the addition of acid, and completely so on saturating the acidified solution with salt. Other salts of the alkalies and alkaline earths acted in a similar manner, so that Reimer was at first deceived when experimenting with baryta-water, because, being more concentrated than lime-water, the coriin remained dissolved in the barium salt formed on neutralising with acid, and it was necessary to dilute before a precipitate could be obtained. The slightly acid solution of coriin gave no precipitate either in the cold or on boiling with potassium ferrocyanide, being thus distinguished from albuminoids. The neutral or alkaline solution showed no precipitate with iron or mercuric chloride, copper sulphate, or with neutral lead acetate; but with basic lead acetate, basic iron sulphate, or an excess of tannin a precipitate was produced. Reimer's analysis showed: Carbon, 45·91; hydrogen, 6·57; nitrogen, 17·82; oxygen, 29·60; and he gives a formula showing its relation to the original fibre, which does not seem supported by sufficient evidence. In all probability coriin is merely an impure degradation-product of hide-fibre or gelatin.

Sitz. Wiener Akad., xxxix. p. 305.

Ding. Polyt. Journ., ccv. p. 153.

Hide Albumin.—The fresh hide contains a portion of actual albumin, viz. that of the blood-serum and of the lymph, which is not only contained in the abundant blood-vessels, but saturates the fibrous connective tissue, of which it forms the nourishment. This albumin is mostly removed from the skin by the liming and working on the beam, which is preparatory to tanning. Probably for sole-leather, the albumin itself would be rather advantageous if left in the hide, as it combines with tannin, and would assist in giving firmness and weight to the leather. It is, however, for reasons which will be seen hereafter, absolutely necessary to get rid of any lime which may be in combination with it. The blood must also be thoroughly cleansed from the hide before tanning, as its colouring matter contains iron, which, by combination with the tannin, produces a bad colour.

The albumins form a class of closely allied bodies of which white of egg may be taken as a type. They are also related to the casein of milk, to fibrin, and more distantly to gelatin. A good deal of information on the class may be found in Watt's Dict. of Chem., 2nd ed., article 'Proteids,' and Beilstein's article 'Albuminaten,' and in Allen's 'Commercial Organic Analysis,' vol. iv.

The most characteristic property of albumins is that of coagulation by heat. The temperature at which this takes place differs somewhat in different members of the group, egg and serum albumin coagulating at 72-73° C. Dry albumins become insoluble if heated to 110° C. for some time. Traces of acid tend slightly to lower, and traces of alkali to raise the temperature of coagulation. Sodium chloride and some other neutral salts favour coagulation. Solutions of albumin become opalescent at a temperature slightly below that at which flakes form.

Albumins are also coagulated by alcohol and by strong mineral acids. Coagulated albumin is only soluble in strong acids and alkalies by aid of heat, and strongly resembles keratin (pp. 56, 68).

Solutions of albumin are lævorotatory to polarised light.

"*Acid*" and "*Alkali*" *Albumins* are formed by the action, in the cold, of dilute acids (such as acetic, hydrochloric) and alkalies on albumin solution. They are uncoagulable by heat, and are precipitated by careful neutralisation, but are soluble in excess of either acid or alkali, or alkaline carbonates. They are thrown out of solution by saturation with sodium chloride or magnesium sulphate. It is doubtful whether albumins combine with either acids or bases, and it is probable that the "acid" or "alkali" albumins are identical with the parapeptones formed in the first stage of peptic digestion.

On putrefaction, or on more severe treatment with acids and alkalies, albumins break down in a way similar to gelatin, and yield almost identical products (see p. 57); amido-acids of the acetic series, and tyrosin (para-oxy-α-amido-phenyl-propionic acid) and aspartic (amido-succinic) acid, being the most important.

Treatment with alcoholic soda (see p. 62) yields peptones similar to those of gelatin.

Paal, Ch. Zeit., 1895, p. 1487.

Heated for some days with dilute nitric acid (1 : 2) all proteids, including albumins, gelatin and keratins, yield yellow flocks of "xantho-proteic acid," a substance of somewhat indefinite composition, soluble in ammonia and in fixed caustic alkalies with production of an orange-red or brownish-red colour.

Millon's reagent gives an intense red coloration when heated with albumins, keratins, or gelatin. The reagent is made by dissolving 2·5 grm. of mercury in 20 c.c. of concentrated nitric acid, adding 50 c.c. of water, allowing to settle and then decanting the clear liquid.

Albumins, previously purified by boiling with alcohol and washing with ether, when dissolved in concentrated hydrochloric acid (sp. gr. 1·196) by aid of heat, give a violet-blue coloration, but the reaction is often somewhat indefinite. Gelatin, chondrin and keratins do not give this reaction.

Treated with a trace of cupric sulphate and excess of caustic potash solution, albumins give a violet, and gelatin and peptones a pink solution (biuret reaction).

Dissolved in glacial acetic acid and treated with concentrated sulphuric acid, albumins and peptones give a violet and feebly fluorescent solution. A somewhat similar reaction is obtained if sugar solution be substituted for acetic acid.

A solution of albumin rendered strongly acid with acetic acid is precipitated by potassium ferrocyanide, salt, sodium sulphate, lead acetate, mercuric chloride, tannin and picric and tungstic acids.

Egg-Albumin is contained in the whites of eggs in membranes which are broken up by beating with water and can then be removed by filtration. When fresh its reaction is slightly alkaline, and it is lævorotatory.

According to Lehmann, white of egg contains 87 per cent. of water, and 13 per cent. of solid matter, the latter being almost entirely composed of egg-albumin. This latter coagulates and becomes insoluble in water on heating to 60° C.

Vitellin (the albumin or globulin of the yolk) is insoluble in water, and is obtained as a white granular residue on extracting undried egg-yolk with large quantities of ether. It closely resembles myosin, the chief globulin of muscle, but differs from other globulins in being soluble in a saturated solution of common salt. A neutral solution of vitellin in very dilute brine coagulates at 70-75° C.

Globulin is an albumin soluble in dilute salt solutions, but insoluble in water.

Yolks of eggs, preserved by the addition of salt, borax, or formalin, are used for dressing skins in the process of "tawing" (see p. 191). For the analysis of such yolks, see L.I.L.B., p. 159. Their most important constituent for the leather-dresser is egg-oil of which they contain about 30 per cent.

Casein, the principal proteid of milk, may be mentioned here in connection with the albumins to which it is closely related, since, though in no way connected with the animal skin, since it is used to some extent as a "seasoning" or glaze for leather, for which it is well adapted, and it is now to a considerable extent a waste product of butter manufacture. It differs from albumins in being very incompletely if at all coagulated by boiling, but separates at once in curdy flakes on the addition of acids (hydrochloric, acetic, butyric), and by the action of rennet. The curd is easily soluble in small quantities of dilute alkalies, lime-water, and salts of alkaline reaction, such as sodium carbonate and borax. If no more than the necessary quantity of alkali is employed for solution, the compound has an acid reaction to phenolphthalein, and like the original milk, is curdled by rennet and dilute acids. Casein may also be dissolved by digestion with diluted mineral or organic acids.

Hair, Epidermis and Glands.—These are all derived from the epithelial layer, and hence, as might be inferred, have much in common in their chemical constitution. They are all classed by chemists under one name, "keratin," or horny tissue, and their ultimate analysis shows that in elementary composition they closely resemble the albumins. It is evident, however, that the horny tissues are a class rather than a single compound.

The keratins are gradually loosened by prolonged soaking in water, and, by continued boiling in a Papin's digester at 160° C., evolve sulphuretted hydrogen, at the same time dissolving to a turbid solution which does not gelatinise on cooling. Keratin is dissolved by caustic alkalies; the epidermis and the softer horny tissues are easily attacked, while hair and horn require strong solutions and the aid of heat to effect complete solution. The caustic alkaline earths act in the same manner as dilute alkaline solutions; hence lime easily attacks the epidermis, and loosens the hair, but does not readily destroy the latter. Alkaline sulphides, on the other hand, seem to attack the harder tissues with at least the same facility as the soft ones, the hair being often completely disintegrated, while the epidermis is still almost intact; hence their applicability to unhairing by destruction of the hair. Keratins give the xanthoproteic reaction with nitric acid, and a red coloration with Millon's reagent, and also resemble albumin, in the fact that they are precipitated from their solution in sulphuric acid by potassium ferrocyanide. By fusion with potash, or prolonged boiling with dilute sulphuric acid, keratin is decomposed, yielding leucin, tyrosin, ammonia, etc. The precipitate produced by the addition of acids to alkaline solution of keratin (hair, horns, etc.), mixed with oil and barium sulphate, has been employed by Dr. Putz as a filling material for leather, for which purpose it acts in the same way as the egg-yolks and flour used in kid-leather manufacture. Eitner attempted to use it for the same purpose with bark-tanned leather, but without much success. Putz has also proposed to precipitate the material after first working its solution into the pores of the leather.

Elastic Fibres.—The elastic or yellow fibres of the hide are of a very stable character. They are not completely dissolved even by prolonged boiling, and acetic acid and hot solutions of caustic alkalies scarcely attack them. They do not appear to combine with tannin, and are very little changed in the tanning process. They are present in hide and skin to the extent of less than one per cent.

Analytical Methods.—The reactions distinguishing the principal skin constituents are summarised in the following table:—

Reagent.	Gelatin.	Albumins.	Keratins.
Cold water	Swells only	Soluble	Insoluble.
Heated in water	Soluble	Coagulate at 72° to 75° C.	Soluble only at temp. over 100° C.
Acetic acid and potassium ferrocyanide to aqueous solution	No precipitate	Precipitate	Precipitate
Millon's reagent	No reaction	Red coloration	Red coloration.
Hot concentrated hydrochloric acid	No coloration	Violet blue	No coloration.

There is no simple method for the quantitative separation of the different constituents of skin. It is, therefore, customary to simply determine the amount of nitrogen which any particular portion of the material may contain, and, as gelatinous fibre, which constitutes by far the greater portion of the true skin, contains 17·8 per cent. of nitrogen, to base the estimation of the amount of skin present upon this figure (see p. 57).

The most convenient process for the determination of the nitrogen is that devised by Kjeldahl, which is most easily carried out as follows:—

A known weight of the substance which contains about 0·1 gram of nitrogen (0·5 gram of skin, or a corresponding quantity of liquor) is placed in a flask of Jena glass, capable of holding 500-700 c.c. together with 15 c.c. of concentrated sulphuric acid. The contents of the flask are then boiled over a small Bunsen flame for 15 minutes, or more, until all the water has been driven off and the material is quite disintegrated; and are then allowed to cool below 100°. 10 grams of dry powdered potassium persulphate is now added, and the boiling continued till the liquid has become colourless.

The operation of boiling should be conducted in a good draught, or in the open air. Before the substance has begun to char it is advisable to place a small funnel in the neck of the flask to prevent, as far as possible, spirting and loss of sulphuric acid.

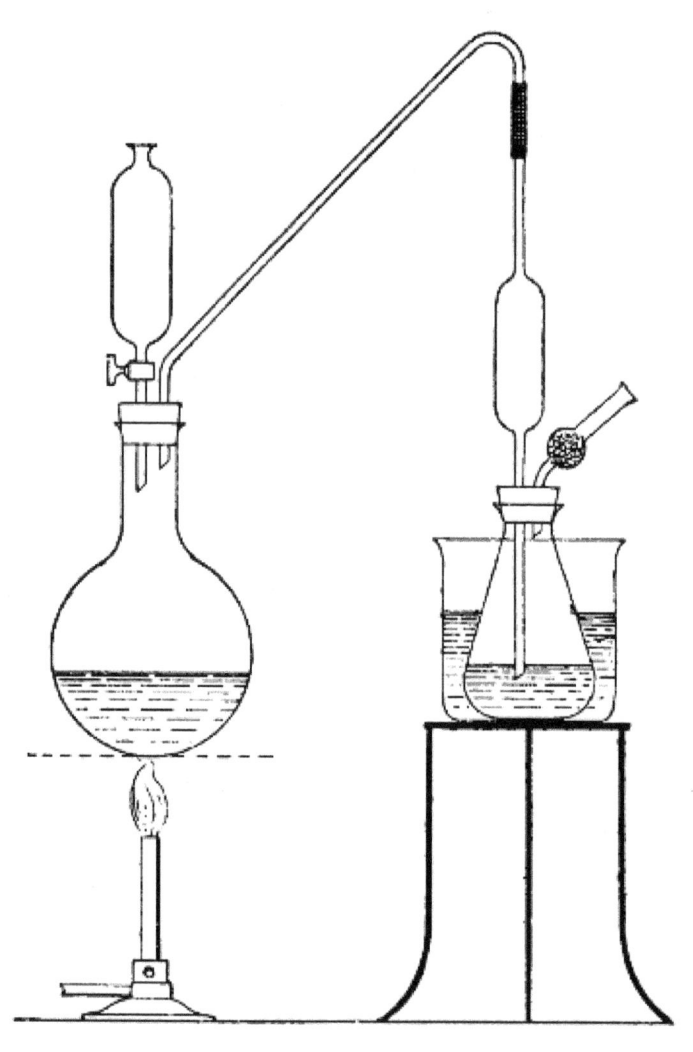

FIG. 18.—Kjeldahl Apparatus.

The colourless liquid is allowed to cool thoroughly, and the flask is then fitted with a tapped funnel and tube, as shown in Fig. 18. This tube must not be less than 4 mm. in diameter, and with the end in the flask cut diagonally to facilitate drops of liquid falling back again into the flask. It rises obliquely for a height of 12 to 15 inches, is then bent over as shown in the figure and connected by a rubber tube to a 100 c.c. pipette, or similarly shaped tube, the other end of which dips just below the surface of a volume of exactly 50 c.c. of "normal" hydrochloric acid contained in a second flask. About 50 c.c. of distilled water is introduced into the flask containing the treated sample, and after this 100 c.c. of a solution of 50 grams of caustic soda in 100 c.c. of water is carefully and slowly run into the flask by means of the tapped funnel with which it is provided. The contents of the flask are now boiled for about half an hour, the normal acid in the receiving flask being kept cool by immersing the latter in cold water. The liquid in this second flask is then titrated with normal sodium carbonate, using methyl orange as indicator. The difference in c.c. between 50 c.c., the volume of acid used, and the quantity of normal sodium carbonate required to neutralise it, when multiplied by $0 \cdot 014$ represents the amount of nitrogen (in grams) in the weight of the substance used for the determination; or if multiplied by $0 \cdot 0786$ shows the weight of hide-fibre in the same quantity of material. Some chemists add copper sulphate, or a drop of mercury before boiling up the substance with the strong sulphuric acid, but the use of such substances introduces complications in the process without, in the case of gelatinous matter, securing more accurate results. It is absolutely necessary that the acids and alkali used should be free from ammonia, and a blank experiment should be made using pure sugar which contains no nitrogen, and a correction applied if necessary for the ammonia they contain.

The ends of the glass tubes should fit closely together, so as to expose the rubber as little as possible to the action of ammoniacal vapour.

"Bumping" is often very troublesome at this stage, and may be prevented by passing a current of steam from another flask, or ammonia-free air through a tube with a capillary opening into the boiling liquid; fragments of pure zinc, of platinum, or broken tobacco-pipe are much less efficient. It is an additional safeguard against the escape of ammonia to fix a small absorption-tube containing fragments of glass to the absorption-flask. The normal acid is run through this tube into the flask, so as to wet the broken glass, and is finally rinsed into the absorption flask before titrating its contents.

Cp. Procter and Turnbull, Jour. Soc. Chem. Ind., 1900, p. 130; also Nihoul, Composition des Cuirs Belges, p. 14 (Bourse aux Cuirs de Liège, Sept. 1901), who advocates the use of potassium permanganate in the oxidation; and Law (Jour. Soc. Ch. Ind., 1902, p. 847).

In place of using 10 grm. of potassium persulphate as described, 10 grm. of ordinary potassium sulphate may be used, and potassium persulphate added in small quantities towards the end of the operation till a perfectly colourless solution is obtained.

<hr size=2 width="26%" noshade style='color:black' align=center>

CHAPTER IX.
THE PHYSICAL CHEMISTRY OF THE HIDE-FIBRE.

The nature of the changes which take place in the conversion of raw hide into leather, and the causes of swelling and "falling" in the various stages of the wet-work and tannage are among the most difficult problems with which we have to deal, and no intelligible explanation can be given without taking into account facts which are among the most recent discoveries of physical chemistry; and of which even yet our knowledge is by no means complete.

We know from our study of the structure of hide, that it consists in its natural state of gelatinous fibres which are soft and swollen with water, and easy putrescible. When these are dried, they contract and adhere to each other, forming a hard and almost homogeneous mass, resembling in degree, a sheet of glue or gelatine. After the tanning process, the fibres are changed in character, though not in form; they no longer absorb water so freely, and in drying they do not adhere together, but remain detached and capable of independent movement. The leather is therefore porous, flexible, and opaque on account of the scattering of light from the surfaces of the fibres, although the individual fibres are translucent. At the same time, chemical changes have taken place which render the fibres incapable of ordinary putrefaction. Our first necessity, therefore, in the conversion of skin into leather is to dry the fibres without allowing them to adhere. This is accomplished in the most primitive mode of leather dressing, by mechanically working fatty substances into the skin as it slowly dries, so as to coat and isolate the fibres, which are loosened by kneading and stretching; while at the same time the fat forms a waterproof coating which prevents them from again absorbing the water which is necessary to putrefaction. Similar results may be produced by causing chemical changes in the fibres themselves, which render them insoluble in water, and consequently non-adhesive; and a sort of leather may even be made by merely replacing the water between the fibres with strong alcohol, in which they are insoluble, and which absorbs and withdraws the water from them, allowing them to shrink and harden, while preventing their adhesion. The merit of having first clearly seen and expressed these cardinal principles in leather production belongs to the now venerable Professor Knapp, who published in 1858 a short paper (*Natur und Wesen der Gerberei und des Leders*) which is a model of clear explanation and practical experiment. Knapp, however, deals mainly with the changes in the condition of the fibre which are necessary to convert it into leather, and not with their physical causes;

and before we can explain the means by which these changes are brought about, we must be acquainted with certain facts and theories about solutions which have become much clearer since he wrote.

The particles (molecules) of all substances are drawn together by attractive forces somewhat of the same character as the attraction of gravitation which holds together the solar system, and which is the cause of weight. It is indeed even possible that these forces are identical. Like gravitation, these molecular attractions increase rapidly in intensity as the distance of the attracting bodies diminishes, so that in solids and liquids, where the molecules are near together, they are immensely powerful, while in gases and vapours they are barely perceptible. These attractions are opposed by the motion of heat, which takes the same part in molecular physics which the energy of planetary motion does in the solar system. In solids, the attractive forces hold the molecules rigidly in position, the motion of heat being limited to short vibrations round a fixed point, the effects of which are visible in the expansion caused by rising temperature. If the temperature is increased, most substances become liquid, a condition in which the particles can roll round each other, but are still held together by their mutual attractions, as the sun holds the earth from flying off into space. If the temperature goes on rising, the orbits of the molecules become greater, the liquid expands, and finally molecules fly off at a tangent out of reach of the attractions of the mass of liquid, and are only diverted from their course by colliding with solids or with other flying molecules, from which they rebound. This constitutes the state of vapour or gas.

The molecules usually consist of *groups* of atoms. Thus in the vapour of water, each molecule contains one atom of oxygen combined with two of hydrogen, and it is only at immense temperatures that this inner grouping is broken up. Naturally, the more complicated and heavier the molecular group, the more easily it is broken up by outside causes into simpler groupings, and molecules may exist in liquids or solids, which break up before they reach the gaseous form. Of such substances the chemist says that they "cannot be volatilised without decomposition." In very rare instances does the gaseous molecule consist of a single atom; even those of the most perfect gases, such as hydrogen, oxygen and nitrogen consist of pairs which are not broken up at any known temperature. The pressure of a gas, and its tendency to expand is due simply to the motion and impact of its flying molecules, and it may be noted that at the same temperature and pressure equal volumes of all gases have the same number of molecules, the lighter molecules making up for their want of weight by their greater velocity. The average velocity of a molecule of oxygen (O_2) at freezing point is 461 meters per second or about that of a rifle-bullet. It must not be taken however, that in any given solid, liquid, or gas, all the molecules at any temperature move at a uniform velocity, but that each individual molecule may vary from moment to moment from rest up to a very high speed, while the temperature of the mass only represents the average. Thus it happens that in all liquids, and even in solids, a certain proportion of the molecules at any temperature will have a speed sufficient to enable them to leave the surface, and take the form of vapour, while a certain proportion will fall back and be caught and retained. Thus every liquid, and theoretically every solid, has a "vapour-pressure," rising with the temperature, and depending on it only, and at the boiling temperature of the liquid equal to that of the atmosphere, or about 15 lb. per square inch, and therefore able to form bubbles in the interior of the liquid. If a little of a liquid is confined in a flask, the flask will become filled with its vapour, and so long as any of the liquid is present, the pressure of the vapour will depend only on the temperature and not at all on the respective quantities of liquid or vapour. Neither will it be affected by the pressure of other vapours or gases present in the flask, the total pressure in which will be the sum of the "partial" pressures of all the gases and vapours present.

Cp. p. 421.

The behaviour of gases and vapours has been described in some detail because it possesses very close analogy to that of substances in solution. The molecules of liquids are held together by attractions which are very powerful over the short distances which separate them, amounting in most cases to many tons per square centimeter of sectional area, but the range over which they act is very small. In the interior of the liquid the attractions on one side of a molecule are of course exactly balanced by those on the opposite side, so that it is free to move within the liquid without hindrance, but at the surface a very small part of the force due to the attractions of the surface-layer is unbalanced and acts as a sort of elastic skin holding the liquid together, and is called "surface-tension." Familiar examples of this are found in the force which supports a drop on the end of a tube, the possibility of laying a slightly oily needle on the surface of water without sinking, and the ability of some flies to walk on water as if it were covered with a sheet of india-rubber. Many liquids will mix or dissolve in each other in any proportions, e.g. water and alcohol; the attraction of the alcohol for the water-molecule being as great or greater than that of alcohol for alcohol, or water for water. In other cases, such as water and oil, or water and petroleum spirit, practically no mixture takes place, their mutual attraction being small; and each retains a considerable surface-tension at the points of contact, though less than that of the free surfaces, since each exerts an attraction on the other. There are also many intermediate cases, such as water with chloroform, carbolic acid, or ether, in which each solvent dissolves a portion of the other, but the two solutions do not mix, but form separate layers. In these cases an equilibrium is attained, in which there is just as much tendency for either of the liquids to pass into as out of the other layer. In this there is an extraordinary resemblance to what has been said of vapour-pressures; and the tendency to pass into solution is often called solution-pressure; and it may be noted that when equilibrium has been reached, not only is the solution-pressure, but the vapour-pressure of each constituent equal in both solutions. Like vapour-pressures, the solution-pressures usually increase with rise of temperature, more of each constituent passing into the other, till at last the composition of the two layers becomes identical, their surface-tensions disappear, and complete mixture takes place. With phenol (carbolic acid) and water this takes place at about 70° C.

Most of what has been said of the mutual solution of liquids is also true of the solution of solids, but the latter may be divided into two very distinct classes, colloids and crystalloids (which, however, shade off into each other). The colloid or gluey bodies are mostly miscible in any proportion with liquids in which they dissolve, and there is no such thing as a definite point of saturation. There are however some which form *jellies* which have great analogy to the partially miscible liquids; there is a mutual solubility, a portion of the solid dissolving to a liquid solution, while the remainder of the liquid dissolves in the solid, increasing its volume, but still retaining the characteristics of the solid state. As the temperature is raised, this mutual solubility generally increases, till at a given point the jelly melts, and complete solution takes place, as in the case of partially miscible liquids. These phenomena are of prime importance in the theory of tanning, but their further consideration must be deferred till a few words have been said about the crystalloids. These are characterised by regular crystalline form, indicating that the attractive forces of their molecules are exerted in definite directions, giving them a tendency to attach themselves together in definite geometrical arrangements. They dissolve in themselves no part of the solvent, but are dissolved by it till an equilibrium is reached in which the tendency of further particles of the solid to pass into the solvent is balanced by that of those already dissolved to attach themselves to the remaining solid, or "crystallise out." Such a solution is "saturated" with respect to the solid residue, but the word has no meaning unless solid crystals are present, and where a body has, as sometimes happens, more than one crystalline form, a solution may be saturated with regard to one of them, and more or less than saturated with regard to another. In "supersaturated" solutions, crystallisation is at once started by the addition of a "seed" crystal of the proper form.

If a crystalloid substance, such, for instance, as copper sulphate, be placed in a solvent (e. g. water), the dissolved salt will gradually spread itself through the whole body of the solvent, though in the complete absence of currents in the liquid, the motion is extremely slow, and years may be taken for the diffusion to rise through a few feet. In many cases salts diffuse through aqueous jellies at the same speed as they would through still water. Colloid substances on the other hand have little or no power of diffusion and mostly cannot pass through jellies at all. This is the reason why tannage with mineral salts is so much more rapid than with vegetable tannins which are of colloidal character, and diffuse through the gelatinous fibres of the hide with extreme slowness.

All dissolved crystalloids do not pass through gelatinous membranes with equal ease, and substances are known, mostly gelatinous precipitates, which do not permit the diffusion of dissolved salts, though they allow water to pass freely. Thin layers of such precipitates form what are called "semipermeable membranes." The existence of such membranes affords us the possibility of direct measurement of the tendency to diffusion, or as it is generally called the "osmotic" pressure of dissolved bodies. Thus a porous earthenware battery-cell may be immersed in a solution of copper sulphate, and filled with one of potassium ferrocyanide. In this way its pores will be filled with a gelatinous precipitate of copper ferrocyanide, which is pervious to water, but impervious to most dissolved substances. If now the cell be filled with a dilute solution of some crystalloid, say sugar, and its top closed by a perforated cork fitted with a vertical tube, and the cell be plunged in water, the latter will pass into the cell, and the dilute solution will rise in the tube to a height of many feet above the water outside. By substituting a mercury pressure gauge for the vertical tube, exact measures of the pressure in the cell can be made, which is the osmotic pressure of the dissolved substance. At first sight it is paradoxical that the water should flow into the solution, apparently against a heavy pressure, but the explanation is simple. Mention has already been made of the enormous internal pressures of liquids produced by the attractions of their molecules. In the solution a portion of this is borne by the dissolved substance, and the water flows in from the outside till an internal mechanical pressure is produced, equal in amount to the osmotic pressure of the dissolved substance. The resemblance of the phenomena of solution to those of vapour-pressure has already been mentioned, and it is found to be even quantitative, since the measured osmotic pressures are exactly equal in amount to those which the dissolved body would produce if it were in the state of vapour at the same temperature and occupying the same volume as the solution. It acts, in fact, precisely as the "partial pressure" of a vapour. There are several indirect ways of measuring the osmotic pressure of dissolved bodies, as for instance, from the lowering of the freezing point, or the raising of the boiling point of the solution as compared to those of the pure solvent, all of which confirm the direct measurements, and show that in a given volume at the same temperature, the same number of molecules will produce the same osmotic pressure whatever their nature, or conversely, that at the same osmotic pressure and temperature equal volumes of any solution must contain the same number of molecules. The use of these facts in determining molecular weight is obvious.

Solution-pressure and osmotic pressure are really two names for the same force; the former being employed to signify the tendency of a solid to dissolve, and the latter the pressure produced by the dissolved body which tends to prevent further solution. Thus, in a saturated solution in contact with its solid, the two pressures are always equal, but exerted in opposite directions.

A curious apparent deviation from this law is however noticed in solutions of salts, acids, and alkalies, and indeed of electrolytes generally; thus a dilute solution of sodium chloride produces an osmotic pressure nearly double that corresponding to the number of molecules of NaCl present; and in fact behaves as if it were a solution of Na and Cl existing separately. Such a solution conducts a current of electricity very readily, while at the same time the chlorine is carried to the positive, and the sodium to the negative pole, where they separate as Na_2 and Cl_2 (the Na decomposing the water present and forming NaOH). In fact, the modern theory of electrolysis asserts that these dissociated atoms are not separated from each other by electricity, but that they exist already separated in the solution of the electrolyte, and merely act as carriers for the electricity, and that the work done by the latter is not that of breaking up the salt-molecule, but of giving its dissociated atoms fresh charges of electricity which enable them to combine as new molecules, and escape from the electrolyte. Complex salts do not always break up into single atoms, thus calcium sulphate dissociates into Ca and SO_4, hydrogen sulphate (sulphuric acid) into 2H and SO_4, and so on. These dissociated atoms and atom-groups are called "ions," and may be monovalent, divalent, and so on; the divalent ion carrying double the electrical quantity or charge of the monovalent. Without discussing the ultimate nature of electricity itself, the matter is most easily pictured by assuming that the molecule of the undissolved salt is made up of an ion with a + charge ("kation," e.g. Na), and an ion with a - charge ("anion," e.g. Cl), by the electrical attraction of which charges they are held together. In the solution these attractions are balanced by those of other ions, so that they can wander freely within the liquid, but in order to take the molecular form of free elements and escape, say as Na_2 and Cl_2, the pair of kations must go to the - pole and give up one + charge, and at the same time a pair of anions must go to the + pole and receive a + charge. Thus the Na and all other kations separate at the − pole, and the Cl and all other anions at the + pole.

From what has been said, it will be obvious that free ions can only exist in solution, and can neither evaporate, nor separate as solids; but that in the liquid they act much like other dissolved molecules, exerting their own osmotic pressure independently of each other or of the dissolved salt, but with the limitation that a solution must always contain at the same time equal numbers of + and − ions. As a solution is diluted, more ions are liberated; as it is concentrated, more recombine to form undissociated salt. This will be made clearer by an example. In a saturated solution of sodium chloride with solid salt present, we have dissolved salt at the solution-pressure of the crystallised salt, and Na and Cl ions at the dissociation-pressure of the saturated salt solution, and neither affect the others. If we now add hydrochloric acid, it has no effect directly on the solubility of the *salt*, but as HCl dissociates largely into H and Cl, it increases the pressure of the Cl ions, and so compels the salt to recombine till the Cl pressure is reduced to its normal amount. This increases the concentration of the undissociated salt-solution, and thus salt is precipitated or crystallises out till the solution is no longer super-saturated with respect to the salt-crystals.

Most chemical reactions, and especially those between acids and bases, are really reactions of the ions. Thus NaOH in dilute solution is mostly ionised into Na and OH, while HCl is similarly ionised into H and Cl. On the other hand, water ionises only very slightly. Hence, on mixture, the H and OH combine and form water, with evolution of heat, while no actual combination occurs between the Na and Cl, so long as they remain in *dilute* solution. For this reason, the heat of neutralisation of all strong acids and bases is the same, independent of their nature, since strong acids, bases and salts are almost completely ionised. The rapidity of action, and consequently what we call the "strength" or "avidity" of an acid or base depends on the number of its free ions in solution; very weak acids and bases are very little ionised, though their salts ionise almost completely in dilute solution. On this depends the explanation of a fact of great practical importance. Hydrochloric acid, a strong acid, is almost completely ionised in solution; acetic, a weak one, very little; while sodium acetate and sodium chloride as salts are both almost completely ionised. If we add hydrochloric acid to a solution of sodium acetate, we shall have sodium-ions, acet-ions, chlorine-ions and hydrogen-ions in the solution. As the pressure of the acet-ions and the hydrogen-ions will be greater than the dissociation-pressure of acetic acid, they will combine to form it, till the pressure is equalised, and we shall have in the solution, free acetic acid slightly ionised, the sodium- and chlorine-ions of sodium chloride, and the sodium- and acet-ions of any excess of sodium acetate left. If the hydrochloric acid were just sufficient to combine with the whole of the sodium, we should have an equilibrium containing much (ionised) sodium chloride and little sodium acetate, together with much free acetic acid, and little hydrochloric. Thus the "strong" acid would displace the weak one.

Taking another example, we add sodium acetate to a solution of acetic acid. As the ionisation-pressure of the acetic acid is much less than that of sodium acetate, and both have a common acet-ion, the ionisation of the acetic acid will diminish, and more undissociated acetic acid will form, till by its concentration the two pressures are equalised. The total quantity of free acetic acid will be unchanged, but a less proportion of it will be ionised, and it will act like a weaker acid. This reduction of the activity of a weak acid by the addition of its neutral salt is often made use of by chemists. Instances in tanning practice are the use of excess of potassium dichromate with chromic acid in the chrome tanning process, the effect of neutral salts in "mellowing" the action of tanning liquors, and the use of salt in "pickling."

Let us now try to apply these facts to the physics of tanning, taking first the simplest cases, where electrolytic dissociation does not take place. We may consider the wet hide as made up of a mass of fibres of gelatine-jelly, with interspaces which are filled with water. In fact, for many purposes of experiment we may substitute for hide, mere sheets of swollen gelatine, so as to avoid the complications introduced by the water or solution mechanically retained between the fibres.

If we place a sheet of dry gelatine in water, it swells, absorbing perhaps seven or eight times its weight of water, but does not appreciably dissolve. A condition of equilibrium is reached when the attraction of the water-molecules for the gelatine is equal to the sum of the cohesive attraction of the gelatine for itself and the internal attraction of the water outside. An increase of the cohesion of the gelatine would tend to make it contract and expel part of the water, and this contraction would tend further to increase both the cohesion of the gelatine, and its attraction on the diminished number of water molecules it contained, and clearly these causes would act in opposing directions. The equilibrium is therefore a very unstable one, and slight causes might be expected to produce great changes in the degree of swelling, which is indeed the case. If we increase the temperature we diminish the cohesion of the gelatine, till at a point it becomes less than its attraction for the water, and the jelly suddenly loses its solid condition and dissolves.

The absorption of water by colloids (including gelatine) is accompanied by contraction of volume (compression) of the water absorbed, and by evolution of heat, and, as has been pointed out by Koerner, it is opposed (and swelling decreased) by increase of temperature. Solution, on the other hand, absorbs heat, and is therefore favoured by rise of temperature.

Beiträge zur wissenschaftlichen Grundlage der Gerberei, Freiberg, 1899.

If we place the swollen jelly in alcohol, it parts with water and contracts. The gelatine and alcohol are not mutually soluble, the sum of the attraction of water for alcohol, and the cohesive attraction of the gelatine is greater than the attraction of the latter for water, and as the alcohol cannot pass into the gelatine, the water passes out, and the jelly contracts. The greater the concentration of the alcohol, the more completely is the jelly dehydrated, and in strong alcohol it may become quite hard and solid. If we like to express the same facts in language more familiar to the modern chemist, but perhaps less clear to the non-chemical reader, we may say that the alcohol exerts an osmotic pressure outside the gelatine, but little or none inside it, and therefore the water is squeezed out. It would be equally true to say that the water passes out of the jelly till its osmotic pressure is equal in both the jelly and the alcohol. The jelly is a true "solid solution" of water in gelatine, and in a solution we may regard either of the two constituents as the solvent. Exact parallels may be found in the distribution of a third substance between two immiscible solvents (see p. 76), say alcohol between water and ether.

The osmotic pressure of water into alcohol may be demonstrated in a very simple way, taking advantage of the fact that a film of jelly is permeable for water but not for alcohol. If the experiment described on p. 78 be made by placing alcohol in a cell previously washed out with a gelatine solution, and the cell be placed in water, the water will pass into the cell, and the alcoholic solution will rise many feet in the vertical tube. The insolubility of gelatine in alcohol may be made use of for its estimation. If three times its volume of absolute alcohol be added to a solution containing gelatine, the latter will separate as a solid mass on a stirring rod, or on the sides of the beaker, and may be washed with further portions of alcohol. The method is useful in the analysis of gelatine lozenges and "jelly squares," roller compositions, hectograph masses, and the like; and for the determination of true unaltered gelatine in glues, and commercial gelatines (see page 60). Many other colloids are however also precipitated by alcohol.

If hide be treated with alcohol, as in Knapp's experiment (p. 74), the action is precisely the same as has been described with gelatine-jelly. The water is withdrawn, first from the spaces between the fibres, and then from the fibres themselves, and the skin dries with the fibres isolated and non-adherent, and is in fact converted into a sort of leather, which, however, returns to raw pelt on soaking in water.

The action of solutions of sugars, glycerine, and the like is in principle similar to that of alcohol, but more complex, since in general these bodies are soluble not only in the water, but in the gelatine or hide-fibre, so that their effect cannot be foretold, though usually it tends towards contraction rather than swelling. In general terms the equilibrium is a balance of the attraction of the water and the sugar for the gelatine, against the sum of their mutual attraction in the solution outside and the resisting cohesive force of the gelatine; and will depend not only on the nature of the substances, but on temperature and concentration.

The action of acids, alkalies and salts on gelatinous fibre is yet more complex, since not only electrolytic dissociation, but most probably actual chemical combination comes into the question. The chemical constitution of gelatine is as yet quite uncertain, but it is known that the molecule contains both amido-groups capable of linking with acids, and carboxyls which will combine with bases (see p. 58). Hence hide-fibre absorbs both acids and bases with great avidity, so much so that the sulphuric acid of a decinormal solution may be completely removed by hide, leaving only water without a trace of acid recognisable by litmus. Alkalies are absorbed in a similar way, and in both cases the gelatine or gelatinous fibre acquires a greatly increased power of absorbing water, and consequently of swelling. Familiar cases of this are the swelling of hide by acid, and by lime, and in neither case can the added substance be removed in any reasonable time by mere washing with water. Hence to free hides from lime or acids it is necessary to neutralise the alkali with acids (see p. 153) or the acid with chalk or alkalies (p. 91). No accurate determination has yet been made of the amount of acid or alkali with which gelatine or hide-fibre will combine, since the matter is complicated by the volume of acid or alkaline solution which is absorbed mechanically, and by the tendency of the compound to partially decompose on washing with water. Experiments made by the author lead to the conclusion that 1 grm. of air-dried gelatine will combine with about 0·025 grm. of actual hydrochloric acid (HCl) when placed in a very dilute solution of the latter, and this compound will absorb 40 or 45 grm. of water while still retaining the jelly state. The maximum swelling, with both acids and alkalies, is obtained with dilute solutions; and with the stronger acids, the outside solution must be almost neutral when equilibrium is attained, increasing quantities of acid diminishing the amount of water absorbed. The same statement is true of the strong alkalies. Thus in both cases, where swelling is desired, the object is defeated by the use of too strong solutions, and the quantity of acid or alkali should be rigidly adjusted to the weight of pelt, and not to the volume of solution.

As regards a physical explanation of the effect of acid and alkaline solutions upon gelatine, anything which can yet be said must be regarded rather as speculation than as actual scientific knowledge. It must also be admitted that while the view that actual *chemical* combination takes place between the gelatine and acids (or alkalies) seems much the most probable, difficulties arise from the fact that different acids apparently do not always combine in proportion to their equivalents, though it is probable that these will prove only apparent anomalies when more accurate means are known of determining how much acid is really combined, and how much merely mechanically absorbed.

Leaving out of account for the moment the question of swelling, a few words must be said about a property of these acid- (and alkali-) gelatine compounds, a knowledge of which is essential to understanding the swelling process. If a mass of acid-gelatine be suspended in pure water, a certain portion of it will be decomposed into neutral gelatine and free acid, and the latter will diffuse into the water. Thus acid-gelatine can only exist in presence of a certain amount of free acid. This dissociation by water is a common property of all salts, and necessarily follows from what has been said of ionisation; but it is only where the combining affinity of the constituents is weak, that it becomes practically perceptible. Water to a *very* small extent ionises to H and OH. If we imagine a salt dissolved in it, such as NaCl, which ionises almost completely to Na and Cl, we see that a certain proportion of NaOH and HCl must be formed by combination with the water-ions. In the case named the quantity is absolutely negligible, since both sodium hydrate and hydrochloric acid are almost completely ionised themselves, but if either the acid or the base is weak (that is little ionised), the process of combination must go on till the acid or basic solution is strong enough to have an ionisation-pressure equal to that of the salt. As this acid or base is no longer in an ionised condition, it may be removed from the solution by volatilisation or diffusion. For instance, if a solution of ferric chloride be confined in a tray of parchment paper, through which it has little power of diffusion, and this tray floated upon water which is frequently changed, the dissociated acid will diffuse through the membrane into the water, and in this way the whole of it may be ultimately removed, leaving nothing but a colloid solution of hydrated ferric oxide in the tray. Actions of this sort, in which the gelatinous fibre of the hide plays the same part as the parchment-paper membrane, have an important share in many of the phenomena of tanning. Thus, in the case of hide swollen with acid, the acid compound with the fibre is somewhat dissociated, and if the hide be hung in water which is constantly changed, the acid diffuses into it, and the whole may be ultimately, though slowly removed. A similar effect is produced in the familiar operation of removing acid from pelt or chromed leathers by paddling with "whitening" (calcium carbonate). The latter is insoluble in water, and therefore cannot penetrate into the hide, but as it instantly combines with any acid which diffuses out, the acid-gelatine compound is rapidly decomposed, since it is only permanent in a solution containing enough free acid to have an ionisation-pressure equal to that of the compound. Similar statements are true of the alkali-gelatine and lime-gelatine compounds.

Probably chrome, aluminium and iron salts are decomposed in this way in mineral tanning, and thus fixed in the hide as insoluble basic salts. Cp. pp. 186, 215.

It will be easier to follow the results of what has been said if we take a concrete case which has been carefully investigated by the author and others; that of the action of hydrochloric acid solutions on gelatine. If a weighed sheet of gelatine be placed in a very dilute solution of the acid, it swells much more considerably than it does in water, a maximum swelling being attained with a concentration of the outer solution of 0·1 to 0·2 grm. of HCl per litre. The swollen jelly has then a volume of about 45 c.c. per gram of the air-dried gelatine, and a concentration equal to about 0·75 grm. of HCl per litre of swollen jelly, or at least about five times that of the outer solution. As the concentration of the latter is increased, the concentration in the jelly also increases, but in a much smaller ratio, while the volume of the jelly diminishes, till, with a concentration of 5 grm. of HCl per litre in the outer solution, the volume of the jelly is only about 18·5 c.c., and its concentration not quite 6 grm. per litre. These facts cannot be accounted for by any theory of simple solution of the HCl in the jelly, since the law of such solutions is that the concentration in each maintains a constant ratio, unless chemical change takes place. It is possible that they might be explained by adsorption (surface attraction), but as it is known that gelatine contains both amido-groups capable of combining with acids, and carboxyl-groups which can combine with bases, it is much more likely that actual chemical combination takes place, and that the apparent irregularities in the amount of acid fixed are due to partial hydrolysis of the compound.

Cp., however, Walker and Appleyard on the 'Absorption of Acids by Silk,' Chem. Soc. Trans. 1896, p. 1334.

The following may be suggested as a working hypothesis. As both water and hydrochloric acid can pass freely in and out of the jelly, it must be in osmotic equilibrium with the outer solution in every respect, and neither the un-ionised hydrochloric acid of the solution, nor the small amount which may be formed by hydrolysis of the gelatine compound can have any effect on the swelling. So long as the outer solution is very dilute, by far the greater part of the acid present is absorbed and fixed by the gelatine, and almost the whole of the outer acid will be ionised, as well as a portion of that in combination with the gelatine. In the latter case, however, the ions will be unable to pass out of the jelly, and will therefore cause an internal osmotic pressure, and the gelatine will swell till the Cl-ions are in osmotic equilibrium with those of the outer solution. At the same time, this internal pressure of Cl-ions will oppose the entry of the Cl-ions (and therefore also of their associated H-ions) from the outer solution, and the acid solution absorbed mechanically will be somewhat less concentrated than that outside. As the concentration of the outer solution is increased, the pressure of the outer Cl-ions will repress the ionisation of the gelatine-chloride, and at the same time its tendency to hydrolyse. Thus the acid actually combined with the gelatine should somewhat increase, but the swelling should diminish, as is actually the case. It is impossible to carry the concentration of the hydrochloric acid much above 5 grm. per liter without causing solution of the gelatine, but the addition of common salt to the outer solution should equally increase the pressure of its Cl-ions, and cause further diminution of swelling, the Na-ions in this case increasing the outside pressure in the same way as the hydrogen ions. In fact the addition of salt in sufficient quantity will reduce the swelling till the gelatine becomes quite solid, and retains only about its own weight of water, while at the same time the apparently combined acid largely increases. This cannot be attributed to any direct dehydrating action of the salt, since concentrated sodium chloride solutions have no dehydrating, but rather a swelling effect on gelatine in the absence of acid, and the concentration of the salt in the outer solution and in the jelly proves precisely the same within the limits of experimental error. Several other facts may be noted, tending to support the explanation which has been given. The tendency to swell gelatine is common to all acids of appreciable strength, and in all cases where the concentration of the acid could be increased to a moderate extent without causing solution of the jelly, the effect of a maximum swelling, diminishing as the concentration of the acid increased, has been observed. Other salts also produce similar effects to sodium chloride; thus the swelling caused by sulphuric acid is repressed by sodium sulphate. Sodium chloride seems to diminish the swelling caused by all acids, but in presence of large excess of sodium chloride, most of the acid in combination with the gelatine will probably be hydrochloric, whatever the acid used to originally produce the swelling. A curious fact observed by the author, is that absolute alcohol, which so effectually dehydrates neutral gelatine, is almost powerless to remove either water or acid from gelatine swollen by hydrochloric acid. HCl is freely soluble even in absolute alcohol, but H- and Cl-ions can only exist in it to a very small extent, so that we may conclude that the acid which causes the swelling and retains the water of the jelly exists either in actual combination with the gelatine, or in an ionised condition.

The acid retained by the gelatine, as measured by deducting from the total contained in the jelly, a quantity equivalent to the volume of solution absorbed, at first rises rapidly to a maximum, then slightly diminishes and remains practically constant. On the theory suggested, it is evident, however, that the absorbed solution must be more dilute than that outside, and the actual combined acid greater than that shown by the above calculation. The "combined" acid, as determined by indicators, shows slight but continuous increase. It is acid to phenolphthalein, but neutral to methyl orange.

Solutions of caustic alkalies are in most respects analogous in their swelling action to those of strong acids. A portion of the alkali is in some way fixed by the gelatine, while another portion is simply absorbed as solution. A maximum swelling effect is also noticed with dilute solutions, which is diminished as the concentration increases. Swelling by alkalies is not diminished by chlorides so far as has been observed, and especially it may be noted that the swelling produced by caustic soda is not diminished by sodium chloride. On the theory which has been suggested there is no reason why alkaline swelling should be reduced by chlorides, since the swelling agent has no Cl-ion, but it is somewhat singular that the sodium salt, having a common Na-ion should produce no repression of the swelling by caustic soda. In the present state of our knowledge no definite explanation can be given, but it is quite possible that the swelling in this case is not produced by the sodium-ion but by some more complex one, or even by the hydroxyl-ion, like most of the characteristic reactions of alkalies. Apparently the gelatin-alkali compound is still strongly alkaline, affecting phenolphthalein indicator like uncombined alkali—an effect which is known to be due to the presence of free HO-ions.

The effect of acids and alkalies has been studied by Procter and others on actual pelt as well as on gelatine, and has been found to be qualitatively, if not quantitatively quite similar to that on gelatine, though from the acid retained mechanically in the interfibrous spaces, exact quantitative determination is more difficult. The amount of swelling produced is not proportional to the strength of the acid, some weak and little ionised acids such as lactic producing larger swelling than stronger acids such as hydrochloric and sulphuric, of which the ionic pressure in the external solution is greater. Dilute solutions generally produce greater swelling than more concentrated, so that where swelling is required without destructive effect on the fibre, dilute solutions of such weak acids are to be preferred, and the presence of neutral salts is to be avoided. On the other hand, where it is desired to remove lime, or to bring the pelt into an acid condition without swelling, the addition of neutral salts, and especially of chlorides is advantageous. A very important application of this principle is the "pickling" of sheep-skins, and especially of sheep-grains, in order to preserve them for export. The principle of this operation is that the skins are first swollen slightly with sulphuric acid, and the swelling is then reduced by salt, either added, or used in a subsequent bath. In practice, salt is now generally also added to the first bath to moderate the swelling. A suitable strength for the "rising solution" is about 80 grm. common salt, and 7·5 grm. sulphuric acid per litre. 100 c.c. of this solution will therefore require about 15 c.c. of $^N/_1$ alkali to neutralise it, and it should be tested after each lot of skins, and maintained at the same strength by suitable additions of acid. The acid absorbed by the skins is mainly hydrochloric, sodium sulphate accumulating in the bath. The salt is not absorbed by the skins in the same way as the acid, but will be continually diluted by the water they bring in, and occasional additions of salt must therefore be made, the density being maintained at about 65° Bkr. (1·065 sp. gr.) After paddling or being stirred in this bath for about ½ or ¾ hour the skins are transferred to saturated brine, and stirred in it till fully fallen in thickness, the density of the liquid being maintained by excess of salt. They may be allowed to remain some hours in the saturated brine with advantage.

Within moderate limits, the strength of the rising liquor is not of great importance, since the skins will only absorb a certain amount of acid (increasing with the concentration of salt). In the second or falling liquor the large excess of salt forces all the acid present into the skins, none diffusing into the bath. Skins may be effectively pickled with very much smaller quantities of acid than those prescribed above, or ordinarily used, and are much easier to tan satisfactorily; but it is said that they are more liable to suffer from mildew. Pickling may also be done by placing the skins in a concentrated brine-bath, and adding a calculated quantity of acid, not exceeding 0·1 grm.-molecule of sulphuric acid per kilo. of dry hide substance, but the method is not economical in practice from the dilution of the bath produced by the water brought in by the skins and the necessity of constant large additions of salt.

Pickled skins must not be brought in contact with water, which by diluting the brine they contain, allows the excess of acid to act upon and destroy the fibre. Even drops of water, accidentally sprinkled on the skins produce this effect, and it is said that it spreads to parts which have not been wet. For similar reasons, it is necessary in tanning pickled skins, at least to begin the process in liquors to which salt has been added, the quantity required being dependent on the amount of acid used in pickling the skins, and where this is reduced to a minimum, it is even possible to tan without further addition of salt than that contained in the skins. The pickling process converts the skins into a species of white leather, and skins tanned in salted liquors after pickling, or by addition of both acid and salt to sumach liquors give good colour, and tough leather with a much diminished consumption of sumach.

The permanency of such leather is somewhat doubtful, but the writer was unable to detect free sulphuric acid in a sample which he examined, and it may be that when no acid is added to the later liquors, that derived from the pickling is expelled by the tannin; but this is very doubtful.

Instead of using salted liquors, the skins maybe "depickled" by a bath of whitening and water, borax, or some other mildly alkaline solution before tanning.

The facts which have been discussed in the preceding pages offer a sufficient explanation of the causes which operate in those deliming processes which depend on the simple neutralisation of the alkaline matters present in the hide, and of the swelling by means of acid which forms a step in the manufacture of many sorts of sole-leather, but they by no means fully elucidate the causes of the much more complete depletion of the pelt brought about by the bacterial products of bates and puers. It has been pointed out (p. 82) that gelatine and hide-fibre in a neutral condition are swollen by water, but that the equilibrium so reached is an unstable one, easily influenced by slight causes. Among these, as has been pointed out by Koerner, the surface-tension between the water and the swollen fibre holds a place; and surface-tensions of this sort are greatly influenced by many substances of the class to which bacterial ferments belong. Many salts also alter the water-absorption of gelatinous fibres, sometimes causing swelling, and sometimes contraction, according to temperature, concentration, and the nature of the salt. Though most salts do not seem to be absorbed by hide-fibre, it is possible, as suggested by Koerner (*loc. cit.*), that in some instances the base may combine with the acid-groups, and the acid of the salt with the basic groups of the gelatine-molecule, while other cases are known in which salts are actually dissociated, and their acid fixed by the affinities of the hide-fibre. An interesting case of this sort was recently proved by Paessler and Appelius, who showed that sulphuric acid was absorbed from a solution of hydric sodic sulphate, and the neutral sulphate left in the solution. Similar reactions undoubtedly occur with some salts of strong acids and weak bases, but this point must be more fully discussed in connection with the theory of mineral tannages.

Beiträge zur wissenschaftlichen Grundlage der Gerberei, Jahresberichte der deutschen Gerberschule zu Freiberg, 1898-9 and 1899-1900.

Wissenschaftliche Beilage des Ledermarkt, 1901, ii. p. 106.

<hr size=2 width="26%" noshade style='color:black' align=center>

CHAPTER X.
WATER AS USED IN THE TANNERY.

Of all the materials employed in tanning, none is of more indispensable importance than water, and its quality has undoubtedly great influence on tanning, though it is constantly blamed for faults and troubles which are really due to the mistakes of the tanner.

Water is chiefly used in tanneries for soaking and washing hides and skins, for making the limes, the bates, and the tanning liquors, for steam boilers, and in dyeing. For all these purposes it should be as free as possible from impurities, but since water is the most universal solvent in Nature, it is never found pure, but always contains mineral matter derived from the rocks and soil through which it has flowed, as well as organic impurities from decaying animal and vegetable matter. Associated with the latter are usually living organisms of putrefaction (*bacteria*) which may affect the quality of the water for tanning even more seriously than the mineral impurities. The purest natural waters are those which have flowed only over hard sandstones and volcanic rocks. Water sufficiently pure for laboratory use can only be obtained by distillation. The steam-water from heating pipes usually contains large quantities of dissolved iron, and often also volatile organic matters from the oil, etc., which finds its way into the boiler. It may sometimes be made fit for use by boiling (which precipitates the ferrous carbonate present), and subsequent settling or filtration. The use of steam-water containing iron is a frequent source of stains and discolorations in the tannery which more than counterbalances the advantage of its softness.

The "hardness" of natural waters is mostly due to the salts of lime and magnesia which they contain, which precipitate soap in the form of insoluble stearates and oleates, which are useless for washing. It is commonly estimated by determining the amount of a standard alcoholic soap solution which must be added in order to produce a permanent froth on shaking. Theoretically about 12 parts of soap (sodium stearate or oleate) are destroyed by 1 part of calcium carbonate or an equivalent quantity of other lime salts, with formation of insoluble lime soaps (calcium stearate or oleate). Really, the reaction is much more complicated, owing to the dissociation of the soap into free alkali and acid-salts on solution in water. Teed estimates that $\frac{1}{3}$ to $\frac{1}{2}$ more is required than the theoretical quantity, and more in hot water than cold. This uncertainty is partially overcome by testing the soap solution against a known solution of calcium chloride. The presence of magnesia also complicates the test and leads to discrepant results.

Journ. Soc. Chem. Ind., 1889, p. 256. Cp. also Allen, ibid. 1888, p. 795.

The methods of determining hardness originated by Hehner (see L.I.L.B., p. 19) are simpler and more accurate than the soap-test, and are to be preferred, except for direct determination of the suitability of a water for scouring with soap. "Degrees" of hardness in England are calculated as parts of $CaCO_3$ per 100,000, or sometimes grains per gallon (70,000 grains).

Hardness is of two kinds, "temporary" and "permanent"; the former being removed by boiling, while the latter is not so removed.

Temporary hardness consists of the carbonates of alkaline earths held in solution by an excess of carbonic acid. Lime combines with 1 molecule of carbon dioxide to form the ordinary normal carbonate (chalk), which is practically insoluble in water. When, however, excess of carbonic acid is present, hydric calcic carbonate (bicarbonate) which is fairly soluble is produced. This is easily demonstrated by passing carbon dioxide into somewhat diluted lime-water, which at first becomes turbid from precipitated chalk, but soon clears by formation of soluble hydric carbonate. If the solution be now boiled, the hydric carbonate is decomposed, and the excess of carbonic acid is driven off as CO_2, and the chalk again precipitated. The reactions are represented by the following equations:—

$$Ca(OH)_2 + CO_2 = CaCO_3 + OH_2. \quad (1)$$

$$CaCO_3 + CO_2 + OH_2 = - \genfrac{}{}{0pt}{}{CaCO_3}{H_2CO_3} \quad (2)$$

Magnesia forms soluble double carbonates in a similar manner, but on continued boiling gradually loses the whole of its carbonic acid, and is precipitated as magnesium hydrate, $Mg(OH)_2$.

One of the most important reactions in connection with temporary hardness is that caused by the addition of calcium hydrate (slaked lime), which forms the basis of Clark's softening process. When an equivalent amount of lime is added to a solution of hydric calcic carbonate, it displaces the water of the "half-bound" carbonic acid, forming a second molecule of calcium carbonate, which is precipitated together with that originally present, as is represented in the following equation:—

$$CaCO_3 - + Ca(OH)_2 = 2CaCO_3 + 2OH_2. \quad (3)$$

H_2CO_3

Hydric magnesium carbonate is also precipitated by lime, but the reaction is somewhat different, the magnesia being removed as hydrate as follows:—

$$\begin{matrix} MgCO_3 \\ H_2CO_3 \end{matrix} + 2Ca(OH)_2 = 2CaCO_3 + 2OH_2 + Mg(OH)_2. \quad (4)$$

It will be noted that 2 equivalents of lime are required to precipitate 1 of magnesia. Two molecules of sodium hydrate (NaOH) or potassium hydrate (KOH) may be substituted for 1 of $Ca(OH)_2$ with similar results, and in some cases it is practically advantageous to use the former, as the sodium carbonate formed in precipitating the temporary hardness reacts again on the permanent, throwing down the lime and magnesia as carbonates. (See p. 101.)

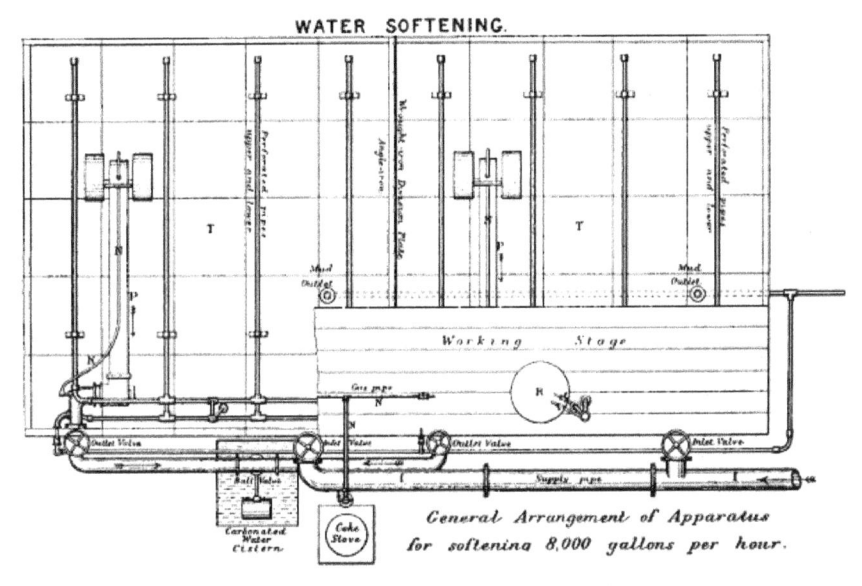

FIG. 19.—Plan of Archbutt and Deeley's Apparatus.

Larger plan (110 kB)

The use of lime for softening temporary hard waters was originally proposed by Thomas Henry, F.R.S., of Manchester, but was first applied as a practical process by Clark, who, after adding the requisite quantity of lime to the water in a mixing vat, allowed it to stand in a large tank to clear by subsidence, the precipitated carbonate of lime taking from 6 to 12 hours to settle. The process in its original form is a perfectly satisfactory one, except for the capacious settling tanks which are required, which in some cases are inconvenient and expensive. Messrs. Archbutt and Deeley have patented a modification of the Clark process, by which the time of subsidence is much shortened, and according to which the precipitated carbonate of lime of previous operations is allowed to remain in the tank, and the fresh charge of water and lime is mixed up with it by means of steam-injectors, which blow in a current of air through perforated pipes at the bottom of the tank, and at the same time very slightly warm the water. The action goes on much more rapidly at a slightly raised temperature than in the cold; and rather curiously, the stirred up precipitate, instead of increasing the time of clearing, settles rapidly and carries down with it that formed in the new operation. It is particularly suitable for treating waters containing magnesia, from which a compound of lime and magnesia is apt to be precipitated in a colloid form which chokes filter-cloths and will not readily settle. After softening, the water is usually "carbonated" by passing the gases produced by burning coke into the floating exit-pipe through which it falls, in order to retain any remaining traces of carbonates of lime and magnesia in a soluble form, and prevent their subsequent precipitation in the pipes. The apparatus is made by Messrs. Mather and Platt, of Manchester, and its arrangement is shown in Figs. 19 and 20.

Journ. Soc. Chem. Ind., 1891, p. 511.

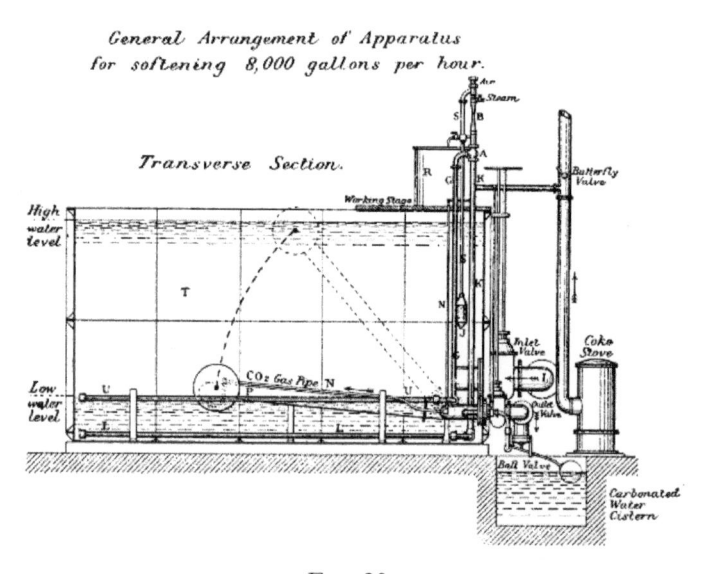

FIG. 20.

Larger section (**115 kB**)

Several modifications of the Clark process have been introduced, in which the precipitation is carried on continuously instead of intermittently. The most important of these is the Porter-Clark, in which one portion of the water to be softened flows through an agitator containing excess of lime, with which it forms saturated lime-water, which is passed slowly up a cylinder where it deposits the excess of suspended lime. The clear lime-water so produced is mixed with a fresh portion of the water to be softened in a second cylinder also provided with an agitator, the proportion of the two liquids being regulated by cocks. The carbonate of lime is at once precipitated, and is removed by passage through a filter press. This process is in successful operation on a considerable scale at Messrs. Hodgsons' tannery at Beverley.

Several other forms of filter have also been employed with success, and also methods in which the treated water traverses tanks with sloping partitions on which the carbonate of lime is deposited. The latter plan was originally patented in France by Gaillet-Huet, and has been introduced into England by Stanhope.

So far as is yet known, from the tanner's point of view, it is hardly necessary to make any distinction between lime and magnesia, either or both of which may be considered simply as "hardness." A hard water probably softens dried hides more slowly than a purer water, though it is possible that the observed difference in the time required may be due in many cases to the lower temperature of wells from which hard water is generally derived. In the actual "limes" the hardness of the water can have no appreciable influence, though if sodium sulphide be used alone for unhairing, a certain waste occurs from temporary hardness which may render it advisable to add a little lime. It is in washing the hides free from lime that the influence of hard water is first distinctly felt. If limy goods, after unhairing, are placed in a water with much temporary hardness, the same action occurs as in Clark's water-softening process, and chalk is deposited in the surface of the hides, making them harsh and apt to "frize" or roughen the grain in "scudding." The common, but not wholly satisfactory expedient is to add a little lime, or better, a few pailfuls of lime liquor to the water before putting in the hides. The best plan is to use a properly softened water. Permanent hardness is not injurious in this way.

Unfortunately it is not the grain alone which is injured by the use of hard water for washing the hides, but on coming into the liquors the precipitated bases combine with the acids and tannins, forming compounds which oxidise and darken when exposed to the air, and which are the commonest causes of stains and markings on all descriptions of leather. Even when goods are drenched or bated before tanning the injury is not prevented, since the weak organic acids which are capable of removing the lime (as such) from the hide have little effect on the precipitated carbonate, which can only be dissolved by the use of stronger acids. It must be noted that the same injurious effect on limed goods is produced by free carbonic acid, which may be present even in soft waters.

When temporarily hard waters are employed for leaching tanning materials, the carbonic acid is displaced by the tannins, which form compounds similar to those just mentioned, which are incapable of tanning, and darken and discolour when exposed to the air. Though the amount of lime present in a liter of even the hardest water is very small, yet in the aggregate of thousands of gallons used weekly in a good-sized yard it amounts to something very considerable, and as the molecular weight of tannins is very high, the quantity destroyed is many times that of the lime present. This loss can be prevented (*a*) by the addition of sufficient mineral acid to convert the temporary into permanent hardness, (*b*) by the use of oxalic acid, which precipitates the whole of the lime as oxalate, or, (*c*) best of all, by softening the water by suitable treatment before use. Each part of temporary hardness reckoned as $CaCO_3$ (L.I.L.B., p. 19), requires 1·26 parts of crystallised oxalic acid or 0·98 parts of H_2SO_4, or say one part of ordinary oil of vitriol of sp. gr. 1·840 per 100,000 parts of water.

As the lime and magnesia of temporarily-hard water is thrown down by boiling, it is deposited in steam boilers as a soft precipitate, much of which can be blown out by suitable sludging; but if oils or fats obtain access to the boiler, a soft, bulky, adherent deposit is formed, keeping the water from the plates, which may become red hot, and lead to collapse or explosion. This effect is not produced by mineral oils, which, on the contrary, tend to prevent adherence of scale to the plates, and as suitable mineral oils are not only cheaper, but much less injurious to the working parts of steam engines than animal or vegetable oils or tallow, they should always be used in preference for cylinder purposes.

Water which is temporarily hard owing to calcium and magnesium carbonates, is unsuitable for *dyeing*, as the carbonates react with basic dyes, precipitating the colour-base, and so rendering a part of the dye useless. Further, as this precipitate is deposited on the skins it causes uneven dyeing and gives rise to spots and streaks. In dyeing with basic dyes, therefore, it is advisable to add sufficient acetic acid to the water before use to exactly neutralise the carbonates present. Of course this treatment is quite unnecessary when acid dyes are employed, as acid is usually added with the dye, and with dyewoods the presence of a little calcium salt is advantageous.

As each "degree" of total hardness represents a soap-destroying power of at least 2 oz. of soap per 100 gallons of water, allowance must be made in making up "fat-liquors" with soap and oil for the loss of soap due to its precipitation by the mineral matter in the water. The sticky lime-soaps are apt to adhere to the leather and interfere with glazing; so that it is much better to employ a soft water.

Permanent hardness of water is generally caused by sulphates of lime and magnesia, and more rarely by chlorides and nitrates. As none of these can be precipitated by lime, permanent hardness cannot be removed by Clark's process, nor can it produce the injurious effect on limed hides which have been attributed to temporary hardness. Neither can the lime and magnesia present combine with the tannins if used for leaching, since they are already fixed by stronger acids, and at most can only act injuriously by slightly lessening the solubility of the tannins. Even this effect cannot be regarded as proved, though it deserves further investigation. Permanent hardness is therefore of little moment as regards the ordinary uses of the tannery, though it has considerable influence in some of the processes of dyeing, and acts very injuriously where soap is used for scouring, as in the washing of sheep-skins for wool mats, since each part of lime reckoned as carbonate destroys at least twelve parts of pure soap (sodium stearate or oleate), producing a sticky and insoluble lime-soap which adheres to the fibre. In sole-leather tanning, permanent hardness is sometimes advantageous, especially if it be due to calcium and magnesium sulphates, and Vignon recommended that sulphuric acid should be added to the water before use in quantity sufficient to exactly neutralise the carbonates which cause temporary hardness, as magnesium and calcium sulphates are not injurious, but tend to plump the hides. It must be remembered, however, that the carbonic acid liberated may still have prejudicial effects on limed hides.

Recent investigations by Nihoul ('Influence de la nature de l'eau sur l'extraction des matières tannantes,' Bulletin de la Bourse aux Cuirs de Liège, Sept. 1901) on the tanning waters of Belgium seem to show that permanent hardness is more injurious in the extraction of tannin than has generally been supposed.

Permanent hardness is most objectionable in waters employed for boiler-feeding, and calcium sulphate is especially so, as it becomes nearly insoluble in water at 150° C. or 55 lb. steam-pressure, and is deposited on the plates as a hard crystalline scale which has to be chipped off with a hammer. Where many boilers have to be worked with a hard water, it is much the most satisfactory to soften the water with caustic soda, or with lime and soda together before it comes into the boiler, but in cases where the plant required would be too costly, boiler-compositions are sometimes used with good effect, though considerable caution is advisable, since some of them affect the plates injuriously. The active constituent of many boiler-compositions is soda-ash or sodium carbonate, which acts by double decomposition with the calcium sulphate, forming sodium sulphate, and precipitating calcium carbonate as a sediment which is easily washed out. Most tanning materials, and even spent tan liquors, will prevent or lessen incrustation if mixed with the feed water, but sometimes corrode the plates if used too freely. This danger is lessened if they are used in conjunction with soda. Heavy mineral oils, either introduced in small quantity with the feed water, or painted on the sides of the boiler when cleaned, are useful in preventing the formation of a coherent scale.

The removal of permanent hardness from water is easily effected in most of the forms of apparatus employed for the softening of water by lime, by using a calculated quantity of sodium carbonate in addition. The reaction is represented in the case of calcium sulphate by the following equation—

$$CaSO_4 + Na_2CO_3 = CaCO_3 + Na_2SO_4.$$

The conversion of magnesium sulphate into carbonate may be similarly effected, but as the latter is somewhat soluble, an additional equivalent of lime must be used to precipitate it as hydrate. Magnesium salts, from their solubility, do not cause scale on boilers (though the chloride is apt to produce corrosion), but they are equally destructive of soap with the calcium salts. Caustic soda will remove temporary hardness, and after becoming converted into carbonate will further react on any permanent hardness present; and its use is therefore sometimes convenient in small softening plants, but it is not more effective, and considerably more costly than a suitable mixture of lime and sodium carbonate. Even with these, Archbutt states that the cost of softening permanent hardness is about ten times as great as that of removing temporary hardness with lime only.

Proceedings of Inst. of Mech. Engineers, 1898, pp. 404-54, in which much valuable information on water-softening is given.

As regards the influence of other impurities, our knowledge is far from complete, but the following are the most important matters likely to be present.

Mud under any circumstances is objectionable. It frequently contains organic slime and organisms which encourage the putrefaction of hides placed in it to wash or soften. It also almost invariably contains iron as one of its constituents, and hence stains leather and gives dark coloured liquors. It is not easily removed by filtration, as large filter-beds are expensive and difficult to keep in order, and much space is required to clear water by subsidence. Some mechanical filter which can be easily cleaned, and used under pressure, offers the best chance of success. The Pulsometer Company make one consisting of sponge tightly packed below a perforated piston. To cleanse the filter a stream of water is passed the reverse way, and the piston raised and worked up and down, either by hand or power, so as to loosen and knead the sponge. Filter-presses, in which cloths, or in some cases sand, are used as the filtering medium, are also well adapted for the purpose. If a water be softened by Clark's or other process the precipitated chalk carries down the mud with it, together with most of the organisms.

Iron is always an objectionable impurity in the tannery, though it is less injurious to the quality than the appearance of the leather produced, and indeed German sole-leather tanners frequently put old iron in the handlers to darken the colour of the leather, and apparently, if not really, to quicken the tannage. It must not be present in waters used for dyeing. Iron oxide is frequently present as a mud merely, and in this case can be removed by filtration. It is rarely in solution in any other form than that of acid carbonate, since sulphate or chloride could not exist in presence of bicarbonate of lime. In this form, iron is precipitated at once by boiling or on the addition of lime, like the temporary hardness due to other bases, in the form of ferric hydrate, and more slowly by oxidation on exposure to the air. The mud produced by softening waters which contain iron must be completely removed by filtration, or subsidence, before the water is used for leaching, or the iron will redissolve in the acids of the liquors. Iron is not perceptibly injurious in the limes, but in the bates and wash-pits sometimes causes stains, which are scarcely visible till blackened by the tanning liquors. In presence of sulphur (from sulphide of sodium or the decomposition of sulphates by the sulphur-bacteria nearly always present in bates and soaks), the stains become bluish or greenish black, and a black deposit is frequently produced on the sides of the pit, in which the threads of sulphur-bacteria (*Thiothrix*) can often be recognised by the microscope. As ferric salts not only combine with the tannins, but are themselves tanning agents (see p. 198), they are rapidly absorbed by leather, and iron is always present in leather ash. (For detection and estimation see L.I.L.B., p. 218.)

Alumina, except as clay, is rarely present in waters, and probably harmless in any water likely to be used in tanning.

Soda is sometimes present in considerable amount, as sulphate, chloride, or carbonate. The sulphate is probably inoperative. The chloride, if present in material quantities, prevents plumping, and may be the cause of thin and soft leather, and in large amounts will greatly impede the proper exhaustion of many tanning materials. Sodium carbonate is sometimes present in considerable quantities, as in some of the waters of the Leeds district. It may coexist with temporary hardness, and produces similar injurious effects. Waters in which it is present cannot have any real permanent hardness. It may be neutralised by the very cautious addition of an acid; or by admixture of a permanent-hard water. It tends to increased plumping in the limes, but neutralises the free acids of the tan-liquors which are necessary in sole-leather tanning.

Copper, lead, and other metallic bases are not likely to be present in any waters used for tanning in quantities sufficient to be injurious.

Sulphuric acid rarely occurs free in water, and then only in such traces as would be harmless for tanning, though possibly injurious to steam boilers. As sulphates it is most common. Alkaline sulphates are not known to have any deleterious action. The sulphates of lime and magnesia are the principal cause of permanent hardness, q.v. Iron sulphate is sometimes found in colliery waters.

Nitrates and nitrites in water are usually the result of "previous" sewage contamination, and are only important as an indication of the possible presence of the putrefactive ferments, and are of little moment in waters only used for manufacturing purposes, while they seem to be even useful in promoting the "working" of bran drenches, by supplying the nitrogen required by the ferment.

Chlorine is seldom or never present in water in the free state, but only in the form of chlorides, most frequently of sodium chloride (common salt), the effect of which has been referred to above, and also at p. 88. The action of other chlorides is probably similar as regards the swelling of hide. *Magnesium chloride* is very objectionable as a constituent of boiler-waters, as it liberates hydrochloric acid at high temperatures, and corrodes the plates at the surface of the water. This injury can be prevented by addition of soda.

Carbonic acid has been referred to under temporary hardness. Its presence in the free state is a matter of some importance to the tanner (see p. 99).

Silicic acid in a soluble form is present in some waters in considerable quantity. Such waters are said to harden leather, but of this the writer has no personal experience.

Few accurate researches have been made on the effect of the impurities of water on tanning, and though, from what has already been said, it will be seen that they are not without effect it is probable that in many cases the water is blamed for troubles which are simply the result of mismanagement, and credited with virtues which are really due to careful and skilful manufacture.

See Nihoul, 'Influence de l'eau sur l'extraction des matières tannantes,' Bulletin de la Bourse aux Cuirs de Liège, Sept. 1901.

The hardness of water, and the dissolved carbonic acid which it contains, are, together with its temperature, the principal factors which determine whether a hide will plump or fall in it. Almost the only accurate investigation of this point has been made by W. Eitner. He placed pieces of hide, unhaired by sweating, and quite flat and fallen, in water for four days at a temperature of 46° F. (8° C.), with the following results:—

1. In distilled water — Scarcely at all plumped.
2. ,, water saturated with CO_2 — Well plumped.
3. ,, ,, with lime bicarbonate, 20° German scale of hardness — Tolerably plump.
4. ,, ,, ,, magnesia bicarbonate, 20° do. — ,, ,,
5. ,, ,, ,, lime sulphate 20° do. — Well plumped.
6. ,, ,, ,, magnesia sulphate, 20° do — Best plumped.
7. ,, ,, ,, magnesium chloride, 20° do. — Not at all plumped.
8. ,, ,, ,, common salt, 20° do. — ,, ,,

(1 German degree of hardness corresponds to 1 of CaO in 100,000.)

Gerber, iii. (1877) p. 183.

The peculiarities which were shown by the hide pieces on removal from the water were maintained throughout the tanning, which was conducted in imitation of the German method, the hide being swollen and coloured through in weak birch-bark liquors, made with distilled water and acidified in each case with equal quantities of lactic acid, and finally laid away, till tanned, in a mixture of oak bark and valonia. No. 6, from magnesium sulphate, was the best; then No. 2; No. 3 was less good, but all the pieces from 1 to 6 were firm, close and of good substance and texture, No. 1 having swelled well in the sour liquor. On the other hand, 7 and 8 scarcely swelled in liquor, but remained flat throughout, and were looser, thinner and of finer fibre. From this experiment it is clear that while sulphates and carbonates exert a favourable influence on plumping, chlorides do the reverse, as they themselves not only do not plump, but they place the hides in an unfavourable condition for the plumping action of acids in the liquors. These experiments are quite borne out by the writer's experience in practice. The water at the Lowlights Tannery, which in dry weather was mostly obtained from beds of what was originally sea-sand, and which consequently contained a very abnormal proportion of chlorides (up to 68 pts. NaCl per 100,000), required special and very careful management to make thick leather, notwithstanding the fact that it contained a considerable quantity of calcium and magnesium sulphates. These facts also indicate the importance of the thorough removal of salt from hides intended for sole-leather. Plumping is not a desirable thing in leather intended for dressing purposes, and it is possible that the use of a small percentage of salt in the liquors or wash waters might in some cases enable bating to be dispensed with. Like a bate, salt would dissolve a small proportion of hide substance (see p. 65). There is no practicable means of removing chlorides from water, but Eitner suggests the addition of a small quantity of sulphuric acid to water containing much temporary hardness (bicarbonates), in order to convert it into permanent hardness (sulphates), which, as stated above, plumps better. The amount required may be calculated from an acidimetric determination of temporary hardness (see L.I.L.B., p. 19). A simple but not very accurate guide, is to add enough acid to purple, but not to redden litmus paper even after moving the latter about in the water for some minutes. In practice the acid must of course be very thoroughly mixed with the water by stirring and plunging. It must be borne in mind that Eitner's experiment was on sweated hides, and that with limed hide, which is kept plump by the dissolved lime retained in the hide, different results as regards carbonic acid and bicarbonates would be obtained. Both these would convert the lime in the hide into chalk, which is insoluble and inert, and the hide would fall, at any rate when the lime was completely carbonated, while hides would remain plumpest in waters most free from substances capable of neutralising lime. From this we may conclude, what may be *a priori* expected, that the purer the water, the plumper limed hides remain in it. In soft but peaty waters, hides fall rapidly, from the neutralisation of the lime by the weak organic acids of the peat. Such waters are dangerous for domestic use from their solvent action on lead, but this danger can be entirely removed by storing the water in limestone reservoirs, or allowing it to flow slowly through a limestone culvert before use. In some towns in the north of England a small quantity of lime is added so as to neutralise the water as it leaves the reservoir and before it enters the mains.

Wherever the conditions of putrefaction or decaying organic matter are present, as in a bate, hides fall rapidly, and in extreme cases even the presence of the stronger acids will not maintain plumpness. Eitner mentions the case of a stream at Vissoko in Bosnia, which was in special repute among the tanners from its power of pulling down hides rapidly, and which took its rise in a common on which the pigs of the town were pastured. The causes of this action are no doubt due to the products of putrefaction, but are somewhat obscure. Bacteria present in water are a frequent source of injury in the soaks, and probably in other stages of the tanning process.

Rain water and the water of streams in mountain districts of hard igneous rock are generally nearly free from mineral constituents. This is the case with the Glasgow water from Loch Katrine, and the Thirlmere water which supplies Manchester. Such water, if cold enough, and free from mud and organic impurity, is the best for almost every purpose in the tannery. Most river-water contains material quantities of mineral matter, though it is usually softer than that of springs or wells.

For further details as to the chemical examination of water, and the methods of determining the amounts of its different constituents, see L.I.L.B., pp. 18 *et seq.*

CHAPTER XI.
SOAKING AND SOFTENING OF HIDES AND SKINS.

As has been explained in the last chapter, hides and skins come into the hands of the tanner either uncured ("green"), as they are taken off the animal, preserved with salt or some other antiseptic, dried, or "drysalted" in which both methods are combined. His object in each case is to remove blood and dirt, and to restore the hide to its soft and natural condition; but the treatment required varies much with the state of the hides.

Fresh hides merely require cleansing from blood and dirt. This is necessary because the blood causes bad colour, and both blood, lymph and adhering dung are sources of putrefaction, which ultimately attacks the grain and fibrous structure of the hide. Hence washed hides keep better than unwashed. Cold water is most desirable, as checking putrefaction. If the water is much over 10° C., or if it is charged with organic matter and ferment-germs; or if, as is too generally the case, the hides are in a partially putrid state when received, the time of soaking must be reduced as much as possible, and it may be necessary to sterilise the water with carbolic acid or creolin (pp. 26, 28). In such cases the use of a wash-wheel, or tumbler, is very desirable, rapidly cleansing the hides and removing adhering dung, which interferes with the liming, and is a serious cause of damaged grain. The American pattern of wash-wheel shown in Fig. 21 is very suitable for the purpose. In no case is it desirable to allow green hides to lie for more than a few hours in water; and unwise treatment at this time is the cause of many troubles, which are only detected at later stages, and which are very difficult to trace to their source. "Weak grain," in which the hyaline layer (p. 50) is destroyed, and which tans a whitish colour; "pricking," or perforation of the grain with small pinholes, which may go on to "pitting" with larger holes, and a general weakening of fibre, with softening and needless loss of weight, are among these results. An instructive instance may be quoted. A large tanner found that his curried leather was affected with small spots and rings of darker colour, which rendered it quite unfit for staining, and which reappeared even when the leather was buffed. When finished as black grain, these spots had a tendency to "spue," or rise as little pimples of resinous matter. Before the leather was stuffed no defect was noticeable to the eye, but either then, or on stripping the grease by a solvent, they could be seen under the microscope as lighter patches of open and porous grain which absorbed more than their share of fat. During the tanning process they could hardly be detected, but in the first colouring they appeared for a few hours as blackish specks almost exactly like those caused by particles of iron or iron-rust. By careful observation they were traced back to the limes; specimens of the limed hide were submitted to Director Eitner, who identified the defect as "*Stippen*," caused by a species of bacteria, which cannot subsist in limes, and which therefore must have been in the soaks. These, which had been somewhat neglected from pressure of work, were cleaned out and sterilised with creolin solution, and the mischief ceased. It is worth noting that the tanner dated the beginning of the trouble from the soaking of some "Spanish" horse-hides, which may have introduced the infection. Several very similar cases have come under the writer's notice.

It is not absolutely necessary to soak fresh hides or skins at all before liming, and where the water is scarce or unfavourable, or the skins tainted or "slipping" hair, it is best to pass straight into a weak lime. In this case the limes must be worked in shifts (see p. 131) and the whole of the oldest liquor run away and the hides rapidly changed into a fresh lime, or the limes will become so charged with organic matter and bacteria that the hides will cease to plump, and may even putrefy.

Salted hides and skins require more soaking and more thorough washing than fresh ones, as it is not only necessary to remove the salt, but to soften and plump the fibre which has been dehydrated and contracted by salting. If goods with salt in them are taken into limes, they will not plump properly, and creases and wrinkles (drawn grain) are formed which no after-treatment will remove. This is especially important in sole leather. In deciding on a method, we must bear in mind that salt is easily soluble, and diffuses rapidly into water or weaker solutions, and that weak salt solutions tend to prevent the plumping of the fibre, while those of about 10 per cent. have considerable power of dissolving the cementing matter of the fibres (p. 65) and so lessening weight and firmness. It may also be noted that though salt is not a true disinfectant (p. 22), salted hides are much less prone to putrefaction than fresh ones, and therefore a longer soaking may be safely given.

Experiments mentioned on p. 89 throw some doubt on the power of salt to prevent plumping in the limes, though the opinion in the text is generally held by tanners.

These conditions point to the desirability of free exposure to water, attained by suspending, handling frequently, or tumbling, and repeated changes to remove the salt. The degree of removal of salt is easily determined by the estimation of Cl in the last wash-water (L.I.L.B., p. 18). American tanners universally soak wet-salted hides three or four days with as many changes of water, and frequently finish by a few minutes in a wash-wheel. Any washing tumbler may be used; but the cheap and simple construction of the American wash-wheel will be easily understood from

Fig. 21. The sides are open, so that hides can be put in or removed between the spokes. The rim of the wheel is generally perforated, for the escape of water which is supplied by a pipe passing through the axis; and the wheel is often driven by a chain or rope round its circumference. No severe mechanical treatment, such as "stocking," is necessary or desirable for green or salted hides.

Dry and dry-salted hides require much longer soaking than wet-salted, the amount naturally depending on the thickness of the hide and the character of drying. Even thin skins when strongly dried require considerable time to soften and swell the fibres, although they soon become wet-through and flexible. Many different methods of soaking have been employed. Sometimes hides are suspended in running water; sometimes laid in soaks which may be either renewed, or allowed to putrefy; sometimes in water to which salt, borax or carbolic acid has been added, to prevent putrefaction; and more recently weak solutions of caustic soda, sulphide of sodium or sulphurous acid have been used with much success.

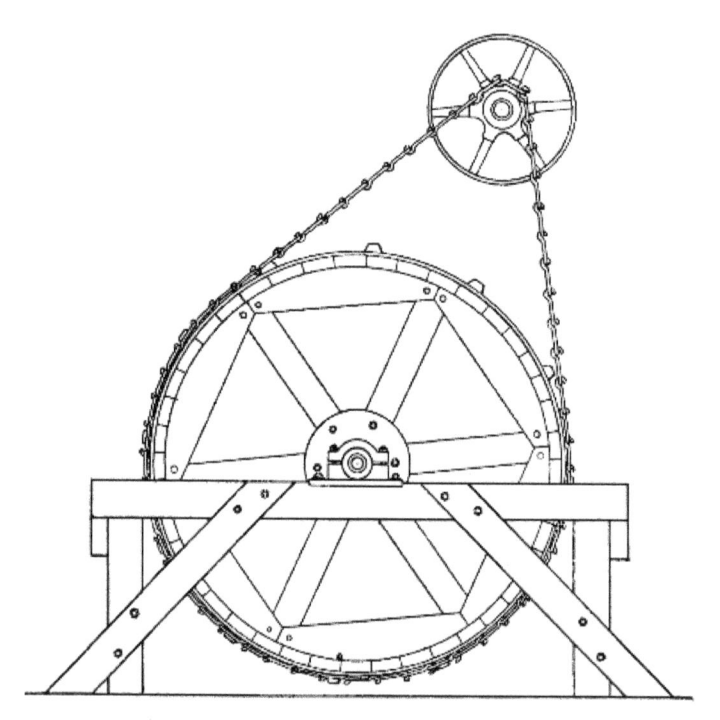

FIG. 21.—American Wash-wheel.

The first of these methods, were it desirable, is rarely possible in these days of River Pollution Acts; of the others, it is difficult to say which is better, since the treatment desirable varies with the hardness of the hide and the temperature at which it has been dried. The great object is to thoroughly soften the hide without allowing putrefaction to injure it. As dried hides are often damaged already from this cause, either before drying, or from becoming moist and heated on shipboard, it is frequently no easy matter to accomplish this. The fresh hide, as has been seen, contains considerable portions of albumin, and if the hide is dried at a high temperature, this may become wholly or partially coagulated and insoluble. The gelatinous fibre and the coriin (if indeed the latter exists ready formed in the fresh hide) do not coagulate by heat, but also become less readily soluble. Gelatin dried at 130° C. can only be redissolved by acids, or water at 120° C. Eitner experimented with pieces of green calf-skin of equal thickness, which were dried at different temperatures, with results given in the following table:—

Sample.	Temperature of Drying.	Remarks.	Time of Softening in Water.	Remarks.	Coriin Dissolved by Salt Solution.
I.	15° C.	In vacuo	24 hours	Without mechanical work	1·68 per cent.
II.	22° C.	In sun	2 days		1·62 ,,
III.	35° C.	In drying closet	5 ,,	Twice worked	0·15 ,,
IV.	60° C.	,,	-	Refused to soften sufficiently for tanning	traces

Gerber, 1880, p. 112.

Hence it is evident that, for hides dried at low temperatures, short soaking in fresh and cold water is sufficient, and, except in warm weather, there would be little danger of putrefaction. With harder drying, longer time is required, and more vigorous measures may be necessary. A well-known tanner recommended a brine of 30°-35° barkometer (sp. gr. 1·035, or about 5 per cent. of NaCl). This has a double action, not only preserving from putrefaction, but dissolving a portion of the hide-substance in the form of coriin, which is undoubtedly a loss to the tanner, though it is questionable if there is any process which will soften overdried hides without loss of weight; since even prolonged soaking in cold water at a temperature which is too low to allow of putrefaction taking place will dissolve a serious amount of hide-substance. Chlorides, however, do not seem well adapted for the purpose in view, from their weak antiseptic power and tendency to prevent swelling. To prevent this Jackson Schulz advised the use of water at 80° F. for soaking during the winter months. Water containing a small quantity (0·1 per cent.) of carbolic acid has been recommended for the purpose, and will prevent putrefaction, while it has no solvent power on the hide, but, on the contrary, tends to coagulate and render insoluble albuminous matters. Borax has been proposed for the same purpose, and, in 1 per cent. solution, certainly prevents putrefaction, and has considerable softening power, but is far too costly. Other methods of chemical softening are described on p. 115.

For some descriptions of hides, and notably for India kips, putrid soaks were formerly much employed, the putrefactive action softening and rendering soluble the hardened tissue. In India the native tanners soften their hides in very few hours by plunging them in putrid pools, into which every description of tannery refuse is allowed to run. Putrefactive processes, however, are always dangerous, as the action, through changes of temperature, or variation in the previous state of the liquor, is apt to be irregular, and either to attack one portion of the hide before another, or to proceed faster than was expected. Hides are also frequently more or less damaged by putrefaction and heating during the process of cure, and these damages are accentuated in a putrid soak. Hence hides in the soaks require constant and careful watching, and the goods must be withdrawn as soon as they are thoroughly softened, for the putrefaction is constantly destroying as well as softening the hides. It is possible that putrefactive softening is less injurious to kips, and such goods as are intended for upper-leather, than to those for sole purposes, as it is generally considered necessary in the former case that a good deal of the albumen and interfibrillary matter be removed, and that the fibre be well divided into its constituent fibrils for the sake of softness and pliability; and thus the putrid soak, if acting rightly, accomplishes part of the work which would afterwards have to be done by the lime and the bate, as the actual fibre of the hide seems less readily putrescible than the softer cementing substance.

Putrefaction is caused, as we have seen, by a great variety of living organisms, each of which has its own special products and modes of action. It is quite possible that, if we knew what precise form of putrefaction was most advantageous, we might by appropriate conditions be able to encourage it, to the exclusion of others, and obtain better results than at present. Putrid soaks (in the old sense) are, however, disused in the present day by all enlightened tanners, as it is recognised that the risks outbalance the advantages, and when drysalted hides are worked, the soluble salts of the cure accumulate to an injurious extent. The modern method, where no chemicals are used, is to give one fresh water at least to each pack of hides or skins. Even in this case considerable putrefaction takes place where the soaking occupies 7 to 14 days, as is the case with kips and hides, and it is probable that the use of chemical and antiseptic methods of soaking will ultimately be generally adopted, both on technical and sanitary grounds.

The use of dilute acids for softening has much to recommend it, their power of causing the fibre to swell and absorb water being quite equal to that of the alkalies, while few, if any, putrefactive bacteria can thrive in an acid liquid. Very dilute sulphuric acid has been used with success to dissolve the alkaline "plaster" of East India kips (p. 39). It has considerable disinfectant power (p. 23), but its action on the hide-fibre is undesirably strong.

Sulphurous acid is much more suitable. Its use for this purpose was patented by Maynard, along with a number of other possible uses, but the patent has now lapsed, and he does not seem to have succeeded in introducing it into practice. Experiments at the Yorkshire College, and also at a tannery on a manufacturing scale, have shown that the method is capable of excellent results. The hides are soaked for 24-48 hours in a solution of sulphurous acid containing about 2 per cent. of SO_2 (for manufacture, compare p. 24; for testing, L.I.L.B., pp. 16, 37), and are then transferred to water, where they swell freely to their full thickness. They may be either limed at once, or first neutralised with dilute caustic soda, ammonia, or sulphide of sodium, which, for dressing leather, is perhaps desirable. No putrefaction takes place, even if they are retained for a considerable time in water, and the acid has little or no solvent effect on the hide-fibre, the strength of which is well preserved. The liming, however, must either be conducted with the aid of sodium sulphide or in old limes, since the sterile condition of the hides renders liming in fresh lime very slow (cp. p. 137). For experimental purposes a ½ per cent. solution of Boakes' "metabisulphite of soda" may be used, to which ¼ per cent. of concentrated sulphuric acid previously diluted with water is gradually added during the soaking, the hides being first withdrawn. For permanent work it will be found much cheaper to manufacture the acid on the spot by burning sulphur.

The use of solutions of caustic soda (1 part per 1000), or of sodium sulphide (1½-3 parts per 1000) as suggested by Eitner, seems at present likely to supersede all other methods of softening from their simplicity and safety. Twenty-four to forty-eight hours in either of these solutions, which may if necessary be followed by a short soak in plain water, seem sufficient to soften either kips or hides. Experiments at the Yorkshire College have shown that solutions of this strength have little or no solvent action on the hide-fibre, but promote its swelling in water so effectively that no mechanical softening is needed (though a slight drumming is advantageous), while putrefaction is almost entirely prevented, so that the solution may be repeatedly used if kept up to its original strength, which is easily determined with standard acid and phenolphthalein (see L.I.L.B., p. 17). Neither caustic soda nor sodium sulphide have any injurious effect on liming, though it may prove somewhat slower than with the older methods, where the epidermis was partially destroyed by the action of putrid ferments. The dilute solutions used are not only less injurious to the hide than those of greater strength, but they are also more effective in softening. Eitner (Gerber, 1899, p. 584) states that when using a solution of caustic soda of 1 part in 1000 strength, the time required to soften some hides was only two days, as against three days for a sodium sulphide liquor, and four days for pure water, and that with the soda solution only about 0·6 per cent of the hide-substance of the skin was dissolved out, whilst when sodium sulphide was used it was 0·7 per cent., and with pure water alone no less than 1·9 per cent. was lost by solution.

The use of moderately warm water (40° C.) in a drum is quite successful in rapidly softening sound hides after they have previously been soaked for some days in cold water; but if they are tainted in the cure, it is very apt to intensify the mischief. Hides which have partially putrefied internally, or which have been exposed to a hot sun while the interior is still moist, are very apt to appear sound while dry, but to blister or go to pieces from the destruction of the fibres as soon as they are limed, and this in spite of even the most careful treatment. For tainted hides, caustic soda is probably preferable to sodium sulphide.

Many chemicals have been patented for softening hides. Sulphide of arsenic is said to be in use, and if dissolved in caustic soda solution would differ little in its effect from ordinary sulphide of sodium. Saltpetre has also been employed, but its effect, if any, was probably merely antiseptic. Ordinary sodium carbonate has been used, but is less effective than caustic soda. Gas liquor and mixtures of this with tar and water were patented by Barron, and probably the first would soften by virtue of its ammonia and sulphides, while tar contains carbolic acid. Probably the most absurd mixture of all was patented by Berry, which consisted of ½ bucket of slaked lime, ½ bucket of wood-ashes, 12 lbs. of potash, 5 lbs. of oil of vitriol, and 4 lbs. of spirit of salt!

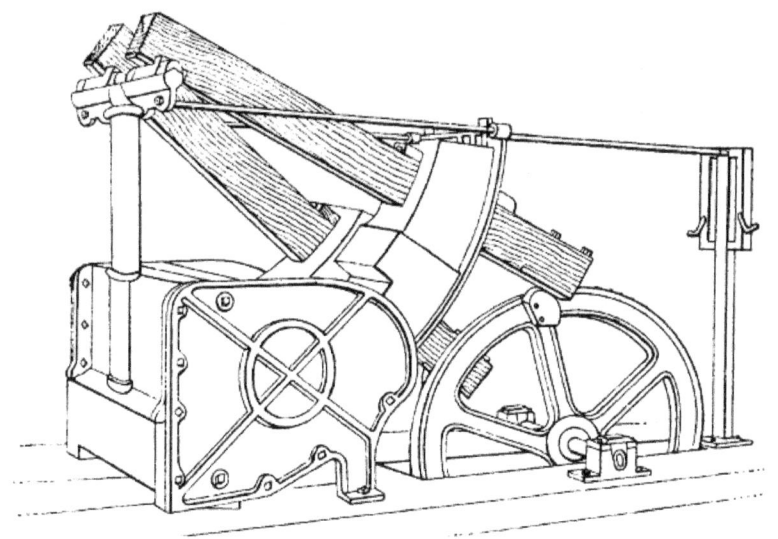

FIG. 22.—Faller Stocks.

Beside merely soaking the hides, it is sometimes necessary to work them mechanically, to promote their softening; this was formerly accomplished by "breaking over" the hides on the beam with a blunt knife. This process is still in use for skins of many sorts, but for the heavier classes of leather is now usually superseded or supplemented by the use of "stocks," or drums. The former consist of a wooden or metallic box, of peculiar shape, wherein work two very heavy hammers, raised alternately by pins or cams on a wheel, and let fall upon the hides, which they force up against the curved end of the box with a sort of kneading action. The ordinary form of this machine is shown in Fig. 22. A more modern form, which seems to possess some advantages, is the American "double-shover," or "hide-mill," seen in Fig. 23. "Crank stocks," similar in form to the faller stocks, but driven by cranks, are sometimes used for softening, but are better adapted to lighter uses.

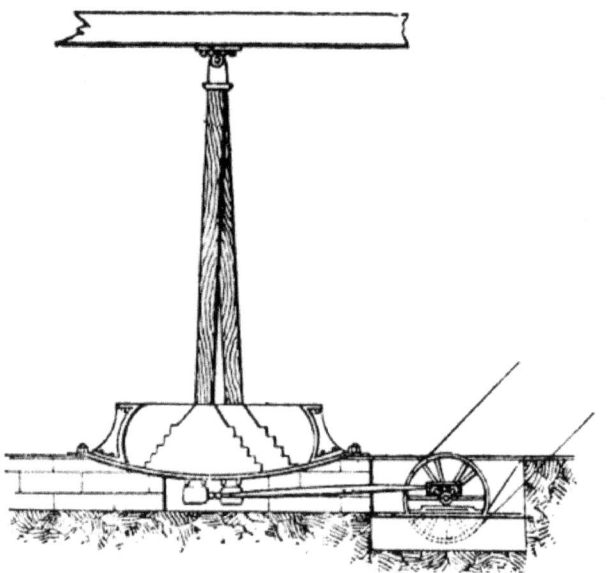

FIG. 23.—American Hide-Mill.

The number of hides which can be stocked at once naturally varies with the size of both hides and stocks, but should be such that the hides work regularly and steadily over and over. The whole number should not be put in at once, but should be added one after another, as they get into regular work. The duration of stocking is 10-30 min., according to the condition and character of the hides. Hides should not be stocked until they are so far softened that they can be doubled sharply, without breaking or straining the fibre. After stocking, they must be soaked again for a short time, and then be brought into an old lime. A small quantity of sodium sulphide added to the soaks or in the stocks has been recommended as of great value in softening obstinate hides, and probably with justice, from its well-known softening action upon cellular and horny tissues.

Tumbler drums of various forms may also be used with good effect for softening purposes, especially for skins, and are much less detrimental than stocking, both as regards the weight and quality of the goods.

For sole leather, and even for kips, the use of stocks has in recent years been entirely discarded by many of the more advanced tanners. If mechanical work is required at all, the drum is preferred, and is sometimes employed after a few days' liming, the goods being first merely softened in fresh water. The use of caustic soda, sodium sulphide, or sulphurous acid renders mechanical softening almost unnecessary.

FIG. 24.—Drum for Washing or Tanning.

The drums employed are in principle like a barrel-churn, and are large cylindrical wooden chambers 6 to 12 feet in diameter, and fitted inside either with shelves like the floats of a water-wheel, or with rounded pegs on which the hides fall. The American wash-wheel figured on p. 111 is a machine of this kind, and one of a more elaborate description is shown in Fig. 24. Drums are not only used for softening, but for tanning, dyeing, and many other purposes in leather manufacture. It is advantageous to be able to reverse the direction of their rotation to prevent the rolling up of the hides.

CHAPTER XII.
DEPILATION.

After the softening and cleansing of the hide or skin is completed, and before proceeding to tan it, it is usually necessary to remove the hair or wool. The earliest method of accomplishing this was by means of incipient putrefaction, which attacks in the first instance the soft mucous matter of the epidermis, and thus loosens the hair without materially injuring the true skin. This loosening of the hair often takes place accidentally in hides which have been kept too long without salting, and is known as "slipping," and is apt to be accompanied by some degree of injury to the grain. The old method of loosening the hair by putrefaction, or, as it is generally called, "sweating," was to lay the hides in piles, usually in some warm and damp place. Occasionally a slight preliminary salting was given to prevent too much putrefaction of the hide. The action in this case, however, was very irregular, and it has been quite abandoned in all civilised countries.

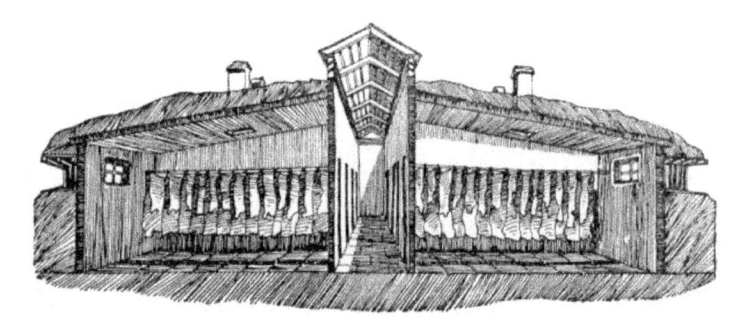

FIG. 25.—Sweat-Pit.

The method which is now used is to hang the hides in a closed chamber, generally called a "sweat-pit," Fig. 25, but usually constructed above the ground-level and protected from sudden changes of temperature by double walls, or by mounds of earth. The hides are hung in the sweat-pit, in small chambers each capable of holding 50 or 100 hides. The temperature is kept at about 15° to 20° C., the air being warmed, if necessary, by the admission of steam below a perforated floor, or cooled by a shower of water from sprinklers, so arranged as not to play directly on the skins, and is thus always kept saturated with moisture. Little if any ventilation is allowed, and a large quantity of ammonia is given off from the decomposition of the organic matter, and no doubt contributes to the solution of the epidermis and the loosening of the hair, as the writer has found that ammoniacal vapours alone very speedily produce this effect.

After 4-6 days of this treatment, the hair is sufficiently loosened to be removed by working the skin over the beam with a blunt knife, or by means of the stocks or hide-mill (see p. 116). Great care and watchfulness are required to avoid injury to the grain by putrefaction.

The hide is in a slimy and completely flaccid and "fallen" condition, and some trouble is occasioned by the hair being worked into the flesh by the hide-mill, to obviate which, a slight liming is frequently given after the sweating. Hides which have been unhaired in this way require to be swollen by acid in the liquors in order to produce a satisfactory sole-leather, as the sweating process does not swell or split up the fibres.

In some European tanneries a similar process, but at a higher temperature, is employed, and it is also largely used for sheep-skins under the name of "staling," but in this case is sometimes conducted in a very rude and primitive manner, and frequently with the result of considerable injury to the pelt.

The great objection to the sweating process, however carefully conducted, is the liability of putrefaction to attack the skin itself, causing "weak grain." Its most advantageous use is for sole leather, as, although the solution of the hide-substance may not be very much less than in the case of liming, the dissolved matter remains in the hide instead of being washed out, and being fixed by the tannin, contributes to the solidity of the leather.

In England, lime is the agent almost universally employed for unhairing, though every tanner admits its deficiencies and disadvantages. It is hard, however, to recommend a substitute which is free from the same or greater evils, and lime has one or two valuable qualities which will make it very difficult to supersede. One of these is that, though it inevitably causes loss of substance and weight, it is also impossible, with any reasonable care, totally to destroy a pack of hides by its use; which is by no means the case with some of its rivals. Another advantage is that, owing to the very limited solubility of lime in water, it is of comparatively small consequence whether much or little is used; and even if the hides are left in a few days longer than necessary, the mischief, though certain, is only to be detected by careful and accurate observation. With all other methods, exact time and quantity are of primary importance, and it is not easy to get ordinary workmen to pay the necessary attention to such details. Again, the qualities of lime, its virtues and failings, have been matter of experience for hundreds of years, and so far as such experience can teach, we know exactly how to deal with it. A new method, on the other hand, brings new and unlooked-for difficulties, and often requires changes in other parts of the process, as well as in the mere unhairing, to make it successful. As our knowledge of the chemical and physical changes involved becomes greater, we may look to overcoming these obstacles more readily.

The universal source of lime is chalk or limestone, which consists of calcium carbonate, and from which the carbon dioxide is driven off by burning in a kiln. Many limestones, however, are far from being pure calcium carbonate, but contain large proportions of magnesia, iron and alumina, the latter perhaps originally deposited in the form of clay with the sediment from which the stone was formed. Such clay limestones when burnt yield natural cements, like oolite and other "hydraulic" limes, which are capable of setting even under water. The presence of magnesia and clay is injurious not only by diminishing the amount of lime present, but by making the lime much more difficult to slake; and iron oxide, though quite insoluble, may become mechanically fixed in the grain of the hide, and may be the cause of subsequent stains. The burning of lime in the kiln is probably not quite so simple an operation as the equations of the text-books would suggest. By mere heating, the carbonate can, it is true, be decomposed, but to do this completely a good white heat is required, which is rarely attained in practical burning, and it is probable that at least a part of the carbon dioxide present is reduced to carbon monoxide by the combustible fuel-gases, and so separated from the lime, for which it has no affinity. Carbon monoxide is the cause of the intensely poisonous character of limekiln gases, the pure dioxide being irrespirable, but not strictly poisonous.

Quicklime, CaO, on coming in contact with water, combines with it with the evolution of considerable heat, becoming slaked or converted into hydrate, $Ca(OH)_2$. This change takes place rapidly and easily when the lime is light and porous, such as is obtained by the burning of chalk or good limestone at a low temperature; but if it has been too intensely heated or "over-burnt," or contains silicates or other salts which fuse at the temperature of the kiln, a compact lime is formed which slakes with difficulty and extreme slowness, thus being lost to the tanner, or leading to the still more serious result of burning holes in the hides by the heat produced by slaking in contact with them. It is stated by Le Chatelier that for dense limes 24-48 hours is frequently required for complete slaking in the cold, while magnesia is still more obstinate, months being sometimes necessary for the complete hydration of hard-burnt samples; and mixtures of lime and magnesia are intermediate in their character. Slaking is greatly assisted by heat, even heavily burnt magnesia being hydrated in about six hours at 100° C. Slaking is also much more rapid in a dilute solution (2 per cent.) of calcium or magnesium chloride. From these facts it is easy to deduce the reason why a suitable quantity of water, neither too much nor too little, is desirable for the rapid and effectual slaking of lime. If too little is used, the lime is only partially slaked, and it is not easy for further portions of water to gain access to the interior of the powdery mass. On the other hand, if it is "drowned" by excess, the temperature is lowered, the process goes on slowly, and the mass does not readily fall into powder, and so fails to be utilised in the liming process. Of all methods of slaking lime, the ordinary one of tipping it direct into the lime-pits is perhaps the most irrational, leading to the formation of unslaked lumps which may burn the hides, and which, together with stones and dirt, rapidly choke the pits with useless matter. The best process is that adopted by builders and in many Continental yards, in which a large quantity of lime is slaked in a shallow tank by throwing on it sufficient water to thoroughly wet it, and after allowing it to heat and fall for 24 hours, adding enough water to convert it into a stiff paste. In this form it may be kept for months without material deterioration. When required for use, a suitable quantity of the paste is dug out, and well stirred with water in a tub or tank before running into the pit when the stones and sand remain in the tank. In this way all nuisance from dust is also avoided. If lime is stored unslaked, it gradually absorbs moisture from the air, falling, and soon becoming dusty and difficult to slake completely, while the traces of carbon dioxide in the air gradually convert it into useless carbonate.

Bull. de la Soc. d'Encouragement, 1895, x. pp. 52-62; Journ. Soc. Chem. Ind., 1895, p. 575.

The solubility of lime in water is very limited, and the figures determined by different chemists do not agree very satisfactorily. The following table gives the result of determinations made by Mr. A. Guthrie in the Author's laboratory, and is probably one of the most accurate:—

100 c.c. of saturated lime water at $5°$ C. contain $0·1350$ grm. of CaO.

,,	,,	$10°$	,,	$0·1342$	,,
,,	,,	$15°$	,,	$0·1320$	,,
,,	,,	$20°$	,,	$0·1293$	,,
,,	,,	$25°$	,,	$0·1254$	,,
,,	,,	$30°$	,,	$0·1219$	,,
,,	,,	$35°$	,,	$0·1161$	,,
,,	,,	$40°$	,,	$0·1119$	,,
,,	,,	$50°$	,,	$0·0981$	,,

,,	,,	60°	,,	0·0879	,,
,,	,,	70°	,,	0·0781	,,
,,	,,	80°	,,	0·0740	,,
,,	,,	90°	,,	0·0696	,,
,,	,,	100°	,,	0·0597	,,

Journ. Soc. Chem. Ind., 1901, p. 224.

It will be noticed that unlike that of most substances, the solubility of lime in water diminishes as the temperature is raised. It is therefore necessary in employing lime-water as a standard solution to take care that it is saturated at a constant temperature. The results given in the above table are those from pure marble lime. Where the ordinary impure limes from limestone are employed, a somewhat stronger lime-water is often obtained. This is difficult to explain, but possibly some double hydrate of lime and magnesia is formed which is more soluble than either hydrate alone. The results harmonise with the old belief of tanners that chalk-lime is milder in its action on skin than that made from less pure limestones. The solubility of any given lime is easily determined by adding it in excess to water in a stoppered flask, and shaking frequently until a solution of constant strength is obtained. A known volume of this solution (which must be clear and free from undissolved lime) is then titrated with $N/10$ hydrochloric acid, using phenolphthalein as the indicator.

Saturated lime-water may be conveniently used as an alkaline standard solution for many purposes, and if kept on excess of lime is always caustic, and varies very little in strength at ordinary laboratory temperatures. The solution is nearly $1/20$ normal, but for accurate work its strength should be exactly determined with $N/10$ acid. 1 liter of pure lime-water at 15° C. should require 471·4 c.c. of $N/10$ acid for neutralisation.

Lime is much more soluble in sugar solutions than in water. Such solutions have been used as standard solutions, and sugar has been added to limes to increase the action on the hides.

The following is the analysis of a lime used in a Leeds tannery, which was made by Mr. G. W. Flower, B.Sc., in the Leather Industries Laboratory of the Yorkshire College:—

Per cent.

SiO_2 and insoluble matter   17·70

Fe_2O_3	6·42
CaO	49·86
$CaCO_3$	14·21
$CaSO_4$	3·01
$CaCl_2$	0·33
MgO	2·09
Organic matter	0·80
Moisture by difference	5·58
	100·00

Journ. Soc. Chem. Ind., 1901, p. 224.

The sample only contained 31·02 per cent. of available lime, the remainder being probably combined with the silica. It also contained an appreciable quantity of iron oxide, which might lodge mechanically in the pores of the skin and become dissolved in later processes, darkening the colour of the leather. The lime was also under-burnt, judging from the amount of carbonate it contained.

For comparison with this, the analysis of a good specimen of carboniferous-limestone lime from Buxton may be given:—

	Per cent.
CaO	91·95
MgO	1·30
CO_2 and moisture	6·75
	100·00

Determination of "Available" Lime.—The practical value of lime for the tanner is easily determined by drawing a sample by breaking off small pieces from a number of lumps of the bulk, coarsely pulverising them in a mortar, and then rapidly grinding a portion as fine as possible, and transferring it at once to a stoppered bottle for weighing. A portion of this, not exceeding 1 grm., is shaken into a stoppered liter flask, which is filled up roughly to the mark with hot and well-boiled distilled water, and allowed to stand for some hours with occasional shaking. When cold it is filled exactly to the mark with cold distilled water, well shaken again and allowed to settle, or rapidly filtered, and 25 or 50 c.c. of the clear liquid withdrawn with a pipette and titrated with $N/10$ hydrochloric or sulphuric acid and phenolphthalein. Each cubic centimeter of $N/10$ acid equals ·0028 grm. CaO. It is generally a very mistaken economy to make use of an inferior lime for tanning purposes, as any saving in cost is discounted by the larger quantity required, the more frequent cleaning of the pits, and the danger of stains and of burns from imperfect slaking.

The action of lime on the hide has already been spoken of to some extent. It is throughout a solvent one. The hardened cells of the epidermis swell up and soften, the mucous or growing layer and the hair-sheaths are loosened and dissolved, so that, on scraping with a blunt knife, both come away more or less completely with the hair (constituting "scud" or "scurf," Ger. *Gneist* or *Grund*). The hair itself is very slightly altered, except at its soft and growing root-bulb, but the true skin is vigorously acted on. The fibres swell and absorb water, so that the hides become plump and swollen, and, at the same time, the "cement-substance" of the fibres is dissolved, and they become split-up into finer fibrils: the fibrils themselves become first swollen and transparent, and finally corroded, and even dissolved. A similar swelling of the fibres is produced by both alkalies and acids, and is probably due to weak combinations formed with the fibre-substance, which have greater affinities for water than the unaltered hide. This swelling is useful to the tanner, since it renders the hide easier to "flesh" (i.e. to free from the adhering flesh) on account of the greater firmness which it gives to the true skin. It also assists the tanning, by splitting up the fibre into its individual fibrils, and so exposing a greater surface to the action of the liquors. This is advantageous in dressing-leather which is afterwards tanned in sweet liquors, and which must have the cement-substance of the fibres dissolved and removed for the sake of flexibility; and, in the case of sole-leather, it is necessary for sake of weight and firmness that the hide be plumped at some stage of the process; but it is probable that this effect is produced with less loss of substance and solidity by suitable acidity of the tanning-liquors. Another advantage of lime is that it acts on the fat of the hide, converting it more or less completely into an insoluble soap, and so hindering its injurious effects on the after tanning process, and on the finished leather. If strong acids whether mineral or organic are used later on, this lime soap is decomposed, and the grease is again set free. In sweated or very low-limed hides this grease is a formidable evil, causing darkening or grease spots on the finished leather.

Cp. p. 84.

This has been questioned, but I have satisfied myself it is correct.

The customary method of liming is simply to lay the hides horizontally one at once in milk of lime in large pits, taking care that each hide is completely immersed before the next is put into the pit, so as to ensure a sufficiency of liquor between them. Every day, or even twice a day, the hides are drawn out ("hauled"), and the pit is well plunged up, to distribute the undissolved lime through the liquor. The hides are then drawn in again ("set"), care being taken that they are fully spread out. How much lime is required is doubtful, but owing to its limited solubility, an excess, if well slaked, is rather wasteful than injurious. Great differences exist in the quantity of the lime used, the time given, and the method of working, not only for various classes of leather, but for the same kinds in different yards. Lime, as we have seen, is only soluble to the extent of about 1·25 grm. per litre, or (as 1 cub. foot of water weighs about 1000 oz.) say 1¼ oz. per cub. foot, or, in an ordinary lime-pit, not more than ¼ lb. per hide. Only the lime in solution acts on the hide, but it is necessary to provide a surplus of solid lime which dissolves as that in the liquor is consumed or absorbed by the hide; and this is especially the case where, as is generally customary, the hides are laid flat in pits, so that no circulation of liquor is possible. Where hides are suspended in lime-water, which is constantly circulated and kept up to its full strength by agitation in another vessel with solid lime, they unhair as quickly as with milk of lime, but the method seems, in the case of lime, to present no special advantage over the ordinary one, if in the latter the hides are hauled sufficiently often to keep the lime uniformly distributed. The case is otherwise in dealing with more soluble depilatories. Various patents have been taken for methods of liming by suspending in liquors, but the idea is now public property, and is largely used on the Continent. It is necessary that the lime which settles to the bottom of the pit should be agitated and kept in suspension, which may be effected either by moving the hides on a frame as in "suspenders" (p. 221), or by agitators acting on the principle of pumps, and raising the liquor and sludge from the bottom. Such agitators have been patented in Germany, but had been in use much earlier in the Author's tanyard. An agitator on the principle of the screw-propeller of a steamship, placed near the bottom of the pit, and protected by a lattice, may also be usefully employed (Fig. 26). Skins are frequently limed in paddles, or stirred up by blowing air into the pit. The latter method is neither effective nor economical in power.

FIG. 26.—Suspension Lime-Pit.

As has been noted, the solubility of lime, and consequently the strength of the lime-liquor, is diminished by rise of temperature, but its solvent action on hide-substance is much increased. As a consequence, the loosening of the hair proceeds much more rapidly in warm limes, but the hides do not plump well, and become loose, hollow and inclined to "pipe" in the grain, and to weigh out badly, and for sole leather the method is therefore in every way disastrous. In the few cases among the lighter leathers where a decided softening and loosening of the texture of the skin is required, it is possible that useful advantage may be taken of this effect; but it would be exceedingly difficult to regulate the temperature of an ordinary lime-pit with accuracy, and better results could probably be obtained with suspenders in which the liquor could be constantly circulated. When limes are very cold, in spite of the greater strength of solution, the action is very much checked, and where goods are frozen into pits in severe weather, there is but little danger of overliming, although the usual time may be much exceeded. It is generally best to work limes at about the ordinary summer temperature, and this is better done in winter by warming the limeyard than by any direct heating of the limes. If lime which has cooled after slaking is used, the water with which limes are made may safely be warmed in midwinter to a temperature not exceeding 20° C.

The quantity of lime used by different tanners, and for different sorts of hides and skins, is very variable, not only according to the effect which it is desired to produce, and the way in which it is used, but from the arbitrary fancy of the user, since its limited solubility renders an excess comparatively innocuous. For sole-leather, the amount recommended varies from under 1 per cent. to 10 or 12 per cent. on the green weight of the hide; but probably 2-3 per cent. is all that can be really utilised, the remainder being wasted. In order, however, to utilise the whole of the lime, very frequent handling or agitation is required to ensure its uniform distribution. It must also be borne in mind that the strength of commercial limes varies from above 80 down to 30 per cent. of available calcium oxide.

Von Schroeder has found that a strength of 6 grams of calcium oxide (CaO) per liter was sufficient, but, in practice, much more is generally added. It is also noteworthy that a perfectly fresh milk of lime must be made much stronger than one which has been used. This is partially due to the fact that some bacterial action takes place in an old lime and that ammonia is formed which assists unhairing, in addition to the effect of the lime itself, and partially because the lime in old liquors remains in suspension for a much longer time, and is thus more evenly distributed.

A method of liming, sometimes known as the "Buffalo method," has been largely adopted for sole-leather in America, and is now used in many Continental yards. It consists in a very short liming and the subsequent use of warm water. The limes are also often sharpened by the addition of a little sodium sulphide or of some other sulphide. Thus, in one large yard in the States, the hides for sole-leather (salted "packers") are limed for 10 hours only with 2 lb. lime and 2½ oz. of sulphide of sodium per side, and after lying overnight in water of a temperature of 35-45° C., are easily unhaired. A Continental firm lime two days in weak fresh limes with a little tank-waste, and then treat with water at 32° C. for 6-8 hours, when the hides are unhaired and returned to the warm water for two hours before scudding. All sorts of combinations between liming and hot water treatment can be employed. The longer and stronger the liming, the lower temperature or shorter time in the water will suffice. The method is much to be recommended for firm sole-leather, but it does not saponify grease or swell the fibres thoroughly, and usually vitriol is used for the latter purpose in a later stage. The hide goes into the liquors practically free of lime, and the loss of hide-substance is much less than in the ordinary method of liming.

A point of probably much greater importance than the quantity of lime used is the length of time during which a lime is worked without change of liquor. An old lime becomes charged with ammonia and other products of the action of lime upon the skin, such as tyrosin, leucin (amidocaproic acid), and some caproic acid, the disagreeable goaty odour of which is very obvious on acidifying an old lime-liquor with sulphuric acid, by which considerable quantities of partially altered gelatin are at the same time precipitated (compare p. 64). Lime has considerable antiseptic power, and a new lime is practically sterile, but very old limes, especially in hot weather, often contain large numbers of active bacteria, which may be seen in the microscope under a good $\frac{1}{6}$-inch objective. Their presence is always an indication that putrefaction is going forward, and if their number be very excessive, the leather out of such limes will generally prove loose, hollow and dull-grained, and in extreme cases hides may be totally destroyed. Spherical concretions of calcium carbonate may also be seen under the microscope, resembling on a smaller scale those found in Permian limestone, and caused perhaps in both cases by crystallisation from a liquid containing much organic matter. It is hardly probable that in many tanneries the ammonia would pay for recovery from the lime-liquors, though it could be easily done by steaming the old limes in suitable vessels, and condensing the ammoniacal vapours in dilute sulphuric acid. Its quantity rarely exceeds 0·1 per cent. of NH_3. For methods of estimation of ammonia, see L.I.L.B., p. 30.

Up to a certain point, it is found that old limes unhair much more readily, and have a greater softening effect than new ones, which is often advantageous for dressing goods; though for sole leather, where weight and firmness are of primary importance, the use of stale limes must be kept within the narrowest limits. In the finer leathers also, such as kid and moroccos and coloured calf, where a sound and glossy grain is desired, the effects mentioned are generally better obtained in other ways, such as by the use of sulphides. On East India kips and other dried hides, which are difficult to soften, and which have great power of resistance to the action of lime, old limes are distinctly useful, but, even there, there are limits which should not be passed. Probably no lime ought to be allowed to go for more than three months at the outside limit without at least a partial change of liquor, and the system of allowing all the limes in a yard to run for twelve months, and then cleaning them all together, is almost the worst which can be planned. A very much better way is to clean the limes in regular rotation, using, if desired, a portion of the old liquor in making the new lime, so as to avoid a too sudden transition. The old liquor is valuable, if at all, for the ammonia and organic matter which it contains, as the amount of lime in solution is not worth considering. The ammonia considerably increases the solvent and unhairing power, while swelling the hide less than an equivalent amount of lime. In some cases it may be desirable to add ammonia artificially for this purpose. In this case it will be cheaper and more convenient to add it in the form of ammonium sulphate than as liquid ammonia. If it be desired to retain ammonia, the lime should be kept covered. Very old limes containing excess of ammonia and lime, sometimes in hot weather cause a transparent swelling of the goods, with destruction of the fibrous texture. The writer has observed a similar phenomenon in very weak and old limes strengthened with sulphides, in which hide was left experimentally for several weeks. The principal effect of the dissolved animal matter is to enable bacteria to thrive in it, which they will not do in a fresh lime, but putrid limes probably also contain liquefying ferments produced by the bacteria present (p. 17), and which dissolve hide. Eitner has published researches on the amount of hide-substance dissolved by limes, in which he shows that the loss of substance in liming sufficiently to unhair is materially greater in old limes than in fresh ones, although during the first two days of liming the new limes are decidedly the most active. As he remarks, this justifies the wisdom of the method, now largely adopted, of working limes in shifts, and beginning the operation in old limes and completing it in fresh ones. (See also p. 131.)

Gerber, 1884, pp. 150, 184.

Gerber, 1895, pp. 157-9, 169-72.

For details of the analytical methods employed, Eitner's original paper must be consulted, but the annexed table (see next page) summarises his results. The letters heading the columns have the following meanings.

A. Hide substance precipitated by neutralisation of the lime with carbonic acid.

B. A further precipitate obtained by slight acidification with hydrochloric acid.

C. Soluble peptones precipitated by hypochlorous acid or mercuric nitrate.

It is obvious that none of these figures represent the *total* dissolved organic matter, and it is to be regretted that this was not determined. It is, however, fairly safe to assume that the table correctly represents the relative solubility in the different liquors. In each case 2 liters of liquor were used for each kilo of green hide. When old liquors were employed, the hide-substance they originally contained was determined, and deducted from the final result.

	Hide Used.	Description of Lime Liquor.	Days Liming.	Hide-substances in Grams per Liter.				Loss per cent. on Dry Pelt.
				A.	B.	C.	Total.	
1	Oxhide	Fresh lime 30 grm. per liter	6	1·068	0·324	2·370	3·762	2·35
2	,,	Ditto	9	2·764	0·540	3·624	6·928	4·14
3	,,	Fresh lime 30 grm., ½ grm. sulphide of sodium per liter	5	0·852	0·172	1·816	2·840	1·75
4	,,	Ditto	8	1·240	0·514	3·846	5·600	3·36
5	,,	5 weeks old lime, through which four packs had passed	2	0·180	0·212	0·988	1·380	0·87

6	,,	Ditto		5	0·868	1·318	3·356	5·542	3·46
7	,,	5 months old lime, with sodium sulphide	-	2	0·196	0·188	0·864	1·248	0·77
8	,,	Ditto		5	0·928	1·198	3·004	5·130	3·06
9	Cowhide	Fresh lime as above	-	5	1·982	0·413	4·501	6·896	4·30
10	,,	Ditto		8	3·132	0·672	5·741	9·545	5·94
11	,,	Fresh lime as above, and ½ grm. sodium sulphide per liter	-	5	1·012	0·403	2·315	4·730	2·96
12	,,	Ditto		8	2·521	0·653	5·026	8·200	4·87
13	,,	Old disused lime	-	5	0·344	0·291	2·341	2·976	1·84

14	,,	Ditto	8	2·119	1·697	6·952	10·768	6·45
15	,,	Used sulphide of sodium lime 4 weeks old	5	..	1·600	1·047	2·527	1·58
16	,,	Ditto	8	0·791	0·519	4·592	5·892	3·43

Hides unhaired.

Taking into account the liming necessary for unhairing only, as shown in the table, it will be noted that the percentage of loss is invariably greater in old limes than in new ones, and less in limes sharpened with sulphide of sodium than where lime alone is used. The only exception to this rule is in No. 15, where a sulphide lime 4 weeks old shows the least loss of any in the time required for unhairing; and indeed sulphide limes if kept strengthened with the requisite addition of sulphide, seem to deteriorate very slowly, No. 8, with a lime 5 months old, showing a result which may still be considered good. Another point especially noted by Eitner is the slight action of old limes during the first stages of liming, as compared with their rapid solvent effect as the hair becomes loosened. The loss in any case does not appear to be so great as the advocates of other unhairing processes have often claimed. If we assume that all the dissolved hide-substance might have made leather, the worst loss on oxhide only limed to the point of unhairing amounts to less than 3½ per cent. on the possible total; and it must be remembered that at least a part of this consists of dissolved epidermis matter, which could not by any possible method have been converted into leather. It will be noted in Nos. 2, 4, 10, 12 and 16, what considerable losses are produced by plumping limes after unhairing, but it must be borne in mind that, in the case of dressing-leather, solution of at least a part of the cementing matter is essential to produce the necessary softness and flexibility. Eitner calculates the dry pelt-weight from that of the green hide on the assumption, based on experiment, that 100 parts of the original skin corresponds to 32 parts of dry pure pelt in green oxhide, 25 parts in green calf-skins, and 56 parts in dried calf-skins. In some of the smaller skins, such as kid worked for glove leather, where great softness and stretch is required, the loss is necessarily much greater than in ordinary dressing-leathers, amounting, in the case of kid, to from 20 to 27 per cent.

The parts taken by the purely chemical activity of the lime, and by the action of bacteria and bacterial ferments in the unhairing process must still be regarded as uncertain. The late Professor von Schroeder carried out a series of experiments on liming and sweating which were characterised by his usual care and thoroughness, and which tend to prove that the chemical action is far more important than the bacterial. He had fresh hides well washed in a tannery immediately after slaughter, and fleshed. The butts were then cut into pieces of about 10 cm. (4 inches) square, and salted in brine repeatedly changed, and finally preserved for use in glass jars in saturated salt solution. He found that when washed free from salt, and placed in a moist chamber at a temperature of 16° C., the hair was sufficiently loosened by bacterial action in four to five days. Pieces placed in the moist chamber without previous removal of the salt only showed signs of sweating after about ten weeks' exposure. Liming experiments were made with similar pieces of salted hide, both after three days' washing to free them from salt, and unwashed, and in both cases the pieces unhaired freely in three to four days. These experiments were varied by using 6, 18 and 30 grms. of lime per liter of water in which about 200 grms. of hide were placed, but neither in the washed, nor unwashed portions was there any material difference in the time required to loosen the hair. Addition of 1 vol. of used lime-liquor to 3 vols. of water in making up the limes was equally without perceptible influence, and careful bacteriological examination of hide and liquors showed that the former was almost sterilised by the intense salting, and that the lime-liquors were practically free from bacteria.

Gerberei-Chemie, Berlin, 1898. p. 646.

Von Schroeder's conclusion that no gain arises from the use of excessive quantities of lime, so long as the solution is kept saturated, is fully justified both by experience and scientific reasoning, but his results with regard to the effect of old liquors and bacteria contradict the conclusions both of practical tanners and of other scientific experimenters.

The different effects of old and new limes are too well known to practical tanners to be discounted by laboratory experiments, even if they were not confirmed not only by Eitner's results, but by a considerable amount of work done in the Author's laboratory and elsewhere; while the necessity of bacterial action is at least rendered probable by the fact that soda solutions, which are completely sterile to bacteria, fail to unhair hides which have not previously undergone some putrefaction (see p. 137). In some experiments undertaken at the suggestion of the Author it was found that a perfectly fresh and sterilised calf-skin which was not unhaired after ten days' liming in sterilised lime-liquor unhaired rapidly on the addition of a bacterial culture to the lime. It is extremely difficult to exclude bacteria, and even where perfectly fresh skins treated with chloroform or carbon disulphide were employed, bacteria were always to be recognised when the skin was ready for unhairing. Von Schroeder's work, is, however, so painstaking and reliable, that these divergent results must be explained as other than experimental errors. With regard to old liquors, it is known that ammonia is a powerful aid to the unhairing process, and it is not certain to what extent the liquors he used were charged with it. It is also certain that old limes containing much organic matter, support bacterial life freely, while 25 per cent. of a possibly not very old liquor would probably be sterilised by the addition of lime and 75 per cent. water. In order to test the matter fairly under exact tannery conditions, the lime should have been made up entirely with old lime-liquor well charged with ammonia and organic matters, instead of with water. It is also probable that the hides had undergone a sufficient amount of bacterial change in the tannery before they came into Von Schroeder's salt solutions, and it is not at all unlikely that the salt solution itself exercised some specific effect on the unhairing. It is also possible that his bacterial cultures were made on gelatine media unsuitable for the growth of alkaline bacteria, and therefore gave blank results. Under these circumstances it is scarcely possible to arrive at any very definite conclusions, and it is obvious that further experiments on these points are extremely desirable.

Sodium and Potassium Hydrates.—From the earliest antiquity, wood-ashes, consisting mainly of potassium carbonate, have been used for unhairing, either alone or in conjunction with lime, and indeed the German name of the process (*Aeschern*) is derived from the fact. In more recent times, caustic soda, either ready formed, or causticised on the spot by the addition of lime, has often been recommended as a substitute for lime. Its action is very similar to lime, but, from its greater solubility, is far more powerful, and probably this has hitherto formed one of the greatest obstacles to its use, since a solution of the strength of lime-water is almost immediately exhausted, while a much stronger one is too violent in its action on the hides. Experiments made in the Author's laboratory show that caustic soda, in solutions of the same strength as lime-water, dissolve considerably less hide substance than the latter, but it is more antiseptic than lime, and does not unhair readily without the aid of bacterial action (cp. p. 137). It also swells more violently, and it is difficult to keep the grain smooth and unwrinkled.

Caustic soda has the great advantage that from its solubility, and that of its carbonates in water, it is much more easily and completely removed by washing than is the case with lime. It has been successfully applied in some instances to soften skins of which the texture is naturally too compact for moroccos and the softer leathers; and is usefully employed in softening dried goods (p. 115). Where caustic soda is required merely to "sharpen" limes, it is best added in the form of sodium carbonate (soda-ash or crystals), which are causticised by the lime in the pits. One-quarter or one-half per cent. on the weight of hides added in this way decidedly increases the plumping power of the lime. It may be noted that in the use of sodium sulphide in conjunction with lime, caustic soda is one of the products of its decomposition, and is probably one great cause of the difference of effect of this material for sharpening limes as compared with red arsenic.

This has been denied, but is probably correct, though the actual reaction is not easy to prove analytically; but the effect on the hide is practically what is stated.

An indirect method of liming has recently been patented by Messrs. Payne and Pullman of Godalming, which is of both scientific and practical interest. From the difficult solubility of lime, and the consequently weak solutions which must be employed, the ordinary process of liming is a slow one. Caustic soda, however, can be used in much stronger solutions without producing injury to the hide, or larger solution of hide substance, and from its great diffusibility, it penetrates very rapidly. Used alone, however, the hide becomes too much swollen for most purposes, and for certain classes of leather at least (e.g. buff and chamois leather) the presence of a portion of lime in the hide appears to be necessary for successful work. If a hide which has been swollen with caustic soda be afterwards treated with a solution of calcium chloride, double decomposition takes place, and caustic lime is formed actually in the interior of the fibre of the hide, while the sodium unites with the chlorine to form common salt. Both solutions may be used in any convenient way, and by the employment of drums, the whole liming process may be accomplished in five or six hours. It is found, however, that perfectly fresh hides treated in this way cannot be unhaired, and the explanation appears to be that in the ordinary liming process, the epidermis is made soluble by the joint action of bacterial ferments and of the alkaline solutions. If sodium sulphide be added to the caustic soda used for unhairing, the goods will unhair without the use of putrefactive means, but the process is difficult to manage without destruction of the hair, and Messrs. Pullman now recommend that all hides or skins for unhairing by their process should be soaked for forty-eight hours in winter, and twenty-four hours in summer in a really putrid stale soak. This necessity constitutes for very many purposes a serious weakness in the method, as putrid soaking is always extremely dangerous to the grain of the hide, and especially so in hot weather. For certain purposes, however, advantage may be taken of the fact that the hide or skin can be fully limed by Pullman's process and the fibres swollen so as to be prepared for tanning without any loosening of the hair, and the Author has seen deerskins which have been treated in this way, on which the hair was perfectly firm, while they possessed a softness and fulness which could not be attained without liming.

Eng. Pat. 2873, 1898.

Messrs. Pullman now recommend that the treatment with their solutions should take place in pits, in preference to drums or paddles, and that the caustic soda should not exceed a strength of one pound in ten gallons (1 per cent.). The hides or calf-skins remain in this for about forty-eight hours, during which they are once drawn and returned, by which time, if the putrid soaking has been properly done, the hair should be fully loosened. The hides are then drained for two hours, and passed into another pit containing a solution of calcium chloride, which should be slightly stronger than the caustic soda, say of about one and a half pounds per ten gallons. The goods remain in this for about forty-eight hours, during which they are drawn once, and are then well washed in soft water (free from temporary hardness) in which they may be kept for some time without injury. As both the caustic soda and the calcium chloride solutions are quite sterile to ordinary putrefactive bacteria, both can be used for an almost unlimited time, and they are conveniently kept up to strength by the addition of strong stock-solutions. These may be made of a sp. gr. of 1·4 (80 deg. Tw.) which gives a strength of about 5½ lb. of caustic soda and 5¾ lb. of calcium chloride per gallon.

In addition to the advantage of considerable saving of time, the effects can be much more easily regulated than in ordinary liming, and the amount of soda (and subsequently of lime) absorbed by the hide can be exactly determined by titration of the liquors. Grease is better removed than by ordinary liming, as soda-soaps are soluble in water, but if this result is to be obtained, the soap must be worked out before passing into the calcium chloride solution, which would otherwise convert it into an insoluble lime-soap. A great gain in many districts is that the process yields practically no effluents and no lime slab, both of which are frequently very difficult to dispose of. The serious disadvantages of the stale soaking, however, have already been mentioned.

In place of applying the caustic soda first, and the calcium chloride subsequently, hides may be first treated with calcium chloride solution, and then with caustic soda, or the caustic soda may be applied to the flesh side of the hide by painting. These modifications are covered by Messrs.

Pullman's patent, but they are willing to grant licences for experiments at a nominal fee.

Alkaline carbonates are much milder in their action on hide than the corresponding hydrates, and although they will unhair hides, in absence of lime, their action is somewhat uncertain and slow. "Polysulphin" (Polysulphin Co., Keynsham) owes its unhairing power principally to the sodium carbonate, and not to the small traces of sulphur compounds which it contains.

Sodium carbonate occurs in commerce in three forms: "soda ash," a more or less pure dry sodium carbonate; "soda crystals," or washing soda, $Na_2CO_3 \cdot 10Aq$, containing 62·95 per cent. of water of crystallisation, and efflorescing in the air; and Gaskell and Deacon's "crystal soda," $Na_2CO_3 \cdot 1Aq$, containing only 14·5 per cent. of water of crystallisation. It must be remembered that where carbonate is used in conjunction with lime it becomes causticised and converted into NaOH.

Sulphides.—The practice of using realgar, or red sulphide of arsenic (Ger. *Rusma*) as an addition to limes for fine leathers is one of considerable antiquity. It has the property of loosening the hair and epidermis structures with less solution of cement-substance than lime alone, and hence produces a leather of fuller and closer texture. It will, however, be convenient to defer the consideration of this agent till after that of some of the more modern and simpler substitutes, such as the sulphides of sodium and calcium. Sulphides of the alkalies and alkaline earths, if used in strong solution, say 5 per cent. or upwards, have the effect of very rapidly reducing the harder keratin-structures, such as hair and wool, to a pulp, attacking first the interior cells, so that the hair crumples up like a string of sausages, and in a few hours, or even, with very strong solution, in a few minutes, the whole mass becomes so completely disintegrated that it can be swept off the hide with a broom, or washed off in a tumbler. At the same time, the action on the substance of the hide, and especially on the cementing substance, is very slight, though the grain is swollen and temporarily rendered somewhat tender. On the other hand, when used in weak solutions, say ¼ per cent. and under, in conjunction with lime, the hair is but little injured, while the hair-roots and dirt are rapidly loosened, and results are obtained very similar to those with arsenic.

Sodium Sulphide ($Na_2S \cdot 9OH_2$).—For the methods of valuation and determination of sodium sulphide, see L.I.L.B., p. 28.

In the Laboratory Book the water of crystallisation is given as 10 Aq. Later researches show that pure crystals of the commercial sulphide only contain 9 Aq., or 67·5 per cent. of water.

Hides suspended in solutions of sulphide of sodium of 2 to 3 per cent. strength unhair rapidly.

For the commoner classes of sole-leather, hair is frequently removed by painting on the hair side with a 15°-28° Tw. (30-40 per cent.) solution of (crystallised) sulphide of sodium thickened with lime, applied with a fibre-brush, and folding the hide in cushions in a damp place, or packing in a tub. The hair is reduced to paste in a few hours. The same effect is produced by drawing the hides through a similar solution without lime, of which sufficient is retained by the hair to destroy it. The workmen must be provided with indiarubber gloves to prevent the caustic effect of the solution on the skin and nails. Skins and lighter hides are conveniently unhaired by painting the mixture on the flesh side, when it will loosen the hair or wool in a few hours without destroying it.

For dressing-leathers and the finer sorts of sole it is best employed as an addition to ordinary limes to the extent of $\frac{1}{4}$-$\frac{1}{2}$ per cent. on the weight of the hides or skins, when the hair is loosened more rapidly than with lime alone, and with less loss of hide substance.

Good samples of sulphide of sodium consist of pale-brown, almost colourless crystals, containing 28 to 32 per cent. of dry sodium sulphide, which readily deliquesce on exposure to air. Fused sodium sulphide can now be obtained, which contains nearly twice as much actual sulphide as the crystalline form. The dark green colour possessed by many samples of sodium sulphide is due to the presence of iron sulphide. If carefully used no serious harm can accrue from its presence. If allowed to stand a short time in solution the iron sulphide will settle out.

Calcium sulphydrate, $Ca(SH)_2$, sometimes called Böttger's *Grünkalk*, is a powerful depilatory, while it has probably less destructive action on the hide-fibre than even the sulphide of sodium, and would no doubt be largely used but for its unstable character. It is probably the principal active product produced by the use of sulphide of arsenic in conjunction with lime, though it is possible that a sulpharsenite may be formed. It may be produced by passing hydrogen sulphide (SH_2), into milk of lime. According to von Schroeder, it is *not* formed by the reaction of sodium sulphide on lime solutions (see note, p. 136). It may be obtained crystallised, and is soluble in water, but is decomposed on boiling. The sulphide, CaS, is insoluble in water, but by the action of steam under pressure it is said to be converted into a mixture of equivalent parts of hydrate and sulphydrate. It may also be dissolved in a solution of hydrogen sulphide, forming a solution of sulphydrate. In this way it might be formed on a large scale from the "tank waste" of the Leblanc soda process.

Gas-lime is principally active on account of the calcium sulphide which it contains, but is very variable in its strength, as both sulphydrate and sulphide are decomposed by the carbon dioxide always present in the gas, forming carbonates. Lime has nearly gone out of use for purifying gas, its place being now taken by iron oxide, but formerly gas-lime was a good deal used for unwooling the small lambskins used for the commoner sort of glove-kid, usually by painting a cream of it on the flesh side, but sometimes by immersing in a strong solution, which of course destroyed the wool. Its place is now taken by a solution of sodium sulphide of 15°-18° Tw. (approximately 30-35 per cent. crystals), thickened with lime to a soupy consistence, the use of which is much to be recommended for unwooling sheep-skins.

The tank-waste from the Leblanc process, consisting principally of calcium sulphide, is, when fresh, quite insoluble, and has no depilatory powers; but when exposed to air and moisture, decompositions take place, resulting in the formation of sulphydrates and polysulphides, which form a solution which has been the subject of several patents for unhairing. Polysulphides alone have probably no unhairing effect, but in conjunction with lime, sulphydrates are formed which rapidly loosen the hair. This fact was the basis of an ingenious and effective unhairing process used very many years ago by Mr. John Muir, of Beith, who, after liming for 24 hours in the usual way, submitted the hides to a pretty strong solution of weathered tank waste for 24 hours, and finally to water for 24 hours, to remove the surplus lime and sulphides. The sulphydrates formed in the hide attacked the hair-roots with little injury to the hair itself, and the hides contained so little lime that they could be tanned for dressing without bating, and made about 10 per cent. more weight than those treated in the ordinary way. Some trouble was occasioned by stains caused by impurities in the tank-waste.

Squire, E. P., 756, 1855; Claus, E. P., 1906, 1855.

A somewhat similar unhairing mixture to that obtained from tank-waste, which is now seldom to be got, was patented by Prof. Lufkin, who mixed equal parts of sulphur and soda-ash with a little water till combined, and then added 8 to 10 parts of lime, slaked and still hot. Schultz states that such a mixture containing 10 lb. of sulphur, will unhair fifty hides in the same way, and in about the same time as an ordinary lime, the pelt being little plumped and easily reduced without bating by a few minutes' wheeling in warm water. By boiling lime and sulphur with water a yellow solution is obtained which can be used in the same way as that from the tank-waste. A further quantity of water can be boiled on the same materials, more lime and sulphur being added as required. Polysulphides appear to have a marked effect in preventing plumping.

Eng. Pat. 2053, 1860.

'Leather Manufacture,' p. 35.

Barium sulphydrate has been put on the market experimentally as an unhairing agent, in the form of a strong solution containing yellow polysulphides, and which deposits crystals of sulphydrate in cold weather. It is more stable than calcium sulphydrate, but, on the whole, does not seem to present any advantages over sodium sulphide.

Realgar or red sulphide of arsenic, As_2S_2, is made by fusing arsenious acid and sulphur. (Orpiment is As_2S_3, but its action is different from that of realgar.) Mixed with lime it produces calcium sulphydrate and possibly hyposulpharsenite. To produce a rapid and complete reaction it must be mixed with hot lime, and the hotter the mixture is made the more powerful is its unhairing action. Milder forms may be made by mixing cold, or with the aid of hot water only. It is used with great advantage in conjunction with lime in varying proportions for unhairing lamb- and kid-skins for glove-kid and other fine leathers, to which it gives the necessary stretch and softness and cleanness of grain, without the loosening of texture and loss of hide-substance which would be caused by an equivalent amount of ordinary liming. For glove-kid about $0 \cdot 1$–$0 \cdot 3$ per cent. of realgar and 5 per cent. of lime is used, reckoned on the green weight of the skin.

For painting the flesh side of calf- and lamb-skins 1 part of realgar is mixed with 10 parts of hot lime, made into a paste with water. Calf will unhair in 8 or 10 hours.

"Inoffensive" unhairing solution contains a large quantity of arsenic sulphide apparently dissolved in caustic soda, although Moret's original patent claimed the use of wool-sweat potash only!

W. R. Earp has suggested the use of compounds of sulphur and arsenic (thio-arsenates, thio-arsenites, etc.), in 5 per cent. alkaline solution. He prefers to add the compounds to the ordinary lime-liquors, or to manufacture them *in situ* by adding the proper quantities of arsenious or arsenic acid mixed with one-third of its weight of sulphur to a solution of an alkaline sulphide in lime-liquor. The pelt is not bated or drenched in the ordinary way, but, after unhairing, is passed directly into the tanning liquor to which sulphurous acid has been previously added.

Eng Pat., No. 2052, Feb. 12, 1886.

There is more danger of injury to the hide from the very prolonged action of weak solutions of sulphides, which tend ultimately to destroy the structure and reduce the fibre to a gelatinous condition, than there is from too concentrated solutions. No danger need, however, be apprehended in the course of any ordinary liming. Arsenical limes are not suited for tainted skins, and they should not be made so strong as to destroy the hair or wool.

For methods of analysis of both old and new lime-liquors, see L.I.L.B., pp. 27 to 34.

Whichever method of loosening the hair be adopted, the actual removal must be effected by placing the hide on a sloping beam with a convex surface, and then scraping it with a blunt two-handled knife (Fig. 27), the workman pushing the hair downward and away from himself. The beam may be either of cast iron or of wood, usually covered with zinc to increase its wearing capacity. The hides after being removed from the lime-pits, are allowed to drain for half an hour or so before the hair is removed, and immediately this operation has been completed, they should be placed in soft water. It is of great importance that the limed hides should not be exposed to the air longer than is absolutely necessary for the removal of the hair, as the carbonic acid present in the atmosphere quickly carbonates any lime contained in the surface of the skin, forming chalk, and leading to uneven tanning at a later stage.

When hide has been insufficiently limed it is often easy to remove the longer hair but excessively difficult to get rid of the short under-growth of the young hairs, which even in properly limed skins can often only be removed by shaving them with a sharp handknife. This difficulty is caused partly by the small resistance which the short hairs offer to the unhairing-knife, and partly by their being more deeply rooted in the skin than the older hairs (see p. 49).

FIG. 27.—Unhairing (Penketh Tannery).

Various machines have been devised to accomplish the removal of the hair, but owing to the rapidity with which it may be worked off by hand, and the fact that the work is not difficult, no machine has as yet come into general use. Hand-work has the further advantage that in those portions of skin where the hair is tighter than usual it may be removed by greater pressure of the knife or by hand-shaving, whereas after goods have been unhaired by machine they must always be examined and any patches of hair removed by hand on the beam. The edges invariably require to be gone over by hand.

Several machines with spiral knives have been introduced for the purpose. That made by the Vaughn Company (Peabody, Mass.) for fleshing is one of the most satisfactory for unhairing, though any other machine of a similar type, and provided with spiral knife-blades, purposely kept blunt, may be used. The Leidgen unhairing machine, shown in Figs. 28 and 29, is one of the latest and most ingenious.

E. H. Munkwitz, Milwaukee.

FIG. 28.—Leidgen Unhairing Machine.

Occasionally goods are unhaired by fulling in the "stocks"; but it is very doubtful whether the saving in labour is not more than counteracted by the loss of weight caused by submitting the hide, while its gelatin is in a partially dissolved condition, to such rough usage.

The use of the wash-wheel (see pp. 111, 118) for the same purpose is much more satisfactory, and may be profitably employed for common goods, especially when the hair has been loosened by painting with a sulphide mixture.

After being unhaired, the hides are "fleshed" on the beam. This work, which consists in removing any small pieces of flesh and fat left by the butcher on the inner side of the skin, should be carefully and thoroughly done; but the closeness of the fleshing required is dependent on the purpose to which the hides or skins are to be applied.

FIG. 29.—Leidgen Unhairing Machine.

It is necessary not only to remove those portions of fat which are easily visible, but also to force out that contained in the loose areolar tissue. The form of knife used in England in fleshing is shown in Fig. 30. It differs from the one used for unhairing in being somewhat broader and heavier, and both its edges are sharp, so that where the flesh is too tight to remove by mere friction of the knife, it may be actually cut away by holding the knife almost flat on the beam, and using the convex sharp edge. The strokes in cutting must not be too broad, or, from the convexity of the beam, the substance of the hide will be cut into in the middle, or flesh will be left at the edges of the stroke. This difficulty is avoided by the flexible knife commonly used in Germany, but in other ways its work is less rapid and effective.

FIG. 30.—Fleshing.

Machines have long been used for fleshing and scudding light goods, such as lamb-, kid-, and goat-skins, and their use for fleshing dressing hides has now become very general in the United States, and is gradually gaining ground in England. The type of machine used for these heavier leathers, varies considerably from that used for light skins, but the general principle is the same. In most cases the working tool of the machine is a cylinder with spiral blades, which are generally arranged right-handed on one half, and left handed on the other, so as not only to scrape the hide in the direction in which the cylinder works, but also to extend it sideways. Much of the efficiency of these machines depends on the exact adjustment of the pitch of the spiral, and in the Vaughn machine, which is probably most in practical use, the blades are so arranged as to form two intersecting spirals, one of steeper pitch than the other. The great difference in the machines for skins and for heavy work, consists in the means adopted to support the skin, and to carry it under the spiral blades.

FIG. 31.—Jones Fleshing Machine.

In the machine invented by the late J. Meredith Jones, the skins are supported upon an india-rubber blanket stretched over two rollers, so that the knife-cylinder works on that part of the blanket which is between them, by which great elasticity is obtained, and this machine has proved most successful in treating delicate skins. In some other forms of machine, cylinders thickly covered with rubber have been substituted for this arrangement. The Jones machine is shown in Fig. 31. For heavy hides the Vaughn machine is most generally used, and may be taken as the type of the rest, as the Vaughn Company certainly originated the semi-cylindrical "beam," which forms a very important feature. Its construction will be seen from Fig. 32.

FIG. 32.—Vaughn Fleshing Machine, front view.

It will be easily noticed that if a hide be thrown over the half-cylinder so that one half hangs outside it, and the other half falls in its hollow, and it be then rotated, the hide is first caught firmly by a spring-clamp, which has been supported above the edge of the half-cylinder by blocks attached to the frame. As the edge rises, it lifts this clamp off the blocks, and thus carries the hide under the spiral knife-cylinder. The blades of this spiral knife-cylinder are ground to a sharp rectangular edge, and partly scrape and partly cut the loose tissue of the flesh. When the half-cylinder has made a semi-revolution, it returns to its original position, and the sizes of the driving pulleys are so arranged that the cylinder travels downwards more rapidly than it rises, in order to economise time, though in both cases the hide is worked upon by the knife-spiral which is rotated at a still higher speed. The hide is of course turned on the beam-cylinder and the other half is similarly fleshed. The beam-cylinder reverses automatically, or may be reversed by hand, and its nearness to the spiral knife is also under control. It is usually covered with a thick sheet of rubber.

It is obvious that machines of this type can not only be used for fleshing, but for unhairing and scudding, by the substitution of suitable knife-cylinders, and in the case of light skins, cylinders fitted with slates are frequently employed for the latter operation. The slate for the purpose must be of a peculiarly fine and even grain, and is mostly obtained from a single quarry in Wales. The Vaughn machine is frequently used in America for fleshing hides after soaking but before they go into the limes, and much is to be said in favour of this method, as the removal of the flesh permits even and uniform action of the lime. It is, however, a distinct disadvantage to the method that the flesh appears rough-looking after tanning, and the method is most suitable in conjunction with the American system of splitting the tanned leather.

In the production of sole-leather, fleshing machines have not as yet come into very general use. This may be accounted for by the fact that if used before liming a rough flesh is produced, which is unsightly on sole-leather, and which cannot well be afterwards improved, while something of the same objection attaches to fleshing after liming, with the added disadvantage that the hide is too much pressed, and is not easy to plump again, so as to make a satisfactory sole-leather.

In America, both sole- and dressing-leathers are usually tanned in sides, the hide being cut down the centre of the back. In England, the hide is usually "rounded" for sole-leather into "butts" or "bends" and "offal," as shown in Fig. 33. The rounding is done by hand with a sharp knife on a table, and in some of the best tanneries frames made of wood or metal are employed, to mark the sizes required. The chief advantage of rounding before tanning is that the different parts of the hide can be differently tanned, and appropriated to the purposes for which they are most suitable. The offal is now frequently split and worked up for light leather, or in other cases is tanned with a cheaper and more rapid tannage than the butts.

FIG. 33.—Diagram of Hide.

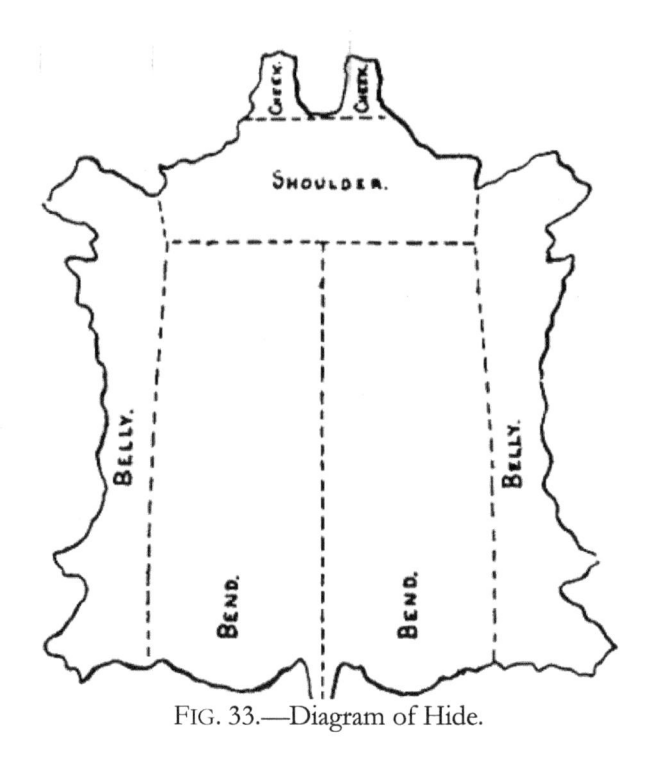

Dressing leather is more frequently rounded after tanning, according to the purposes for which it may be required.

CHAPTER XIII.
DELIMING, BATING, PUERING AND DRENCHING.

Although lime is in many respects the most useful and satisfactory means of loosening hair from hides and skins, it is of the greatest importance that it should completely removed when it has done its work, since its action on tannins is most injurious, and it is often harmful in tawing. For soft leathers it is also necessary that the skin should be brought from a swollen to a soft and flaccid condition.

In practice this is mainly accomplished for dressing leathers by bating, puering and drenching; while sole-leather and strap-butts are only too frequently left to chance, and to the natural acidity of the tanning liquors.

Bating consists in handling, or steeping the goods in a weak, fermenting infusion of pigeon- or hen-dung for a time usually extending over some days, and is applied to the heavier classes of dressing leather, such as "common" and shaved hides, kips and calf-skins.

Puering is a very similar process, applied to the finer and lighter skins, such as glove- and glacé-kids and moroccos, in which dog-dung is substituted for that of birds, and, as the mixture is used warm and the skins are thin, the process is generally complete in a few hours at most. Neither bating nor puering are very effective in removing lime, and seem to act principally by some direct effect of the bacterial products on the swelling of the pelt.

Drenching is occasionally used (e.g. on calf-kid) as a substitute for bating or puering, but more frequently follows the latter, and serves to cleanse and slightly plump the skins before tanning, and complete the removal of lime. The drench-liquor is an infusion of bran made with hot water, and allowed to ferment under the influence of special bacteria, which are always present in vats used for the purpose, and which develop lactic and acetic acids.

It will be noted that all these methods are fermentative, and their effect is not simply the chemical one of removing the lime, but the bacterial action leads also to solution of the cementing substance of the hide-fibres, and produces a marked softening effect on the leather, together with considerable loss of hide-substance. In the manufacture of the softer leathers this effect is generally desired, and no process would be satisfactory which did not produce it; but in other cases, such as harness- and strap-butts, firmer and heavier weighing leathers would be preferred, if it were known how to make them. The putrefactive processes would be gladly relinquished, if satisfactory substitutes could be found, not only on account of their offensive character, but because of their uncertainty and danger to the goods; and even if lime only were removed, the necessary softness could often be obtained by appropriate liming and tanning.

It will be best, therefore, to deal first with the purely chemical methods which aim only at removal of lime, before considering those involving bacterial action. Unfortunately, the chemical problem is not so simple as it might at first sight appear. The alkaline lime clings obstinately to the hide-fibre, and can only be removed very slowly, if at all, by mere washing. On the other hand, the use of any excess of strong acid is absolutely precluded, because of its powerful swelling effect on the pelt, in the tanning of which it would prove even more injurious than the lime, making dark-coloured and brittle, or tender, leather. This effect is not to be avoided by the use of even very dilute solutions of strong acids, since the affinity of hide-fibre for them is so strong that it will abstract practically all the acid from even a decinormal solution, leaving it quite neutral. What is required is an acid of extremely weak affinities, forming soluble lime salts, and obtainable at a low cost; or, on the other hand, a salt of some weak base which could be displaced by lime, and which would not act injuriously on the pelt. With certain precautions, and in special cases, however, the stronger acids may be used successfully.

In the cases of sole- and belting-leather no softening is desired, and formerly tanners usually contented themselves with a very perfunctory washing in water, trusting to the acids present in the liquors to complete the removal of the lime. Even pure distilled water effects this removal very slowly and imperfectly, owing to the strong attraction of the lime for the fibre; and if "temporary hard" water is used, the lime present in the hide combines with that present in the water and is precipitated as chalk in the surface of the hide. This may be prevented by previously adding a small quantity of lime or lime-liquor to the water before use to soften it (see p. 95); but unless this is very carefully done, the free lime present in the water prevents it from removing any from the hide. The safest way is not to add lime direct to the water, but to change the latter gradually, so as to allow the lime already present to soften the new portion of water.

A much more efficient method is to suspend the butts in water to which small portions of diluted acid are successively added till the lime is nearly, but not quite, neutralised. If carefully used, sulphuric acid is perhaps as good as any, but, of course, any excess will spoil the colour or "buff" of the leather.

The use of sulphuric acid for this purpose was patented by H. Belcher of Wantage (No. 14,943), but was used some years previously in several tanneries known by the author.

Acetic, formic, and lactic acids are safer than sulphuric, but are somewhat costly, and must not be used in appreciable excess. Crude pyroligneous acid may be used, and it has a considerable antiseptic effect owing to the phenols, etc., which it contains. Hydrochloric acid is not suitable for sole-leather, on account of the bad effect of chlorides on plumping. Sulphurous acid is perhaps the best, and its acid properties are so weak that slight excess does little harm, but the neutral calcium sulphite is insoluble, and to actually dissolve the lime the hydric sulphite must be formed, which can only occur in presence of excess of the acid. Unless such excess is used, the colour of the pelt in the early liquors is apt to be somewhat greyish. Probably a very good method would be to suspend the butts in a solution of sulphurous or some other acid of about $N/20$ strength, sufficiently long to remove all lime from the surface and slightly to plump it but not to penetrate to the centre of the hide, which should then be suspended in water until any excess of acid had been taken up by the unneutralised lime still present in the middle of the butt, which at the end of the operation should be rather alkaline than acid. The course of this, or any other bating operation can be followed by cutting the hide, and moistening the cut surface with alcoholic solution of phenolphthalein, which is turned red, or pink, by the least trace of free lime.

Manufacture of sulphurous acid, see p. 24; testing, see L.I.L.B., p. 37.

In using mineral acids it is of great importance that they should be perfectly free from iron, and that the vat employed should contain no iron which could become dissolved, since, if present in the bating liquid, it is sure to be fixed by the hide, especially if the quantity of acid used is insufficient to neutralise the whole of the lime.

Besides the direct use of mineral acid which has been described, sulphuric, or still better, oxalic acid may be very advantageously employed in precipitating lime from used bating liquids containing weak organic acids, or other lime solvents, so as to restore their original activity. Not only is the bate economised by being used repeatedly, but some of the organic products dissolved from the hide have themselves considerable power of removing lime. Putrefaction should not be allowed to take place; but many of the organic acids which have been proposed for bating belong to the aromatic series, and have considerable antiseptic power. Where organic acids are employed, the presence of their neutral lime-salts in the liquor, resulting from previous operations, will reduce the swelling action of the acid on the skin, without diminishing its power of removing lime (cp. p. 81).

In place of sulphuric acid, some tanners have employed a material advertised under the name of "boral." This substance consists simply of sodium anhydrosulphate melted up with about one-seventh of its weight of boric acid, the quantity of which is, however, too small to have appreciable influence as an antiseptic, while it is said to form insoluble borates with the lime present, which are sometimes a source of subsequent trouble.

There is no reason why ordinary sodium bisulphate should not be used for the purpose, and its action is more mild than that of sulphuric acid itself, but great care must be taken that no nitric acid is present, as is frequently the case in the crude product obtained in the manufacture of nitric acid from sodium nitrate, and known in commerce as "nitre-cake." The presence of a trace of sodium chloride would not be disadvantageous for dressing leather, but would tend to prevent plumpness in sole. Paessler and Appelius have recently shown that raw hide absorbs sulphuric acid from sodium bisulphate, leaving the neutral sulphate in solution.

'Wissenschaftlich-Technische Beilage des Ledermarkt,' 1901, p. 107.

Boric (boracic) acid, though used to a slight extent for a number of years past, has recently come much into favour as a deliming agent, for which purpose it is in many respects particularly suitable. Sole-leather may be improved in colour by giving a short bath in 1½-2 per cent. boric acid solution to remove surface-lime. In this case the acid is best applied just before the hide enters the suspenders. Boric acid may also be suitably employed on hides which have been bated. It then acts as a drench and removes traces of lime still left in the hides, so that the liquors have a more even effect on them. Experience has shown that the skins should never be allowed to lie for any length of time in the boric acid solution in a motionless condition, as this tends to produce patches of partially delimed skin, which cause irregular colour. It is best to keep the skins in fairly constant motion in a paddle or by frequent handling. Boric acid has considerable influence in preventing drawn grain in the early liquors, but if it gets into the forward liquors it renders the leather loose and light (cp. p. 229, and L.I.L.B. p. 37).

Borax has also been suggested as a deliming agent, and as it is chemically an acid salt, it has naturally some deliming effect, but it cannot compare with boric acid in either price or efficiency.

Both boric acid and borax are antiseptics (see p. 25).

In the employment of either sulphuric, boric, or any other acid forming calcium salts of limited solubility, it must be borne in mind that if the solution is repeatedly re-strengthened, it will become saturated with the lime-salt, and although the acid will still combine with the lime and render it neutral, it will no longer remove it from the hide. Under these conditions, sulphuric acid may cause the deposition of crystalline calcium sulphate in minute nodules between the fibres. Calcium borate may be similarly deposited, and has the further disadvantage of becoming decomposed by the tanning liquors, which form dark compounds with the lime. In using sulphuric acid alone it is therefore best to renew the water each time. When it is used in conjunction with some other acid, forming very soluble lime salts, this danger is not to be apprehended, while oxalic acid precipitates the lime almost completely from the solution.

It is to be borne in mind that in all cases of using acids, any carbonate of lime present on the pit sides or elsewhere will be decomposed, and the carbonic acid will become dissolved in the liquor, and unless acid is used in sufficient quantity to remove the whole of the lime, may tend to fix the remainder as carbonate. In the case of dressing leather there is less danger of this, as warm water is generally used, in which little carbonic acid dissolves. It is probable that some of the coal-tar acids which have been advertised for bating dressing leather might be advantageously employed for sole. Hauff's "anticalcium" (see pp. 29, 163), would appear to be very suitable for this purpose, and if the liquor were regenerated by the addition of sufficient sulphuric acid to neutralise the lime dissolved from the hide, might be used repeatedly, and would not then prove expensive; while its sterilising power would be very advantageous to the proper swelling of the butts in the handlers, since nothing tends to check plumping so much as putrefactive action.

Turning from sole to dressing leather, mineral acids are very successfully employed for "pulling down," the goods being thrown into a paddle containing warm water of about 30°-35° C., and the calculated quantity of sulphuric or hydrochloric acid, previously largely diluted with water, is then added in two or three successive portions at intervals of perhaps ten minutes. The acid must in no case be sufficient to neutralise quite the whole of the lime. Goods treated in this way can be further bated, puered, or drenched as required by the ordinary methods, if they are not sufficiently soft. If too much acid has been used, and the skins show signs of swelling, they may be brought down by the addition of a little ammonia, borax, or even soda.

In many cases the addition of salt in small quantity to the acid liquor will tend to deplete the hides, and at the same time prevent any injurious action of the acid. Ammonium chloride may also be used with advantage (see p. 159). A solution containing about 15 per cent. of salt and 0·3 per cent. of sulphuric acid, with some molasses, has been a good deal used in the States as a bate, and seems to answer well on some classes of goods, but the acid and salt are apt, ultimately, to find their way into the liquors and destroy tannin. The process is well suited for chrome-leather, and may also be usefully applied in cases where goods have become "wind-blasted" or otherwise impregnated with carbonate of lime, since in presence of salt the acid can be used in sufficient excess to dissolve the carbonate. Vegetable acids may, of course, be used in conjunction with salt in the same way. The salt does not neutralise the acid, but simply controls the swelling of the skin, and if acid has been used in any material excess, the first part of the tanning must be done in salted liquors, or the acid neutralised with ammonia, sodium carbonate, or chalk, previous to tanning, as, otherwise, the goods will plump up in the liquors, and be tender when tanned (cp. p. 91).

Lactic acid has recently come largely into use as a deliming agent. It is best known as the acid which gives a characteristic taste to sour milk, and is the chief product of the lactic ferment. It may be very successfully used for neutralising the lime left in the skins after the depilation, but, if used in excess, it tends to plump or swell the leather very strongly, being one of the best plumping agents known. When used for deliming, a solution of 2 lbs. in 100 gallons is very suitable. It may, in many cases, be substituted for the bran-drench with advantage, and is much more rapid and less dangerous in hot weather, but the effect is not in all respects identical.

On the manufacture of lactic acid by fermentation, see Claflin, Journ. Soc. Chem. Ind., 1897, p. 516. Campbell states that practically pure cultures of the lactic bacteria are obtained by continued culture in milk. These cultures employed as a ferment for drenches have given good results in the Yorkshire College Experimental Tannery.

When lactic acid is used for bating, or drenching, the operation should always be conducted in a paddle, and the liquid works more satisfactorily if it is at a temperature of 30-35° C. As regards cost, it will be found that in practice it is not appreciably more expensive than dung or bran. About an hour's paddling will generally suffice, if the right quantity of acid has been used, but in some cases it is best to add the acid in several portions and take more time.

The estimation of the amount of lactic acid in the commercial article may be carried out by diluting exactly 9 grms. with about ten times its volume of water, and then titrating it with normal caustic soda as described in L.I.L.B., p. 16, for acetic acid. As each c.c. of normal alkali is equivalent to ·090 grm. of lactic acid it will represent one per cent. of real lactic acid in the sample. If other acids are present, they are of course included. Commercial lactic acid is usually of about 50 per cent.

It is important that the lactic acid should be free from iron, a dilute solution should give no blue coloration on addition of either potassium ferrocyanide or ferricyanide. Acid perfectly free from iron is now easily obtained.

Formic acid in 60 per cent. solution, formed synthetically by the combination of carbon monoxide with caustic soda and the subsequent decomposition of the sodium formate so produced, has recently been brought into commerce at a cheap rate, and will probably form a satisfactory substitute for acetic acid in the deliming of hides and many other technical operations.

Instead of acids, many neutral salts may be used to neutralise lime, and in sole-leather, it is not generally disadvantageous to leave the lime in the hide, so long as it is in an insoluble and fixed condition, and combined with an acid which cannot be displaced by tannin. Thus phosphates, or oxalates of sodium or ammonium will convert the lime into insoluble phosphate, or oxalate, setting free sodium- or ammonium-hydrate which form soluble tannates and other salts which are easily washed out of the hide. Zinc sulphate will form sulphate of lime and zinc oxide in the hide, and seems worth further experiment for sole-leather, but must be free from iron. Alum, or sulphate of alumina, would similarly form calcium sulphate and alumina, but the tanning effect of alumina salts is too great to admit of their general use for bating. Ammonium sulphate will form calcium sulphate with liberation of ammonia.

For dressing leather, the use of ammonium chloride would be still more advantageous, and it is a powerful bating material, converting the lime into calcium chloride with the evolution of ammonia, which has but little plumping power, and which is easily washed out. Ammonium chloride has been very successfully used in calf-kid manufacture as a preparation for drenching, instead of puering, which was formerly in vogue. As, however, only about ¾ oz. per dozen skins was employed, the cleansing must have mainly depended on the warm water with which it was used, and the free ammonia evolved.

The use of ammonium chloride as a bate was patented by Zollickoffer in 1838.

A bating liquor which was proposed by the writer, and which has been used with some success on harness-leather, is made up with a ¼ lb. of good white ammonium chloride (sal ammoniac) and a ¼ lb. of Boakes' "metabisulphite of soda" per hide, and for successive packs sufficient sulphuric acid to neutralise the ammonia formed, together with a small quantity of metabisulphite and ammonium chloride to restore that carried out by the hides is added. It is probable that this would also answer well for deliming sole-leather as it entirely removes lime without pulling down the hides much, and they would remain still plumper if ammonium sulphate were substituted for ammonium chloride, while the sulphuric acid might be safely increased till the liquor was but slightly alkaline when the bating was finished. About 2-4 oz. of good white oil of vitriol is required per hide, but the exact quantity will depend on the mode of liming, and the amount of washing the hides receive before going into the bate, and can therefore be only ascertained by experience. As no free sulphuric acid can exist in the liquor so long as the quantity of metabisulphite is maintained, there is no practical danger of spoiling the leather if the acid be in slight excess. The quantities given may in most cases be advantageously diminished, since it is not always advisable in practice to remove the whole of the lime, which in small quantity renders tannage and penetration of the liquor much more rapid, either by acting as a mordant to the tannin, or by temporarily neutralising it and diminishing its astringent action on the hide-fibre.

Turning to dressing leather, we find that the use of cold water alone has been practically abandoned in this country, though the finest French calf is produced by repeated soakings in cold water with alternate workings over the beam, sometimes extending to nine or more. In this case, from the lengthened exposure to waters which are only gradually renewed it is probable that putrefactive action takes place, and that a sort of bating is effected by the decomposing products of the hide itself; in fact, in many French yards, bran-drenches have been introduced to supplement the action of the water alone. Waters differ greatly in their power of removing lime from skin. Slightly acid and peaty waters, and those in general which contain much organic matter, are much more powerful in reducing than those which are purer (cp. p. 107).

Warm water has much more effect in removing lime than cold, since the heat lessens the risk of dissolved carbonic acid, and seems to have a direct depleting effect on the pelt. A good tumbling in warm soft water will remove a great deal of lime, and is an excellent preparation for bating, but heat must be used cautiously, and should never exceed 30°-35° C.; some skins, such as seals, being very readily tendered by its action, while others, especially sheep-skins, will stand a comparatively high temperature.

The use of a solution of carbonic acid for removing lime has been patented by Nesbitt, who takes advantage of the fact that calcium carbonate is soluble in excess of carbonic acid (p. 94). The gas, which he generates, as for soda water, by the action of acids on chalk, or limestone, is received in a gasholder, and forced by a compressing pump into the vessel containing the hides, which is preferably a rotating drum lined with copper, and capable of bearing a pressure of about three atmospheres. The invention excited considerable interest on its introduction, as the gas is, certainly, quite uninjurious to the hides, and it was claimed that it enabled the grease and dirt to be better removed than by the ordinary methods. Further experience has shown, however, that the removal of the lime is far from complete, since, for success, it is not only necessary to bring it into solution, but to wash it out with carbonic acid solution under pressure, as on exposure to the air, solutions of lime in excess of carbonic acid rapidly deposit calcium carbonate. At the present time, the only tannery in which to my knowledge the process is in use is that of Messrs. Mossop and Garland, of Capetown, who state that it answers very well for harness-leather when a pure lime made by calcining sea-shells is used for liming, but is not satisfactory with ordinary stone lime. It is difficult to account for this on chemical grounds. Gluestuff may be treated very satisfactorily by simply blowing carbon dioxide, or washed and cooled lime-kiln- or furnace-gases, into an open pit in which the material is kept agitated. In this case, however, there is no need for the actual removal of the lime, so long as it is carbonated and its caustic character destroyed. Carbonic acid does not decompose lime-soap, and hence sets free no fatty acids, which, together with grease, are the main cause of the turbidity of glue, and the process therefore yields a more brilliant though darker coloured glue than does treatment with sulphurous acid.

Eng. Pats. 7744 and 12,681, 1886.

Several acids of the aromatic series have been from time to time recommended as deliming agents, and generally possess the merit of acting at the same time as powerful antiseptics. In this connection it may be well to mention the solution of 1 per cent. of phenol and 2 per cent. of boric acid used by Dr. Parker and the writer for preparing and preserving skins for colour tests (L.I.L.B., p. 133). This answers very well as a bate even when much diluted, and may be rendered cheap enough for use in practice by the employment of a good commercial carbolic acid instead of pure phenol, and the use of sulphuric acid to remove lime from the solution and render it capable of repeated employment. The carbolic acid should not be too dark in colour, and should be carefully dissolved, or "carbolic" stains will result.

"Cresotinic acid," a mixture of impure acids obtained from cresols in the same way as salicylic acid is manufactured from pure phenol, was introduced as a bate and unhairing and deliming agent by J. Hauff, of Feuerbach. He also claims the use of hydrochloric acid to liberate the acid after it has been combined with lime in the deliming process. It is only soluble to the extent of about 1 in 800 of water, so that, even if used in excess, no dangerously strong solution is formed, but it has a tendency to slightly swell, and somewhat harden, the hides or skins, so that it is perhaps more suitable for sole than dressing leather. It has also powerful disinfectant properties (see p. 29).

Eng. Pat. 14,889, 1888.

Compare also Journ. Soc. Chem. Ind., 1889, p. 954.

Hauff states that a solution of 18 lb. of cresotinic acid in 500 gallons of water at 30° C. will bate one lot of 50 heavy hides, and that the same liquor may be used continuously, by adding 4-5 lb. more cresotinic acid for each successive 50 hides. For bating glove-leather, Hauff recommends the use of 5 kilos. cresotinic acid dissolved in 1000 liters of warm water for every 500 kilos. of wet skins, to which is added ammonia nearly sufficient to neutralise the cresotinic acid, leaving the solution still slightly acid to litmus paper; and he also advises the addition of 5 kilos. of ammonium chloride or sulphate. The goods are paddled in this solution for about half an hour.

"Oxynaphthoic acid," the corresponding mixed acids of the naphthols (p. 30), has also been patented by Hauff as a bate, since cresotinic acid sometimes acts too powerfully on light skins. He mentions that mixtures of this and cresotinic acid, or salicylic acid, may also be used. Oxynaphthoic acid requires for its solution 20,000 to 30,000 parts of water.

Eng. Pats. 10,110 and 12,521. Journ. Soc. Chem. Ind., 1889, pp. 124, 809; 1890, p. 85.

A mixture of the α and β mono- and di-sulphonic acids of naphthalene has also been patented for bating, under the name of "Acrilene bating and puering acid." 150 calf-skins, weighing 880 lb., were pured in a 3 per cent. solution of the α acid, and gave 266 lb. of leather as against 255 lb. from a lot of similar weight treated with hen-dung, and this gain was more than maintained on stuffing, while the shoulders were plumper and fuller. This patent appears to anticipate a part of Hauff's claim mentioned in the next paragraph.

Burns and Hull, Eng. Pat. 8096, 1891; Journ. Soc. Chem. Ind., 1892, p. 48.

More recently Hauff has patented, under the name of "anticalcium," a mixture of impure sulphonic acids of various cresols and hydrocarbons. This is cheaper than cresotinic acid, and like it, possesses considerable antiseptic powers. One-half to one-quarter per cent. solution will keep hides uninjured for a considerable time, but at this strength it plumps considerably, and seems more suitable as a deliming agent for sole-leather than as a bate for dressing-leather, though it may replace drenching. No doubt, by the use of warm water, and avoidance of excess of acid, skins could be pulled down satisfactorily, or the plumping could be controlled by addition of salt, but the disinfectant powers of the acid would render further treatment with an ordinary bate or puer very difficult.

J. Hauff, Eng. Pat. 22,546, 1894; Journ. Soc. Chem. Ind., 1895, p. 170, Gerber, 1895, p. 133.

The "C. T. Bate," manufactured by the Martin Dennis Chrome Company, is of a very similar character; and is in the form of a greyish crystalline paste, consisting mainly of sulphonic acids of naphthalene and probably other hydrocarbons. It is very possibly made by sulphonating coal-creasote oils, which contain much naphthalene and phenanthrene. The following directions are given by the company for its use.

"1. After unhairing and fleshing from the lime, the skins should be thoroughly washed with water (preferably warm) so as to remove as much lime as possible.

2. If, in the liming process, the sulphide of sodium is used in combination with the lime, it will render the lime more soluble and therefore more easily removed with water.

3. The more completely the skins are cleansed with warm water the less will be the quantity of bate required.

4. After washing, the skins should be thoroughly worked on the beam, especially on the grain.

5. A solution of C. T. Bate is now prepared in the proportion of from one-half pound to one pound of bate in 100 gallons of warm water (90° F.). In making the solution do not have the water over 140° F. Under no circumstances boil it.

6. If the hides or skins have been treated as above indicated, one pound of bate should be sufficient for 400 pounds wet hide, washed from the limes. The hides or skins are placed in the bating solution and worked for an hour. They are then allowed to rest in the solution with occasional stirring for some hours or over night.

7. The length of time that the bating should continue will depend upon the degree of softness and pliability required in the leather. For instance, for sole-leather fifteen minutes is sufficient; for satin leather thirty minutes; for glove-leathers four to six hours or even longer.

8. On removing the skins from the bating solution it is sometimes desirable, especially for the finer grades of leather, to wash them in warm water and again work them over the beam. They are then ready to be placed in the tanning liquors.

9. In preparing the bating solution for the second pack, draw down the old solution one-third and replace with fresh water; then add in solution just one-half the quantity of bate used at first, and so on with each succeeding pack.

10. When fresh white limes are used toward the end of the liming process, and a manure bate is deemed necessary to reduce the harshness of grain caused by the fresh lime, it is very beneficial to give the skins from the

manure bate a drench of C. T. Bate, thereby arresting the bacterial action of the manure bate, preserving the grain, besides cleansing, bleaching and neutralising the skins preparatory to placing them in the tanning liquors.

11. Again, when it is considered desirable to use a manure bate, it is good practice to treat the skins as above indicated (down to item No. 7), and then place them in the manure bate. By this previous treatment the antiseptic action of the C. T. Bate tends to arrest the destructive bacterial action of the manure bate, thereby lessening the risk of damage to the grain. In all cases where the value of the leather is dependent on the quality and perfection of the grain, this is an important advantage to gain."

All these coal tar "bates" are rather suitable to replace drenching than bating or puering, as their effect is mainly that of removing lime. From their antiseptic character they are very useful in stopping the effects of putrefaction, and preventing ferments being carried into the tanning liquors, and skins may safely be kept at least for some days in weak solutions, but any necessary fermentive puering or bating should usually be done before and not after their use.

A writer in the 'Gerber,' 1875, p. 279, recommends the use of dilute solution of sulphide of sodium as a bating agent. Possibly it removes lime as sulphydrate, and the writer named seems to have obtained good results with glove lamb-skins. In experiments made at the Yorkshire College, a solution of 4 grm. per litre used on 40 grm. of pelt was found to plump it considerably, but probably a much weaker solution might be sufficient and more satisfactory. Polysulphides, such as "liver of sulphur," or the yellow solution obtained by boiling dilute sodium sulphide or sodium hydrate solution with excess of sulphur, have great power of "bringing down" the pelt, and seem well worthy of experiment as bating agents.

In India, the pods of the babool (*Acacia arabica*) are much used as a bate, the infusion being allowed to ferment. In their dry state they contain about 12 per cent. of an easily changeable tannin, which does not precipitate lime-water, and which by fermentation is very probably converted into gallic acid. The use of gallic acid itself as a bate has been patented by Albert Hull, and would undoubtedly accomplish the removal of the lime if used in sufficient quantity; but as he only uses a solution of 25 mgr. per litre (one part in 40,000) any effect must be mainly due to the washing with water. Gallic acid forms dark oxidation products with lime.

Eng. Pat. 14,595, 1889.

Of the fermentive methods of removing lime, "drenching" with fermenting bran-infusions is the simplest in theory, and has been very carefully investigated by Mr. J. T. Wood. It will, therefore, be convenient to consider this process first, although it is frequently employed as a means of cleansing and slightly plumping the skin after the lime has been removed by puering or bating. In calf-kid manufacture, however, it is now used without previous puering, and in some other cases it is substituted for the use of dung bates. The most important of the active ferments are two species of bacteria, named by Wood *Bacterium furfuris* α and β, which are very similar in their form and action (see L.I.L.B., p. 264), but produce a somewhat better fermentation together than separately. They are shown in Figs. 34 and 35.

Journ. Soc. Chem. Ind., 1890, p. 27; 1893, p. 422; 1897, p. 510; Brit. Assoc. Rep., 1893, p. 723.

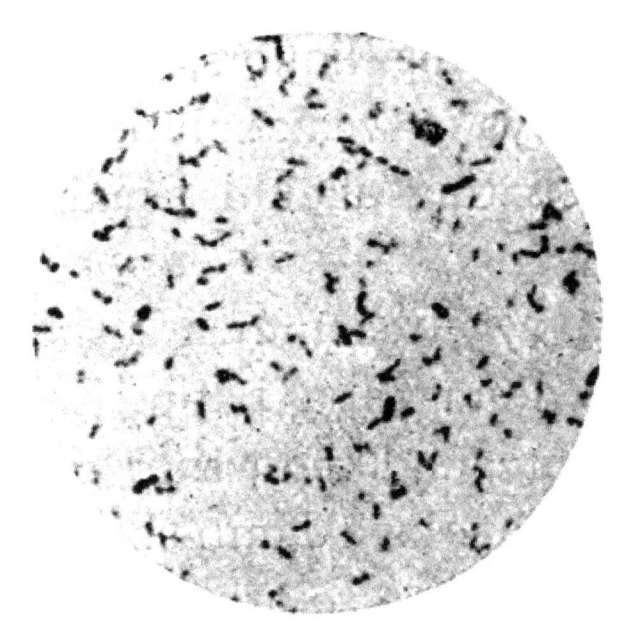

FIG. 34.—*Bacterium furfuris* α.

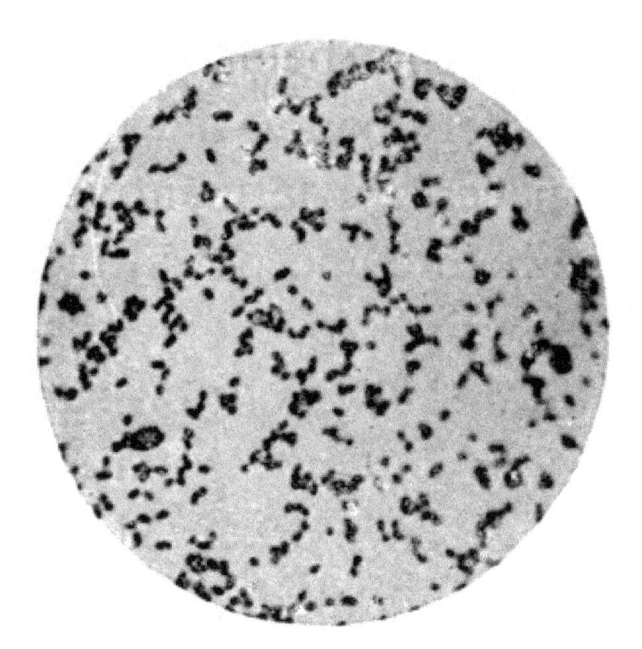

FIG. 35.—*Bacterium furfuris* β.

Neither species has any direct action on the hide substance, but ferments the glucose produced by the action of the cerealin of the bran on the starch which is present. A considerable quantity of hydrogen, with carbon dioxide, nitrogen and small quantities of hydrogen sulphide, are produced during the fermentation, together with lactic and acetic, and traces of formic and butyric acids and amines. Active drenches contain 1-3 grm. of mixed acids per liter, to which they owe their action, a perfectly satisfactory drenching being produced by an artificial drench containing 0·5 grm. of glacial acetic acid and 1 grm. of lactic acid (sp. gr. 1·210) per liter in which the skins were worked for 1½-2 hours, while 12-16 hours would have been required in the ordinary drench. An experimental drench gave the following results on analysis:—

Formic acid 0·0306 grm. per litre

Acetic acid 0·2402 ,,

Butyric acid 0·0134 ,,

Lactic acid 0·7907 ,,

Total 1·0749 ,,

It is probable that other organisms are capable of producing similar fermentations, and it is not certain that in all tanneries the same ferments are present. Mr. A. N. Palmer states that at the Cambrian Leather Works at Wrexham, he has been unable to detect lactic acid in the drenches, all the acids present being of the acetic series.

The drench-ferments investigated by Wood are incapable of attacking or injuring the hide, and, in his opinion, when the skin is attacked, it is generally due to putrefactive and gelatine-liquefying organisms introduced from the bates, or from the air in hot sultry weather. Drenching takes place most safely and satisfactorily at temperatures not exceeding 30°-35° C., when the process is usually complete in 12-24 hours. In hot sultry weather a butyric fermentation of an active character sometimes suddenly takes the place of the normal one (Ger. *Umschlagen*), the skins swell rapidly, become translucent (*glasig*) and finally dissolve to a jelly. If tanned in the swollen condition, tender and useless leather results, and the injury, once begun, proceeds with alarming rapidity, skins being sometimes completely ruined in a few hours. Prompt action is therefore necessary, and the first step to take is to add salt, which checks the fermentation, and acts in the same way as in the pickling process, controlling the action of the acid, and producing a sort of tawing. Such skins will yield sound leather, though the grain is apt to be somewhat drawn. If the skins can be immediately got out of the drench, the acid may be neutralised by the cautious addition of ammonia, soda, or whitening to the water in which they are placed, preferably in a paddle, and if they are insufficiently drenched they may then be paddled in tepid water, though this is hardly likely to be needed, as the effect of the acid is to remove the lime very completely. The objection to the use of whitening, which otherwise is the safest and best material to employ for removing acid from pelt, is that it is apt to become mechanically fixed in the grain, and, thus, to produce bad colour with vegetable tans. For white or chrome leather it would do no harm. Precautions to prevent the recurrence of the injury are to keep the temperature of the drench low, and to free the bran from flour by washing in two or three cold waters, before adding to it the hot water with which the actual drench-liquor is made, since the flour, or at least its starch, is the source from which the butyric acid, as well as the lactic, is formed. In cold weather, where drenching is proceeding in a normal way, the flour is useful, since it is the natural nutriment of the drench-ferment; and, in England, flour is frequently added purposely to the bran to increase the activity of the drench. To retain the flour, the bran may be washed first with boiling water, which gelatinises the starch and makes it adhere to the bran, and, according to Eitner, removes a sticky fatlike matter from it, and fits it better to remove the fat of the skin. After soaking in hot water for two hours, it is washed in several cold waters and infused at about 40° C. for use. Many tanners use the bran without previous washing, but if much flour is present it rises to the top with the gas evolved by the fermentation, and forms a pasty mass on the skins, which interferes with even drenching.

Gerber, 1882, p. 246.

The quantity of bran used in ordinary drenching is very variable, but about 4 parts per 1000 of water used and from 5 to 10 per cent. on the weight of pelt may be taken as an average quantity, more being frequently employed. The temperature may vary from 10° up to about 30°-35° C., and the time inversely from days or weeks down to two or three hours, according to the temperature of the drench, the amount of ferment present, and the thickness and character of the skins. The skins are usually thrown into the freshly prepared drench, to which a few pailfuls of old drench-liquor is frequently added as a ferment. Fermentation soon sets in, and the gas evolved causes the skins to float to the surface; this is called the "working" of the drench. Thin skins may be sufficiently drenched after once rising, while thick ones require to be put down two or three times. A certain sign of sufficient drenching is the appearance of small blisters on the grain, caused by the evolution of gas in the substance of the skin. When these are seen the drenching should be at once discontinued, as otherwise the blisters will increase in number and burst through the grain, causing minute holes or "pricks" (one of the many forms of the complaint called in German *Pikiren* or *Piquieren*). When a bubble of air is enclosed in a fold of the sufficiently drenched skin and pressed, it raises the grain without actually separating it from the substance of the skin. The properly drenched skin also falls easily in folds when held between the hands either lengthways or crossways, and if thin, the skin tightly stretched over the hand shows grains of bran underneath it as little lumps, round which the skin clings to the hand. The drenched skin should not be transparent, but white and soft; and when pressed should retain the mark of the finger. Some experience is required to determine certainly the point of sufficient drenching, which, of course, varies with the character of the skins, and the kind of leather which is to be produced; and the feel of the skin to a practised hand is one of the most important criteria.

A writer in the 'Gerber' divides drenching into three classes—"sweet," "alcoholic" and "sour." Sweet drenching is done in a bath of tepid bran-water, made by infusing in hot water and drawing the clear liquor off the bran, which settles to the bottom. The skins are only allowed to remain in 2-3 hours, or not long enough for fermentation to set in. The process is only suited for very thin or soft skins, which will not stand any further loosening. The use of bran-water has the advantage of saving the labour of "branning," or removing adhering bran with the knife on the beam, but it is doubtful if unfermented bran has much actual effect. Bran-water can, however, be used for drenching by fermentation, and for small glove-lamb has largely superseded the older method. The mechanical action of the bran in cleansing the pelt is however often useful. In sour drenching the bran is allowed to steep and soften in cold water for many hours, and boiling water is then added till the temperature is raised to 75° C., and it is allowed to infuse with frequent stirring for some hours, and after cooling to 45° a considerable quantity of old drench-liquor is added as a ferment. If the drench is used warm (30°-35°, or, in cold weather, even 40° C.), the skins only remain in 1-3 hours, but if cold the drenching can be extended over a period of 2-3 days, the skins being frequently handled. This modification is suitable for glacé-kid and the harder sorts of skins, but glove-lamb are always treated by the warm and rapid process. What the writer in the 'Gerber' describes as the "alcoholic" bran-drench is probably the method of fermentation investigated by Mr. Wood, in which ordinary inflammable gases, but no alcohol, are produced.

Gerber, 1888, p. 257.

A normal drench plumps the goods slightly, but if it contains much of the putrid ferments carried in from the bate or puer the skins fall in it as they would do in a bate. To increase this effect, putrid soak-liquor is sometimes added to the drench, but with doubtful advantage.

In drench-liquors the total acidity may be determined by titration with lime-water or $N/10$ caustic soda, with phenolphthalein as indicator; and the volatile acids may be distilled off as described under the analysis of tanning liquors (L.I.L.B., p. 126). For more complete methods of analysis the reader is referred to Messrs. Wood and Willcox's paper on the "Nature of Bran Fermentation."

Journ. Soc. Chem. Ind., 1893, p. 422.

Drenches are said to "work" somewhat better if made with water containing nitrates, and this is quite probable; but the necessary nitrogen can easily be supplied if required by the addition of a very small quantity of saltpetre.

Wood is of the opinion that the ferments found in bran do not originate in the drench itself, but come from the bated skins, as the drench-bacteria soon die out without finishing the fermentation, and constant renewing of the nutrient material is necessary (cp. p. 18).

Bating and puering, though differing practically in many ways, are identical in theory, and most of what follows applies to both of them. The action is much more complex than that of the drench, involving both chemical reactions and those of organised and unorganised ferments, and it is a matter of no little difficulty to say what proportion of the observed effect should be ascribed to each of these agencies.

Formerly, the principal effect was attributed to organic salts of ammonia and its homologues, and to amido-acids which combine with lime. Phosphoric acid is also present, and if any exists in the form of soluble salts, it will combine with lime, and render it insoluble and inactive. It is probable, however, that most if not all the phosphoric acid is already in the form of tricalcium phosphate, and therefore without effect.

It is now, however, recognised that the effects of these chemicals are of no importance as compared with the products of bacterial action, and the researches of J. T. Wood have cleared up much that was until recently quite inexplicable.

Journ. Soc. Chem. Ind., 1894, p. 218; 1895, p. 449; 1898, pp. 856, 1010; 1899, pp. 117, 990.

Much effect has been ascribed to the digestive ferments, such as pepsin and trypsin, which are present in fresh dung. It is known that the animal organism secretes these in considerable excess of its requirements, but it is doubtful whether any exist undecomposed, even in fresh dung; though they are apparently more resistant to putrefaction and decomposition than would *a priori* have been expected of such complex organic compounds, and there is therefore a possibility of their existence in the dung, even as it comes to be used in the tannery. Both pepsin and trypsin are enzymes (see p. 16), and belong to the great class of albuminoids. They are soluble in water, but insoluble in alcohol, and hence are precipitated by the addition of the latter to their solution, but are not altered by it, and regain their activity on solution in water. By heat they are coagulated and decomposed, and their activity permanently destroyed.

Pepsin is the active principle of the secretion of the glands of the stomach, and large quantities are prepared for medical use as an aid to digestion from the stomachs of pigs. Pepsin only acts in slightly acid solution, and, though fresh bate liquor is slightly acid to litmus, it speedily becomes alkaline from the lime of the skins and the ammonia present, so that the action of pepsin in a bate can only be a very limited one. Wood compared the action of a 1 per cent. solution of pepsin, acidified with 0·2 per cent. of hydrochloric acid, with that of a dogs' dung puer liquor, both at the temperature of 40° C. At the end of one hour the skin in the pepsin-solution was considerably fallen, but that in the puer-solution was almost dissolved. Since the solution here employed was much stronger than is likely to occur in practice, and the conditions much more favourable to its action, it may be assumed that the practical effect of traces of pepsin in the bate may be neglected.

Journ. Soc. Chem. Ind., 1894, p. 220.

Trypsin or *pancreatin* if present, is more likely to have an effect, since it is active in neutral and in alkaline solutions. It is the product of the pancreas, and is largely concerned in intestinal digestion. Chemically it much resembles pepsin, but is more resistant to heat, retaining its power of digestion after heating to a temperature of 160° C. in a dry condition. Its warmed solution dissolves fibrin almost instantly, and in large quantity, and peptonises gelatin and hide-fibre, so as to render them soluble in water. Wood found that a 1 per cent. solution of pancreatin acted far more rapidly than a solution of pepsin of equal strength. At 40° C. in neutral solution, the skin fell rapidly, and the action continued even in the cold. In 15 hours the liquid was swarming with minute bacteria. At the suggestion of the Author, the experiment was therefore repeated, with the addition of 15 per cent. of chloroform, which prevented the development of bacteria, while it did not stop the action of the pancreatin. The skin fell as before, but in neither case had it the peculiar touch of puered skin, nor were the characteristics of the leather produced from it the same. We may therefore conclude that, though trypsin may contribute to the action of the bate or puer, it can only do so in a minor degree, and that the principal effect of the bate or puer is due to other causes. It is certain, however, that fresh bird-dung, and probably that of all animals, contains ferments capable of liquefying gelatin. An instance of this is found in the observation, common in glue manufacture, that if the dropping of a sparrow falls on a cooler full of solidified gelatine size, it will liquefy a track quite down to the bottom of the cooler. Trypsin, or at least the secretion of the pancreas, as well as the gall from the liver, have great power of wetting and emulsifying fats, and this has possibly something to do with the action of the bate in enabling the skins to be cleansed of fat.

Loc. cit. and Beilstein, iii. p. 1308, 2nd ed.

Bacterial fermentation and its products are however the main factor in the action of puers and bates, and on this subject we owe most of our knowledge to the work of J. T. Wood, since, though Popp and Becker have worked over much of the same ground, they have not nearly so freely published their results.

Wood showed that a fresh puer liquor, even when boiled for half an hour and so freed from living organisms and albuminoid ferments, has still considerable action on a limed skin, though much less than the unboiled puer. He found that this action was principally due to amines and their compounds with organic acids, which removed lime, but did not remove the interfibrillary substance or give the proper feel of puered skin. A very similar result was obtained with aniline (phenyl-amine) hydrochloride in 1 per cent. solution.

A considerable variety of bacteria from dung and other sources were cultivated in various media and their puering power tested, but though greater than that of the unorganised chemical compounds such as amine salts and organic acids, it was in no case equal to that of an ordinary puer, or sufficient for practical use. When, however, a small quantity of the amine salts obtained from the puer were added to a mixed bacterial culture the effect on the skin was almost as rapid and considerable as with an actual puer.

In order to determine whether the puering effect was due to the direct action of the bacteria or to their enzyme-products, the latter were separated from a filtered puer solution by adding it to a large volume of 98 per cent. alcohol in which the enzymes are insoluble. When redissolved in water, they had a decided puering effect, and a solution of 0·5 grm. of the mixed enzymes and 0·5 grm. of the mixed amine hydrochlorides in 100 c.c. of water at 350° C. brought down a piece of limed sheep-skin in thirty minutes exactly like a puer. The action is therefore dependent on the mutual action of the enzymes and amine salts, but as the separation of these would be too costly for practical use, and the puering proved more effectual when they were formed in contact with the skin by active bacteria, Wood adopted the method of preparing a suitable sterilised nutritive liquid, which was inoculated before use with a mixed culture of suitable bacteria. For laboratory purposes a suitable culture-medium was obtained by digesting 10 grm. of gelatine with 5 grm. of lactic acid (reckoned water-free) and 100 c.c. of water for three hours in a closed vessel on the water-bath. The resultant solution was neutralised with sodium carbonate and diluted to 1 litre with addition of a small quantity of potassium phosphate.

The bacteria of fresh dog-dung were not found to possess a satisfactory puering effect, but those from dung which had been fermented a month (as in practice) gave a result nearly equal to actual puer. A still better result was obtained by a mixed culture from the roots of wool loosened by sweating. The bacteria were principally of two species, of which neither separately was capable of satisfactory puering; but which together acted more rapidly than an actual puer. These bacteria do not liquefy gelatine.

During the course of his experiments, Wood found that filtered puer solutions were less active than turbid ones and that their activity was increased even by the addition of inert substances, such as kaolin.

Wood attributes the differences in action between dog-dung and bird-dung not only to different bacteria, but to the fact that in the latter case the urinary products, and especially uric acid are contained in the dung.

From the results of these and similar researches, Wood in England, and Popp and Becker in Germany succeeded in producing a practical artificial puer, which they now manufacture in conjunction under the name of "Erodin."

"Erodin" consists of a solid nutrient medium and a liquid "pure culture" of the bacteria necessary to effect the required bating or puering.

The following are the directions for working with erodin bate, as supplied by the manufacturers:—

"For 100 lb. of wet skin washed ready for bating, about 1 lb. of erodin is required. Or in the metric system, 1 kilo. wet skin requires about 10 grm. erodin. The strength or concentration of the bate must not fall below 3 grm. per litre of bate liquor, i.e. ½ oz. per gallon.

For preparing the bate a sufficiently large cask or tub carefully *cleaned* and steamed out is placed near the bating paddle. The cask should be fitted with a steam pipe easily screwed on and off, and also furnished with a *clean* cover.

The requisite quantity of erodin is weighed out and put into the tub with fifty times its weight of water, and the whole brought up to a temperature reaching but not exceeding 40° C. (104° F.) by direct admission of steam, thoroughly stirred, and the pure culture of *Bacillus erodiens* added to the mixture. The temperature must not be allowed to fall below 25°C. (87° F.), and a little steam should be admitted first thing in the morning, again at noon, and in the evening, to bring the temperature up to 40° C. (104° F.).

A practical mode of procedure is as follows:—On Friday make up and start fermenting twice as much erodin as will be required for a day's work. This is allowed to remain under the above-mentioned conditions until Monday. On Monday half the amount will be used for bating; this is replaced by an equivalent amount of fresh erodin powder, dissolved in fifty times its weight of water, which is added to the already fermented erodin in the tub. Proceed in this way each day until the following Friday, when there will be left in the tub sufficient erodin for one day. This is put into a smaller tub for use on Saturday, and the cycle of operation begun again.

One pure culture of *Bacillus erodiens* should be used for every 11 lb. (5 kilos.) erodin powder or less quantity.

Suppose the amount of erodin required for a day's work to be 11 lb. (5 kilos.), then on Friday 22 lb. (10 kilos.) erodin must be mashed as above described in 110 galls. (500 litres) water, 2 pure cultures added, and allowed to ferment until Monday.

On Monday half of this is used, and to the remainder 11 lb. (5 kilos.) erodin and 55 galls. (250 litres) water is added. This is repeated on Tuesday, Wednesday and Thursday; and on Friday half is used and the remainder put into a separate cask for use on Saturday, and in the mashing cask a fresh quantity of 22 lb. (10 kilos.) erodin with 110 galls. (500 litres) water is made up for use next week.

Mr. Wood has found that in many cases it is unnecessary to start afresh at the end of each week, but that additional quantities of erodin solution with the accompanying bacterial culture may be added continuously to the stock-tub as required. In puering, the concentrated solution from the tub may be diluted with 4 to 6 times its volume of warm water. The diluted liquor should usually only be used for one pack of skins.

On Saturday the remainder of the old mash is used up.

In case this mode of procedure is for any reason not suited to the conditions of work, erodin may be used by making up every day a fresh quantity with fifty times its weight of water, adding the pure culture, and allowing it to ferment three days before use." In some cases the solution may be used for several consecutive packs, merely adding water and a small quantity of erodin without a new culture.

Erodin is being used most successfully in several large works both in England and abroad, and on calf-skins and sheep-skins has proved quite as effective and much safer than dog-dung; the skins coming out clean and free from stains. It has been a good deal used in the experimental tannery of the Yorkshire College, and has proved a satisfactory substitute for puer, but with the present bacterial cultures can only be employed warm, and does not answer used cold like the ordinary pigeon-dung bate. No doubt a suitable bacterial medium and culture can be found for cold bating, which for thicker leathers is often preferable to puering, and experiments in this direction are being undertaken.

From the multiplicity of germs present, and the adaptability of the dung infusion as a nutrient medium for any putrefactive organisms which may gain access to it, the bating and puering process is necessarily a dangerous one for the goods, always leading to loss of weight, and, if the process is carried on too long, to the more or less complete destruction of the skins. Loss of weight, however, in greater or lesser degree is inevitable, and indeed necessary where a soft leather is to be produced. If the skins are allowed to lie in the bate or puer liquor, mud, containing organisms, and zoogloea-forms of bacteria settle in the folds, and produce marbled markings, streaks and lines by the destruction of the grain surface (hyaline layer). Black or bluish stains are also often produced, known as bate-stains, and either due to bacterial pigments, or in some cases, to the action of evolved hydrogen sulphide on iron present from salting or other sources. Frequent change of position is therefore necessary, especially when the liquor is active from being used at a high temperature, but it does not seem to be desirable to keep the skins in constant motion, and if puering is done in a paddle, it should only be run at intervals.

T. Palmer determined in experiments on pigeon-dung bates that there is considerable loss of nitrogen during the process, and recommended bating in pits from which the air was excluded as much as possible, both as effecting a considerable economy in the dung, and in excluding false ferments, which, he concludes, are mostly aerobic. It is not improbable that the method is advantageous, since it has been shown by Roscoe and Scudder that liquefaction of gelatin only takes place in presence of oxygen, and its partial exclusion would therefore lessen the risk of overbating, and consequent damage and loss of weight.

Leather Trade Circular, 22nd Sept., 1891; 1887, p. 667; and Sanford, Journ. Soc. Chem. Ind., 1893, p. 530.

Starting from the presumption that bating and puering are, in the main, bacterial processes, more or less successful attempts had been made previous to those of Wood, Popp and Becker, to substitute other fermenting substances for dung; and probably these efforts failed in many cases, not so much because they were wrong in principle, as from want of knowledge of the necessary details, such as the use of proper ferments, and the provision of suitable culture-media. Guano, prepared horse-flesh, urine, yeast, and fermenting vegetables have all been tried. A solution of glucose or treacle of about 10 per cent., to which 3 per cent. of pasty dog-puer is added about a week before use, was tried many years since in a morocco-factory, at the suggestion of the writer, as at least a partial substitute for puer, and is still in use there. The mixture keeps for some time in an active state, and is added to the puer liquors in the same way and in approximately the same proportions as the dung paste. Similar in principle is the solid bate supplied by an American firm, in which glucose is mixed with a small amount of nitrogenous matter and phosphates, together with a lactic ferment, and which only requires dissolving in warm water some little time before use. Its results are good for some purposes, but rather resemble those of a drench than a bate. In a similar way, puer may be added to bran-drench liquors, and induces in them a fermentation which brings the skins down much lower than the ordinary drench. It is probable that a weak glucose solution, with traces of mineral constituents similar to Cohn's solution (see L.I.L.B., p. 269) and "set" with sour milk, or fermenting drench-liquor, might in some cases be used with advantage for drenching, with a saving of cost. A writer in 'Hide and Leather' describes a bate in which two parts by weight of glucose are dissolved in about 25 parts of water, and fermented, for about three days, till a foam gathers on the top, with about one part of old bran drench-liquor, or 0·1 part of pressed yeast, and then made up with water to 1000 parts. The goods are bated 24-36 hours at a temperature of about 35° C, and the bate is strengthened for a second pack with about one-fifth of the original glucose, a new bate being made at the end of a week, and set with one part per thousand of the old one. A short bating of say 10 hours produced very nice harness-leather, but the general tendency was to make the goods looser and more spongy than a dung-bate. It is obviously not a matter of indifference whether old drench, or yeast, is used to start the fermentation, since in the latter case only alcohol could be produced directly by the ferment introduced, though this might be fermented later, by other accidental organisms, into acetic acid. These mixed bates, containing glucose, are however probably wrong in principle, since the true puering and bating bacteria will not thrive in presence of acids, and require nitrogenous nutriment.

As regards the relative effect of dog- and hen- or pigeon-dung bates, the chief of the published experiments are those made by W. J. Salomon at the Vienna Versuchsanstalt für Lederindustrie, in which he determined the relative solvent power of equal quantities as being, for dog-dung 2½, for pigeon-dung 2, and for hen-dung 1. It is obvious that these figures, though interesting, must be taken with some reserve, as the composition even of pure dungs is by no means constant, depending on the feeding of the animals, and adulteration is common. The writer has heard stories of a certain dealer who used to fabricate his product from clay by the aid of a popgun, though he does not vouch for the statement! It is generally held that the action of bird-dung is more penetrating, but less softening and loosening than that of dog-dung, which is thus generally used for descriptions of leather where great softness and stretch are required. It is to be remembered in this connection that bird-dung bates are generally used cold, and hence are much slower in their action, which allows them time to penetrate thicker hides more uniformly. Few analyses of the dungs used in leather manufacture have been published, and these mostly with a view to manurial value. Schulze gives the result of forty analyses of pigeon-dung as follows:—

	Min. per cent.	Max. per cent.	Mean. per cent.
Water	3·80	40·00	21·00
Nitrogen	1·47	5·04	2·53

Phosphoric acid	1·00	2·77	1·79
Potash	0·71	2·57	1·46

One sample contained 43·3 per cent. of sand!

Tech. Quart., 1892, v. p. 81.

Der Landwirt, 1895, li. p. 301.

Wood quotes the following:—

Hen-Dung.

	Per cent.
Water	60·88
Organic matter	19·22
Phosphates	4·47
Calcium carbonate and sulphate	7·85
Alkaline salts	1·09
Silica and sand	6·69

Dog-Dung.

Water	31·0
Ca	43·0
Na, K, Mg	0·8
PO_4	3·4
CO_2	7·5
Organic matter	14·2
Traces Fe, Cl, Si, loss	0·1

Journ. Soc. Chem. Ind., 1894, p 220.

Containing nitrogen equal to 0·74 per cent. of ammonia.

This was apparently a sample from a dog fed on bones; that from the kennels, which is more commonly used in leather manufacture, contains much less lime; a sample analysed by Wood gave 4·7 per cent. mineral matter, 9·7 per cent. organic, and 85·6 per cent. of water, part of which was no doubt added.

Analysis.—Little or no attention has been paid to the analysis either of dungs for bating purposes, or of the bating liquors, and although the total cost of manure bates is a high one, it is evident that such low- priced and irregular articles will not pay for elaborate analysis. Probably in some cases it would be worth while to make a determination of moisture and organic and mineral constituents by drying and ignition. Where a further investigation is desired, the determination of the soluble matter by filtering and evaporating a portion of the solution to dryness, and that of the nitrogen by Kjeldahl's method (see p. 70), would be advisable, and of course in the future, when the subject is better understood, a bacteriological examination may be useful. If it is desired to estimate the solution of hide-substance in the use of bate or drench liquors, the determination of the nitrogen in a measured quantity by Kjeldahl's method will afford the best basis of calculation, allowance being made for the nitrogen present in the original bate liquor. Hide-substance contains about 17·8 per cent. of nitrogen. In many cases, simple weighing of the solid residue, left on evaporating the liquor to dryness and drying for several hours at 100° C., with subsequent ignition to determine lime and other mineral matters, will suffice.

The quantity of hen- or pigeon-dung used in bating hides is very variable, but may be stated at from 12 to 60 litres per 1000 kilos of raw hide, in at least 2000 litres of water. The bate is generally used cold, the hides remaining in it 4-8 days, with frequent handling; but some tanners, especially in the United States, prefer bating in a paddle or drum at a temperature of about 35° C., in which case the time must be diminished to a few hours. The dung is best infused with warm water in a separate vessel, and allowed to ferment for at least a week without use, when it will be found to swarm with micrococcus-chains. Only the clear liquor should be run into the bate-pit, the sediment and dirt being thrown away, or used as manure. In this way the danger of stains and flaking is much reduced. Bates may be mended with fresh portions of dung-infusion for several successive packs of hides, but should not be used too long, as they gain in solvent power by the dissolved hide-substance and the increased fermentation, and the method is not without risk.

This seems to have been first suggested by T. Palmer, Eng. Pat. 13,636, 1886.

After bating, the hides are usually "worked" ("scudded," "fine-haired") on the beam, to remove dirt and grease, but in America a wash in the wash-wheel is often considered sufficient. Goods are occasionally "stocked" (p. 116) from the bates, but this is not to be recommended, as it is likely to drive out much of the partially dissolved hide-substance and produce undue looseness and loss of weight.

It is difficult to give any definite marks of sufficient bating other than the soft and fallen feel of the hides, which is easily recognised by a practised hand. One of the earliest signs of commencing overbating is the occurrence of bluish patches, or a bluish tinge somewhat similar to an iron-stain, which, if slight, generally disappears in a few days after the hides are taken into the liquors. Hen- and pigeon-dung is probably best kept air-dried, though, if very wet, or for convenience for immediate use, it may be kept in paste like dog-dung.

Dog-dung should never be allowed to lie exposed to the air, or it putrefies and turns black, the bating ingredients are destroyed, and it will not puer the goods which turn black and putrid without softening. Dung should, therefore, be mixed to a paste with water and kept in tanks, so as to be but little exposed to the air, when it will retain its puering properties for a long time unaffected. Fresh dung should be allowed to ferment for at least a week before use. No accurate statement can be made as to the quantities required. Eitner states that 1-1½ pails of dung-paste (say 14-20 litres) is sufficient for 200 medium to large lamb-skins for glove-kid. It should be sufficient to make the water quite turbid, but not thick or soupy. For lamb-skins a temperature of 18°-20° C. is suitable, which may be raised in very cold weather to 25° C., to allow for cooling. The time required is from two hours for the thinnest slink skins, to 12-14 hours for strong ones. It is well to use wooden, and not iron, utensils for handling the dung, and it should be strained through a coarse cloth after diluting with water. As has been remarked, it is not desirable to keep the skins in constant motion in the puer; they should be stirred or paddled for the first 20-30 minutes, and then for 10 minutes every hour for five or six hours, after which they can be allowed to lie for a longer period without injury. Puering is sufficient when the skins feel quite soft and flaccid, hanging in folds in any direction and allowing the flesh to be scraped off with the finger-nail.

Wood recommends that, for the puering of sheep-skins, dung should be allowed to ferment one month before use, and states that it deteriorates if kept over three months. The puering products are the result of the successive action of many sorts of bacteria, and Wood is of opinion that those actually concerned in puering originate from the air, or from the vessels in which the dung is stored, and are not present in it when excreted. Borgman advises that the dung should be kept in a dry condition, and only made into a paste between a fortnight and three weeks before use, by covering in a clean cask with cold water, and on the following day mixing to a smooth paste with a clean wooden "poss-stick," made from wood free from tannin. The cask should then be covered up, and allowed to rest undisturbed till required. Clean extract-casks are very suitable for the purpose, if carefully and repeatedly steamed out, and Borgman advises that a regular series should be arranged, so as to supply the dung required, the date of mixing being carefully marked on each cask. Throughout the process the utmost cleanliness should be observed, and the casks should be carefully steamed out as soon as emptied. Immediately before use the dung-paste should be heated by steaming nearly but not quite to boiling point, care being taken to avoid the introduction of condensed water containing iron, and the dung thoroughly mixed with a large quantity (say 100 gallons) of water at 45°-50° C., allowed to settle, and drawn off through a basket, and strained into the puering paddle through a second basket lined with coarse open canvas (such as is used by plasterers to cover windows while the plaster is drying). A further quantity of warm water should be poured on the residue in the mixing tub, and used for diluting that in the paddle to the proper volume. The temperature of the liquor may reach 42° C. before the skins are introduced. The liquor should be of a light colour, greenish to brownish yellow; if darker, it indicates decomposition of the dung by improper storing, or too long fermentation, and will be liable to cause staining and injury to the skins. About 33 liters of dry dung is required per 100 kilos. of wet skin prepared for puering (33 gallons per 1000 lb.). Dry dung should be of yellow to brown colour, dark brown or black dung is spoiled and unsuitable for use. Wet dung is more difficult to judge, but very dark brown or black should be rejected, as well as that with a very strong smell, indicating that it has already fermented. Borgman's directions bear the stamp of experience and common sense, and the book as a whole repays study.

'Die Feinleder-Fabrikation,' Berlin, 1901, p. 69.

Borgman recommends that the skins should be warmed by paddling for some time in water of about 40° C. to which a couple of pails of puer-paste have been added, before bringing them into the puer, the temperature of which they should reduce to perhaps 38° C. The puered skins should feel silky on the grain, and even somewhat slippery, and when pressed between the finger and thumb a dark impress should be left, and the flesh should be tender and easily scraped off. The requisite condition will, however, vary somewhat with the kind of skins, and the purpose for which they are intended. After puering, the skins may be paddled for half an hour in water of about the same temperature as the puer.

CHAPTER XIV.
ALUM TANNAGE OR TAWING.

We have now followed the raw material up to the final stage of preparation for its actual conversion into leather, and it remains to consider the means by which that important change is produced. Though as yet the vegetable tanning process is most largely used, and possesses the greatest commercial importance, the use of mineral salts has long been known, and, through the advent of chrome tanning, has placed the permanent supremacy of the vegetable tannins in considerable doubt. Not only the importance of mineral tanning processes, but their greater simplicity from the scientific side, justify their consideration before those of vegetable origin.

In the previous chapters it has been shown that to produce a permanent leather, it is not only necessary to dry the fibres in a separate and non-adherent condition, but so to coat them or alter their chemical character that they are no longer capable of being swelled and rendered sticky by water. All salts which produce a contraction or dehydration of the fibre similar to that caused by alcohol are capable of the first effect in a greater or less degree. Many sulphates, and particularly those of sodium and magnesium, though they will not alone produce leather, will so far contract the fibres as to greatly hasten tanning by vegetable tanning materials, and they are therefore capable of useful application in quick tanning processes, especially where tough and light-weighing leathers are aimed at, which may be subsequently weighted and solidified by further treatment. Strong solutions of ammonium sulphate are almost as strongly dehydrating as alcohol, and will produce white leathers very similar to those formed by pickling, a fact which is certainly of considerable commercial importance. None of these salts, however, can form a complete leather in themselves, but require the assistance of metallic salts which will permanently fix themselves in the fibre, and diminish or destroy its attraction for water. Many substances have this power in a greater or less degree, but all those of commercial importance belong to the group of which aluminium, iron and chromium are representative, and which are capable of producing salt-forming oxides of the formula M_2O_3 (e.g. alumina, Al_2O_3). Manganese, of which the salts of this type are very unstable, has very slight tanning power, while titanium, which in many ways is allied to the group, though it does not strictly belong to it, has recently been patented as a tanning agent. For the present, however, we may limit our attention to the three metals first named.

Alumina and its salts demand the first attention, not only as having been used for leather manufacture in very early times, but as being still important commercially. The metal aluminium is now well known, and its oxide, alumina, Al_2O_3 is abundant in nature, combined with silica in the form of clay and bauxite, as fluoride in combination with sodium fluoride in cryolite, and in some cases as a native sulphate. Alum-shale, which was formerly the principal source of alum, is a bituminous clay containing much iron sulphide, and which when calcined yields aluminium sulphate. As aluminium sulphate does not crystallise readily, and was difficult to free from iron, potassium sulphate was added to the liquor obtained by leaching the calcined shale, from which, after concentration by boiling, potash-alum, a double sulphate of potassium and aluminium, $Al_2(SO_4)_3, K_2SO_4, 24Aq$, was easily crystallised out. Alum is now usually made by decomposing clay or bauxite with sulphuric acid, and ammonium sulphate is generally substituted for the potassium salt, yielding ammonia-alum, a double sulphate of aluminium and ammonium of similar constitution to potash-alum. Ammonium alum is easily distinguished from the potassium salt, by the strong smell of ammonia which it evolves on the addition of caustic soda or lime. So far as is known, there is no practical difference in tanning effect between the two salts, and ammonium alum is cheaper, and slightly stronger, its molecular weight being 906, as against 948 for the potassium salt. Either alum dissolves readily in cold water to the extent of about nine parts in 100 of water, and more easily, and to a much larger extent in hot water, from which the excess crystallises on cooling. It is said that for purposes of leather manufacture, alum solutions should not be boiled, and, though it is improbable that this produces any change, it must be remembered that chrome alum on boiling really does undergo decomposition to free acid and a more basic salt, indicated by change of colour from violet to green, from which it slowly returns to the violet form on cooling.

Alums are only valuable in leather manufacture in proportion to the aluminium sulphate which they contain, the potassium or ammonium sulphate taking no part in the reaction, and since improved methods have rendered possible the production of aluminium sulphate practically free from iron, it has largely taken the place of alum, than which it is both cheaper and stronger. Crystallised aluminium sulphate, $Al_2(SO_4)_3, 18Aq$, has a molecular weight of 666, which is of equal value to 906 of ammonia-alum, and 948 of potash-alum. Iron is the most objectionable impurity in both alums and aluminium sulphate, and may be detected by the addition of potassium thiocyanate, which will produce a red colour, or potassium ferrocyanide (yellow prussiate of potash), which will produce a blue. As the iron may be present in the ferrous condition, it is safer first to boil the alum solution with a few drops of nitric acid or bromine water. For more accurate determination of iron see L.I.L.B., pp. 20, 136.

No satisfactory leather can be produced with a solution of alum or aluminium sulphate alone, the skin drying horny, and incapable of softening by stretching. In practice, salt is always used in addition, the proportion being very variable, but averaging about half the weight of alum, or two-thirds the weight of sulphate of alumina employed. The mode of action of the salt has long puzzled chemists, and it has been supposed that its use was to convert the aluminium sulphate into chloride, a reaction which takes place to some extent, but which fails to explain the production of a soft leather, since aluminium chloride, though freely taken up by the skin, produces no more satisfactory leather than aluminium sulphate. The real explanation is found in Chapter IX. Alumina is a weak base, which readily gives up its acid to the pelt, becoming converted into a basic salt (see p. 187). The acid not only swells the pelt, and renders it incapable of producing a soft leather, but the swollen pelt is less ready to absorb the alumina salt, and so remains undertanned. The addition of salt prevents the swelling effect of the acid, and produces a partial pickling of the skin (p. 89), which, in conjunction with the tanning effect of the basic alumina salt formed, yields a satisfactory leather, though one which is readily affected by washing. If instead of adding common salt to the alum solution, an alkali such as soda is added, it combines with a portion of the acid, forming sodium sulphate, while the alumina remains in solution as a "basic salt." As the term "basic salt" must be frequently employed in connection with mineral tannage, it may here be explained. Basic salts are compounds intermediate between the normal salt, in which the whole of the base is combined with acid, and the hydrated oxide in which the whole is combined with OH groups. Thus aluminium chloride, Al_2Cl_6, is a normal salt, in which the whole of the combining powers of the aluminium are saturated with chlorine: aluminium hydrate, $Al_2(OH)_6$, is the hydrated oxide, and Al_2Cl_5OH, $Al_2Cl_4(OH)_2$, and so on are basic salts in which successively more of the Cl is substituted by OH. Generally, as a salt becomes more basic, its solution in water becomes more unstable, and very basic salts are either insoluble, or are precipitated from their solutions by very trifling causes, such as boiling, dilution, or the attraction of animal or vegetable fibres; separating into free acid and either hydrate or a still more basic and insoluble salt. On this property depends their importance in tanning and dyeing, many of the metallic mordants being solutions of basic salts. Basic salt solutions are formed in various ways, the most common being the direct solution of a hydrated oxide in a solution of the normal salt, or the neutralisation of a part of the acid of the normal salt by the addition of a stronger base. This is what takes place on the addition of soda to an alum solution. If the soda is added in excess, the whole of the alumina is precipitated as hydrate, or as an insoluble basic salt, but if a proportion not exceeding about four parts of crystallised sodium carbonate be dissolved separately, and added *slowly with constant stirring* to the ten parts of alum dissolved in water, no precipitation will take place. In this solution leather can be tanned, either with or without addition of salt, the alumina is taken up more freely than from the normal alum, and the leather is more easily softened, and more resistant to water. In fact such leather bears a strong resemblance to the chrome tannages, standing a great deal of washing, and considerable temperatures without returning to a pelty condition. The more basic the solution that is used, the fuller and softer is the leather produced. The alumina-salt taken up by the skin from such basic solutions is always basic, while that absorbed from alum or alumina sulphate is *apparently* the normal aluminium sulphate. It is probable however that the actual tanning salt is in both cases basic, and that the acid is fixed as free acid, as in the pickling process, as the proportions of acid and base found in the residual liquor are somewhat variable.

Basic alumina solutions have hardly taken the place in practice which they deserve, though they were described by Knapp in 1858 and have since been patented by Hunt, but the patent (probably invalid) has been allowed to lapse. A good stock solution for practical use is made by dissolving 10 lb. of sulphate of alumina in 10 gallons of water, and 4 lb. of washing soda in 4 gallons, and gradually mixing the latter with the former. Salt can be used in addition if desired, and flour and egg-yolk may also be added.

'Natur und Wesen der Gerberei,' Braunschweig, 1858.

In curing small skins, where it is not desirable for the fur to come in contact with the liquid, or in the tawing of wool rugs, it is often convenient, after freeing the skin as much as possible from blood and dirt, and adhering flesh, to stretch it on a frame, or nail it out on a board, and apply a strong alum-and-salt solution, as hot as the hand will bear, with a sponge, repeating the operation till the skin is struck through. About 1 lb. of alum and ½ lb. of salt per gallon is a suitable strength. In place of applying the solution, powdered alum and salt is sometimes rubbed into the wet skin. Alumed goods should generally be dried out rapidly, and finally at a good temperature, as this tends to fix the tannage, which is also made more permanent and resistant to water by keeping the skins for a month or more in the alumed condition, an operation known as "ageing." When first dried, alumed goods are invariably stiff and horny, and, to give them softness, must first be damped back to a half-dry condition, and then gradually softened by mechanical means. "Staking," and "perching" are the usual methods, the first consisting in drawing the goods vigorously over a bluntish blade fixed on the top of a post, and the second in fixing the skins on a horizontal pole (the "perch"), and working them with the "crutch stake," a tool formed somewhat like a small shovel with a semicircular blade, in place of which a "moon-knife" (a round blade somewhat like a broad thin quoit) is often fixed in a wooden crutch. The tools, and mode of using them are shown in Figs. 36 and 37. Machines, described on p. 192, are now generally used for these operations. After the first staking or softening, the skins are allowed to become nearly dry, and are then staked a second time. Some judgment is required as to the precise degree of moisture in each case: in the first instance the skins must be sufficiently damp to yield without injury to the mechanical stretching, but in this state they retain sufficient moisture to enable the fibres again to adhere on drying; and at the second staking or perching, they must be damp enough to allow these fibres to be again loosened without violence, and dry enough to prevent their again adhering.

The process shown in Fig. 37 is not actually "perching," but "grounding," in which a moon-knife with a sharp turned edge is used to reduce the thickness of the skin on the perch, at the same time as it stretches and softens it.

FIG. 36.—Staking White Leather.

FIG. 37.—Grounding with the Moon-knife.

The following slight sketch of the manufacture of calf-kid will serve to illustrate the practical manufacture of the finer alumed or "white" leathers. The raw material is in England mostly large market-calf, though salted and dried skins are sometimes employed. After sufficient soaking or washing in water, they are limed without arsenic or other sulphides, in limes which must not be allowed to grow stale or putrid, until the hair can be easily removed. After unhairing and fleshing in the usual way, they receive a few days in a pretty fresh lime, in order to plump them, and are then freed from lime gradually but as completely as possible, by successive steepings and washings in water softened by a mixture of that already used on other goods and by working on the beam. This acts as a partial substitute for puering with dung, which is now no longer used on calf-kid. The goods are next drenched in the ordinary way, 3-4 % of bran being used, and the goods allowed to rise two or three times in the drench, which should be conducted with the usual precautions (p. 167) to avoid the danger of butyric fermentation in hot weather. The goods should come out of the drench free from lime, and unswollen by acid, but full, white, and soft. The tanning (or "tawing" as it is usually called in the case of alumed goods) is done in a rotating drum with a mixture of alum or sulphate of alumina, salt, flour, egg-yolk, and olive oil. About 5 per cent. of flour, 2·5 per cent. of alum, 1 per cent. of salt, the yolks of 25 eggs, or 1½ lb. of preserved egg-yolk, 2 oz. of olive oil, and 1¼-1½ gallon (12-15 lb.) of water are required per 100 lb. of wet pelt. The flour is first made into a smooth paste with a little water, the egg-yolk, somewhat diluted with warm water and strained, is mixed in together with the oil, and finally the alum and salt solution is added at such a temperature as to bring the whole mixture to blood-heat (38° C.). The length of drumming depends on the thickness of the skins, several hours being required for very thick ones, but care must be taken to stop and ventilate the drum at frequent intervals, so as to prevent the skins becoming hot by friction. This part of the process was formerly accomplished by treading with bare feet in a tub. After tawing, the goods are allowed to lie in piles over-night, or are sometimes laid in tanks for a day or so with any that remains of the tawing paste, to complete the absorption of the salt and alum, and are then frequently split with the band-knife machine, though it would be better, as is often done on the Continent, to split them before tawing, the materials of which are not only costly, but unfit the splits for many purposes for which they might be employed. The drying should be rapid, but is best done first at a moderate temperature, or in the open air, and then in a rather hot stove. They may now be allowed to "age" from one to three months, but it is usually better before ageing to do the first part of the finishing process, consisting of damping back, staking, and if necessary, shaving. Machines are now almost invariably used for the staking, the principle of which may be described as that of a pair of tongs, carrying one or generally two staking blades on one limb, and a roller on the other which closes on the skin, and presses it against and between the blades, while the tongs are drawn backwards, allowing it to slip through. Fig. 38 illustrates the Slocomb, one of the most popular machines of this type. After staking and ageing, the skin is soaked in water till thoroughly wet in all parts. This not only softens the skin, and prepares it for dyeing, but takes out the superfluous alum and salt, and at the same time a good deal of flour and egg. To replace these, "re-egging" is necessary, and while some manufacturers give egg-yolk, or egg-yolk and flour only, many add a proportion of salt, and sometimes also of alum. This is done before dyeing, if the skins are to be blacked on the table, but as tray-dyeing (see p. 406) would again wash out the egg, the re-egging is deferred till after dyeing if this process is resorted to. Before dyeing, the skins receive an alkaline mordant to overcome greasiness, and enable them better to take the colour. In former times this was usually stale urine, but this has mostly been superseded by solutions of "hydroleine" (a washing powder), or of soap rendered more or less alkaline with ammonia. Eitner gives the following recipe, viz. ½ lb. Marseilles soap dissolved in boiling water, 5 or 6 egg-yolks added, and the whole made up to 4 gallons with water and ¼ lb. potash bichromate. The colour used is infusion of logwood or its extract, or two-thirds logwood and one-third fustic, which is best extracted without alkali, a small quantity of soda or ammonia being afterwards added. It is fixed and darkened by a wash of iron-liquor or a solution of 1 of ferrous sulphate in 75 of cold water. After being again dried, the skins are sometimes grounded with the moon-knife, softened again by staking or perching, for which a machine with inclined or spiral blades attached to a drum and working on a sort of leather apron is often preferred to machines of the Slocomb type, and rubbed over on the grain with a composition containing oil, wax, etc., and are finally ironed with a heavy flat-iron, to give them a fine and smooth surface. Eitner gives a recipe for the gloss:—1 kilo gum arabic, ½ kilo yellow wax, ½ kilo beef-tallow, ¾ kilo Marseilles soap, 1 liter strong logwood infusion, and 5 liters water. The water is brought to a boil in an earthen pot, and then the soap, wax, gum, and tallow are added successively, each being stirred till dissolved before adding the next, and lastly the logwood. After boiling for an hour, it is allowed to completely cool, being incessantly stirred during the whole process. After ironing the goods are rubbed over with a final gloss, for which Eitner gives the following recipe:—8 liters olive oil, 500 grm. tallow, 500 grm. yellow wax, 500 grm. rosin, 500 grm. gum arabic. (No water is given in the recipe, but the gum arabic is presumably softened in water.) The mixture is cooked for two hours in an earthen pot till the water is evaporated, and allowed to cool with constant stirring. The skins are then rubbed with a flannel with a very small sprinkling of French chalk, and are ready for sale.

FIG. 38.—The Slocomb Staking Machine.

The manufacture of glove-kid is quite similar in principle to that just described, but varied in detail to suit the softer and more delicate skins employed, to give greater softness, and especially the quality of stretching in any direction without springing back, which is so characteristic of the leather. Lamb-skins are the principal raw material, though genuine kid is also employed for the best qualities. The manufacture varies much with the quality and character of the goods. The skins, which are mostly dried, are soaked in clean and cool water for three to four days, according to age and thickness. Common qualities (small imported slink lambs) are often unhaired by dipping in or painting with a paste of gas-lime, lime and sulphide of sodium, or lime and red arsenic, so as to destroy the wool. Better skins are sometimes unhaired by painting on the flesh with lime alone or in mixture, and in other cases ordinary lime-pits are used, with limes, which are most usually strengthened with red arsenic, which is added to the lime while hot from slaking (cp. p. 142).

The calcic sulphydrate (and perhaps sulpharsenite) thus formed hastens the unhairing, and preserves the gloss of the grain. Well conducted glove-kid establishments avoid as much as possible the use of old limes, which produce a loose, porous leather, with a rough, dull grain. The liming lasts on the average ten days, and is of the greatest importance. It is essential that the inter-fibrillary substance should be dissolved, that the leather may have the quality known in Germany as *Stand*, that is to say, may be strongly stretched in either length or breadth without springing back. It also depends upon the liming (and this is of special importance in the case of lamb-skins), whether the tissue of the fat-glands is well loosened, so that the fat, either as such, or as lime- or ammonia-soap, may be readily and completely worked out. Skins in which this is neglected can never be properly dyed.

When the hair (or wool) is well loosened, the skins are rinsed in water, and then unhaired on the beam with a blunt knife. The water employed in washing should not be much colder than the limes, or it will prevent the hair from coming away readily. The wool or hair is washed and dried for sale. The skins are thrown into water, to which a little lime-liquor has been added, to prevent precipitation of the lime in the skins by the free carbonic acid of the water, which would have the effect of making them rough-grained.

Next comes the first fleshing (*Vergleichen*) or "levelling." By this, the loose cellular tissue on the flesh-side is removed, together with the head, ears, and shanks; and the flanks are trimmed. The skins are then again thrown into water softened with lime-liquor as above described, and then into a puer of dogs'-dung. This is prepared by stirring up white and fermented dogs'-dung with boiling water, and straining it through a sieve or wicker basket. The puer must be used tepid, and not too strong. The skins "fall" (lose their plumpness) in it rapidly, and become extremely soft and fine to the touch; and the fat-glands, remaining hairs, and other dirt, can now be very readily scudded out.

Too strong puers, or too long continuance in them, produce evident putrefactive effects on the skins. (See also p. 181.)

When the skins come out of the puer, they are stretched and worked on the flesh with a sharp knife, and any remaining subcutaneous tissue is removed. This constitutes the second fleshing. They are then rinsed in warm water, and beaten with clubs in a tub, or worked in a tumbler-drum, in either case with a very little water only; and finally brought into a tank of water, not too cold, and kept in constant motion with a paddle-wheel.

The skins are next cleansed on the grain-side by working on the beam with plates of vulcanite set in wooden handles, so as to remove fat, lime- and ammonia-soaps, and other lime compounds, together with all remaining hair or wool. The skins are now a second time washed in the "paddle-tumbler," first in cold, and then in tepid water; and after allowing the water to drain from them, they are transferred to the bran-drench.

This is prepared by soaking wheaten bran in water at about 50° C., and diluting with warm water. Sometimes the mixture is strained, and the bran-water only used, to save the trouble and cost of removing adhering particles of bran from the delicate skins. Sufficient of the liquid must be employed to well cover the skins, and the temperature may range from 50° F. (10° C.) to 68° F. (20°C.). These conditions are favourable to bacterial activity, which comes into play, and, on the one hand, evolves acetic and lactic acids, which dissolve any remaining traces of lime, and on the other, loosens and differentiates the hide tissue, so as to fit it to absorb the tawing solution. Much care is required in the management of the bran-drench, especially in summer, since the lactic readily passes into the butyric fermentation (see also p. 167). The tawing mixture is composed (like that employed in the fabrication of calf-kid, q.v.) of alum, salt, flour and egg-yolks, in a quite thin paste. A small quantity of olive oil is also generally used. The skins are either trodden in it with the feet, or more generally put into a tumbler-drum with it. Kathreiner pointed out, some years ago, that a mixture of olive-oil and glycerine might be partially substituted for the egg-yolks, in both the tanning and dyeing of glove-kid leather.

Gerber, i. (1875) p. 170; ii. (1876) p. 664.

The tawed skins are now dried by hanging on poles, grain inwards. Rapid drying in well-ventilated, but only moderately heated rooms is essential to the manufacture of a satisfactory product.

The dry leather is rapidly passed through tepid water, and after being hung for a very short time, to allow the water to drain off, is trodden tightly into chests, and allowed to remain in them for about 12 hours, so that the moisture may be uniformly distributed. It is then trodden on hurdles (German *Horden*) composed of square bars of wood, joined corner to corner, so as to make a floor of sharply angular ridges. The next operation is stretching with the "moon-knife"; after which the leather is dried nearly completely, and staked again.

This completes the tawing process. The goods are now "aged" as in calf-kid manufacture. Before dyeing they are washed with tepid water to remove part of the tawing mixture, and especially, superfluous alum and salt, and are re-egged much like calf-kid, before dyeing if the latter is done by brushing, and after if in the dye-tray or paddle. Aniline colours are more used than formerly, especially for topping and brightening the natural colours, but the dyewoods and other mordant colours are still largely employed. The leather is first prepared with an alkaline mordant (stale urine, ammonia, etc.) (cp. p. 413), then repeatedly brushed with or dipped in the dyewood liquor, and a wash ("striker," German *Ueberstrich*) containing some metallic salt is generally applied, with the object either of bringing out the special tone required, or of making the colour more lively and permanent. The striker is usually a solution of one of the so-called "vitriols": "white vitriol" (zinc sulphate), "blue vitriol" (copper sulphate), "green vitriol" (iron sulphate), or occasionally other salts.

After the dyeing, the skins, if dipped, are wrung out and re-egged; if brush-dyed, sleeked out with a brass or ebonite sleeker to get rid of superfluous water. They are then dried in an airy room. Before staking (stretching), the skins are laid or hung in a damp cellar, or in moist saw-dust. They are staked twice: once damp, and once nearly dry; and are finished by glassing or ironing.

Skins which are much damaged on the grain, or otherwise faulty, are smoothed with lump pumice on the flesh side, or fluffed with fine emery on the fluffing wheel. They are then dyed on the flesh side, mostly by dipping, but occasionally with the brush, in which case, the method described is slightly modified.

Tawing with alum and salt is frequently employed for commoner and stronger leathers, such as aprons (of sheep-skin), leather for whip-lashes, laces for belts, and "skivers" for capping chemists' bottles. The process is practically the same as for calf-kid, except that no egg, and little flour is used. Often flour is entirely omitted, and the goods may then be alumed in tubs, in which they are merely handled, as the alum solution penetrates quickly. Goods which are required white are frequently handled or tumbled with a milk of "whitening," both to improve the colour, and to neutralise any acid present, and fix the alum by rendering it more basic. Alumed goods can be stuffed with greases, either by hand or in the drum, after thorough softening by staking.

Alum, and other salts of alumina are frequently used in combination-tanning with vegetable materials (see Chap. XVII.). "Green" leather for laces, "dongola," and "dog-skin" glove-leathers are made in this way. Glazed kid for ladies' shoes must be slightly vegetable-tanned on the surface, or it will not glaze, but this is frequently accomplished by the use of materials in the dye-liquor containing tannins.

CHAPTER XV.
IRON AND CHROME TANNAGES.

Iron tannages may be very shortly dismissed, as their practical interest is at present either historical or prospective, but iron salts enter in so many ways into the chemistry of leather manufacture, that their properties must be briefly considered. Iron exists in salts in two states, the ferrous, and the ferric, in the first of which it is divalent, and in the second trivalent. Thus ferrous chloride is $FeCl_2$; ferrous oxide, FeO; ferrous sulphate, $FeSO_4$; ferrous hydrate, $Fe(OH)_2$. The compounds of ferrous iron are mostly green, like ferrous sulphate ("green vitriol," "copperas"): exposed to air and moisture, they easily absorb oxygen, and pass into the ferric form. Ferric chloride is $FeCl_3$ (or, as it is sometimes written without much reason, Fe_2Cl_6), ferric hydrate $Fe(OH)_3$, ferric oxide Fe_2O_3, ferric sulphate $Fe_2(SO_4)_3$, and so on. The atomic weight of iron is 56. Ferric salts are mostly yellow or orange, ferric hydrate is yellow-brown, and on ignition is converted into deep red ferric oxide, which is very difficultly soluble in acids. Ferric salts in contact with more easily oxidisable matters, readily give up oxygen, and pass into the ferrous state; and especially does this happen in the presence of organic matter, under the influence of sunlight. Thus iron-salts often act as carriers of oxygen, and oxidisers of organic matter, absorbing oxygen from the air, and giving it up again under the influence of light or heat. There are several other oxides of iron which do not form salts, and there is a ferric acid, apparently corresponding to chromic acid, which is so unstable that it has been very imperfectly investigated.

Ferric salts correspond in structure to those of alumina, and like these are powerful tanning agents, and readily form basic salts, while the ferrous salts have no tanning effect until they become oxidised, when they form basic ferric salts. Ferric salts are characterised by giving blue-black or green-black compounds with tannins, and with many other allied bodies, while the corresponding ferrous compounds are mostly colourless, though they rapidly oxidise and darken.

Ferric iron, like alumina, forms an "alum," a double sulphate of iron and potassium, $Fe_2(SO_4)_3K_2SO_4$, 24Aq, forming fine pale-violet crystals, but dissolving to a yellow-brown solution. (It must be distinctly understood that iron-alum and chrome-alum contain no alumina, but are simply called alums because of their similarity of constitution, iron or chrome taking the place of the aluminium. Iron-alum, in conjunction with salt, can be used for tanning, giving a pale buff-coloured leather very similar to an ordinary alum leather. Thus the presence of a small quantity of iron in an alum used for tawing is of no consequence, except as affecting the colour of the leather. In impure sulphate of alumina such as "alumino-ferric," it, however, generally exists in the green ferrous state, and only acquires tanning properties on oxidation. Without common salt iron-salts are still less satisfactory tanning agents than those of alumina under the same conditions, as the acid is yet more loosely held, and though basic ferric salts are taken up in considerable quantities by hide, the leather produced is thin, and usually brittle. Professor Knapp devoted much study to the production of a commercial sole-leather by basic iron-salts; and took several patents, which did not prove practically successful, though the brittleness was to some extent overcome by the incorporation of compounds of iron with organic materials such as blood and urine, of iron-soaps, and of rosin and paraffin in the leather. Like most mineral tannages, the process was far more rapid than that with vegetable materials. Knapp's basic tanning liquor was made by the oxidation of ferrous sulphate with a small quantity of nitric acid. Patents have also been taken for the oxidation of ferrous sulphate by peroxide of manganese in presence of sulphuric acid, which produces basic ferric sulphate in mixture with manganese sulphate, which has also some tanning properties. Attempts have also been made to tan by treatment of the hide with solutions of ferrous sulphate, and subsequent exposure to the air, in order to oxidise the iron on the fibre and convert it into a basic ferric salt, but have not proved of any commercial value.

The principal use of iron at present in leather manufacture is in dyeing blacks (see p. 413), but in this case, its feeble hold upon acids in the ferric state, and its tendency to act as an oxidising agent, or oxygen carrier, renders the blacks somewhat unstable, and is frequently injurious to the leather. There is also little doubt that the presence of ferric salts in leather blacks has a great tendency to cause the resinification of the oil, known as "spueing," by promoting its oxidation.

Chrome tannages, from a practical point of view, stand on a very different footing to those which have just been mentioned; having established their position in the manufacture of almost all sorts of light leathers, in competition with all the older methods, and making a serious claim to a share in the production of belting and even of sole leathers.

Chromium is a grey, and very infusible metal, which chemically much resembles iron in its compounds, and has an atomic weight of 52, or a little over. Like iron, it possesses a divalent and a trivalent form, but the divalent has so strong an affinity for oxygen, and passes so readily into the trivalent form, that until easier means are found for its preparation, it is of little practical interest. Its salts are blue. On the other hand, salts of the trivalent form, corresponding to the ferric salts of iron, are very stable, and powerful tanning agents. They are mostly green, but violet modifications are known, corresponding to the violet crystals of iron-alum, but of a much deeper tint. There is also a hexavalent form, probably corresponding to that of iron in the unstable ferrates, but in the case of chromium, of considerable stability. Its oxide is chromic anhydride, CrO_3, commonly called chromic acid, which combines with bases, and especially with the alkalies to form yellow or orange-red salts, and the anhydride itself is almost crimson in the solid form, though dissolving to orange or yellow solutions. Chromic acid though it hardens and preserves animal tissues, has no tanning properties till it becomes reduced to chromic oxide. There is also a higher, but very unstable oxide, perchromic acid, possibly corresponding to persulphuric acid, which is soluble in ether to an intensely blue solution. The name chromium is derived from the intense colour of many of its compounds.

Our supplies of chromium are derived from chrome-iron-ore, a mineral which contains oxides both of chrome and iron. This is furnaced with a mixture of lime, and soda or potash, when it absorbs oxygen from the air, the chromium becoming converted into chromic acid which combines with the alkali present, while the iron remains undissolved as ferric oxide. Lixiviating the mass, and evaporating the solution, lime and potassium or sodium chromates are obtained, according to the alkali used, and on adding sufficient sulphuric acid to combine with half the base, potassium or sodium dichromate (or as it is commonly called "bichromate") can be crystallised out. Potassium dichromate is most commonly made, because it crystallises well, and is not deliquescent, but sodium dichromate is somewhat cheaper, though less convenient. Dichromates, at least in the crystallised state, are not hydric salts like bisulphates, but anhydrochromates corresponding to the potassium anhydrosulphate obtained by fusing ordinary bisulphate, and to fuming sulphuric acid. Thus the formula of potassium dichromate is

CrO_2OK

-       O   , or $Cr_2K_2O_7$

CrO_2OK

and its molecular weight is 294, while that of sodium dichromate, which is similar in constitution, but crystallises with 2Aq, is 298. The molecular weight of CrO_3 is 100. Chromic acid, and acidified potassium dichromate are powerful oxidising agents, and are used as such in many processes, and especially in the manufacture of alizarine. If sulphuric acid be used in molecular proportions, the product of the reaction is chrome-alum: $4H_2SO_4 + Cr_2K_2O_7 = 3O + 4OH_2 + K_2Cr_2(SO_4)_4$. This, like ordinary alum, crystallises with 24Aq, and hence has a molecular weight of 998. It forms dark purple, almost black crystals, which are a fine garnet-red by transmitted light. In cold water it dissolves to a violet solution, which becomes green on boiling, but very slowly resumes the violet condition when cold. This change, which is not uncommon in chrome solutions, is probably due to a partial decomposition into free acid and a basic salt, the basic salts of chromium being generally green. It has been noticed that raw pelt swells much more in the green, than in the violet solution. Being derived from waste products, chrome-alum is often a cheap and valuable source of chromium for chrome tanning.

For the analysis of chrome compounds see L.I.L.B., p. 141 *et seq*. Chrome oxide, and basic chrome salts, when strongly ignited, become insoluble even in concentrated acids, and their analysis is therefore attended with some difficulty. If, however, the ignited residue (for instance a leather-ash) be finely powdered, and intimately mixed with a fusion-mixture consisting of equal parts of pure calcined magnesia and pure dry sodium carbonate, and ignited (preferably over a Teclu burner), in a platinum crucible, in which it is occasionally stirred with a platinum wire, it will be quantitatively converted into chromate, which may be dissolved in acid, and estimated with potassium iodide and thiosulphate in the usual way. If it is desired at the same time to estimate sulphuric acid, it is sometimes preferable to substitute lime or calcium carbonate for the magnesia, which is apt to be contaminated with sulphates.

Chrome is not only of importance in tanning, but in dyeing; on account of its power of forming insoluble colour-lakes with many mordant colouring matters. For this purpose normal or basic chromic salts are sometimes used, sometimes chromic acid or dichromates, the latter acting not only by yielding chrome-oxide on reduction, but as oxidising agents to the colouring matters. Most of the colours produced with chrome mordants are of dark shades, that with logwood being deep violet or black. The mordanting power of chromium is important in the dyeing of chrome leather. Bichromate of potash is often used in dilute solution for darkening the shade of leather dyed with other materials, but is not to be recommended on account of its destructive action on the leather.

Numerous patents have been taken for processes of chrome tannage. The first practical method was described by Professor Knapp in 1858 (see p. 210), though he did not recognise its value. Some of the patents have a historical interest, though of no importance. Among these may be mentioned that of Cavallin, a Swedish apothecary, whose object was dyeing rather than tanning, but who treated raw hide with a solution of bichromate, which was afterwards reduced on the fibre by one of ferrous sulphate. The leather produced is dark reddish brown, and tender from the amount of basic ferric salt formed at the same time. Mr. J. W. Swan, well known in connection with photographic processes, and electric lighting, also patented a process of chrome tannage (as an addendum to a patent on carbon printing), in which the chromic acid first fixed in the pelt was reduced by "oxalic, or other suitable acid." Although it is possible to produce leather within the lines of the patent, the strongly acid reaction of the reducing agent renders it unsuitable for practical use. The first chrome tanning process which made any show of practical success, was that patented in 1879 by Heinzerling, which was acquired in this country by the Eglinton Tanning Company, and also worked under their license for a short time by the Yorkshire Tanning Company at Leeds. Though the process was not commercially successful on any considerable scale, it possesses points of interest which make a brief description desirable. The hides or skins, after preparation in the usual way, were treated in a mixed solution of salt, alum (or aluminium sulphate), and potassium bichromate, but no systematic attempt was made to reduce the chromic acid to a tanning form, the product being, at first at least, merely an alum tannage, coloured, and perhaps somewhat hardened with chromic acid, though on keeping for a length of time, reduction gradually took place at the expense of the hide-fibre, and of the fats employed in currying, so that the leather internally became greyish-green, and really chrome-tanned. Specimens of the early products of the process, preserved in the museum of the Leather Industries Department at Leeds, have now all undergone this change, but are still tough and flexible, showing that the rapid tendering of the Heinzerling leather, which was one of the causes of its failure, must have been due to some error in manufacture, and was not inherent in the process. Interesting, historically, is the fact, that at an early stage in the life of the patent, a specimen of the leather was submitted to the late Professor Hummel, in order that he should suggest some means of overcoming the disagreeable yellow colour of the product. He reduced it with a bisulphite, and coloured it with an aniline dye, and a piece is still in the possession of the Yorkshire College, and in perfectly sound condition. If legal publication of this experiment could have been proved, it would have invalidated the important Schultz patents under which most of the chrome-kid of the United States has been manufactured. As bearing on modern chrome-tanning, the most important reaction in the process is that of the alum with the bichromate. It has been shown by Heal and Procter that pelt absorbs practically no chromic acid from bichromate, unless it has been previously set free by acidification. When however alum, or sulphate of alumina is added, its sulphuric acid liberates the chromic acid, leaving a basic alumina salt in solution, and this fact has been utilised in some modern tanning processes.

Journ. Soc. Chem. Ind., p. 251, 1895.

The first really important advance in practical chrome tanning was made by Augustus Schultz, in 1884. Schultz was not a tanner, but a chemist, employed by a New York firm of aniline colour merchants, and his attention was accidentally drawn to leather by a friend who asked him if it were possible to produce a leather for covering corset steels, which would not rust them as ordinary alumed leathers do. The process which he adopted was probably suggested by a method then recently patented for the mordanting of wool by chrome oxide, and depended on the power of the pelt to absorb free chromic acid (as it does all other free acids), and the subsequent reduction of the latter on the fibre to a basic chrome salt, which produced the tannage. The reducing substance employed was the free sulphurous or thiosulphuric acid of an acidified solution of sodium thiosulphate (hyposulphite), and as it was not certain which of the two acids was the really active agent, Schultz duplicated his patent, so as to cover both. Though he made no claim in his patent to having discovered the best proportions of his ingredients, those which he specified have proved practically useful after allowing for the modifications required by different skins, and slightly different methods of working. His first bath consisted of a solution of 5 per cent. of bichromate of potash, and 2½ per cent. of concentrated hydrochloric acid (or 1·25 per cent. of concentrated sulphuric acid), reckoned on the wet weight of the prepared pelt, and dissolved in sufficient water for convenient use in the paddle or drum which was to be used in the process. In this bath the skins were worked till they took a uniform yellow colour throughout, but without any tanning effect being produced. They were now freed from superfluous chrome liquor by draining or "putting out," and transferred to the second bath, which consisted of 10 per cent. of "hypo" and 5 per cent. of hydrochloric acid similarly dissolved. In this, they rapidly took a duck-egg green colour from the reduction of the chromic acid; and when this was uniform throughout the skin, the tannage was complete. The exact quantity of water is not of great importance, and good results can be obtained with anything varying from 20 to 50 gallons per 100 lb. of pelt (200 to 500 per cent.) if time be allowed for the weaker solution to act. The quantities of "hypo" and hydrochloric acid given for the second bath are often somewhat insufficient, and have to be slightly increased to complete the reduction. The reactions which take place are represented by the following formulæ, in which the weights of the materials taking part in the reaction are also given below the symbols. In the first bath—

Potassium dichromate.		Hydrochloric acid.		Potassium chloride.		Chromic acid.		Water.
$K_2Cr_2O_7$	+	2HCl	=	2KCl	+	$2CrO_3$	+	OH_2
294	+	73	=	149	+	200	+	18

As ordinary concentrated hydrochloric acid does not contain more than about 30 per cent. of actual HCl, about 2·5 parts would be required to completely decompose 2·94 parts of dichromate, while in Schultz's formula 2·5 parts of hydrochloric acid are used to 5 parts of dichromate. This excess has been found useful in the production of a good leather, both to prevent accidents from an overdose of hydrochloric acid, and because of the modifying effect of an excess of neutral salt on the action of the chromic acid (cp. p. 82).

Acid of S.G. 1·16 (32° Tw.) contains 31·5 per cent. of HCl by weight or 36·6 grm. per liter, and therefore is practically 10 × normal strength. Acid of S.G. 1·2 (40° Tw.) contains 39·1 per cent. or 469 grm. per liter.

The reactions which take place in the second bath are somewhat complicated. Eitner, in a valuable series of articles on chrome tannage, which have been appearing in the 'Gerber' since January 1900, states that even better results are obtained by using the hydrochloric acid in slight excess, as the action of chromic acid (in the presence of the potassium chloride of the chrome-bath) is not swelling but hardening to the skin, and the slight swelling action of the hydrochloric acid tends to counteract this, and also to facilitate the subsequent reduction. The two views are not contradictory, as the excess of bichromate behaves to the hide as an alkaline salt, which also produces a slight swelling effect, and it is quite probable that better results are attained when the solution is either alkaline or acid, than when the potassium chromate is exactly decomposed. Eitner recommends the use of four parts by weight of bichromate, and four parts of the strongest hydrochloric acid, dissolved in 400 parts of water, for each 100 parts of wet pelt, which should yield about 40 parts of dry leather. He states that if such a bath be used, it may be safely and economically exhausted by a second pack of skins, which is impossible in a bath containing excess of unacidified bichromate. He gives the following explanation of the successive changes which take place when acid is gradually added during the reduction, but points out that in practice the reactions always to some extent go on simultaneously.

Gerber, p. 297, 1900.

In the first stage, very slight acidification is required, and if the skins have been chromed with excess of hydrochloric acid, may be altogether dispensed with. The skins become brownish from the conversion of the chromic acid into so-called "chromium dioxide" (probably really a basic chromic chromate, $Cr_2CrO_4(OH)_4$, which on ignition leaves Cr_3O_6); no sulphurous acid is liberated, or sulphur deposited, but sodium tetrathionate is formed in the bath, and the reaction may be represented as follows:

(1) $3CrO_3 + 6HCl + 6Na_2S_2O_3 = 3Na_2S_4O_6 + 6NaCl + 3OH_2 + Cr_3O_6$.

Further addition of hydrochloric acid brightens the colour of the skins, while the liquid still remains clear, and chromium chloride is formed instead of chromic chromate, the main reaction being:

(2) $2CrO_3 + 12HCl + 6Na_2S_2O_3 = 3Na_2S_4O_6 + 2CrCl_3 + 6NaCl + 6OH_2$.

On still further addition of hydrochloric acid, sulphur is separated according to the following equation, and is deposited partly in the skins, and partly in the bath:

(3) $2CrO_3 + 6HCl + 3Na_2S_2O_3 = 3Na_2SO_4 + 3S + 2CrCl_3 + 3OH_2$.

After complete reduction, and consumption of the free hydrochloric acid, further reactions take place at the expense of the excess of thiosulphate which should be present, resulting in the production of basic chromic salts, and the further deposition of sulphur, mostly within the skin, as shown in the following equations:

(4) $Cr_2(SO_4)_3 + Na_2S_2O_3 + OH_2 = 2CrOH.SO_4 + SO_2 + S + Na_2SO_4$.

(5) $2CrCl_3 + Na_2S_2O_3 + OH_2 = 2CrOH.Cl_2 + SO_2 + S + 2NaCl$.

The thiosulphate bath therefore not only reduces, but precipitates sulphur in the skin, and reduces the chromic salt to a basic state. In boiling solution, thiosulphate precipitates the whole of the chromium as chromic oxide, but in the cold, and in presence of free sulphurous acid, it only reduces to a basic salt. Eitner does not consider the possibility, which certainly requires investigation, that instead of basic salts, sulphite-sulphates are formed at least in the first instance. Such salts of one base and two acids are quite possible, and it is very probable that in the use of chroming baths containing organic acids, they have considerable influence on the tannage.

The free sulphur which is liberated is partially deposited on and among the fibres of the leather, and adds to its softness, and also acts chemically on the oils used in "fatliquoring," so that it is probably one of the main causes of difference between the products of the Schultz or "two-bath" method, and the "one-bath" processes subsequently to be described.

It does not fall within the scope of this book to describe in detail the working methods for the production of the different kinds of chrome leather, but a few precautions common to all forms of the process may be named. It is not absolutely important in all cases that goods should be completely freed from lime before chrome-tannage, but in this case a sufficiency of acid must be allowed in the first bath to neutralise the lime introduced. Pretty thorough liming is generally advisable, to plump and separate the fibres, but as a rule the bating or puering of goods for chroming should not be excessive, but should be planned not to remove more than is absolutely necessary of the hide-substance, as the chrome tannage is in its nature soft and light, and does not lend itself to artificial fillings, such as the flour and egg-yolk of the calf-kid process. Skins are sometimes freed from lime by "pickling" (p. 89), and pickled skins may be chromed without depickling, which will be done by the dichromate, but in this case the acid contained in the skins must be considered in the composition of the chroming bath. Skins, indeed, which are pickled with a sufficiency of acid may be chromed in a neutral dichromate bath, and this is sometimes a convenient mode of procedure. To prevent drawing of the grain during tanning, skins not unfrequently receive a preliminary tannage with alum, or sulphate of alumina, and these materials, together with salt, may be introduced into the chroming bath, in which case they will liberate a portion of the chromic acid, as has been mentioned in connection with the Heinzerling process. Alum, chrome-alum, and acid salts, such as sodium bisulphate, may be substituted for the acid in the chrome bath, but organic acids must not be used, as they would reduce the chromic acid. The quantity of free chromic acid in the chrome bath is of the most vital importance to success, as it, and not the dichromate (which may be present in considerable excess), regulates the amount of chrome taken up by the skin, and the subsequent degree of tannage. It is very possible to injure leather by overchroming, rendering it rough, harsh and even tender. If a bath containing excess of bichromate is to be re-strengthened, it may be assumed as a rule that all the free chromic acid has been absorbed by the skins, and while it is merely necessary to restore the strength of the dichromate to its original amount, the full quantity of acid must be used which would be required in preparing a new bath. Where, as in Eitner's acid chrome bath, the whole of the chromic acid is liberated, the bath may be exhausted by a second pack of skins. Many tanners, in order to avoid the complications of remaking a bath, run away their chrome liquors after once using, containing all the excess of dichromate which has been used. With proper chemical control, this should not be necessary, and is objectionable, not only from its wastefulness, but on account of the very poisonous character of the unreduced bichromate. Even weak dichromate solutions, especially if warm, are liable to cause painful and obstinate eruptions on the hands, but this rarely occurs to tanners, as the poisonous action of the solution is removed on reduction. It is well, however, to arrange that men who handle skins in the chrome bath, should subsequently also work in the reducing bath. Methods of analysis of used chrome liquors are given, L.I.L.B., pp. 142 *et seq*. Those for the determination of acidity are not however easily applicable in the presence of alum and salts of chromic oxide.

Goat-skins for glacé kid need thorough puering to produce a smooth grain.

The skins, on coming from the chroming bath may be allowed to lie for some time without serious injury, but should be carefully protected from the action of light, which reduces the chrome at the expense of the skin, and renders the subsequent tannage irregular. It is found that skins, if brought into a weak or neutral reducing bath, are apt to "bleed" or lose chromic acid, which is reduced wastefully in the bath. On the other hand a strong "hypo" bath is apt to draw the grain and contract the skins, owing to the tannage taking place too suddenly. A somewhat strong "hypo" bath is therefore often employed as a preparatory "dip," the skins being simply drawn through it to fix the chrome on the surface, piled on a "horse" and subsequently reduced in a bath of ordinary strength. The tendency to bleed is lessened, but at the expense of the pelt, by the reduction which takes place if the skins are allowed to lie overnight in the chromed state. Eitner states that skins chromed in an acid bath (i.e. where the whole of the chromic acid is in a free state) show little tendency to bleed. After reduction, the skins are well washed with warm water, and their subsequent treatment is the same as that of skins tanned by the one-bath process, which is subsequently described (see p. 211).

Naturally in practical work, the reduction cannot be made to proceed rigidly in the definite steps described by Eitner on p. 206, but all go on in different proportions together, though by supplying the acid in proper quantities, and at proper intervals, they may be made in the main to follow in the given order. Both on this account, and because neither the exact amount of chromic acid in the skins, nor the sulphurous acid lost by escape into the air can be exactly determined, the reduction cannot be conducted on theoretical principles, but the best conditions must be empirically determined. Eitner states that 12 parts of thiosulphate dissolved in 400 parts of water, and 6 parts of (40 per cent.) hydrochloric acid are sufficient for 4 parts of bichromate per 100 of wet pelt employed in the chrome bath, of which not more than one-half to two-thirds is absorbed; and that if equal parts of bichromate and acid are employed in chroming, the acid used in reducing may be lessened to 5 parts. In this case it must not be forgotten, that if the partially exhausted chrome-bath is used for a second pack of skins, which are afterwards finished in a bath of full strength, nearly the whole quantity of bichromate used in making up one bath will be absorbed by the skins. The amount of acid consumed in reduction will be greater, the more rapidly it is added, owing to increased escape of sulphurous acid. It is better to add the acid, previously diluted with water, in 8 or 10 successive portions, more rapidly at first, and more slowly during the latter half of the operation, each portion of acid being added as soon as no further change of colour appears to be caused by that already given. These changes are the more rapid the lighter the goods. The colour darkens at first to olive-brown, then gradually becomes green, and finally blue, and when this colour is uniform throughout the thickness of the goods, no further acid need be added. For goods which have been chromed in an acid bath, Eitner states that no acid will be needed for the first twenty to thirty minutes. It is important to have a sufficient excess of thiosulphate in the bath when reduction is complete, in which case the goods may be left for some hours or overnight in the bath, to complete "neutralisation," but Eitner prefers to use a fresh bath of 1½ parts of thiosulphate in 400 parts of water for this purpose, the bath being used, after settling, for making up the reduction bath for the next lot of goods, for which 1½ parts less thiosulphate is used. The goods must be kept in motion during reduction, either in a drum or a covered paddle.

In a paper on "*Die Natur und Wesen der Gerberei*" published by Professor Knapp, in 1858, he describes clearly a chrome tanning process with basic chromic chloride, formed by the addition of sodium carbonate to a solution of the normal salt, but he expressly states that the product was not more resistant to water than the ordinary alum tannages. How he fell into this error is hard to explain, for leathers produced according to his directions, resist not merely washing in cold but boiling water. As soon as the Schultz process proved successful, many attempts were made to evade the patent by the use of other reducing agents than the "hypo," and other salts of sulphurous acid which it covered. Among these, the use of hydrogen sulphide, and acidified solutions of alkaline sulphides, and especially of polysulphides, proved capable of practical use, though less convenient than thiosulphate, but were soon acquired by a combination, the Patent Tanning Company, together with Schultz's original patents.

"Liver of sulphur" or solutions, made by boiling sodium sulphide or soda with excess of sulphur.

Under these circumstances, Martin Dennis, either by fresh discovery, or otherwise, revived the original process of Knapp, which he patented almost word for word, and offered a basic chrome tanning liquor for sale, without further restrictions on its use. This liquor was made by dissolving precipitated and washed chromic hydrate (easily prepared by precipitating chrome-alum solution with excess of alkali) in hydrochloric acid to saturation, and adding washing soda until the solution was rendered sufficiently basic. Such a solution may be used on skins prepared in the ordinary way, by diluting with water, and strengthening as the tannage proceeds, like a vegetable tan-liquor. It is doubtful if the patent is a valid one, as it was known that the use of such a solution was not new, and it was only granted in America on the representation, which has since been found to be mistaken, that chlorides alone were applicable for tanning, while Knapp had not restricted his statement to these salts. In reality chlorides and sulphates seem equally suitable, but to produce similar results the former must be made more basic than the latter. In any case the patent cannot cover the general principle of basic tanning, but only the particular liquor and mode of preparation specified. It was soon afterwards shown by the writer, that a good chrome tanning liquor might be prepared by direct reduction of dichromate with sugar in presence of such a limited quantity of hydrochloric acid as to produce a basic salt. Suitable proportions are 5 mol. HCl to 1 mol. potassium dichromate, which produces a salt approximately $Cr_2Cl_3(OH)_3$. The solution is easily made by dissolving three parts of dichromate in a convenient quantity of water, adding six parts by weight of concentrated hydrochloric acid, and then cane-sugar gradually till a green solution is obtained, when the whole may be made up to one hundred parts, and will be approximately of the same strength as a 10 per cent. solution of chrome-alum. A little heat may be needed to start the reaction, but too much should be avoided, as considerable heat is evolved by the oxidation; and as much carbonic anhydride is produced, which causes the solution to effervesce briskly, the vessel used should be of ample size. In place of cane-sugar, a good quality of glucose may be used, but some samples contain some impurity which produces a violet solution which will not tan satisfactorily. This liquor is in regular use in many tanneries, producing a good quality of chrome calf, but is somewhat variable in its effects according to the temperature employed in its preparation, and it appears to have no real advantage over a simple solution of chrome-alum, rendered basic by soda and with some addition of salt. A somewhat similar preparation is Eberle's "chromalin," in which some organic substance, probably crude glycerine, is used to reduce the bichromate. The organic matters, and especially the organic acids which result from the oxidation of the sugar or glycerine, are not without influence on the tanning properties of the liquor. Of course these solutions may be rendered still more basic by the addition of sodium carbonate. A good stock-liquor, of approximately the same strength as that above described, is made by dissolving 10 parts of chrome-alum in 80 parts of tepid, but not hot water, and adding with constant stirring a solution of $2\frac{1}{2}$ to $3\frac{1}{2}$ parts of washing soda in 10 parts of water. The chrome alum dissolves somewhat slowly without the aid of heat, and the solution is best made either in a small drum driven by power, or by suspending the crystals in a basket near the surface of the liquor, so that the saturated solution can descend.

Martin Dennis, U.S.A. Pat. 495028, 1893; and 511411, 1893, 7732, 1893. E. Pat. Gallagher.

Leather Trades Review, Jan. 12, 1897.

Compare Eberle's German patents, 119042, 1898, and 130678, 1899. The last of these appears to be anticipated, at least as regards the use of glucose, sugar and starch, by the writer's publication in 1897 above cited.

Leather Trades Review. Later investigations have shown that the temperature of the water is unimportant if alkali be added, but chrome-alum dissociates to some extent in hot water, and comparative experiments have shown that solutions of the normal salt made with the aid of heat act on skin as if more acid than those made in the cold.

Eitner has pointed out the important effect that differences of basicity have on the tanning properties of chrome solutions. Normal chrome sulphate or chrome-alum colours the leather quickly and equally throughout, and swells the pelt on account of its practically acid character, but gives a thin and lightly tanned leather, from which much of the chrome washes out, unless it is at once "neutralised" in alkaline solutions. As the chrome solution is made more basic, the tannage penetrates more slowly, but is heavier and more thorough, the colour is darker and bluer, and much less of the chromic salt is removed by washing with water. When the basicity becomes excessive, the solution becomes unstable, and decomposes on dilution with water into a very basic salt which is precipitated, and a more acid solution than that given by a moderately basic salt. The effect of such solutions on the leather is very unsatisfactory, producing the bad effects both of too acid and too basic salts. The pelt is apt to be swollen and lightly coloured by the more acid salt, but at the same time the actual tannage proceeds very slowly, and in extreme cases it is difficult to tan through, while the surface becomes over-tanned, and the grain often tender and even brittle from the incrustation of precipitated basic salt. Eitner likens the effect of the more acid liquors to the quickly penetrating and lightly tanning vegetable tans, such as gambier, and that of the more basic to the heavier tannages, such as valonia; and within limits, advantage may be taken of these facts in adjusting the liquors to the character of the leather it is desired to produce. In sulphate liquors, he considers the salt $CrOH.SO_4$ as most suited to general use, and in the case of chrome-alum, this is produced by the use of 286 parts of soda-crystals, or 106 parts of dry sodium carbonate (1 molecule) to 998 (or practically 1000) parts by weight (1 mol.) of chrome-alum. (In using washing soda, care must be taken to employ *clear* crystals of the salt, and not those which have become white by loss of water.) In place of soda, Eitner makes a similar basic liquor by boiling 1000 parts of chrome-alum with 248 parts (1 mol.) of sodium hyposulphite until the whole of the liberated sulphurous acid is driven off, and the sulphur deposited. In comparative experiments by the Author, no difference could be detected between the tanning effects of the two solutions, and that with soda is both cheaper and more easily made. If the solution with hyposulphite is not boiled, a more acid liquor results, in which part of the chromium is combined with sulphurous acid, forming an unstable compound which may prove useful in certain cases.

Gerber, 1901, pp. 3 *et seq.*

Eitner states that he has made chrome-solutions of various types, containing organic compounds in combination with the chrome-salt, which combine with the leather, producing a fuller and softer tannage, but he gives no details as to their preparation, as they are made commercially by the "Erste Oesterreichische Soda-Fabrik" at Hruschau. The writer has found that in some cases by the addition of say 3 parts of sugar, or still better of glucose, to 10 parts of the chrome-alum in making up the basic liquor, a much fuller and plumper leather is produced, which dries perfectly soft, even without staking or fat-liquoring; and it is probable that many other organic compounds may be found which produce similar effects. The addition of very small quantities of even neutral tartrates or lactates, and probably of many other organic salts or acids, have a remarkable effect in lowering the apparent basicity of the solution, and it is possible that these may also be usefully employed in combination with very basic liquors. It is highly probable that the unsatisfactory tanning liquors produced by direct reduction with some samples of glucose are due to the presence of small quantities of some organic acid produced during the oxidation. It has been found that these solutions may be made to tan by the liberal addition of soda. It is probable that more satisfactory results in chrome-tanning will be attained by the direct addition of known organic substances to basic liquors of definite constitution, than by the somewhat uncertain products of organic oxidations.

The quantity of salt to be added depends on the qualities desired in the leather, and upon whether chloride or sulphate liquors are employed; salt in chloride-liquors increasing the softness of the leather, but in excess tending to flatness, while in sulphate-liquors it practically diminishes their basicity by converting the chromium sulphate into the equivalent chloride, which, as Eitner points out, behaves as a less basic salt, and hence but little advantage is to be gained from its use. It is best to begin with a very weak liquor, to avoid drawn grain, and for the same purpose a preparatory tannage with alumina salts, or an addition of alum or sulphate of alumina and salt may be made to the first liquor, as the attraction of the chrome salt for the fibre is sufficient to produce a chrome tannage, even in presence of excess of alumina salts. 10 lb. of chrome alum will tan about 100 lb. of wet pelt, but more must be used for the first parcel; as to avoid loss of time, the skins may be tanned out in a pretty strong liquor. The bath has a tendency to become acid by use, and before strengthening, it may be necessary to add some more soda solution. Very little additional salt is required, as it is only absorbed by the skins to a small extent, probably as chromic chloride. As the liquors gradually become charged with sulphates, it is best to work them out like bark liquors, and not to go on strengthening the same liquor indefinitely. If old liquors are used for green goods, it is not necessary to neutralise them with soda before use, as Eitner has shown that less basic liquors colour more evenly and with less tendency to produce drawn grain.

Basic chrome liquors, such as have been described, may also be used in chrome combination tannage. It is generally best to let the light vegetable tannage precede the chrome, and lightly tanned skins, such as "Persians" and East India kips, acquire many of the qualities of chrome-tanned leather by the treatment. The effect is still further increased by a previous detannisation of the leather with alkaline solutions (see p. 241). Several firms beside Dennis now supply basic chrome liquors ready prepared for use.

The time of tannage will of course vary with the thickness of the goods, and for calf-skins will usually extend over some days, though it can be much quickened by drumming. The tannage is generally best accomplished in the paddle, but can be carried out by frequent handling in pits or tubs, or, where very smooth grain is important, by suspension. When the goods come out of the final liquor, they may be allowed to lie in pile for twenty-four hours, or even for some days, with advantage, as the surplus chrome liquor is pressed out, and the tannage becomes more complete. They are then washed with plenty of warm water, till it ceases to be coloured with chrome. They may be kept for an almost unlimited time in a wet condition, as they do not bleed, and have little tendency to heat even in pile. They have now reached the stage at which we left the "two-bath" leather, and the subsequent treatment may be the same in both cases.

Although by both processes, the chrome-salt fixed in the fibre is of a decidedly basic character, it still contains enough acid to act injuriously on the leather in course of time, and to lead to serious inconveniences in its subsequent treatment. Before proceeding further, this access of acid must be removed or neutralised, and it is not too much to say that most of the troubles experienced in the fat-liquoring arise from neglect or mistake in the washing and neutralisation. The difficulty in the process arises from the fact that while the acid should be reduced to a mere trace, it must not be entirely removed, as chromic oxide itself does not seem capable of tanning, and at any rate the effect of excess of strong alkalies is at once to render the leather hard and pelty. Borax is one of the safest neutralising materials, about 3 per cent. on the wet weight of the pelt being required, in not more than ½ per cent. solution. Eitner recommends the use of silicate of soda, which, sold as a solution of S.G. 1·5, is somewhat stronger and much cheaper than borax. Hyposulphite of soda and whitening together neutralise more rapidly and completely than either alone. Other salts of weak acids may also be used, the acids exercising a regulating influence which prevents neutralisation going too far. Sodium carbonate or bicarbonate, or ammonia may also be used, but with these it is difficult to get even "neutralisation," or to avoid the risk of carrying the process too far. Even a thorough drumming with a milk of "whitening" (calcium carbonate) is effective. With the latter there is no danger of overdoing the process, but in some cases the adhering whitening and precipitated calcium sulphate are troublesome in later operations. In any case the neutralising should only be carried so far that the skins show no acid reaction to litmus paper.

Procter and Griffith, Journ. Soc. Chem. Ind., 1900, p. 223.

It is probable that one of the great causes of difference between "one-bath" and "two-bath" leathers is the presence of free sulphur in the latter. This may also be introduced into "one-bath" leather, by treating it in the wet chromed state, without washing out the chrome liquor, with excess of a solution of hyposulphite, or of an alkaline polysulphide, which at the same time will neutralise the skin. The more acid the chrome liquor, the greater the quantity of sulphur which will be introduced. The simplest means of distinguishing "two-bath" from "one-bath" tannages is to test for the presence of sulphur, by wrapping up a silver coin, with a piece of the leather in paper, and leaving the parcel for an hour in the water-oven, or some other warm place, when the presence of sulphur will be shown by the blackening of the coin. Of course a sulphurised "one-bath" leather will give the same reaction.

The leather must now be dyed and fat-liquored. Which of these two operations should be first undertaken will depend on circumstances. Most leathers dye more easily before fat-liquoring, but as many dyes are soluble in the alkaline fat-liquor, a good deal of colour is often lost. This may be compensated by dissolving a suitable aniline (acid) colour in the fat-liquor. "Bluebacking" is generally done before fat-liquoring by drumming with methyl-violet, or some other aniline colour (with or without logwood, which gives alone a very dark violet). Any shaving or splitting required must of course be done before bluebacking.

The fat-liquor is an emulsion of soap and oil, which for chrome leather should be as neutral as possible, if the neutralising has been thorough; but if any acid be left on the skins, a neutral fat-liquor will be precipitated as a greasy mass. This can sometimes be remedied by the addition of a little ammonia or borax, or by re-fat-liquoring with soap solution only, but if the washing of the skins has been incomplete, and soluble chrome-salts remain, the mischief is almost irretrievable, as sticky chrome-soaps are formed, often coloured with the aniline violet, which adhere to the skins, and which can scarcely be removed by any solvent which does not injure the leather. As regards the soaps and oils used, there is considerable latitude: 1½ per cent. of castor-oil soap, and ¾ per cent. of castor or olive oil on the wet weight of the pelt has done good service in my hands, but many manufacturers employ soft soaps, curd soaps, etc., with castor, olive, cod or neatsfoot oil, and sometimes sod-oil or degras. Eitner considers olive-oil and olive-oil potash soap the most suitable, and particularly warns against the use either of drying oils or of oils containing tallow (such as neatsfoot), which are not only apt to cause a white efflorescence, but to give the leather a disagreeable rancid smell. Fish-oils are unsuitable, but mineral oils are often useful constituents of fat-liquors. Wool-fat also makes a good fat-liquor, but is unsuitable for goods which are to be glazed. "Turkey-red oil" (which is sulphated castor) may be used as a fat-liquor, simply mixed with warm water, without soap, and has been recommended where delicate colours are to be dyed after fat-liquoring; but it is said to have an unsatisfactory after-effect, hardening and tendering the leather. Some soaps made from the saponifiable part of wool grease, such as "Lanosoap," also act well in conjunction with olive, castor, or other oils. Where leather is to be glazed, the amount of fat-liquoring must be kept very moderate. Fat-liquors should be thoroughly emulsified, and are generally used warm. They penetrate better if the leather is partially dried by sleeking out, or pressing, or cautious "samming," but the leather must not be completely dried out before fat-liquoring and dyeing, unless it has been previously treated with glycerine, glucose, treacle or some deliquescent salt, which will enable it to be wet back. Chrome leathers are not "waterproof," as has often been stated, unless rendered so by treatment with soaps and greases, and are apparently easily wetted, but the fibre will no longer absorb water after thorough drying, and consequently will neither dye nor stuff satisfactorily. In order to enable chrome leather to be kept in an undyed condition, glycerine or syrup is sometimes mixed with the fat-liquor, but as the watery portion of this is not generally completely absorbed, the process is somewhat wasteful. Mr. M. C. Lamb avoids this difficulty by applying a solution of glycerine to the grain-side with a sponge after fat-liquoring. In this case the leather may be dried sufficiently for staking or shaving without risk.

Chrome leather can be dyed by many of the acid aniline colours without a mordant. Basic colours are only fixed when the leather has been first prepared with a vegetable tannin, gambier, or a mixture of gambier and sumach being the most suitable. Considerable care must be employed in the application of tannins to chrome leather, as they have a tendency to harden it and diminish its stretch, or even to render it tender, but traces of tannin in the dye probably facilitate glazing. Before dyeing, it is advantageous to fix the tannin with tartar emetic, or for browns and yellows, with titanium potassium oxalate solution, which itself gives a good yellow-brown with tannin. In place of employing the tannin and titanium salt in two separate baths, they may be combined, using a weight of the gambier or tanning extract (oakwood, chestnut, etc.) about equal to that of the titanium salt, or titanium tanno-oxalate solution may be used. Chrome leather may be dyed with the various dye-woods, which are mordanted by the chromium present, but the colours are mostly dull, that of logwood being nearly black. A good black of a very permanent character is obtained by dyeing with logwood, and saddening with a hot solution of titanium oxalate in the drum. A little iron-alum added to the chrome liquor in tanning will facilitate dyeing the skins black with logwood and help it to penetrate through the leather, which is sometimes desired. Several aniline blacks, and notably the "corvolines" of the Badische Anilin und Soda Fabrik, Casella's "leather black C," and Claus & Rée's chrome-black give very satisfactory blacks by brushing or dyeing.

Chrome skins may be glazed in the ordinary way with blood or albumen mixtures under glass or agate, but require good pressure and repeated seasonings and glazings, and much care is required in fat-liquoring. The glazing is often assisted by the previous application of barberry juice (épine vinette) or of lactic or tartaric acid solution with a trace of sugar. Much of the difficulty which has been experienced in glazing chrome leathers is due either to the natural fat of the skin, or to oils used in fat-liquoring in excessive quantity or of unsuitable character.

CHAPTER XVI.
PRINCIPLES OF THE VEGETABLE TANNING PROCESSES.

The processes employed in the production of leather with the vegetable tanning materials vary extremely according to the class of leather which is being produced, both in the materials selected and in the time required. In sole-leather tanning, where thick hides are used, and where diffusion is the only force acting to carry the tannin into the hide, many months are frequently needed, while with thin skins, and with the aid of mechanical motion, which circulates the tanning liquid between the fibres, the process is often complete within a few hours. Differences in the strength of the liquors according to whether hard or soft leathers are to be produced, and the mutual action of the acids naturally present in the liquors, and of the tan, have also a determining effect upon the quality of the product.

The simplest form of tanning in principle is probably the old-fashioned method of sole-leather manufacture. For this purpose, the hides are usually "rounded" or trimmed after liming, unhairing and fleshing, so that the most valuable part, the "butt," can be tanned separately from the "offal." The butts are usually washed in water to remove a portion of the lime, considerable care being required at this stage to avoid carbonation and fixation of chalk by means of free carbonic acid, or hydric calcium carbonate (temporary hardness) in the water employed, or by the free carbonic acid of the air. This somewhat primitive process can at best only remove a small portion of the lime, since so long as the lime remains in the caustic condition, it is very obstinately held by the hide-fibre. Advanced tanners now frequently employ weakly acid baths, in addition to washing, in order to produce more complete deliming, and this effects a very considerable improvement of colour in the early liquors. The use of lactic acid (free from iron) or boric (boracic) acid in solutions of about 4 lb. per 100 gallons, in which the butts are kept in motion, are among the safest and most satisfactory ways of removing surface-lime and improving the colour, but even the stronger mineral acids may be used successfully with caution (see Chap. XIII.).

Whether acid be used or not, the butts are now usually suspended in deep pits containing old and nearly exhausted tan liquors. These liquors contain a certain amount of lactic and acetic acids, derived by fermentation from the sugary matters of the tanning materials, and also in some cases, weak acids originally present in the materials themselves. These acids are most important to successful tannage, and their effect is twofold; in the first place, they neutralise and remove any lime which still remains in the butts;

and, secondly, they bring the butt into a slightly acid condition, in which it remains plump and swollen in the liquors, while the tannin gradually penetrates and tans the fibre. If, as frequently happens, especially in modern yards where extracts are very largely used, the natural acid of the liquors is not sufficient for this purpose, the lime combines with the tanning matters, and the butts either become discoloured at once, or darken by exposure and oxidation, when they come to be dried, while the pelt remains flat and insufficiently swollen. To avoid this trouble, resort is sometimes had to artificial acidification of the liquors. As a general rule, it may be stated that it does not answer to mix the stronger mineral acids directly with the liquors, but lactic and acetic acids may be used, or even oxalic acid may be added to the suspenders in such quantities as to precipitate and remove the lime which they contain, setting free the organic acids with which it had been combined. The use of oxalic acid should never be pushed further than this, as it has a most powerful swelling action on the hide; and goods which are too much swollen by acids tan dark and brittle.

After the hides have remained from ten days to a fortnight in the suspenders, they are usually laid in pits called "handlers" which are worked in series of 6, 8, or 10 pits, containing the same number of packs of goods. The weakest liquor from the youngest pack is run to the suspenders daily, a new and stronger liquor is run to the pit, which now becomes the head of the series, into which the oldest and most tanned pack of butts is moved; and the next takes its place and liquor, and so on down the series, the youngest pack finally occupying the place which had previously been taken by the last but one. In this way each pack receives a change of liquor of regularly graduated strength; and during the time which it remains in the handlers, passes from a strength of perhaps 20° Bkr. (sp. gr. 1·020) to one of about 40° Bkr. (sp. gr. 1·040). During this part of the process the butt is completely or nearly coloured through, and is then ready for the "layers."

In the forward handlers, dustings of ground bark or other tanning material are very frequently given, and the layers only differ from these in having much heavier dusting, stronger liquors, and being allowed to remain undisturbed for greater lengths of time, ranging from a week up to a month or even six weeks, as the tannage progresses. The handler-liquors are principally from the old layers, though they are frequently made up with weak liquors from the leaches, and strengthened with extracts or gambier.

Very varied materials are used in the manufacture of sole-leather. Oak-bark is one of the oldest, and as regards quality one of the most satisfactory, but it is costly, not only on account of its weakness in tannin but from the light weight of leather which it gives. Valonia is one of the favourite materials, giving heavy weight and a solid leather, in which it deposits a great deal of bloom. Oakwood, chestnut-wood, and hemlock-bark extracts are now very largely consumed, principally in strengthening the layer-liquors; the great object being not only to lessen the cost in material, but to save time, and produce greater weight and firmness. The layer-liquors in some yards where extract is used, reach strengths of even 120° to 150° Bkr. (sp. gr. 1·12 to 1·15), while in pure oak-bark yards it is difficult to get above 30° or 35° Bkr.; and even these figures are only reached by repeatedly strengthening the same liquor, in which large quantities of non-tanning substances accumulate. The opinion of the most intelligent tanners is, however, that better results are attained by a regular change of liquor, even if the apparent strength is less.

When the leather has remained a sufficient time in the layers to have attained all the weight and solidity of which it is capable, it is washed up in a clear and somewhat weaker liquor or even in warm water, and taken into the shed to be dried and finished. As this finishing is almost purely mechanical, and scarcely comes within the scope of the present volume, a very brief sketch must suffice.

FIG. 39.—Wilson's Striking Machine.

The mode of finishing which was formerly, at least, in vogue in Lancashire and Cheshire may be taken as a type of the best work. (In the present day, the various methods are so widely known that they have ceased to be local, and are varied according to the quality and tannage of the goods.) The butts, which in earlier times were largely bark-tanned, are taken wet from the pits, and scoured on a rounded beam or "horse" with stone and brush, till the bloom is completely removed, and are then lightly oiled on the grain, half dried ("sammed"), laid in pile to temper, and "struck out" with the "pin," a two-handled tool of triangular section shown in Fig. 29. The use of this tool has now been largely superseded by Wilson's striking machine Fig. 39, in which knives or sleekers (or stones and brushes), held in jointed arms, are made to work on the butt, which is extended over a slowly rotating cylinder. The object of the pinning is not so much to remove bloom or dirt, which has been previously effected by the scouring, as to smooth and flatten the grain. After further drying, a second pinning is generally given, and the goods are then twice rolled, first with a light weight, and somewhat moist grain, and then more heavily with the grain nearly dry. This was formerly accomplished by a sort of box or car, heavily loaded with weights, supported on a smooth brass roller of about 5 inches diameter and 9 inches long, and manipulated with a long wooden handle on a floor of hard wood, or zinc plates. One type of the machines which have now almost entirely replaced this primitive contrivance is shown in Fig. 40, but is principally used for offal and common classes of goods. For better work, traversing rollers, such as Wilson's ingenious double bed roller shown in Fig. 41, are to be preferred. After rolling, the goods are dried pretty rapidly by the aid of moderate heat, and, after polishing with a brush (hand, or machine, Fig. 42), are ready for sale. It may be pointed out that although the tools are different, the process is almost the same as that used for "*vache lissée*" in France and Belgium, and closely resembles that of currying harness leather except that the "stuffing" with fats and oil is omitted.

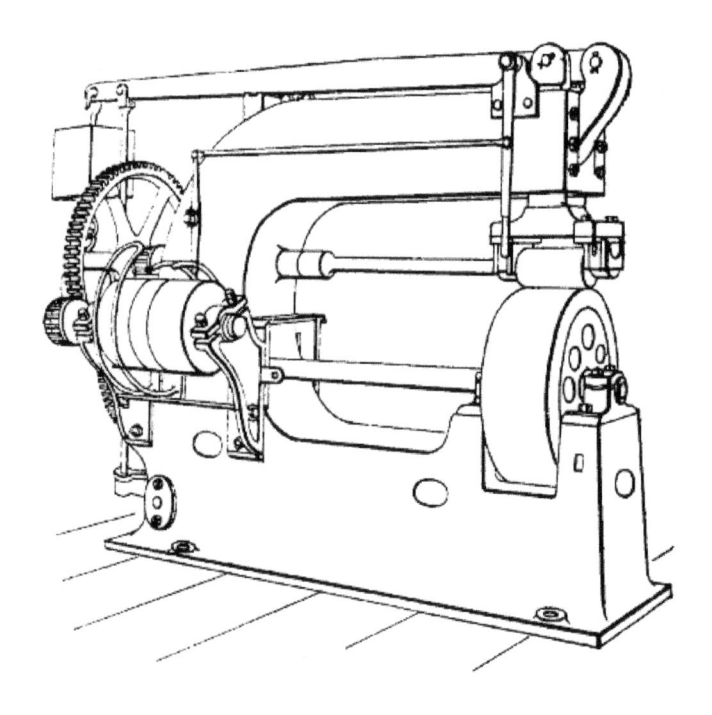

FIG. 40.—Offal Roller.

In contrast with the rather elaborate method just described, we may place the American finish of red hemlock sides, which are tanned throughout with a material which yields no bloom. On these, the scouring and "striking" is altogether omitted: the goods are completely dried out from the pits, which is found to fix the dark-coloured liquor, and result in better colour; they are then damped back, and tempered, and heavily rolled under a rapidly moving pendulum roller, which polishes at the same time that it smooths the leather. The saving of cost by so simple a process is not inconsiderable.

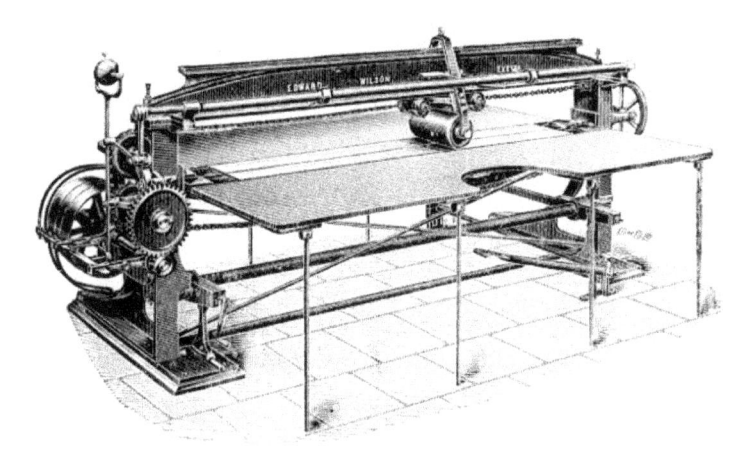

FIG. 41.—Wilson's Double-bed Butt Roller.

In the West of England, much heavy leather is still manufactured from South American hides, which are tanned with a large proportion of valonia; and which consequently are heavily bloomed. No attempt is made to remove this bloom, which would too much lessen the weight and firmness, but the goods, after a light oiling to preserve the colour, are hung up and partially dried, and are then laid in pile to temper. The grain side is now wet with soap and water, with which a little oil is often mixed, and the bloom is "struck in" with the pin or machine; a somewhat blunt pin being used, or a blunt tool in the striking machine; which is held at such an angle as to smooth and compress the grain without taking too much hold on it. After a little further drying, the striking is generally repeated, the goods are washed over with water, and rolled "on." They are now coloured with a mixture of pigment colour, generally containing a large proportion of whitening, or sometimes of French chalk coloured with ochres, chrome-yellow and orange, or whatever may suit the tint preferred by the tanner, or best imitate the colour of a clean-scoured tannage, and usually mixed with size and oil, or sometimes with oil and tan liquor. This mixture is well rubbed in, and smoothed over with a cloth, and then polished by brushing, when the goods are "rolled off," rapidly dried, and again brushed. If the work has been well done, it is not easy to distinguish from clean scouring, and is much cheaper.

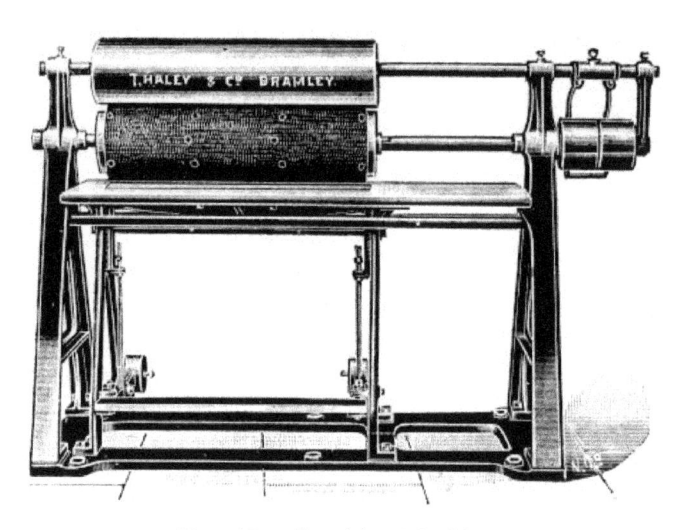

FIG. 42.—Brushing Machine.

A method intermediate between this and the first described, and which was formerly much used in London, was to proceed as above, but using more water and holding the pin in the first striking so as to scour out as much bloom as possible, and assisting this by the free use of water and the brush. Instead of using an opaque pigment-colour, the goods were generally coloured either between striking and the first rolling, or between the two rollings, with a transparent colour, such as dissolved annatto, or a mixture of aniline dyes, so as to conceal the traces of bloom, and to render slight damages to the grain less conspicuous.

The principles of the manufacture have been fully explained in previous sections, up to the time when the goods are taken into the tanning liquors. At this stage complicated reactions take place between the lime in the butts, the free vegetable acids in the liquors, and the tannins; and on the right adjustment of these three factors much of the success of the operation, and indeed of the whole manufacture depends. If the lime is in excess of the acids present, it forms insoluble compounds with the tannins in the surface of the hide. If these are protected from the air, they are generally redissolved as they advance into more acid liquors, but they readily become oxidised into dark-coloured matters, which can no longer be removed. Their presence in the finished leather is one of the great causes of darkening in drying. If the hide in the limy condition has been exposed either to the carbonic acid of the air, or to free carbonic acid, or acid calcium carbonate dissolved in water ("temporary" hardness, p. 94), a precipitate of calcium carbonate will be formed in the surface, which is much more difficult to remove than free lime, and which is perhaps the most common cause of the stains and discolorations which are so serious a source of loss to the sole-leather tanner. These stains may, if not too much oxidised, be removed by treatment of the tanned leather with weak warm sulphuric acid, but this remedy brings other evils in its train, and should not be required. The great remedy is to keep the goods from the time of unhairing till they go into the liquors, under water in which there is always a trace of caustic lime, or which at any rate are free from carbonic acid. In deliming sole-leather with acids, it is best to give the full dose of acid required, at once, and not gradually, so that it may act most powerfully on the exterior, and remove any carbonates present, before it penetrates to and becomes neutralised by the excess of lime in the interior. This is exactly the reverse of what is advisable with dressing leather, where the object of the tanner is to remove lime as uniformly and completely as possible, without excessive acidity of any part. Of course hides should not, even in the case of sole-leather, be allowed to go into the liquors while any acid swelling of the surface remains, but this will soon disappear if the goods are suspended for a time in cold water after deliming, unless excess of acid has been used (cp. p. 153 *et seq.*).

If the proportion of free acid in the suspender liquors is as it ought to be, it is probably rather advantageous than otherwise for a little lime to remain in the interior of the hide, as it keeps the pelt in a plump condition during the first stages of colouring, quickens the penetration of the tannin, and lessens the tendency to "drawn" or wrinkled grain, which arises when the goods go into the liquors in a flat or fallen condition. The causes of drawn grain are often a little obscure. Of course that case needs no elucidation in which the hides are submitted to the tanning liquor in a creased or wrinkled condition, which is simply fixed and made permanent. This may arise, either from carelessness in handling the goods before taking into the suspenders, or from the way in which they are slung to the sticks, which often draws them into long wrinkles, afterwards difficult to remove. Drawn grain in general, however, arises from the grain-surface becoming tanned and fixed in area, while the substance of the hide is in a more extended condition than that which it assumes as tannage proceeds. Hides in a flat and unswollen condition are thinner, the fibres are slenderer and looser than when swollen, and consequently the hide has a larger area. If, after the grain is tanned, the substance of the hide becomes contracted in the liquor, either by swelling with acids, or by the direct action of the tannin on the interior fibres, the grain is certain to be shrivelled, like the skin of a dried apple. A similar effect, produced in a mechanical way, may always be noted where a hide has been coloured hanging grain-side out over a pole, so that the surface is extended at the bend, on which long wrinkles are formed as soon as it is straightened.

A hide in a slightly alkaline condition colours, and even tans more quickly than one which is acid. In presence of a trace of lime, and deficiency of free acid in the suspender liquor, tannages of valonia and bark give the butt a sort of lemon-yellow colour, which is not in itself injurious, and which disappears as the hides advance into more acid liquors, but which is a sign of danger, as showing that no excess of acid exists in the suspender-liquors. Gambier gives pelt perfectly free from lime a pale buff colour, but where lime is present, the colour is always reddish, and much darker, and this coloration does not disappear so readily as that with valonia, so that if gambier is to be used in the first liquors, care should be taken to remove all lime from the surface. The only known tannin which gives no insoluble compound with lime is that of the babool pod (sometimes called "gambia-pod"), which is frequently used in India as a bate, and which would probably prove very useful in colouring liquors (pp. 165, 288).

When sole-leather first goes into liquors, it is generally swollen with lime to some extent. If the liquors contain, as they usually do, sufficient free acid (acetic, lactic) in addition to the tannins, these combine with and neutralise the lime, and the pelt, without absolutely becoming flat and thin, loses its firmness, and becomes soft and spongy. This is a favourable condition for the absorption of tannin, but care should be taken not to allow the pelt to be squeezed or pressed, or water will be squeezed out, and the pelt will not easily resume its plumpness. As the tannage proceeds, both the tannin and the acid of the liquors penetrate deeper into the pelt, the former tending to contract and the latter to swell the fibres. Thus a given quantity of acid will cause the greater swelling, the less tannin is present; and therefore in strong tanning liquors more acid is required. The presence of certain products of bacterial putrefaction has a great but unexplained effect in preventing hide from swelling with acids; and in hot weather, much better swelling is obtained by sterilising and deliming the hides with one of the coal-tar products mentioned on pp. 30, 162. Boric acid may also be satisfactorily used for this purpose, but should not be allowed to get into sole-leather liquors, as it tends to produce a soft and loose tannage, and from its inorganic and indestructible character, is apt to accumulate in a yard in which it is used. The same reasons render unadvisable its introduction into any liquors which are to be returned to the leaches even in the tannage of dressing leather, though its presence in the colouring liquors is otherwise very useful in lessening the astringency of the tannins ("mellowing the liquors"), and making a fine grain. Its mode of action is by no means clearly explained, but is in some way connected with its tendency to produce "conjugated acids" (L.I.L.B., pp. 37, 46).

The so-called "mellowness" of old liquors requires a word of comment. It is well known to practical tanners, that old liquors are much less liable to produce drawn grain, and a harsh surface, when used to colour green goods, than liquors, even equally weak, which have been made from fresh materials. This is probably due, in part at least, to more than one cause. Most natural tanning materials contain tanning matters of varied degrees of astringency and power of attaching themselves to the leather-fibre. It is obvious that if a tanning liquor is used, the most astringent and energetic tannins will be first removed from it, leaving those of a milder character. It is also known that the presence of neutral alkaline salts of weak acids has considerable influence in producing mellowness; the addition, for instance, of sodium acetate has a marked effect. This effect is probably due in the first place to the action of neutral salts in diminishing the energy of weak acids (see p. 81), and secondly to the fact, that their bases combine to some extent with the tannins; and that, as was perhaps first pointed out by the writer, such tannins are, as it were, partially paralysed in their action on hide (p. 339). Sodium sulphite acts powerfully in this way, and may perhaps prove of technical value in temporarily diminishing the astringency of liquors in quick tannage. Borax has a similar effect, but is too alkaline, and, unless used with extreme caution, spoils the colour of the liquors by causing oxidation. It is probable that similar causes explain the mellowness of palmetto extract, which contains large quantities of alkaline salts, and of some extracts which have been treated with sulphites, when used undiluted in drum tannage. The addition of free acid will generally restore these tannins to an active condition.

As the tannage proceeds and penetrates further into the hide, the liquors are used stronger, as the outside, once tanned, is to a large extent protected from their action, and it is only by continuously increasing the strength of the liquors that more tannin can diffuse into the interior, since diffusion only takes place from a stronger into a weaker liquor. The liquor in the interior of the butts is always exhausted of tannin so long as any part of the hide-fibre remains untanned, but as the layer of tanned fibre between this and the outside gets thicker, a greater difference is required to maintain a reasonable rate of exchange, just as a greater head of liquor is required to maintain a flow of liquor through an increased number of percolation-leaches. If the strength of the liquor outside be allowed to fall off, this graduation of strength from the outside to the inside of the butt is disturbed, and takes some time to re-establish. As the liquors become stronger in tannin, they may also become somewhat stronger in acid, since, as has been stated, the two act to some extent in opposition to each other. The acid-swollen fibre absorbs the tannin more slowly than if it were in more neutral condition, but it absorbs it apparently in larger quantity, and at any rate, makes a firmer, solider, and less flexible leather.

It has been mentioned that in the latter stages of the process, solid tanning materials are generally strewed between the butts in the tanning liquor. It may be pointed out that many materials vary in their tanning effect, according to whether they are used in solid form or merely in liquors. It has been shown by Youl and Griffith that such materials as valonia, oakwood and chestnut extracts, and myrobalans, which contain both gallotannic and ellagitannic acids, lose strength rapidly when kept in the form of liquor, the ellagitannic acid becoming decomposed with separation of insoluble ellagic acid. Now it is just this ellagic acid, which deposited *in* or *on* the leather, gives weight, solidity and bloom, and the investigation points out not only an important source of loss in the tanning industry, but also, why valonia, which in sole-leather tannage is known to give hard and heavy leather, can be used in large quantities on dressing leathers in Yorkshire, with gambier, in the form of liquor, giving a soft and mellow leather almost destitute of bloom. If weight and solidity are required from the use of such materials, it is obvious that they must be brought into immediate contact with the leather to be tanned, so that as large a part of the bloom as possible is deposited in, and not outside the leather. With many other materials, such as hemlock, quebracho, and mimosa, which yield no bloom, but "difficultly soluble" tannins (reds or phlobaphenes), the same rule holds, since in contact with the hides, the small proportion of these materials which is soluble in the liquors, is replaced from the materials as rapidly as it is absorbed by the leather, while, when liquors or extracts only are used, the greater part of these solidifying and weight-giving constituents remain unutilised in the spent tanning materials. At the same time, the long "layers" afford an opportunity for the acetic and lactic fermentations to go on which are the principal source of the natural acidity of liquors. It must be understood that what are called layers in England, are not to be identified with the *Sätze*, but rather with the *Versenke* of the German tanner, the former being layers given in much the same manner as was current in England 150 years ago; in which the leather, with thick layers of tanning material between it, is laid into the empty pit, which is afterwards filled up with liquor, often of a comparatively weak character. In such layers, the acidification, and the solidification of the leather both go on to a still greater degree; the acid formed, apparently gradually penetrating to the heart of the leather-fibres, and producing a solidity, and cheesy texture which can hardly be obtained by layers of the English kind; which nevertheless have the advantage in rapidity and cheapness.

Journ. Soc. Chem. Ind., 1901, p. 428.

In drying sole-leather, one of the great objects which must be aimed at is to remove the dark coloured liquor, with which the goods are saturated, from the surface, and to prevent further portions of it from finding their way there from the interior. If a strip of filter-paper be allowed to rest with one end in a basin containing a little liquor, and be placed in a draught of air, the exposed end of the paper will rapidly become dark brown or black, the liquor which evaporates there being constantly replaced by fresh portions sucked up by capillary attraction from the basin. A similar action is constantly seen, when filtering liquors through paper, if the latter be allowed to project above the edge of the funnel. Precisely the same effect occurs, perhaps increased by the oxidation of the tannins, on the edges and other parts of a butt which are most exposed to draughts of air. The use of oiling the grain is not only, to a certain extent to protect it from oxidation, but also to check evaporation, and the consequent accumulation there of the dark-coloured solids contained in the liquor. A very similar result is attained by wetting the grain-side, and allowing as much of the evaporation as possible to take place from the flesh.

The process of sole leather tanning has been discussed in considerable detail on account of its simplicity and importance. It is now time to point out in what respects the tannage of the lighter leathers differs from it in principle. Taking the case of ordinary dressing leathers, such as kips and shaved hides, the first point to remember is that these goods come into the liquors not merely almost entirely deprived of lime by bating, but in a very flat and fallen condition from the action of the bacterial ferments of the bate. As a general rule in this country the colouring is done in paddles, but where a very smooth grain is required, the use of suspenders is to be recommended, and in America is largely adopted. Indeed in the States the entire tannage of much of the cheaper leather is done in suspension, and the sides are only removed from the laths to which they have been nailed, when they are required for splitting. It is obvious, from what has been said of sole leather, that as the hides are brought into liquors in a very fallen and extended condition, the grain will be likely to be wrinkled; and indeed this is sure to be the case unless, by suspension, the hide is more or less kept in tension till its fibres are fixed by tanning. The free motion in the paddle favours the formation of a "pebbled" grain, since the hide is bent now this way, now that, and minute wrinkles and creases are formed in all directions. For many purposes, and especially if a grain is afterwards to be raised by "boarding" the curried leather, this graining in the paddle is not disadvantageous, so long as it is not excessive. In some other cases it causes much trouble and labour to the currier before it is removed, and if the English tanner and currier are ever to compete with the American in smooth grain finishes, it will be necessary for them to obviate this source of wasted labour. The graining is the less considerable, and the easier to remove, the weaker and more mellow are the liquors employed in colouring and the more gradually their strength is increased.

The production of a soft leather depends on the fibre being tanned in a fallen and unswelled condition. It is for this reason that bating is in many cases essential, though where somewhat firmer leathers are required, mere reduction of the swelling by removal of the lime is sufficient. For the same reason, no acid-swelling is permissible either before tanning, or in the liquors, and though liquors for soft leathers must be rather acid than alkaline, they are incapable of removing any large quantity of lime, and for the best results, the deliming must be complete before tanning. As mere bating or puering is mainly designed to reduce swelling by the action of bacterial products (p. 172), and is not a very efficient means of removing lime, it is desirable where it is employed, to supplement it by some more active deliming process. In the lighter leathers, drenching (p. 166) generally fulfils this purpose and many of the more intelligent tanners now give bated hides a bath in boric acid before tanning, which not only removes the last traces of lime without acid-swelling, but checks the bacterial fermentation, and prevents its introduction into the liquors. In gambier tannages, a decidedly better colour is obtained by this treatment (p. 228).

In most cases the production of bloom is not desired in dressing leather tannage, and is prevented by relying chiefly on liquors, and avoiding the use of bloom-giving solid materials, which include most pyrogallol tannins. Dressing leather tannages can frequently be advantageously hastened by drumming: which by continuously bending the leather in all directions, constantly widens and contracts the spaces between the different fibres, and, as it were, pumps the liquor through the skin. The softness of dressing leathers is increased, and the hardening action of acids present in the liquors is prevented by the addition of salt, or of some sulphates (sodium, magnesium, ammonium) which exercise a sort of pickling action on the fibre, and prevent its swelling, but at the same time tend to light weight and a somewhat empty tannage. It by no means follows that a hide or skin which is thoroughly coloured through, is really fully tanned; as, though the fibres may be actually tanned or coated on the surface, time is required for the tannins to penetrate them to the centre. This incompleteness of saturation is often found in drum tannages. Such leathers are generally tough, and gain weight and softness in currying. In order to "carry grease" well, that is, to absorb a large quantity without appearing greasy, it is essential that the fibre-bundles should be thoroughly split up or differentiated; and the degree to which this is attained largely depends on the extent of liming. There is also considerable difference in different tannages, as to the amount of grease which they will carry.

It is now not uncommon to combine a degree of alum or chrome tannage with vegetable tannage in the finer dressing leathers. For further information on this the reader must be referred to the next chapter.

The finest sorts of leather such as goat, calf, sheep and seal for bookbinding, upholstery and the like, are mostly tanned with sumach; paddles and drums being largely used to quicken the operation. Leather tanned with sumach has been proved by the researches of the committee of the Society of Arts on the decay of bookbinding leathers to be the most durable leather for this purpose, some other tanning materials of the pyrogallol class coming near it in this respect, while all catechol tannages are found peculiarly liable to destruction by the action of sunlight, dry heat, gas fumes, and traces of sulphuric acid from other sources, although in many cases more durable than the pyrogallol tannages when exposed to mechanical wear and moisture, as is the case with shoe-leather (p. 298). East India sheep- and goat-skins (so-called "Persians") are tanned with the catechol tannin of turwar or cassia bark.

Soc. of Arts Journ., 1901, p. 14.

FIG. 42a.—Interior of Light Leather Tannery.

The finer leathers of which we are now speaking are almost invariably prepared for tanning by puering with dog-dung, and drenching with bran, as colour and softness are the special characteristics aimed at. A somewhat interesting style of tannage is occasionally used for sheep-skins (roans), and calf-skins, in which the skin is sewn into a bag, flesh side out, with only a small aperture left for filling at one of the shanks. It is then turned grain-side out, and filled with strong sumach liquor, and a little leaf sumach, and floated in a bath of warm sumach liquor. After a short immersion, the skins are piled on a stage, so that the liquor is pressed through them by their weight; and when partially empty, they are refilled and the process repeated. The time of tannage is very short, not exceeding about twenty-four hours, and the leather produced is very soft.

CHAPTER XVII.
COMBINATION OF VEGETABLE AND MINERAL TANNAGE.

In very early times leathers were produced, which were partly tanned with alum, and partly with vegetable materials. One of the earliest of these was probably the Swedish or Danish glove-leather. The principle has long been applied to the production of certain very tough and flexible leathers known as "green leather," and used for "picker-bands" for looms, laces for belting, "combing-leathers" and some other purposes where softness and toughness are of principal importance. About twenty-five years since, it was applied in America by Mr. Kent to the manufacture of an imitation of glazed kid, which he named Dongola leather; and since that time, the method in various modifications, has taken a considerable place in the manufacture of the finer leathers for shoe purposes, especially in the United States.

Alum-tanned leathers, as has been already stated, are remarkable for softness and toughness, and the mineral (crystalloid) tannages have the power of penetrating and isolating the individual fibrils of the skin in a much greater degree than the vegetable tannins, and hence are less dependent than the latter on a previous isolation produced by liming. On the other hand, they give much less plumpness and solidity, and more liability to stretch, and are less resistant to the action of water; and are, as a general rule (to which some chrome-tannages are an exception), incapable of producing a soft leather without mechanical softening (staking) after the tannage is completed. Purely mineral tannages have always a woolly fibrous structure, and never the firm and compact flesh which is required in leathers which are to be "waxed," or finished on the flesh side to a smooth surface, and as they communicate more or less of these peculiarities to combination-tannages, the latter are mostly used, either for grain-finish, or for uses where a soft and velvety flesh-side is required, as in the case of "ooze-" or "velvet-" calf. On the other hand, the partial use of vegetable tannage communicates to them a degree of plumpness, fulness and resistance to water which is not possible to alum-tannages pure and simple, and a softness which is not easily obtained in vegetable tannage without the use of large quantities of fats or oils. A preliminary mineral tannage also greatly increases the rapidity of the penetration of the vegetable tans, by isolating the fibres, and rendering them less gelatinous. Once a leather is *thoroughly* tanned by vegetable materials, it is little affected by subsequent treatment with alumina, or even with chrome; and on the other hand, though chrome and alumina leathers are still capable of absorbing considerable quantities of vegetable tannins, they always retain, in a degree, the qualities which the mineral tannage has communicated to them. The resulting leathers are thus not only modified by the different proportion of vegetable and mineral tannages which have been given, and by the properties of the particular vegetable tannage used; but by the order in which the several treatments have been given, and always retain, to a considerable extent, the characteristics of that which has been first applied. We have thus in our hands a powerful means of modifying the character of our leather to suit the special requirements which it is to fulfil.

So long as tanners were restricted on the one hand, to the ordinary methods of stuffing tanned leathers with oils and fats, and on the other to the use of egg-yolk, which had long been common in alum-tannages, combination-tannage remained of but secondary importance, and it was the application of the method of "fat-liquoring" by James Kent to his Dongola leather, which gave them the place they now possess, by providing a cheap substitute for egg-yolk, and enabling the tanner to obtain softness and resistance to water, without producing the greasy feel which is common to curried leathers. The process of fat-liquoring has already been mentioned in connection with chrome leathers, to which it was subsequently applied, and we shall return to it, after having given some further details of the methods of tannage.

In the first place we must consider briefly the mutual action of the mineral and vegetable tannages on each other. It has been pointed out by Eitner, and also mentioned (p. 339) in connection with the decolorisation of extracts, that the addition of say ½ per cent. of alum, or aluminium sulphate to tanning liquors, lightened their colour, not only by giving a degree of acidity to the solution, but by precipitating a portion of the less soluble and more darkly coloured tannins. Chrome-alum, and basic chrome salts produce a similar effect, though from their marked colour, the lightening of the solution is not so easily observed. It is therefore advisable if these salts are to be used in actual mixture with the vegetable tans, to allow the solution time to subside, or to filter off the dark-coloured precipitated matters. Larger quantities than ½ per cent. of the alum do not appear materially to increase the effect just described.

A second effect produced by these mineral salts on vegetable tannins, is in many cases to develop mordant colouring matters which are present; and thus, since most of these colouring matters are yellow, to produce a yellower leather than would be obtained with the vegetable material alone. This effect is very marked in the cases of sumach, gambier and quebracho. The compounds which these colouring matters form with chrome are mostly of a darker shade than those with alumina, tending to olive, and therefore chrome-combination leathers are generally dull in colour.

Potassium dichromate, especially if acidified, generally oxidises and precipitates tannins, and darkens their colours, so that it is not practical to follow a vegetable tannage by the two-bath chrome process; and though the reverse order may be pursued, the single-bath chrome process, and that following and not preceding the vegetable tannage, generally gives the best results. If lightly tanned leathers, such for instance as the imported East Indian tannages, with babool or turwar barks, be treated with a basic chrome tanning liquor, such as is described on p. 215, so large a proportion of chrome will be absorbed, that the leather will possess most of the characteristics of a genuine chrome leather.

Combination-tannages for glove-leathers, such as the Danish and Swedish leathers already alluded to, are generally first tawed with alum and salt, with or without addition of flour and egg-yolk, and are then coloured, and more or less tanned with vegetable materials. That employed on the original Danish leather was willow bark (of *Salix arenaria*). In France, where this willow is not found, the bark of the commoner *Salix caprea* was substituted; and as it is much weaker in tannin, additions of oak-bark or sumach to supply the deficiency, and of madder to give a redder colour were made to it. The dyeing of these leathers is frequently combined with the tannage, dyewoods or dyewood liquors being mixed with the tanning liquors. In the manufacture of glazed French kid, indeed, the process is so arranged, by brushing on dye-liquors mixed with tannins, as merely to tan the grain-surface, which is necessary to enable it to be glazed by friction, leaving the substance of the leather of purely alum tannage.

On the other hand, in the "green leathers" (so-called from their greenish-yellow colour, and largely made in the West Riding of Yorkshire), the hides usually receive a light gambier tannage, extending over a week or so in weak gambier liquors in handlers, and are then "cured" by handling in hot and strong solution of salt and alum, in which they are finally left all night, and then dried rapidly without washing out the alum, much of which consequently crystallises on the surface. This is slicked off, and the leather damped back, and heavily stuffed with sod-oil. If, however, the combination-tannage is properly carried out, it will stand liberal washing without losing the necessary alum, and of course a tougher and more satisfactory, though somewhat lighter weighing leather results. It is in many cases a better plan to combine the two tannages in one bath, mixing the alum and salt with the gambier, and handling or paddling the goods in the mixture. This is the plan usually adopted for Dongola leather, in the United States. For skins which are to be glazed, it is important that the *surface* should be tanned with the vegetable material, and the goods are therefore worked into gambier liquors, to which the salt and alum are only added after the tannage has made some little progress; while for dull Dongola, intended rather to imitate calf-kid, it is best for the alum and salt tannage to begin first. For goat-skins for glazed Dongola kid, about 4 lb. of block gambier, ½ lb. of alum, and ¼ lb. of salt are used per dozen, and the tannage occupies in all about twenty-four hours.

After the skins are tanned, they are thoroughly washed out with tepid water, to remove loose alum and gambier, and are then ready for fat-liquoring. As in the case of chrome leather, it is of great importance that this washing should be done thoroughly, as any remaining alum which diffuses into the fat-liquor, will cause it to curdle. If the washing is thorough, the more neutral the fat-liquor and the better; but a somewhat alkaline soap-solution is less liable to curdle. The original fat-liquor used by Mr. Kent was the alkaline liquor which had been used in washing the surplus oil from chamois leather (see p. 380), but now soap- and oil-solutions are generally made specially for the purpose. Most of the remarks in the chapter on chrome tannages are applicable in this case, but probably fat-liquoring is somewhat easier than in the case of chrome. Mixtures of either soft soap or curd soap with cod, sod, and olive oil are frequently employed. Sesame oil also seems well adapted for the purpose. The better these are emulsified, and the more satisfactory is the result; a cylinder of zinc or copper fitted with a plunger, something like that of a "Lightning Egg Beater," but covered with perforated zinc, or wire gauze, does very good service as an emulsifier on a small scale.

Another method is to melt the soap with just sufficient water to make it pasty, and to incorporate the oil thoroughly with the mass, which is afterwards dissolved in hot water. Oils are the most easily emulsified when they are somewhat acid. For this reason rancid olive oils are often used for the Turkey-red process, but a similar effect can be obtained by adding a small quantity of candlemaker's oleic acid to the oil before mixing. The addition of sulphated castor oil (Turkey-red oil) also helps emulsification, and is in itself a very good softening agent. One of the commonest mistakes in fat-liquoring is the employment of too strong an emulsion—even so small a quantity as ½ per cent. of soap, and half that quantity of oil, reckoned on the wet weight of the well-drained leather, will produce a very notable softening effect. Of course, for dull finishes, much larger proportions may be used. Not only combination-tannages, but those entirely vegetable, can be fat-liquored with excellent effect, and the process is now largely used for coloured calf, and other leathers, which are required soft and nourished, but without any appearance of greasiness. Leathers absorb the fat-liquor most readily if put into it in a sammed or partially dried condition, but even if quite wet, they soon take up the whole of the oil and soap on drumming, leaving only a little clear water in the drum. Goods may be blacked while still wet with fat-liquor, but should generally (except in the case of chrome leathers) be dried out before dyeing, as this fixes the oil and soap in the fibres.

Many coloured leathers are now made by a process which may be considered a combination of the Dongola process itself with the ordinary process of vegetable tanning, the goods being coloured and partially tanned as if for a vegetable tannage, and then finished in Dongola liquors with alum, salt and gambier. Very good leathers are made in this way in the United States, with a tannage begun in suspension in hemlock bark liquors.

Imitations of Dongola leather are made by treating East India sheep or goat with alum liquors, and afterwards fat-liquoring (if necessary) and finishing like genuine Dongola leather. The treatment is most effective, if a portion of the original tan be removed by washing with warm water, with a little borax, ammonia, or even soda, and the goods then alumed with a "neutralised" or basic alum solution such as that described on p. 187. Goods treated with a basic chrome-liquor, like that used for the one-bath chrome process, p. 212, are almost converted into chrome-tanned goods, and will even stand some degree of boiling. The use of a liquor made like the Martin-Dennis liquor, by dissolving chromic oxide in hydrochloric acid, was the subject of an American patent which in this country is owned by Wichellow and Tebbutt, but which expires in 1903.

East India sheep and goat are generally so heavily oiled with sesame oil (up to 30 per cent. of their weight), that it is desirable in many cases rather to diminish than increase the oil, which may be done by washing with soap solutions, preferably before aluming.

Eng. Pat. Jensen 13126, 1889.

Chrome-combinations may also be made by retanning goods tanned by either of the chrome processes with vegetable materials, of which gambier seems the most suitable. The use, even of very weak liquors of sumach and most other tanning materials, deprives chrome leather of its stretch, and if carried to excess, readily makes it hard and tender.

CHAPTER XVIII.
VEGETABLE TANNING MATERIALS.

As has been stated in the previous chapter, our knowledge of the chemistry of tannins is not sufficiently advanced to render possible any strictly chemical classification, while an additional complication arises from the fact that very different tannins may coexist in the wood, bark, fruit, galls, etc. of the same plant. It therefore seems best to follow the example of Prof. Bernardin in his 'Classification de 350 matières tannantes,' and arrange the plants under the orders of the natural system of botany, as has already been done by von Höhnel and A. de Lof. In the following pages, only those materials which from their high percentage of tannin, or from some other cause, are of commercial interest or value, are included, as the tannins are so widely distributed in the vegetable kingdom, that any exhaustive list would be quite out of the question.

Gand, 1880.

'Die Gerberinden,' Berlin, 1880.

'Matières tannantes,' Halle aux Cuirs, Paris, 1890. See also 'Agricultural Ledger,' 1902, No. 1 (Government Printing Office, Calcutta, 6d.), by Mr. D. Hooper, which contains much valuable information.

Tannins are not confined to any particular part of the plant, though they are usually most abundant in barks and fruits. Insect-galls are often very rich in tannin, usually gallotannic acid; while in several cases woods are of commercial importance from their cheapness, though the percentage of tannin they contain is not generally high. The function of tannins in the vegetable economy is not well understood. In some cases they are probably a waste product of plant-life, and may help to ward off attacks of insects. They usually exist as cell-contents, and as vegetable cells have frequently thick and impermeable walls, and the diffusive power of tannins is low, much time is required for extraction, unless the cells have been previously crushed or broken.

It would be beyond the scope of this text-book to describe in detail the structures of the tannin-yielding parts of plants; but barks are of such general importance, that some particulars seem desirable.

The detailed structure of bark varies greatly in different trees, though its general principles remain unaltered. One of the best short accounts of these is given by Prof. H. Marshall Ward on page 199 of his little book on 'Timber and some of its Diseases,' and further information may be found in Van Tieghem's 'Traité de Botanique' and other works on structural botany.

Macmillan & Co.

With regard to detailed structure of various tanning barks, 'Die Gerberinden' of von Höhnel is one of the best authorities.

'Die Gerberinden,' Berlin, 1880.

The inner surface bark of a young tree, or twig, consists of a layer of soft and living cells resting on the outer surface of the wood, and called the *cambium*. These cells multiply by division (cp. p. 12) and produce from their inner surface the successive annual layers of wood, and on their outer a fibrous tissue called the bast (*phloem*), consisting of lengthened cells, and tubes with perforated divisions (sieve-tubes) which convey sap, and mostly run in the direction of the branch, but are crossed transversely by cells in a line with the medullary rays of the wood. All these cells when first produced in the cambium-layer have thin and soft cellulose walls, but the inner layer forming the wood becomes lignified, or hardened, by deposits of lignine on the interior of the cell-walls, while their contents of living protoplasm disappear. The outer layer forming bast remains much softer and more fibrous, and retains its vitality longer. The outer surface of the young branch is covered by a thin layer of flat cork-like cells forming the epidermis, developed from the growing tissue of the bud, beneath which is a layer of growing cells frequently called the *cork-cambium*. This produces, on its inner side, a layer of soft, juicy, thin-walled cells (*parenchym*), which are living and capable of growth, and contain protoplasm and often chlorophyll, to which the green colour of young twigs is due. This layer at first rests on the bast. On the outer side, the cork-cambium produces corky layers beneath the epidermis. The section of an oak-twig is shown in Fig. 43.

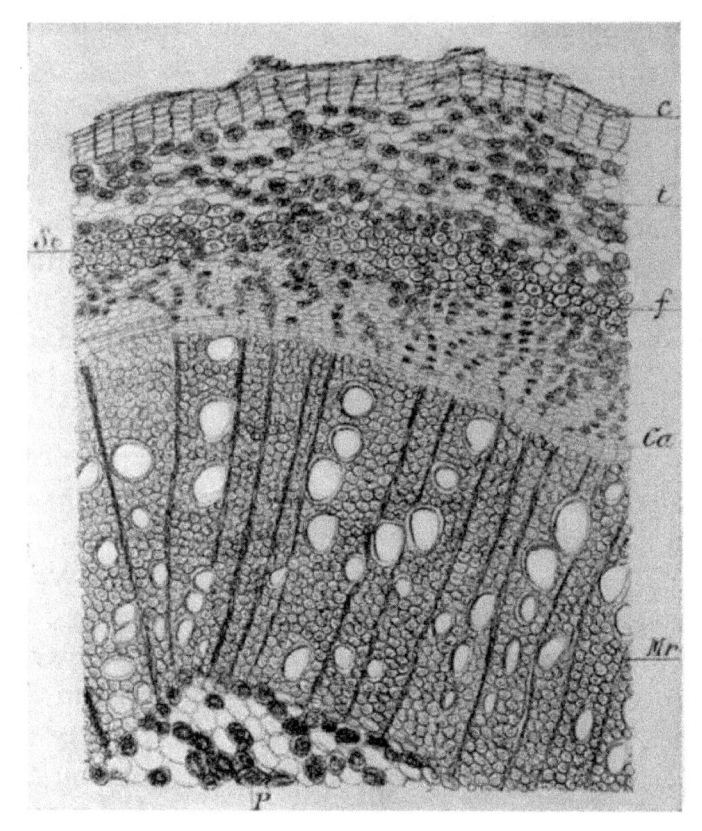

FIG. 43.—Section of Oak Twig, drawn by Prof. Bastin: *c*, corky layer; *t*, tannin-cells; *St*, stone-cells; *Ca*, cambium; *Mr*, medullary ray; *P*, pith.

As the tree grows, it is obvious that the corky epidermis which grows in thickness, but not in breadth, must become distended and finally ruptured. In some cases the surface is renewed by fresh corky layers constantly developed below it, and then the bark remains smooth and unfurrowed, as in the beech and young oak, or in the birch, from which thin corky layers are continually peeling; or it may produce a thick layer of cork, as in the cork-oak. In many cases, and especially in older trees, the outer or primary layer of cork-cambium ultimately dies for want of nourishment, and a fresh cork-producing layer is developed in the still living parenchym. As cork is practically air- and water-proof, the new layer cuts off from its source of nourishment and kills all the parenchym exterior to it. In some cases this peels off, as in the Oriental plane (*Platanus*), but usually it forms a constantly increasing coat of dead tissue forming the "ross" or "crap" (Ger. *Borke*), which as it cannot increase in breadth, becomes deeply fissured as the tree becomes old. In some cases the new growing layer or secondary cork-cambium forms a complete coating parallel with the first, but more often it consists of a series of arcs convex towards the tree and cutting the primary cork-cambium at various places, so as to divide the tissue outside itself into scales. Later on the process repeats itself, new arcs forming inside the first, and cutting off further portions of the parenchym. In this way the cork-forming layer gradually sinks deeper and deeper into the bark, till it frequently passes even into the bast-layer, and very complicated arrangements of tissue result, in which corky layers from the secondary cork-cambium are interspersed with bast-cells and sieve-tubes.

As a rule the outer and dead part of the bark contains but little tannin, though to this there are exceptions, as, for instance, in the hemlock and Aleppo pines. It always contains a large proportion of dark colouring matters (reds, phlobaphenes, p. 297).

Cork consists of thin, and often roughly cubical cells, which are filled with air, while tannin is usually contained in somewhat similar cells with thicker walls. The walls of many vegetable cells are perforated with fine holes, and become thickened by internal deposits of hard ligneous matter which sometimes almost fill the entire cell ("stone-cells"). Bark-cells often contain starch-granules, frequently of peculiar and characteristic forms (which are easily recognised by the blue colour produced on treating the preparation under the microscope with a drop of a solution of iodine in potassium iodide), as well as crystals of oxalate of lime and other matters. These, and the form and arrangement of the cells as seen in sections under the microscope, form useful marks of recognition of the various barks. Tannin is most easily detected by staining, before cutting sections, with a solution of ferric chloride in absolute alcohol.

Apart from microscopic characteristics, the external appearance of barks, both to the naked eye and by the aid of a lens, forms a valuable means of recognition. The arrangement of the bast and corky layers, the remains of epidermis, or the form and character of the fissures, and of the lenticels or small corky protuberances which take the place of stomata in the epidermis, should be observed.

Space does not permit of any detailed account of the structure of fruits, wood and leaves, which are also cellular structures in many respects resembling the bark. The cuticles of leaves, and especially the stomata or breathing pores, and the hairs are often very characteristic. (Cp. Plates III. and IV., and p. 272.)

Valuable hints may also be obtained from the chemical reactions which are described on p. 70 *et seq.*, L.I.L.B.

BOTANICAL LIST OF TANNING MATERIALS.

The percentage of tannin given where the source of information is not stated must in many cases be regarded as uncertain, many analyses having been made before the introduction of modern methods, but those quoted as having been done in the author's laboratory are of recent date and have been made by the latest methods.

CONIFERÆ, Pines, Cypresses, mostly containing Catechol tans, yielding reds.

Abies excelsa, Lam. (*Pinus Abies, Pinus Picea, Picea vulgaris*, Link.), Norway Spruce. Fr. *Faux sapin*; Ger. *Fichte, Rottanne*. The source of the so-called larch-extract, and a principal tanning material of Austria. Contains 7-13 per cent. of a catechol-tannin and much fermentable sugar, and on this account is useful for swelling and colouring, but does not tan heavily. English and Scandinavian bark does not seem much utilised. Best bark 2-8 mm. thick; smooth, yellow inside, with reddish-brown ross outside. For detailed description of structure see von Höhnel, 'Die Gerberinden,' p. 35.

Abies pectinata, Silver Fir. Fr. *Sapin*; Ger. *Edeltanne, Silbertanne, Weisstanne*. Used to a limited extent, but apt to be confused with spruce. Contains 6-15 per cent. iron-blueing tannin. Used in Styria, Austria, Russia. Without "ross," but silver-grey and smooth outside. (Von Höhnel, 'Die Gerberinden,' p. 40; 'Gerber,' 1875, p. 375.)

Abies (Pinus, Tsuga) canadensis, Hemlock Fir (Fig. 44). The principal American tanning material, and source of hemlock extract; averages 8-10 per cent. of a catechol-tannin, but variable, 18 per cent. reported, possibly from a different species. Abundant in Canada and the Northern and North-western States of America. The bark of old trees, which is principally used for tanning and extract-making, is 2-4 cm. thick, smooth and yellow within, greyish and deeply fissured without. The ross, which is red and thick, contains a considerable quantity of tannin, with much dark-red phlobaphen. It does not differ in structure from the inner living and yellow "flesh." The bark is easily recognisable by its well-marked concave lamellæ of cork, cutting off successive layers of "ross" of several millimetres in thickness. (Von Höhnel, *ibid.*, p. 42.)

FIG. 44.—Hemlock Fir (*Tsuga canadense*).

Bastin and Trimble's American Coniferæ, American Journal of Pharmacy.

Abies alba (*Picea alba*), White Spruce, North America. In character of tree and bark very similar to Norway spruce.

Larix europæa D.C. (*Abies* or *Pinus Larix*), Larch. Fr. *Mélèze*; Ger. *Lärche*. Contains 9-10 per cent. pale catechol-tannin, mild and suitable for light leathers. Used, especially in Scotland, for basil tannage.

Pinus halepensis, Aleppo Pine. An important tanning material of the Mediterranean coasts. The outer bark, stripped like cork from the living tree (*Scorza* or *Cortegia rossa*), is a deep red tannage, and contains about 15 per cent. of tannin very similar to hemlock. It is largely used in the island of Syra. The inner and fleshy part of the bark, only obtained when the tree is cut, is *Snoubar* or *Snobar* bark, containing up to 25 per cent. of lighter coloured tannin. This bark is reddish brown, and pretty smooth on both sides, except for shell-like depressions on the outer surface. The "scorza rossa" is dark red-brown internally, grey and irregular outside, frequently very thick, and divided into successive layers of 1-2 mm. thickness by cork lamellæ. (Von Höhnel, *ibid.*, p. 44.) In appearance the tree resembles the Scotch fir.

Pinus tæda, America; *P. Laricio*, Austrian Pine; *P. maritima*, Mediterranean; *P. Cembra*, Alps, Tyrol, 3-5 per cent.; *P. sylvestris*, Scotch Fir. Ger. *Kiefer*, Fr. *Pin sauvage*, 4-5 per cent. *P. longifolia* Roxb., India, 11-14 per cent.

Juniperus communis, Juniper. Bark used in Russia.

Podocarpus elongata and *Thunbergii*, Cape of Good Hope; *Geelhout*, Yellow woods.

Phyllocladus trichomanoides, New Zealand; *Tanekahi, Tarsekahi, Kiri-toa-toa*, "Golden Tan." Used in dyeing glove-leather. Tannin, 30 per cent., gives green blacks with iron.

P. asplenifolia, Tasmania, Celery-topped Pine; 23 per cent. *Phyllocladus* belongs to Yew family.

LILIACEÆ.

Scilla maritima, Squill. Tannin stated from 2-24 per cent. More valuable for pharmacy.

PALMÆ.

Areca catechu, Betel-Nut Palm of India. Yields a species of cutch of no importance for tanning.

Sabal serrulata, Saw Palmetto of Florida (Trimble). ("Dwarf" palmetto is *S. Adansonia*.) Palmetto root has been much talked of as a tanning material; and makes a light-coloured leather.

An extract is now made from the roots of the Saw Palmetto, which grows freely in the Southern States of America, and is especially abundant on the east coast of Florida. The plant is an evergreen, the stem growing flat along the ground, being held in place by numerous roots each the size of a pipe-stem. The leaves are fan-shaped and ribbed, and two to three feet in diameter. In its hardihood the palmetto resembles a weed, as the leaves may be cut off quite close to the stem without damaging the plant, which will grow freely on poor sandy land which is worthless for other purposes. The average yield is stated to be about 10 cwt. to the acre, but in good seasons and with rich land, over a ton per acre has been obtained.

The air-dried leaves contain about 13 per cent. of tannin, but the results obtained by different chemists vary from 5 to 20 per cent. Possibly these variations are caused by the different amounts of moisture in the various samples.

The leaves must be treated with a solution of caustic soda, to remove the glossy siliceous shield which covers them and prevents their being easily extracted. After the tanning matter has been extracted the remaining fibre can be profitably disposed of to paper and rope manufacturers.

As the supply of palmetto is very large it is likely that it will, to a considerable extent, substitute the employment of gambier, and in the United States the extract has already met with a considerable sale. Samples of the extract examined by the Author analysed from 16-22 per cent. of tanning matter, and several per cent. of mineral matter, and produced a very soft and mellow leather of good colour. The extract contains noticeable quantities of common salt, and organic salts of soda which leave sodium carbonate on ignition.

Cocos nucifera, the Cocoa-nut Palm, also contains tannin in roots.

CASUARINÆ.

Casuarina equisetifolia L. (*laterifolia* Lam.); *Filao* bark, Reunion; *Tjamara laut*, Java; Casagha or Tinian Pine, Ceylon. Widely distributed in Southern Asia, bark used for tanning and dyeing. Tannin gives blue-blacks with iron. Several other species very similar in structure and properties. (Von Höhnel.) Hooper found 11-18 per cent. of tannin.

MYRICACEÆ.

Myrica Gale, Sweet Gale, or bog-myrtle.

Myrica (Comptonia) asplenifolia, U.S.A.; "Sweet Fern." Covers millions of acres in Michigan. Yields 40 per cent. of "extract." Leaves 4-5 per cent., roots 4-6 per cent. tannin, according to season (Trimble). Has been much talked of, but in Prof. Trimble's opinion is not likely to prove of much importance.

Myrica nagi (Hind. *Kaiphal*), India, contains 13-27 per cent. of tannin in the bark, and a colouring matter, myricetin, identical with that of sumach. Leather tanned with it is of a somewhat reddish colour which is much brightened by sumaching, and converted into a pale yellow by treatment with alum. It promises to be a valuable tanning material.

Perkin and Hummel, Trans. Chem. Soc., 1896, p. 1287.

BETULACEÆ.

Alnus glutinosa, Common Alder. Fr. *Aulne*; Ger. *Erle*. Contains 16-20 per cent. iron-green tannin, with much red colouring matter; old barks as low as 10 per cent. Colour develops during and after tannage. Used alone it gives a red, hard and brittle leather, but with galls, valonia, etc. it produces a satisfactory tannage. Its principal use is to furnish gunpowder-charcoal, and it is possible the bark might be obtained from powder-factories, if the use of gunpowder is not superseded by nitro-compounds. (Von Höhnel.)

Alnus maritima, Hannoki, Japan; and *A. firma*, Minibari. Fruits (*yashi*) contain 25 per cent. tanning matter (iron-blueing), and little colouring matter. Used in Japan for dyeing and tanning. *A. nepalensis* and *A. nitida* used in India. Several other species of *Alnus* contain tannin.

Betula alba, White or Common Birch. Fr. *Bouleau blanc*; Ger. *Birke*. Inner bark used in Scotland (in conjunction with larch for tanning sheep-skins), Norway, Russia, etc. It contains only 2-5 per cent. of iron-greening tannin, and much fermentable sugar. By far the most important use of birch bark in tanning is to produce the birch-bark tar used to give scent and insect-resisting power to "Russia" leather (*Youft*; Ger. *Juchten*). The outside bark consists of thin layers of cork, often white with a crystalline deposit of betulin, which when distilled yields the odorous oil. The distillation is a dry one, and tarry products accompany the true oil, and at first give a strong empyreumatic smell to the leather, which it loses by keeping, while the true "Russia" odour remains. This "ageing" may be hastened by hanging the leather in a hot stove. If the oil is distilled in a current of steam, or with petroleum ether, the tarry matter passes over, while the matter giving the true odour remains in the retort (p. 372).

Betula lenta, American Black Birch. The bark and twigs distilled with water yield an essential oil, which is almost pure salicylate of methyl, and largely substituted for oil of wintergreen (*Gaultheria procumbens*), with which it is chemically identical. Used for perfumery, and as a rheumatism remedy. Often erroneously spoken of as the source of "Russia" oil. A mixture of a trace of wintergreen oil with sandal-wood oil considerably resembles the "Russia" scent (p. 373).

CUPULIFERÆ.

Castanea vesca, True or Spanish Chestnut. Fr. *Châtaignier*; Ger. *Kastanie*. Abundant in Italy, South of France and Corsica, where it forms great forests. Bark said to be nearly as strong in tannin as oak (up to 17 per cent., de Lof), but not much used in tanning.

Wood only contains 3-6 per cent. tannin, but is the source of the valuable chestnut extract, first employed for dyeing, and introduced as a tanning agent by Aimé Koch. The strength of extract is of course very variable, even for the same density (see p. 339), but it usually contains from 28 to 32 per cent. of tannin.

The tannin gives blue-black with iron, but is not identical with either oak-bark or gall tannins, but apparently a mixture, or possibly a methylated derivative of the latter, and identical with oakwood tannin, or so nearly so as to be indistinguishable; it may also be identical with divi tannin. Decolorised chestnut extracts, sometimes mixed with quebracho and other materials, are often sold as "oakwood" or "oak-bark" extracts. The extract gives a firm leather, with a good deal of bloom if used strong, and a more reddish tint than valonia. The extract often contains dark colouring matters, and the colour of leather tanned with it is readily darkened by traces of lime derived from calcareous waters or imperfectly delimed hides. Like all wood-extracts it tans rapidly, the colour penetrating first, and the tan following, but, according to Eitner, it does not, alone, make full or solid tannage, perhaps from want of acid-forming matters, but answers particularly well in combination with spruce-bark. It is largely used in England for sole-leather in combination with valonia, myrobalans and other materials.

The higher the temperature of extraction, the more colouring matter is contained in the extract in proportion to tannin matter and the greater is its viscosity. Much colouring matter remains undissolved if the extract is dissolved in cold water, but there is, in addition, a loss of tanning power, the colouring matter being also capable of combining with hide. It has in fact been used for tanning by dissolving it in solutions of borax or alkaline salts. By improved methods of manufacture the colouring matter has been much reduced.

The chestnut is an important food tree, the nuts forming a considerable part of the food of the inhabitants of Corsica and Sardinia, and even of Italy.

Oaks.

Almost all species of oak contain useful quantities of tannin in the bark, and probably in the wood. Most if not all oaks yield catechol-tannins with, probably, some mixture of ellagitannic acid.

Quercus robur, Common Oak. Fr *Chêne*; Ger. *Eiche*. It is frequently separated into the two subspecies:—

Quercus pedunculata. Commonest oak of lowlands, England, Ireland and Scotland. Acorns in bunches or spikes on a stalk ⅙ inch long, hence Ger. name, *Stiel-Eiche*. Leaves sessile or short-stalked. In favourable situations, said to yield about 2 per cent. more tannin than *Q. sessiliflora*, but this is doubtful. It is the commonest oak in Slavonia, and the source of commercial oakwood-extract.

Q. sessiliflora, Ger. *Traubeneiche*. Common in hilly districts, and scattered throughout the country. Acorns in bunch on the branch, or with very short stalk; leaves on stalk ½-1 inch long.

Of English barks, Sussex and Hampshire are considered the best, and contain up to 12-14 per cent. of tanning matter; a coppice bark from Wastdale, Cumberland, is however, recorded to have yielded 19 per cent. tanning matter (Hellon).

Probably each of the two varieties of oak gives best bark where it thrives best (v. Höhnel).

Belgian bark is sometimes equal to English, and contains 10-12 per cent. tanning matter. Dutch bark as exported is generally inferior and not cleaned; Swedish is bright, but very poor.

Oak-bark contains a tanning matter, quercitannic acid, giving green-blacks with iron salts, and possibly containing both catechol and pyrogallol groups, but its constitution is not fully understood. It yields both red anhydrides and ellagic acid; and gallic acid has been obtained by the action of hydrochloric acid, though not by fermentation in the tannery. The tannin is not a glucoside, but the fact that a sugar, lævulose, is also present in the bark has led some observers to erroneous conclusions regarding the constitution of the tannin. The unpurified infusion of the bark of *Q. robur* gives a blue-black with iron-salts, from the presence of a colouring matter; but those of most other oaks give green-blacks.

Most tannin is contained in the living part of the bark. The yield diminishes in trees over twenty-five years, and coppice barks, from absence of ross, are often strong, and also contain less colouring matter and more fermentable sugar.

Warm and rich soils seem to yield the best barks.

The brighter the colour of the fresh cut "flesh," the better the bark. Dark brown inner side shows that bark has been exposed to rain, which deteriorates strength and colour; but a very light colour is thought by some to indicate poorness in tannin. White lichen is said to be a mark of poor bark, and probably indicates a damp and unfavourable situation.

Oaks are generally cut when the sap is rising (15th April to 15th June), and the buds open and new soft cells begin to grow, for the bark is then more easily detached.

Experiments in France have shown that the bark of timber felled at other seasons may be loosened by steaming, and it is said there is no practical loss of tannin. Superheated steam, produced in a small boiler in the woods, is used.

The bark is peeled with tools of various forms, the branch and knotted places being loosened by beating with a mallet. The bark must be peeled immediately the tree has been felled.

The peeled bark, in pieces up to three feet long, is laid on hurdles sloped in such a way that the rain runs off as much as possible, and in this way it is dried, but in wet seasons is much damaged. Bark so dried in the woods often retains 40-50 per cent. water, and must be stacked or stored so as to allow of further drying.

English bark is sometimes sold in "long rind," and sometimes "hatched" or chopped in pieces about four inches long. Belgian and Dutch barks are generally hatched. Belgian tree bark is "cleaned" (and cleanings often mixed back with bulk), Dutch bark is not cleaned. Much sand and dirt is contained in most Continental bark: screenings of Belgian bark yielded a black liquor, and contained so much sand that they would not even burn!

Oak-bark extract is occasionally offered for sale, but is not usually genuine or of good quality, except that of the American chestnut-oak, *Q. prinus*, from which an excellent extract has been manufactured in the Alleghanies. Factitious extracts often contain myrobalans and quebracho.

FIG. 45.—Turkey Oak (*Quercus cerris*).

Oakwood contains only a very small percentage (from 2-4 per cent.) of a tannin, practically identical with that of chestnut, but different to that of oak-bark. It is stated by de Lof to reach 9-14 per cent. in old heart-wood; but this is doubtful. The wood retains the tannin in its interior for a long time. Wood of a Roman bridge built at Mainz 55 B.C. is stated by de Lof to have still contained 2·14 per cent. tannin in 1881 A.D. A good deal of imitated oakwood extract is undoubtedly made from chestnut wood, and unfortunately no very satisfactory way of distinguishing it is known, though oak-bark extract can be distinguished from oakwood by giving a precipitate at once, even in dilute solution, with bromine-water, while the wood gives a brown precipitate only after long standing. Precipitation by bromine-water is a general characteristic of catechol tannins, and hence a mixture of quebracho (a cheap catechol tan) with chestnut would simulate oak-bark in this respect. If a few drops of the non-tannin solution or an alcoholic extract from the "total soluble" of extracts containing quebracho or other catechol tannins be treated with concentrated sulphuric acid in a test-tube, a deep crimson will be produced, especially at the surface of the acid, which remains pink on dilution with water. With pyrogallol derivatives, such as genuine oakwood, a yellow or brown only is produced (J. Hughes). The test is very delicate. Another distinction is that bark extracts contain perceptible traces of manganese, but this cannot be relied on as many wood extracts also contain some, probably derived from the twig and branch bark which is used along with the wood. Oakwood extract is now manufactured on an enormous scale in Slavonia, and is used both by sole- and dressing-leather tanners, chiefly to increase the strength of the layer liquors. The extract is also used to increase the weight of leather after tannage by mopping on the flesh-side. All the best oakwood extract manufacturers contract to sell on analysis and colour estimation, and good Slavonian oakwood extract generally contains 26-28 per cent. of tanning matter, giving a tintometer measurement of 4-5° red, and 20-25° yellow, when a solution containing ½ per cent. of tanning matter is measured in a 1 cm. cell. For particulars of the manufacture of concentrated extracts see p. 337.

FIG. 46.—Cork Oak (*Quercus suber*).

Q. cerris, Turkey Oak. Ger. *Zerreiche*. Common in southern Europe, a fine tree, but bark inferior to *Q. robur*. Fig. 45.

Q. pubescens. Fr. *Chêne velu*; Ger. *Weiss-* or *Schwarzeiche*. In mountain districts and scattered in Southern Europe, about equal to *Q. robur*.

Q. ilex, Evergreen Oak. Fr. *Chêne vert, Chêne yeuse*; Ger. *Grüneiche, Steineiche*; Span. and Ital. *Encina*. South Europe, Algeria. Said to be somewhat stronger in tannin than common oak, yielding 5-11 per cent. of a rather darker coloured tannin, but well adapted to sole-leather. Good bark is smooth outside, without fissures, short in fracture.

Q. Suber, Cork Oak. F. *Chêne liège*; Ital. *Sughero, Suvero*. (Figs. 46, 47.) The outer bark is cork; the interior bark contains 12-15 per cent. of tannin which is redder than that of ordinary oak. Trees at first produce an irregular cork, sold as "virgin cork" for ferneries, etc. After this is stripped, later growths are more uniform, and fit for use; tanning bark is only obtained when the tree is cut down. Bark is rough but pale-coloured on both sides and about 1 cm. thick; interior like ordinary oak, but more strongly furrowed. Produced chiefly on Mediterranean coasts, and formerly largely used in Ireland.

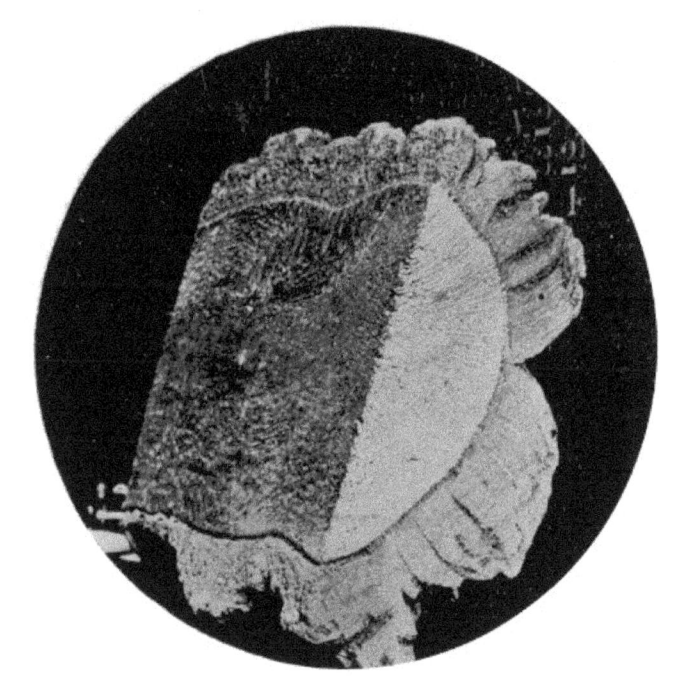

FIG. 47.—Section of Cork Oak, showing cork, inner bark and wood.

Q. pseudosuber, African Oak. Fr. *Chêne faux liège*. Algeria. Not stronger than English oak, but with more colouring matter, hence strikes quickly through leather. Bark very thick.

Q. Mirbecki. Fr. *Chêne Zeen*. Algeria. Rapid growth. Bark contains 8 per cent. of tannin.

Q. Tozæ. Fr. *Chêne tauzin*. Pyrenees and S. France. Bark contains 14 per cent. of tannin.

Q. coccifera, Kermes Oak. Fr. *Kermes, Garouille* (Fig. 48). South Europe and Algeria. Root bark is called "rusque" or "garouille"; averages 10-18 per cent. tannin, but trunk bark does not exceed 11 per cent. This tree is the food of the kermes insect, used for dyeing scarlet before the introduction of cochineal. Garouille is principally used in the south of France, giving a firm sole-leather of a disagreeable odour and dark brown colour.

FIG. 48.—Kermes Oak (*Quercus coccifera*).

Q. Ægilops (and probably other species—*Q. macrolepis, græca, Ungeri, coccifera*), Valonia. Fr. *Valonée*; Ger. *Valonea, Ackerdoppen, Orientalische Knoppern*. Best Smyrna contains up to 40 per cent., Greek 19-30 per cent., Candia valonias up to 41 per cent., and Caramanian (probably not *Q. Ægilops*) 17-22 per cent. of tannins which are at least principally pyrogallol derivatives and which give blue-blacks with iron, no precipitate with bromine-water, and which deposit a great deal of bloom consisting of ellagic acid.

FIG. 49.—Valonia Oak (*Q. Ægilops*).

Q. Ægilops (Fig. 49) is said to be most abundant in the highlands of Morea, Roumelia, Greek Archipelago, Asia Minor and Palestine, while *macrolepis* forms large forests in many parts of Greece, and especially on the lower slopes of Mount Taygetos. In Asia Minor the fruit ripens in July-August, when the trees are beaten and acorns left on the ground to dry. They are afterwards gathered, and carried on camels to stores in the towns, and thence by camel and rail to Smyrna, where they are placed in heaps 5-6 feet deep in large airy stores, and allowed to ferment and heat for some weeks, when the acorn, which contains but little tannin, contracts and falls from the cup, and is used for feeding pigs. This fermentation is risky, and if carried too far the cups become dark-coloured and damaged. The acorn contains a considerable amount of fermentable sugar.

When ready for shipment, the valonia is hand-picked, the largest and finest cups (prima) going to Trieste, the second selection to England (Inglese), and the remainder, known as "natural," also coming largely to England. The "Inglese," although inferior in appearance to the very large selected cups, is, of course, less costly, and gives an equal yield of tannin.

In 1887, Smyrna exported about 23,000 tons to England, and 16,000 tons elsewhere, principally to Austria, Germany and Italy. The largest known crop is stated at 70,000 tons in Asia Minor, and 14,000 in Greece, but the average yield is considerably less than this.

The beard contains considerably more tannin than the cups, sometimes over 40 per cent. It is often sold separately at the same or a lower price, and in Smyrna is known by the Turkish name *tirnac* (Ital. *trillo*).

In Greece the best valonia is collected (in April?) before the cup is matured and while it still encloses the acorn, and is known as *chamada* (It. *camata* and *camatina*). The colour of these kinds is excellent and the percentage of tannin high. Mainly used by dyers, but often worth attention for tanning where colour is important. In camatina the acorn is completely covered in the cup, while in camata it is partly exposed.

The next quality, *rhabdisto*, is beaten down by sticks in September-October (hence name), while after the first rains the fruit falls and turns black, and is called *charcala*. It contains but little tannin, and is not generally collected.

Sometimes valonia is attacked by a sort of honeydew, probably caused by an aphis, which renders it very sticky, and perhaps more liable to heat, but does not in itself damage its tanning properties.

The lighter the colour, the heavier the weight, and the thicker the scales of the beard, the better the quality usually proves, but analysis is the best guide. Caramanian valonia is very inferior.

The tannin contained in valonia is especially suitable in the manufacture of sole-leather. It deposits much bloom, and if used as a dusting material, has the characteristic of making the leather solid and compact, but leaves the grain somewhat rough and hard to work. In mixture with gambier and other materials, it is an excellent tannage for dressing leather, and with proper management deposits little or no bloom (cp. p. 231).

Q. infectoria (Fig. 50) is the source of the "Turkish" or Aleppo galls. Galls are caused by insects, principally of the genus Cynips, or gall-wasps, which lay their eggs in different parts of plants, and in some way cause an abnormal growth of the bud, leaf, or other part.

FIG. 50.—Gall Oak (*Q. infectoria*).

Aleppo galls are developed from the young shoot of the oak, are best before the insect has escaped, and contain in this stage up to 50 or 60 per cent. of gallotannic acid. When the insect has developed and escaped, the galls are of course perforated, much lighter, and more porous. These galls and those of *Rhus semialata* are the principal sources of the tannin of commerce.

The *Q. infectoria* also bears a large gall like an apple, "Apples of Sodom," or "rove," caused by a different insect. This, in a crushed condition, has been somewhat largely used as a tanning material, and contains 24-34 per cent. gallotannic acid.

English oaks have several species of galls and oak-apples, but they do not seem to be of much value for tanning.

FIG. 51.—Chestnut Oak (*Q. prinus*).

Knoppern are galls produced on the immature acorns of various species of oaks, principally *Q. Cerris* in Hungary, and were formerly largely used there for tanning, as they contain up to 35 per cent. gallotannic acid. They are now less abundant, and have been largely replaced by valonia, sometimes called *orientalische Knoppern*. Like all purely gallotannic materials, they naturally give a soft and porous tannage, ill-adapted for sole-leather purposes, which has led to the Austrian practice of drying, or rather stewing, the leather in very hot and damp stoves, which make it hard and brittle.

Chinese and *Japanese galls* are the product of the action of an aphis on a species of sumach, and will be mentioned again under sumachs (*Rhus*).

Djaft, *dchift*, *jift*, or *jaft* is a material apparently of Eastern origin, and said to be derived from an oak of Kurdistan. Dark red scales or fragments, origin uncertain, very astringent and darkish tannage, liquor when spilt dries whitish, apparently from crystallisation of some sort. It contains a large amount of tannin. It appears very irregularly in commerce and the writer would be glad to obtain further samples and details of origin. He once used 6 or 7 tons successfully in sole-leather tannage. It has also been attributed to a shrub allied to the *Cæsalpinias* (p. 286).

The most important American oaks are—*Q. prinus* (*castanea, monticola*), the Chestnut or Rock Oak (Fig. 51). About equal to our oak in strength, bark very thick, and infusion strongly fluorescent, especially in presence of ammonia. Source of chestnut-oak extract. The most important tanning oak-bark of the United States.

Q. alba, or "white oak," is perhaps the most widely distributed and abundant of any of the American oaks, and very closely resembles the European *Q. robur*.

Q. tinctoria or *nigra*, Black or Quercitron Oak. Poor as a tanning material, but used for dyeing yellow, and for modifying the colour of hemlock tannages. The dyestuff, *quercetin*, is closely allied to that of fustic, and gives yellows with alum and tin mordants.

A good deal of information is given by Trimble on American oaks and other tanning materials.

'The Tannins,' vol. ii., Lippincott, Philadelphia, 1894.

Important Indian oaks are *Q. glauca*, *Q. lamellosa* and *Q. incana*; bark of last said to yield 22 per cent. of tannin.

SALICACEÆ, Willows.

The bark of various willows, especially *Salix arenaria* and *Russeliana*, is used for tanning in Russia, and for Danish glove-leather. Some contain up to 12-14 per cent. of an iron-blueing tannin. They impart a strong odour to leather, but different to that of birch-tar oil, and the scent of genuine Russia leather is due to a combination of both. In many cases the bark peeled off osiers for basket-making is employed. A Russian willow (species unknown), in the form of thin bark of osiers or small branches, gave 9·5 per cent. tannin when examined in the Leather Industries Laboratory of the Yorkshire College; and willow barks certainly demand more attention than they have received in England as tanning materials for fine leathers. *Salix caprea* has been used in France for glove leathers, but is weaker than *S. arenaria*.

Poplars belong to the same natural order, and have been used for tanning, but their barks at the most contain 2-3 per cent.

POLYGONACEÆ, Docks.

Most members of this family contain tannin.

Rumex hymenosepalum, Canaigre, Gonagra (Cana agria), Red Dock, wild pie-plant (Fig. 52). Common in sandy alluvial plains of Mexico and Texas, and considerably resembling rhubarb. Its tuberous roots resemble those of the dahlia, and contain, when air-dried, 25-30 per cent. of a catechol tannin, probably allied to that of mimosa. Undried, the roots contain about 68 per cent. of water and only 8 per cent. of tannin. When well harvested by slicing thin and rapidly drying, it gives leather a bright orange colour, and, it is said, considerable weight and firmness, and is thus specially suitable for use in retanning and finishing light goods and harness leather. Besides tannin, the root contains a yellow colouring matter, and about 8 per cent. of starch, of which the granules are very variable in form and size, but mostly oval or elongated. They do not stain readily with iodine till they have been well washed, or treated with dilute sulphuric acid. Both the starch and tannin are contained in large and somewhat thin-walled cells, and the sliced material is easily extracted at low temperatures. Greater heat gelatinises the starch, and extracts a darker colour. The best temperature for extraction is between 30° and 50° C. (see p. 348).

FIG. 52.—Canaigre (*Rumex hymenosepalum*). 'New Commercial Drugs and Plants,' T. Christy.

The root is most readily grown from tubers or portions including the crown, as the plant seeds sparingly. Sandy soils, subject to inundation or irrigation, seem best suited to its culture. In California and Arizona the growth begins in October or November with the winter rains, blooming about the end of January, while the leaves die down in May and the roots remain dormant during the summer. It is not important at what time the roots are harvested, and they seem to improve in percentage of tannin up to the second year, after which they become darker and deteriorate.

The harvested crop should be sliced into thin pieces and rapidly dried at a low temperature, or still better, converted at once into extract. This is already done on a considerable scale at Deming, New Mexico. The residue after extraction is used in America as cattle-food; and might no doubt be also applied to the production of alcohol.

Planting takes place in autumn, in rows, say 30 inches apart, with 10 inches between each root. Roots for "seed" should be kept in the ground or stored in dry sand. This should yield a crop of 10 tons per acre in an average season.

References.—Report U.S. Commissioner of Agriculture, 1878, pp. 119 *et seq.*; Trimble, Am. Jour. of Pharmacy, p. 395, 1889; Canaigre, Bull. No. 7, Arizona Agr. Expt. Station, 1893; 'Canaigre or Tanner's Dock,' Bull. No. 105, University of California, Berkeley, Cal.; 'Canaigre Tannin,' Trimble and Peacock, Philadelphia, 1893; 'Report to the German Leather Trades Association,' by V. Schroeder, 1894; 'Il Canaigre,' E. Andrieis, Turin, 1899.

Rumex maritima, or *maritimus*. Central Europe, England, Ireland. It is said by de Lof to be found in California, where it is used by the Indians for tanning; but he probably confounds it with canaigre. De Lof found its roots, wet, to contain 6 per cent. and after drying, 22 per cent. of tannin, together with starch and an acid allied to malic.

Several English docks contain tannin; the writer had a sample of leather tanned with dock-root (very possibly *R. aquaticus*), many years old, but still soft and close in texture, and of excellent quality.

Polygonum amphibium. Said to grow on thousands of acres (?) on the lower Missouri. Roots contain 22 per cent., branches 17 per cent. of tannin. *P. amphibium* is a common English and European plant, with spikes of pink flowers, growing in marshes and ponds. Probably this is the *Polygonum* analysed by Fraas, who found 20-26 per cent. tannin.

Polygonum Bistorta. Common in damp places in England. Bistort, Snakeweed, called "Eastermer giants" in Cumberland, where the young leaves are used for making herb-puddings. Fraas found 16-21 per cent. tannin in the roots.

Other species are known to contain much tannin. Perkin found a red colouring matter in *P. cuspidatum*, a native of India and China, commonly grown in gardens as a foliage plant (Journ. Chem. Soc., 1895, p. 1084). *P. tinctorium*, used as a source of indigo in China and Japan.

Coccoloba uvifera, Seaside Grape of West Indies; source of West Indian kino. Whole plant rich in tannin.

LAURACEÆ, Bay Family.

Persea, or *Laurus lingue*. Bark used in Chili for tanning Valdivia leather. (According to Arata, *Laurus caustica*.) A tree 25-30 feet high and 2 feet in circumference. Bark rough outside, and whitish, with an aromatic smell and taste, brittle and easily ground, contains 17-19 per cent. of a catechol-phloroglucol tannin, greening iron salts (Journ. Chem. Soc., 1881, p. 600). About 60,000 heavy hides are tanned yearly with this bark in Valdivia and district, and mostly sent to Hamburg. The hides are thick and scarcely tanned through, colour fair, leather soft and porous.

Persea Meyerina N. and *Laurus Pneumo*. Said to be also used in Chili.

SANTALACEÆ.

Osyris compressa (*Fusanus compressus*, *Colpoon compressum*, *Thesium Colpoon*), "Cape Sumach," "*Pruim Bast*," leaves and bark, Cape of Good Hope. Leaves contain about 23 per cent. of tannin and form a useful substitute for sumach; but the tannin is not identical, and is of the catechol class, resembling gambier.

O. arborea. Northern India. Leaves rich in tannin.

Fusanus acuminatus (*Santalum acuminatum*), "*Quandony*." Australia. 18-19 per cent. tannin, dark coloured.

Exocarpus cupressiformis. Australia. Bark contains 15 per cent. tannin.

DAPHNOIDÆ, Spurge Laurels.

Daphne Cnidium L., "*Garou*." Algeria. Used for dyeing and tanning.

PROTEACEÆ.

Banksia serrata, Heath Honeysuckle. Australia. Specimen examined contained 11 per cent. tannin; according to Maiden it reaches 23 per cent.

Banksia integrifolia. Queensland. Bark contains 11 per cent. tannin.

Grevillia striata. Australia. Bark contains 18 per cent. tannin.

Leucospermum conocarpum. *Kruppelboom*. Knotted Tree. Cape of Good Hope. Said by de Lof to contain 22 per cent. of tannin; but a specimen examined by the Author yielded 10·9 per cent. on analysis.

Protea mellifera. Sugarbush. *Suikerbosch*. Cape of Good Hope. Contains 25 per cent. tannin, according to de Lof; but Palmer found 18·8 per cent.

Protea grandiflora. *Waagenboom*. Cape. Contains 25 per cent. tannin (de Lof); 15·9 per cent. (Palmer); 15·6 per cent. (Procter).

Protea speciosa. Cape of Good Hope.

Leucadendron argenteum, Silver Tree, *Silverboom*, *Witteboom* Cape of Good Hope. Bark said to contain 16 per cent. tannin (de Lof); a specimen examined by the Author yielded 9·2 per cent.

Brabium stellatifolium, *Wilde Amandelboom*, Wild Almond.

PLUMBAGINÆ.

Plumbago Europea, Leadwort. Fr. *Dentelaire*. A garden plant in England, native in France; contains much tannin, especially in the root-bark.

Statice coriaria, Marsh Rosemary. South of Russia. Roots up to 3 metres long and 2-12 cm. thick; used by Kalmucks for tanning sheep-skins; contain 22 per cent. of tannin (de Lof).

Statice limonum, Sea Lavender. Coasts and salt marshes of Europe and America. Richer in tannin than *S. coriaria*; used in France, Spain and Portugal.

Several other species contain tannin. These plants are allied to "Thrift" (*Armeria*).

MALPIGHIACEÆ.

Byrsonima spicata, Antilles, "Tamwood."

Byrsonima coriacea, Jamaica, "Golden Spoon."

Byrsonima chrysophylla, etc.

Malpighia punicifolia, Nicaragua, "Nancite"; "Mangrutta." Bark contains 20-30 per cent. of light-coloured tannin.

POLYGALACEÆ, Milkwort Family.

Krameria triandria, Rhatany, Peru.

The root is used in medicine, and is stated to contain 40 per cent. of tannin.

Wittstein found only 20 per cent. of an iron-greening catechol-phloroglucol tannin allied to tormentil tannin, in the root-bark, the only active part of root.

ANACARDIACEÆ.

Loxopteryngium Lorenzii. Span. *Quebracho colorado.* South America, especially Argentine Republic; the highest proportion of tannin occurring in the wood from Gran Chaco district. Wood contains on an average about 20 per cent. of a red, difficultly-soluble tannin, yielding "reds," and containing catechol and phloroglucol. The tannin is not very soluble in water, and hence can only be used in weak liquors, but is very astringent, and gives a firm, reddish leather. The wood also contains a catechin and a colouring matter, fustin, identical with that of "young fustic." It is imported into England, and more largely to Havre and Hamburg, in logs, which are there chipped like logwood, and either used direct for tanning, or made into extract. A very cheap tan. With alum it gives a yellow colour. The extract usually dissolves to a fawn-coloured turbid solution. Many quebracho extracts are now made completely soluble by treatment with alkalies or sulphites (cp. p. 338).

See P. Arata, Journ. Chem. Soc., 1878, A, p. 986; 1881, A, p. 1152; and Perkin and Gunnell, Trans. Chem. Soc., 1896, 1303.

"Quebracho" means "axebreaker," and is consequently applied to a variety of hard woods. Its specific gravity is 1·27-1·38, and it therefore sinks in water.

Pistacia lentiscus, Ital. *Pistacio*, Fr. *Lentisque*. Sicily, Cyprus, Algeria. Small myrtle-like leaves contain from 12-19 per cent. of a catechol-tannin, and are very largely used in the adulteration of sumach. Leather tanned with sumach adulterated with this material darkens and reddens on exposure to light and air, and for this reason its use in many cases is decidedly injurious. In Cyprus and the East it is known as "*Skens*," Ital. *Schinia*, Fr. *Poudre de Lentisque*, in England, often called Cyprus sumach. (Cp. p. 272.)

P. orientalis, terebinthus, vera, etc., India, Mediterranean. Various aphis galls, 30-40 per cent. tannin. A sample of galls of *Pistacia vera*, "*Gool-i-pista*," India, recently examined in the Author's laboratory, contained 30 per cent. of a light-coloured tannin.

Schinus molle, "Molle," Buenos Ayres. Leaves only used; said to contain 19 per cent. tannin.

S. Aroeira, Brazil. Said to contain 14 per cent. tannin.

Rhus coriaria, Sicilian sumach. Ital. *Somacco*. (Fig. 53.) A shrubby bush, of which leaves and small twigs are used.

FIG. 53.—Sicilian Sumach (*Rhus coriaria*).

Mostly propagated by suckers from older plants, which are planted in rows about two feet apart in early spring, and pruned to 6-8 inches. Bushes begin to bear the year after planting, though the strength is not so good as from more mature plants. Cropping is either by pruning off shoots, or gathering leaves by hand; in the latter case shrubs are pruned in winter. The leaves are dried either in the fields, or on covered threshing floors, where they are afterwards separated from the stems by beating. Some is exported in this state, as "leaf" or "baling" sumach, but most is ground to fine powder under edge-runners. "Ventilated" sumach is winnowed to remove dust and sand, which often contains iron. "*Mascolino*" is the best sumach from

Palermo and district; "*feminella*" consists of weaker sorts from other parts, and is generally used for mixing.

The different varieties of sumach are classed as follows:—

			Relative Market Value.
Sumach	for	baling	2·5
,,	,,	grinding	2·3
,,	from	yearling plants	1·5
,,	,,	ends of branches collected in autumn	1·0

To prepare these different grades for ultimate consumption, they are ground in mills similar to those employed for crushing olives, that is, in which two large stone wheels follow each other, revolving upon a circular bed, the whole construction being about the same as the Spanish or Mexican *arrastre*. The sumach thus pulverised is passed through bolting-screens to separate the finer from the coarser particles.

After the sumach leaf has been subjected to the first process of trituration, the coarse remaining portions are re-ground and the product added to that which has been already obtained. The still unpulverised residue known as *peduzzo* is sifted, and the coarser and ungrindable parts are used as fuel, while the finer are mixed with the partially-ground, small, leaf-bearing branches (*gambuzza, gammuzza*), and ground again.

Palermo is the principal seat of the sumach trade. The material is generally bought from the small growers by middlemen, who hold it till market conditions are favourable. The quotations are always in *tarì* of 42·5 centimes per *cantar* of 79·342 kilos, which are obsolete even in Sicily, and have to be reckoned into *lire* (francs) and kilos. Consequently 1 tarì per cantar equals 0·53565 lira per 100 kilos.

In 1894, the prices delivered at the mills were about 41-42 tarì for mascolino, 37-38 tarì for femminello, 14-18 tarì for brusca, and 10 tarì for stinco, per cantar; the lira being worth about 9*d*.

Cf. 'Kew Bulletin,' No. 107, pp. 293-6.

Sumach has been introduced into Australia, and is said to thrive well in the dry plains of the Wimmera district.

Sumach often contains much sand, and sometimes particles of magnetic iron ore, which cause black stains, and may be collected by a magnet, and which dissolve in dilute hydrochloric acid without evolution of hydrogen, to a yellow solution. Metallic iron, which is also attracted by the magnet, dissolves in hydrochloric acid with effervescence to a colourless or green solution.

Good sumach contains at least 25-27 per cent. of tannin. The Author has analysed samples of undoubted genuineness containing as much as 32 per cent. of a tannin, principally gallotannic, with some ellagitannic acid, and a colouring matter (myricetin) identical with that of *Myrica nagi* (p. 250), which gives yellows with alumina and tin mordants, and is fugitive to light.

Sumach is the best tanning material known for pale colour and soft tannage, and is hence used for moroccos, roans, skivers, etc., and also for brightening leathers of darker tannages, such as mimosa, gambier, the colouring matters of which warm sumach liquors seem able to dissolve.

In the report of the Society of Arts Committee on bookbinding leathers, it is stated on abundant evidence, that sumach-tanned leathers are less affected by light and gas-fumes, and less liable to decay than those of any other known tannage.

Soc. Arts. Journ., 1901, p. 14.

Sumach is frequently adulterated with the ground leaves and twigs of *Pistacia lentiscus* ("schinia" or "skens"), *Coriaria myrtifolia* ("stinco"), *Tamarix africana* ("brusca"), *Ailantus glandulosa*, *Vitis vinifera* (leaf of the common grape vine) and some other species of the Rhus family, but *Pistacia lentiscus* is used to a much larger extent than any of the others. *Pistacia*, *coriaria*, and *tamarix* all contain considerable quantities of tannin, though less than genuine sumach, and of a different chemical constitution.

The most satisfactory method of detecting these adulterants is by microscopic examination, none of the chemical methods proposed being very satisfactory; though, as many of the added matters contain catechol tannins, while those of sumach are purely pyrogallol derivatives, the method proposed by Hughes for the detection of quebracho in oakwood by the reaction of concentrated sulphuric acid (p. 296) might render good service, and any sumach infusion which was rendered turbid by bromine-water would at least be open to grave suspicion.

PLATE III.

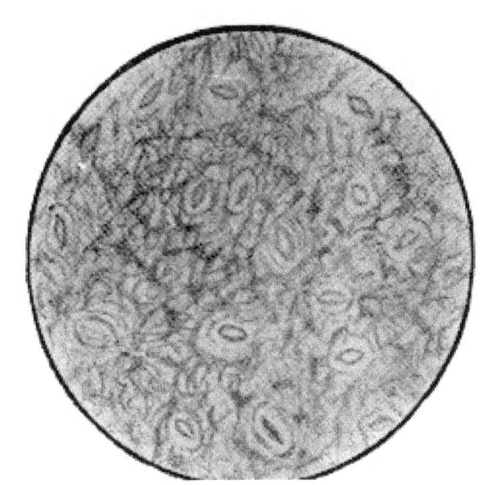

Ailantus glandulosa.

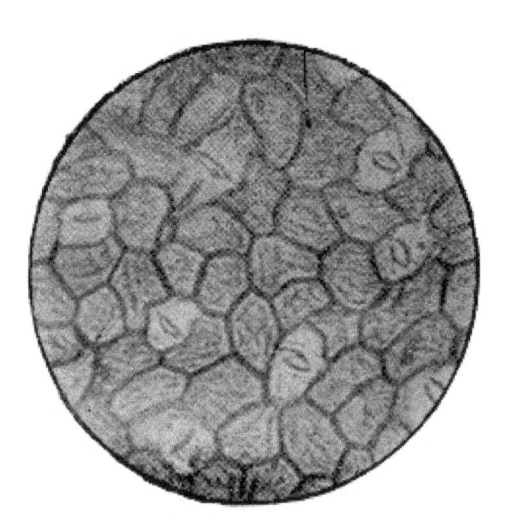

Coriaria myrtifolia.

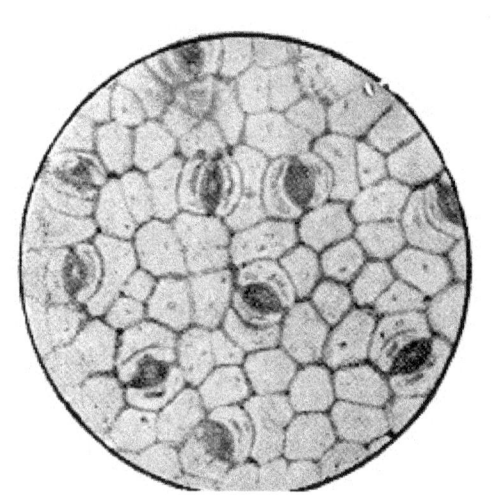

Colpoon compressa.

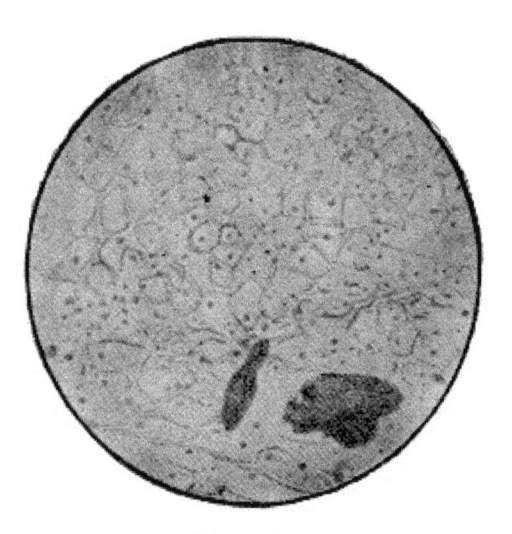

Rhus cotinus.

PLATE IV.

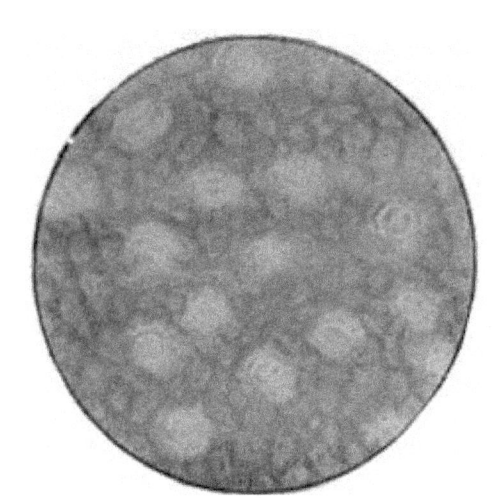

Pistacia lentiscus.

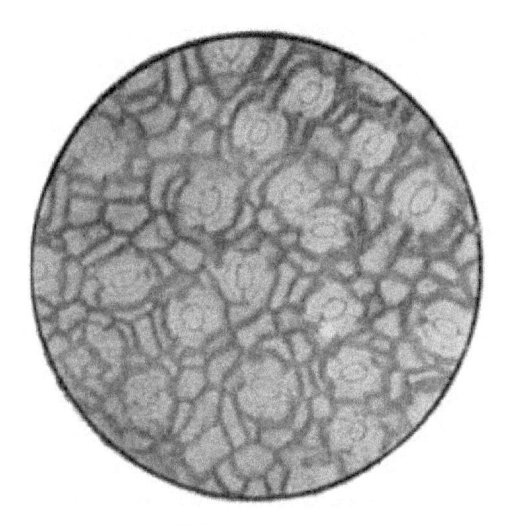

Rhus metopium.

Rhus coriaria.

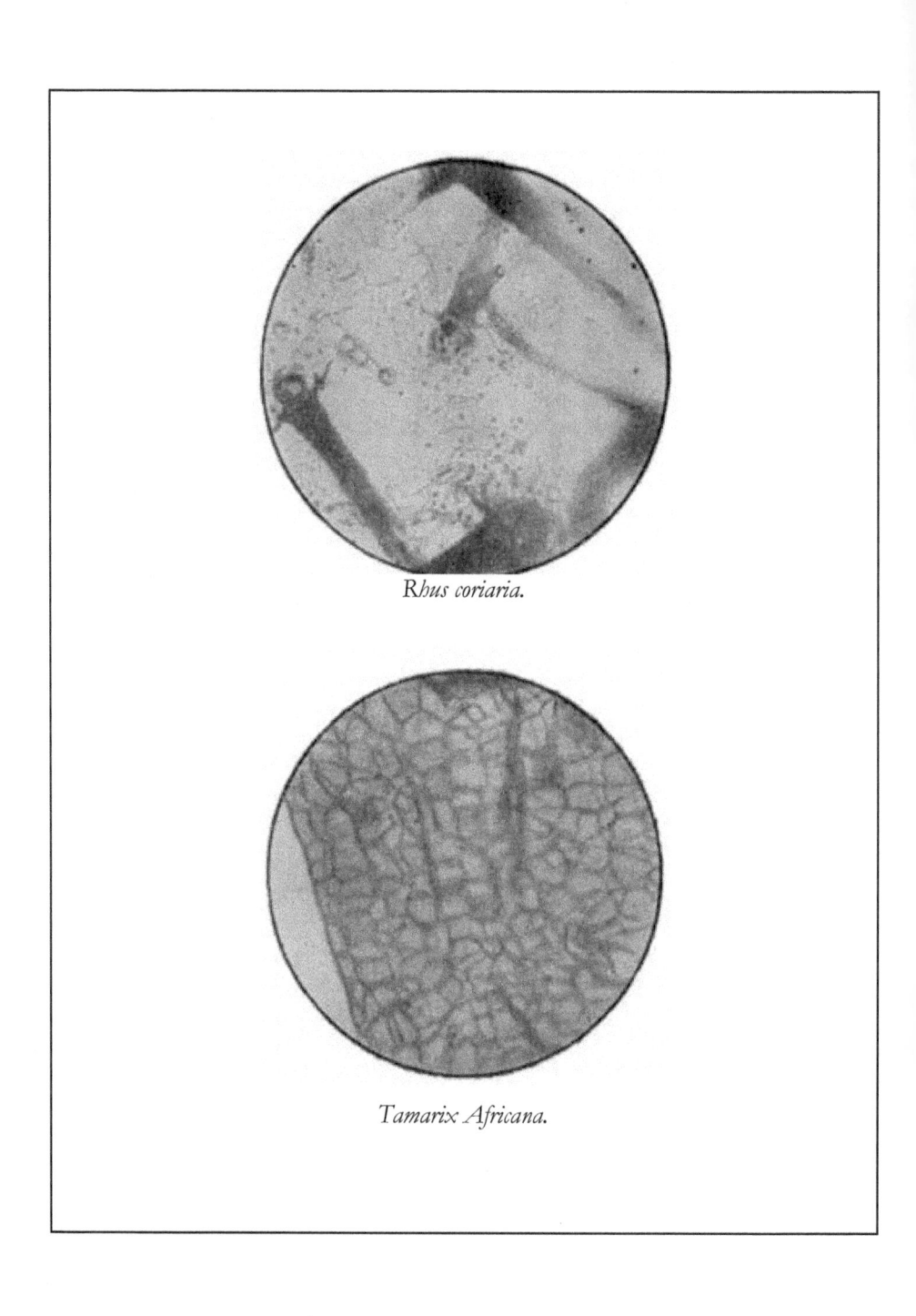

Tamarix Africana.

The most important work on the microscopic structure of the tissues of sumach and its adulterants was done by Andreasch, when during the later stages of his last illness he was obliged to winter in Sicily. His work will well repay study, but unfortunately does not admit of useful abstraction here. A very useful investigation was also made in the Author's laboratory by Messrs. M. C. Lamb and W. H. Harrison, as regards the treatment and examination of the leaf-cuticles, which renders the detection of mixture comparatively easy. For details, the original memoir must be consulted, but if the suspected sumach be gently warmed for a few minutes with strong nitric acid, its more delicate leaf structure is entirely destroyed, and after washing and neutralising with sodium carbonate the strong cuticles of the leaves of the more common adulterants, "schinia" (*Pistacia lentiscus*), "stinco" (*Coriaria myrtifolia*), "brusca" (*Tamarix africana*), and *Ailantus glandulosa* are uninjured, and easily recognised. Examination is rendered easier by dyeing the cuticles; safranine, acid green, Bismarck brown, and naphthol yellow being suitable for the purpose. Mr. Lamb's photographs of the cuticles are reproduced on Plates III. and IV., but if possible, it is most satisfactory to compare the suspected sample direct with known specimens of the adulterants.

'Sicilianischer Sumach und seine Verfalschung,' Wien, 1898.

'Sumach and the Microscopic Detection of its Adulterants,' Journ. Soc. Dyers and Colorists, March 1899.

FIG. 54.—American Sumach (*Rhus glabra*).

R. glabra, Southern States, U.S.A. (Fig. 54). Very largely used in the States to take the place of Sicilian sumach. A sample collected by the late Professor Trimble, and analysed in the Leather Industries Laboratory, contained 25 per cent. of tannin and produced a leather of very much darker colour than Sicilian.

R. typhina, "staghorn" or Virginian sumach, contains 10-18 per cent. of tannin. A sample from same source as above contained 13 per cent.

R. cotonoides, U.S.A. The analysis of a sample of this material gave 21 per cent. of tanning matter, and leather tanned with it was almost equal in colour to that from *R. glabra*.

Other sorts found in States: *R. semialata* (5 per cent. tannin); *R. aromatica* (13 per cent. tannin); *R. metopium* (8 per cent.); *R. copallina*, *R. pumila*, *R. canadensis*; *R. toxicodendron* is the well-known "poison ivy," a climbing plant which causes a severe and irritating eruption if touched.

R. glabra and *R. copallina* are chiefly recommended for extended cultivation in the United States.

In Virginia, the leaves are collected and cured by the country people, and sold and delivered to owners of mills for grinding. Their particular object being to secure the largest possible quantity of product at the lowest cost, little attention is given to the quality obtained, or the manner of collecting. The most intelligent dealers in the raw material urge upon collectors to observe the following particulars:—To ensure a maximum value for tanning purposes, the leaf should be taken when full of sap, before it has turned red, has begun to wither, or has been affected by frost. Either the leaf-bearing stems may be stripped off, or the entire stalk may be cut away, and the leaves upon it allowed to wither before being carried to the drying shed; but care must be observed that they are neither scorched nor bleached by the sun. When wilted, they are carried to a covered place, and spread upon open shelving or racks to dry, avoiding the deposit in any one place of a quantity so great as to endanger the quality of the product by overheating and fermentation. Sumach should be allowed to remain in the drying-house for at least one month before sending to the market; in case of bad weather, a longer period may be required. When ready for packing for shipment, it should be perfectly dry and very brittle, otherwise it is likely to suffer injury in warehouses from heating and fermentation.

Buyers of sumach leaves for grinding depend largely upon colour for the determination of the value; the leaves should, therefore, when ready for market, present a bright-green colour, which is evidence that they have suffered neither from rain after being gathered, nor from heating during the process of drying. Leaves having a mouldy odour or appearance are rejected. The Virginian crop reaches 7000-8000 tons, and is collected at any time between July 1st and the appearance of frost.

There is an important difference in the value of the European and American products. The proportion of tannic acid in the latter is generally lower than that found in the former, which is much preferred by tanners and dyers. By using Sicilian sumach it is possible to make the finest white leathers, while by the employment of the American product, the leather has a disagreeable yellow or dark colour, apparently due to a colouring matter, which exists in larger quantity in the American variety than in the Sicilian.

Experiments upon the presence of colouring matters made by treating an infusion of sumach with a solution of gelatine, gave the following results:—

Virginia,	mixed,	collected in	June,	gave	A nearly white precipitate.
,,	,,	,,	July,	,,	A decidedly yellowish-white precipitate.
,,	R. copallina	,,	August,	,,	A dirty-yellow precipitate.
,,	R. glabra	,,	,,	,,	A very dirty-white precipitate.
Fredericksburg, mixed		,,	,,	,,	A dirty-yellow precipitate.
Sicilian		,,	,,	,,	A slightly yellowish-white precipitate.

For the purpose of tanning white and delicately coloured leathers, therefore, the collection should be made in June; while for tanning dark-coloured leathers, and for dyeing and calico-printing in dark colours, where the slightly yellow shade will have no injurious effect, the collection may be made in July. It appears that for all purposes, the sumach collected after the 1st of August is inferior in quality.

Experimental results as regards percentage of tannin obtained by collecting sumach at different seasons showed:—

					Per Cent. of Tannic Acid.
Virginia, mixed,		collected in June,		gave	22·75
,,	,,	,,	July,	,,	27·38
,,	R. glabra	,,	August,	,,	23·56
,,	R. copallina	,,	,,	,,	16·99
Sicilian,	R. coriaria	,,	,,	,,	24·27

It is evident, therefore, that in order to secure the maximum amount of tannic acid, the sumach should be collected in July, but the colouring matter of the leaves has an important influence upon the value of the product. The leaves of the upper extremities of the stalks are always richer in tannic acid than those of the base; and the increase of age of the plant is accompanied by a general diminution of this acid.

The mill used for grinding sumach leaves consists of a heavy, solid, circular, wooden bed, 15 feet diameter, with a depression around the edge a few inches deep and 1 foot wide, for the reception of the ground sumach from the bed, and two edge-rollers, weighing about 2500 lb. each, 5-6 feet diameter, and provided with numerous teeth of iron or wood, thickly inserted. In Europe and in some parts of the Southern States, sumach is still ground by stones revolving on a stone bed, and the sifting is often done by hand.

FIG. 55.—Venetian Sumach (*Rhus cotinus*).

R. cotinus, Venetian sumach. Fr. *Arbre à perruques*; Ger. *Perrukenstrauch* (Fig. 55). More important as a dyeing than as a tanning material, its twigs and wood, "young fustic," containing a large proportion of a colouring matter (fisetin), which with tin and alumina mordants dyes bright yellows; and much resembles, but is not identical with the myricetin present in *R. coriaria*. Its leaves, known as Turkish or Venetian sumach, contain about 17 per cent. of tannin, and are used for tanning.

Perkin and Allen, Trans. Chem. Soc. 1896, 1299.

R. pentaphylla, "Tezera," Algeria, is used by the Arabs for tanning goat-skins.

R. Thunbergii, Kliphout, Cape of Good Hope. A sample of the bark analysed in the Author's laboratory contained 28 per cent. of tanning matter. A valuable tanning material, of reddish colour. The tannin is of the catechol class.

Several other species of Rhus are used in tanning. *R. semialata* yields Chinese and Japanese galls, containing up to 70 per cent. gallotannic acid. They are caused, not by a fly, but by the attack of an aphis, as are those of the allied Pistacia. The aphides pass their asexual stage inside the gall, which is large and thin-walled. A similar aphis-gall is found on the American sumach. A specimen of the leaves examined at the Yorkshire College yielded only 5 per cent. of tannin.

See Flückiger and Hanbury, 'Pharmacographia.'

Mangifera indica, Mango, widely distributed in the Tropics. Bark and leaves rich in tannin, which gives green-blacks with iron.

CORIARIACEÆ.

Coriaria myrtifolia, French sumach (of which there are four kinds—*fauvis, douzère, redoul* or *redon*, and *pudis*). A poisonous shrub of South of France; leaves used for tanning, and as a sumach adulterant under the name of "stinco"; contain about 15 per cent. tannin. (Cp. p. 272.)

Coriaria ruscifolia bark, the *tutu* of New Zealand, contains 16-17 per cent. of tannin.

Other Coriarias merit examination, and are known to contain much tannin.

RUBIACEÆ.

Rubia, Madder, allied to Galiums, which are almost the only English representatives of the family. The coffee- and cinchona-plants are foreign representatives.

Nauclea, or *Uncaria gambir*. East Indies. (Fig. 56.) A climbing shrub, source of "gambier," or "Terra Japonica"; also called "Catechu," in common with several other solid extracts. Gambier is first described by the Dutch trader Couperus, in 1780; plant introduced in Malacca, 1758; plantations established in Singapore in 1819.

Culture is mainly by Chinamen, and is very rude; it yields rapid return, but under the treatment to which it is subjected a plantation is worn out in ten to fifteen years. Cropping commences three years after planting, and is continued two to four times annually, with little regard to fitness of shrubs, the plant being cropped till it has barely leaves left to support existence. It is found advantageous to combine pepper-culture with that of gambier, the spent leaves form a good protection for the pepper-plant roots, but they have little actual manurial value.

FIG. 56.—Gambier Shrub (*Nauclea gambir*).

Cropping is done with a knife called a *parang*, while a larger knife is used for chopping the leaves and twigs before they are put in a boiler, in which they are heated with water till the liquid, which is constantly stirred during the operation with a wooden five-pronged stirrer, becomes syrupy. The leaves are then brought out with a wooden fork, and allowed to drain on a tray, so that the liquor runs back into the boiler. The coarser matter still remaining in the boiler is removed with a strainer like a racquet, and the finer by straining the liquor through a perforated cocoanut shell into small shallow tubs, where it is allowed to cool with constant stirring with a cylindrical wooden bar, which is worked up and down with a rotary motion until the catechin crystallises. When quite cool the pasty mass is turned out of the tub, cut into cubes with sides 1 inch long with a hoop-iron knife, and dried on bamboo trays in racks under sheds, or sometimes smoke-dried with wood fires.

Good cube gambier is an earthy-looking substance and is dark outside, but pale within from crystallisation of catechin. Catechin is not itself a tanning material, but is apparently converted into a tannin by drying at 110°-126° C., when it parts with a molecule of water. It is very probable that a similar change occurs in the tannery. The tannin is a catechol-phloroglucol derivative, less astringent than most of this series, and of pale colour. (See p. 297.)

A commoner quality, called "block-gambier," instead of being cut into cubes, is run into large oblong blocks of about 250 lb. weight, which are wrapped in matting and exported in a pasty condition. These contain 35-40 per cent. of tannin, as estimated by the hide-powder method, while the best cubes reach 50-65 per cent. Besides the forms named, various others are made, principally for native use in chewing with betel-nut in the form of small biscuits, or in thin discs ("wafer gambier") by running the pasty mass into bamboos and cutting the cylinder so formed into thin slices. These forms are usually light in colour, and very rich in catechin.

For details of the chemistry and employment of gambier, see pp. 228, 231, 239, etc.

APOCYNACEÆ.

Aspidospermum quebracho. Sp. *Quebracho blanco*. Brazil. Bark contains aspidospermin, an alkaloid used in medicine, but both bark and wood are poor in tannin.

Quebracho colorado, see ANACARDIACEÆ, p. 269.

ERICACEÆ, Heath Family.

Arctostaphylos (or *Arbutus*) *uva-ursi*, Bearberry. Used in Russia, Finland; twigs and leaves said to contain 14 per cent. tannin. Often adulterated with leaves of *Vaccinium vitis-idæ* or Cowberry.

Arbutus unedo, Common Arbutus. Leaves, fruit and bark used on Mediterranean coasts.

VACCINIÆ.

Vaccinium Myrtillus, Bilberry. Used in Piedmont.

SAXIFRAGEÆ.

Weimannia glabra L., "Curtidor" bark. Venezuela.

Weimannia macrostachys D.C. Reunion.

Weimannia racemosa, New Zealand Towai or Tawheri bark.

These species contain 10-13 per cent. of iron-blueing tannin, and have been practically used, but are not of much importance.

TAMARISCINIÆ.

Most of the members of this group are poor in tannin, but several species have galls which are rich.

Tamarix africana, Egypt, Algeria. Galls containing 26-56 per cent. tannin. The small twigs are collected in Tunis, and when dried and ground are imported into Sicily to be used for the adulteration of sumach under the name of "Brusca," and contain about 9 per cent. of tannin. (Cp. p. 272.)

T. articulata, Morocco, yields galls produced by aphides, called in Arabia *Takout*, and stated by Vogel to contain 43 per cent. of tannin.

Tamarix gallica, used in Spain and Italy.

OXALIDEÆ.

Oxalis gigantea, source of *churco* bark, Chili. A thin, brittle, dark red bark, mostly about 2 mm. thick, cork and ross entirely absent. The bark is brittle, and the cells thin. It contains about 25 per cent. of an easily extracted, dark red tannin, giving green-blacks with iron. The bark has been incorrectly attributed to *Fuchsia macrostemma*. (Cp. Von Höhnel, 'Die Gerberinden,' p. 125, and this book, p. 284.)

COMBRETACEÆ.

Several families of this genus contain trees rich in tannin, but most important are the Myrobalans (often, but incorrectly, written Myrabolams or Myrabolans), the unripe fruit of various species of Indian *Terminalia*.

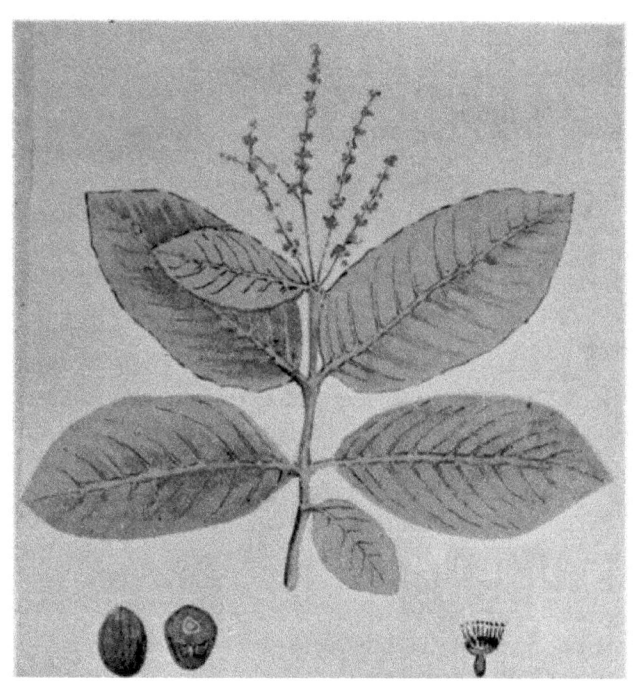

FIG. 57.—Myrobalan Tree (*Terminalia Chebula*).

T. Chebula (Fig. 57), a tree 40-50 feet high, and yielding good timber, is the source of all the ordinary varieties, which differ only in the district from which they are obtained, and the state of maturity of the fruit. The nuts contain from 30 to 40 per cent. of tannin. Of the various sorts, probably those known as Bombays are least unripe, while "lean greens" are the most so. The unripe fruit is the richest in tannin. "Bombays" have a smooth skin in coarse wrinkles, and when cut are porous and light coloured. "J's" (Jubbalpores) and "V's" (Vingorlas), have finer and shallower wrinkles, and are harder, solider and consequently darker looking, but do not give a darker liquor, while "lean greens" are greener, have less yellow colouring matter, and consequently more nearly approach in character to sumach, which the tannin in many respects resembles, though probably containing more ellagitannic acid in proportion to gallotannic acid than the latter.

The "nuts" should be bright in colour, not worm-eaten, nor "waxy" or soft. If kept in a damp place they rapidly absorb moisture, and fall into the "waxy" condition, in which they are very difficult to grind, sticking to and choking the cutters or beaters of the mill.

Neither the large hard stones nor their kernels contain tannin, but the latter have an oil which gives a peculiar odour to leather. The tannin exists in large and rather thickly-walled cells, and is not very easily extracted; the skin is wrinkled, but the uncrushed nuts swell up to their original plum-like form when placed in water for some time. The bark is almost as rich as the fruit, and the tree also yields galls.

T. Belerica yields Beleric or "Bedda nuts," which are downy, rounder and larger than ordinary myrobalans, and contain about 12 per cent. of tannin, used as adulterant of ground myrobalans. A sample of solid extract made from the bark of T. Belerica contained 70 per cent. of tannin.

T. tomentosa has downy nuts, containing about 10 per cent. of tannin, bark stated by de Lof to contain 36 per cent. of tannin. A sample of solid extract contained 56 per cent. of tannin. The bark contains about 11 per cent.

There are several other Indian species.

T. Catappa, "Badamier bark" of Mauritius, contains 12 per cent. of tannin.

T. mauritiana, "Jamrosa bark," said to contain 30 per cent. of tannin.

T. Oliveri, Malay Archipelago, yields "Thann leaves," from which an extract is made as a cutch substitute. A sample of the extract from Burmah examined recently in the Author's laboratory, contained 62 per cent. of tannin. The tannin is a catechol derivative, differing from that of *Acacia catechu* in containing no phloroglucol (p. 297).

A sample of bark from Mandalay contained 31 per cent. of tannin, while the leaves from the same tree contained 14 per cent.

Emblic myrobalans, see p. 293.

RHIZOPHORACEÆ, Mangles or Mangroves.

Rhizophora Mangle, and other allied species, Mangrove or Mangle, *Manglier, Paletuvier, Cascalote*, grows on tropical coasts all round the world. The barks vary much in strength, from 15 up to 40 per cent. in different species (see *Ceriops*). Leaves, used in Havana, are said to contain 22 per cent. tannin. According to Eitner, the younger plants contain the highest proportion of tannin. *R. Mangle* seems to yield a bark inferior to several other species.

All trees growing in swamp, and of the same character of growth as mangrove, are called "Bakau" in the East Indies (Anglice, mangrove) and various species of *Ceriops* yield the best tanning bark. A tidal mangrove swamp at low water is a tangle of arched roots like inverted branches on which the trees are supported.

The catechol-tannin, which is easily extracted, is of deep red colour and allied to that of the mimosas. In admixture with other materials the red colour has a much smaller effect, and mangrove bark is now largely used in combination with pine, oak and mimosa.

Several other species are also rich in tannin, and used in different parts of the world under the name of mangle, as are also several species of *Conocarpus* belonging to the *Combretaceæ*.

Rhizophora mucronata. India and Burmah. Bark varies considerably; David Hooper, Indian Museum, Calcutta, gives 26·9 per cent. of tannin. Dr. Koerner (Deutschen Gerberschule, Freiberg) analysed two samples in 1900, one containing 48 per cent. and the other 21 per cent. of tannin; two samples from the British Imperial Institute recently examined by the Author showed only 4·5 and 6·1 per cent. of tannin respectively.

Ceriops Candolleana, Bakau or *Tengah* Bark, East Indies. *Goran*, Bengal. Contains up to 27 per cent. of tannin and yields an extract which promises well as a substitute for cutch, to which, for dyeing purposes it is nearly or quite equal. The solid extract contains up to 65 per cent. tannin, making a good but dark red leather.

Ceriops Roxburghiana, a somewhat larger tree, also growing in the Sunderbans, bark very similar in strength and character to the above.

ONAGRACEÆ, the Œnothera Family.

Fuchsia excorticata, the only deciduous tree of New Zealand. Contains 5 per cent. tannin.

Fuchsia macrostemma, Chili. Yields Tilco or Chilco bark. Churco bark has been incorrectly attributed to this plant, but it is certainly derived from an *oxalis*, as stated by the Kew authorities. (Cp. von Höhnel, 'Die Gerberinde,' p. 125.)

GUNNERACEÆ.

Gunnera scabra (Pangue?), Pauke, Chili. Used occasionally in the tanning of goat-skins.

MYRTACEÆ.

Eucalyptus globulus, and other species of *E.* common in Australia, and introduced into Algeria and Southern Europe (gum-trees), are more or less rich in catechol-tannins, their sap being the source of Botany Bay or Australian kinos, which contain up to 79 per cent. tannin. Several species of *Eucalyptus* afford astringent extracts; those from the "red," "white," or "flooded" gum (*E. rostrata*), the "blood-wood" (*E. corymbosa*), and *E. citriodora*, being quite suitable for replacing the officinal kind. The gum is chiefly obtained by woodcutters, being found in a viscid state in flattened cavities in the wood, and soon becoming inspissated, hard and brittle. Minor quantities are procured by incising the bark of living trees; a treacly fluid yielding 35 per cent. of solid kino on evaporation is thus obtained. The gum is imported from Australia, but there are no statistics to show in what quantity.

Compare Journ. Soc. Chem. Ind., 1902, p. 159.

Eucalyptus longifolia bark, the "woolly-butt" of Australia, contains 8·3 per cent. of tannic acid, and 2·8 of gallic. The "peppermint" tree contains 20 per cent. of tannic acid in its bark. The "stringy-bark" (*E. obliqua*) gives 13½ per cent. of kinotannic acid. The Victorian "iron-bark" (*E. leucoxylon*) contains 22 per cent. of kinotannic acid, but is available only for inferior leather.

Myrtus communis, and several other myrtle species, contain a considerable amount of tannin in the bark and leaves.

GRANATACEÆ.

Punica Granatum, Pomegranate. Peel of fruit employed in Spain and the East as substitute for sumach, containing up to 25 per cent. of tannin. Bark said to contain 22 per cent. tannin. *Balaustines*, wild pomegranates, East Indies. Fruit, said to contain 46 per cent. tannin.

ROSACEÆ.

Tormentilla erecta, *Potentilla tormentilla*. Root variously stated to contain 20-46 per cent. tannin. Red coloured leather, formerly used in Orkneys, Shetland, and Faroe Islands, and in some parts of Germany.

Sorbus or *Pyrus Aucuparia*, Mountain Ash. Bark said to be stronger than oak.

Many other plants of the family contain tannin, among others the strawberry.

PAPILIONACEÆ.

Butea frondosa. This (with *Pterocarpus marsupium*) furnishes East Indian kino. The flowers are used in India as a dye, under the name of Tesu. Bark fairly rich in tannin.

'Dictionary of Economic Products,' I.B., p. 944; Hummel and Cavallo, Proc. Chem. Soc. 1894, p. ii.

Agricult. Ledger, 1901, No. 11, Gov. Printing Office, Calcutta.

Pterocarpus or *Drepanocarpus senegalensis* is the source of African kino, which contains up to 75 per cent. of tannin.

Cæsalpinia coriaria, Divi-divi. A tree of 20-30 feet, native in Central America, introduced successfully in India, but principally imported from Maracaibo, Paraiba and Rio Hache. The dried pods contain 40-45 per cent. of a pyrogallol-tannin, mainly ellagitannic acid, and would be a most valuable tanning material, but for a liability to fermentation and sudden development of a deep red colouring matter. The causes are not well understood, but apparently the risk can be materially lessened by use of antiseptics. If used in strong liquors it gives a heavy and firm leather, but is principally employed as a partial substitute for gambier on dressing leather. Used in rapid drum-tannage for light leathers, an excellent colour may be obtained. It is said to give an especially firm and glossy flesh. Leather tanned with it, even when of outwardly good colour, has often a blueish-violet shade within, perhaps due to the development of a colouring matter allied to that of logwood. The seeds do not contain tannin, which lies almost free in the husk of the pod. The pods are about 3-4 cm. long, dark outside, and curl up in drying to an S-shape.

C. digyna, Tari or *teri* pods. Occurs in Prome, Toungoo, Bassin, Mynang and other parts of India and Burmah, where it is used as a drug. The pod-case is said to yield over 50 per cent. of tanning matter. A sample from Burmah, kindly sent by the Imperial Institute, examined by the Author in 1900, contained 24 per cent. of tannin, but after removing the seeds the remaining pod-cases yielded 44 per cent. of tannin on analysis. *C. digyna* promises to become a valuable tanning material if it proves free from the tendency to ferment which is so troublesome in divi-divi. It has been introduced into England under the name of "white tan," which yields a leather quite as white as sumach; but the supply seems at present uncertain.

C. cacolaco, Cascalote, Mexico. Pods rich in tannin (up to 55 per cent., Eitner). Pods larger and fleshier than divi, seeds smaller, tannin similar.

The pods of several other Cæsalpinias are used in tanning, sometimes under the name of "Algarobilla," which is simply a diminutive of Algaroba, the carob, or locust-bean, derived from Arabic *al Kharroba*, and applied to several small pods. (See *Balsamocarpon* and *Prosopis*.)

C. (or *Balsamocarpon*) *brevifolia*, Chili, ordinary Algarobilla. Fig. 58. One of the strongest tanning materials known, containing an average of 45 per cent. of a tannin very like that of divi, but less prone to discoloration. The tannin lies loose in a very open skeleton of fibre, and is easily soluble in cold water; the seeds contain no tannin. If not allowed to ferment it produces a very bright-coloured leather.

Algarobilla has been attributed to *Prosopis pallida*, but this appears incorrect. Several species of P. are known to yield tanning pods; those of *P. Stephaniana* of the desert of Kaschan, in Persia, are *dschigh dschighe*, perhaps identical with *dchift* or *jaft*. (See p. 263.) Bark of *P. spicigera* used in Punjab.

C. (or *Hæmatoxylon*) *campechianum*, Logwood, Central America. In addition to colouring matter, and a glucoside which it yields on oxidation, this wood contains about 3 per cent. tannin. Its principal use is in dyeing blacks with iron or chrome mordants. (See p. 413.)

FIG. 58.—Algarobilla (*Cæsalpinia brevifolia*).

'New Commercial Drugs and Plants,' No. 5, T. Christy.

C. echinata yields "Brazil-wood." (See p. 413.)

C. Sappan, Sappan-wood, India.

Cassia auriculata, *Turwar* or *Tanghadi* bark, Southern India. Used for tanning so-called "Persian" sheep- and goat-skins, contains about 17 per cent. of a catechol tannin. Leather tanned with it is of a pale yellow colour, but rapidly reddens in sunlight. Cp. p. 235.

C. fistula, India. Husk of pod, 17 per cent. tannin. The pulp of pod is used as an aperient.

C. elongata and *lanceolata*. Senna leaves. Upper Egypt.

C. Sophora, "Bali-babilan."

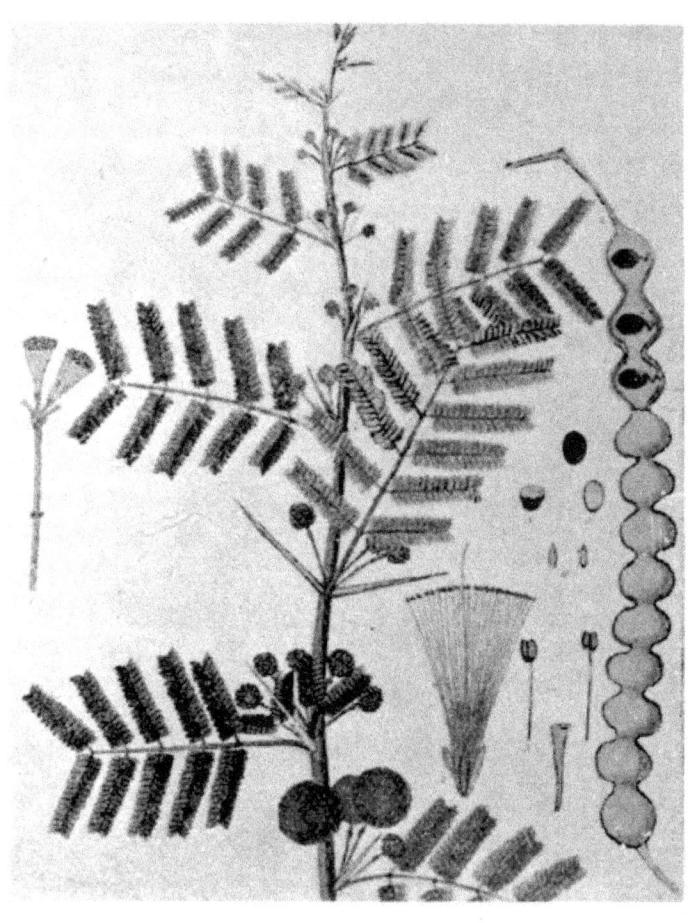

FIG. 59.—Babool (*Acacia arabica*).

MIMOSEÆ, a Tribe of Leguminosæ.

Acacia arabica, "Babool," "Babul," India, Egypt. Fig. 59. Bark contains about 12-20 per cent. of catechol tannin; one of the principal Indian tanning materials, used for kips and heavier leathers. Pods, used in India for bating, contain about same amount of tannin as bark, but of a different kind, that of the bark being a catechol-tannin, with a good deal of red colouring matter, while the pods contain a paler tannin allied to divi, which is not precipitated by lime-water. In Egypt the pods are called *bablah*, a name which is also applied to pods of *A. cineraria* and *A. vera*, and others. They are used for dyeing glove-leathers.

A. nilotica, Egypt. Pods called *neb-neb* or *bablah*.

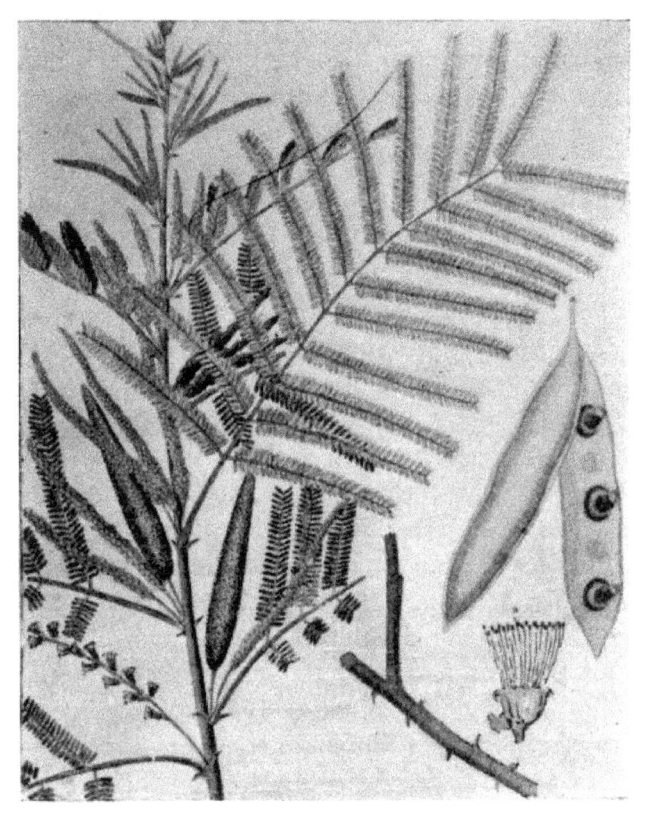

FIG. 60.—Cutch Tree (*Acacia catechu*).

A. catechu, India. The wood yields cutch or "dark catechu." A lighter coloured variety called *kath*, containing much crystallised catechin, is also made in India, and principally used for chewing with betel. *A. catechu* is a tree 30-40 feet high, common in India and Burma, and also in tropical East Africa, where, however, it is not utilised. In Southern India, *A. suma* is also used for the same purpose.

Trees of about 1 foot diameter are cut down, and the wood (some state the heart-wood only) is reduced to chips, and boiled with water in earthen jars over a mud-fireplace. As the liquor becomes thick and strong, it is decanted into another vessel, and the evaporation continued till the extract will set on cooling, when it is poured into moulds made of leaves or clay, the drying being completed by exposure to the sun and air. "Kath," or pale cutch, is made in Northern India, by stopping the evaporation at an earlier point, and allowing the liquor to cool, and crystallise over twigs and leaves thrown into pots for the purpose. It contains a large proportion of catechin, apparently identical with that of gambier, but its tannin is much redder. Good cutch contains about 60 per cent. tanning matter, but is principally used for dyeing browns and blacks with chrome and iron mordants. It contains quercetin, a yellow colouring matter (p. 263).

A. leucophlea, India and Java "*Pilang*." Pods and bark equal to *A. arabica*.

Australia abounds in acacias (mimosas), many of which are used in tanning, but vary greatly in strength, not only according to species, but probably also by situation and growth. Probably the best information is to be found in a pamphlet on 'Wattles and Wattle-Bark,' by J. H. Maiden, F.L.S., published by the Department of Public Instruction at Sydney, 1890. His analyses were made by the Löwenthal process, and can only be roughly compared with those by the hide-powder method. The analyses given are by the I.A.L.T.C. method, and mostly on samples furnished by Mr. Maiden.

A peculiarity largely developed in the mimosa family is the tendency for the true leaves to be suppressed, and their place taken by the flattened and expanded midrib (phyllode). Thus leaves of two very distinct forms are common in the genus, and some acacias, as *A. heterophylla*, may have both forms on the same branch. Compare *A. pycnantha* and *A. decurrens*.

The Australian mimosas have been naturalised in India, and grow freely in the Nilgiri Hills, but the bark does not appear to be utilised.

The most important species are as follows:—

A. pycnantha. (Fig. 61.) "Broad-leaved" or "Golden Wattle," South Australia. One of the strongest tanning barks known. A sample marked "special," analysed in the Yorkshire College, contained 50 per cent. of tannin; another sample marked "ordinary" contained 40 per cent.

FIG. 61.—Broad-leaved Wattle (*Acacia pycnantha*).

FIG. 62.—Green Wattle (*Acacia decurrens*).

A. longifolia, the Golden Wattle of New South Wales, only contains half as much tannin as *A. pycnantha*.

A. mollissima, with its two varieties *A. decurrens* (Fig. 62) and *A. dealbata*, are among the most important of the Wattle family commercially. Two samples of the former marked "Green Wattle" showed 36-39 per cent. of tanning matter; another sample marked "Sydney Green Wattle," contained 41 per cent. A sample of *A. decurrens*, the second variety, was much weaker, showing only 12 per cent. on analysis.

A. penninervis (Hickory bark) is said to be particularly hardy, but its strength seems to vary. A sample from Bateman's Bay contained 38 per cent. of tanning matter.

A. binervata, another "Black Wattle" contains up to 30 per cent. tanning matter, as does also the "Weeping Willow," *A. saligna*. The latter is poisonous, and is said to be used for killing fish.

A. prominens, the bark of which resembles that of the Golden Wattle, *A. longifolia*, in appearance contains only 14 per cent. tannin.

The cultivation of wattles in Australia has been somewhat neglected, but would render possible the utilisation of many acres of land lying waste, or which have already been exhausted and rendered unfit for the growth of cereals. It requires so little attention as to make it very profitable, and wattle-growing and sheep-grazing can be combined satisfactorily after the first year, when the young trees in the plantation have reached the height of 3-4 feet. In Natal the Australian wattles, especially *A. mollissima*, have been acclimatised and cultivated with success, and large quantities of excellent bark are now exported to England. African wattle-barks usually contain about 30 per cent. of tannin.

Wattles grow in almost any soil, even the poorest, but their growth is most rapid on loose, sandy patches, or where the surface has been broken for agricultural purposes. When the soil is hard and firm, plough-furrows should be made at a regular distance of 6-8 feet apart, and the seeds dropped into these. The seed should be sown in May, having been previously soaked in hot water, a little below boiling temperature, in which they may be allowed to remain for a few hours. It should be dropped at an average distance of 1 foot apart along the furrow, in which case, about 7200 seeds would suffice for one acre of land. The seed should not be covered with more than about ¼ inch of soil.

On loose sandy soil, it might even be unnecessary to break up the ground in any way; the furrows may be dispensed with, and the seed sown broadcast after the land has been harrowed. After the plants have come up, they should be thinned so that they stand 6-8 feet apart. When the young trees have attained the height of 3-4 feet, the lower branches should be pruned off, and every effort afterwards made to keep the stem straight and clear, in order to facilitate the stripping, and induce an increased yield of bark. It is advisable that the black and broad-leaved kinds should be grown separately, as the black wattle, being of much larger and quicker growth, would oppress the slower-growing broad-leaved one. Care should be taken to replace every tree stripped by re-sowing, in order that there should be as little variation in the yield as possible. In Victoria, the months of September-December are those in which the sap rises without intermission, and the bark is charged with tannin. Analysis proves that the bark from trees growing on limestone is greatly inferior in tannin to that obtained from other formations, differing 10-25 per cent.

The following are South American mimosas:—

A. cavenia, Espinillo. Bark, contains 6 per cent., pods, 18-21 per cent., or more of tannin.

A. cebil, Red Cebil. Bark, contains 10-15 per cent.; leaves, 6-7 per cent. tannin. Argentine Republic.

A. Guarensis, Algarobilla of Argentine Republic. Bark, pods and flowers said to be used for tanning.

A. timbo, Buenos Ayres.

A. curupi, Curupy bark.

A. angico, or *Piptadenia macrocarpa*, Brazil, yields "angica bark," a sample of which contained 20 per cent. of tanning matter when analysed recently in the Author's laboratory.

"White Bark," South America, probably an acacia, bark internally very similar to angica, if not identical.

A. horrida, "Doornbosch," Cape of Good Hope, contains 8 per cent. of tannin.

Inga feuillei, "Paypay," Peru. Pods said to contain 12-15 per cent. of tannin (doubtful). Several other species of *Inga* known to contain tannin.

Elephantorrhiza Burchellii, Elandsboschjes, Tugwar, or Tulwah, South Africa; a papilionaceous plant. The air-dry root contains 12 per cent. of tannin, and a great deal of red colouring matter. The roots are several feet long, and about 2 inches in diameter, growing by the sides of rivers.

The following additions may be made to the above list:—

EUPHORBIACEÆ.

Cleistanthus collinus, "Kodarsi," Deccan. Bark stated to contain 33 per cent. of tannin.

Phyllanthus emblica, India, yields emblic myrobalans, which in immature condition contain considerable tannin. Leaves (18 per cent.) and bark used for tanning.

Phyllanthus distichus and *nepalensis* both yield tanning barks.

COMBRETACEÆ.

Anogeissus latifolia, India. Bark and leaves rich in tannin.

GUTTIFERÆ.

Garcinia mangostana, India. The rind of the mangosteen fruit contains much tannin.

CHAPTER XIX.
THE CHEMISTRY OF THE TANNINS.

The essential constituents of tanning materials are members of a large group of organic compounds known as "tannins" or "tannic acids," which are widely distributed throughout the vegetable kingdom, and said to have one representative among animals, in the body of the corn-weevil. Their use in vegetable physiology is as yet uncertain, and indeed they appear in some cases to be waste products of organic change. The tannins, though varying considerably in their chemical constitution, and in many important characteristics, are all marked by the power of precipitating gelatine and some allied bodies from their solutions, of converting animal skin into the imputrescible material known as leather, and of forming dark-coloured compounds with ferric salts which are often utilised as inks. They are also precipitated by lead and copper acetates, stannous chloride, and many other metallic salts, and form insoluble compounds with many organic bases, such as quinine, and with the basic aniline colours. They are possessed of feeble acid character.

All tannins are soluble in water to a greater or less degree; they are also soluble in alcohol, in mixtures of alcohol and ether, in ethyl acetate, acetone, and a few similar solvents, but are not dissolved by dry ether alone, nor by chloroform, petroleum spirit, carbon disulphide, nor benzine.

As the tannins are uncrystallisable, and incapable of being distilled without decomposition, they are exceedingly difficult to obtain in a state of purity, and, owing to the considerable differences in their character, no one method is equally applicable to the whole group. As their successful separation requires considerable chemical training, and experience, detailed description is outside the scope of the present work, but some particulars of the more important methods employed are given on p. 43, L.I.L.B.

Their chemical constitution is complex and in most cases imperfectly understood, but all the natural tannins which have been investigated prove to be derivatives of the trihydric phenol, pyrogallol, or of the dihydric phenol, catechol, the latter of which is often accompanied by a trihydric phenol, phloroglucol, which is isomeric with pyrogallol. The phenols are, themselves, a class of derivatives of benzene, C_6H_6, in which one or more of the hydrogen atoms are replaced by OH groups. Common phenol or "carbolic acid" is their simplest representative. Many of them, including pyrogallol and catechol, are used as photographic "developers." The phenols on replacing another hydrogen by carboxyl (CO.OH) form true acids, of which salicylic corresponds to common phenol, protocatechuic to catechol, and gallic to pyrogallol; and the tannins are apparently complicated acids, in which one of the two latter acids is linked to a second molecule of the same or another acid as an anhydride, in some cases possibly with the addition of phenols or other organic groups. For more detailed information, see L.I.L.B., p. 45. Gallotannic acid is apparently digallic acid, in which two molecules of gallic acid are linked together after giving up the elements of a molecule of water. Natural gallotannic acid and many other tannins are glucosides, or at least contain glucose, which in many cases can be removed by purification.

From what has just been said, it is obvious that a classification of the tannins according to constitution, is at present impracticable, not only from our imperfect knowledge, but from the difficulty of separating and determining the products of their decomposition. It is not, however, difficult to distinguish the catechol- from the pyrogallol-tannins by their chemical characteristics, apart from actual separation of the phenols, and the division is important as it is marked by certain broad differences in their properties which affect their use in tanning.

The catechol-tannins, dissolved in water, yield a precipitate when bromine-water is added till the solution smells strongly of it. The precipitate is occasionally crystalline, but generally amorphous, and of yellowish or brownish colour. When the infusion of tannin is very weak, the precipitate is sometimes only slight, or forms slowly. Pyrogallol-tannins give no precipitate with bromine-water. Another reaction, which is generally characteristic of catechol-tannins, is that if concentrated sulphuric acid is added to a single drop of the infusion in a test-tube, a dark red, or crimson ring is formed at the junction of the two liquids, and on dilution with water, the solution is generally pink. Pyrogallol-tannins on the other hand give a yellow, or at most a dark brown ring, which dilutes to a yellowish solution. This reaction is of great delicacy, which may be further increased by the use of an alcoholic instead of an aqueous extract. It is often given also by the non-tannin residue of catechol-tannins which is left after treatment with hide-powder, in which case it is probably due to the presence of catechins allied to the tannins. With ferric salts (preferably a solution of iron-alum), pyrogallol-tannins give blue-blacks, while catechol-tannins generally give greenish blacks, though the reaction is apt to be rendered uncertain by the presence of colouring matters, or perhaps in some cases by the constitution of the tannin. Thus aqueous infusions of common oak-bark (*Quercus robur*) give a decidedly blue black with iron, though the tannin is a catechol one, and the purified tannin gives a green-black. Most of the barks of American oaks, such as *Q. prinus*, give green-blacks without purification. The Australian mimosas generally give dull purple-blacks with iron-salts, though they all contain catechol-tannins. The iron test was first proposed by Stenhouse as a means of classification. Trimble has shown that while the purified pyrogallol-tannins only contain about 52 per cent. of carbon, the catechol-tannins have about 60 per cent.

'The Tannins,' ii. p. 131.

Only two tannins of the pyrogallol group have been definitely distinguished, though it is very possible that more exist. These are ordinary tannic acid of gall-nuts (probably digallic acid), which yields gallic acid when heated with dilute acids, or by the action of certain unorganised ferments or zymases (p. 16) which are generally present in tanning materials; and ellagitannic acid (usually present in greater or less proportion in mixture with the gallotannic acid), which, under the same conditions yields "bloom" (an insoluble deposit of ellagic acid), as one of its products. Hence it happens that most pyrogallol tannins deposit "bloom" on leather, though in very different proportions, gall-nuts and sumach giving very little, and myrobalans, valonia and divi-divi a great deal. English oak-bark deposits a good deal of "bloom" on leather, though it is certain that its principal tannin is a catechol one, but it is possible that the blue-black which it gives with iron salts may be due to the presence of ellagitannic acid, though gallotannic acid is known to be absent. The tannins of oakwood, chestnut and valonia are principally if not entirely pyrogallol derivatives, closely allied to, if not identical with the two just named, but, if so, very difficult to obtain in a pure condition. It is noteworthy that so wide a difference exists between the various products of the oak; galls, bark, fruit and wood yielding tannins of very varied properties. The tannin of other galls, such as those of the sumach and pistacio, generally contain gallotannic acid, even when, as in the last case, the remainder of the plant yields catechol-tannins.

The tannins of the catechol group appear to present much more variety than the pyrogallol-tannins, though it is possible that many apparent differences may be due to the presence of impurities. It is, however, at least certain that the tannins of gambier and cutch contain phloroglucol as one of their constituents, while it is absent from most other tanning materials. Its presence is easily detected by moistening pine-wood (a deal shaving) with an infusion of the tannin in question, and applying a little concentrated hydrochloric acid, when after a few minutes, a bright red or purple stain is produced. The catechol-tannins, on boiling with acids, yield no gallic acid, or bloom, but generally a deposit of "reds," insoluble in water but soluble in alkaline liquids, and in alcohol, and which are closely allied to resins, and especially to the red resin known as "dragon's blood." These reds are anhydrides of the tannins, that is, are produced from them by the abstraction of water; and are consequently formed by any agency which tends to remove water, such as long boiling or high temperature. The lower anhydrides (that is, those from which least water has been abstracted) are not wholly insoluble, but form the "difficultly soluble" tannins which are naturally present in many materials. They are much more readily soluble in hot than in cold water, which is one of the causes why liquors made by the aid of heat generally give darker colour to leather than those extracted cold. They exist in large quantity in hemlock extract and quebracho. Attempts have been made to utilise their alkaline solutions for tanning, but without much success; though alkalies or alkaline sulphites are frequently used to obtain "soluble" quebracho extracts (p. 338).

Many catechol tanning materials, and especially gambier, cutch and quebracho, contain in addition to the tannin, considerable portions of colourless bodies called catechins, which are only slightly soluble in cold water, but readily in hot, and which crystallise out on cooling. These bodies do not tan, but are in a sense the source of the tannins, which appear to be their first anhydrides, the reds being formed by the successive loss of further molecules of water. These bodies very probably ultimately become converted into tannins by changes in the tanyard. The change may be brought about very rapidly by heating to a temperature of 100 to 120° C. The catechin of gambier, by crystallising on and in the leather, is the cause of a trouble known as "whites," which is common where gambier is largely used.

Some doubt exists as to the exact temperature at which catechins become converted into anhydrides, and Perkin puts it higher than that stated.

An unfortunate peculiarity, apparently common to all catechol-tannins, is that, however light-coloured the leather produced by them, it darkens and reddens rapidly by exposure to strong light, and ultimately becomes quite friable and rotten. Cp. pp. 234, 272.

Cp. Report of Committee on Leathers for Bookbinding, Journ. Soc. of Arts, 1901, p. 14.

Wagner, a German chemist, attempted to classify the tannins into "physiological" tannins, which were produced in the natural growth of the plant, and "pathological" which were caused by the attack of insects such as the gall-wasps, and he further ventured the assertion that only the former class were capable of producing leather. It has since been shown that the tannins produced in galls are identical with some of those found in healthy plants, and galls themselves have been used in tanning from very ancient times. It is only necessary to remind the reader of the use of Turkish gall-nuts, in place of sumach, which was common in the East in the tannage of moroccos, and of the "Knoppern," or oak-galls formerly so largely used in Austria as a tanning material for sole leather. It is true that the tannin of galls is not very suitable for the latter purpose, consisting as it does mostly of gallotannic acid, which, giving no solid deposit of bloom or reds, is incapable of making a heavy or solid leather. Pure gallotannic acid itself produces a very white and soft leather.

The class to which the tannins of the different tanning materials belong is mostly mentioned in the Botanical List (Chap. XVIII.), but it may be well here to specify a few of the most common. Galls and sumach contain gallotannic acid with a little ellagitannic; myrobalans, valonia, divi-divi, algarobilla, oakwood and chestnut are all pyrogallol-tannins giving ellagic and gallic acid among their decomposition products. All the pine barks, including the American hemlock, and the larch, all the acacias and mimosas, including the Indian Babul (*Acacia arabica*), the oak barks (though not the oak wood, fruits, or galls), quebracho wood, cassia and mangrove barks, canaigre, cutch and gambier are catechol-tannins, and the two last contain phloroglucol, of which minute traces are also present in many other catechol-tannins (p. 297).

Cassia auriculata, or "turwar" bark, is the ordinary tannage of the East Indian or "Persian" sheep- and goat-skins, largely used in bookbinding, but which redden and decay very rapidly.

Gallotannic acid, and several artificial tannins with the characteristic reactions of the class have been produced in the laboratory, but there is no present prospect of their manufacture at prices which can in the faintest way compete with those of natural production.

Tanning materials frequently contain mordant colouring matters, often derived from the same phenols as the accompanying tannins. They also usually contain gums, starch and glucose. Oak bark contains lævulose which is not combined with the tannin. Many tannins, however, exist in nature in combination with the sugars as glucosides, which are easily decomposed by the action of acids or by fermentation. These sugary matters are important as furnishing by fermentation the acetic and lactic acids of tanning liquors.

CHAPTER XX.
THE SAMPLING AND ANALYSIS OF TANNING MATERIALS.

Although the analysis of tanning materials falls more properly within the scope of a book for chemists than one intended primarily for tanners, and though it has been treated at considerable length in the 'Leather Industries Laboratory Book,' a slight sketch must now be given of the methods in general use, since it is of great importance that at least the principles on which they are based should be understood by all to whom they are of practical interest, and also because an approximate analysis of a tanning material by the hide-powder method is within the scope of any intelligent tanner who will provide himself with the necessary implements. Much attention has been paid to the subject area by the International Association of Leather Trades Chemists, and also by the American Official Association of Agricultural Chemists, and as the methods prescribed by one or other of these are with very little exception employed by all qualified chemists throughout the world, their directions, corrected up to date, are given in Appendices A and C. As, however, these directions are addressed to chemists already familiar with the usual course of analysis, a somewhat fuller explanation must here be given.

It must specially be insisted on, that absolute adherence to the methods given is essential to obtaining concordant results, and little points of manipulation which appear in themselves unimportant, are frequently the result of long experience and careful discussion. The members of the International Association, especially, are bound by their rules to make note in their analytical reports of any deviation, however small, from the prescribed process.

The first step in the analysis of any material is to draw a sample truly representing the bulk, which is often by no means easy, while failure to accomplish it is probably the cause of more errors and disputes than any inaccuracy of the method of analysis itself. In very many cases, chemists are blamed for discrepancies which really exist in the samples supplied to them. The chemists of the International Association only hold themselves responsible for the accuracy of their analyses when the sampling has been done strictly according to the rules prescribed by their Association. On this account, all important samples should be drawn in the presence of a principal, or some other responsible person.

In liquid extracts, the thorough mixing of the liquid is of the greatest importance. Most extracts contain a portion of "difficultly soluble" tannins (see p. 297), which slowly settle to the bottom, or adhere to the sides of the cask; from which such expedients as merely rolling a full cask are quite inefficient to dislodge them. In fact nothing but taking the heads out of a sufficient number of casks, and actually stirring them with a suitable plunger, which should be specially applied to the sides and bottom, or emptying the entire contents of the casks into a tank in which the whole can be adequately mixed, is really thoroughly reliable, though at times it is necessary to be content with less satisfactory methods. In any case, when it is probable that samples must be submitted to more than one chemist, the whole should be drawn at once, thoroughly mixed and divided, and sealed in separate bottles, and in dividing a sample the same care must be taken to ensure complete mixture, as in drawing the original sample.

Solid and pasty extracts, such as quebracho, cutch and gambier, are still more difficult to sample fairly, as the outside is almost invariably much drier than the interior. Generally the only way is to select such portions as are thought fairly to represent the bulk, to chop them into moderately small pieces, mix and seal in an air-tight tin, leaving it to the chemist to draw from these the smaller sample required for analysis. Gambier is best sampled with a tubular tool like a cork-borer, designed by Mr. Kathreiner, Fig. 63, which should be passed completely through the bale, or the cylindrical sample of gambier cannot be withdrawn. The same tool may also be used for sampling sumach in bags, if the damage to the bag is not objected to. If such a tool is not available, the only fair way to sample gambier is to cut slices completely through the bale with a clean fleshing knife. In any case it is of the utmost importance that the sample once drawn, should be mixed as rapidly as possible, and at once enclosed in an *air-tight* box or jar, sealed and labelled.

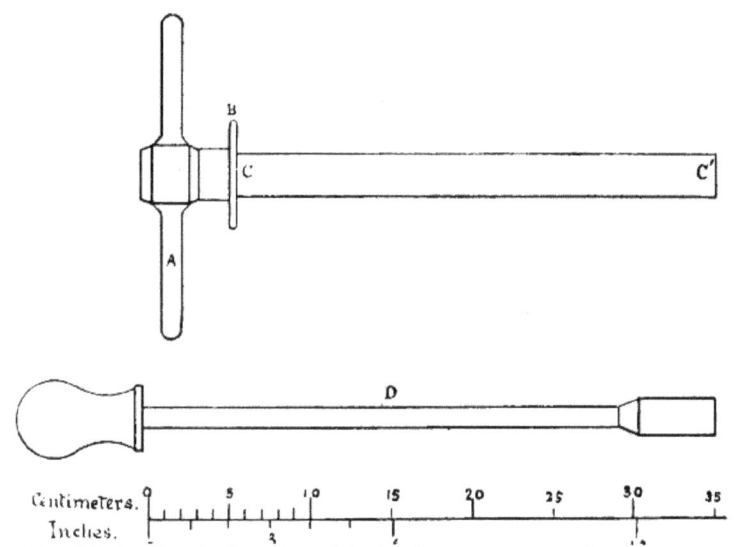

FIG. 63.—Kathreiner's Sampling Tools. A, strong cross-handle; B, guard-disc; C C´, brass tube sharpened at C´; D, brass or wooden plunger.

Dry tanning materials, such as bark and valonia, require judgment in selecting samples which fairly represent bulk. If they are of a nature which do not readily separate into dust and fibre, a good method is to grind a sufficient quantity in an ordinary bark-mill, and after well mixing, to draw the sample from the ground portion. In other cases it is best to empty a sufficient number of bags one upon another in layers on a smooth floor, and to take out a section down to the floor. In such materials as valonia and divi-divi, the dust or beard is usually much stronger than the average of the pods or cups.

The same sort of precautions are required in drawing the still smaller sample required for analysis from the larger original sample, but these are sufficiently detailed in the directions of the I.A.L.T.C. given in the Appendix. As materials usually require finer grinding than can be managed with the mills employed in the tannery, a suitable mill must be provided, and one of the simplest, at a moderate price, is a No. 4 drug-mill made by A. Kenrick and Sons, Limited, West Bromwich, Fig. 64. Coffee mills are seldom strong enough for the purpose, but if nothing better is available, the sample must be *thoroughly* dried before grinding, and its loss of weight noted, and taken into account in calculating the analysis, care being taken that the sample after grinding is so preserved that it cannot re-absorb moisture. Valonia, myrobalans and even barks, may before grinding be broken with a flat-faced hammer, on a thick cast-iron plate, with raised edges to prevent loss from flying fragments.

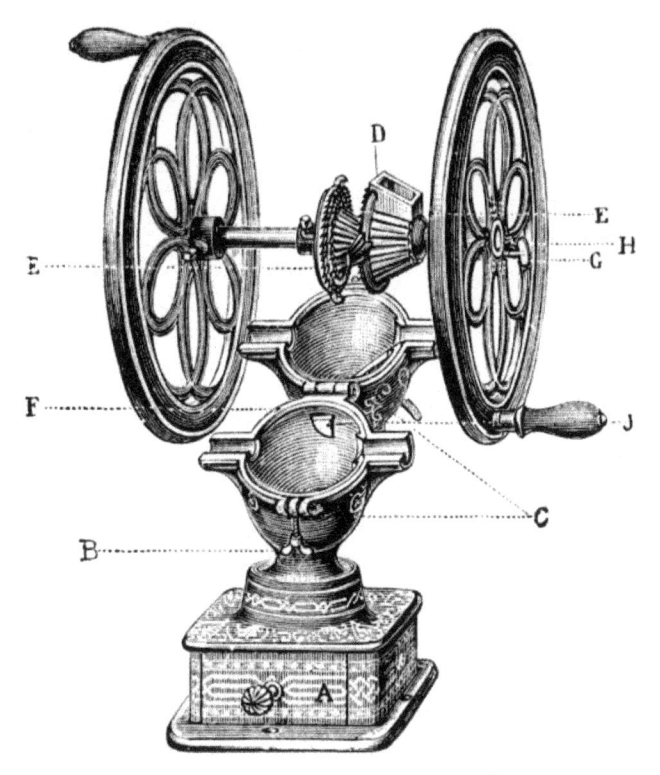

FIG. 64.—Kenrick's Drug-Mill.

Preparation of solution for analysis.—As the method of analysis only gives satisfactory results when the quantity of tanning matter in the solution is within certain limits, the International Association prescribes that it must be such as to contain between 3·5 and 4·5 grms. of tanning matter per liter, or as near as possible, on the average, to 4 grms. If, as will rarely happen, the strength of a material is quite unknown, it may be necessary to make a trial test to ascertain the quantity of substance to be used, but the following table gives the quantity with sufficient accuracy for most ordinary materials.

TABLE SHOWING THE AMOUNT OF DIFFERENT MATERIALS
TO BE WEIGHED OUT FOR ANALYSIS
TO MAKE UP ONE LITER OF SOLUTION.

Barks, etc.

	Grams.
Algarobilla	9
Canaigre	15
Divi-divi	9
Hemlock bark	16
Mimosa bark	11
Myrobalans	15
Oak-bark	30
Oak-wood	100
Quebracho wood	20
Sumach	15
Valonia	15
Valonia beard	11

Extracts.

Oak-wood, sp. gr. 1·2 or over	15
Chestnut ditto	14
Quebracho (solid)	6
Quebracho (liquid)	9 to 13
Gambier (block)	10
Gambier (cube)	7

The best method of weighing out exact quantities may be here described for those to whom it is not already known, as much time may be wasted by attempting it unsystematically. The material is of course weighed in a basin, which together with the weight which is desired of the material, is exactly counterpoised by weights in the other pan. Where many weighings of the sort have to be made, it saves time to keep one particular basin for the purpose, which should be properly marked; and to make a counterpoise of lead or brass exactly equal to it in weight, so that it is only necessary to add weights corresponding to the quantity required to be weighed out. Supposing now, that it is a liquid extract which is to be weighed, a sufficient quantity is introduced into the basin with a pipette, to slightly exceed the required weight. The pipette is now emptied, and a small quantity is withdrawn with it from the basin. If the basin is still too heavy, the pipette is emptied, and the process repeated until the basin is too light. The true weight now lies between that in the basin and the small quantity retained in the pipette, from which extract is added till the basin is again over-weighed, and the same process is repeated, each time reducing the margin, till a sufficient approximation is obtained. It is not necessary in weighing out the sample, to be accurate to a single milligram; but with practice, this amount of accuracy is easily attained. If the material is solid, a spatula is substituted for the pipette. The weighing of liquid or pasty extracts should be as rapid as possible, as they lose weight on the balance by evaporation.

Porcelain basins may be indelibly marked by writing on them with an ordinary iron ink, and heating strongly with a blowpipe.

Liquid extracts are most easily dissolved by placing a large funnel in the neck of a liter flask, and after pouring a little boiling water into the flask, holding the basin inclined in the funnel, and washing out its contents with boiling distilled water from a glass wash-bottle, or a perfectly clean copper kettle, till the flask is filled to the mark. The flask is now covered with a small beaker, which must hang loose on its neck, without resting on its shoulders, and is rapidly cooled by placing it under a cold water tap, to a temperature as little above 15° C. as possible, and is then filled up to the mark on the neck with cold water, and well mixed by shaking very thoroughly.

Solid or pasty extracts are dissolved in a beaker by stirring with successive quantities of boiling water, which are poured off into the flask, leaving the undissolved matter in the beaker. When the flask is nearly full, if any small portions remain undissolved or insoluble, they may be rinsed into it with the last portions of hot water, and the flask is now cooled and mixed as already described.

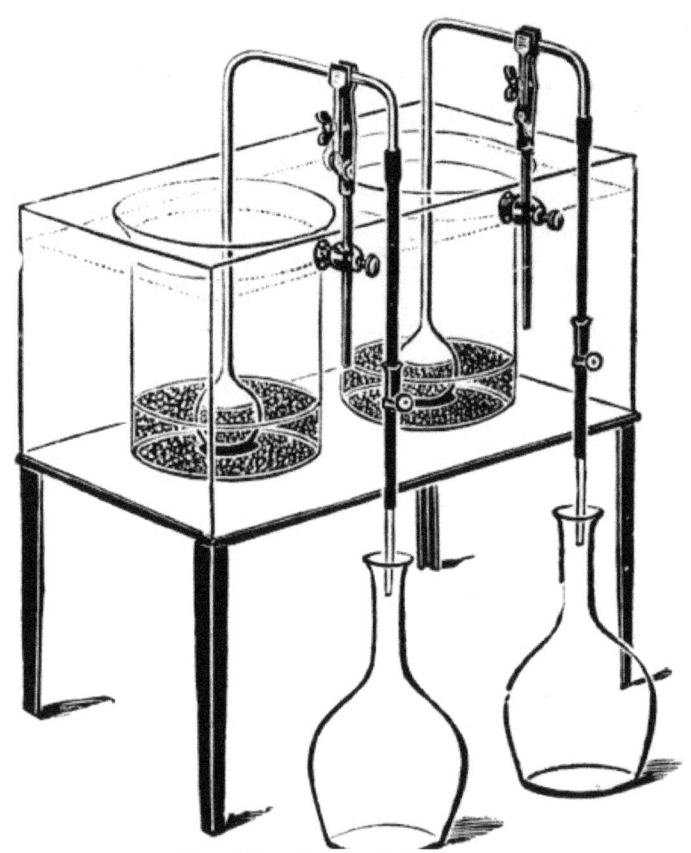

FIG. 65.—Procter's Extractor.

Extraction of solid materials, such as barks, or valonia, is more difficult, but the following is a convenient method, which has been recognised as official by the International Association. An ordinary beaker, of about 200 c.c. capacity, but which may be varied in size according to the weight of the material which it is necessary to treat, is placed in a water-bath, as shown in Fig. 65. A thistle-headed funnel, the stem of which is bent twice at right angles, and of which the head is covered with a piece of fine silk gauze (such as is used by millers) to act as a strainer, is placed in the beaker and held in position by a clamp as shown in the figure. To the free end of its stem a piece of glass tube, six or eight inches long, is attached by indiarubber tube, which is provided with a pinchcock to regulate the flow of liquid. Fine silver-sand, freed from iron and soluble matters by washing first with hydrochloric acid, and then very thoroughly with water, is now poured into the beaker, so as to surround the head of the funnel to about half an inch in depth; and the weighed quantity of tanning material is next introduced. It is best to cover the material with cold water, and allow it to stand all night, but in case of haste, water of 30° to 50° may be used, and the extraction proceeded with after the material is thoroughly soaked. Percolation is started by sucking the syphon, and allowing the liquid to drop slowly into a liter flask, the temperature of the water-bath being maintained by a Bunsen burner, and the beaker being refilled as it requires it with water at the desired temperature. At least 500 c.c. must be percolated before the temperature is allowed to exceed 50°, after which, except in the case of sumach and canaigre, which should be begun about 30°, and at no time allowed to rise above 50°, the temperature may be raised to boiling point. At least 1½ hour should be employed in percolating 800 to 900 c.c. and if the material is not then practically exhausted, the liter flask must be withdrawn, and an ordinary ungauged flask substituted, into which the percolation is continued till the material is exhausted. The very dilute liquor in the second flask is now boiled down till its volume is sufficiently small to be added to that in the liter flask, a small funnel being placed in its neck during ebullition, to prevent spirting and the access of air. Under no conditions must the stronger liquor of the first part of the percolation be boiled down, as this would involve destruction of tannin. The solution is now cooled, and made up to the mark as has been before described. Most ordinary materials may be practically exhausted by the liter of water if percolation is slow, and the trouble of evaporation may thus be avoided.

The material should be kept in an even layer, and if necessary the surface may be stirred at intervals with the thermometer or a glass rod.

Total soluble matter.—The solution of which the preparation has been described, must now be filtered, the size and kind of paper, and exact method of filtration prescribed by the International Association being strictly adhered to. All papers and methods of filtration absorb traces of tanning matters, and but few will give a clear filtrate with such solutions as those of quebracho and hemlock extracts; and to obtain uniform results exact uniformity of method is essential. Deviations from the exact method, in the case of quebracho, easily cause discrepancies of several units per cent. in the result. The object of rejecting the first portions of the filtered solution is to prevent, as far as possible, errors which would arise from the absorption of tannin by the paper, and to insure a clear filtrate. 50 c.c. of the clear filtrate is now measured by an accurate pipette, and evaporated to dryness in a weighed porcelain basin, on a steam-bath, in order to determine the "total soluble." This and succeeding operations should be done in duplicate, even if this has not been the case in making up the original solution, which is certainly desirable.

Methods of correction for absorption of filter-papers have been worked out in the Author's laboratory, and adopted by the last conference of the International Association. Cp. Collegium, pp. 145-158, 1902, and App. A, p. 477.

Ordinary light porcelain basins, generally of about three inches diameter, are employed for evaporation, which takes place somewhat more rapidly if they are flat-bottomed (saucer-shaped). In place of porcelain, thin glass basins of hemispherical form may be used, and, but for the cost, platinum would be better than anything else. Aluminium and nickel basins have been tried, but are slightly attacked by some liquors, and hence are more liable to vary in weight, though they have the advantage in rapidity of evaporation. Evaporation takes place most quickly if the steam-bath can be placed in a draught of air, so as to rapidly carry away the vapour formed, but the basins must be protected from dust. Under favourable circumstances, evaporation of 50 c.c. in porcelain basins occupies one to one and a half hour. An ordinary pan fitted with a lid of thin copper perforated with holes of two and three-quarter inches in diameter, makes a useful water-bath; but where much work is done, it is desirable to have a rectangular bath of thin sheet copper, taking a single, or at most a double row of basins, and fitted with the usual appliance for keeping the water at constant level; or with a supply of steam from a boiler, and an overflow for condensed water.

As soon as the contents of the basins appear completely dry, they may be transferred to the drying oven. The most satisfactory form is one in which the basins are placed in a closed chamber, surrounded by steam at the atmospheric pressure, and at the same time subjected to a vacuum maintained by a water-jet air-pump; but as this apparatus is somewhat costly, it will probably only be provided in laboratories which make a speciality of such work. Next to the vacuum-oven, an air-oven, heated by a gas-burner, and with its temperature controlled by a mercurial regulator to 100-105° C., gives the best results, and it is also the cheapest; but considerable care and some scientific knowledge are required to work it satisfactorily. In intelligent hands good results may be got from the small "breakfast cooker" gas ovens made by Fletcher of Warrington, which are placed on an iron plate heated by a gas burner, the supply of gas to which is regulated by a thermostat, or mercurial gas-regulator, inserted, together with a thermometer, through holes drilled in the top. The basins must not be placed too near the bottom of the oven, which must be protected by a perforated metal plate supported perhaps one inch above it, to prevent radiation and to distribute the hot air. Any cold air required for ventilation should be admitted below this plate, and care should be taken to exclude the products of the burning gas. Contact of the basins with any heated part of the metal-work should be carefully avoided, and they are best supported on grid-shelves covered with wire gauze or perforated metal, so as to allow of free circulation of air. If perforated zinc is used, it must be well supported, as it is much softened at the temperature used. The least satisfactory appliance in skilled hands, but probably the most easy to work by the inexperienced, is the ordinary water- or steam-oven. It is impossible, in this apparatus, to raise the temperature of the interior fully to boiling point, and below this gambier, quebracho, and other solutions containing catechins (p. 298), dry very slowly. On the other hand, so long as it is kept boiling and supplied with water, the temperature is necessarily constant, and there is no danger of overheating, which easily occurs in ovens heated directly by gas. Such ovens are often fitted with openings at the top for use as a steam-bath. To get the best results, the basins must be as freely exposed as possible to the air in the interior of the oven (in no case must basins be set one inside another, except in the exsiccator for cooling), and little or no ventilation from the outside is required, as only traces of moisture remain after evaporation on the steam-bath; so that, after an hour's drying, any ventilators may safely be closed. As a good deal of cooling takes place through the door, it is best to protect it with some non-conducting material, such as asbestos millboard, which may be attached with rivets, or even with ordinary paper-fasteners. One to one and a half hours will be required to dry to constance in the vacuum-oven; two to three in the air-oven at 105°; and probably about four hours in the water-oven, except in the case of gambiers, which may require somewhat longer. Too long heating is disadvantageous, as the residues begin to oxidise and gain in weight. As soon as it is judged that the basins will be constant in weight, they are withdrawn from the drying oven, and at once placed in an exsiccator (a glass vessel with an accurately fitted lid, which should be slightly greased, in the bottom part of which is placed either dry calcium chloride or concentrated sulphuric acid, to absorb the moisture of the air it contains). In this they are left till thoroughly cold, which if several basins are put in together, may require half an hour. They are then weighed accurately, but as rapidly as possible; returned to the drying oven for half an hour; and replaced in the exsiccator. The exact weight of each basin, as it comes in turn to be weighed, is now placed on the balance before removing the basin from the exsiccator, so that it can be seen instantly if there is loss or gain of weight, before it has time to absorb any moisture from the air. The weight should not be more than a milligram or so less than at the first weighing; if weight has been gained, it is caused by oxidation, and the first weight should be taken as correct if it is certain that the basin was then perfectly cold; a very slight amount of warmth easily reducing the apparent weight by several milligrams. If material loss has occurred, the basin must of course be returned to the oven, and re-weighed in another half hour; but with experience, this should rarely be needed.

It is necessary that the balance used should weigh accurately to milligrams; and it must carry at least 50 grm. on each pan; while it is more convenient that it should carry 100 or more, it is always possible with a little ingenuity, to manage within 50 grm.; and if a cheap balance must be used, the smaller size will probably be more accurate. Balances of this sort can now be got for two or three pounds, though it is in all respects better to obtain one of first rate quality, which should cost about ten pounds. The balances of Verbeek and Peckholdt, of Dresden, from their simplicity and rapidity of weighing, have given great satisfaction in technical work in the Yorkshire College. Whatever economy be exercised in the choice of the balance, it is essential that the set of weights should be of the greatest accuracy, and especially that all the weights of one denomination (10 grm., 1 grm., etc.), should accurately balance each other. Even after all precautions are taken, it is desirable that those weights which are in duplicate should receive distinguishing marks (e.g. with a centre-punch), and should always be placed on the scale in the same order; and, not only on account of possible inaccuracy, but to save time, it is desirable to reject basins which are so nearly of an even weight (20, 25, 30 grm.) that when weighed with the residue (0·3-0·4 grm.), a change of the larger weights may be required, since it is to be remembered that any error of the weights employed is concentrated on the small weight of the residue.

After deducting the weight of the empty basins, the weight *in milligrams* of the two residues of 50 c.c., which should be practically alike, are added together, and the sum divided by the weight *in grams* of tanning material used; which gives the percentage of "total soluble matter."

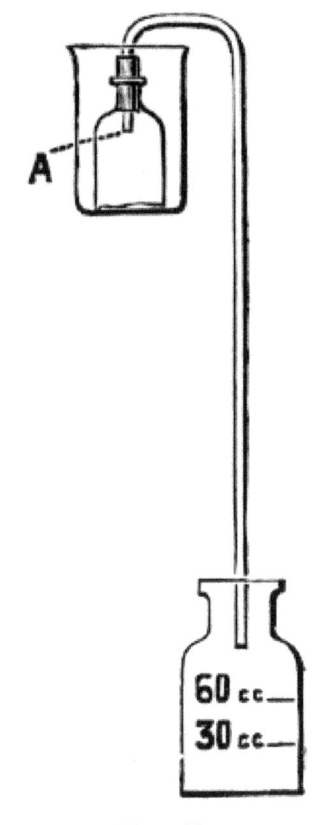

FIG. 66.
Hide-powder Filter.

Non-tannins.—It is now necessary to determine the proportion of the "total soluble" which consists of "non-tanning matters," that is, of substances not removed from the solution by treatment with hide-powder. The so-called "tanning matters" removed, include colouring matters and some other substances, which though absorbed by hide, are certainly not tannins in a strictly chemical sense. (See note, p. 480.)

According to the method of the International Association, the apparatus shown in Fig. 66 is employed for this purpose. The glass bell is carefully and uniformly stuffed with hide-powder, care being taken that no channels are left, especially at the sides, through which the liquor can reach the syphon without traversing the hide-powder. Before filling the bell, the short leg of the syphon-tube should be loosely plugged with cotton-wool (of which a little is allowed to project from the end), in order to prevent the powder from gaining access to the tube. The powder is retained in its position in the bell by a piece of muslin held by an indiarubber band, and the bell is then placed in a beaker or tumbler as shown in the figure; and filtered liquor is gradually added, as it is absorbed by the powder, till the whole is uniformly wetted. The liquor which was first filtered through the paper, and rejected for "total solubles," may be used for this purpose, and it is not necessary that it should be absolutely clear. The syphon is now gently sucked, and the filtrate is allowed to fall, drop by drop, into a gauged cylinder. The first 30 c.c. which collects is rejected, since it contains traces of dissolved hide-substance even from the purest hide-powder; and the next 50 c.c. should give no turbidity if a few drops are mixed either with clear tannin solution (absence of dissolved hide-substance), or with the first 30 c.c. (absence of tannin). This 50 c.c. is used for determination of non-tannins, by evaporation and drying precisely as has been described in the case of "total soluble." Some chemists, with very accurate balances, prefer to evaporate only 25 c.c., which effects a little saving of time in evaporation; but in any case the whole of the 50 c.c. must be allowed to run through the filter before it is measured, as the filtrate varies somewhat in solid contents as the filtration proceeds. The filtration and evaporation should be done in duplicate. The weight of the residue is calculated into percentage as "soluble non-tanning matters" precisely as has been described for the "total soluble"; and when subtracted from the latter, the remainder is the percentage of "tanning matters." If the hide-powder now employed by the English members of the International Association (manufactured by Messrs. Mehner and Stransky in Freiberg in Sachsen), be employed, no difficulty will be found in the filtration. This powder is quite neutral, and contains between 10 and 20 per cent. of cellulose to render it more absorbent. It does not swell in the filter, and hence should be stuffed into the bell almost as tightly as possible, about 10 grm. being required. If the bell is properly filled, the filtration should altogether take about one hour, but if the liquid runs too fast, it must be regulated by a pinchcock on the indiarubber tube of the syphon. If other powders are used, which often contain acid, and swell very much in the bell, the filling is much more difficult, and while the sides of the bell must be closely packed, great care is requisite to keep the powder loose in the centre, or the filter will not run. One point requires mention with regard to neutral hide-powders. If an extract which has been rendered soluble by the addition of alkalis or sulphites (p. 388) be analysed with a perfectly neutral powder, it has been shown by Paessler and Appelius that a part of the tannin combined with the alkali will not be absorbed, while with acid powders, the whole will be estimated.

Wissenschaftliche Beilage des 'Ledermarkt,' 1901, p. 107.

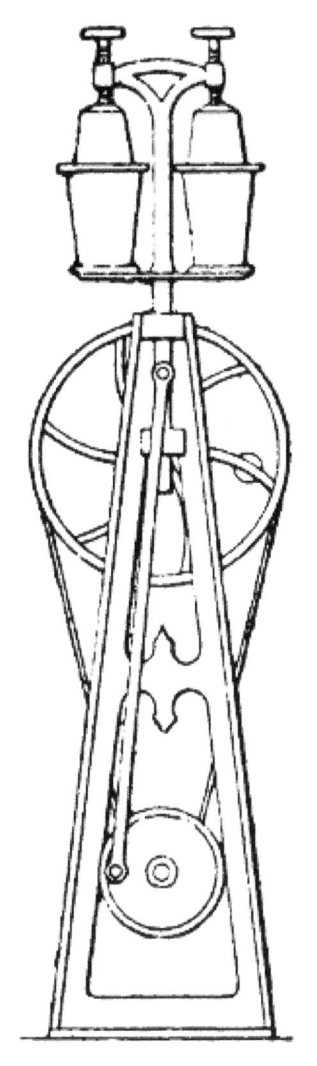

FIG. 67.
American Milk-shaker.

The "shake-method" adopted by the American Association of Official Agricultural Chemists, possesses some advantages, especially in the analysis of used liquors which, from the acids they contain, are apt to give somewhat too high results by the filter method (see App. B, page 480). It has the further advantage of being much less dependent than the filter-method on the quality of the hide-powder employed. It has therefore been accepted by the International Association as permissive for all tanning materials, and as compulsory for used liquors (see App. A), and must therefore be briefly explained. It can be carried out successfully with somewhat inferior hide-powders to those required for the filter, but generally gives results 1 or 2 per cent. lower in tannins than the latter. A special shaking machine must be employed, capable of thoroughly agitating a mixture of hide-powder and the liquor to be analysed; and if many analyses have to be done, it is convenient that it should be driven by power, as otherwise the work becomes somewhat laborious. A machine called a "milk-shaker," Fig. 67, employed in the mixing of summer drinks, is generally used. The quantity of powder required for the analyses to be made (about 8 grm. of ordinary air-dried powder for each determination, with say 5 grm. added), is stirred in a large beaker with 25 times its weight of distilled water, and allowed to soak for 24 hours, 1·5 per cent. of chrome-alum previously dissolved in water being added at the beginning of the operation, and 1·5 per cent. more not less than 6 hours before its end. The powder is then washed by squeezing through linen, and the washing is continued till the wash-water no longer gives a precipitate with barium chloride; and is then well squeezed out in linen, preferably with the aid of a press. The damp squeezed powder is now roughly weighed, to determine approximately what quantity it is necessary to take, to give 7·5 grm. of the original dry powder to each estimation (air-dried powder contains about 15 per cent. of moisture), and a portion is accurately weighed in a basin, and dried, first on the water-bath, and then in the drying oven, to determine its moisture by loss. The approximate amount of powder required for each determination—if possible a round number of grams—is now weighed into as many bottles of about 300 c.c. capacity as determinations are to be made, 100 c.c. of the filtered liquors, prepared as before described, are introduced into each bottle, and the bottles are then each shaken for 10 minutes (Mr. Alsop states that in his experience 5 minutes is sufficient). The contents of the bottles are now filtered through funnels, the stems of which are plugged with pure cotton-wool, and the liquor is returned till a clear filtrate is obtained, of which 50 c.c. is evaporated as in the International method. It is now necessary to accurately correct the residue obtained, for the amount of water carried in by the wet powder. The loss of weight of the powder which has been dried, divided by its wet weight, gives the water contained in each gram of wet powder, and this multiplied by the weight of wet powder added to the liquor, gives the weight in grams (or volume in c.c.) of water which has been added to each 100 c.c. of liquor. Consequently, if the residues found be multiplied by this weight plus 100, and the product divided by 100, the weight will be obtained which should have been given by 50 c.c. of undiluted but detannised liquor; and from this the non-tannins are calculated exactly as in the case of the residues from the filter process. Of course, in practice, a factor is found, by which it is simply necessary to multiply all the residues, to correct them to undiluted weight. The process sounds somewhat complicated, but in reality, where a large number of determinations have to be made, is quite as quick, if not quicker than the filter method; which it is quite possible it may ultimately supersede, as much attention is being devoted to its improvement.

Having determined the tanning, and soluble non-tanning matters of the materials, it remains to determine the moisture, and the insoluble which make up the whole. To determine moisture, a quantity, not exceeding two or three grams of dry solid materials, or half a gram of moist or liquid extracts, is weighed into a basin, and dried in the same way as has been described for the residues, only that a considerably longer time will be required before constancy is attained. The object of employing so small a quantity of liquid extracts is to abridge this time, and the consequent oxidation, as much as possible, as the extract soon forms a hard skin on the exterior, which renders further drying very tedious. It is advantageous to add a little alcohol to liquid and semi-liquid extracts, and so dilute them that by inclining the basin they can be distributed in a thin layer over its sides, while at the same time the alcohol facilitates the evaporation of the water. The weight of the dried residue in the basin is the "total solids," while the loss is the "water"; and these can be converted into percentages by multiplying by 100 and dividing by the weight of substance originally taken. An alternate method, which is frequently convenient with extracts, is to pipette off 50 c.c. (in duplicate) of the dissolved and well-mixed extract-solution *before filtration*, and dry exactly in the same way as for "total soluble." The sum of the two residues in milligrams, divided by the weight of extract taken for analysis, gives the "total solids"; subtracting this from 100 leaves the "water," while the difference between the "total solids" and the "total soluble" is the percentage of insoluble matter. Two further points must be noted. If the total solids are determined by the first method, and the total soluble in the ordinary way, in an extract which contains no insoluble matter, it frequently happens that they differ by 0·1 or 0·2 per cent., owing either to the difficulty of driving off the whole of the water, or to slight oxidation of the total soluble residue. On the other hand, if the second method is adopted, a small amount of "insoluble" is invariably found, even in perfectly soluble extracts, which is due to the absorption of tannin or colouring matter by the filter paper. On the correction of this error, see Collegium, 1902, pp. 145-158, and App. A, p. 477.

As the value of a tanning material often depends very much on the paleness of its colour, it has become customary to specify in contracts the intensity of colour of a solution of it containing one-half per cent. of tanning matter (as measured by the I.A.L.T.C. method of analysis), in a glass cell of one centimeter thick, by comparison with standard coloured glasses in the tintometer. On the method of making the measurement see L.I.L.B., p. 131.

NOTE.—All the apparatus named in this chapter can be obtained of Messrs. Reynolds and Branson, Commercial Street, Leeds; or of Messrs. Portway, Jamaica Road, S.E.; and of most other dealers in chemical apparatus.

<hr size=2 width="26%" noshade style='color:black' align=center>

CHAPTER XXI.
GRINDING OF TANNING MATERIALS.

Before the tannin they contain can be extracted, most materials require to be ground, almost the only exceptions to this rule being divi-divi and algarobilla, in which the tannin is very loosely contained. Extracts, whether solid or liquid, merely require to be dissolved in water or liquor, in which they are, for all practical purposes, perfectly soluble. With the less soluble extracts it is generally preferable to dissolve at a temperature of 50° to 60° C. with vigorous stirring.

The actual method of grinding, and consequently the machinery employed for the purpose, vary not only with the material to be ground, but with the method of leaching adopted, as it is essential that the mass of ground material should be completely permeated by the liquor employed in leaching; and if it be ground too finely, or subjected to too much pressure on account of the height to which it is piled in the leaches, it is apt to form a compact and clay-like mass, the interior of which remains unextracted.

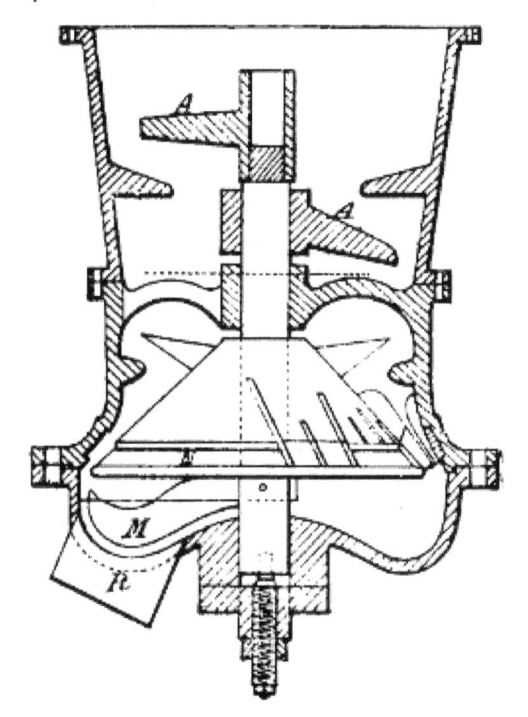

FIG. 68.—Cone-Mill.

In the laboratory, where thorough extraction must be completed in a few hours, the material can hardly be too fine; but on the larger scale a much coarser product must be used, and leaching requires days, or sometimes even weeks, and is then seldom successful in removing all the tannin. It is probable, however, that in the future these mechanical difficulties of extraction will be overcome; and the material will then be as finely divided, and as completely extracted on the large scale, as it is in the laboratory at the present time.

One of the earliest methods of grinding oak-bark, and which is still used for sumach (p. 271) consists in crushing it under large circular edge-stones, frequently turned by a horse. This process was very slow and inefficient for barks, and both it and horizontal millstones similar to those used for wheat were long ago superseded by iron or steel mills on the same principle as the ordinary coffee-mill.

These mills, Fig. 68, consist of a "bell" or inner cone, covered with blades or teeth arranged at a slight angle to the vertical section of the cone, and which are made finer and increased in number towards its lower and wider part. This cone rotates within an outer hollow cone or casing, also provided with blades or teeth which are sloped slightly in the opposite direction to those of the inner cone, so as to meet them at an angle, like the cutting-blades of a pair of scissors, and the angles of the cone are so chosen that the blades approach each other more closely towards their base. The outer cone is fixed, and is provided with a hopper like a coffee-mill, while the inner cone is so rotated on its axis that bark placed in the hopper is screwed down between the two, and cut finer and finer till it reaches the lower edge, when it drops out. The blades or teeth are usually cast in one piece with the metal cones, and sharpened when required by chipping with cold chisels. This operation should not be conducted in the mill-house, or small chippings of iron may get mixed with the bark, and cause stains on the leather. This form of mill, which is run in England at about 30 revolutions per minute, and at nearly three times this speed in America, works very well with dry material, but clogs badly if it be appreciably damp. On this account it is always well to run the mill with a fairly slack belt which will slip before exerting sufficient pressure to break the machine, as in such operations as grinding, safety clutches are of but little use.

A type of mill varying somewhat from the above, consists of a pair of discs or very obtuse cones, the inner one of which runs on a horizontal axis. The teeth are generally arranged in concentric rings and interlock with each other. The material to be ground is fed at or near the centre of the fixed disc, and escapes at the edges. The construction of this class of mill will be easily understood from Fig. 69. Very small pieces of iron or steel which get caught between the teeth will often result in the breaking of the latter, and the formation of iron dust, which is a serious objection to the employment of this type of mill (to which the Schmeija "Excelsior," the Glaeser "Favorita," and the "Devil Disintegrator" of the Hardy Patent Pick Co. belong) for grinding barks.

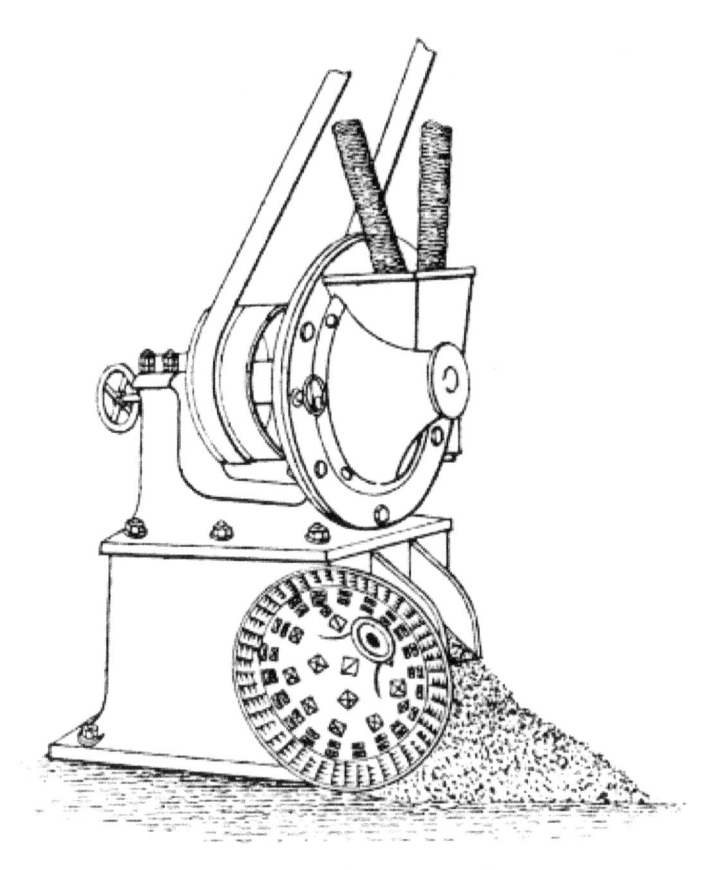

FIG. 69.—"Excelsior" Mill.

Myrobalans and mimosa-barks have proved especially troublesome to grind, the former from the hardness of the stones of the fruit, and a tendency to clog the mill, and the latter from their combined hardness and toughness. "Disintegrators" of various patterns are now made, which are capable of grinding both these materials satisfactorily, and but for their liability to cause fire, and the large proportion of fine dust which they make, are usually to be preferred to toothed mills. In spite of their disadvantages, however, they have come very largely into use, on account of their efficiency in grinding obstinate materials. Disintegrators work on the principle of knocking or beating the material to powder, by means of very rapidly revolving beaters, which, in the smaller machines, are driven at 2500 to 3000 revolutions per minute.

The first disintegrator was made by Carr and consisted of two concentric cylinders or baskets of steel bars, rotating in opposite directions at a very high speed. The material was fed between these and was dashed to pieces by being thrown against the bars and the outer casing.

FIG. 70.—Disintegrator.

A simpler form was soon introduced by Carter, in which only one axis was employed, carrying radial beaters which dashed the material against the serrated outer casing, a portion of the circumference of which was fitted with gratings, through which the ground material was thrown as soon as it was sufficiently reduced in size, the fineness of the grinding being regulated by changing the grates as required. This type of disintegrator is, with slight variations, made by all the leading makers of tanners' machinery; and one form is shown in Fig. 70, and a similar but smaller machine, opened to show construction, in Fig. 71.

In the more modern machines the sides as well as the circumference of the casing are frequently corrugated in order to increase the action on the material.

Mills running at such high rates of speed as 3000 revolutions per minute will grind most hard substances, such as stone or brick, without injury, but pieces of iron among the tanning material are apt to cause damage, and various magnetic devices have been employed for separating this metal, but with only partial success. In the best mills, therefore, the beaters and inner casings are constructed so that they can be easily replaced, and the damage is then rarely serious.

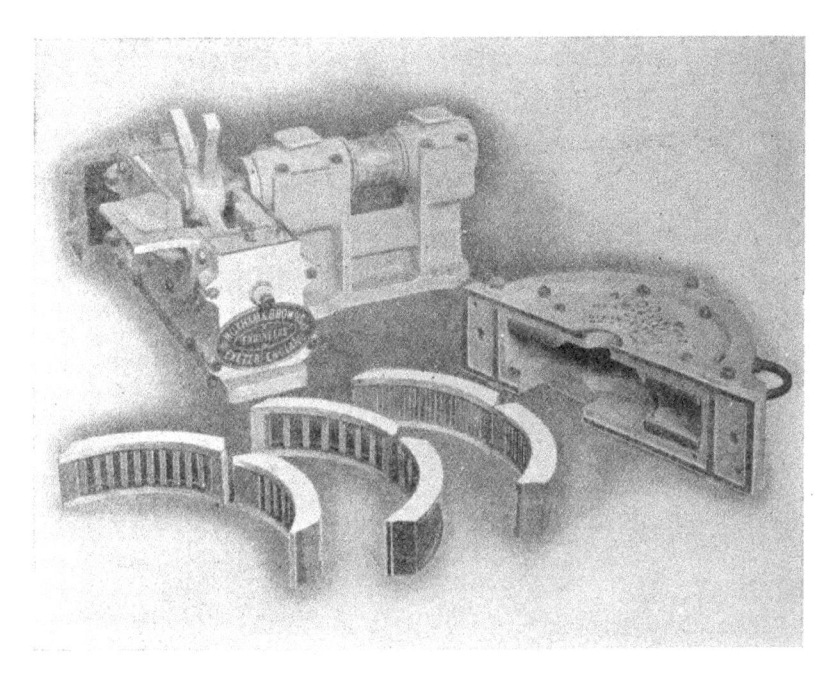

FIG. 71.—Disintegrator opened, showing construction.

In order to avoid vibration, the discs and beaters of all these high-speed mills must be balanced with great accuracy. This is best accomplished by removing the spindle from the mill, and allowing it to roll on two levelled straight-edges, and then filing or chipping the beaters on the heavy side until it will remain indifferently in any position.

A new form of disintegrator has been recently brought out in America by the Williams' Patent Crusher and Pulveriser Company, in which a series of discs are keyed to the main shaft, to the circumference of which a number of sets of "hammers" are suspended by means of hinge-bolts. Each of these steel bars, or hammers, has a free arc movement of 120°, and when the machine is in motion take a position divergent from the centre on account of the centrifugal force. After striking a blow against any material fed on to a plate serving as an "anvil," the hammers recoil, and, after passing any material which is not shattered by the blow, again resume their normal position, leaving the next set of hammers to beat against the unground material. The hinged suspension of the hammers imparts a degree of flexibility to the mill which is not found in any other machine of this character, and lessens the risk of serious damage to the machine by the introduction of pieces of metal along with the bark. The makers claim that this machine can be repaired more rapidly and with less expense than any other disintegrator of equal power on the market. Considerable improvements have recently been made in the details of its construction. Fig. 72 shows a section of this mill. Of course only the end hammers of each set can be seen in the figure.

FIG. 72.—Section of Williams' Crusher.

When myrobalans or valonia is to be used for leaching, it is generally better to crush it between toothed or fluted rollers, rather than to grind it finely, as the cellular structure is just as completely broken up, and the flakes formed by crushing allow of much freer percolation than when the material is powdered by the disintegrator, while the consumption of power is also less. The general construction of the machine will be easily understood from Fig. 73, and it is only necessary to point out that the small upper roller acts mainly as a "feed" to the larger crushing rolls.

In the best mills, the rollers are made up of a series of toothed steel discs on a square axis, and are on this account easily replaced or sharpened when they have become broken or worn.

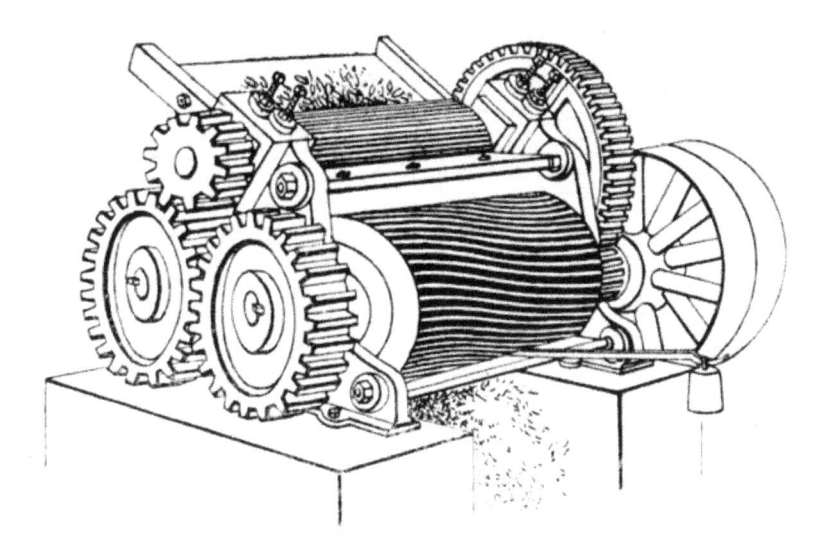

FIG. 73.—Myrobalans Crusher.

Several mills have been introduced in America in which the bark is sawn or rasped by toothed discs like circular saws, but these are only capable of dealing with barks of a brittle nature, and are immediately choked by tough materials like the bark of the mimosa or oak. A better form of mill, but one which is, to some extent, subject to the same disadvantage, is the "shaving-mill," in which blades are fixed like plane-irons upon a disc, cones or cylinder, and are rotated at a high speed against the material which is fed against them by toothed rollers at such an angle that the shavings are cut diagonally to the grain. These shaving-mills are largely in use in America for hemlock-bark, with which they are particularly successful. The principle of the machine is exactly the same as that of the machines used in cutting oakwood, quebracho, and the different dye woods. One type of shaving-mill is illustrated in Fig. 74.

FIG. 74.—Shaving Mill.

It frequently happens that the material is delivered from the mill in a very unequal state of division, and it is sometimes necessary to screen it and thus separate the coarser portion either for use in the leaches or for re-grinding, while the finer portion is more suitable for "dusting." With disintegrators, which deliver the bark with considerable impetus, the screening can be accomplished by placing a screen diagonally below the mill, through which the finer parts are projected. It is, however, essential that this screen should be quite smooth on its upper surface and very strong, as ordinary wire gauze is immediately cut through by the impact of the material. What are called "locked wire screens" in which the wires are supported by being actually twisted round the transverse bars are very suitable. Where the circumstances will not permit of screening in this way, cylindrical rotating screens, or nearly horizontal screens vibrated by an eccentric may be used. The latter are cheaper to erect and have the advantage that they take up less room, and by having lengths of wirework or perforated steel of different coarseness, the material may be separated into more than one degree of fineness.

FIG. 75.—Bark-Breaker.

Oak-bark as it is taken off the trees is usually in lengths of perhaps three feet, and it is necessary to cut or break it into smaller fragments before it can be ground in most of the machines just described. This is frequently done by hand by chopping the bark into pieces about four inches long, and the operation is known as "hatching." Machines on the principle of the chaff-cutter, consisting of a fly-wheel with curved blades radially attached to it, are sometimes used. Instead of "hatching" it, the bark is frequently broken by passing through toothed rollers fitting into each other, and often attached to the mill; the construction of this machine will be readily understood from Fig. 75.

In Belgium, and some other bark-producing districts, the adhering moss and dead outside bark are usually removed before hatching, but apparently these impurities are frequently re-mixed with the bark after the hatching is completed! As such barks often also contain much clay and dirt, it is generally expedient to pass the hatched bark over a coarse screen before letting it enter the mill, so as to remove the greater part of such rubbish, since, if left in the bark, it produces black and unsatisfactory liquors.

In drawing up policies for fire insurance, it is usual to charge a higher rate where disintegrators are used to grind the tanning material, as owing to the amount of dust and the production of sparks by the striking of the steel parts of the machine on any chance piece of flint or metal which may get into it, there is a greater liability to fire than with toothed mills, although with proper precautions the risk is really small. (Cp. p. 446.)

All disintegrators act like ventilating fans, and suck in air with the material, blowing it out again with great force at the periphery. This air is heavily laden with dust from the tanning material which is extremely irritating to the lungs. The difficulty is to some extent remedied by an air-channel or flue (generally cast in the casing of the machine) connecting the discharge with the feed-opening so as to convey the air back to the disintegrator. The air is thus circulated through the arrangement, but some is always drawn in from the external atmosphere and driven out with the ground material, and it is advisable that the chamber into which it is discharged should be provided with some means of filtering the air before it escapes. One convenient method is to have a large flannel bag which is blown out by the air like a balloon and out of which the dust can be shaken when the machinery has stopped. Another efficient method is to have one of the walls or the ceiling of the chamber made of canvas or of sacking; but in any case the air should be allowed an escape where a little dust will not cause annoyance.

Chain-Conveyors.—While, in England, the ground material is usually carried from the mill to the leaches in barrows or baskets, in America the use of conveyors is practically universal, and there is no doubt that they effect a great saving of labour at a comparatively small cost.

The most practical conveyor for tanning materials consists of a trough through which an endless chain passes, carrying scrapers. The chain generally used for this purpose is one consisting of square links fitting into each other and capable of running over toothed wheels. These chains are made by several firms in America, and in England by the Ewart Chain Conveyor Co., of Derby, who supply not only plain links but also those having projections to which buckets, scrapers and a variety of attachments may be fixed.

FIG. 76.—Chain-Conveyor.

In many cases the trough is V-shaped with the chain running in the angle; in others flat-bottomed as in the illustration, or rectangular. The scrapers may consist either of metal or of wood; and where materials have to be carried up a steep incline buckets instead of scrapers should be employed. The arrangement of such a conveyor is illustrated by Fig. 76.

A useful form of conveyor for dry materials consists in a woven cotton belt running in a smooth trough and with laths riveted across it at intervals. These laths should project slightly beyond the edges of the belt so as to prevent wear. Care must be taken with belts of this sort that the material does not get between the belt and the pulley.

Chain-carriers are often used for conveying the spent tan to the furnaces from the leaches, and occasionally for carrying skins.

Several other kinds of conveyor are in use in corn-mills, spiral or worm conveyors which work on the screw principle being very largely used for carrying corn. They are not very suitable for tanning materials on account of the coarseness of the latter, by which the friction is greatly increased; they are however occasionally used. Those built up of separate blades are specially to be avoided.

An ingenious form of conveyor has been recently introduced from Germany, and consists of a light trough supported on steel springs and vibrated longitudinally by means of an eccentric in such a way as to shake the material from one end of the carrier to the other; the velocity of motion of the trough being less in the outward than the return stroke, so that the material is carried with it as it moves forward and slides over it in its return. It is obvious that the principle may also be applied to screening or sifting.

CHAPTER XXII.
THE EXTRACTION OF TANNING MATERIALS, AND THE MAKING OF EXTRACTS.

Leaching.—The material, having been reduced to a suitable state of fineness, is ready for extraction. This requires a considerable amount of time, as the tannin is contained in cells whose walls are of a wood-like substance (cellulose and lignine), through which the water diffuses but slowly. Hence, unless the material be very finely ground, a long soaking will be necessary before it becomes "spent." It should be the aim of the tanner to have his barks, etc. ground so finely that they may be extracted as rapidly as possible, and yet not be so fine that they settle to a compact mass in the leaches and so prevent circulation. Using the present methods of extraction on the large scale it is necessary to have the material only somewhat coarsely ground or crushed, so as to render its percolation practicable; but it is quite possible that in the near future some better mechanical means will be found of treating the dust and other excessively finely ground matter so as to bring about a very rapid extraction.

Up to perhaps 150 years ago, no attempt was made to leach the tanning material, which was simply strewed in layers between the hides, and moistened with water. Leaching originated in England, and was first applied merely to complete the exhaustion of the material which had been already used for layers; but the use of even weak liquors instead of water in the layers was found so advantageous, that new material was soon applied to make stronger infusions. The earliest form of leach was simply a pit with a perforated wooden "eye" or shaft down one corner, in which a pump could be placed to remove the liquor without being choked with solid matter. This was considerably improved by the addition of a perforated "false bottom" to the pit, with which the eye communicated. The perforations of the latter were found unnecessary, and it now serves simply for pumping through, or for the manipulation of a plug in a hole communicating with an underground "trunk" leading into a pump-well. The false-bottom is best made of laths about 1 inch thick and 2 inches wide, cut slanting so as to be wider on the upper than the lower surface, which makes the spaces between them less liable to choke. The laths are nailed on cross-battens with copper nails, which should be long enough to clinch, ¼-inch to ½-inch spaces being allowed between the laths according to the fineness of the ground material. The lattice-bottom should be in at least two sections, so as to allow of its easy removal for cleaning, and should rest on detached blocks, which are best nailed to the underside of the battens. A space of 2 inches to 3 inches below the false bottom will prove sufficient if it is cleared every time the pit is emptied, but not otherwise. Clearness from obstruction both below the bottom and between the laths themselves is very important in securing free running in the "press leach" system about to be described. A section of the latticed bottom is shown in Fig. 77. The laths are easily cut by employing a circular saw with a tilted table, and turning the board at each cut. No advantage is gained by planing them.

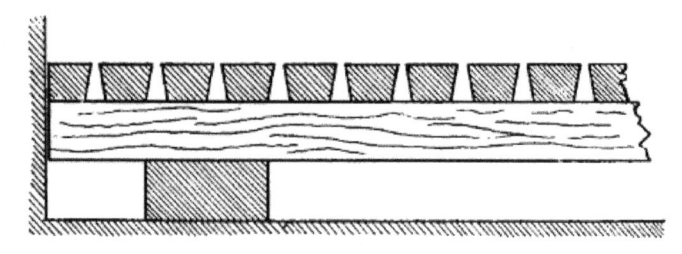

FIG. 77.—Section of Leach-Bottom.

As a strong liquor cannot be made by the use of a single leaching-pit, a series of pits are now always employed, and it is the leaching, systematic or otherwise, which determines how much of the total tannin will be thrown away and lost in the "spent tan." In the case of properly extracted materials the "spent tan" will not contain more than one per cent. of tanning matter, but the degree of extraction which is profitable is dependent on the tanning material employed and the class of leather to be produced.

The system of leaches now considered to be the best is based on the "continuous" process of extraction. Of its different forms, the "press-leach" is the simplest and in most cases is all that is required.

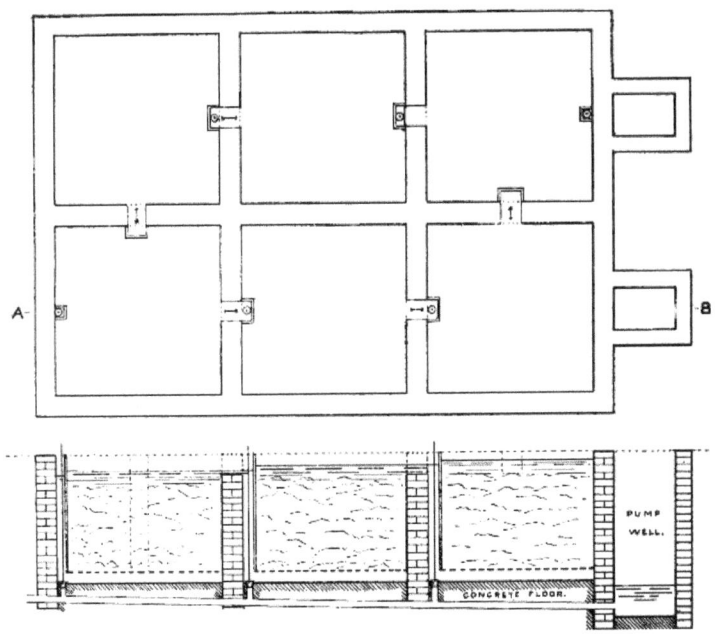

FIG. 78.—Plan and Section of Battery of Press-Leaches.

A plan and vertical section of the leaches is shown in Fig. 78. Assuming that the leaches have been working for some time and that the liquor in the strongest leach has been run off to the tan-pits, or in the case of manufacturing extracts to the decolorising tanks or evaporator, the last vat in the series is now filled with water or spent liquor, which may be heated by steam if desired, and this water, which completes the exhaustion of the material in this vat, forces the liquor forward in the whole series, so that it gets stronger and stronger as it passes from vat to vat. The very weak liquor remaining in the last vat is now pumped into a spare pit, or on to the next stronger vat, pressing the liquor forward as before; the vat is emptied of the spent material and refilled with new, and now becomes the head leach; and the strongest liquor is pressed on to it by running water or weak liquor on the weakest vat.

As regards the construction of such a "battery" of leaches, details will differ according to whether the usual English square sunk pits, or the American form of circular tub-leaches is employed. In the former case the vertical spouts connected with the space under the false bottoms are usually made of wood, like the old fashioned "eye," and placed at one side or corner of each pit, and connected with the top of the next pit by a short trough which may be open above or covered as preferred. Both eyes and cross troughs must be of ample size, so as not to check the running of the liquor, and for a set of six or eight leaches, the bottom of the cross trough should be at least 10 or 12 inches below the actual top of the leach, which should not be filled with material above that level. The object of this is to allow of a sufficient fall from the first to the last leach. Means must be provided for the temporary closing of the cross-trough between the vats which form the first and last leach. On a very small scale, this may be done with a plug; sliding wooden doors are convenient, but difficult to keep tight. A hinged or sliding door held against an indiarubber facing by a wedge or toggle-joint would seem a practicable device.

If round tub-leaches are employed, the vertical connection may be similarly made with a wooden trough, but copper tubes are almost essential for the cross connections. If a vertical copper eye in the centre of the leach be provided for boiling, or for emptying the leach (p. 334), it may be utilised for the upflow by connecting it with the cross pipe with a thin copper pipe of large diameter, which must be movable for the purpose of casting the leach. A joint like that of a stove-pipe will probably prove sufficiently tight, but if necessary may be made tighter by rolling an indiarubber ring over it.

Six to eight leaches is generally a sufficient number to form a press-leach "battery." If more are connected in one series it will usually be necessary to assist the circulation, either by pumping an intermediate leach, or by one or more pumps on the Holbrook system, in which a power-driven pump of simple construction is fitted in the eye of the leach. It is hardly necessary to note that the liquor must run *downward* through the leaches, and *up* through the vertical pipes, in order to prevent mixture of the weaker with the stronger liquor.

Several additions and modifications to the system have been made with a view of obviating the so-called "channel difficulty." There is always a fear on the part of some tanners that the liquid in the leaches may push the material aside and form channels through it, thus preventing proper extraction of the tanning matter. In the author's opinion this evil has been greatly exaggerated, as, unless the liquid be pumped from the leaches at a very rapid rate while they are in circulation, it is not at all easy for the formation of such channels to take place. In any case it can be entirely avoided by turning over the material in the leaches occasionally, so as to lighten it somewhat and rearrange it a little.

It may also be pointed out that the provision of a proper system for pressing or circulating leaches does not prevent their being pumped off as frequently as desired, though this is generally to be avoided, since when the leach is emptied of liquor, the material tends to settle into a compact mass, which is not easy to percolate, and which is liable to shrink from the sides of the pit, thus causing the very trouble which it is desired to avoid. There are some advantages in taking the first and strongest liquors off the material in a separate tank, and then finishing the exhaustion in the press leaches, since many materials swell, and pack tightly when they are first wetted, but on the whole the method hardly pays for its added cost.

The press-leach system as above described is well adapted for the requirements of tanners, as its first cost is very small in addition to that of the construction of the leaches themselves; it extracts the bark well, and saves much labour in pumping, and greatly lessens the tendency of the pumper to miss pits in the series, to save time, when the master's eye is not on him. Another advantage which is often important, is that when the leaches are full, much more than a single liquor can be run from the head-leach without pumping on; and similarly when they are run down to their lowest level, much more than a single liquor can be pumped on to the worst leach before it overflows. As the leaches flow slowly in comparison to the rate at which liquors can be pumped by a good steam pump, it is very advantageous to allow the pump to discharge into a liquor-tank raised to such a height that the liquor can be run from it into any leach at a suitable rate for the circulation, and it also enables liquors to be pumped without waiting till room has been found for them in the leaches. Similar tanks are very useful in running liquors for the yard, and especially for the suspenders in a sole-leather yard, enabling circulation to be kept up during the night, and at other times when the pumps are not running. They may also be used as filters for the suspender liquors by fitting them with false bottoms covered with a layer of nearly spent tan. The liquors may be distributed to the different pits and leaches by means of canvas hose-pipes, or, what is often more convenient, by overhead troughs, carefully levelled, and fitted with discharge valves where required. The latter are conveniently made of lead in a hemispherical form, resting on an indiarubber washer supported by a light brass casting, or a suitably turned rebate in a block of wood. (Cp. p. 457 and Fig. 79.) Such valves if good indiarubber is used, wear well, and are absolutely tight.

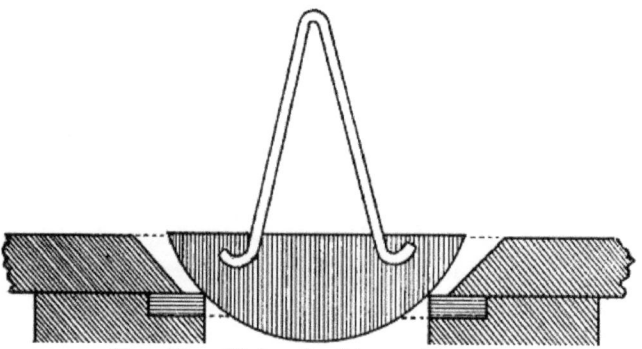

FIG. 79.—Valve for Liquor-Troughs.

In England, leaches are usually sunk in the ground, and are frequently made of brick and cement, or of large Yorkshire flagstones. Such leaches are somewhat costly but very durable. Square wooden pits, puddled outside with clay, are also used, and last well with cold, or even warm liquors, but will not stand direct steaming, the wood gradually bending, and allowing the clay to leak into the liquor, causing black stains. The large round vats of thick pine, and often holding 10 or 12 tons, which are generally used in the United States, stand boiling much better, and are frequently supported above a tramway or conveyor, into which the spent bark can be discharged through a manhole in the bottom. If this method is adopted, it must be remembered that bark, and indeed most other tanning materials, will not run through a hole like corn, but must be cast into it, so that unless the vat is of great depth, it is simpler and almost as easy to cast over the top. If the manhole is used, a central hole must be made in the false bottom, and this must be surmounted by a copper pipe made in sections of two or three feet, and reaching to the top of the leach. When the pit is to be emptied, the top length is removed, and the tan shovelled down the hole until the second length is reached, and the process repeated. The central pipe serves also for the circulation of the liquor when the pits are boiled, and may be used as the ascending pipe for circulating on the press-leach system.

The question of the influence of temperature on extraction is discussed on p. 344, but except where a pale colour is all important, it is generally profitable to use a moderate degree of heat in extraction. In the opinion of the writer (which is supported by a vast amount of careful experiment) only the nearly exhausted leaches should be heated, not merely to avoid discoloration, but to extract the maximum amount of tannin. In American tanneries the boiling is frequently done by copper coils fixed below the false bottoms of the vats, but such coils are very costly, and, where weak liquors only are to be heated, seem to present no advantage over a well-arranged system of heating by direct steam in which care is taken that dry steam only is used, and that all water condensed in steam pipes, and usually containing iron, is removed by effective steam-traps. If steam is blown into cold liquor through an open pipe, a very disagreeable rattling and vibration is produced, which is not only annoying, but is very injurious to the leaches. This evil may be avoided by the use of "silent boiling jets" on the principle of the steam-jet water-raiser; and, following a suggestion of the writer, these jets may be used at the same time to circulate the water through the tanning material of the nearly exhausted vat, and so wash out the last traces of tan. The simplest way to accomplish this is to lower the boiling jet, directed upwards, and connected with a movable steam-pipe, into the eye of the leach (which is preferably central) so that the heated water flows over its top, and percolates downwards through the material to be washed. Two forms of these boiling and mixing jets made by Messrs. Körting are shown in Figs. 80 and 81.

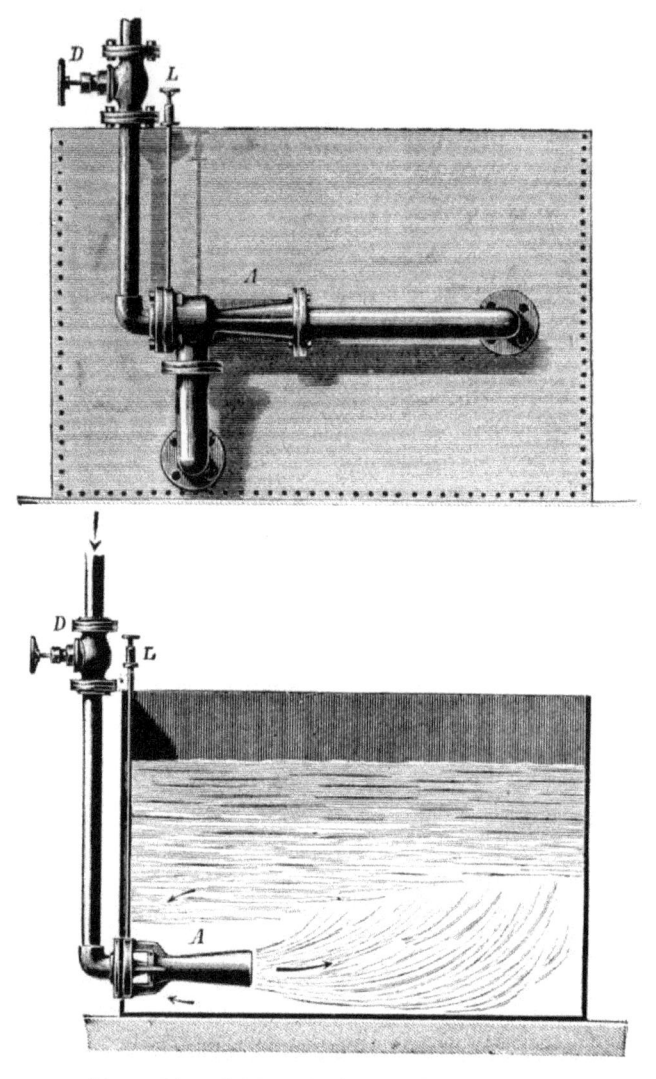

FIGS. 80 and 81.—Boiling and Mixing Jets.

Batteries of closed copper extractors, worked on the press system, and similar to those used in extracting sugar from beetroot, have frequently been advocated, but are very costly, and have no other advantage over open vats than that the liquor can be forced through the series by pressure, instead of circulating by gravity. No advantage is gained by boiling under pressure, since even boiling in open vats has been shown to destroy tannin, darken the colour of the liquor, and increase the amount of insolubles, and higher temperatures are still more injurious.

Heating the weakest leach in the press-leach system promotes the even circulation of the liquor, since the warm weak liquor is much lighter than the colder and stronger liquors in the forward leaches, and so floats on the top, and presses the stronger liquor uniformly downwards. It also has the advantage that the liquors are cooled before they are strong enough for the yard, while in tanneries where all the leaches are heated, expensive tubular coolers are often employed. As the liquor cools, much of the colouring matters and reds dissolved in the hot liquor separate, and are filtered out by the tanning material, so that much brighter and lighter coloured liquors are obtained.

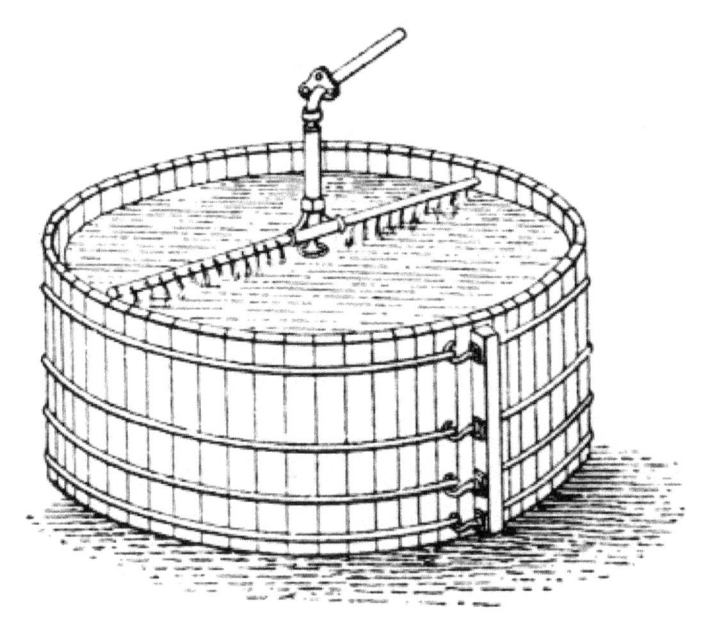

FIG. 82.—Sprinkler-Leach.

Sprinkler-Leaches, Fig. 82, were formerly used in many tanneries and extract factories, especially in the United States. They were introduced by Allen and Warren, and yield a liquor which is at first very strong, but which becomes very rapidly weaker as the running is continued. These leaches are similar in principle to the mashing-tub and sparger of the brewer, but the process is not well adapted for tanners' use, as the material is left too much exposed to the air, which is apt to cause oxidation and loss of tannin. It is also extremely difficult to completely exhaust the material without using an impracticably large volume of water. Sprinkler-leaches are arranged so as to spray the liquor, or water, on to the top of the solid material which is to be extracted at such a rate that it flows out just as rapidly as it flows into the vat. Some idea of the great amount of oxidation and consequent loss of tannin which takes place in this form of extractor may be obtained when it is remembered that this same method is now used for the destruction of sewage matter by spraying it on to beds of coke so that it may be mixed with as much air as possible before it is attacked by the bacteria of the coke-beds (see p. 473), and also to oxidise weak alcohol to acetic acid in the "quick vinegar process."

So far as extraction is concerned, there is no difference in principle between the methods adopted by the tanner and the extract manufacturer, though the latter usually works on a larger scale, and not unfrequently, in order to increase his output, or the gravity of his extract, employs a higher temperature. This is probably justified by practical considerations in the manufacture of extracts from very low-grade materials, such as oakwood, which only contains 2 to 3 per cent. of tanning matter, or even of chestnut wood which is somewhat stronger, but it is one of the causes why decoloration of the battery liquor is generally necessary.

Dried blood is chiefly used as the decolorising agent, but a paste of blood-albumen has been recently placed on the market, which is said to be free from several of the disadvantages attending the use of the crude material.

The liquor to be decolorised is run into a mixing vat fitted with a steam coil capable of raising the temperature of the liquid to at least 80° C., and usually provided with a simple rotary stirring gear. The liquor, as run into the mixing vat, must not have a temperature of more than 48° C. (118° F.) nor a strength of more than about 20° Bkr. (sp. gr. 1·020).

The blood or albumen dissolved in a little water, is added to the contents of the vat, which are then well mixed, and the temperature is raised to 70° C. when the albumen coagulates and carries down much of the colouring matter. The solution is run into another tank where the precipitate is allowed to settle, and the clear liquor is then drawn off for the evaporation. The muddy portion, about 8 inches in depth, is pumped through filter-presses (which can be cheaply constructed of wood), the clear liquors going to the evaporators and the press-cakes being dried for manure.

In addition to blood-albumen, several other substances, such as lead acetate (sugar of lead), salts of alumina, casein and other albuminous matters have been employed in the decoloration of extracts, but they are by no means so efficient as albumen.

Decolorising always causes a loss of tanning matter, some of this being carried down with the precipitated colouring matter; and is for this reason to be dispensed with whenever its use is not really necessary. It may often be avoided by careful extraction at moderate temperatures, and this is especially to be aimed at in the case of strong tanning materials, which easily yield battery liquors of much greater strength than 20° Bkr., and which thus, if they can be sent direct to the evaporator, save cost in evaporation, which is often an important consideration.

Another method which is frequently used to brighten the colour of extracts, is treatment with sulphurous acid. Dilute sulphurous acid solution may be used for extraction, but a more common method is to pass sulphur dioxide gas into the liquor before concentration. Sulphurous acid acts partly as a weak acid, in decomposing compounds of the tannins and colouring matters with bases, such as lime, iron, copper, but more actively by reducing oxygen compounds and preventing oxidation. Bleaching in this way does not actually destroy or remove the colouring matters, which are apt to reappear on exposure to the air, either in the liquor, or perhaps more often in the leather tanned with it, so that the gain is frequently more apparent than real. If present in any considerable quantities, sulphurous acid may also cause inconvenience by its swelling action on the pelt, but is mostly expelled in concentration.

Another process should perhaps also be mentioned here, though not strictly a means of bleaching. Several tanning materials, and notably quebracho and hemlock, contain large quantities of "difficultly soluble tannins," which render the liquors made from their extracts turbid on cooling. These tannins form soluble compounds with alkalis and with alkaline sulphites, in the latter case probably setting free the sulphurous acid and combining with the base. This has been taken advantage of in a recent patent in which quebracho and other extracts are rendered soluble by heating in closed vessels with bisulphites, sulphites, sulphides, or even caustic alkalis; and many "soluble quebracho extracts" made on this principle are now on the market. In this case, even where bisulphites are used, the greater part of the sulphurous acid, after serving its purpose in preventing oxidation, escapes in course of manufacture, and the extracts remain neutral or alkaline. There is no reason that such extracts should not prove serviceable in tanning, but it has recently been shown by Paessler that the alkaline tannin is not absorbed by neutral hide-powder, and it therefore may lead, not only to discrepancies in analysis, but in case of drum-tannage, where no acid is naturally present, to failure to utilise the whole of the tannin, though, when added to ordinary liquors, the acids contained in the latter will set free the tannins.

Lepetit, Dollfus, and Gansser, Eng. Pat. 8582, 1896.

The use of ferrocyanides has been suggested as a means of precipitating iron and copper present in extracts, and it may also be pointed out, that with many red-coloured tanning materials, such as hemlock and quebracho, the addition of small quantities of alum to the tanning liquor effects considerable improvement in colour, not only by precipitating a part of the difficultly soluble "reds," but by developing the yellow colour of certain colouring matters (quercetin, myricetin, etc.) which may be present. Such an addition does no harm in the case of soft leathers, but would probably be injurious in a sole-leather tannage.

The liquors, whether direct from the leaches or from the decolorising vats, must next be concentrated by evaporation (Chap. XXVI.), to sirupy consistency for liquid extracts, or until they will become nearly solid on cooling, if a solid extract is required. As has already been stated, the action of heat tends to cause a loss of tannin and a darkening of colour by decomposition and the formation of insoluble reds. To reduce this loss to a minimum, the weak liquors are evaporated with as little access of air and at as low a temperature as possible, and these conditions are best obtained by the use of steam-heated vacuum pans.

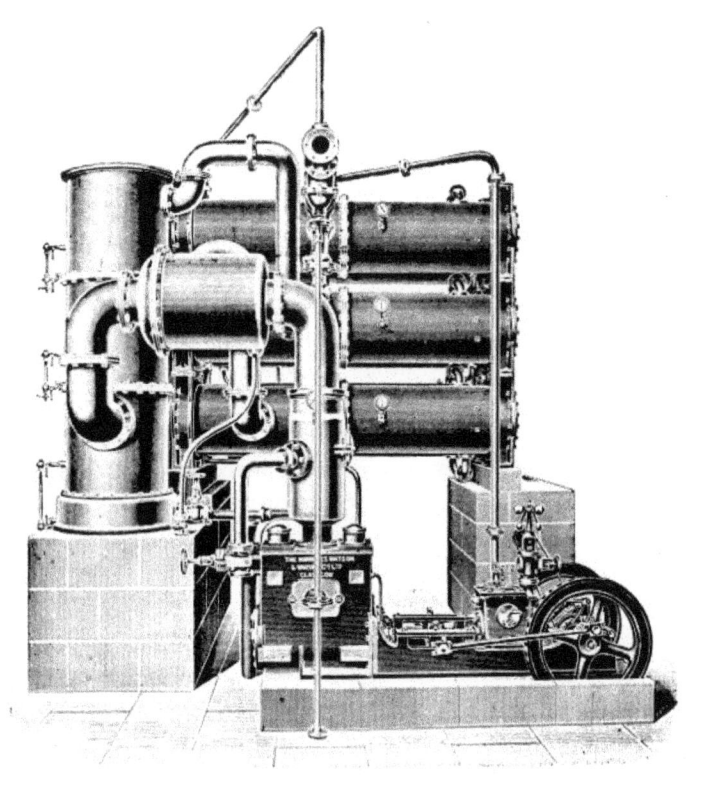

FIG. 83.—Triple-effect Yaryan Evaporator.

For concentration to gravities not exceeding 1·200, the Yaryan apparatus made by Mirrlees, Watson and Yaryan, of Glasgow, is that most employed. The general arrangement of a "triple effect" machine of this make is shown in Fig. 83, and the internal construction in Fig. 84. Each body consists of a strong casing into which steam is admitted, and which is traversed by copper tubes which terminate in a separating chamber at the further end, which is maintained at a low pressure by an air-pump. The liquid to be evaporated is admitted into the tubes, and is immediately converted into spray by the steam generated from it, and swept forward into the separating chamber, from which it is withdrawn by a pump. The steam before going to the air-pump (or, in the case of "multiple effects," to the next body), is passed through a "catch-all," to separate any spray still retained in the steam. Thus the liquor to be evaporated will pass through the entire apparatus in four or five minutes, and may be concentrated from a gravity of 1·02 or 1·03 to that of 1·20 without ever having been heated above 70° C. (160° F.). Unless fuel is very cheap, which is often the case where the spent tanning material can be used to raise steam, it is advisable to use a double or triple effect, in which the steam from the evaporation of the weakest liquor in the first body is used to heat the second, which is maintained at a lower vacuum, and so on. In this way the steam is made to do nearly double or triple duty. As the steam from the extract-liquors contains acids which corrode iron, it is necessary to have the casing as well as the tubes made of copper in all bodies in which it is employed. Iron must, in fact, be carefully avoided in every part of apparatus which comes in contact with extract-liquor or its vapour. Besides the Yaryan, there are several other evaporators in which the spray principle is more or less completely employed. The simplest of these consists in substituting for the heating coil of an ordinary vacuum-pan a copper steam-box traversed by vertical tubes open at both top and bottom. This is immersed in the liquid to be evaporated, which enters at the bottom of the tubes and is sprayed out at the top. Paul Neubäcker, of Danzig, constructs a pan on this principle with a very ingenious arrangement for the destruction of foam, which seems worth attention.

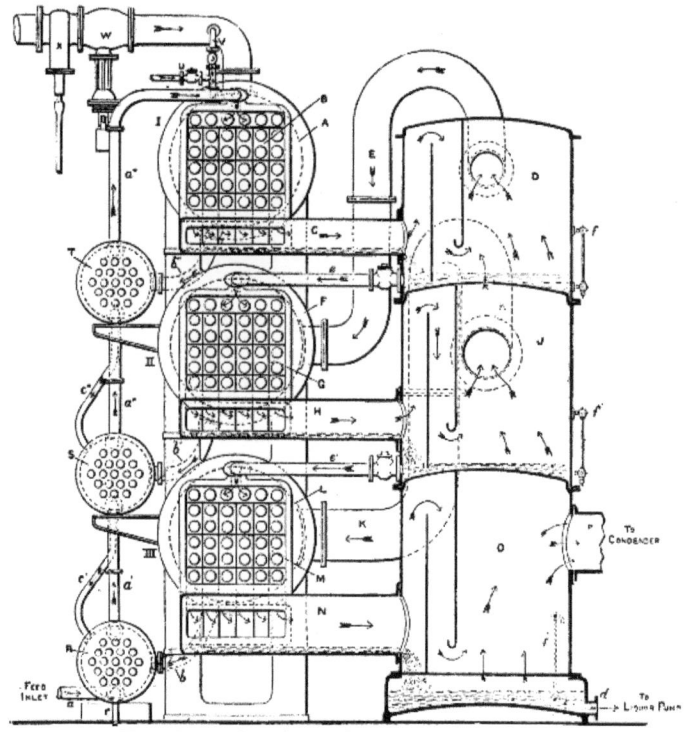

FIG. 84.—Section of Yaryan Evaporator.

Larger section (160 kB)

It is unfortunately impossible to carry the evaporation of extracts much further than sp. g. 1·2 with spray apparatus, as thicker liquors are apt to clog the tubes, which are then difficult to clean, so that even liquid extracts are usually finished in vacuum-pans of the ordinary type, which may also be arranged in multiple effect.

In the case of a solid extract, the evaporation must be carried on until it is as thick as can be run from the apparatus. To do this satisfactorily, stirrers must be provided to keep the extract in motion so long as it is in the pan. The thick, hot, liquid extract is then run into boxes lined with paper, or other suitable material, where it is allowed to cool and to solidify.

The pan for the final evaporation of solid extracts should be planned so as to allow of easy cleaning and ready access to its interior, so that if accidentally the evaporation is carried so far that the liquid will not run out, the clearing of the pan may be a comparatively easy matter. It is also important that the extract-exit should be of large size. Probably a broad and somewhat shallow pan, heated merely by a steam jacket, and fitted with rotating stirrers, is the most suitable.

The Use of Extracts in the Tannery.—One of the great attractions of extracts is that they save the trouble and cost of leaching, and as the extract manufacturer makes this his specialty, he can often extract more tanning matter from a material than the tanner who has no means of concentrating his weak liquors. The extract manufacturer also can employ methods of decoloration which would be impracticable to the tanner, and so enable the latter to obtain better colour than if he employed the raw material. By the use of extracts a tanner can strengthen weak liquors without trouble, and with definite quantities of materials; and by using extracts for this purpose the tanner is enabled to use up the weaker liquors of his leaches and so employ more water and obtain better extraction of his solid materials than if he used them alone. In the case of very weak materials like oakwood, the difficulties of making liquors of sufficient strength for tanning without evaporation are so great as to render such materials useless to the tanner for his own extraction, and their carriage even for short distances may amount to more than their total value. Even with much richer materials, extraction effects a saving if the carriage is a long one, as it rarely pays to import any material containing less than about 25 per cent. of tanning matter. Even when the strength of the natural material is considerable, as in the case of quebracho, extraction may be profitable if from its hardness, or other reasons, the material is difficult for the tanner to handle. For long voyages, and especially from the tropics, solid extracts are more suitable than liquid, as the expense of casks is saved, and the danger of fermentation is lessened. As it is impossible for the tanner to judge by appearance or consistency of the strength or value of extracts, they should always be bought and sold on the analysis of the particular shipment or parcel by a competent chemist. For directions for sampling see pp. 301, 475.

Extracts simply require to be dissolved in a suitable quantity of water or weak liquor at an appropriate temperature, to obtain a liquor of any required strength. Some extracts are completely soluble in cold water or liquor, but most dissolve better by the aid of heat. 40°-60° C. (100°-140° F.) is generally sufficient, and probably no advantage can arise from temperatures over 80° (180° F.). Boiling should be avoided, as it facilitates the formation of insoluble "reds" with consequent loss of tanning matter and darkening of colour. The extract should be run into the vat in a thin stream, and continuously plunged up; where large quantities of extract are to be dissolved, a mechanical agitator is advantageous. A "silent boiling jet" (p. 335) may be used, fitted into a small casing immersed in the liquor and open at both ends, and the extract run into the current it produces.

Whether in the manufacture of extracts, or for direct use in the tannery, the temperature at which tanning materials are extracted is of prime importance. It is a common mistake to assume that the largest amount of tannin is extracted by boiling. Mr. A. N. Palmer has pointed out that this is by no means the case, but that each material has an *optimum* temperature of extraction, at which more tannin is extracted than at any other; and the question has been carefully investigated by J. G. Parker and the author, with results which are given in the following tables. For many purposes the colouring matter which accompanies the tannin is a serious disadvantage, and it is usually most extracted at the higher temperatures; and on this account it is necessary for the tanner who will work his leaches economically to ascertain at what temperature he can extract the largest amount of tannin combined with no more colouring matter than he can permit to enter his leather. Most materials are satisfactorily extracted at 50°-60° C., but as a general rule it is best to begin cold or nearly so, and only raise the temperature as the extraction proceeds. The tables show the percentages of tanning matter, and the amount of colour (as measured by Lovibond's tintometer), obtained by extracting materials in a Procter's extractor (p. 306 and L.I.L.B., p. 102) so long as any colour or tannin could be obtained.

Journ. Soc. Ch. Ind., 1895, 635.

BELGIAN OAK BARK.

Temperature of Extraction.	Tanning Matters absorbed by Hide.	Soluble Non-tanning Matters.	Per cent. of Tannin on Maximum Yield.	Colour of ½ per cent. Solution in ½ inch Cell.		Per cent. of Colour on Maximum Yield.
				Red.	Yellow.	
°C.	per cent.	per cent.		deg.	deg.	
15	5·9	5·1	61·9	8·6	23·1	57·4
15-30	6·8	5·5	70·7	9·2	26·4	64·5
30-40	8·0	5·5	83·5	11·6	30·4	76·1
40-50	8·2	5·7	84·2	12·0	32·1	80·0
50-60	8·5	5·8	87·6	12·5	36·0	84·0
60-70	9·1	5·9	95·5	13·1	38·1	92·7

70-80	9·2	6·0	95·7	14·7	38·9	98·7
80-90	9·6	6·0	100·0	14·0	36·9	93·2
90-100	9·6	6·1	100·0	14·0	41·2	94·6
Boiled ½ hour	9·1	6·6	93·7	15·0	42·6	100·0

MYROBALANS.

Temperature of Extraction.	Tanning Matters.	Soluble Non-Tannins.	Per cent. of Tannin on Maximum Yield.	Colour of ½ per cent. Solution in ½ inch Cell.		Per cent. of Colour on Maximum Yield.
				Red.	Yellow.	
°C.	per cent.	per cent.		deg.	deg.	
15	28·5	12·8	79·2	1·09	4·9	97·4
15-30	30·1	13·6	83·6	1·00	4·1	82·5
30-40	32·3	14·3	89·8	1·03	4·1	82·7
40-50	33·5	13·6	93·0	1·03	4·2	84·4
50-60	34·7	14·4	96·4	1·03	4·4	87·6
60-70	34·8	14·4	96·6	1·03	4·5	89·3
70-80	34·9	14·9	96·8	1·10	4·7	94·1
80-90	35·1	15·0	97·4	1·16	4·8	96·7
90-100	36·	14·9	100·0	1·12	4·9	97·0

| Boiled | 35.4 | 15.5 | 98.1 | 1.26 | | 4.9 | 100.0 |

Smyrna Valonea.

Temperature of Extraction.	Tanning Matters.	Soluble Non-Tannins.	Per cent. of Tannin on Maximum Yield.	Colour of ½ per cent. Solution in ¼ inch Cell.			Per cent. of Colour on Maximum.
				Red.	Yellow.	Blue.	
°C.	per cent.	per cent.		deg.	deg.	deg.	
15	25.5	19.1	70.5	2.5	6.0	0.3	74.6
15-30	29.1	18.3	74.5	2.5	6.4	0.3	78.0
30-40	33.6	18.1	86.2	2.3	6.4	0.3	76.2
40-50	35.5	18.1	86.2	2.3	6.5	0.3	74.6
50-60	39.1	16.6	100.0	2.0	6.0	0.3	76.2
60-70	38.6	17.0	99.0	2.0	6.8	0.3	84.7
70-80	38.8	17.5	99.5	2.1	7.4	0.4	84.7
80-90	36.9	17.2	95.0	2.2	7.6	0.4	84.7
90-100	36.6	17.0	94.0	2.4	7.8	0.5	90.6
Boiled	35.4	17.6	90.6	3.0	8.2	0.6	100.0

GREEK VALONEA.

Temperature of Extraction.	Tanning Matters.	Soluble Non-Tannins.	Per cent. of Tannin on Maximum Yield.	Colour of ½ per cent. Solution in ½ inch Cell.			Per cent. of Colour in ½ per cent. of Tannin Solution.
				Red.	Yellow.	Blue.	
°C.	per cent.	per cent.		deg.	deg.	deg.	
15	16·0	13·0	64·0	2·9	6·3	0·3	67·3
15-30	18·1	12·6	72·4	3·0	6·6	0·3	70·0
30-40	21·1	12·0	84·4	2·8	6·5	0·3	68·0
40-50	23·6	12·1	94·4	2·4	6·6	0·3	65·9
50-60	24·8	12·4	99·2	2·7	7·0	0·4	71·6
60-70	25·0	12·6	100·0	2·9	7·3	0·5	75·8
70-80	24·6	12·5	98·4	3·1	7·9	0·6	82·3
80-90	24·0	12·5	96·0	3·4	8·1	0·6	85·8
90-100	23·6	12·6	94·4	3·5	8·8	0·7	92·0
Boiled	22·6	13·0	88·8	3·9	9·4	0·8	100·0

Natal Mimosa.

Temperature of Extraction.	Tanning Matters.	Soluble Non-Tannins.	Per cent. of Tannin on Maximum.	Colour of ½ per cent. Solution in ½ inch Cell.		Per cent. of Colour on Maximum.
				Red.	Yellow.	
°C.	per cent.	per cent.		deg.	deg.	
15	21·2	11·6	66·2	2·6	4·1	51·1
15-30	29·0	9·8	90·6	3·0	4·1	54·2
30-40	30·1	9·8	94·0	3·0	4·4	56·5
40-50	30·2	9·8	94·4	3·1	5·0	61·8
50-60	30·4	10·4	95·0	3·9	6·5	79·9
60-70	31·5	10·6	98·4	4·2	6·5	81·6
70-80	32·0	10·8	100·0	4·2	7·0	85·5
80-90	30·8	11·2	96·2	4·9	7·4	93·8
90-100	30·1	11·8	94·0	5·3	7·8	100·0
Boiled	29·4	12·0	91·8	5·7	7·2	98·4

Sumach.

Temperature of	Tanning Matters.	Soluble Non-Tannin	Per cent. of Tannin	Colour of ½ per cent. Solution in	Per cent. of Colour

Temperature of Extraction.	Tanning Matters.	Soluble Non-Tannins.	Per cent. of Tannin on Maximum.	Colour of ½ per cent. Solution in ½ inch Cell.		Per cent. of Colour on Maximum.
				Red.	Yellow.	
°C.	per cent.	per cent.		deg.	deg.	
15	14.2	17.8	70.0	1.6	5.4	63.6
15-30	17.6	18.1	86.7	1.4	4.3	51.8
30-40	18.5	18.1	91.1	1.3	4.4	51.8
40-50	20.1	18.5	99.0	1.4	4.4	52.9
50-60	20.3	19.1	100.0	1.5	4.7	56.5
60-70	19.0	19.4	93.6	1.7	5.6	66.6
70-80	18.0	19.9	89.1	1.9	6.2	72.8
80-90	16.9	21.1	83.2	2.3	6.8	82.7
90-100	16.6	22.3	81.7	2.6	7.0	87.7
Boiled	15.2	24.0	74.8	3.3	7.7	100.0

QUEBRACHO WOOD.

Temperature of Extraction.	Tanning Matters.	Soluble Non-Tannins.	Per cent. of Tannin on Maximum.	Colour of ½ per cent. Solution in ½ inch Cell.		Per cent. of Colour on Maximum.
				Red.	Yellow.	
°C.	per cent.	per		deg.	deg.	

		cent.		.		
15	7·6	2·2	35·0	8·9	14·1	71·3
15-30	10·1	2·4	46·5	6·4	10·7	68·7
30-40	11·8	2·4	54·4	5·9	9·6	65·2
40-50	15·1	2·4	69·5	5·3	8·4	60·0
50-60	16·5	2·4	76·0	5·4	8·5	60·4
60-70	17·4	2·4	80·0	5·6	8·2	59·9
70-80	19·1	2·7	88·0	6·4	8·6	67·4
80-90	21·7	3·0	100·0	6·4	9·4	74·3
90-100	19·5	3·0	89·8	6·6	9·8	100·0

MANGROVE BARK (*Ceriops*).

Temperature of Extraction.	Tanning Matters.	Soluble Non-Tannins.	Per cent. of Tannin on Maximum.	Colour of ½ per cent. Solution in ½ inch Cell.		Per cent. of Colour on Maximum.
				Red.	Yellow.	
°C.	per cent.	per cent.		deg.	deg.	
15	13·0	10·4	61·6	14·2	20·8	64·7
15-30	16·1	10·4	76·3	16·1	21·7	69·8

Temperature of Extraction	Tanning Matters absorbed by Hide	Soluble Non-Tanning Matters	Per cent. of Tannin on Maximum Yield	Colour of ½ per cent. Solution in ½ inch Cell			Per cent. of Colour on Maximum Yield
				Red.	Yellow.	Total.	
°C.	per cent	per cent.		deg.	deg.	deg.	
30-40	17.4	12.5	82.4	15.8	23.0		71.7
40-50	18.5	11.4	87.7	16.5	33.5		73.8
50-60	20.3	10.3	96.2	16.0	23.4		72.8
60-70	20.0	11.4	94.7	17.5	31.2		90.0
70-80	20.4	11.2	96.7	16.5	28.3		82.8
80-90	21.1	10.8	100.0	15.4	24.6		73.8
90-100	20.2	11.4	95.7	23.0	34.1		100.0

CANAIGRE ROOT (three years old).

Effect of Different Temperatures.

Temperature of Extraction.	Tanning Matters absorbed by Hide.	Soluble Non-Tanning Matters.	Per cent. of Tannin on Maximum Yield.	Colour of ½ per cent. Solution in ½ inch Cell.			Per cent. of Colour on Maximum Yield.
				Red.	Yellow.	Total.	
°C.	per cent	per cent.		deg.	deg.	deg.	
15	21.1	13.0	78.7	1.6	4.1	5.9	41.5
15-30	26.2	12.5	85.6	1.6	3.8	4.4	38.0
30-40	28.1	12.5	91.8	1.4	3.7	5.1	35.9
40-50	30.5	13.1	99.6	2.1	4.2	6.3	44.3

50-60	30·6	13·6	100·0	2·4	4·8	7·2	50·7
60-70	27·2	14·1	88·8	2·5	5·0	7·5	52·7
70-80	26·4	14·6	86·2	2·8	6·1	8·9	62·6
80-90	23·2	14·8	75·8	3·1	6·9	10·0	70·4
90-100	22·8	14·8	74·5	4·3	7·4	11·7	82·4
Boiled ½ hour	19·2	12·3	62·7	5·6	8·6	14·2	100·0

CUBE GAMBIER.

Effect of Different Temperatures.

Temperature of Extraction.	Tanning Matters absorbed by Hide.	Soluble Non-Tanning Matters.	Per cent. of Tannin on Maximum Yield.	Colour of ½ per cent. Solution in ½ inch Cell.			Per cent. of Colour on Maximum Yield.
				Red.	Yellow.	Total.	
°C.	per cent.	per cent.		deg.	deg.		
15	46·8	21·8	78·0	2·5	7·8	10·3	57·2
15-30	48·8	21·0	81·3	1·7	8·0	9·7	54·9
30-40	50·2	22·0	83·7	1·7	8·6	10·3	57·2
40-50	51·9	23·0	86·5	1·7	8·8	10·5	58·3
50-60	51·	20·3	91·9	1·7	8·9	10·6	58·8

	1						
60-70	55·6	20·3	92·7	1·9	9·4	11·3	62·7
70-80	55·7	20·3	92·8	2·2	10·1	12·3	68·3
80-90	55·8	21·2	93·1	2·3	10·6	12·9	71·6
90-100	56·1	22·0	93·3	2·8	11·6	14·4	80·0
Boiled ½ hour	60·0	20·0	100·0	3·2	14·8	18·0	100·0

BLOCK GAMBIER.

Effect of Different Temperatures.

Temperature of Extraction.	Tanning Matters absorbed by Hide.	Soluble Non-Tanning Matters.	Per cent. of Tannin on Maximum Yield.	Colour of ½ per cent. Solution in ½ inch Cell.			Per cent. of Colour on Maximum Yield.
				Red.	Yellow.	Total.	
°C.	per cent.	per cent.		deg.	deg.		
15	30·1	27·4	50·1	2·6	8·1	10·7	33·5
15-30	34·8	26·2	69·6	2·4	8·0	10·4	34·0
30-40	40·8	27·2	81·6	2·0	9·0	11·0	55·0
40-50	44·8	27·6	89·6	2·4	9·8	12·2	61·0
50-60	46·8	27·8	93·6	2·4	10·1	12·5	62·5
60-70	47·	27·6	94·6	2·5	10·6	13·2	66·0

70-80	47.4 3	27.6	94.7	2.8	10.9	13.7	63.5
80-90	47.6	27.3	95.2	3.2	11.6	14.8	74.0
90-100	48.2	27.1	96.4	3.8	12.8	16.6	83.0
Boiled ½ hour	50.2	26.4	100.0	5.0	15.0	20.0	100.0

CHAPTER XXIII.
FATS, SOAPS, OILS AND WAXES.

Fats and oils constitute a large class of substances, of animal or vegetable origin, which may be solid, pasty or more or less viscous liquids, but which in the latter case are commonly known as "fixed" or fatty oils, to distinguish them from the volatile, or essential oils, which may be distilled without decomposition, and which are the source of most of the odours of plants, and of quite different chemical constitution. The term "oil" is also applied to various products of mineral origin, and especially to those derived from petroleum, on account of their similarity in appearance and physical properties to the fixed oils, though, chemically, they form a very distinct class. The waxes are another group somewhat closely allied to the fats; and there are certain fixed oils, such as sperm oil, which though very similar in appearance and properties to the fatty oils, are chemically members of the group of waxes.

As it is obvious that there is no chemical distinction between the fats and fatty oils, except that of melting-point, it will be convenient to treat them together; especially as what is a solid fat in one climate may be an oil in another. Palm and cocoa-nut oils are cases in point, as the first is buttery, and the second a hard fat in this country, though they are both liquid in tropical climates.

For more detailed information on the chemistry of fats and oils, the reader must be referred to the 'Leather Industries Laboratory Book,' sect. xviii., or to the larger manuals devoted specially to the subject by Lewkowitsch, Jean, and others, or the very excellent section on oils in Allen's 'Commercial Organic Analysis,' vol. ii.; but a few general facts must be recapitulated.

The true fats contain carbon, hydrogen and oxygen, but no nitrogen. They are all compounds of glycerin with organic acids which are generally termed "fatty acids," and which resemble in many of their characteristics the fats themselves. Glycerin is a very weak base, of the nature of an alcohol, and consequently, when a fat is heated with a solution of one of the caustic alkalis, the fatty acid combines with the latter, and the glycerin is set free. The salts thus formed are denominated "soaps." The reaction with stearin (glycerin stearate), the principal constituent of hard animal fats, is shown in the following equation.

| Stearin | Sodium | Sodium | Glycerin |

$$\underset{}{(C_{17}H_{35}CO.O)_3C_3H_5} + \underset{}{3NaOH} = \underset{\text{stearate}}{3C_{17}H_{35}CO.ONa} + \underset{}{C_3H_5(OH)_3.}$$
hydrate

If a soap is treated with an acid stronger than its own, the latter is set free, while the new acid combines with the base. The following equation, for instance, shows the action of hydrochloric acid on the stearic soap.

$$\underset{\text{Sodium Stearate}}{C_{17}H_{35}CO.ONa} + \underset{\text{Hydrochloric acid}}{HCl} = \underset{\text{Stearic acid}}{C_{17}H_{35}CO.OH} + \underset{\text{Sodium chloride}}{NaCl.}$$

If any soap be dissolved in hot water, and sufficient hydrochloric or sulphuric acid added to render the solution acid, the latter will turn first milky, and (if it be kept warm) the fatty acid will finally rise in an oily layer to the surface, which in many cases will harden, as it cools, to a solid mass. The amount of fatty acid in a soap may be roughly determined by weighing 25 grm., dissolving in 50 c.c. of boiling water, and adding excess of acid, and allowing the reaction to take place in a graduated cylinder, or a flask with a graduated neck, in a vessel of boiling water. When the fatty acid has risen to the top, its volume may be noted, and each c.c. may be roughly reckoned as $0·9$ grm. (For more detailed methods cp. L.I.L.B., Sect. XVII.).

Soaps are insoluble in strong caustic alkaline solutions, and therefore saponification (as the decomposition of fats by alkalis is called), does not readily take place in them, and for this reason the soap-boiler generally dilutes his caustic soda solutions to a strength not exceeding 18° Tw. (sp. gr. $1·090$) in gravity, and separates the soap at the end of the operation, by the addition of brine, in which it is insoluble. An easier method, and one which is often useful for the preparation of small quantities of special soaps for fat liquors and the like, is as follows. 10 lb. of a *good* caustic soda, free from common salt, is dissolved in 4 gallons of water, and 75 lb. of oil or fat is warmed to about 25° C. or just sufficiently to render it liquid, and the soda solution is added in a thin stream, with constant stirring, which must be continued until the mass becomes too pasty. It is now set aside in a warm place for at least twenty-four hours, during which saponification gradually takes place. For leather purposes, a neutral soap, with a slight excess of fat, is generally advantageous, so that the fat may be increased to 80 lb.; or, in place of this, the operation will be facilitated by the addition of 5 lb. of commercial oleic acid. If soft soap is desired, 14 lb. of caustic potash may be used in place of the 10 lb. of caustic soda. The hardness or softness of soaps varies to some extent with the fat used, but potash soaps are always much softer than the corresponding soda soaps. It is obvious that with soaps made in this way, all the glycerin remains mixed with the soap. If, on testing, the soap does not prove to be free from caustic, it may be re-melted, which will generally complete the reaction. Before attempting to work with large quantities, a laboratory experiment is desirable, using 10 grm. of soda in 40 c.c. of water, and 75 to 80 grm. of oil or fat. The neutrality or freedom of the soap from caustic alkali may be tested by touching a freshly cut surface with an alcoholic solution of phenolphthalein, which the least trace of caustic soda or potash will render pink.

Carpenter, 'Soap, Candles and Lubricants,' p. 144.

If solutions of soaps are mixed with those of salts of the heavy metals or of the alkaline earths, a mutual decomposition takes place, the acid of the salt combining with the alkali of the soap; and the fatty acid with the metallic base, to form a metallic soap. Most of these soaps are sticky masses, insoluble in water, but not unfrequently soluble in turpentine or petroleum spirit, if previously thoroughly dried, so that some of them have been applied to the production of varnish. Alumina soaps are occasionally used to thicken mineral oils, or render them more viscous. The general reaction of the stearin soap with calcium sulphate is shown in the following equation, though in practice it is sometimes more complex:

Stearin soap	Calcium sulphate		Sodium sulphate		Calcium stearate
$2C_{17}H_{35}CO.ONa$	+	$CaSO_4$	=	Na_2SO_4	+	$(C_{17}H_{35}CO.O)_2Ca$

This is the reaction which causes the curdling of soap by hard water, page 93.

True fats cannot be distilled alone without decomposition. When distilled in a current of steam, some undecomposed fat passes over, but the greater part is broken up into free fatty acid and glycerin; and hydrocarbons practically identical with mineral oils are also formed.

Fats and oils are insoluble in water, and in most cases only sparingly soluble in alcohol, but freely soluble in ether, petroleum spirit, benzene, and most other hydrocarbons, as well as in chloroform, carbon tetrachloride, and carbon disulphide. Petroleum spirit, often called benzine, is largely used for their extraction, and for de-greasing leather, and removing grease from clothes. In the laboratory, carbon disulphide, or carbon tetrachloride is to be preferred. Castor oil is an exception to the rule, owing to the large proportion of oxygen which it contains, being readily soluble in alcohol, and very sparingly in petroleum-spirit; and other oils, when oxidised, usually become more soluble in alcohol, and less so in hydrocarbons.

Oils vary much in their tendency to "dry," or become converted into solid or sticky resin-like substances. This tendency is greatest in some of the seed oils, and least in olive oil, and the oily part of animal fats (tallow oil, neatsfoot oil). Sperm oil, a "liquid wax," is also very free from this tendency, but all fish oils possess it in a greater or less degree. It is not due to evaporation, but to the absorption of oxygen by the fatty acid. The tendency to oxygen-absorption, and consequently to drying (and, in the case of leather-oils, to "spueing"), is measured analytically by the "iodine-value," the absorption of iodine being proportional to that of oxygen, while it is much more easily measured.

There are no simple tests by which the purity of oils can be determined, though in a few cases the presence of particular oils can be detected. The mixing and adulteration of oils is now a science, and those who practise it are well acquainted with the customary tests, and take care to adjust their mixtures so as to meet them. Taste and smell however, with practice, often furnish useful indications.

Natural oils and fats are invariably mixtures of the glycerides of several fatty acids, and their qualities depend simply on the character of these glycerides and the proportions in which they are mixed. The fatty acids form several groups, differing in their degree of "saturation," or, inversely, in their power of taking up oxygen, on which their tendency to drying depends. The members of any one of these groups resemble each other strongly, differing principally in melting points, density, and other physical characteristics.

A "saturated" compound is one, the constituents of which are present in such proportions that all the combining affinities of each are satisfied by the others. Iodine value, see L.I.L.B., p. 176, and Jour. Soc. Ch. Ind., 1902, p. 454.

Saturated Fatty Acids.—Stearic acid, $C_{18}H_{35}O.OH$, and palmitic acid, $C_{16}H_{31}O.OH$, are the most important. At ordinary temperatures they are hard, white, crystalline bodies, and melt at 69° and 62° C. respectively. They do not, under ordinary circumstances, absorb any oxygen, nor iodine, and are very little liable to chemical change. Together with oleic acid, they are the principal acids of tallow and other animal fats, while palmitic acid and some lower members of the same group are more common in vegetable oils. Free stearic acid is an important constituent of the "distilled stearines" used in currying; while "oleostearine" consists mainly of the neutral fats or glycerides of stearic and palmitic acids.

Liquid Fatty Acids, Non-drying.—Of these, oleic acid is much the most common and important; its glyceride, olein, forming the liquid part of animal fats, and being the principal constituent of vegetable non-drying oils. Olive oil consists almost entirely of olein, with a little palmitin. The formula of oleic acid is $C_{18}H_{33}O.OH$, thus differing from stearic acid in having two less atoms of hydrogen. The "bonds" or affinities corresponding to these two atoms are linked together, but can separate, and attach two atoms of iodine, bromine, or chlorine, or one of oxygen. The iodine-value of pure olein is 83·9 (that is, 100 grm. absorb 83·9 grm. iodine); and that of olive oil about 83. Any oil with a higher "iodine-value" than olein must contain drying oils, though a lower value does not necessarily indicate their absence, if palmitin or other saturated acids are also present.

Unsaturated Liquid Fatty Acids.—Of these there are several groups, differing in their degree of saturation, and also probably in their structure. Their glycerides, together with olein, and sometimes palmitin, are the constituents of the seed oils, the drying tendency of which depends on their proportion of unsaturated acids, and the particular group to which they belong. The fish oils contain a peculiar group of unsaturated acids, together with olein, and usually stearin and palmitin, like the other animal fats. Linolenic acid, $C_{18}H_{29}O.OH$, one of the acids of linseed oil, has six hydrogen atoms less than stearic acid, and therefore three double linkings, and will take up six atoms of iodine. Its theoretical iodine-value is 274, while linseed oil itself often has an iodine-value exceeding 180. The iodine-value of cod-liver oil is sometimes nearly as high. Both oils therefore contain other acids less unsaturated than linolenic.

The "spueing" of leather is due to the absorption of oxygen and consequent resinification of the oils, and therefore all drying oils, however pure, are capable of producing it, though some are more liable to do so than others (cp. pp. 363, 365, 366, 368, 390).

Linolenic acid, and probably other allied acids, become converted by absorption of oxygen into solid varnish-like substances, which are important to the tanner, as furnishing the principal constituents of japans for leather. The unsaturated acids of fish oils seldom give hard varnishes, though menhaden oil (page 367) is sometimes used as paint-oil for outside work.

Most fats are liable to become rancid by exposure to the air, acquiring a disagreeable taste and smell, and an acid reaction from the liberation of the fatty acids. The changes which take place are somewhat complex.

The fatty acid of castor oil is of peculiar constitution, being an oleic acid in which one of the hydrogen-atoms is replaced by a "hydroxyl" or OH group. The solubility of castor oil in alcohol has already been alluded to. It does not dry, and is an excellent oil for lubricating heavy machinery. It is sometimes adulterated with "blown" oils, which are made from non-drying, or slightly drying seed oils, like cotton-seed or rape, by blowing air through them in a warmed condition. Under this treatment they increase greatly in viscosity and density and in their solubility in alcohol, but do not acquire the other valuable properties of genuine castor oil.

The "foots" or sediments which oils deposit on standing, sometimes consist of animal or vegetable fibres, or mucilage combined with water, but often are simply the harder fats, stearin, palmitin, etc., which crystallise from the oil on cooling. In this case they are re-dissolved on warming the oil. Such oils, which like neatsfoot and tallow oils become turbid in cold weather, are styled "tender."

NON-DRYING FATS AND OILS.

Tallow (Fr. *Suif*; Ger. *Talg*) is the fat of various mammalia, principally of the ox and sheep, but occasionally also of the goat. The mixed fat obtained from all parts of the carcass is known as "rendered tallow," while that obtained from the region of the kidneys (suet) is harder. A substance commonly referred to as "pressed tallow" or "oleo-stearine" is obtained by pressing ordinary tallow, in cloths, in the hydraulic press. The more liquid portion which is expressed is tallow-oil, the finer qualities of which are used in making margarine. Oleo-stearine must not be confounded with the "distilled stearine," obtained from Yorkshire grease by distillation and pressure (page 359), nor with candlemakers' "stearine," which is a mixture of free stearic and palmitic acids.

Pure tallow is white and tasteless, but much of that sold is yellowish and of a disagreeable, slightly rancid flavour. Mutton tallow is usually harder and whiter than that of beef. Goat tallow has a characteristic odour, as have the recovered stearines and other waste greases from glue-works. Buck tallow, which is particularly hard, has now been largely replaced by oleo-stearine.

Beef tallow melts at about 40° C.; mutton tallow at 45°.

In chemical composition, tallow consists chiefly of a mixture of the triglycerides of palmitic, stearic and oleic acids; its hardness diminishing with the increase of the last.

Tallow should, when melted, be perfectly clear, turbidity indicating the presence of water or other foreign matters, due either to carelessness in the manufacture or, possibly, adulteration. Traces of phosphate of lime, or fragments of animal tissue, may be present as accidental impurities; lime, on the other hand, is sometimes added to thicken the tallow and enable it to retain more water; starch, china clay, whiting, heavy spar, etc., are also occasionally employed. Tallow has been not infrequently adulterated with the distilled fatty acids from wool grease. When this is the case, crystals of cholesterol (see L.I.L.B., p. 181) may be detected by examination of the unsaponifiable matter of the mixture under a microscope. It would also give the tallow an unusually high "acid-value."

Methods for the proximate analysis of tallow are given in the 'Laboratory Book,' pp. 189 *et seq.*

The fats produced by the boiling of fleshings for glue, and by the pressing of sheep-skins, are of the nature of soft tallows. If the fleshings are delimed with acid, and boiled fresh, the grease is generally of good colour, and with little unpleasant odour, but contains traces of free fatty acids derived from the decomposition of the lime-soaps. If the fleshings have been dried and the lime carbonated, the grease will generally be brown, and more or less rancid; but the lime-soaps are not decomposed, unless the "scutch" or refuse be treated with acid, when a further yield of grease is obtained. The grease from sheep-skins is generally somewhat brown, and often smells of the volatile acids and other constituents of the tan-liquors, especially if larch bark has been used. These greases are usually much improved in appearance and odour, if well washed by boiling or steaming on water, or by blowing a mixture of air and steam through them, or sometimes even by mere heating to a sufficient temperature to evaporate the water and drive off the volatile matters. By allowing the grease to cool slowly, so as to favour crystallisation, till it is of a soupy consistency, and then pumping through a filter press with woollen cloths, the more liquid is separated easily from a more solid portion, and both may in many cases be used in leather manufacture, the tallow for currying, and the oil in place of neatsfoot oil.

Horse-fat, and especially that from the fatty portions of the neck (Ger. *Kammfett*), as well as various other animal greases, are used in the manufacture of leather. They differ from tallow chiefly in that they have a lower melting-point, and contain more olein in proportion to the stearin and palmitin than true tallow, and are consequently somewhat softer. Though often almost white, these greases are sometimes darkened in colour by the products of putrefying animal matter, but this does not, as a rule, interfere with the oil being used for leather dressing. They are usually so cheap that they are but little adulterated; means of determining their purity are, however, given in L.I.L.B., p. 191.

Neatsfoot oil is a yellowish, nearly odourless oil, of bland taste, which is largely employed in the dressing of calf-kid. It has a similar composition to tallow oil and the other oils obtained by subjecting the soft animal fats to great pressure at a low temperature. It is often adulterated with bone oil, lard oil and cotton-seed oil, and occasionally with mineral oil and recovered wool-grease.

As neatsfoot oil is somewhat costly, curriers may with advantage often use ordinary animal greases (horse-fat, etc.) after they have had the harder tallow extracted by cooling and pressure, the product thus obtained being, chemically, the same as neatsfoot oil, and in every respect as suitable, while it is much less liable to adulteration.

The true neatsfoot oil is prepared by boiling the feet of cattle, and sometimes of sheep and horses, with water, and skimming off and clarifying the oil which is thus obtained.

The physical and chemical characteristics of this oil are described in L.I.L.B., p. 192.

Wool-Fat (Fr. *Suint, oesype*; Ger. *Wollschweissfett*) is a grease of high specific gravity, exsuded from the sebaceous glands of the sheep, together with organic salts of potassium. It is obtained by extracting wool with solvents; or by washing with alkaline solutions, from which it is recovered by precipitation with acid, and subsequent hot-pressing of the "magma," or, more recently, by evaporating the scouring liquor to small bulk, and centrifugating. Wool-fat is characterised by its low percentage of glycerides, the fatty acids which it contains being mainly combined with higher alcohols (bodies of alcoholic structure, but of a waxlike consistency), and chemically it is rather a wax than a true fat. Among the alcohols which it contains is included a marked percentage of cholesterol and isocholesterol. It is difficultly saponifiable, requiring to be heated to 105-110° C. with alcoholic potash under pressure; and even then about 44 per cent. of alcohols remain, which are incapable of further saponification. Care must therefore be taken not to assume that unsaponifiable matter in greases which may contain wool-fat is necessarily mineral oil. For details of analysis see L.I.L.B., p. 194.

Pure wool-fat is nearly white, of salve-like consistency and very slight smell, with a density of 0·973 at 15° C. Crude wool-fat is yellow or brown, with an unpleasant and very persistent characteristic smell. Both the pure and the crude wool-fat have an extraordinary power of emulsifying with water, which makes them very valuable as substitutes for dégras in stuffing greases. Lanoline (and several other preparations under different names) are mixtures of purified wool-fat and water, of which lanoline contains about 22 per cent.

"Yorkshire grease" differs from crude wool-fat, in being recovered from the waters employed in scouring woollen cloths, as well as wool, and hence contains the free fatty acids of soaps used in scouring, as well as the "oleines," etc., used in oiling the cloth, and although it often contains much wool-fat, it is occasionally destitute of this substance.

Holden Fat consists of ordinary wool-grease mixed with fish oil, and is used either as a substitute for, or in admixture with dégras (q. v.).

Distilled Wool Grease is produced by distilling crude Yorkshire grease with steam. Most of the glycerides are broken up, but many of the free fatty acids, alcohols and waxes distil over unchanged, though a considerable part is decomposed into volatile hydrocarbons strongly resembling mineral oils. The distillate is separated by cooling and pressure into a liquid "oleine" and a solid "stearine." The latter forms a very valuable stuffing-grease which, in England, largely takes the place of the "oleo-stearine" used in the United States—with which, however, it must not be confounded.

Distilled Stearine, prepared as above described, is a pale yellow-to-brown fat, which varies in hardness and in its melting point according to the conditions of its preparation. It has a characteristic odour which is very persistent, and it consists largely of free stearic and palmitic acids; most of the liquid hydrocarbons formed by distillation being removed with the "oleine."

Olive Oil (Fr. *Huile d'olive*; Ger. *Olivenoel, Baumoel*) finds extensive use in leather dressing, and especially in the manufacture of "fat-liquors" (pp. 217, 240). It is extracted from the fruit of the olive tree by pressure, and of late years from the residues by extraction with carbon disulphide. Although it chemically resembles tallow and lard oils very strongly, its adulteration with these substances may usually be detected, at any rate roughly, by the taste and odour of the oil. It is principally characterised, from a chemical point of view, by containing the glyceride of palmitic but not that of stearic acid, and by having a much larger proportion of olein to solid glycerides than most of the non-drying animal oils. At low temperatures, olive oil solidifies to a product which can be separated by pressure into a solid tallow-like fat, and a fluid oil consisting essentially of tri-olein.

Olive oil is the type of a non-drying vegetable oil, but though it does not thicken materially on exposure, it becomes rancid somewhat rapidly, and is thus rendered unsuitable for lubrication. Unless the acidity is excessive it does not appear to spoil the oil for leather manufacture, and for some purposes is actually an advantage as aiding emulsification. Free acids in oils may be removed by shaking with sodium carbonate solution.

Olive oil always contains some free acid; which is of importance in the preparation of fat-liquors, as it facilitates the production of an emulsion. This quality may be increased by the addition, when necessary, of a little oleic acid.

Olive oil is frequently adulterated with other vegetable oils. Probably the most useful criterion is the iodine-value, which is raised by the addition of any seed oil. Examination in the refractometer also affords useful indications. Cotton-seed, sesame and arachis (earth-nut) oils are the most frequent adulterants of the better qualities, and in many cases may be recognised by special tests.

Castor Oil (Fr. *Huile de ricin*; Ger. *Ricinusoel*) is the oil expressed from the seeds of *Ricinus communis*, and is a transparent, colourless or pale yellowish liquid, having a faint odour and a disagreeable taste. At a low temperature it thickens and deposits slightly, and at -18° C. it solidifies to a pale yellow mass.

Castor oil is distinguished from all other natural fixed oils by its high density (0·960 to 0·964) and viscosity, and by its solubility in alcohol and its insolubility in petroleum ether. Genuine castor oil is completely soluble in an equal volume of absolute alcohol, or in four times its volume of "rectified spirit" at the ordinary temperature. It is practically insoluble in petroleum ether, but can dissolve an equal measure of that liquid.

For the purpose of the leather manufacturer, the ordinary hot-pressed oil, such as is used for lubricating machinery, is quite as good as the more costly cold-pressed oil which is used for medicinal purposes. It is generally imported in tins holding about 40 lb. of oil. Castor oil, and castor-oil soap made as described on p. 352, are very good for fat-liquors, seeming to interfere with dyeing and glazing less than most other oils. Boots oiled with castor oil may be blacked at once, and will take a good polish.

The only oils which are usually mixed with castor oil are "blown" or oxidised seed oils, or resin oil. Any other oils would so seriously lower the specific gravity as to render their use impracticable. For the detection and estimation of these the 'Laboratory Book' should be consulted, or if fuller details are required the reader is referred to Benedikt and Lewkowitsch's 'Oils, Fats and Waxes,' or to Allen's 'Commercial Organic Analysis,' vol. ii.

Sulphonated castor oil or Turkey-red oil is now largely used for "fat-liquoring," for which it was probably first employed by the author, about 1890. This material—which must be carefully distinguished from the olive oil preparation which is also used for dyeing cotton a Turkey-red colour—is made by treating castor oil with one-quarter of its weight of strong sulphuric acid (specific gravity 1·8), adding the latter in very small quantities at a time, and taking care that the temperature of the mixture at no time exceeds 35° C. The mixture is then allowed to stand for twenty-four hours, with occasional stirring, and is washed with its own volume of water, allowed to stand until the water has all separated, and the oil is then syphoned off. If desired, the oil may be further washed once or twice with a solution of strong brine, but this is of doubtful advantage, and should in no case be excessive. The washed oil is finally neutralised by the cautious addition of one-hundredth of its volume of strong ammonia solution (sp. gr. 0·880).

If properly prepared, Turkey-red oil (sulphonated castor oil) will, when *largely* diluted with water, bear the addition of ammonia to alkaline reaction without showing any turbidity even on standing several hours. If a turbidity is produced, it indicates that the castor oil used was impure and contained some oil rich in stearin.

The alcohol test described on p. 360 may also be applied, as the oily layer will be entirely soluble if castor oil alone was used in the preparation of the red oil.

Turkey-red oil usually contains about 50 per cent. of fatty acids (Allen).

Linseed Oil (Fr. *Huile de lin*; Ger. *Leinoel*) is used by leather manufacturers in the preparation of the japan for making "patent leather," and to some extent also in currying, for oiling off levants and moroccos, though for these purposes it has been largely superseded by mineral oils. It is obtained from the seeds of the flax plant, *Linum usitatissimum*, chiefly grown in Russia and India. The Russian oil is usually mixed with the oil from hemp to the extent of about 20 per cent., while that from India, being grown as a mixed crop with mustard and rape, is never perfectly pure. The Baltic oil is considered best for japans, and is improved by storing for a considerable time in tanks in a warm place.

When obtained by cold pressure of the seeds, linseed oil is of a bright yellow colour; if a higher temperature be used in the extraction the oil is more or less brown, and tastes much more acrid. On exposure to air, linseed oil turns easily rancid, absorbs oxygen, and if spread out in a sufficiently thin film it dries to a neutral substance (linoxyn), which is insoluble in ether. This property is the one on which the chief value of linseed and other "drying oils" depends.

Linseed oil is chiefly adulterated with other seed oils, cottonseed being the most often used for this purpose, though menhaden and various other fish oils are occasionally employed. As the density of raw linseed oil varies between 0·932 and 0·936 at 15° C., the addition of other seed oils or of mineral oil would cause an appreciable lowering of this figure, whilst rosin or rosin oil would raise it. A judicious admixture of both mineral and rosin oils would give a product of normal density. Fish oils can be detected by their characteristic smell, especially on warming.

Various methods have been proposed for judging the quality of linseed oil, but none of them are perfectly satisfactory. The best oil is that which dries the most perfectly; but the rapidity of the drying, and the consistency of the dried product, are most important factors which must also be taken into account. The iodine-valve, which is a measure of the drying power, should not fall much below 180.

A satisfactory practical test, recommended by Allen, consists in mixing the oil with three times its weight of genuine white lead, and covering a perfectly clean glass surface with the paint. An exactly similar experiment is made simultaneously with a standard sample of linseed oil, and the rates of drying and the characters of the coating of paint compared.

Commercial Organic Analysis, ii. p. 122.

J. Muter has simplified this test by merely flooding a plate of glass with the oil and then exposing it to a temperature of 38° C. (100° F.) in a good current of air. The time required for drying, to such an extent that the coating will not come off when lightly touched, is noted, and compared with standard samples of oil. By applying the finger at intervals to different parts of the film surface the progress of the drying can be readily observed.

Kathreiner states that this method is a useful test for fish and liver oils, those which dry most rapidly being specially liable to "spue."

Boiled Oils.—Its capacity for thus drying is much enhanced by heating, with addition of "driers," to a temperature of 130° C. and upwards, while passing a current of air through the oil and then increasing the temperature until the oil begins to effervesce ("boil"). Large quantities of linseed oil are now treated in this way for use in the arts. The driers used are metallic salts, principally those of lead and manganese, which apparently act as oxygen-carriers. Litharge was formerly most commonly used, but its place has been taken to a considerable extent by acetate, borate and resinate of manganese. From 1 to 2 per cent. of either litharge or manganese borate may be used, though less quantities produce a marked effect. Apparently litharge gives the most rapid drying, and manganese a much paler colour. Linseed oil is usually darkened by boiling, and increases both in actual weight and in specific gravity and viscosity. The chemical reactions which take place in boiling are not well understood, but it is in the main a process of oxidation and polymerisation, perhaps accompanied by the formation of anhydrides of the fatty acids, and a portion of the drier remains dissolved in the boiled oil. These driers may be detected by boiling an ounce or so of the oil with dilute hydrochloric acid, allowing the mixture to separate into two layers and then syphoning off the lower into another vessel, and testing for metals (lead, manganese, zinc) or acids (boric, oxalic, etc.).

Cp. F. H. Thorpe, Abst. Jour. Soc. Chem. Ind., 1890, 628, from Technology, Quart., iii. pp. 9-16.

Black japan for patent leathers is made by boiling linseed oil, without blowing air through it, for at least seven or eight hours, with Prussian blue, or with oxides of iron. The japan is brownish rather than blue in colour, and it is probable that the Prussian blue serves merely as a source of iron oxide, which acts both as a colouring matter and a drier. Other driers, such as litharge, are sometimes added, and for coloured enamels other pigments are substituted for the Prussian blue.

Cotton-seed Oil (Fr. *Huile de coton*; Ger. *Cottonoel or Baumwollensamenoel*) is now expressed in enormous quantities in the United States, on the continent of Europe and in Great Britain. The crude oil contains a very characteristic colouring matter which, though naturally ruby red, is sometimes so intense as to make the oil appear to be nearly black. This colouring matter causes the oil to produce stains, and is therefore removed by a process of refining, and a product of a straw- or golden-yellow colour is thus obtained. The refining is usually effected by shaking the crude oil with a cold 5 per cent. solution of caustic soda, using about ten times as much oil as soda solution.

Cotton-seed oil is, on account of its price, seldom or never adulterated, but is itself frequently employed as an adulterant of olive and neatsfoot oils. It is a semi-drying oil, and unsuitable for most purposes in leather manufacture. For a description of its characteristic properties, both chemical and physical, the reader is referred to Lewkowitsch's 'Oils, Fats and Waxes,' or to Allen's 'Commercial Organic Analysis,' vol. ii.

Sesamé Oil (Fr. *Huile de sésamé*; Ger. *Sesamoel*; Teel oil, Gingeli oil) is another seed oil, usually of paler colour than cotton-seed oil, but resembling it in having scarcely any odour, and possessing a bland and agreeable, though not very characteristic taste. It is often used as an adulterant of olive oil.

Sesamé oil is a non-drying oil, which does not easily turn rancid. When present in other oils, it may be detected by agitating 10 c.c. of the sample with 5 c.c. of concentrated hydrochloric acid in which $0 \cdot 1$ grm. of white sugar has previously been dissolved. After shaking together for at least ten minutes, the oil and acid are allowed to separate, when, if sesamé oil be present, the acid layer will have a marked rose colour, the intensity of which increases with the amount of sesamé oil in the sample (Baudouin's test).

Sesamé oil is largely used in India for oiling tanned sheep- and goat-skins ("Persians"), and has the characteristic property of being assimilable in large quantities by leather without the latter appearing oily. East India tanned skins often contain 25 and even 30 per cent. The oil is applied to them in the wet condition before they are dried. It is easily detected in the oils extracted from these skins by Baudouin's test. The oil seems well adapted for many purposes in leather manufacture.

Cod Oil (Fr. *Huile de morue*; Ger. *Leberthran*) is by far the most important oil used by leather manufacturers, and is obtained from the liver of the common cod-fish (*Gadus Morrhua*) and several other members of the genus *Gadus*. The chief seats of the cod fishery are the coasts and banks of Newfoundland, Nova Scotia, the Gulf of St. Lawrence, the coasts of Norway, Denmark and Germany, the Dogger Bank in the North Sea, and the shores of Alaska in the Pacific Ocean.

The oil was formerly obtained by keeping the livers of the fish in large wooden vats, stirring constantly until so much decomposition has taken place that the cells containing the oil burst, and the oil thus released rises to the surface and is skimmed off with wooden ladles. The crude oil is allowed to deposit any suspended matters by sedimentation in a tank, and is then poured into casks ready for sale. The "brown oil" so often used by tanners is obtained by boiling the solid matter left after extracting the oil as above in iron tanks until all the water has evaporated; the oil thus liberated is then strained off, clarified and put into barrels.

The purer qualities of cod-liver oil are now obtained by boiling the livers with water and skimming off the oil which rises to the surface. Three grades are on the market at the present time: medicinal, or ordinary bright; an inferior "light brown"; and "dark-brown," or "tanners' oil." It is probable that these steam-extracted oils are much more liable to "spue" than those extracted by the old method at a higher temperature, since Eitner has shown that seal oils extracted at a low temperature spue badly, but lose the tendency if heated for some time to 250-300° C.

Gerber, 1880, p. 244.

Genuine cod oil, as suitable for use in leather manufacture, is always more or less brown in colour, of specific gravity about 0·928, and refractive index 1·482. At present prices it can only be adulterated with other fish oils, rosin, or mineral oil, or with water, gelatine or mucilage. Of these, rosin oil and petroleum are the most frequently employed in sophistication.

An inferior variety of oil, known as "coast cod," made from the livers of various fish, such as ling, haddock and hake, is also sold, but, as it is frequently mixed with oils from other fish refuse, it has a very poor reputation.

Cod oil, together with most of the other oils obtained from fish livers, has the property of producing an intense reddish-violet colour when a drop of strong sulphuric acid is dropped upon ten or fifteen drops of the oil contained in a white porcelain tray or saucer. The reaction succeeds still better, if, instead of the oil itself, its solution in chloroform, carbon disulphide or tetrachloride is employed. This test, although very useful for the detection of liver oils when they are present in oils of a totally different character, such as rape or olive oils, does not in any way indicate whether a sample of fish oil is pure or otherwise. A very similar reaction is given by cholesterol which is present in wool-fat.

Shark-liver Oil (Fr. *Huile de requin*; Ger. *Haifischthran*) is obtained from the liver of the "basking shark," or "ice-shark," chiefly caught off the coast of Norway; but the livers of the dog-fish and several allied fish also are sometimes substituted.

Shark oil has been employed in tanneries as a substitute for cod-liver oil, but, according to Lewkowitsch, and to Allen, it is no longer employed in England. From its pale colour it is probably principally used to improve the appearance of darker oils. According to Eitner, its use causes leather to "spue" badly if not previously heated.

Gerber, 1886, p. 266.

Shark oil is characterised by the very notable proportion of unsaponifiable matter which it contains, which is of the same character as that of sperm oil, and not easily removed from its soap solution by petroleum ether. It gives a strong violet-blue coloration with concentrated sulphuric acid, the reaction being even more marked than with cod-liver oil itself, and of a bluer violet.

Whale Oil (Fr. *Huile de baleine*; Ger. *Wallfischthran*) is extracted from the blubber of various species of whale, and often contains traces of spermaceti, the substance which characterises the oil from the sperm whale. This yields on saponification higher alcohols, which are found in the unsaponifiable matter; but in ordinary whale oil the total unsaponifiable matter seldom exceeds 1½ to 2 per cent. Whale oil is largely used on the Continent for "chamoising" (q.v.), and is consequently a constituent of dégras. It is much less oxidisable than cod.

Seal oil (Fr. *Huile de phoque*; Ger. *Robbenthran*) is obtained from the common rough-coated seal, abundant in the Arctic regions. It bears a strong resemblance to both whale and fish oils, and cannot be detected in mixtures of these. The Swedish "Dreikronenthran" (Three Crown Oil) is a mixture of seal and fish oils. As genuine seal oil only contains about ½ per cent. of unsaponifiable matter, its adulteration by mineral or resin oils may be detected by a determination of the matter extracted by petroleum ether after saponification of the oil (see L.I.L.B., p. 178).

There is no simple test by which the purity or otherwise of a sample of oil can be determined, as the dealers know all the best tests which the users could try, and fake up their oils accordingly. For instance, if petroleum is to be added surreptitiously to a cod oil, the decrease in specific gravity of the oil caused by this addition would be corrected by the addition of a suitable quantity of soap or rosin oil, which would scarcely affect the colour, taste or odour of the sample. The only satisfactory method of detecting adulteration is to submit the oil to a complete chemical examination, and for this purpose L.I.L.B., pp. 156 *et seq.*, or the larger text-books already named may be suitably consulted.

Menhaden Oil (Porgie oil, Straits oil) is largely used in certain districts as an adulterant or substitute for cod oil. It is obtained from the *Alosa Brevoordia* or *menhaden*, a member of the herring family, about a foot long. The fish is caught on the Atlantic coast of America, and is so plentiful that it is very doubtful whether cod oil can ever compete with it successfully in price. The fish are boiled in steam kettles, the oil squeezed by hydraulic presses, clarified, and bleached by exposing to the sun in shallow glass-covered tanks. An inferior grade is known as "Bank oil." Menhaden oil is chiefly characterised by its very high "specific temperature reaction" (L.I.L.B., p. 169) which is about 306. It is not a good leather-oil, being very liable to "spue."

Many other varieties of oil extracted from the bodies, and not from the livers only of fishes, are classed as *fish oils*. Menhaden oil is the principal of these; but Japanese oil, sardine and herring oils, and those obtained from the refuse of other fish are scarcely less important, though as they are derived from such different sources it is not possible to quote any definite characteristics by which they may be identified when mixed with more valuable oils. They are usually very liable to "spue."

Fish Tallow, which, according to Eitner, is a good and cheap substitute for dégras, is the solid grease obtained from different kinds of fish oil by subjecting them to a low temperature and separating the matter which is thus precipitated, or (as in China and Japan) the solid fat which is extracted at the same time as the oil from the body of the fish. Formerly fish tallow was only obtained from and with Japanese train oil, but it is now obtained from whale blubber. This latter yields a very pure form of the tallow, which does not need any rectification; but the Japanese variety, which is obtained from fish of the herring family, contains a sort of fish glue, which greatly deteriorates the quality of the product. By careful purification, however, this glutinous matter may be removed, and the refined product has none of the leather-staining properties so characteristic of the crude tallow. The refined tallow is sold in square flat cakes, melts at 42° and is not quite so stiff as ox tallow.

Dégras and *Sod Oil* are products of chamois-leather dressing (p. 378) which are used in currying. Skins are treated with marine animal oils, and submitted to oxidation, and the surplus and partially altered oil is recovered.

In the French method, whale and seal oils as well as liver oils are used, and the oxidation is slow and gradual, and the residual oil, being liquid, is recovered by pressure, and constitutes *moellon*, of which the first pressing (*première torse*) is the best. This is never sold for currying in its original purity; but, mixed with further quantities of fish oils, tallows, and sometimes woolfat, it constitutes the ordinary dégras of commerce. The additions, though they lower the value, are not to be considered as simple adulterations, since the *moellon* alone would be less suitable for the purpose. After removal of as much oil as is possible by dipping in hot water and pressing, a further quantity is recovered by washing with solutions of potash or soda, from which it is separated by addition of acid, and constitutes a lower quality of degras. The *moellon* is of such value as a currying material, that factories are run in which chamoising is carried on solely for its production, the skins being oiled and oxidised repeatedly, till reduced to rags.

In the English method of chamoising, liver oils are almost exclusively used, and the oxidation is much more rapid and intense, the skins being packed in boxes or piled, and allowed to heat. The product obtained in this way is much more viscous, and can only be recovered by scouring with alkalis; and the product, recovered with acid, constitutes sod oil. In many English factories, a modified method is now adopted, and a product recovered by pressure, which scarcely differs from *moellon*.

An important peculiarity of dégras and sod oil is its ready emulsification with water, which from its mode of preparation, it always naturally contains, and which should be present in a good dégras to the extent of not less than 20 per cent. Such a mixture, containing water, is a sort of natural fat-liquor and is absorbed much more perfectly by the skins than an oil alone. Sod oils, however, are frequently "evaporated," or deprived of water by heating above 100°, with the object not only of effecting a fancied improvement, but of getting rid more completely of the sulphuric acid which the water is apt to contain. This makes them more homogeneous, and consequently much darker in colour. It is not easy to neutralise the acid in an aqueous sod oil by direct addition of alkali; possibly ammonia is best adapted for the purpose; or a suggestion, I think due to Eitner, may be adopted, of incorporating a small quantity of a suitable soap. In any case, very complete mixture is required. If the sulphuric acid used in recovery has been insufficient for complete neutralisation of the alkali, the dégras or sod oil will naturally contain soaps, and sometimes also free alkali. Free acid and free alkali are both injurious to leather, the former if anything the more so, darkening the colour, and even rendering the leather tender. When dégras is used in mixture with other fats, care should be taken not to raise the temperature of the mixture so high as to drive off the water, to which a good deal of its special efficacy is due.

The chemical changes which take place during the chamoising process are as yet incompletely understood. A large proportion of the glycerine is dehydrated during the "heating," forming acrolein (acrylic aldehyde), to the action of which it is very possible that the actual conversion of the skin into leather is due, while the fatty acids also undergo oxidation. Dégras therefore always contains considerable quantities of oxidised fatty acids, which are sometimes associated with nitrogenous products from the skins, and which are soluble in alcohol, but insoluble in petroleum ether. To these products Simand gave the name of *Degrasbildner* (dégras-former, Fr. *dégragène*), and it has been considered a measure of the quality of the degras, but its exact value and function is rather doubtful. According to Simand, a genuine dégras should contain not less than 15 to 20 per cent. of the dégras-former as estimated by his method, calculated on the dry oil, and a smaller percentage is also present in the original fish oils. (For method of estimation see L.I.L.B., p. 182).

As the process of dégras manufacture is obviously mainly one of oxidation, many attempts have been made to produce it by direct oxidation of fish oils, without the agency of skins, both by blowing air through the oil, and by addition of oxidising agents such as nitric acid. Eitner states that such oxidised oils are more liable to "spue" than the original oils, as they already contain large quantities of resinised products; but this is certainly not true of all artificial dégras, some of which answers its purpose perfectly as a currying material, though it is very probably justified in other cases. Of course the methods of successful manufacturers are kept as profound secrets.

Dégras and sod oil, when deprived of water, are dark and viscous oils, of high specific gravity (0·945-0·955), and therefore heavier than the oils which have been employed in their manufacture.

WAXES, as has already been stated, differ in their chemical character from true fats, in that their fatty acids, which are mostly of high molecular weight, are combined, not with glycerine, but with alcohols, also of high molecular weight and of wax-like consistency. Most waxes are solid bodies of high melting point, but some oils, especially sperm and bottlenose oils, are chemically liquid waxes; woolfat contains a considerable proportion of waxes; and many marine oils, such for instance as shark-liver oil (p. 366), contain waxes in smaller quantity in mixture with true fatty oils.

Sperm Oil (Fr. *Huile de cachalot*; Ger. *Spermacetioel, Walratoel*) is obtained from the sperm whale, an inhabitant of the Antarctic seas. "Arctic sperm" (Ger. *Doeglingthran*) is a very similar oil obtained from the "Bottlenose whale." These oils are very fluid, do not dry, and are excellent lubricating oils for light machinery, and also good lamp oils. They contain little if any glycerides, and about 40 per cent. of unsaponifiable solid alcohols, which are soluble in ethyl-alcohol, and must not be confused with ordinary unsaponifiable mineral oils, which are frequently used as adulterants in mixture with fatty oils to adjust gravity and the "saponification value." Mineral oils are liquid, and insoluble in alcohol. Sperm oil is the lightest of ordinary oils, its gravity being only about 0·880 at 15° C. From its price it is particularly liable to sophistication. It is used in leather manufacture in the finishing of some fine leathers, and sometimes as a constituent of fat-liquors. Spermaceti, a wax also obtained from the sperm whale, is an occasional constituent of leather polishes.

Beeswax (Fr. *Cire des abeilles*; Ger. *Bienenwachs*) is one of the most important waxes for the leather-dresser. As is well known, it is obtained from the honeycomb of the ordinary bee. It is a yellowish solid body, fairly plastic when fresh, and of "waxy" feel. At low temperatures it is brittle and of fine granular texture, and when pure is almost tasteless. It is often bleached by repeated melting and exposure to sunlight. As wax always contains a considerable amount of pollen it may be identified when in admixture with other substances by means of the microscope.

Beeswax is almost insoluble in cold alcohol, but boiling alcohol dissolves out the contained cerotic acid, which crystallises from it on cooling. Wax is saponified by alcoholic potash, but the resulting myricyl alcohol (about 54 per cent.) is not capable of further saponification.

Beeswax is frequently adulterated. Water and mineral matters (ochre, gypsum, etc.) also flour, starch, tallow, stearic acid, Japan wax, carnaüba wax, resin and paraffin-wax are among the substances most commonly used in its sophistication.

The detection of these, and especially of the other waxes, is so difficult that it will not be described here. The reader is, however, referred to Benedikt and Lewkowitsch's 'Oils, Fats and Waxes,' for further information.

Carnaüba Wax (Fr. *Cire de carnauba*; Ger. *Cearenwachs, Carnaubawachs*) has come largely into use recently owing to the advent of the coloured leather shoe. As it is a very hard wax it has become very popular with boot polish makers, its low price being also in its favour. Carnaüba wax is an exudation from the leaves of *Copernica cerifera*, a palm indigenous to Brazil, and is, on this account, often known as Brazilian wax. It is difficult to saponify, and with different experimenters has yielded very varied results on analysis; it is generally agreed, however, that it is a complicated mixture of several of the higher alcohols and acids.

Japan Wax is not a true wax, but a fat consisting of glycerides. It is a pale yellow, hard, waxy substance obtained from the berries of a sumach (*Rhus succedanea*, etc.). At ordinary temperatures its specific gravity is exactly that of water, and it melts at 56° C. Any admixture with other fats would lower the melting point, but japan wax is often adulterated with 15 to 30 per cent. of water. It is chiefly valuable to leather dressers as a substitute for beeswax on account of its lower price.

VOLATILE OR ESSENTIAL OILS.

These oils are distinguished from those described in the previous section in that they are capable of distillation without undergoing any serious amount of decomposition. They occur to some considerable extent in nature, but those of most importance to the leather trade are produced by the decomposition of more complicated materials.

Birch Oil is by far the most important of this class of oils so far as the leather-dresser is concerned, since it is the substance which gives to "Russian leather" its characteristic odour.

The oil is obtained by destructive distillation, and the process by which the peasants conduct this is one of the rudest that can be imagined. A cauldron is filled with dry birch-bark, closed, and heated over a fire. The vapours which are evolved are carried, by means of a pipe, to another vessel which is buried in the ground, and are there condensed. The dark-brown liquid (birch-tar) is allowed to cool, and the liquor which rises to the surface skimmed off. The tar is sometimes distilled, and an oil is thus obtained which does not give the true birch-oil scent very strongly though occasionally sold as a refined oil. The true odorous substance is evidently of very high boiling point and remains mainly in the tar.

The birch tar is almost entirely used for giving leathers a "Russian" odour, for although it smells somewhat strongly of tarry products, the oils causing this smell are far more volatile than the birch scent itself, and therefore disappear on storing the leather a short time. Tar obtained from various species of pine is sometimes substituted for birch tar, but it may readily be distinguished from the latter by the odour and the difference in the specific gravity. Birch tar has a specific gravity of $0 \cdot 925$ to $0 \cdot 945$, whilst fir tar has one of $1 \cdot 02$ to $1 \cdot 05$; thus the former floats on water while the latter sinks if it be entirely free from enclosed air. Fir tar, too, gives up a yellow colouring matter to water shaken up with it, while birch tar leaves the water colourless. Birch tar has a distinctly acid reaction, and must not be kept in iron vessels. (See p. 251).

The leaves and twigs of American black birch when distilled with water or steam, yield an oil which is practically identical with that of *Gaultheria procumbens* (wintergreen), and consists almost entirely of methyl salicylate. It is clarified, and to some extent decolorised, by filtration through woollen blankets and redistillation. A ton of brushwood is said to yield about four pounds of oil. This oil has quite a different odour to that of the real Russian oil, and cannot be used in the scenting of "Russia" leather. Sandalwood oil with a little black birch or wintergreen oil is sometimes employed for scenting small fancy articles and bears considerable resemblance to the true "Russia" leather odour. Black birch, aniseed, sassafras and various other essential oils are occasionally used in small quantities as preservatives, and to cover disagreeable odour in blood-seasonings, cements and other products used in the leather trade. The methods employed for their detection and estimation do not, however, come within the scope of a work such as the present one. Most essential oils have considerable power as antiseptics, and in preventing mildew and the attacks of insects.

Mineral Oils and Waxes.

This class of bodies is totally different in chemical constitution from the true oils and waxes, containing neither glycerides, fatty acids nor alcohols, but consisting of carbon and hydrogen only, approximately in the proportion of one atom of the former to two of the latter. They occur in underground lakes, from which they are obtained by springs or borings; or in shales, from which they are separated by distillation. It is commonly supposed that they have been formed, at some remote period of the earth's history, by the decomposition of animal and vegetable matters, at a high temperature and under great pressure.

Oils from wells or springs are technically called "petroleum oils," those from shale, "paraffin" oils, but chemically, there is no definite distinction.

The mineral oils and waxes are largely capable of being distilled without decomposition, but if heated to high temperatures, are readily "cracked" or broken up into simpler and generally more volatile compounds—a fact which is employed in the production of gas, and the utilisation of some of the heavier products.

They differ greatly in their gravity and boiling-point, but not much in their ultimate composition, consisting largely of saturated or nearly saturated hydrocarbons (cp. p. 354), and hence are little liable to oxidation, and acted on by few chemical reagents. From their constitution they are of course unsaponifiable, and in this way can be separated from fats and oils with which they have been mixed. (For particulars of the method see L.I.L.B., p. 178.)

The heavier mineral oils are a good deal used in mixture with other oils and fats, for stuffing leathers, those of a specific gravity of 0·880-0·900 being usually most suitable. They are quite incapable of "spueing," and are useful in lessening that tendency in other oils with which they are mixed. They have not, however, the same affinity for the leather fibre as some of the true oils, and are to a certain slight extent volatile, and should generally be used in mixture, rather than alone.

Most mineral oils, when held so that a strong light (daylight or electric light rich in ultra-violet rays) falls upon them, show a green or violet fluorescence or "bloom." This is very persistent, even when the oil is mixed with a large volume of other oils, and is often relied upon as a means of detecting them when used as adulterants. The test is, however, not infallible, since the effect is due to impurities which may be removed by purification, or masked by the addition of such substances as nitrobenzene or nitronaphthalene, and it also occurs in the hydrocarbon products produced in the distillation by steam of animal oils, and is occasionally seen to some extent even in oils which have not undergone distillation.

Vaseline and Vaseline Oil are the most viscous and densest of the petroleum oil products. They probably differ from the solid paraffins in chemical constitution, though their ultimate composition is almost the same. They are often useful constituents of stuffing greases.

Paraffin Wax consists of a mixture of hydrocarbons similar in chemical constitution to the paraffin and petroleum oils, but of higher boiling point, and solid at ordinary temperatures. Its hydrocarbons are mostly saturated, and hence very stable bodies, and little liable to oxidation. They are completely unsaponifiable, and unaffected by boiling with alcoholic potash, and in most cases by boiling with strong sulphuric acid, by which they may be separated from animal and vegetable waxes or fats with which they have been mixed. They are quite incapable of resinising by oxidation, or of causing "spueing" in leather. They are soluble in petroleum spirit, carbon disulphide and most of the ordinary solvents of fats, but insoluble in alcohol.

Paraffin wax separates from the liquid oils by crystallisation on cooling, and the remaining liquid which adheres is removed by hydraulic pressing, as in the case of tallow. The hardness and melting point vary according to the extent to which the pressing has been carried, and the temperature at which it has been done. The paraffins of higher melting point are as a rule the more costly.

Pure paraffin wax is a white, more or less hard and brittle substance which does not melt so easily as ordinary fats, and is on this account used in stuffing certain kinds of leather, hardening the stuffing grease, and making the leather feel less oily. When melted, paraffin wax forms a thin liquid, more resembling an ordinary petroleum lamp oil than the viscous vaselines and leather oils. On ignition it burns with a bright somewhat smoky flame, and leaves no ash behind. It is found on analysis when mixed with other waxes or oils in the "unsaponifiable matter" (see L.I.L.B., p. 178).

Ozokerit is a natural paraffin material used for the manufacture of cerasin candles, which sometimes occurs in the vicinity of petroleum springs, especially in Galicia. It is of pale yellow colour when pure, and has then a melting point of about 70° C. Its chief impurities are petroleum oils, water and clay. These are removed by melting the ozokerit, decanting off the clear oil, and filtering it through fine animal charcoal. If liquid oils are present the material is treated with alkali or with strong sulphuric acid, and is pressed before filtering through charcoal. The refined product is termed "cerasin," and is of a more waxy and less crystalline texture than ordinary paraffin wax.

The Resin Oils are derived from resins, and *mainly* from colophony or common pine rosin, by destructive distillation. Their specific gravity ranges from 0·96 to 0·99, but their chemical composition is very imperfectly understood, and appears to be by no means constant. Like the mineral oils they are "unsaponifiable," but often contain small amounts of soap-forming material (resin acids).

The detection and estimation of resin oils is often a matter of considerable difficulty, but further particulars on this point will be found in L.I.L.B., p. 180. From their cheapness, they are considerably employed as adulterants of other oils, and their high gravity makes them convenient to adjust the gravity of mineral oils when used for this purpose, as the latter are usually lighter than the fatty oils. As currying oils, they are not particularly suitable, though often employed in stuffing picker bands, and other heavily greased leathers. They have considerable antiseptic powers, and for this reason are useful in leather greases, preventing heating, and checking mildews.

Resin itself is occasionally used as an addition to stuffing greases, and is said to increase the waterproofness of the leather, and to give it a drier feel. In mixture with about half its weight of paraffin wax, and with a little grease if necessary to soften the mixture, it is often used in waterproofing mixtures, which can be made to melt at 50° to 60° C. Leather will bear immersion in the melted mixture without scalding if thoroughly dried in a hot stove at a temperature of not less than 50° C. before dipping. Any great increase of the proportion of paraffin wax causes the rosin to separate. Rosin consists mainly of free acids which easily combine with alkalies and alkaline carbonates in boiling. It is hence largely used in the manufacture of soaps on account of its cheapness, and to render them more soluble in water. The rosin acids are not so strong as many of the fatty acids, and rosin soaps are therefore somewhat strongly alkaline. Rosin soap, precipitated among the ground paper pulp in the rag engine, by addition of alum or sulphate of alumina, is largely used as a sizing for common papers.

CHAPTER XXIV.
OIL TANNAGES, AND THE USE OF OILS AND FATS IN CURRYING.

The conversion of skin into leather by the agency of oils and fats is probably one of the most primitive methods, and is used in different ways suited to the skins and fats which are available, by savage races in all quarters of the globe. In its simplest form, it consists merely in oiling or greasing the wet skin, and kneading and stretching it as it slowly loses moisture and absorbs the fat. Under these conditions, the fibres become coated with a greasy layer, which prevents their adherence after they are once separated by the mechanical treatment. At the same time some chemical change takes place in the fibre itself, which has a part in its conversion into leather varying in importance according to the method and fat employed, and of which the chemistry will be best discussed after some slight sketch has been given of the methods themselves.

The most complete sort of oil-leather is that produced by "chamoising," or oil-dressing with marine oils, a process applied to the ordinary "chamois" or "wash-leathers" (now made from the flesh-split or "lining" of the sheep-skin), and to the manufacture of "buff-leather" for military purposes. The process varies somewhat according to the character of the leather, but the manufacture of the common wash-leather may be taken as a type. For this purpose the sheep-splits are freed from the loose and fatty middle layer (p. 51) by "frizing" with a sharp knife on a beam similar to that used for fleshing (Fig. 30, p. 147), but much more steeply inclined. The process is rather one of scraping than cutting, and was originally adopted to remove the grain from the deer-skins which were largely used for glove-leathers, since oil-dressing does not easily penetrate a skin with the grain surface intact. The fleshes are usually delimed by drenching, but removal of fat is unimportant. After being well drained, they are "stocked" for some time with sawdust till they become partially dry and porous, the common "faller" stocks shown in Fig. 22, p. 116, being generally employed. During the stocking, care must be taken that the goods are not overheated by the friction produced. When the skins have become opaque from the inclusion of air between the fibres, they are, according to the Continental method, shaken out and oiled on the table, and after folding into bundles, are put back in the stocks. In England, the oil is usually added to them during the stocking, in small quantities, which become rapidly and evenly distributed by the motion of the skins. In England, cod oil is almost exclusively employed, but on the Continent, a considerable proportion of seal and whale oils is used. As the goods are apt to heat, not only from friction, but from the oxidation of the oils employed, they are removed from the stocks at intervals, and allowed to cool, usually hung on hooks exposed to the air. In France this exposure to the air is much more considerable than in England, the skins being hung for eight or twelve hours after each stocking. The drying rooms are kept moderately warm, and a good deal of oxidation of the oil takes place in them, which materially affects the character of the product, and especially of the residual oil or dégras, which is afterwards squeezed out of the skins and used for currying (p. 368). Great care is required to prevent any parts of the skins becoming dry before they are completely saturated by the oil, which causes hard and transparent patches which the oil will not afterwards penetrate. After each exposure to the air, the skins are oiled on the table and returned to the stocks. The stocking has to be continued for many hours, even for wash-leather; and as it proceeds, the skins lose the smell of limed skin, and acquire a peculiar mustard-like odour from the volatile products of oxidation of the oils. When the skins are completely saturated, they are, according to the English method, packed in boxes, and allowed to heat spontaneously by oxidation of the oils, during which great care is required, especially at the outset, that the heat does not rise so high as to destroy the skins. To prevent this, they are removed at intervals from the boxes and spread on the floor to cool, and then re-packed, and this treatment is continued until the oxidation is complete, and the skins cease to heat. During the heating, large quantities of volatile and very pungent products are given off, and especially acrolein (acrylic aldehyde, from the dehydration of the glycerine), which is excessively irritating to the eyes. The German method is not unlike the English, but in France, the packing in boxes is omitted, and the oxidation is completely effected in warm stoves in which the goods are hung on hooks. The heating in this case is much more moderate, and the oil less thickened, a result which may be partly due to the different oils employed, and which leads to differences in the subsequent treatment of the leather.

In the French process, the oily skins are dipped in hot water and wrung or hydraulic pressed, the expressed oil constituting *moellon* or *dégras* (p. 368), and the skins are afterwards washed in a hot soda or potash solution, from which a further portion of an inferior *dégras* is recovered. In the old-fashioned English method, the oil became so thickened that it could not be pressed out, and the whole was removed by washing with soda or potash solution, from which it was recovered by the use of acid, constituting "sod oil" (p. 369.) Now many English manufacturers adopt a modified method, and remove a good deal of their oil by pressure.

Buff leather, much used for military accoutrements, is made in a similar manner to chamois, from ox or cow hides, the grain of which is frized off.

The bleaching, both of buff and chamois, is done by exposing to the sun in a damp condition, the skins being watered as required with water or fat-liquor, or the alkaline emulsion of *dégras* obtained in washing the skins. It may also be bleached by oxidising agents, such as permanganate of potash or acidified sodium peroxide. If permanganate is used, the leather is treated in a solution of perhaps 5 grm. per liter till of a deep brown colour, and then in a solution of sulphurous or oxalic acid till the colour is removed.

Messrs. J. and E. Pullman, of Godalming, make a species of buff leather, which they style "Kaspine" leather, by treating limed and drenched hides or skins in a drum with a very dilute solution of formaldehyde ("formalin") rendered alkaline with sodium carbonate (Eng. Pat. 2872, 1898). The change to leather takes place very rapidly, and the leather is afterwards treated with soap solutions of fat-liquors, to feed and soften it. It is almost indistinguishable from genuine buff leather, except from the fact that it is white throughout, and needs no bleaching. It is finding considerable application for military purposes.

A type of leathers which bear a close chemical relation to oil-leathers, is that including "Crown," "Helvetia," and fat-tanned leathers. The first leather of the sort was invented by a German cabinet-maker named Klemm, by whom the secret was sold to Preller, who manufactured it in Southwark, under the name of "Crown" leather. Klemm used flour, ox-brains, butter, milk, and soft fat, which was made into a paste with water, and spread on the limed, drenched and partially dried skins, which were rolled into bundles, and drummed in slightly warmed drums for some hours; taken out, again dried slightly, and coated with the mixture, and again drummed. For thick hides the process was repeated a third time, drumming in each operation for about eight hours. The leather was used for laces, picker-bands, light belts, and other purposes where great toughness and flexibility were required. It was found by further experience (if indeed, it was not known to Klemm himself) that the only really essential ingredients of the mixture were the soft fats and flour; and even the latter could, for some sorts of leather, be dispensed with. It was further ascertained that only the gluten or albuminous part of the flour was absorbed by the leather, the starch serving mainly to facilitate the emulsification of the fats. The proportions used in the paste are about seven parts of flour, seven parts of soft fat such as horse grease, two parts of tallow, four parts of water, and a little salt or nitre to act as an antiseptic. Other greases, such as mixtures of tallow and oil, can be substituted for the horse grease, and pipe-clay or ochre may to some extent take the place of the flour, while soap may also be added. The similarity of the mixtures used to the tawing paste in calf- and glove-kid dressing (pp. 191, 196) is obvious, and Klemm had an earlier process in which the operation just described was preceded by a slight alum tannage, and which was almost identical in its detail with the methods now in use for the production of so-called "rawhide." On the other hand it is nearly allied to the production of "Riems," or raw-hide straps in South Africa, for which a long thong is cut spirally from a hide, and wound into a sort of skein which is suspended from a crossbar, with a heavy weight at its lower end, and oiled and twisted, with frequent changes of position, until the water is dried out, and the thong is saturated with fat, forming a very tough and durable leather. A similar material can be made by fulling or otherwise working grease into a raw hide prepared for tanning. Eitner examined samples of "Crown-leather" chemically, by removing the gluten of the flour with an alkaline solution, and found that an imperfectly chamoised leather remained, which when restuffed with fat, was much less full, and carried a much smaller quantity of grease than before.

Gerber, 1878, p. 2.

Various theories have been proposed to explain the reaction which takes place in the production of oil-leathers. Knapp supposed that it was merely a case in which the smallest fibrils of the hide were coated with the products of the oxidation of oils, and so prevented from adhering together, and protected from the action of water by the sort of waterproof coating which was formed. This explanation is scarcely feasible in the face of the fact that chamois leather can be treated even with hot dilute solutions of the caustic alkalies without destruction, while cotton fibres waterproofed by treatment with drying oils have their coating entirely removed by treatment with alkalies. Lietzmann supposed that the whole of the gelatinous fibres were removed in the liming and subsequent treatment, and that the finished leather consisted only of the skeleton of yellow or elastic fibre which exists in the skin, and which is remarkable for its resistance to heat, acids and alkalis. Unfortunately the proportion of these fibres does not exceed about 6 per cent. of the total, so that they are quite insufficient to account for the production of the leather. We now know, however, that aldehydes, including the acryl-aldehyde, which is evolved in the oil oxidation of chamoising (and which is covered by Messrs. Pullman's patent) are capable in themselves of converting gelatinous substances into a material identical in its properties, and especially in its power of resisting hot water and alkaline solutions, with the fibre of chamois leather. In all cases where perfect chamoising is produced, intense oxidation takes place, and oxidisable oils are used which will evolve acrylic and other aldehydes. Where oils of little drying power are employed, as in the case of Crown- and other fat-leathers, only an imperfect chamoising occurs, and we are therefore justified in attributing the special qualities of chamois leather to a natural aldehyde tannage. On the other hand, there is no doubt that the coating of the fibres with oxidised oil-products really occurs, and is probably a powerful factor in the leathering of Crown-leather, and other similar products which are not washed out with alkaline solutions. Knapp proved by treating raw pelt which had been dehydrated with alcohol (p. 74) with a very dilute alcoholic solution of stearic acid, that a thin coating of stearic acid on the fibres would confer great softness and considerable resistance to water. Even where no stearic or other fatty acid is purposely added to alcohol used for dehydrating pelt, traces are present from the decomposition of the natural fat of the skin, and there is little doubt that this is the cause why such alcohol-leathers are much more difficult to wet back again to the state of pelt than would *a priori* be expected; and why hide-powder dehydrated in this way is unsuitable for use in the hide-powder filter (p. 311) from its non-absorption of water.

FIG. 85.—Scouring large Seal-Skins by Hand.

It is not within the scope of the present volume to describe in detail the processes used in currying, many of which are purely mechanical, and of no theoretical interest, whatever their practical importance; and with which the writer hopes to deal fully in a future book. The leather is usually scoured with stone, brush and sleeker to free it from "bloom" and loose tan (Fig. 85); or by machines such as Fig. 86; and is often reduced in thickness by shaving by hand (Fig. 87), or by machine (Fig. 88). In place of shaving, hides and skins are frequently split into two or more thicknesses. This is done by various machines, of which the "bandknife" shown in Fig. 89 is the most important; the cutting tool being a thin steel belt stretched like a bandsaw and sharpened on one edge by an emery-wheel.

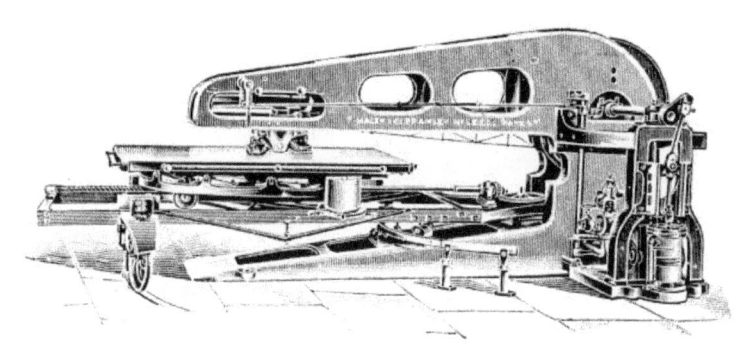

FIG. 86.—Scouring Machine.

CURRYING SHOP, LEATHER INDUSTRIES DEPARTMENT, YORKSHIRE COLLEGE.

Something must be said here about the function of the oils and fats used in currying, and their general method of application. It is obvious that the possibility of coating the finest fibrils of leather with a fatty layer is not restricted to raw hide, but is present, sometimes even in a higher degree, in tanned or tawed leathers, in which the fibres are already so far isolated as to make the access of the fat easy. Even the possibility of an aldehyde-tannage is not excluded, where the fibre is not already completely saturated with other tanning agents or where these agents, from their nature, have not so firm a hold on the fibre as to be incapable of being displaced by the action of aldehydes. It is therefore obvious that we may apply some of the ideas which we have formed with regard to oil-tannages to the action of fats upon tanned leather. In the first place, it must be remembered that gelatinous matters are as a rule insoluble in fats; and *vice versa*, that fats are incapable of penetrating dry and solid gelatinous fibres. If the skin becomes dry in the chamoising process, that part remains raw. It may therefore be concluded that fats and oils have little power in themselves of isolating the fibrils, and that this must be accomplished by other agencies, since if they are still adhering together, the fats cannot penetrate them. Hence the necessity of moisture, which keeps the fibres soft and divisible; and with raw hide, the importance of powerful mechanical treatment, which will work the minute globules of fat between the fibrils. In the case of tanned leathers, the last condition is less important, since the fibres are already isolated by the tannage, and capillarity assists the penetration. Even in this case the distribution of the fat is much assisted if it is already in a state of fine division (emulsification), and if the surface-tension (p. 76) between it and water is low, as is the case with dégras and other partially oxidised oils. On this rather than on any special chemical affinity probably depends the importance of the "dégras-former" and other products of oxidation which are present in dégras; and the difference in penetrating power of different oils. So long as oil remains in an undivided condition, so long can it be squeezed out, and the leather will feel and appear greasy; while, when it is thoroughly emulsified, and adherent to the fibre, it can no longer be expelled by mechanical means. No doubt the different power of different tannages to "carry grease" without appearing greasy, is also related to the degree of isolation of the fibrils, and their surface tension with regard to fats. We may judge that the more readily an oil can be emulsified, the more freely and completely it is likely to fix itself on the leather fibre.

FIG. 87.—Hand Shaving.

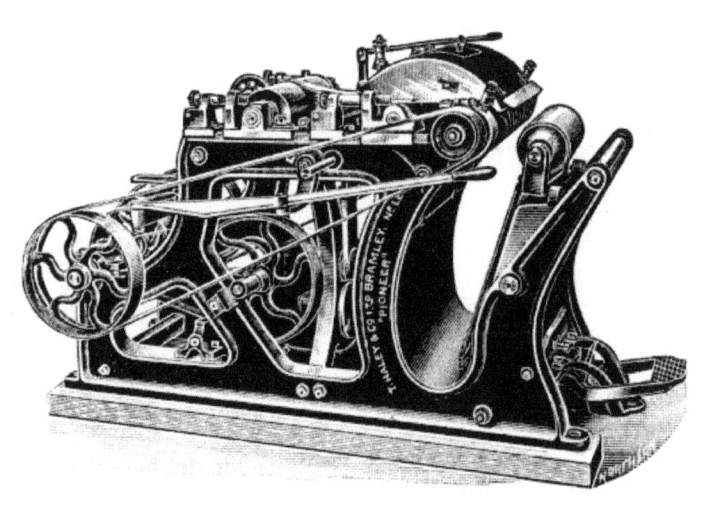

FIG. 88.—Shaving Machine.

It is a practically invariable rule that the leather-fibre must be wet when it is stuffed. The surface-tension between the water and the fats is less than that of either with regard to air; and therefore, as the water dries out of the small interstices of the leather, the fat follows it in, and gradually takes its place. Generally speaking, the amount of water should be such that some exsudes in minute drops when the leather is pinched, that is, that not only the minutest spaces between the fibrils are filled, but even the larger ones between the fibre-bundles to a considerable extent.

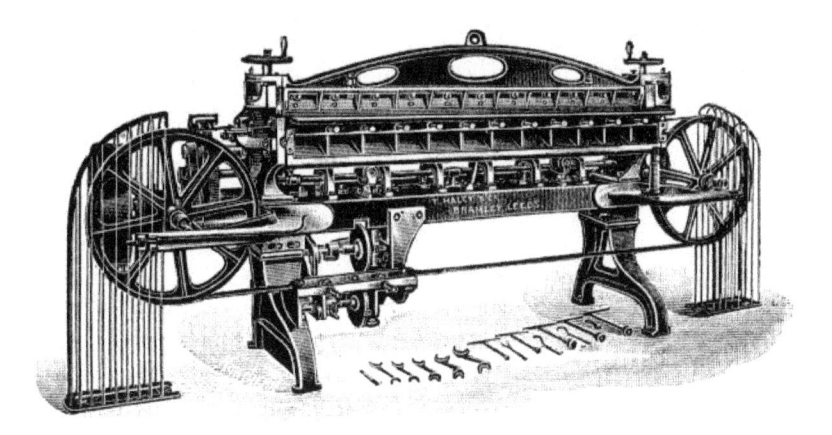

FIG. 89.—Band-Knife Splitting Machine.

In "*hand-stuffing*," the leather is now coated on the flesh side, or occasionally on both sides with "dubbing," which is a pasty mixture of fats usually mainly composed of cod-oil and tallow, which is applied rather thickly with a brush and smoothed down with the fleshy part of the forearm. When such constituents are melted together, the harder fats dissolve in the oils, and as the mixture cools, much of the hard fats again crystallise out. To make a good dubbing, the cooling fats must be stirred continuously till this has taken place, as otherwise the mixture separates into little globular masses of crystals with liquid oil between them, instead of forming a uniform body of salve-like consistency. The proportions of the hard and soft constituents of the dubbing should be adjusted to the season, and to the temperature at which the drying of the stuffed leather is to take place, so that on the one hand, the dubbing will not melt and run off, and on the other, that it should not solidify more than is necessary, as only the liquid solution which remains entangled among the crystals can be absorbed by the leather. The solid crystalline fats remain on the surface, and are scraped off by the sleeker in finishing, as "table-grease," which is generally re-melted and used over again. It does not answer, in hand-stuffing, to carry this re-use too far, as the table-grease contains only the harder parts of the fat, with a continually increasing proportion of stearic acid, so that if a dubbing be made continuously of table-grease and oil, in the end little but the latter will be absorbed by the leather; while where fresh tallow is used, a portion of its softer constituents remains dissolved in the oil. The principal function of the harder fats is the mechanical one of retaining the oil on the surface of the leather; and to a certain extent they may be replaced by other solids, such as steatite ("French chalk"), or perhaps other pulpy materials. The use of a portion of soft fat, such as bone-fat, or the better sorts of glue-grease, is quite practicable, especially if mixed with the harder table-grease.

The drying of hand-stuffed leather should be slow, to allow time for the absorption of the grease; and the temperature should be so regulated as to keep the dubbing in a soft but not liquid condition. In winter, if the temperature of the outer air be raised sufficiently for this, the drying will be too keen (cp. p. 426) and the water will be dried out before the grease is properly absorbed. It is therefore best, in cold weather, to maintain the ventilation mainly by circulating the air in the room, with little admission from the outside, and in extreme cases even artificial damping of the air may be advantageous. Sometimes the tendency to mildew during slow and warm drying is very troublesome. This may be prevented by the addition of antiseptics to the stuffing grease. Carbolic acid and creasote are effective, but generally objectionable from their smell; rosin oil has considerable antiseptic power, and mineral oils also in a less degree. Probably α-naphthol would prove an efficient remedy, as it has little odour, and its antiseptic properties are very strong, but it has not been tried by the writer. (Cp. Chapter V.)

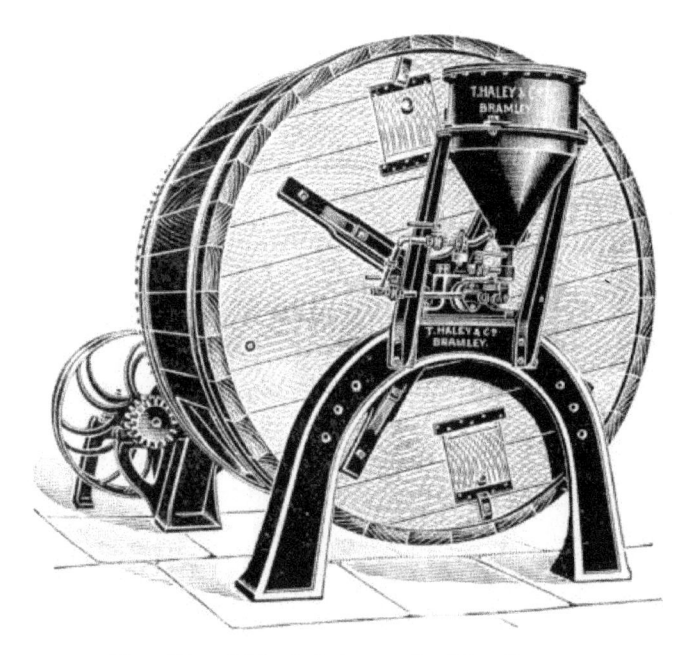

FIG. 90.—Haley's Injector Stuffing Drum.

In *drum-stuffing* the conditions differ materially from those of hand-stuffing. The goods, in a damp condition, are placed in a drum (Fig. 90), which has been heated by steam to as high a temperature as the leather will safely stand. Cold damp leather may be stuffed in a drum heated to 60° C. and the grease may be run in at the same temperature. The grease should generally be melted and mixed at a somewhat higher temperature. Sometimes steam is merely blown into the drum before introducing the leather, to heat it to the required temperature; sometimes a steam-coil is placed in the drum itself. A more modern method, which is now largely used in the United States, is to heat by hot air, which is circulated by a fan over an external steam heater and through the drum. The drum is set in rotation, and the stuffing grease in a melted condition is run in through the hollow axle, or if this is not provided, it is introduced through the door, and the rotation is maintained for twenty to thirty minutes. During the last few minutes the door is frequently replaced by an open grating or cold air is drawn through the drum by means of the fan, in order to cool the goods, which are set out with the sleeker on the table while yet somewhat warm, and dried under much the same conditions as have been described with regard to hand-stuffed goods.

In drum-stuffing, the hardness of the grease is limited by its melting-point, which must not be so high as to damage the leather, but it may be soft as is desired. As the grease is forced by mechanical means into the interior of the leather, there is no danger of its running off, but the drying must take place at such a temperature as to keep it at least in a partially soft condition, as the drumming only forces it into the coarser spaces of the leather, and does not complete its distribution on the fibre. By the use of exceedingly hard greases, such as "stearin" (p. 359) and oleo-stearin (p. 356), sometimes with additions of paraffin wax, it is possible to introduce immense quantities of grease, and yet to obtain a leather which will board up to a good colour. In America, it is not unusual to reckon 100 or even 115 lb. of greases to 100 lb. of leather weighed dry after scouring, or estimated from its wet weight; and the whole of this is absorbed, scarcely anything coming off in "setting." The leather, as it comes from the drum, is dark brown, but when bent sharply in "boarding" to form the grain, after cooling and drying, the very hard and crystalline fats crumble into white powder, and the leather takes a light and pretty colour. Such leather would of course darken at once if it were held to the fire, but would again brighten on cooling and breaking up with the "board." Some portion of liquid fats, such as dégras or fish oil, should be contained in the stuffing grease, as the solid fats alone will not penetrate to the heart of the fibres, but will leave the leather dry and harsh.

By drum-stuffing, it is possible to incorporate solid matter with the leather, and barytes (ground heavy-spar or barium sulphate) was formerly much used for this purpose, but has now been nearly abandoned. Glucose is still used as an adulterant of leather, but is not introduced in the drum, but by painting the goods with syrup before stuffing. It not only adds weight, and gives the leather a lighter colour than an equivalent quantity of grease, but at the same time lessens its toughness, and ought to be prohibited in England, as it already is in Germany. On the detection of adulteration of leather, see L.I.L.B., p. 212. Drum-stuffing is in this country mainly applied to shoe-leathers, but in America, with the hot-air drum, is coming into increasing use for harness, and even belting.

A method of stuffing is used in Germany for heavy belting and the like, which appears at first glance to contradict the axiom that leather must be stuffed wet. It is called *Einbrennen* (to burn in), and consists in first drying at a high temperature (50° C.), to ensure the absence of all moisture, and then either pouring hot melted tallow over the leather on a table, and holding it over a brazier, to allow the grease to sink in, or dipping it completely in a bath of melted tallow. The exception is only apparent, because, though the leather is at this stage completely saturated with tallow, it is only after wetting and drumming that it attains the flexibility due to true stuffing. Similar methods are applicable to alumed leathers, and even to chrome-leather; and so-called "waterproof" or "anhydrous" leather is made by immersing thoroughly dried leather in a bath of 2 parts of resin and 1 of paraffin, or some similar mixture. If the leather is not first thoroughly dried, it is scalded and destroyed by the hot grease.

The most troublesome defect to which stuffed leathers are liable, is known as "spueing," and is of two kinds, of which the first and less serious (perhaps more properly distinguished as "striking out") consists of a white efflorescence rather like incipient mould, which is easily wiped off, but generally reappears. This is due to the crystallisation of the harder fats, and especially of the free fatty acids, on the surface of the leather, and is almost sure to occur in greater or less degree when the hard fats such as tallow or stearine are combined with a non-drying oil such as neatsfoot, or when soft fats are present in the leather. It is sometimes combined with actual mildew, from which it is rather difficult to distinguish, even under the microscope, and may even be caused by fungoid plants, which not only mechanically expel the fats by their growth, but probably promote their rancidity and the separation of the crystalline fatty acids. It is at most only a defect of appearance, and does not in any way injure the leather. It is constantly present in calf-kid, from the neatsfoot oil used in finishing, and is in this case rather liked by the buyers, who for some reason regard it as a proof of quality. A very similar appearance may be caused by the use of solutions of barium chloride, alum or other mineral salts, for weighting or other purposes; but is persistent when the leather is held to the fire, while the crystallised fatty acids at once melt and disappear. The fatty acids are at once removed by a drop of benzene or petroleum spirit; but unaffected by water, while with water-soluble salts the reverse occurs.

The second form of spueing is of a much more troublesome character, and makes its first appearance as minute spots or pimples of resinous matter, raised above the surface of the leather, which if removed, generally reappear, and which may become so bad as to form a sticky resinous coating over the whole surface. The exsuded matter consists of the oxidised products of oxidisable oils, but the cause of its appearance is not always easy to explain. The currier generally attributes it to adulterated oils, and it must be admitted that some oils almost invariably produce it, but it appears occasionally when only the purest and absolutely genuine cod-oil has been used. It can only be produced from drying or semi-drying oils, which include all the ordinary fish oils and most of the vegetable seed oils, but can never arise from tallow or stearine, from mineral oils or vaseline, or from genuine non-drying oils, such as tallow, neatsfoot, sperm, or mineral oils, nor, probably, from rosin oil. It is favoured by causes which promote the oxidation of oils, such as moist heat with limited access of air, and by the presence of oxygen-carriers, such as iron-salts in blacks, and possibly also by the presence of free acids. A large amount of free fatty acid in the oils themselves is suspicious, not only because the free acids oxidise more freely than the neutral fats, but because their presence is an evidence of the tendency to rancidity and change in the oil. It is also said to be caused by previous mildewing of the leather, and certainly often occurs where the grain has been rendered porous by bacterial action in the soaks, limes, or bates, probably from the greater quantity of oil absorbed by these parts. While it is easy to say which oils may possibly spue, there is no known chemical test which will foretell whether a given sample is likely to do so under ordinary conditions. Eitner states that seal oil extracted at a low temperature is very liable to spue, but that when heated for a considerable time to a temperature of 250°-290° C. it darkens in colour and loses the tendency. This is probably true of many other marine oils; and may be one cause of the frequent trouble with modern oils, many of which, especially the lighter coloured kinds, are extracted by steam at a temperature below boiling point. It is very probable that one effect of heating to a considerable temperature is to dehydrate and separate albuminous or gelatinous matters which are present in the fresh oils, and which probably increase their tendency to decomposition. Many of these substances separate as "foots" from oils during long storing, and such old oils are said to be less liable to spue than those of recent manufacture.

Gerber, 1880, p. 243.

If oxidisable oils are used upon leather, they "dry" upon the fibre, and if a sufficiency of non-drying constituents are not present at the same time, the leather will ultimately become hard, and may even crack from hardening of the fibre. Mineral oils are not liable in this way to form a hard coating on the fibre, but as they are slightly volatile, though of very high boiling point, they may ultimately evaporate, and leave the leather insufficiently nourished. From their low surface-tension, they have great powers of capillary penetration, as is witnessed by the way that lamp oils "creep" over the surface of the lamp, but they have less affinity for water than the more oxidisable oils, and probably do not combine so intimately with the leather-fibre. They are probably better used in combination with other greases than alone. The admixture of solid paraffin with stuffing greases has the tendency to make the leather feel less greasy and drier than it otherwise would; and crude turpentine and rosin are said to have a still greater effect in this direction.

The water which is required for satisfactory stuffing may in some cases be introduced into the stuffing grease as well as into the leather. The effect of dégras is largely due to the water with which it is intimately mixed, and when dégras or sod-oil is deprived of that which it naturally contains, by heating it to too high a temperature, either before or after its mixture in a stuffing grease, its efficacy is greatly lessened.

Fat-liquoring (pp. 217, 239) may be considered a special case of stuffing, in which the oil is very perfectly emulsified with a large quantity of water. In this way, very considerable quantities of oil may be introduced into leather without giving it the least greasy feel. Egg-yolk contains about 30 per cent. of an oil chemically very like olive, but with a larger proportion of palmitin, and may be considered as a very perfect natural fat-liquor, containing also some albumen which serves as "nourishment" for the leather. If a means of emulsifying olive, lard, or tallow oil (with the addition of a little palm oil) with albuminous matter as perfectly as in the egg could be discovered, the problem of an egg-yolk substitute would in all probability be solved. Milk and cream are also natural fat-liquors.

CHAPTER XXV.
DYES AND DYEING.

Before the discovery of artificial organic dyestuffs, the only colouring materials known to industry were those of mineral and direct organic origin; and on this account the dyeing of leather was formerly subject to great difficulties and limitations.

The discovery of the means of artificially preparing an organic dyestuff (mauve) by Perkin some forty-five years since, opened up a new field for research, and since that time, the list of commercial dyes has so increased that there is now scarcely a tint or shade which cannot be accurately matched and reproduced by the coal-tar colours. These colours are often spoken of as "aniline dyes" owing to the fact that many of them, and especially the earlier ones, have been derived from aniline, one of the products of coal-tar; but more recently, a considerable number of important colours have been prepared from other constituents of the tar, and it is therefore more correct to term the whole of the dyes obtained, either directly or indirectly, from coal-tar, the "coal-tar colours."

The coal-tar colours are generally soluble in water, or mixtures of water and alcohol, and the majority of them combine with the fibre of the leather without the use of any mordant, so that in most cases it is only necessary to apply a solution of the dye direct to the leather, though their suitability for the purpose varies considerably. A few which are only soluble in oils or hydrocarbons, are not suitable for leather-dyeing, though they may sometimes be utilised in conjunction with fats in currying; and there are also certain colours which are not applied to the fibre ready formed, but are developed on it by subsequent chemical treatment, and which have only been applied to a limited extent to leather.

A number of the coal-tar dyes, which are produced in the crystalline form, have a totally different colour when solid to that of their solutions, and to the colour they produce when dyed. A well-known instance of this is magenta or fuchsine, which forms glistening green crystals, while in solution it is a brilliant red dye. The colours of the crystals are usually complementary to those of the solution, thus several blues have the appearance of metallic copper, and violets, such as methyl-violet, are greenish-yellow, generally with a pronounced metallic lustre. This peculiarity is the cause of the defect in dyeing known as "bronzing," in which the dye, when applied in too concentrated a form, takes a surface-shimmer of its complementary colour.

The coal-tar colours are mostly either "acid" or "basic." The former are the salts of organic colour-acids with inorganic bases (generally sodium) and are usually readily soluble in water, but frequently do not fix themselves on the fibre till the colour-acid is set free by the addition of some stronger acid to the bath, and in many cases the free colour-acid is of different colour to its salts. The "basic" colours are salts of colour-bases (organic bases of the nature of very complicated ammonia-derivatives) with acids (mostly hydrochloric, sulphuric or acetic). Most of those in commercial use are soluble in water, though a few require the addition of alcohol. The colour-bases themselves are usually insoluble in water, and therefore precipitated by alkalies, and in some cases they are also colourless. The basic dyes have generally greater intensity of colour than the acid dyes, but large classes of them are very fugitive when exposed to light, and in strong solution many others are very liable to "bronze," a defect which is generally less marked with the acid colours.

It has recently been shown by Lamb (see App. D, p. 498) that many basic colours are much faster to light on leather than on textiles.

As it is not obvious at first sight whether a given dye is acid or basic, a reagent to distinguish them is useful. For this purpose a solution of 1 part of tannic acid and 1 part of sodium acetate in 10 parts (by weight) of water is conveniently employed, which gives coloured precipitates with basic dyes, but is not affected by acid ones. The fact that basic dyes are precipitated by tannins influences their use in leather dyeing, not only as regards their fixation on the leather-fibre by the tannin which it contains, but as the cause of their precipitation in the dye-bath if great care is not taken to avoid the presence of tannins in a soluble form. The use of the sodium acetate is to combine with the mineral acid of the colour-salt, which if left free would prevent complete precipitation, substituting for it acetic acid, which is much weaker, especially in presence of excess of sodium acetate (cp. p. 81).

In using the terms "acid" and "basic" with regard to dyes, it is not to be understood that the dyestuffs as employed are acid or alkaline in the sense that vinegar is acid, and soda basic, but merely that the actual colour-constituent of the salt is in the one case of an acid nature, and set free by stronger acids, and in the other case is basic, and liberated (and often precipitated) by stronger alkalies.

There are several general theories with regard to the fixation of colours in dyeing organic fibres, and it is probable that no one of them affords a complete explanation in all cases. One holds that the action of dyeing is mechanical rather than chemical, the colour adhering to the fibre by surface-attraction; another, that an actual chemical compound is formed between the dye and the dyed material or one of its constituents; and a third, the "solid solution" theory of Witt, is in a sense intermediate, holding that the colouring matter is actually dissolved in the dyed fibre. The idea of a solid solution, strange at first, offers little difficulty on consideration. The colouring metallic salts in tinted glasses exist obviously in solution in the melted glass, and can hardly be said to change their condition in this respect when the glass becomes solid. Gelatine, indiarubber, and perhaps all other colloid bodies, absorb water or other liquids without losing their solid form, and these liquids may fairly be said to be dissolved in the solid. All animal and vegetable fibres are in this respect like gelatine, and during the process of dyeing are swollen with water. It is quite easy to dye a mass of gelatine throughout with most water-soluble dyestuffs. (Compare on these points what is said in Chapter IX. on the physical chemistry of hide-fibre.) The distinctions between solution and molecular surface-attraction on the one hand, and certain forms of chemical combination on the other, are not wide ones, and probably all three theories are true in different cases, and shade off into each other by imperceptible gradations. The subject of leather-dyeing is, in fact, a very complicated one, since we are not dealing with a fibre of uniform composition, but with one which has had its structure (both chemical and physical) altered by the processes to which it has been subjected during its conversion into leather.

Although, strictly speaking, the constitution of the gelatinous fibre of the skin is unknown, we are quite justified in stating that, like the amido-acids which are important proximate products of its decomposition, it contains both acid and basic groups, and is therefore capable of attracting both bases and acids. It is well known, for instance, that the neutral fibre is capable of withdrawing sulphuric acid from a decinormal solution with such vigour that the residual liquid is neutral to litmus paper; and it will also absorb caustic alkalies with perhaps equal avidity.

Procter, Jour. Soc. Chem. Industry, 1900, p. 23.

Cp. Chap. IX.

It is thus readily dyed by colouring matter of either basic or acid character, and in many cases will even dissociate their salts, dyeing the characteristic colour of the free dyestuff, but possibly at the same time fixing the liberated base or acid with which the colouring matter has been combined. Many tanning processes consist in a somewhat analogous fixation of weak bases and acids, and it is, therefore, to be anticipated that they will profoundly modify the colour-fixing properties of the original fibre, as indeed proves to be the case. Exactly what the result of a particular tanning process in this respect will be is less easy to foresee.

In the ordinary vegetable tanning process, the tannins, which are of acid nature, are freely fixed by the fibre. It is, therefore, not surprising that vegetable-tanned leather most readily fixes the basic colours, especially as these form insoluble compounds with the tannic acids, so that it is quite probable that the dyeing is mainly effected by the formation of tannin-colour-lakes on the fibre, rather than by actual fixation of the colour-base in combination with the original matter of the skin. It is noteworthy, however, that even fully tanned skin has by no means lost its attractions for acid colouring matters, many of which will dye it even without the presence of free acid, though it is possible that the tannic acid performs the function of saturating the alkaline base with which the colour acid has been combined.

It should be pointed out that while the substance of animal skin consists practically of gelatinous fibres, it is covered on the outer surface with a thin membrane of extreme tenuity, called the hyaline or glassy layer (p. 50) which, in the living animal, separates the true skin from the epidermis. This layer, the chemistry of which is quite unknown, reacts to colouring matters differently from the gelatinous fibres, and probably is less absorbent for basic colours, and more so for the coloured anhydrides of the tannins, and perhaps for acid colours generally, than is the true skin. As a result, it colours more darkly in tanning, and less so in dyeing with basic colours, and as it is extremely liable to damage in the preliminary operations of removing hair and lime by the tanner, this irregularity of colouring is a serious disadvantage which is most marked with the basic colours. Small quantities of lime left in the skin are also probably important causes of irregular dyeing.

Mordants are chemicals used to enable the fibre to fix dyes for which it would not otherwise have sufficient attraction, and hence are generally substances which have affinity both for the fibre and the dye. Thus cotton, which does not itself attract the basic colours, is mordanted for them by a solution of tannin, which it attracts, and which, in its turn, attracts and fixes the colours. In many cases, however, the function of mordants is more complex, not merely fixing the dyestuff, but often modifying, or even producing its colour. Thus tannin dyes black on an iron mordant, though it is itself colourless. Such mordants may be applied *after* the colouring matter, where it has sufficient attraction for the fibre to be taken up alone, but does not produce the required colour. This process is often called "saddening," as the colour is generally darkened. A familiar instance is the use of iron solutions to darken or blacken tannin or logwood. There is scarcely any distinction in theory between mordants of this class and the constituents of dyes which are successively applied to the leather in order to produce the colouring matter on the fibre. Among these may be mentioned several mineral salts which were formerly employed in leather dyeing, though their use is now nearly obsolete. Iron salts are easily fixed by leather, whether tanned or tawed, and in the former case produce a dark colour by action of the tannin. On subsequent treatment with a solution of potassium ferrocyanide, a deep blue is formed (Prussian blue). If copper acetate or ammoniacal solution of copper sulphate be substituted for the iron salt, a deep red-brown ferrocyanide is produced. Yellows are sometimes dyed by first treating tanned leathers with lead acetate, which is fixed by the tannin, and then with potassium bichromate, by which yellow lead chromate is produced. A more important use of lead is in the so-called "lead-bleach," which is really a white pigment-dyeing with lead sulphate. The tanned leather, after washing, is first treated with a solution of lead acetate (usually "brown sugar of lead" of about 4 grm. per liter), and subsequently with a dilute sulphuric acid of about 30 grm. of concentrated acid per litre, and then thoroughly washed to free it from acid. The process is often used as a preparation for dyeing pale shades, as many of the aniline dyes are easily fixed on the bleached leather, but is subject to the disadvantage attendant on all pigments containing lead, of becoming rapidly darkened by traces of sulphur or sulphuretted hydrogen, such as are constantly contained in lighting gas, or arise from the putrefaction of organic matters. The use of acid is also liable to cause early decay of the leather.

A large proportion of the coal-tar colours contain amido-groups (NH_2 groups) which, when treated on the fibre with nitrous acid (or an acidified solution of sodium nitrite), become "diazotised" (converted into —N : N— groups with elimination of OH_2). On further treating the diazo-compound with solutions of amines or phenols, combination takes place, and new azo-colours are formed in or on the fibre, often remarkably fast to washing or rubbing. Since these qualities are less important in leather than in textiles, and the process is moreover somewhat delicate, and the nitrous acid is apt to injuriously affect the leather, these processes have been little used in leather-dyeing, and are only mentioned here for the sake of completeness.

The use of the natural polygenetic colours in dyeing leather of vegetable tannage, which was once universal, is gradually disappearing, except for the production of blacks. Leather cannot be very satisfactorily mordanted for these colouring matters; but they have some natural attraction for the leather itself, and are generally dyed first, and their colours afterwards developed by metallic mordants such as iron, chrome, tin salts, and alum, which act not only on the absorbed dyestuff, but frequently on the tannin and colouring matters derived from the tanning materials. For black-dyeing, the use of coal-tar colours, either alone, or to deepen the colours produced by iron, is gradually extending. Claus and Rée's "Autho-black," the

"Corvolines" of the Badische Co., and Casella's "Naphthylamine Black," "Aniline Grey," and "Naphthol Blue-black" may be mentioned as useful colours. As coal-tar blacks are mostly dark violets rather than dead blacks, their colour may be deepened by the admixture of suitable yellows or browns, and this has already been done in one or two of the colours named. Apart from the coal-tar colours, black dyeing is generally produced by the action of iron (and chrome), either on the tannin of the leather itself or on logwood. As the leather is frequently greasy, and the satisfactory formation of a tannin- or logwood-lake can only take place in presence of a base to absorb the liberated acid of the iron salt, the skins are either brushed with, or plunged in, a logwood infusion, rendered alkaline with soda or ammonia, or the tanned leather receives a preliminary treatment with weak soda or ammonia solution. As such solutions act powerfully on tanned leathers, rendering them harsh and tender, great care must be taken to avoid excess. The effect of this alkaline treatment is not only to assist the wetting of the greasy surface, but to prevent too deep penetration of the dye, by causing rapid precipitation of the colour-lake. In recent times, however, leathers are sometimes demanded in which the colour goes right through, and in this case it might be well to reverse the treatment, beginning with a weak solution of a ferrous salt, perhaps with addition of sodium acetate or potassium tartrate, and finishing with alkaline logwood, as without alkali the full colour is not developed. The use of iron salts is not very satisfactory in regard to the permanence of the leather; and in this respect it is of great importance that they should not be used in excess, and that any strong acids they contain should be saturated with permanent bases, and if possible washed out. Leather-surfaces blacked with iron almost invariably ultimately lose their colour, becoming brown if tannins, and red if logwood has been employed, and at the same time the leather surface usually becomes brittle or friable. This is to a large extent due to the effect of iron oxides as oxygen-carriers. Exposed to light, they become reduced to the ferrous state, oxidising the organic matters with which they are combined, and in the dark they re-oxidise, and the process is repeated. It is therefore of the first importance that excess of the organic colouring matter should be provided, and that the quantity of the iron should be as small as possible, and in stable combination. These points are greatly neglected in practice, especially where blacking is done by the application of iron salts without logwood, when the evils mentioned are intensified by the actual removal of part of the tannin of the leather, and perhaps by the combination of ferric oxide with the skin-fibre itself, forming a brittle iron-leather. Treatment with alkaline sumach-, gambier- or logwood-solutions, both before and after the application of the iron, would lessen the evil. Iron-logwood blacks are much less permanent, and fade more rapidly under the influence of light and air than iron-tannin blacks. The use of iron-blacks on curried leathers seems considerably to increase the tendency to "spueing," a defect due to oxidation of the oils (see p. 390). Copper salts mordant logwood a very dark blue, which is much more stable than the iron compound, and hence are often used advantageously in mixture with iron salts. In practice, iron blacks are generally oiled in finishing, and this renders them more permanent, both by protecting the lake from air and by forming iron soaps which are stable. The use of actual soaps in blacking and finishing is not unknown, and probably deserves more attention. Hard soaps of soda and stearic acid, form an excellent finish where a moderate glaze is required, the soap jelly being applied with a brush very thinly, allowed to dry thoroughly, and polished with a flannel or brush, or glassed. Many acid colours are soluble in such soap jellies, which may thus be employed for staining. Similar but harder finishes, and capable of being glazed to a high polish, are made by dissolving shellac with dilute borax or ammonia solutions. Both of these finishes are useful in lessening the tendency of iron blacks to smut or rub off, a failing which is due to the precipitation of loose iron-lakes on the surface, instead of in combination with the fibre, and is particularly obvious where "inks" or one-solution blacks are employed, or where the mordant and the colouring matter solutions are allowed to mix on the surface of the leather. Such "inks" are generally made with a ferrous salt and logwood or tannin, together with some aniline black, and the colour-lake should only be formed on oxidation. Chrome is not much employed in blacks with vegetable tannages, as it only produces blacks with logwood, the chrome compounds of tannins having no colouring value; and bichromates used at all freely being very injurious to the leather.

1 of caustic soda in 10-15 of water, boiled with 8 of stearic acid till clear, cooled to 25° C. and diluted with 400-800 water, with constant stirring, till the white jelly of suitable consistence is obtained. Somewhat similar, but harder preparations may be made with waxes, or fatty acids still higher than stearic.

5 parts of shellac digested warm with 100 water and 3 of ammonia fort., or 1 of borax. If the solution is used as a "seasoning" for glazing, the waxy matter which separates on standing should be mixed by shaking before use. As a varnish, a stronger solution should be used and the wax skimmed off.

In dyeing blacks on other than vegetable tannages, however, chrome becomes of importance, as logwood is principally employed, though sometimes in conjunction with tannin, and often with addition of quercitron or fustic, to correct the bluish shade of the logwood-chrome or logwood-iron lake. It must not be overlooked in practice, that if ferrous salts are mixed with bichromate solutions, the latter are reduced, and the iron is oxidised to the ferric state.

In alumed leathers the fixing power of the original hide-fibre is much less affected than in vegetable tannages. Whatever may be the truth with regard to the latter, there is little doubt that physical influences are at least as important as chemical ones in the production of mineral tannages. The amount of the tanning agent absorbed is greatly influenced by the concentration of the solutions, and in ordinary alum tawing much of the alumina may again be removed by free washing. In this case, the sulphate of potash present takes no part in the operation, but the alumina salt is absorbed apparently as a normal salt. Alum or alumina sulphate alone is incapable of producing any satisfactory tannage without the assistance of common salt, the quantity absorbed being small, and the fibre becoming swollen by the action of the acid. In presence of salt the absorption is greater, and the swelling is prevented. The explanation of this is not to be found in the formation of aluminium chloride, for though this undoubtedly takes place, it has been shown that the action of aluminium chloride without salt is not more satisfactory than that of alum. It has long been known that salt prevents the swelling action of acids on skin, although it does not lessen the absorption of acid; and the fact is capable of explanation on modern osmotic theories (cp. p. 89). The skin so treated is found to be converted into leather, but if the salt be washed out, the acid is retained by the skin, which returns to the state of acid-swollen pelt. It is probable, therefore, that although the acid and alumina are absorbed in equivalent proportions to each other, they are really dissociated, and attached to different groups in the gelatine molecule, and that the effect of the salt is to allow the absorption of the acid without swelling, and, osmotically, to increase the dissociating power of the pelt. If, in place of a normal alumina salt, a basic salt is employed, such as may be obtained by partial neutralisation of the sulphuric acid with soda, satisfactory tannage may be accomplished without salt, a basic compound is absorbed, and the leather is much less affected by washing. In the analogous case of chrome tannage, this basic compound may be still further deprived of its residual acid, by washing the tanned skin with alkaline solutions, leaving a leather which is extremely resistant even to hot water; and a somewhat similar result may be obtained with alumina, though with more difficulty, as apparently a very small excess of alkali destroys the qualities of the leather. (Cp. p. 187.)

The results on dyeing are almost what might have been foreseen. While ordinary alumed leather absorbs both acid and basic dyes readily, the basic chrome leather has practically lost its affinity for the latter. Both chrome and alumina leathers readily absorb vegetable tannins, thus supporting the view that the acid-fixing groups of the gelatine molecule are still unsaturated (tannins are capable of tanning pelt swollen with sulphuric acid and apparently of expelling the acid). In the case of chrome leather the effect of re-tanning with tannins is greatly to lessen its stretch, and if carried too far, to destroy its toughness, but it at once becomes capable of fixing basic dyestuffs. This property is frequently made use of in dyeing, but the effect on the leather must not be disregarded where softness and stretch are important, as in the case of glove-leathers. Polygenetic dyes are, of course, fixed on alum- or chrome-leathers by the alumina- or chrome-mordant, though apparently the bases are not present in the most favourable condition for fixing colours. Thus logwood extracted without alkali dyes tanned leather yellow, alumed leather violet-blue, and chrome leather blackish-violet, and some of the alizarine group dye very well on chrome as its resistance to hot water allows much higher temperatures to be used than with most other leathers. The tannin contained in dyewoods has the effect of lessening the stretch of chrome leathers.

Something should perhaps be said on the dyeing of oil and aldehyde leathers, but the subject has as yet been scarcely treated scientifically, and our practical knowledge of the subject is insufficient to justify theorising. (See, however, p. 496.)

Defects in the colour of the finished leather are due to a variety of causes, but many are produced by want of cleanliness and system during the dyeing itself. The greatest care is needed in this respect, and in brush-dyeing a different brush should be used for each different colour, as it is impossible to thoroughly remove all traces of dye by the ordinary methods of cleansing.

Irregular and surface dyeing sometimes occurs owing to too rapid fixation of the colours; while in other cases the affinity of the dye is too small to allow of reasonable exhaustion of the bath. Addition of salts of weak acids, such as potassium hydrogen tartrate (tartar), or of those like sodium sulphate, which form hydric salts, lessen rapidity of dyeing with acid colours; while acids generally increase it, and it is also often increased by addition of common salt, which lessens the solubility of the dye. Weak acids, such as acetic or formic, or acid salts, such as sodium bisulphate, are generally to be preferred to sulphuric acid as an addition to the dye-bath; and if the latter is used, great care is desirable in its complete removal. There is no doubt that the rapid decay of leather bookbindings and upholstery is largely due to the careless use of sulphuric acid in "clearing" and dyeing the leather; and even if it is fully removed, it has saturated all bases such as lime, which are naturally present in leathers in combination with weak acids, and which would otherwise act as some protection from the sulphuric acid evolved in burning coal gas.

See Report of Committee of Society of Arts on Bookbinding Leathers, 1901.

"Bronzing," the dichroic effect produced by light reflected from the surface of many colouring matters, complementary to that transmitted by them and reflected by the surface of the dyed material, is not peculiar to basic colours, but is generally more marked in them than in acid ones. Basic colours, from their great affinity for tannins, and consequent rapid dyeing, are apt to dye irregularly, and without sufficiently penetrating the leather, and if the soluble tannin is not wholly washed out of the skins previously to dyeing, it bleeds in the dye-bath, and precipitates insoluble tannin-lakes, which waste colour and adhere to the surface of the leather. The inconvenience of basic colours due to their too rapid fixation may sometimes be lessened by slight acidification of the dye-bath with a weak acid, such as acetic or lactic. The acid may be still further "weakened" if desired, by the addition of its neutral (sodium) salt. The precipitation of tannin-lakes in the bath may be prevented by previous fixation of the tannin with tartar emetic, titanium potassium oxalate or lactate, or some other suitable metallic salt.

The fading of the colours of dyed goods by exposure to light is a defect which has been much more investigated in the textile industries than in leather manufacture, though in the latter case, and especially with regard to bookbinding and furniture leathers, it is of even greater importance. It is probable that no colours are actually unaffected by strong sunlight, but in many cases the action is so slight that it may practically be disregarded; some of the coal-tar colours, and especially some of the alizarines, being practically permanent, while others, and particularly the aniline colours belonging to the triphenylmethane group, such as magenta, are so fugitive as to be practically bleached by a week of strong sunlight. Chrysoidine and the eosins are also very bad in this respect. The fastness of colours to light is a good deal influenced by the material on which they are dyed, and but little has yet been published of the results of direct experiments on leathers, but Mr. M. C. Lamb has been for some time engaged in a research of this nature, and the subject is now receiving a good deal of attention in other quarters. Experiments are easily made by exposing samples to sunlight under glass or in a south window, a part of the leather being covered with wood or thick brown paper for comparison. The results are often complicated by the tendency of all leathers tanned with tannins of the catechol group, and especially with turwar bark (p. 298), mimosa and quebracho, to darken and redden in sunshine, or even by exposure to diffused light. Pure sumach tannages are nearly free from this defect, and are also much less easily destroyed by the action of gas fumes (sulphuric acid), and the other injurious influences to which books and furniture are often subjected.

See App. D., p. 488, 498, and Journ. Soc. Chem. Ind., 1902, pp. 156-158.

Cp. Report of Society of Arts Committee on Bookbinding Leathers, 1901.

Want of fastness to friction or rubbing is a defect generally more important in textiles than in leather, where it is often prevented by glazings or other finishes applied to the surface; but in some cases, and, especially in black leather, it is apt to be annoying. If suitable colours are used, the defect is generally due to the precipitation of loose colour on the surface, either by the too free use of mordants, or the dyeing of basic colours on leathers which have not been sufficiently freed from loose tannin. It is also often caused by "flaming" or the application of colour mixed with the "seasoning" used in glazing, to hide imperfections in the dyeing, or vary its colour. Colour applied in this way is only mechanically fixed on the leather, and is easily removed by moisture, staining articles with which it comes in contact.

A very similar defect may be caused by incomplete washing of the dyed leather, which leaves loose dye from the dye-bath in the goods. To avoid it in glove-leathers, where its occurrence would be particularly annoying, the natural mordant colours are still largely in use, which being precipitated on the fibre in an insoluble form by the mordant or "striker" (generally a metallic salt) are little liable to come off. Basic colours may be fixed by a subsequent treatment with tannin, or by topping with certain acid colours such as picric acid. Some few colours, and especially Martius or "Manchester" yellow (dinitronaphthol) are volatile at a low temperature, and therefore liable to "mark off" or stain any materials with which the dyed fabric, even in a dry state, is placed in contact.

FIG. 91.—Dyeing in the Tray.

The practical dyeing of leathers varies considerably according to whether they are tanned with vegetable materials, chrome, alumina salts, or chamoising. Vegetable-tanned leathers are dyed either by hand in the "dye-tray," or in the drum or paddle, the two latter methods being now largely employed. The dye-tray is a shallow vat, about 10 inches deep, and large enough for the goods to be laid flat in it. In the English method, one or two dozen skins, or even more, are dyed at a time, being turned over in the tray by hand, the undermost pair being drawn out and placed on the top (Fig. 91). The method is convenient where only a small number of skins are to be dyed to one particular shade, which is more easily matched as the goods are always under observation, and it has the further advantage that, if desired, the grain sides only of the skins can be coloured, by "pairing" or "pleating" them before dyeing. For this purpose two skins of equal size are laid together flesh to flesh (pairing), or each skin is doubled down the back, flesh side in (pleating), and pressed firmly together with a sleeker on the table, when the skins adhere so closely that if carefully handled, no colour penetrates between them during the dyeing, except a little round the edges. This effects considerable economy of dye-stuff, as the fleshes would absorb a good deal, and for some purposes, an undyed flesh is preferred. In dyeing in the paddle or drum, the skins are merely placed loose in the dye-liquor, so that the fleshes are dyed equally with the grain sides. Paddle-dyeing has the advantage of effecting a considerable saving of labour, as compared with the dye-tray, in which constant handling, which often lasts an hour or more, is required. It also allows of almost equal facility in examining the colour of the skins, which is very important when dyeing to shade; but it is less economical in dye-stuff, as not only the flesh sides are dyed but a much larger volume of liquor is used, and as the dye-bath can never be entirely exhausted, more dye is run away in the used liquor. Drum-dyeing is much less expensive in this respect, as the volume of liquor may be very small, and from the efficiency of the motion, the dyeing is very thorough, and penetrates deeply into or through the skin, which in many cases is advantageous, but it is difficult to dye to exact shade, since the skins can only be examined by stopping and opening the drum. Most dyes are more readily fixed at high temperatures, and in this respect the drum has an advantage over all other methods, as once heated it retains its heat with very little loss to the end of the operation, while both in the paddle and the dye-tray the liquor is rapidly cooled, and special methods of maintaining the temperature complicate the apparatus, and require great care to avoid overheating. It is usually best to work at the highest temperature which the goods will safely bear, and this varies to some extent with the class of goods, chrome tannages and chamois leather being peculiar in standing almost any temperature short of boiling. With vegetable tanned leather 50° C. may be taken as a maximum; but cold wet skins may safely be introduced rapidly into a liquor heated to 60°, as they will cool it sufficiently.

The Continental method of dyeing in two trays may be mentioned here, as it produces very rapid and even dyeing, with considerable economy of dye-stuff, and the principle is capable of application to other methods where a large number of skins have to be dyed to the same colour. As generally carried out, two trays are employed, each about 4 feet long, 18 inches wide, and 10 inches or a foot deep, and these are usually made with a sloping bottom, or propped up in such a way that the dye-liquor all runs to the further side of the tray. A single pair of skins is usually dyed at once (in about 6 liters (5 qt.) of liquor for sheep and goat). To begin with, the first tray is filled with a very weak liquor, and the second with one of about half strength. The goods are entered in the first tray, turned a few times, and passed into the second; the liquor in the first is run away, and it is re-filled with one of the full strength, to which the goods are then transferred, and dyed to shade. The second tray is much reduced in strength by the skins, and now serves as the weak liquor for a fresh pair, which in its turn passes into that from which the goods have been dyed out, and then into a new liquor; each pair of goods thus passing through three baths, of which the last is of full strength, and which quickly brings up a full and even colour. In the ordinary English method, the goods must, for the sake of economy of dye-stuff, be dyed out in a nearly exhausted bath, which is a tedious operation, the last stage of dyeing often taking a time far longer than that required to bring the goods nearly up to shade, and even then failing to produce a good and full colour. This evil may be lessened by adding the dye-stuff in several successive portions, as the bath becomes exhausted, but cannot be altogether avoided with a single tray, if any reasonable exhaustion of the bath is to be attained. At first sight it seems a very slow process to dye the goods in single pairs, but this is to a great extent compensated by the rapidity with which they take on colour. In the Continental system, the dyes, mostly of the coal-tar series, are used as strong solutions, and each new dye-bath is made up by filling the tray with a definite volume of hot water and adding a measured quantity of the dye-solution.

The re-use of partially exhausted dye-baths is generally limited to cases where either single dyes, or mixtures of very equal affinity for the leather are employed, since where dyes of unequal affinity are employed, one is more rapidly removed than the other, and the shade of the dye-bath is altered. Many dyes sold as single colours are really mixtures, and alter in shade if successive quantities of leather are dyed in their solutions. Basic dyes are also apt to be precipitated by traces of tannin washed out of the goods, and thus rendered unfit for use a second time. This may be avoided by suitable preparation of the goods (see p. 411).

Such mixtures may often be detected by putting a drop of their solution on blotting-paper, when the dyes form differently coloured rings according to their more or less rapid fixation by the paper, or by dusting the dry dye *very* thinly on wet blotting-paper, when each particle produces its separate spot.

Much of the success of practical leather-dyeing depends on proper selection and preparation of the goods. Sound uninjured grain is a matter of first importance; no satisfactory dyeing can be expected on skins which through carelessness in soaks, limes, or bates, are tainted by what is known as "weak grain," caused by destruction or injury of the delicate hyaline layer, which forms the natural glaze and outer surface of the skin (p. 50). For such goods, "acid" are to be preferred to "basic" dyes, the latter having an especial tendency to dye darker and deeper where the grain is imperfect. Goods of different tannages and colours should never be dyed together, as they are certain to produce different shades in the same dye-bath. Tanned skins which have been dried, especially if they have been in stock for some time, should be thoroughly softened by soaking in tepid water and drumming, a temperature of between 40° and 45° C. being most advantageous. Skins, such as calf of mixed or bark tannage, must now be freed from all bloom by scouring with brush and if necessary with slate or stone, but great care is requisite to avoid injury to the grain. A little borax or other weak alkaline solution assists in removing bloom. Fresh sumach-tanned skins merely require setting out with a brass sleeker, but those which have been long dried often dye more evenly and readily if they are re-sumached.

Dark coloured tannages, such as Australian bazils, and East India sheep and goat tanned with cassia bark, are always improved by sumaching, and if for light colours, by first stripping a portion of the original tan by drumming for a quarter of an hour with a weak ($1/4$ per cent.) solution of soap powder or borax at a temperature of 30° to 35° C. and then passing (after well washing in warm water, but with as little exposure as possible to the air) through a weak sour of sulphuric acid of 1-2 per cent. The acid should now be as thoroughly removed as possible by washing in water, and the goods should be sumached. The process, and especially the use of sulphuric acid, is always deleterious to the skins, and is one of the causes of the early decay of coloured bookbindings and furniture leathers. Lactic, formic, or acetic acid may be substituted for sulphuric with safety, and the risk of injury from sulphuric, which generally is only apparent after the lapse of a considerable time, is a good deal lessened by adding to the sumach liquor a small quantity of potassium tartrate, sodium acetate or lactate, or some other salt of a weak organic acid, which is thus substituted for the much more dangerous sulphuric. Except in cases of absolute necessity for the production of light shades, the use of sulphuric acid should not be resorted to, and then only for goods which are not expected to possess great permanence. For light shades for bookbinding and upholstery, good sumach-tanned leathers and organic acids only should be employed. Alkaline treatment also demands great caution, as excess of strong alkalies is very injurious to the leather. Another objectionable method for the preparation of leather for very light shades, is the use of the lead-bleach described on p. 399.

The sumaching is best done in a drum, at a temperature of about 40°. Lamb advises that 1 to 2 lb. of sumach per dozen is sufficient for calf, and recommends running in this liquor for two or three hours. The skins are then rinsed in water to free them from adhering sumach, and set out on a table with a brass sleeker, and are now ready for dyeing with "acid" dyestuffs. If "basic" dyes are used, thorough washing in several tepid waters is necessary to free them from the loose tannin; and if deep colours are to be dyed, it is better, instead of too much washing, to fix the tannin, which then serves as a mordant for the colour. For blues, blue-greens, or violets, this is done with a solution of "tartar emetic" (antimony potassium tartrate, of 5 to 20 grm. per liter according to the amount of tannin to be fixed, often with addition of some common salt), which produces no alteration in the colour. For browns, yellows, deep reds, or yellow-greens, it is advantageous to use titanium-potassium lactate or oxalate (2 grm. per liter), which in combination with the tannin produces a very permanent yellow coloration on which the basic colours dye freely. In many cases the titanium salt is best applied after dying with one of the dyewoods (Dreher).

The basic colours usually require simple solution in hot water before adding to the dye-bath, and are used in quantities of 0·5 to 2·5 grm. per liter of dye-bath, according to their colouring power, which varies a good deal, and to the depth of shade required. The solutions should not be boiled, and some colours are injured by too high a temperature. Some colours dissolve incompletely, and require filtration through a cotton cloth. As basic colours are precipitated by calcium carbonate, it is important that "temporary" hard waters should be neutralised with acetic or lactic acid till they faintly redden litmus; and in the case of colours which, from their attraction for the leather fibre, dye too rapidly, and consequently unevenly, better dyeing is often obtained by the use of a small excess of acetic acid, which also increases the solubility of the colour. Too much acid, however, will prevent the proper exhaustion of the bath. Some few colours, now little used, require to be dissolved in the first instance in a little methylated spirit; and the addition of spirit will often assist dyeing and staining where the leather is slightly greasy, though considerations of cost generally prevent its use.

Sodium sulphate is not unfrequently added to dyeing baths to improve equality of dyeing; and with some of the cotton dyes common salt is used to lessen their solubility and facilitate the exhaustion of the dye-bath.

"Acid" colours usually dye better if acid is added to the bath, to liberate their colour-acids, and for this purpose sulphuric acid is generally used in weight about equal to that of the colour used. Its use is, however, objectionable, in this case, for the same reasons as in bleaching, since it is impossible by mere washing to remove it entirely from the leather, which it ultimately rots when concentrated by exposure to a dry atmosphere or high temperature; and it is better to use formic or acetic acid to the extent of two or three times the weight of the dye-stuff. Sodium acid sulphate may also be used, but is probably more objectionable than an organic acid. Many acid colours, however, dye quite satisfactorily from a neutral bath. The acid colours are used in somewhat similar quantities to the basic, but are generally inferior in colouring power, though they dye more evenly, especially on defective grain, and are often more permanent to light.

Mention has already been made of the polygenetic or mordant dye-stuffs, which are still used to some extent for dyeing glove-leathers, and of which logwood is important in dyeing blacks. Fustic and Brazil-wood (peach-wood) are not quite gone out of use among old-fashioned dyers, even for dyeing moroccos and other coloured leathers of vegetable tannage. Peach-wood, with a tin mordant (generally a so-called "tin spirits" made by dissolving tin in mixtures of hydrochloric and nitric acid) was formerly much used in dyeing cheap crimsons, but is now quite displaced by the azo-scarlets. The acid tin-solutions were frequently very injurious to the leather.

The wood-infusion, rendered slightly alkaline with soda, ammonia or, formerly, with stale urine, is usually dyed first on the leather, and followed by the mordant "striker"; ferrous or ferric solutions, and potassium bichromate being used for dark colours, and tin salts, or sometimes alum, for the brighter ones. The mordant is sometimes added to the dye-bath towards the end of the operation, but is better used as a separate bath, as it is apt to produce a precipitate of colour-lake on the surface of the skin, which rubs off on friction. In some cases, and especially in black dyeing, the strong infusion of dye-wood, and the necessary "striker" are successively applied by brushing instead of in the dye-tray.

Logwood and Brazil wood are both Cæsalpinias closely allied to divi-divi. Logwood is *Cæsalpinia* (see p. 287) *Campechianum*. Its colouring matter is hæmatoxylin, a substance nearly allied to tannins, and almost colourless; which on oxidation gives hæmatin, which dyes a yellow-brown, only developing other colours by the aid of mordants. Logwood chips are extracted by boiling or heating under pressure for some time with water;

and as hæmatin gives dark purplish-red compounds with alkalies, soda or stale urine is frequently added under the mistaken belief that it produces a better extraction, but really leads to waste of colouring matter by oxidation. It is best to extract with water alone, and add any necessary alkali to the infusion before use. 1-2 lb. of wood per gallon is frequently employed in making the infusion, and as this proportion of water is quite insufficient to properly extract the wood, the residue should be boiled with one or more further quantities, which are employed in turn for extracting fresh portions of wood. Logwood dyes best at high temperatures, and especially in the case of chrome leather with which a temperature of 80° C. may be safely used. The presence of a trace of a salt of lime is advantageous, and with very soft waters a little lime water or chalk may be added to the logwood liquor.

In blacking skins, the strong infusion is rendered slightly alkaline with sodium carbonate or ammonia, and brushed undiluted on the leather. If employed as a bath, a somewhat weaker infusion is used, and the leather is frequently treated first in an alkaline bath, to which a small quantity of potassium bichromate is often added. The object of the alkali is not only to assist in the formation of the colour-lake, by saturating the acid set free from the iron-salt used as a striker, and thus to prevent the colour from penetrating the leather too deeply, but, at the same time, to overcome the resistance to wetting caused by grease or oil which the leather may contain. It must thus be used more freely when stuffed leather is to be blacked, but excess should be carefully avoided, as it easily renders the leather tender and brittle. The potassium bichromate oxidises the hæmatoxylin, or the ferrous salt subsequently applied, and forms a nearly black chrome-logwood lake.

The iron solution is generally either of ferrous sulphate of perhaps 5 per cent. strength, or commercial "iron-liquor," which is a "pyrolignite" or crude acetate of iron, containing catechol-derivatives and other organic products from the distillation of wood, which act advantageously, both as antiseptics, and in preventing the rapid oxidation which occurs when pure ferrous acetate is used. Iron-liquor is generally to be preferred to ferrous sulphate ("green vitriol"), as the sulphuric acid of the latter, unless completely neutralised by the alkali employed in preparation, acts in the end disastrously on the leather. Commercial iron-liquor is often adulterated with ferrous sulphate, which may be detected by its giving a precipitate with barium chloride. Great care should be taken not to use iron in excess of the logwood or tannin present, as it otherwise takes tannin from the leather itself, making it hard and liable to crack, while any uncombined iron acts as a carrier of oxygen, giving up its oxygen to the colouring matter or tannin with which it is in contact, and again oxidising from the air, and so causing "spueing" or oil-oxidation, and other evils.

Good blacks which are more permanent than those with logwood, may be obtained by merely treating leather containing an excess of oak-bark tannin or sumach, first with an alkaline solution (not at the most stronger than $2\frac{1}{2}$ per cent. of liquid ammonia, or 5 per cent. of soda crystals), and then with iron-liquor. If it is not certain that the leather contains excess of a suitable tannin, a tannin-solution must be employed like the logwood infusion, or the leather must be sumached. The addition of some sumach to logwood liquor is often advantageous, and a blacker (i.e. less blue) black, especially on alumed leathers, is obtained by using a proportion of fustic. Solutions made by boiling 10 per cent. of cutch with 5 per cent. of sodium carbonate give good blacks with iron-liquor, and do not make the leather tender, and they can be used in mixture with logwood. Many commercial logwood extracts contain chestnut-wood extract as an adulterant.

Instead of dyeing in the bath, it is very common, especially for the cheaper leathers such as linings, and coloured leathers of the commoner sort, to apply the colour by brushing (commonly called "staining"). Many colours, however, which dye well with time and warmth, are inapplicable in this way, and only those should be used which have a strong attraction for the leather, and hence go on well in the cold. If "acid" colours are employed, it is essential to select those which can be used in neutral solution, or at most with addition of some mild organic acid such as formic or acetic, since, as the leather is not washed after staining, the sulphuric acid would remain in it, and would ultimately destroy it. Where leathers have a hard and repellent surface, the addition of a little methylated spirit to the dye is often very useful. The colours are used in solutions of from $\frac{1}{4}$ to 1 per cent., which should be quite clear and free from sediment. Difficultly soluble colours must be used in weak solution, or the dye kept warm while in use. Dye-solutions will not generally keep for any great length of time without change.

Before staining, the leather must be carefully "set out," or otherwise made as smooth as possible, and the staining is generally done after most of the other operations of currying or dressing have been completed. Staining is best begun with the leather in a slightly damp or "sammied" condition, and the colour is applied evenly with a softish brush in two or three coats, the leather being slightly dried after each. As a rule the more coats are applied, the more even is the work; but to save cost of labour it is common on cheap goods to be content with two, of which the first is given, preferably with a weaker solution, to the dry leather. Where the leather is "weak-grained" it is sometimes advantageous to size it first with a weak solution of gelatine, gum tragacanth, or linseed mucilage, and similar solutions are often used to fix the colour and give a higher gloss. The stearine-glaze mentioned on p. 401 may also be used for this purpose, and a weak solution of it is sometimes employed as a vehicle for the acid colours. Acid yellows and browns may also be dissolved in the undiluted glaze where only a pale colour is required, or to heighten the colour of leather already stained. A list of suitable colours for staining is given in the Appendix, p. 486.

It rarely happens in leather dyeing that the required colour can be given by the application of a single dye, most of the shades now required being produced by mixtures. It is, therefore, necessary to say a few words on the theory of colour combinations.

White light is of course composed of a mixture of all the spectrum-colours, and can be separated into them by the prism. It is probable, however, that the eye is only capable of three distinct colour-sensations, and that all the colours we perceive are represented by the excitement of these in different proportions, the actual colour-sensations being red, blue-green, and violet. If we interpose a piece of yellow glass between the eye and white light, the violet and blue are absorbed, and the remaining red and green rays combine to produce the sensation of yellow. If pure blue glass is used, the red is absorbed, and we have blue as the result of the remaining mixture of green and violet. Red glass absorbs the whole of the green, and greenish-blue, allowing red and much of the violet to pass. Thus, if we combine blue and yellow glass, only the green is allowed to pass, and similarly with red and blue glass, green and blue is cut out, and only the violet remains. Thus red, yellow, and blue are frequently called the primary colours, and by combining all three in equal proportions all colours are cut out, and black or grey results. The blue and violet which are stopped by yellow glass are those colours which would produce the sensation of violet-blue, and hence the latter is called the "complementary colour" of yellow, and so on with the rest. It will be noted that all the colours of coloured objects are produced by absorption of a part of the light, and therefore coloured bodies are always darker than white ones, and where a colour is mixed with its complementary in suitable proportion, all colours are absorbed and black or grey is produced.

The subject of colour is too complicated to be adequately treated here; and for fuller information, readers are referred to Abney's 'Colour Measurement and Mixture,' S.P.C.K., London, 1891. It may, however, be pointed out that, while the true primary colour-sensations are unquestionably red, blue-green and violet, and by mixture of *light* of these colours, all other colours, including white, can be produced; the primary pigments or dyes are red, yellow, and blue; the effect being produced in the former case by the addition of colours, and in the latter by their subtraction.

Colours which are made by mixing two primary colours are generally called "secondary"; while the duller tints made by the addition to these of black, or of a complementary colour which produces black, are called "tertiary." Any primary colour is complementary to the secondary colour produced by mixing the other two primaries and *vice versa*. The following tabular arrangement shows at once the effect of colour mixing.

PRIMARY.	SECONDARY.	TERTIARY.
Red		
	- Orange	with Black. Brown.
Yellow		
	- Green	„ Olive, Sage.
Blue		
	- Purple (Violet).	„ Puce, Maroon.
Red		

Theoretically, *any* colour may be obtained by mixture of the primaries, and that this is possible to a great extent is shown in the success of modern "three colour" printing, by which pictures are obtained in natural colours by the use of three primaries only; but in practice few colours are quite pure, and if two very different colours are mixed, it is difficult to avoid the production of tertiaries. The most brilliant colours are generally produced by dyeing with the nearest colour which can be obtained to that required, and shading with another which is near, but on the other side of the desired tint.

Thus if we want to produce bright shades in dyeing, we must avoid the introduction of complementary colours. A bluish red mixed with a reddish blue will produce a bright shade of violet, but if we mix an orange-red with a greenish-blue, we introduce yellow into the mixture, and obtain a dull maroon or puce according to the proportion of the other colours. In a similar way, the introduction of a blue dye will dull a bright orange to a brown, and a little of a yellow dye will dull a bright purple to a maroon. This fact is frequently used in producing the quiet shades of colour often required from the most brilliant dyes. If to a bright orange we add black, or a blue dye which as its complementary produces black, we convert it into a brown. If instead of blue we use green for dulling, we give the brown a yellower shade, since the green produces black at the expense of the *red* of the orange. Violet similarly used gives a redder brown, since it produces black by combination with the *yellow*. This shading, if small in amount, is frequently done by direct mixture of a suitable dye, but if considerable, it is generally better to top one colour with another. Thus a blue, topped with a powerful orange, will produce a Havanna brown. For dark colours, it is frequently convenient to produce a dark ground with some cheap dye, such as logwood and iron or chrome, and to top it with a bright shade of the colour required. In this way cheap dark blues and greens can be easily produced. For reds and browns, mixtures of logwood and Brazil-wood, or Brazil-wood and fustic may be used, topped with coal-tar colours. Tanning materials, such as quebracho and mangrove extracts, which give browns with bichromate, are also employed on cheap goods. It is also frequently wise to dye with a basic colour and top with an acid one, or *vice versa*; as in many cases the one fixes and combines with the other, and an increase of fastness is obtained.

Morocco and many other coloured leathers are finished by damping the surface of the dried leather with a very dilute "seasoning" of water, milk, and blood or albumen, allowing the leather to become quite or nearly dry, and polishing by friction under a cylinder of agate, glass, or wood in the glazing machine. Many leathers are also grained by printing from engraved or electrotype rollers, or by "boarding," or a combination of the two. "Boarding" consists in pushing forward a fold in the leather on a table with a flat board roughed underneath, or lined with cork, in a way which is difficult to describe, but which in skilful hands wrinkles or "grains" the skin in a regular pattern.

The colour of a dyed skin is much altered by finishing and especially by glazing, which always darkens and enriches the colour. In dyeing to pattern, it is useful to glaze a little bit of the rapidly dried skin by friction with a smooth piece of hard wood for comparison, and a portion of the pattern may also be wetted for comparison with the wet skin. Colours which look full and even in the dye-bath, often go down in a most disappointing manner on drying, though to some extent they regain intensity on finishing.

In comparing the dyeing value of colours, the most practical way is to make actual dyeing trials with equal or known quantities of the colours and of water. Such trials may be made, either by "turning" the samples in photographic porcelain trays, kept warm in a water-bath (a "dripping tin" may be used for the purpose, the trays being supported a little above the bottom on tin supports soldered to the tin), or the leather may be hung from glass rods, by hooks of copper wire, in glass vessels (square battery jars), also placed in a water-bath. The leather samples should be of equal *surface* in every case; for suspension, pieces of "skiver" (sheep-grain) of 8 by 4 in. or 20 by 10 cm. are very convenient. These may either be "pleated" or suspended by the two ends grain side out, with a short glass rod to weight the fold, and keep them flat. The weight of colour used for a sample 8 in. by 4 in. multiplied by 54 times the area of a single skin in feet, will give approximately the weight of colour needed per dozen; which is, however, a good deal influenced by the mode of dyeing, and the quantity of water used.

In dyeing on the large scale, iron, zinc and even copper are to be avoided, the latter acting very injuriously on many colours, and on the whole wooden vessels are to be preferred. Though these become deeply dyed, they become very hard, and if well washed with hot water, and occasionally with dilute acid, they may be cleansed so as to give up no colour in subsequent dyeing operations, though of course it is not desirable, if it can be avoided, to use the same vessel for very different colours. Zinc rapidly bleaches many colours, especially while wet and slightly acid, and discharge-patterns may often be produced by pressing the wet leather on perforated zinc plates.

CHAPTER XXVI.
EVAPORATION, HEATING AND DRYING.

Questions of evaporation, whether for raising steam, or for the concentration of tanning extracts and other solutions are of considerable importance in the tanning industry, and as the same natural laws which apply to these equally govern the drying of leather, it is convenient to study the theory of the whole subject in one chapter, rather than to divide it, and place each part in a different portion of the book.

The modern conception of evaporation and vapour pressures has been described on page 75, but it will be necessary to recapitulate a little. It is a well-known fact that most liquids, if left exposed in an open vessel, gradually disappear by evaporation into the air, even at ordinary temperatures. If the vessel is heated sufficiently, the liquid "boils"; that is, bubbles of vapour are formed in it, and escape, and the evaporation is therefore much more rapid. To avoid complication, let us first imagine a liquid sealed in a glass flask, which contains no air, but which is only partially filled by the liquid. It has been pointed out that the motion of heat by which the molecules of the liquid are agitated, enables some of them to break away from the attraction by which liquid particles are held together, and pass into the form of gas or vapour, which will fill the empty part of the flask. This evaporation will, however, soon reach a limit, since the vapour cannot escape from the flask. The flying molecules of vapour produce pressure by striking the walls of the flask, while a proportion of them will strike the surface of the liquid, and again be caught and retained by its attraction; and as the pressure rises, the number of these necessarily increases till a point is reached when as many fall back and are retained (or "condensed"), as those which evaporate, and the pressure will then remain constant. The amount of the pressure will vary with the nature of the liquid, and will be the greater the more volatile it is, or, in other words, the less the power of its internal attraction. It will also increase with rising temperature, which, by increasing the velocity of motion of the molecules, renders their escape from the liquid easier, and their recapture more difficult. It will not be at all affected by the volume of vapour or the size of the flask, but so long as any liquid is present, it will depend merely upon the nature of the liquid, and the temperature. If the flask is large, more of the liquid will evaporate till the same pressure is reached. If at the outset the flask is not empty, but filled with air, it will make no difference to the pressure or quantity of the *vapour* in it, which will be added to that of the air, whatever that may be. If the sealing of the flask is broken so that it is open to the atmosphere, air and vapour will escape, or air will pass in, till the total pressure is equal to the atmospheric pressure outside, (about 15 lb. per square inch). As, however, the vapour in the flask is always renewed by evaporation, so that the full vapour-pressure of the liquid is maintained, the "partial" pressure (as it is called) of the *air* in the flask will be less than that of the outer atmosphere by the amount of the vapour-pressure, which makes up the difference. Once this balance is attained, evaporation will go on very slowly in the flask, as it can only replace the small quantity of vapour which escapes. If, however, the vapour is removed by blowing fresh air into the flask, it will rapidly be replaced in the old proportion by fresh evaporation. Thus goods in a close room will dry only very slowly, even if the temperature is high, unless the moistened air is replaced by dryer air from the outside by some effective system of ventilation. In absence of this, evaporation only becomes rapid when the temperature of the liquid is raised to its "boiling point," that is, when the vapour-pressure becomes slightly in excess of that of the atmosphere, so that the freshly formed vapour can push out that already in the flask or chamber into the outer air, and at the same time, bubbles can be formed in the interior of the liquid by the escaping vapour. As the vapour-pressure of a liquid rises continuously with increasing temperature, and its boiling point is defined as that temperature at which it is equal in pressure to the air (or vapour) in contact with it, it is evident that the boiling point must entirely depend on the pressure. Thus the boiling point of water in a boiler at a pressure of 55 lb. per square inch above the atmosphere is 150°C., and in a partial vacuum equal to 5·8 inches of barometric pressure, is only 60° C., a fact which is made use of in the concentration of extracts and other liquids at a low temperature in the vacuum-pan. (Atmospheric pressure is taken at 30 inches or 760 millimeters of the barometer or 14·7 lb. per inch, or 1·033 kilos per square centimeter.)

If a piece of iron is placed over a powerful gas-burner, it will go on getting hotter till its temperature is nearly or quite equal to that of the gas-flame. On the other hand, a pan of water, in the same condition, once it has reached its boiling point, becomes no hotter till all the water is evaporated. It is evident that the whole available heat or energy of the gas-flame is consumed in converting the water into steam. We might convert a proportion of this energy into mechanical work, by using the steam in a steam engine; but even without this, work is actually being done by the escaping steam in raising the weight of the atmosphere, and in overcoming the attractive force which holds the particles of water together in the liquid form. It is of course known to everyone, that energy may change its form, as from heat to work, but that it cannot be destroyed, diminished or increased; and therefore the whole of the work performed in converting the water into steam is again recovered as heat when the steam is condensed. In this connection a clear distinction must be made between *quantity* of heat, and *temperature*, which in popular language are often confused. It is for instance obvious that if we mix a pound of water at boiling temperature with another pound at freezing point, the temperature is altered to 50° C., but the total *quantity* of heat is unchanged. It is equally clear that no change in quantity of heat takes place when 1 lb. of mercury at 100° is mixed with 1 lb. of water at 0°, though in this case, owing to the small capacity of mercury for heat, the common temperature would only be raised to about 3°. We must therefore have some measure of heat apart from the mere direct indications of the thermometer, and that most generally used is the quantity of heat required to raise 1 kilo of water 1° C. (kilogram-calorie). In England the heat required to raise 1 lb. of water 1° F. is also in use as a unit. The k.-calorie is equal to 3·97 (very approximately 4) lb. × F. units. For our purpose it may be taken that 100 k.-calories of heat are required to raise 1 kilo or liter of water from freezing to boiling temperature. If, however, the water is actually frozen, we require 80 k-calories merely to melt the kilogram of ice without perceptibly raising its temperature, and when the water is raised to 100°, 536 calories of heat are still necessary merely to convert it into steam at the same temperature. To melt 1 lb. of ice requires 144 lb. × F. units, to raise it to boiling point 180 more, and to evaporate it 965 additional. The quantity of heat required for actual evaporation varies a little at different temperatures, being somewhat larger at lower temperatures, but the total heat required to raise water from the freezing point, and convert it into steam at *any* pressure is nearly constant, being 635 calories at atmospheric pressure, and only about 650 calories, or 1180 lb. × F. units at 50 lb. per sq. inch. The quantity of heat evolved by the combustion of 1 lb. of good coal is 13,000 to 15,000 lb. × F. units; or of 1 kilo, 7200 to 8300 k-calories, but in raising steam in a good boiler coal will only evaporate 10 times its weight of water at 100° (5360 calories or 9650 lb. × F. units), the remaining heat being lost. 1 horse-power (33,000 foot-pounds per minute) in the best engines requires about 1½ lb. of coal or 15 lb. of steam per hour, but in those of worse construction may run up to many times that amount. As, even theoretically, not 20 per cent. of the total heat can be converted into mechanical work in a "perfect" engine working at 75 lb. pressure, it is often economical to use waste steam for heating or evaporation, and where this can be done profitably, the additional cost of the mechanical power is very small.

A gram-calorie of one-thousandth part of the above is also in use for some scientific purposes, but the kilogram-calorie only is used in the following pages.

This is equal to 76·04 kilogrammeters per sec., but the metrical horse-power is only taken at 75 kilogrammeters in France and Germany.

In evaporating liquids in the open pan 536 calories is required to evaporate 1 kilo of water already raised to boiling temperature, and a larger amount for salt-solutions, and it makes comparatively little difference whether this is done at 100° or at a lower temperature. Where, however, evaporation is done in *vacuo*, considerable economy can be effected by what are known as multiple "effects," in which the steam from one vacuum-pan is employed to boil a second under a reduced pressure, and consequently boiling at a lower temperature. This principle can be practically applied to as many as five or six successive "effects," the weaker liquor being usually evaporated at the highest temperature and lowest vacuum in the first "effect," by the exhaust steam of the engine used for the vacuum pumps, while the steam from the first effect heats that of the next higher concentration, and so on. In the Yaryan evaporator (p. 339), the boiling liquid is sprayed through coil-tubes, thus exposing an enormous surface to evaporation, and the whole concentration of any given portion of liquid takes place as it passes through the apparatus, which does not, even in multiple effects, occupy more than 4 or 5 minutes; and without the temperature of the liquid ever rising above 60° or 70° C. In the case of liquids, like sugar- and tannin-solutions which are liable to chemical change from continued heating, the shortness of the time is a very great advantage. The number of effects which it is desirable to use depends greatly on the cost of fuel as compared to the largely increased cost of the apparatus. 1 lb. of coal employed in raising steam will evaporate $8\frac{1}{2}$ lb. in a single-effect Yaryan, 16 lb. in a double-effect, $23\frac{1}{2}$ lb. in a triple, $30\frac{1}{2}$ lb. in a quadruple, and 37 lb. in a quintuple-effect apparatus.

Where liquids are evaporated in the open air at temperatures below boiling, it is advisable by some means to spread the liquid in a thin film, so as to expose a large surface, which must be continuously removed by agitation, so as to prevent the formation of a skin. A good apparatus for this purpose is the Chenalier evaporator (Fig. 92), which consists of steam-heated copper discs rotating in a trough containing the liquid, which is taken up by buckets attached to the rims of the discs, and poured over their heated surfaces. In other forms, the liquid is allowed to trickle over steam-heated pipes or corrugated plates. Such evaporators should be placed in a current of air so as to rapidly carry off the vapour formed. Their use is very objectionable for liquids, like tannin-liquors, which are injured by oxidation, and they are not nearly so economical as vacuum-pans.

The drying of leather depends on the same laws as the evaporation of liquids, but demands special consideration from its very different conditions of temperature and supply of heat. It is important to remember that evaporation cannot go on unless the vapour-pressure of the liquid to be evaporated is higher than that of the vapour in contact with it, and that air-pressure does not prevent evaporation, so that if we sweep away the stagnant vapour with dry air, evaporation will go on as quickly as in vacuo, except that the liquid cannot boil. We must also bear in mind that evaporation consumes quite as much heat at low temperatures as in a steam boiler, and that this heat must generally come from the surrounding air, the temperature of which it reduces.

FIG. 92.—Chenalier Evaporator and Glue Coolers.

The rapidity of evaporation, and the quantity of moisture which can be taken up by a given volume of air depends on the vapour-pressure, which increases with temperature. The relation between the two, and the weight of water in grams per cubic meter which can be dissolved in dry air is given in the following table. (Grams per cubic meter is practically equivalent to ounces per 1000 cubic feet. Vapour-pressure is given in millimeters of mercury of the barometer, p. 422.)

VAPOUR PRESSURE OF WATER.

Temperature, °C	-10	-5	0	5	10	15	20	25	30	35	40
°F	14	23	32	41	50	59	68	77	86	95	104
Pressure, mm.	2·2	3·2	4·6	6·5	9·1	12·7	17·4	23·5	31·5	41·9	54·9
Grams per cb. m.	2·4	3·4	4·9	6·8	9·3	12·8	17·2	22·8	30·1	39·2	..

Air is practically never dry, and in damp weather is frequently saturated with moisture to the full extent corresponding to its temperature. In England the average quantity of moisture contained in the air throughout the year is 82 per cent. of the total possible, and even in the driest summer weather it is never less than 58 per cent. So long as the water is in the form of vapour, the air remains quite clear and does not feel damp; in fogs, the air is not only saturated with moisture, but contains small liquid particles floating in it. Of course when the air is really saturated with moisture, it has no drying power whatever.

As is evident from the table, the amount of water which can be dissolved in a given volume of air rapidly increases with temperature. Air at 0° C. is only capable of containing 4·9 grams per cubic meter, or not much more than 20 per cent. of what it can contain at 25° C. It hence rapidly increases in drying power as it is warmed, and consequently the air in a warm well-ventilated drying room in winter is generally much drier, and has greater capacity for absorbing moisture than the open air in the driest summer weather. This is the principal cause of the tendency to harsh and irregular drying by the use of artificial heat; and may be remedied by a proper circulation of the air by a fan without too frequent change with the colder air outside. On the other hand the use of a little artificial heat in damp summer weather, when the air is saturated with moisture, may be quite as necessary as in winter. The amount of moisture in the air is most easily ascertained by a device known as the "wet and dry bulb thermometers." This consists of two thermometers mounted on a board; one of which has the bulb covered with muslin, and kept moist by a lamp-wick attached to it, and dipping in a vessel of water. The temperature of the wet bulb is lowered by the heat consumed in evaporation, and the difference of its temperature from that of the dry bulb is proportionate to the drying power of the air. This may be approximately calculated in grams per cubic meter by multiplying the difference by 0·64 for Centigrade or 0·35 for Fahrenheit degrees; and if deducted from the total capacity for moisture corresponding to the temperature of the *wet* bulb as given in table, p. 426, will give the actual moisture in grams contained in a cubic meter of air; but for practical purposes, all that is necessary is to find by experience the temperature and difference between the wet and dry bulbs, which gives the best result for the drying required, and to maintain it as nearly as possible by regulation of the heating and ventilation. Cheap forms of the instrument are made for use in cotton-mills, where it is necessary to maintain a certain degree of moisture; or it may be improvised from two chemical thermometers which agree well together. Distilled (rain or steam) water should be used to moisten the bulb, or it will quickly become coated with lime salts, and it should be placed in a draught, or its indications will not be accurate.

It is of course obvious that not only the wet thermometer, but the wet hides or skins are cooled by evaporation, and they, in their turn, cool the air with which they are in contact, which not only becomes moistened, but is lessened in its capacity for moisture by cooling, and thus rapidly reaches a condition when it can absorb no more moisture. It is thus necessary to maintain its temperature by artificial heat, or to replace it constantly by fresh air from the outside, and which of these expedients is most economical will depend on the temperature of the air outside as compared with that which it is required to maintain. If the outside air is sufficiently warm, and not saturated with moisture, it is generally best to use it in large quantities without artificial heat, wind usually supplying the necessary motive power for its circulation. Wet goods from the pits may thus be dried to a "sammed" condition by any air which is not saturated, and above freezing point; though the drying will often be slow. For drying "off," artificial heat is generally necessary, since the attraction of the fibre for the last traces of moisture is very considerable, and to remove it the drying power of the air must be considerably higher than that required for the evaporation of free water. In drying stuffed leather a temperature must generally be maintained sufficient to keep the fats employed in partial fusion, and so permit their absorption by the leather, while at the same time the drying must be gradual, or the water may be dried out before the fats have time to take its place. This is generally best attained by the use of artificial heat, and ventilation by circulating the air by a fan without its too frequent renewal, especially in cold weather. Frequently air which has been heated and used for drying off finished goods, and so partially saturated with moisture, may be used with advantage for wet goods, or for other purposes where a more gentle drying is required. If the temperature is low outside, the amount of heat consumed in heating cold air to the temperature required may be very considerable. The weight of a cubic meter of air at $0°$ C. and atmospheric pressure is $1·293$ kilos, and its specific heat at constant pressure is $0·2375$ of that of water. Therefore to heat a cubic meter of air at ordinary pressure and temperature $1°$ C. will require the same amount of heat as that used to heat $0·3$ kilo of water to the same extent, or in other words $0·3$ of a k.-calorie. If steam-heating is used, 1 kilo of good coal burnt under the boiler should heat about 1800 cubic meters $10°$ C., or 1 lb. should heat 52,000 cubic feet $10°$ F., assuming that the condensed water is not cooled below $100°$ C. These seem large volumes, but if we reflect that a 48-inch Blackman fan may move 30,000 cubic feet per minute, we shall realise that the cost of coal in heating air is not inconsiderable.

Commercially-dry leather generally, if unstuffed, contains about 15 per cent. of residual moisture, which varies in amount with the weather, and can be more or less completely removed by drying at high temperatures. If leather has been over-dried, it only slowly regains its weight on exposure to cold air. Commercial disputes not unfrequently arise on the dryness of leather. In the opinion of the writer, a customer can only claim that the leather should be sufficiently dry not to lose weight when exposed to dry air at the ordinary temperature and degree of dryness of a warehouse or factory, and claims based on re-drying in hot drying rooms are distinctly fraudulent.

We must now consider the heat consumed by the actual evaporation of the water in the leather. The actual evaporation of water already raised to 100° C. consumes 536 k.-calories, but the evaporation of water which has not previously been heated so far consumes more heat, and we may take that required at ordinary temperatures as in round numbers 600 k.-calories per kilo, or 1080 lb. × F. units per lb. Disregarding small fractions, this is equivalent to the cooling to the same temperature of an equal weight of steam in the heating pipes, and this, as we have seen, demands about $\frac{1}{10}$ of its weight of coal for its production from water already heated to 100° C.

The cooling takes place, in the first instance, in the leather, the temperature of which is reduced like that of the wet-bulb thermometer; and this in its turn cools the air in contact with it. Thus in air-drying without artificial heat, the whole heat must be supplied by the air and the loss reduces its capacity for moisture, greatly increasing the volume required. This is not of much consequence in open-air drying, since even a light wind will supply air in enormous volume. A moderate breeze of ten miles an hour moves about 15 feet or 4½ meters per second. When, however, the air must be moved by fans, the power required becomes important. The evaporation of 1 kilo of water at summer temperature will cool about 2000 cubic meters, and that of 1 lb. 32,000 cubic feet of air 1° C.

In calculating the ventilating and heating power required in fitting up drying rooms, it is usually necessary to ascertain that required under the most unfavourable circumstances, and then add a liberal margin to cover errors and accidents. As the calculations are, in consequence of the many varying conditions, somewhat complex, it may be convenient to give as examples the quantities of air and heat required to evaporate 1 kilo (2·205 lb.) of water under different ordinary conditions, and these may serve as a basis of calculation of the drying power which must be provided for different tanneries.

1. *Indifferent Open-Air Drying.*—Air at 10° C. (50° F.), wet-bulb thermometer 7° C. (44·3° F.), indicating a total capacity for moisture of about 2 grm. per cubic meter; air not to be cooled beyond 7·75° C. (46° F.), leaving a residual capacity for moisture of 0·5 grm. per cubic meter. Each cubic meter will therefore take up 1·5 grm. of moisture, and as 1 kilo contains

1000 grm. we have 1000⁄1·5 = 666 cubic meters per kilo required to absorb moisture; and 600⁄2·25° × 0·3 = 888 cubic meters reduced 2·25° to furnish the 600 cal. required for evaporation. Total air used 1554 cubic meters or 54,900 cubic feet.

2. *Drying with Heat.*—Outside-air at 10° saturated with moisture, heated to 20° C. (68° F.) acquires a capacity for 7·9 grm. per cubic meter. If we assume that a drying capacity of 2 grm. per meter is required to complete the drying, we have an effective capacity of 5·9 grm.

1000⁄5·9 = 170 cubic meters or 6000 cubic feet, and to heat this 10° C. will require 510 cal. Evaporation of 1 kilo will consume 600 cal. Total heat 1110 cal.

3. *Drying with Heat.*—Outside-air at 10° as above, heated to 25° C., giving an effective capacity for moisture of 13·5 - 2·0 = 11·5 grm. per cubic meter.

1000⁄11·5 = 87 cubic meters or 3070 cubic feet. To warm this 15° requires 391 cal.; and 600 cal. added for evaporation gives a total of 991 cal.

Comparing 2 and 3 we see that the higher temperature is more economical, where it can be allowed, than the lower, both in air and heat, though this is partly compensated by the greater loss of heat by cooling of the building, etc., which it entails.

4. Air at 0° C. heated to 20° requires about 97 cubic meters, or 3430 cubic feet of air, and a total of 1180 cal.

5. Air at 0° C. and heated to 25° C. requires 63 cubic meters or 2230 cubic feet, and a total of 1075 cal.

6. Air at -15° C. (5° F.) requires 4·5 cal. per cubic meter to raise it to 0° C., and acquires a capacity for drying of about 2 grm. per meter.

We will apply these figures to a drying room arranged with a screw-fan with a central division, or two floors, so that the air can be either circulated or replaced with fresh air from the outside at will (see Fig. 94, p. 435). Such a room with 100 feet of length clear of space required for fans, air passages, and heating pipes, and 20 feet × 8 feet in section, should hang about 800 medium butts, weighing say 12½ kilo (27 lb.) each, and when wet from the yard, containing the same weight of water. A 48-inch Blackman fan, under these conditions would probably move say 20,000 cubic feet (565 cubic meters) of air per minute, at the cost of 2 or 2½ horse-power. This, in a room of the section named, would give an average velocity of 125 feet per minute or rather under 1½ miles an hour; not at all too much to keep the air freely circulating among closely hung leather. If we assume that these butts are to be dried in a week (practically 10,000 minutes) under the conditions of No. 2, the 10,000 kilos of water they contain will require

1,700,000 cubic meters of air, or about 170 cubic meters per minute, or about $3/10$ of the air must be fresh every time it passes through the fan. 1 kilo of water requiring 1110 cal. must be evaporated per minute.

Under the conditions of No. 4, only 97 cubic meters of air per minute would be required, or about $5/6$ might be circulated without change, but the total heat required would be about the same, 1180 cal. Under the conditions of Nos. 4 and 6 some 1620 cal. per minute would be employed. It is hardly necessary to provide for the full amount of heat required by No. 6, since in this country such conditions occur but seldom, and never for more than a few days at a time, and during such a period, much less heat would suffice to carry on the drying at a slower rate, and keep out the frost.

Beside the heat required for actual drying, it is necessary to provide for that lost by the building during cold weather, and this is much more difficult to calculate. If, by arranging the outlet for moist air on the pressure side of the fan, the internal pressure of the building be kept a little lower than the outside, there can be no loss by escape of hot air, any leakage being inwards, and supplying a part of the change of air which, we have seen, is necessary. In a brick building with glass windows, the loss of heat is far less than in the old-fashioned wooden louvre-boarded structure, and where fan-drying is in constant use, the brick structure is much to be preferred. Frequent windows, with casements horizontally pivoted at the centre, will supply enough air for favourable conditions of air-drying, and when the weather is bad, resort is had to the fan. Most modern drying rooms in the Leeds district are built upon this plan. Where louvre-boarded structures must be used for fan-drying, the sides should be made as tight as possible in winter by sheets of canvas or sail-cloth nailed on, for which purpose old sails can be bought in seaport towns at reasonable rates, a few louvre-boards only being kept open for the admission of air in suitable positions.

Box, in his 'Practical Treatise on Heat' puts the loss through walls in brick buildings for a difference of 30° F. (16·6° C.) between inside and outside temperatures, at the approximate amounts shown in the following table.

E. & F. N. Spon, Ltd., London.

LOSS OF HEAT THROUGH WALLS.

Thickness of Wall in Inches.	K.-calories per Sq. Foot per Hour.	—
4·5	1·76	Stone walls must be about one-half thicker, to afford equal warmth with brick ones.
9	1·44	

| 14 | 1·20 | The loss from glass windows |
| 18 | 1·06 | amounts to 3 or 4 k.-calories per square foot per hour. |

If the building is of several stories, the loss to the roof in the intermediate ones need hardly be taken into account, but if the ceiling is not tight, and open to the roof, the loss may be great, but difficult to estimate. If we consider the drying room already described, the total area of the walls and ceiling is about 4000 feet, and to maintain its temperature 30° F. above the atmosphere at 1·2 cal. per sq. foot would require 4800 cal. per hour or 80 cal. per minute, a very small amount compared to that consumed in drying.

The following table calculated from data given by Box will give some idea of the amount of steam or hot-water piping required for heating. The sizes given are for the internal diameter of the pipe, allowance being made for the increased heating surface of pipes of ordinary thickness. Small pipes are considerably more effective in proportion to their surface than large ones, and for high-pressure heating 1½ or 2-inch wrought-iron pipes are to be recommended as in many ways preferable to cast iron. The gilled or ribbed pipes now often used are also advantageous as giving a greatly increased heating surface.

HEAT GIVEN BY STEAM-PIPES.

Steam Pressure, lb. per sq. in.	Temperature of Pipe.	K.-calories per hour per foot run of Pipe.		
	°F.	2 in.	3 in.	4 in.
52	300	102	137	169
35	280	92	121	148
21	260	81	106	130
10	240	68	92	113
2·5	220	59	81	97
	210	54	72	89
	200	49	66	81
	190	45	60	74
	180	40	54	67

| | 170 | 36 | 49 | 60 | |

The temperature of the air to be heated is understood to be 60° F.; at lower temperatures the quantity of heat given off by the pipes would be greater, and at higher temperatures less; the amount being approximately proportional to the difference of temperature between the air and the hot pipes. It is also important to note that the table refers to steam-pipes in still air, and that if placed in a powerful draught, (as immediately before or behind the fan), their heating effect may be at least doubled. This has not been considered in the following calculations.

Applying these figures to the estimate of 1110 calories per minute required for drying in our building, and assuming 80 calories per minute for the loss of heat through the walls, we have a total of about 71,400 calories per hour, and to obtain this would require 736 feet of 4-inch pipe at 220° F. (heated by exhaust steam) or 700 feet of 2-inch pipe heated to 300° F. by steam at 52 lb. pressure.

If we adopt the estimate of 1620 calories of No. 5 and 6, we shall require 1050 and 1000 feet of the two pipes respectively, and this covers approximately the worst conditions. We must, however, remember that these estimates are made for continuous drying during the twenty-four hours, and that if the fan and steam are only applied during a portion of this time, the supply both of air and steam must be proportionately increased, or the time of drying correspondingly lengthened.

It is very desirable, however, that the fan should be driven by a small separate engine, the steam for which will only form a small proportion of that required for heating, and of which the whole of the heat will be recovered, since even that utilised in driving the fan will again be converted into heat by the friction of the air, and will therefore cost nothing. This arrangement will enable the drying to proceed so long as the necessary steam is maintained, which in bad weather can easily be done by the night watchman. It may also be pointed out that, during a great part of the year, the goods can be dried to a "sammied" condition without heat, or in the open air, or in the case of dressing leather, a considerable part of the water can be removed by pressing or squeezing, effecting a further economy.

FIG. 93.—Blackman Fan.

It must be left to the reader to apply the same calculation to other sorts of leather than sole, but it may be pointed out that the essential point, as regards heating and ventilation, is the weight of water to be evaporated in a given time, and that the actual size and shape of the drying room is unimportant, so long as adequate heating and circulation of the air between the leather is secured; and these remarks also apply to the particular form of fan or other ventilation employed, and to the means of heating. As the quantity of heat consumed is very considerable, it is well to look out for sources of waste heat which can be employed, or for means by which the heat of the fuel can be more directly and completely utilised than it is in raising steam. Thus a large amount of heat can sometimes be obtained by passing air through pipes or "economisers" fitted in a chimney-flue; or gilled stoves or "calorifers" may be used in a separate chamber to directly heat the air which is drawn in by the fan.

These pipes should be provided with scrapers to remove soot as in Green's economiser, or their efficiency will be much diminished.

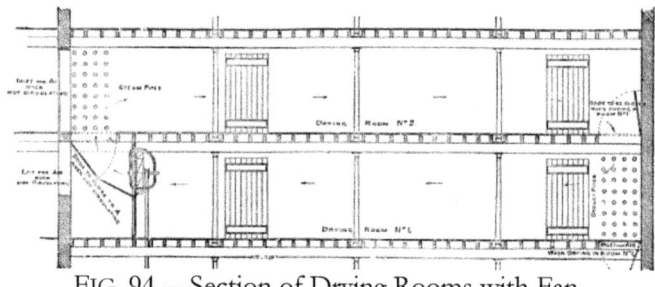

FIG. 94.—Section of Drying Rooms with Fan.

Large section (150 kB)

Figs. 93 and 94, furnished by the James Keith and Blackman Co., Ltd., give a good idea of the construction of screw fans, and the general principle of arrangement of fan drying rooms, the air in this case being circulated in opposite directions on two floors, and the amount of change being regulated by the shutters at A, etc. The grouping of pipes at the ends of the two floors which it shows is in general a good arrangement, but the length between them should not be too great, or the drying will be unequal in different parts of the room. Sometimes this is convenient; thus if most of the heat be supplied to the air coming fresh from the inlet on the upper floor, the damper and colder air of the lower room can be continuously used for drying wet goods from the yard, and the upper reserved for drying off the finished leather. A disadvantage of this plan is that open air drying can seldom be utilised except in an elevated building; and even when it is adopted, means should be provided for heating the lower room in cold weather. In place of two floors, it is obvious that a single floor may be divided into two compartments by a longitudinal partition. Whatever pipes are grouped at the ends of the building, it is advisable to arrange sufficient to prevent frost, against the walls, or in the old-fashioned way on the floors beneath the leather, but not too close to it, and protected by a wooden lattice on which the workmen can stand, which removes the risk of accident from wet leather falling on the hot pipes. The latticed space should be open at the end facing the air current, so as to receive a portion of the draught, which will become heated and ascend, its place being taken by damp and cold air from the leather, to be re-warmed. Water-vapour in itself is lighter than air, but the contraction produced by the cooling of evaporation more than compensates this, and the damp air is therefore heavier than the dry. The arrangement of hot pipes near the ceiling of a drying room, which has been borrowed from some American tanneries, is wrong in principle, unless the air is forced in at the upper part of the room, or the upper floor is latticed, and only acts in other cases when the air is thoroughly mixed and circulated by mechanical ventilators; while pipes near the floor will continue to produce a certain amount of circulation of the air, even when the fan is not running. In protecting pipes by lattices care should be taken not to confine them too closely, or their heating effect will be seriously diminished. In fan-drying, leather should be hung edgeways to the current of air, so as to allow of its free and uniform passage between. In the case of sole leather the butts or bends are conveniently suspended by S-hooks of brass or iron wire, to hooks or nails fixed in the joists. If gangways between the leather must be left in the direction of the draught, they should be closed at intervals in the length of the room by curtains or shutters, so as to deflect the air-current into the leather.

Screw fans like the Blackman can be used either to suck or to blow the air, though the former is preferable where it can be arranged, because it produces a more uniform current in the room. On the blowing side the air issues with considerable velocity in a sort of cone, but little coming through the centre of the fan, while that near the edges spreads rapidly from its centrifugal motion. This is rather advantageous where the fan blows into an open room, but involves waste of power where it discharges into narrow and square air-ways. The ends of the vanes of the Blackman are turned in at the rim of the fan to prevent this tangential discharge, but it is probable that where a fan is to *blow* into a room, it would be more advantageous to put it on the inner side of the wall, and without curved ends to the vanes, so as to distribute the air as widely as possible. A somewhat similar result would be attained with a Blackman, by placing it in a position the reverse of that for which it is intended, and running it also the reverse way; but its "efficiency" might possibly be lessened.

Screw-fans are good for moving large volumes of air at comparatively low velocities, and against little or no resistance, but they are quite unsuitable for forcing air against high resistance, or through narrow channels, and for this purpose centrifugal fans like the Capel (Fig. 95) are much more suitable, and mechanically more efficient. In any case there is much loss of power in forcing air through narrow airways, and if a screw fan must be employed for the purpose, the channel should be as large in section as the area of the fan, and all sharp angles in its course should be avoided. There is great loss of power where a current of air or water has to pass suddenly either from a wider to a narrower channel, or the reverse, and in both cases the resistance is diminished by making the enlargement or contraction gradual or "bell-mouthed." Thus a pipe conveying water at a given head into or out of a cistern will discharge a much larger quantity, if the ends are bell-mouthed, than if it terminates abruptly. For the same reasons, air suffers considerable resistance if it has to pass suddenly into, or out of a larger space, such as a drying room; and unnecessary partitions, and other abrupt changes of dimension in the current should be avoided. Curves should also take the place of angles as much as possible.

FIG. 95.—Capel Centrifugal Fan.

Systems in which air is drawn or forced over systems of heating pipes by a centrifugal fan, and then distributed through comparatively small airways among the leather which is to be dried are in some cases convenient and advantageous. Among these may be mentioned the Sturtevant and the Seagrave-Bevington. There can be no valid patent on the general principle of heating by distributing air in this way, but only on the particular arrangement or appliances used in the special case. Centrifugal fans should be considerably larger in diameter than in axial length, those with long vanes of small radius being wasteful in power from the insufficient supply of air to the centre. There is also no reason why, in some cases, centrifugal fans should not be substituted for screw-fans in drying on the system which I first described, especially in cases where the air has to encounter considerable resistance, as for instance in traversing a filter to remove dust. One of the best filters for this purpose is a table of wire-gauze covered to a depth of 3 or 4 inches with loose wool. Hair or cheaper fibrous materials may be substituted for the wool, but are less efficient. The air must of course be sucked downwards through the gauze. When the wool becomes dirty, it may be washed, if possible in a wool- or hair-washing machine, and again spread on the table in a damp condition, as it will quickly be dried by the current of air. Flannel is also useful where the wool-filter is impracticable, but requires frequent washing.

Apart from wind, natural ventilation is seldom to be relied on for drying on any considerable scale. Heated air is, of course, lighter than cold, and this is the cause of chimney-draught, but to get a good circulation in this way, a high shaft, and high temperature is required. Nevertheless, in one of its best forms, the method has been a good deal used in America, in the so-called "turret-dryer," a building of seven or eight stories in height, constructed of wood with latticed floors, and heated by steam-piping at the bottom, where the air is admitted. The method is not likely to be much used in this country, as apart from the questions of cost of building, fire-risk, and trouble of raising and lowering the leather, a good draught will only be obtained when the outer temperature is low in comparison to that inside, and in our milder and moister climate the conditions are not nearly so favourable as in the United States. As the air is rendered heavier by the cooling of evaporation to a larger extent than it is lightened by the water vapour, there is a tendency in drying by upward ventilation for the warm air to form local upward currents, while the cold and damp air falls back; and from this irregularity of flow, it is difficult to saturate the air equally. This may be avoided by downward ventilation, in which the warm air is admitted at the top of the drying room and the cold and damp air allowed to escape at the bottom. This fact suggests that in using systems of drying such as the Sturtevant, it would be better to place the distributing pipes at the top rather than the bottom of the room, but in this case care would have to be taken that there were no openings left by which the air could escape at the top of the room without descending through the leather. If this be avoided, the warm air will float on the top of the colder and damper, and press it uniformly down and out. I believe the merit of first having applied the principle of downward ventilation to leather-drying is due to Edward Wilson of Exeter. It is necessary that the hot air should be *forced* in at the top, or the cold air *sucked out* from the bottom; and the mere placing of hot pipes near the top of the room (p. 436) will not cause the required circulation. Wilson placed his heating pipes in a partitioned space at the side of the room, at the bottom of which cold air was admitted from the outside, which escaped into the room at the top. As the temperature of this side chamber was high and the air consequently light, an upward current was produced in it, though probably somewhat inefficiently, as the height of the column of heated air could only be small. Assisted by a fan, and circulating a part of the air, the method should give good results, especially over two (latticed) floors. As the air could not be satisfactorily heated in its downward course, the method would not be suited for more than about two floors, and the drying in the lower room would be cool and gentle.

One or two points in the practical arrangement of steam-pipes may be mentioned, as they are often overlooked even by professional engineers. The steam must *always* be admitted at the highest point in the system, and there must be a steady descent, without hollow places where condensed water can accumulate, to the steam-trap by which it is removed. In horizontal pipes, about 1 inch descent in 100 is sufficient. If water accumulates, there is not merely serious danger in case of frost, but during use, by the sudden condensation of the steam, a vacuum is frequently formed, into which the water is shot like the liquid in a "water hammer," producing violent and noisy concussions, and in some cases even fracture of the pipes, or loosening of their joints. If high-pressure steam is used, a very small supply-pipe will feed a considerable system of heating pipes or radiators, but with exhaust steam, great pains should be taken to have pipes of ample size, to avoid back-pressure on the engines. In both cases it is often convenient to arrange the pipes, not as a continuous line, in which drainage is generally difficult, but in parallels like the bars of a gridiron. With high-pressure steam, there need be no fear, if the pipes are kept clear of air by allowing a little escape through small air-taps, of the steam failing to find its way to all parts of the pipe, as a vacuum is produced by condensation in proportion to the heat given off. With exhaust-steam, no steam-trap is desirable, but any steam not condensed should escape freely into the open air or a chimney (after separating condensed water), and it is well to render the resistance in all the pipes of a gridiron approximately equal, which may be done by admitting steam at one corner, and allowing it to escape at the opposite (diagonal) one. In the arrangement of steam-pipes in parallels, the practicability of repair to one pipe or joint without interfering with the others must always be considered. If screwed wrought-iron pipes are used, each parallel must be provided with a bolted flange, or "running socket," to permit of unscrewing. The difficulty of accurately adjusting the lengths of the several parallels must be considered, especially with flanged metal pipes, and also their motion by expansion when hot, which amounts to 1 or 2 parts per 1000 of length according to the temperatures of steam and air. Expansion-joints with stuffing boxes are costly and troublesome, and apt to leak, and may in many cases be avoided by suitable arrangement of the pipes. Thus instead of having the pipes rigidly fixed at both ends, one end of the system may be left free to move, each pipe being separately returned to an exit pipe at the same end but lower in level than the supply; or a single exit pipe may be thus returned, its expansion and contraction being practically the same as that of the heating pipes. In moderate lengths of wrought-iron pipe, sufficient relief may often be obtained from the flexure of the pipe, if in some part of its course it is carried at right angles to its general direction, which is often necessary for other reasons. If pipes are laid in long lengths, the loose end should be supported on rollers or short pieces of pipe, so as to avoid moving the supports or straining the pipe in expansion.

It is useless to attempt to regulate the temperature of low pressure steam-pipes by turning down the steam, since, so long as the pipe is supplied with sufficient steam to fill it, its temperature cannot be less than 100°, and even with high-pressure pipes, the power of regulation by altering the steam-pressure is very limited. It is far better to arrange the pipes or radiators in groups, from some of which the steam can be turned off entirely when less heat is needed. It must not be forgotten that if these discharge into a common steam-trap, it will be necessary to turn off their exits as well as their steam supply, or steam will come back into them from the other pipes, and probably prevent the escape of condensed water. In some cases it is more convenient to give the several sections independent exits or steam-traps.

Many good steam-traps are now on the market, depending either on the expansion and contraction of metals, or on floats in a closed box, which open a valve as the water accumulates. Traps of the latter class with closed copper balls are to be avoided, as the ball is sure eventually to become filled with water. Several traps have been devised in which an open vessel is used as a float, which is always kept empty by the discharge of the water through a pipe dipping into it.

The condensed water from steam-pipes is rarely suitable for use in the tannery, from the dissolved and suspended iron-oxide which it contains, from which it can only be freed by boiling and filtering, or treatment with precipitants (p. 95). Its most appropriate use is generally return to the boiler. Systems were formerly in vogue by which it was allowed to run back to the boiler as it condensed, but these could only answer when the pressure in the pipes was equal to that in the boiler, which is rarely the case. It must generally be forced in by the feed-pump or injector.

Hot water has often been advocated in preference to steam for heating, but is more costly, as it requires a separate boiler, and much larger pipe-surface for the same effect. Its only important advantage is that the pipes maintain their heat for some time, even when the fire has gone down, while steam-pipes cool at once if steam is allowed to go down in the boiler. In any considerable tannery, however, this will seldom or never be the case, since if a good pressure of steam is up at night, when the fires are banked up, the boiler will in itself contain a large reserve of heat, and, of course, working pressure will be required before the engines can start in the morning. Hot water systems require careful planning to obtain reliable and uniform circulation.

CHAPTER XXVII.
CONSTRUCTION AND MAINTENANCE OF TANNERIES.

As few architects have specially studied the construction of tanneries, and in most cases much of the arrangement depends on the knowledge of the tanner himself, a short chapter on the subject will not be out of place.

In the selection of a site, a clay or loamy soil is to be preferred to a gravelly or sandy one, as lessening the liability to leakage, and waste of liquor. Perhaps, however, the first consideration of all is the possibility of drainage and disposal of effluent waste liquors and washing waters, since it is now rarely possible to run these, without previous treatment, into a river or stream. Some information is given in Chapter XXVIII. on the methods of partial purification which are available to the tanner, but these are always costly and troublesome, and the possibility of running direct into a sewerage system, or a tidal river is of great advantage. Under the Public Health Act, authorities are bound to receive manufacturing effluents into their sewers if the latter are of sufficient capacity, and the effluents not such as either to damage the sewers, or interfere with the processes of purification adopted by the authority. This act is in many districts practically superseded by special legislation, but tanners' effluents are generally received into sewers if freed from solid matter. When mixed with other sewage, they do not interfere with irrigation or bacterial treatment. In selecting a site within a sewered district, regard must be had to the possibility of causing a nuisance to the neighbourhood by foul smells. Really injurious smells should not be caused by a properly conducted tannery, but it is difficult to avoid odour, and a single badly disposed neighbour may cause infinite trouble and expense.

Another important consideration is the water supply, since for the large quantities used in a tannery, town water is generally very expensive. With regard to quality and impurities of water information may be found in Chapter X.; but, as a general rule, the softer and purer the supply the better. It is also of great advantage when the source is at such a level that the water can flow into the tan-yard, or at least into the beam-house, without pumping. Filtration too, when needed, is much facilitated by a sufficient head of water.

Commercial facilities, such as nearness to markets and sources of supply of raw materials, and the availability of rail and water carriage are of an importance at least equal to the points already considered, but hardly come within the scope of this work.

The site chosen, the next question is the arrangement of the buildings. It is very doubtful, where ground is not inordinately expensive, whether it is wise to erect drying-sheds over the pits. In case of fire, very serious damage is done to liquor and leather by the heat and burning timber. If the turret form of drier be decided on, strong foundations are required, and the ground-floor or basement is occupied with heating apparatus; if fan-drying, no lofty buildings are needed, and the drying rooms are conveniently placed over the finishing and currying shops; and, on the other hand, the tan-house may be easily and cheaply covered with slated roofs, with nearly vertical sections of glass, to the north if possible, like a weaving-shed, through which sufficient light for convenient work and cleanliness is admitted. The direct rays of the sun should be avoided, but in the writer's opinion the balance of advantage is largely in favour of a liberal supply of light. Iron roofs are unsuitable, since the moisture condenses on, and rusts them; and particles of oxide fall into the liquors, and cause iron-stains.

Good ventilation along the ridge of the roof should be provided, wherever there is any steam or hot liquor used; or the condensed moisture soon leads to decay.

In arranging the general plan of the buildings, much depends on local circumstances; but as far as possible, they must be so arranged that the hides and leather work straight forward from one department to another with as little wheeling or carrying as possible; that the buildings where power is used be near to the engine so as to avoid long transmissions, which are very wasteful of power; and that the different buildings be so isolated as to diminish the risk of the whole being destroyed in case of fire.

A chapter on the construction and maintenance of tanneries and leather works would be incomplete if it did not refer to the very important question of Fire Insurance. To an extent this may be regarded as a fixed charge against any business, very much in the same way as local and imperial rates. It is not, however, to be lost sight of, that to some considerable extent the amount of insurance premium is regulated by the insured himself. If a man conducts his business in unsuitable and badly constructed buildings; if attention is not paid to some of the elementary hazards connected with a fire outbreak; he must not blame the insurance companies for the demand of what he considers an excessive premium. If this faulty construction and imperfect equipment of buildings pertain to any considerable extent throughout a given trade where the process is more or less hazardous, it is futile to appeal to insurance companies, which, after all, are merely commercial and not charitable institutions, for a reduction in the rates. The only standard to guide the company is the loss-ratio, and given a high loss-ratio, there must be a corresponding premium paid.

With regard to fire insurance, I am much indebted to Mr. A. W. Bain, of Leeds for valuable information.

There is, however—thanks to modern science—a method available whereby the great bulk of fires may be checked in their inception; an appliance, automatic in its operation, and of proved efficiency. This appliance is known as the sprinkler. A system of water-pipes is fixed under the ceilings of the building to be protected, to which are attached sprinkling jets at suitable intervals, each of which is closed by a valve held in place by a joint of fusible metal, which gives way if the temperature rises beyond a given point. There are two or three recognised patterns approved by the Fire Offices Committee after patient investigation and practical test. These appliances have now been at work for something like fifteen years in this country. One of the first trades to recognise their utility was that of the cotton-spinner. At one time serious fires in the cotton trade were of frequent occurrence. Now—owing to the efficient fire appliances—while fires may be as frequent in their inception as formerly, they are stopped at such a stage as to prevent any considerable loss. The consequence has been that the cotton-spinner, at one time the owner of a highly-rated risk, and one which few companies cared to insure, is now in the position of having his business eagerly sought after, and large discounts offered him off the charges he was once called upon to pay.

More important still is the consideration to him that his business is not so liable to be interfered with or stopped as the result of fire. There are, it is estimated, at the present moment, no less a proportion than 90 per cent of the cotton-spinners whose premises are protected by sprinkler installations.

Other hazardous risks such as corn-millers', woollen and worsted manufacturers', saw-millers', engineers', are adopting these appliances freely, and it is a matter of surprise that so very few tanneries or currying shops—so far as I have been able to learn, not more than twelve—have done the same. The consequence is that the loss-ratio in tannery risks still retains its unenviable notoriety: the rates for fire insurance have risen considerably, and as a result the tanners' profits are correspondingly less. Considering the extent and importance of many of the tannery risks throughout Great Britain, one can only express surprise that these appliances have been so little adopted.

The construction of a new tannery demands serious attention from an insurance standpoint. The boiler-house should be a detached building; the grinding of bark and myrobalans should be conducted in buildings isolated from the general works; in fact no better advice could be given to a tanner, either in the construction of new premises, or the rearrangement and remodelling of old, than to consult an experienced insurance man, whether official or broker, as to the best means of constructing and arranging to secure the most favourable terms.

Another point which should be provided for, and which is often overlooked, is the feasibility of future extension without serious changes of arrangement. It may be taken as a probability of the future, even if it be not already a fact, that small tanneries cannot be made to pay, and that if a business succeeds, its extension will prove desirable; and in an ill-planned yard this may involve either entire reconstruction of a very expensive and inconvenient sort, or the separation of new departments, so as to involve serious increase of carrying. A good arrangement is that of a long front building serving to connect the whole, behind which the various departments are erected at right angles leaving room for extension backwards as required.

As regards the first of these conditions, if the various soaks, limes, bates, and handlers are well arranged, it is hardly necessary to do more than draw the goods from one pit into the next throughout the whole of the process. To, and from the layers, the goods must generally be carried or wheeled. In the sheds, if it be a sole-leather tannery, the butts should first come into turrets or open sheds for the rough drying; then into a room sheltered from draughts to temper for striking. The striking machines or beams should be in an adjoining room, or immediately below; then a small shed-space for drying before rolling; next the roller room; and then the warm stove for drying off. If two of the latter can be provided to be used alternately, it will allow the goods to be aired off without taking down, and they may then be immediately handed or lowered into the warehouse, without fear of over-drying, which is sometimes difficult to avoid where leather must be taken direct out of the hot drying-room. The same principles are easily applied in yards for lighter leathers.

To lessen loss of power in transmission, the engine should be near the centre of the main range of buildings, with perhaps the grinding machinery on one side, and the leather finishing on the other; but this would be rather liable to increase the fire-risk. A very good plan would be to have the engine-house in the centre as suggested, but separated from the buildings on each side by brick gables; and with the boiler-house behind it, and under a separate roof, say of corrugated iron. If it be impossible to have the engine near its work, it is in most cases better to employ a separate high-pressure engine, which may be within a glass partition, and will work all day with scarcely any attention. The loss of power in carrying steam for moderate distances through sufficiently large and well-clothed pipes is much smaller than that of long lines of shafting. The writer has known cases where fully half the indicated power of the engine was consumed in friction of the engine, shafting and belts. High-pressure engines are as a rule to be preferred to condensing for tannery use, since the waste steam can generally be employed for heating, and both the first cost and that of maintenance are smaller. Where much fuel is used, it is quite worth while to have the cylinders indicated occasionally, both running light, and driving the machinery; much information is gained in this way as to the power spent on the various machines, and very frequently large economy is effected by proper adjustment of the valves. To work economically, an engine should be of ample power for all it has to do; and adjusted to its work, not by lowering the pressure of steam, or by checking it at the throttle-valve, but by setting the slide-valves to cut off as early in the stroke as may be. As to how early this is possible, an indicator-diagram will at once give information. If the whole of the waste steam can be used profitably for heating purposes, economy in the working of the engine is of little consequence, but, otherwise, it is very injudicious, for the sake of a little saving in first cost, to put in an old or inferior engine, which has to be dearly paid for in waste of fuel. In the choice of an engine, the advice of an expert engineer is desirable, since many engines which are mechanically well made, are uneconomical through the faults of a rule-of-thumb design. In this respect the English engine-builder is frequently inferior to his better trained continental competitor.

In place of using small steam engines to distribute power, electric driving deserves consideration. For long drives the loss of power is much less than that of shafting, and by concentrating the whole production of the power in one large and well-constructed engine, the cost per horse-power can be much reduced. While large and well-constructed engines may develop 1 horse-power at a cost in coal of $1\frac{1}{2}$ lb. per hour, it is not uncommon to use 12 lb. for the same output. In tanneries, however, the power used bears a much less proportion to total expenses than it does in the textile and many other trades. The first cost of electric driving is somewhat high. Motors of the "armoured" or iron-cased type must be used in all positions where they are subject to wet or dust. It must be borne in mind that an electric motor will not start against a heavy load, as it only develops its full power at a high speed, and if it receive the full pressure of the current before this is attained, its coils will probably be burnt out, unless saved by the melting of its safety-fuse. A similar danger is incurred, if the motor is brought up by overloading while the current is on. It is therefore generally necessary to connect a motor with its work by a belt which is only brought on to the working pulley when its full speed is attained.

In some cases the use of gas-engines is convenient and economical; for though gas from town-supplies is an expensive fuel, the best gas engines give a higher mechanical efficiency than steam-engines, and they work with very little attention.

In arranging shafting, moderate speeds, say 100-150 revolutions per minute, should be chosen for main lines, and when higher speeds are necessary, they should be got by light and well balanced counter-shafts, with wrought iron or wooden pulleys. (Cp. p. 452.) In calculating speeds, it must be remembered that they vary inversely as the size of the pulleys. Thus a 3-feet pulley running at 100 revolutions will drive a 2-foot pulley at 150 revolutions, and a 12-inch one at 300. Of course the higher its speed, the more power any shaft will transmit, but increased friction and wear and tear soon limit this advantage. The velocity of a belt in feet per minute is obtained by multiplying the number of revolutions per minute by the girth of the pulley in feet or by its diameter multiplied by $3\frac{1}{7}$, or more accurately, 3·1416.

Pulleys should always be of ample breadth for the power they have to transmit; and it is more economical, both in power and cost, to use broad single belting than the same strength in double. If the pulley will not take a belt broad enough for the work it has to do, a second belt may be made to run on the top of the first, as suggested by Mr. J. Tullis, and will do its share of the work. Belts should be washed occasionally with soap and tepid water, and oiled with castor or neatsfoot oil; but if of sufficient breadth, should not require the use of rosin, or adhesive materials, to make them grip the pulley. Chrome-leather belts should be kept thoroughly oiled. They have a much greater adhesion than vegetable tannages, and this is increased by oiling. Good chrome belting is much stronger than bark-tanned; and is unaffected by damp or steam, but generally stretches somewhat more. Makers of machines often err in constructing their driving pulleys too small both in breadth and diameter.

The horse-power which a belt is capable of transmitting obviously varies extremely with circumstances, but may be approximately calculated by the formula $a.v/66000$, where a is the area of contact of the belt with the smallest pulley, and v its velocity in feet per minute. Another rule is, that at a velocity of 1000 feet per minute, each inch of breadth of belt should transmit $2\frac{1}{2}$ horse-power on metal pulleys, or 5 on wooden ones, on which the adhesion is greater. Adhesion may also be increased by covering the pulleys with leather or indiarubber. Both rules assume that the belt is of ample strength. One horse-power would be transmitted by a belt running 1000 feet per minute with a pull of 33 lb. A good single belt should not break with a much less stress than 1000 lb. per inch of breadth, and should stand about $\frac{1}{10}$ as much as a working stress.

The following table gives the experimental breaking stresses and extensions of some leathers. It may be noted that 1 square inch sectional area is equal to a belt 4 inches wide × ¼ inch thick; and that *kilos per cm²* × 14·22 = lb. per inch².

Breaking Stresses of Leather.

	Kilo per sq. centimetre.	Lb. per sq. inch.	Stretch per cent.
Belting leather, layer system	283	4,030	25·4
,, ,, Durio system	298	4,240	21
Well-tanned chrome leather	740	10,500	32·5
Over-tanned chrome leather	234	3,330	23
Stuffed alumed leather	835	11,900	38·3
Alumed "rawhide"	921	13,100	31·4

'Gerber,' 1900, p. 73.

Good English tanned belting leather breaks at from 4500 to 5500 lb. per sq. inch sectional area.

Over-tanned leathers are less tough, whether of vegetable or mineral tannage, than those somewhat lightly tanned, and the tensile strength of leather varies considerably with the part of the hide from which it is taken, that from approximately over the kidneys being the strongest. Even thick and tough leather is easily torn if a cut or nick is once started, and all holes used in jointing belts should be carefully rounded. Glucose, and the use of acid in bleaching both lessen the toughness of belts, and they may also be rendered tender by the heat evolved in slipping on a pulley.

Countershafting and high-speed machinery, such as disintegrators, striking machines of the Priestman type, etc., should run without material jar or vibration. If this occurs, it is generally a sign that the running part is not equally balanced. In this case the shaft or spindle must be taken out of its bearings, and supported on two exactly horizontal straight-edges, on which it will roll till the heaviest part is downwards; and weight must then be taken off or added till it will lie in any position. In this way the writer has had to add fully 2 lb. of iron to balance the drum of a striking machine before equilibrium was secured, and a most troublesome vibration prevented. Of course all machinery should be supported as solidly as possible; and if circumstances permit, most machines are better on a ground floor. In placing bark mills, however, it is frequently convenient to fix them at a higher level, so that the ground material may be sent down shoots by its own weight to the required places. An alternative plan is to set the mill on the ground over a pit, and to raise the ground material with a bucket-elevator. This may be done successfully by letting the material fall directly from the mill into the buckets; but otherwise it must be thrown in with a shovel, as buckets will not pick up ground bark, even from a hopper; and in any case such elevators are apt to be troublesome. In a grinding plant designed by the writer, the unground material was filled on the basement floor into an iron barrow, which was wheeled into an iron sling working between upright guide-rails like a hoist. On pulling a brake line, the barrow was raised to the top of the building, and its contents were tipped into a large hopper, after which the barrow righted itself, and descended for another load. In the bottom of the hopper was a sliding shover, which forced the material on to vibrating screens, by which it was guided either into a disintegrator, or crusher-rolls, at pleasure. Both these discharged through iron spouts into large hoppers on the outside of a brick gable, from which powdery materials like myrobalans and valonia could be run direct into barrows or trucks. It is very desirable that such hoppers should be separated from the main building by a fireproof partition. Fires may occur from hard substances getting into disintegrators along with the bark, etc. and if this occur with a dry and dusty tanning material, it is not unlikely that it may result in an explosion such as sometimes happens in flour mills, in which the fire is rapidly conveyed along spouts, and into chambers filled with dusty air. Insurance companies generally charge an extra rate for disintegrators, and it is very desirable to keep the mill-house structurally apart from other buildings, either by actual separation or by the introduction of brick gables dividing the roofs. On the whole, however, mills of the coffee-mill type are probably quite as dangerous as disintegrators; since if they become partially choked, the heat caused by friction is very great.

In America, the fire-risk from mills is often lessened or prevented by the introduction of a jet of steam into the chamber or spout by which the mill discharges, but this is only permissible if the tanning material is conveyed at once to the leaches or yard.

The use of chain-conveyors for handling tanning material both wet and dry is practically universal in America, though comparatively rare in England. Various forms are used, the most common consisting of a chain of square links of malleable cast iron which hook into each other, so that a broken link can be immediately replaced (see p. 325). At intervals special links are inserted, which can be had of various patterns, for the attachment of scrapers or buckets. The endless chain runs in a trough of rectangular or V-shaped section, and is driven by a toothed wheel, over which it runs like a belt. In some cases the returning half of the chain can be utilised to bring back the spent tan on its way to the boiler house. For dry materials, cotton or leather belts with short wooden cross-laths attached, may often be used satisfactorily in place of the chain.

For lubricating purposes, mineral oils of high density are not more dangerous than animal or vegetable, but rather the reverse; as, though they are possibly more inflammable, and make more smoke, their mixture with cotton-waste and other porous materials is not spontaneously combustible, as those of vegetable and animal oils occasionally are. The danger of spontaneous combustion is very considerable when heaps of leather shavings or cuttings containing fish-oils are allowed to accumulate in warm workshops, and, especially near steam-pipes. Heavy mineral oils should always be used as cylinder-oils in high-pressure engines, in preference to other oils or tallow, since they are not decomposed by steam, and do no harm if blown into the feed-water, but serve to loosen and prevent scale and deposit. Ordinary oils and tallow, on the other hand, when submitted to the action of high-pressure steam, are separated into glycerin and fatty acids (see p. 351), and the latter corrode the valve faces and seatings, and are liable with "temporary hard" waters to form a very dangerous porous deposit in the boilers, which often leads to overheating of the tubes.

Next to the machinery, the pits demand special consideration. The chapter on the subject in the late Mr. Jackson Schultz's book on 'Leather Manufacture,' is well worth attentive study as giving American practice on the subject.

The old-fashioned method of sinking pits is to make them of wood, and carefully puddle them round with clay, which should be well worked up before use. It is of no use to throw it in in lumps and attempt to puddle it between the pits, which will not be made tight, but probably displaced by the pressure. Such pits, if made of good pine and kept in constant use, are very durable, some of the original pits at Lowlights Tannery, constructed in 1765, having been in use till 1889. Loam mixed with water to the consistence of thin mortar may also be employed, the pits being filled up with water, to keep them steady, at the same rate as the loam is run in. Probably the best materials for pit-sides are the large Yorkshire flagstones. Where these are not attainable, very durable pits may be made of brick, either built with Lias lime, and pointed with Portland cement, or built entirely with the latter. Common lime cannot be used, as it spoils both liquors and leather; and even cements with too large a percentage of lime are unsatisfactory. Brick and common mortar are, however, suitable for lime-pits, and for these Mr. C. E. Parker's plan of constructing the bottom of cement, the ends and sloping hearth of brick, and the sides of 3-inch planks bolted together is also very satisfactory (Fig. 96).

The writer has constructed wooden pits in two ways. In the one case, after making the excavation, beams were laid in a well-puddled bed of clay; on these a floor of strong tongued and grooved deals was laid, and on this the pits were constructed of similar wood to the floor, and puddled round with clay. In the second case the pits were built like large boxes above ground, and when finished, lowered on to a bed of clay prepared for them, and then puddled both around and between. It may have been due to defective workmanship in the first case, but those made on the last-named plan, which is that adopted from very early times, certainly proved the tightest and most satisfactory. Mr. Schultz describes a plan as the Buffalo method, in which a floor is laid as just described, and grooves cut with a plane for the reception of the sides, which are formed of perpendicular planks, each end and side being finally tightened up by the insertion of a "wedge plank." Owing to the perpendicular position of the side-planks such pits would be difficult to repair in the common case of decay at the top.

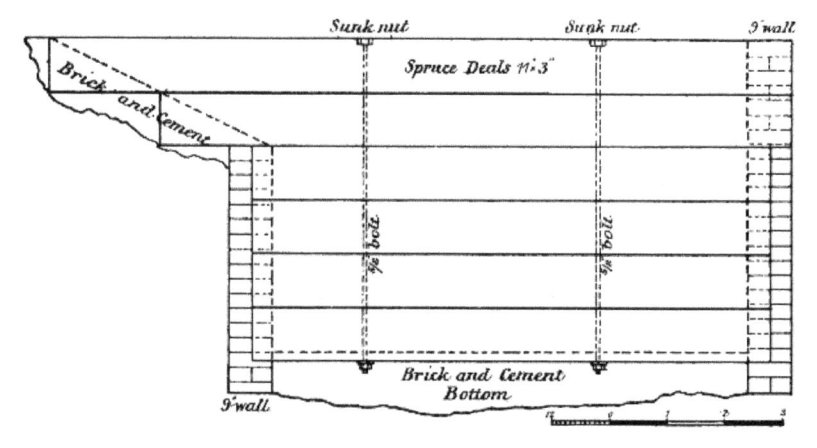

FIG. 96.—Mr. C. E. Parker's construction of Lime-Pits.

If bricks be used, great care must be taken that the cement is not merely laid so as to fill the joints towards the two surfaces of the wall, as is the habit of modern bricklayers, but actually floated into all the joints so as to make the wall a solid mass; or leaks can hardly be avoided. Hard pressed bricks are best, and should be tested as to whether they discolour liquor. Cement-pits are very good, and, though not particularly cheap in material, which must be of the best, are readily made by intelligent labourers under good supervision. The first step is to lay a level floor of good concrete, in which glazed pipes for emptying the pits may be embedded; care being also taken that all joints in these are thoroughly tight, since future repairs are impossible. The next step is to make frames, the exact length and breadth of the pits required, and perhaps 15 inches deep. These are arranged on the floor where the pits are to be, and the intervening spaces are filled with concrete of perhaps 1 of cement to 3 or 4 of crushed stone or brick. Rough stones and bricks may also be bedded in the concrete as the work goes on, to help to fill up. After the first layer has set, the frames may be raised and a second added, and so on. The work is generally finished by floating over it, while still damp, a little pure cement, to give a smooth surface. Before using, the cement should be tried on a small scale, to be sure that it does not discolour leather or liquors, and the pits should always be seasoned with old or cheap liquor before actual use.

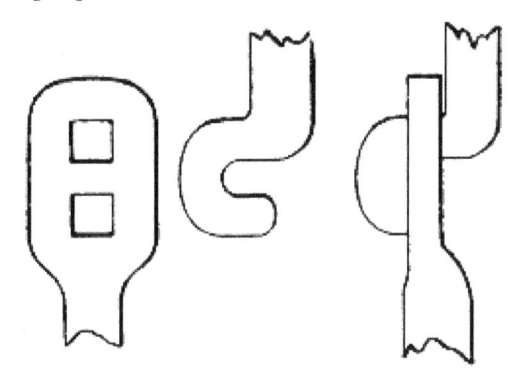

FIG. 97.—Cleaning Rod Joint.

If possible, both leaches and handler-pits should be provided with plugs and underground pipes, communicating with a liquor-well some feet below their levels. Glazed fire-clay is very suitable both for pipes and plug-holes, which should be in the pit corners. If fire-clay blocks for plug-holes cannot be obtained, they may be cast in good cement, the wooden mould being soaked with hot paraffin wax to prevent adhesion. Means must be provided for the ready clearing of the pipes when choked with tanning materials. A good plan is to let each line of pipes end in a liquor-well large enough for a man to go down. As it is almost impossible to make plugs fit without occasional leakage, it is not well to run pits with very different strengths of liquors to one well, but the layers, handlers, and different sets of leaches should each have their own, so as to avoid mixture. A good means of clearing pipes consists in a series of iron rods 3-4 feet long, connected by hooks fitting into double eyes, as shown in Fig. 97. It is obvious that in a narrow pipe or drain, these cannot become disconnected. Pipes may often be forced out by fitting a strong delivery-hose of a steam-pump into one of the plug-holes.

It is, as Schultz points out, of questionable advantage to lay wooden troughs under the alleys for supplying liquor to each pit, since it is almost impossible to preserve them from decay; but the same objection would not apply to glazed pipes, jointed with pitch or cemented. A good and cheap plan in practice, is to let the liquor-pump, or a raised liquor-cistern, discharge into a large and quite horizontal trough raised 6 or 7 feet above the level of the yard, and provided with plug-holes at intervals, from which the liquor can be run into the various pits by short spouts or sailcloth hose. In place of plugs in the raised trough, a simple and convenient valve devised by the writer may be advantageously employed. A lead weight is made by casting in a hemispherical tin basin of about 5 inches diameter and 2 inches deep in the centre, a loop of strong brass wire with turned up lower ends, being suspended in the middle, so as to become fixed in the lead. To prevent adhesion, the tin must be previously burned off, and the basin well blackleaded. This weight forms the valve, which rests in use on a 6-inch washer of good indiarubber with a 4-inch hole, which is held by a wood block against the bottom of the trough, through which a 5-inch hole is cut. The valve is raised by a lever or cord, and is absolutely water-tight in use. It is shown in section in Fig. 79, p. 333.

It is very advantageous in practice, instead of pumping direct into the pits, to have one or more tanks, into which liquor can be delivered by the pump, and which are sufficiently raised to allow it to be run from them into the horizontal distributing troughs which have been mentioned. This is specially important with regard to liquors for leaches and suspenders which are worked on a circulating system, since they do not run very quickly, and much time is lost in pumping out pits, if the speed of the pump has to be regulated by the rate at which the liquor will circulate. It also enables liquors to be run through suspender- and rocker-pits during the night or at meal-times while the machinery is standing; and it is often useful on beginning work in the morning, to have an empty tank into which the first liquor can be pumped.

Direct-acting steam-pumps without fly-wheels are very unsatisfactory for tan-yards, since they are usually uncertain in their action, difficult to run slowly, and apt to "hammer"; and they are also costly in steam, which cannot be used expansively. Steam-pumps with fly-wheels, operating the steam-valve by an eccentric, are free from these defects, and though more costly at the outset, soon save the difference in lessened repairs and consumption of steam. Pumps with a capacity of 8000 gallons per hour are very suitable, and can be used with a 3-inch hose pipe; smaller sizes are decidedly more liable to choke with tanning material. Rubber mitre-valves work satisfactorily, and do not choke frequently, but are costly, and easily damaged by hot liquors. On the whole brass clack-valves are the most satisfactory, but the hinge-pins, instead of fitting neatly in circular sockets, should be held in slots, allowing the back of the valve to rise half an inch, when it will clear itself of small hard myrobalan stones and suchlike things, which getting under a more tight-fitting hinge would prevent the valve closing, and so stop the pump. Whatever valves are employed, means should be provided for easy access without unscrewing too many bolts. If the several valve-chambers of the pump are closed by a single cover with an indiarubber washer, the spaces between them which make the joint should be faced with brass or gun-metal, as, if the least leakage takes place over an iron surface, the friction and solvent power of the liquors soon eat away the metal and render a good joint impossible. Where colour is of first importance, it is well to have the whole pump of gun-metal, but in any case the working cylinder should be brass-lined, and the piston and rod, and the valves and seatings should be of brass or gun-metal. Spring-rings are far better than pump-leather and are unaffected by hot liquors; chrome leather, however, will stand a good deal of heat. Double-acting force-pumps have practically superseded the older single-acting double or triple pumps. Instead of direct driving with a steam cylinder, it is sometimes advantageous to drive by belt, but at least one steam pump should be provided, so that pumping can be done when the main engine is not running, and the speed of the pump can be regulated to the work, which is impossible in a belt-driven pump. Steam pumps are sometimes very useful as fire engines.

Centrifugal pumps are very suitable for tannery work, where the liquor is drawn from a well, but are not well adapted for use with suction-pipes. If the form with vertical spindle is adopted, which is sunk below the liquor in the well, the pump fills itself, and needs no foot-valve, but unless the well is very large, or some convenient means is devised of withdrawing the pump, repair or cleaning is difficult. If the horizontal pattern is used, which is above the ground, repair, cleaning, and driving is much easier, but a foot-valve is necessary, which may itself give trouble, and some convenient means, such as a pipe from a raised tank, should be provided for filling the pump with liquor, as, unlike suction pumps, centrifugals will not start unless full, although they raise very large quantities when running, and from their steady flow, will deliver much more through a given pipe than an ordinary reciprocating pump with the same power. In selecting the pump, care should be taken that the pattern allows ready access, not only to the foot-valve, but to the body of the pump.

It is seldom satisfactory to use windbores or strainers to prevent tanning material getting into a pump, as they speedily become choked; and it will be found better, after taking such precautions as are possible, to have the pump and valve of ample size and suitable construction to pass what comes with the liquor. The writer has known a mop-head pumped and delivered through a 3-inch hose without stoppage, by a Tangye fly-wheel steam-pump with brass clack-valves such as have been alluded to.

Pulsometers have not, in the experience of the writer, proved satisfactory in tanneries, warming and diluting the liquor, consuming much more steam than a pump of the same power, and becoming easily choked. For the same reasons, steam-jet water-raisers are not to be recommended except where raising is to be combined with heating, as in some leaching devices (p. 334).

CHAPTER XXVIII.
WASTE PRODUCTS AND THEIR DISPOSAL.

The products which are of no direct value to the tanner and currier in the manufacture of leather, and which are nevertheless obtained in fairly large quantities, are of very varying characters. In the present chapter, the most important of them will be described, and some of their uses mentioned.

Hair is removed from the skin of the animal in the process of depilation (p. 143) in the form of a wet sodden mass, containing a considerable amount of lime when the skin has been through the lime-pits.

As white hair is the more valuable, care should be taken in the unhairing to keep it separate from the coloured. It is washed first in plain water to get rid of as much of the lime as possible, and then in water containing a little acid. Hydrochloric acid is often used for this purpose, but sulphurous acid (p. 25) is preferable as it has a slight bleaching action on the hair. The acid neutralises and renders soluble the lime which still remains in the hair, so that it can be easily removed by washing with water. In many tanneries, hair-washing machines are used. The washed hair is dried by laying it out on frames; or preferably, the greater part of the water is first removed by a centrifugal drier, or by pressing, and the drying is completed in a drying room, the temperature of which is a few degrees higher than that of the outside air, and which is provided with a fan or some other appliance for mechanical ventilation. Tables of wire gauze on which the hair is spread, and through which the warm air of the room is drawn by a centrifugal fan, are the most effective.

Coloured hair is sometimes washed and treated like the white hair, but is usually sold direct to plasterers, in which case there is no necessity to remove all the lime and other impurities which the hair contains. A considerable amount of hair is also sold to iron founders, who use it in preparing cores and in loam-casting. The loose lime may be effectively beaten from dried hair by passing it through a disintegrator with one of the grates removed.

Fleshings and Glue-stuff.—The various scraps of fat and flesh, more or less free from actual hide substance, are usually worked up for glue, though if they cannot be sold for a fair price it will pay to boil them in order to recover the fat they contain. If this is to be done, the fatty portions may be thrown out at the beam and not mixed with the fleshings as in the ordinary way. Before boiling, the fat is treated with sulphurous, sulphuric or hydrochloric acid, sufficient to neutralise the lime present. The boiling should be carried on very gently, so as to allow the fat to rise without emulsifying with the gelatinous matter. For boiling, open steam may be used, but in this case the size formed will have little value; on the other hand, if sulphurous acid has been used and a wooden vat with a copper steam-coil be employed, really good glue may be obtained, and the slight trace of bisulphite which it may contain will prevent its putrefaction. Except under special conditions it will not pay to make glue on a small scale in England, as its value depends much on its appearance, and the necessary plant is somewhat expensive. In some places, however, size can be sold to advantage. Fig. 98 shows a glue-boiling plant.

After separation of the fat by skimming, the clear size is run off from the residual matter into wooden cooling troughs about 5 feet long by 9 inches deep and 15 inches wide, in which it is allowed to set (Fig. 92, p. 425). Great care is required that both size and coolers are quite sweet and free from putrefaction, the coolers being frequently washed with sulphurous acid solution or fresh milk of lime. The jelly is cut out in blocks, and sliced into cakes of appropriate thickness by means of a series of frames like slate-frames which fit over the block of glue, and between which a wire or thin blade stretched on a saw-frame is inserted to cut the glue into sheets. In some factories a machine is used, with a series of parallel blades against which the glue-block is pushed. The sheets are afterwards separated by girls and laid to dry on nets, on which they are frequently turned. When dry, the cakes may be washed with warm water to remove any adhering dirt, but this causes some loss of weight, and in many cases it pays better to dry in a stove until quite hard, then grind in a disintegrator and sell as "size-powder," in which appearance counts for little if the colour and strength of the size are good.

FIG. 98.—Glue Boiling.

Fat.—The fat, whether obtained in the manufacture of glue, or by boiling the fleshings and shavings for its recovery alone, is skimmed from the surface of the heated liquor, and should afterwards be freed from gelatinous matter by washing it with hot water in a tub and running off the upper layer after allowing the water to settle out. The fat thus obtained is a light-coloured grease of buttery consistence.

There are various other sources of waste fats which may be considered here. If glue is made from dried glue-stuff without previous treatment with acid, the fat skimmed off the pans, though dark in colour, will be neutral or alkaline, and a considerable additional quantity of fat and free fatty acids may be obtained by reboiling the "scutch" or refuse with open steam in lead pans with the addition of water and enough sulphuric acid to render the contents of the pan distinctly acid. This grease will be dark and of unpleasant smell from volatile fatty acids, but its odour may be to a considerable extent improved by blowing air and steam through it, and washing with water, or by heating to a temperature somewhat above the boiling-point of water for a considerable time. The same sort of treatment may be applied to the fat pressed out of sheepskins, and to that obtained by boiling currier's shavings with water and a little acid.

Recovered fats may be separated into a tolerably firm grease suitable for use instead of tallow in currying, and an oil not unlike neatsfoot oil, by melting, allowing to cool slowly to a soupy consistency to promote the crystallisation of the harder fats, and forcing the mixture through flannel cloths in a filter press. The temperature at which the filtration should take place is generally 20-25° C. The oil is, of course, "tender," or liable to solidify in cold weather; and the more so the higher the temperature at which filtration takes place. The tallow is obtained in cakes. If from fresh fleshings, it will be white and with little odour, but that from dried glue-stuff is usually brown and of unpleasant smell, while recovered grease from curriers' shavings or "moisings" is always dark in colour.

If the fleshings are to be sold wet, they should be preserved in a sweet lime liquor; if to be dried, they are washed carefully in a fresh lime, spread on frames, and frequently turned over so that they may dry evenly and rapidly. Heat, if employed at all, is in most cases only used at the end of the drying operation, but some tanners dry from the first in a room the temperature of which is a few degrees higher than the normal, and which is provided with good ventilation. For the purposes of the glue manufacturer, the roundings and larger pieces are more valuable than the fleshings, and should be treated with correspondingly greater care by the beamsman and his assistants.

Bate-Shavings are very valuable as sizing materials. They should be well washed in water, or with a very dilute solution of sulphurous acid, and are then laid out in thin layers to dry. They may also be partially dried by pressing between latticed boards in a screw or hydraulic press, and are then best finished as cakes. On the manufacture of sulphurous acid compare p. 25.

Horns are usually kept until the "slough," "pith," or internal bone can be knocked out, having become loosened through drying and putrefaction. If kept dry, practically no longer time is required, and the smell and other annoyances incidental to storing in a damp place are avoided. The sloughs may be removed by steaming, but the horns are somewhat damaged by this treatment. The sloughs are principally ground for "bone-meal," but some are boiled for glue, either without preparation, or after decalcifying with dilute hydrochloric acid.

The actual horn itself, which is quite incapable of making glue, is used chiefly in the manufacture of combs, buttons, and similar articles. The value of horns is to a considerable extent dependent on their size, small horns being unprofitable to work up for the articles above mentioned.

Spent Tan.—The tan as it is obtained from the leaches after extraction has, naturally, no value for the tanner except as a fuel. Spent tan cannot be profitably sold as manure, as its worth in this respect is extremely small. In those places where white lead is still made by the Dutch process, oak-bark is used to cover up the earthen pots, and commands a good price. It is, however, essential that oak-bark only should be used, as many other tanning materials give off products which injure the colour of the white lead. The quantities of tan used for hot-beds, and for deadening the noise of traffic in the streets, are so small that they are of no practical account in the disposal of this product. Spent tan is not nearly so good as wood for the manufacture of paper, and an attempt to distil it and thereby obtain pyroligneous acid and wood-spirit did not result in any commercial success. On the Continent, fine-ground tan is usually pressed into briquettes for use as domestic fuel, but it would be hard to obtain a market for these in England.

On the whole, in spite of its low heating value, spent tan is best utilised as a fuel. For this purpose specially constructed furnaces are necessary on account of the dampness of the tan, and its low calorific value, which varies, however, with the particular materials: thus while oak-bark and valonia are only poor fuels, hemlock and myrobalans are much better on account of the resin and lignine they contain.

The first successful furnaces for raising steam with wet tan were introduced in the United States, and consisted of large arched combustion chamber with abundant grate-area, and with four or six feed-holes in the fire-brick top which formed a floor on which the spent tan was laid, and where to some extent it was dried by the waste heat. The flames and furnace gases were conducted under the boilers, the flue being very large and deep so as to collect the light ash which was drawn in great quantities from the furnace, and the gases then returned through the tubes of the boiler, afterwards passing down the sides and going to the chimney. The wet fuel was fed in through the firing holes alternately, so that only a part of the grate-space was covered at once with wet fuel; which was speedily ignited by the heat from other parts of the furnace, and especially from the vaulted arch. The large grate-area was a necessity not only on this account, but because of the light weight of the fuel and its low calorific power, which involved the need of burning a large volume. Fig. 99 represents a furnace of similar principle constructed by Messrs. Huxham and Browns. Furnaces of this type are, the author believes, still largely in use in the United States, but in Germany "step-grates" sloping from the furnace-doors towards the back, are now preferred. In these the combustible material rests upon the flat surfaces of the grate, while the air enters by the spaces between the steps without the fuel being able to fall through. Fig. 100 represents the furnace on this principle constructed by the Moenus Co. of Frankfort.

 Detailed drawings and particulars are given in Jackson Schultz's 'Leather Manufacture in the United States,' New York, 1876.

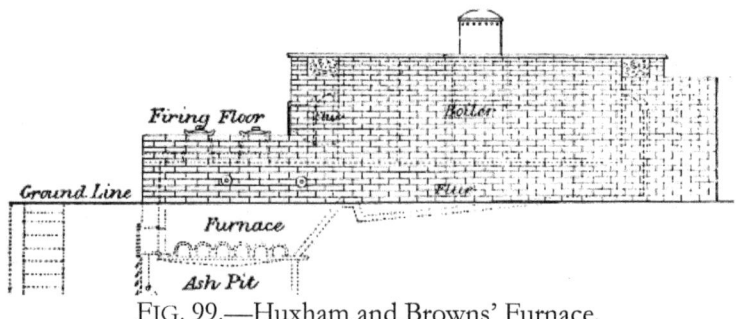

FIG. 99.—Huxham and Browns' Furnace.

The essential conditions which are to be observed in the proper burning of the tan are a sufficiently large grate-area, a correct and sufficient supply of air, and a combustion-chamber of very high temperature. It is consequently not possible to burn tan very successfully in an ordinary Lancashire or Cornish boiler, since not only the grate-space is too limited, but the water of the boiler prevents the upper part of the furnace from attaining a high temperature; and it is therefore difficult to get the damp tan rapidly into vigorous combustion. The difficulty may to some extent be overcome by mixing the tan with a proportion of coal, and by closing the ash-pit and employing a forced draught unless the chimney is a very powerful one. In this way large quantities of tan may be burnt, but without effecting any great saving of coal. The heating power of the tan is improved by the partial removal of its water by pressing, and this is almost essential where a special furnace is not employed.

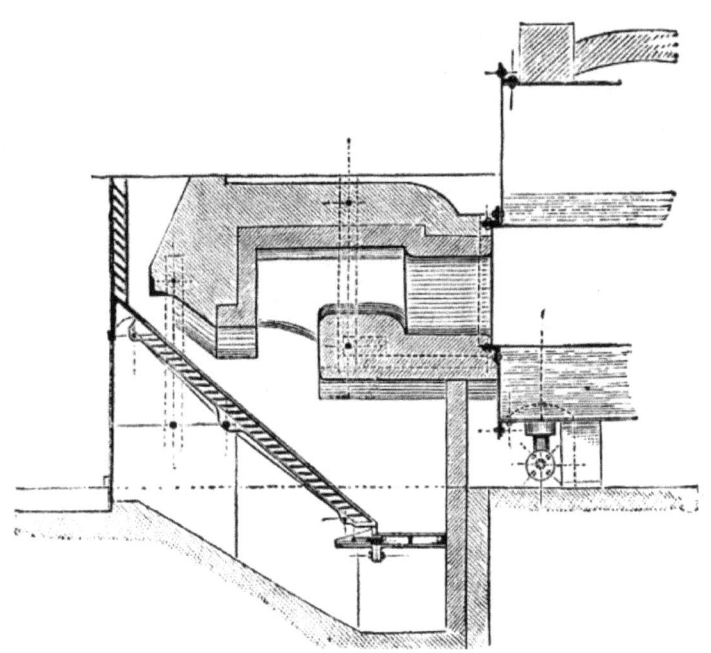

FIG. 100.—Moenus Step-grate Furnace.

The answer to the question as to whether tan should be used as fuel in the wet state in which it is obtained from the leaches, or whether it should be previously pressed, depends upon the nature and quantity of the tan. Where abundant quantities of a fairly good material such as hemlock bark are to be disposed of, the cost of pressing is an unnecessary expenditure; but if it is desirable to obtain the highest value from the fuel, or if the furnaces are not well constructed for burning very wet fuels, it will be profitable to press the tan. Hydraulic presses have been used for this purpose, but those now commonly employed consist of powerful rollers arranged in the same way as those of the valonia-crusher (p. 322). The pressure is given by levers loaded with weights or fitted with powerful springs. The liquid which runs from these presses is of little value, as it contains such large quantities of finely divided material that it is almost impossible to filter it, and if run upon the leaches it chokes them and prevents their proper circulation. Much of the cost of pressing is caused by the labour of feeding it to the press, and this may be greatly reduced by the use of mechanical conveyors (p. 325) from the leaches. A tan press is shown in Fig. 101.

FIG. 101.—Tan Press.

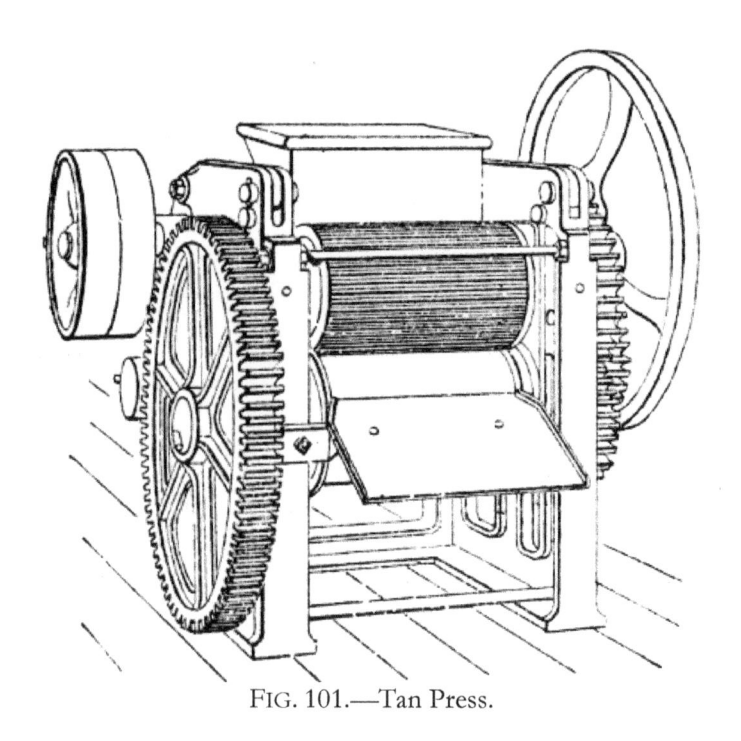

Sewage and other Waste Liquids.—The waste liquors from the different liming, bateing, puering, tanning, washing and other soaking processes are, without any doubt, the most troublesome of any of the side-products which are obtained in the manufacture of leather. In former times they were simply run into the nearest stream, but nowaday the various sanitary authorities and other similar bodies will only permit comparatively pure waters to be turned into a public stream or watercourse.

Various methods of effecting the necessary purification of the waste liquors from tanneries have been proposed at different times, and have been used with varying degrees of success. These methods may be divided into three heads: precipitation, followed by filtration or sedimentation land-treatment; and bacterial purification.

The first of these depends on the power of certain substances, such as alumina and oxide of iron, to carry down organic matter with them if precipitated in solutions containing it. The method usually consists in adding a sufficient quantity of lime to render the waste liquid slightly alkaline, and then treating it with some crude salt of aluminium or of iron. By this means a precipitate of aluminium or iron hydrate is formed, which encloses within itself a considerable proportion of the organic matter of the liquid, and after settling to the bottom of the precipitation-tank is drawn off as "sludge." Various chemicals are sold under fancy names, such as "alumino-ferric," "ferrozone," etc., and have a composition not very dissimilar to that of crude sulphate of iron or alumina. In some cases by-products, such as the acid liquors used in preparing iron articles for "galvanizing," can be used with advantage.

In the case of the waste liquors from a tannery, the use of these chemicals may often be avoided if sufficient care be taken in regulating the proportion of the various liquids which are to be mixed together and run into the settling tank. As tanning matter combines with lime and dissolved hide-substance to form a heavy brown insoluble precipitate, it is clear that if care be taken to have rather more waste lime-liquor mixed with the waste tan-liquors than is necessary to throw all the tan out of solution, a very considerable amount of purification of the effluent will have taken place without any cost whatever to the tanner. Hence, if the proportion of waste lime is small in comparison to that of the tanning liquors, an extra addition of lime may be necessary in order to precipitate the tannin.

The precipitation- or settling-tanks are usually square or rectangular vessels or pits, the size of which varies with the quantity of liquid to be treated, but the depth of which rarely exceeds six feet. They may be divided into two classes—the "intermittent," and the "continuous." In the former class the tank is filled with the mixed waste liquids, taking care that such a sufficiency of lime is present that the mixture is faintly alkaline to phenolphthalein paper, and is then allowed to rest until the suspended matter has settled down to the bottom of the tank, when the clear, or almost clear upper liquid is drawn off, the remainder being the "sludge"; some means must also be employed to prevent the passage of scum and floating matters. In the case of the intermittent process it is advisable to have two tanks, one of which is being filled while the other one is settling or being emptied. With the continuous process the liquids are run into the tank in the proportions calculated to give a maximum amount of purification, as described above, but as they enter very slowly the undissolved matter soon settles, and consequently the liquid may be continuously run out at the further end of the tank. This plan, though it does not yield such good results in the hands of unskilled workmen, is yet useful in many cases, as only one tank is absolutely necessary. It is desirable that in running off the tanks, the effluent should be taken as near the surface as possible, by means of a hinged pipe attached to a float, or some equivalent device; and care is required, as the tank gets low, to avoid the escape of any of the sludge.

For continuous settling the tanks are usually long and somewhat shallow rectangular ponds, into which the previously well-mixed precipitating liquid flows through a wooden trough fixed across one end and as long as the breadth of the tank, and perforated with holes to allow the uniform and quiet influx of the liquid, which finally escapes by a similar trough crossing the opposite end of the tank. In front of the exit-trough a "scum board" must be placed, which is a simple plank dipping slightly below the surface of the liquid, so as to prevent any oil, scum or other floating matter from passing out of the tank along with the clear effluent. Whether the intermittent or continuous system is employed, the effluent should in most cases be afterwards passed through a bacterial filter-bed, or treated by land filtration before it is allowed to flow into a stream or river. Tannery effluents are usually received into sewers without further treatment than mixing and settling to remove solid matter, and many authorities are satisfied with the removal of merely such coarse suspended matters as might choke the sewers. Where continuous precipitation-tanks are used, they must be emptied at frequent intervals, and the sludge run on to cinder-filters, to part with most of its water. These filters are conveniently placed at a lower level than the settling tanks, and it is generally necessary to return the effluent from them for further precipitation and settling. Several types of continuous settling tank with upward flow have been devised by Mr. Candy and others, which are very suitable for use where space is limited; but otherwise less costly constructions are often sufficient. Apart from the question of obtaining an effluent sufficiently good to satisfy the sanitary authority, the treatment of the sludge is one of the greatest difficulties in the purification of effluents. It is usually very bulky, easily putrescible, and therefore difficult to dry; it is of little value for manure; and if allowed to remain long wet, its smell is very offensive.

It has been mentioned that in most cases the liquid, and in every case the sludge, must be freed from solid undissolved matter by filtration. This may take place through open filters or through filter-presses. The open filters generally consist of a pit with an exit at the bottom for the filtered liquid. This pit is filled with either stones and sand, with clinker, ashes or coke. Most tanners use clinker and ashes, as they do not cost anything; and the material should be so arranged that while the lowest layers are very coarse, the surface of the filter-bed should be of the finest material. As soon as this has become covered with so thick a layer of solid matter that the filtration proceeds too slowly, the top surface of the filter may be removed with a rake (taking care to remove as little of the ashes or sand as possible), and burnt, or dried and used as manure. In some cases, filter-presses are used which are composed of grooved or perforated plates with cloths between them through which the liquid is forced by pressure. The solid matter remains behind in the form of a comparatively dry "cake." The filter-cake, dried if desired, is sold as manure, for which it is in many ways very suitable. Although they work much more rapidly than do the open filters, the cloths so soon become rotten and have to be replaced, that the open ash-filter is on the whole the most convenient for the tanner's use. It will be readily understood that apparatus of this kind, though very efficient on a small scale, is quite out of the question when many thousand gallons of liquid have to be filtered daily, and so can only be effectively applied to "sludge."

No system of chemical precipitation has as yet proved entirely satisfactory. Undoubtedly a great deal of purification is effected by this means, but in most cases the "purified" liquid is still too impure to be turned into a stream, though for various reasons this is often permitted by the authorities.

A great advance was made in the purification of effluents when manufacturers were compelled by law to allow the effluent from the precipitation-tank to filter through land set apart for that purpose. In this case certain hardy cereals were sown on the land, which was watered as often as possible with the effluent. This latter, after soaking through the land, was drained off into the nearest stream. Although in many ways this treatment was satisfactory, it had the disadvantage of being very expensive, especially in the neighbourhood of large towns where the price of land is high, and, in addition to this, the conditions necessary for success were far from being correctly understood, so that the land often became "sewage-sick" or waterlogged, and ceased to purify the effluent. It was not until the researches of bacteriologists proved that the purification by land-filtration was mainly due to the bacteria in the soil, that any really satisfactory solution of the problem could be found, but the question has now been to a considerable extent simplified by the introduction of "bacterial treatment."

Bacteria, considered from the point of view of their action on organic matter, are often classified as "anaerobic" and "aerobic," though many species are capable of existing under both conditions (Cp. L.I.L.B., Section XXIV.). The anaerobic bacteria thrive only in the absence of air, and their chemical action consists in breaking down the organic matter on which they feed into simpler, and generally more soluble forms, by processes which do not involve oxidation. The aerobic bacteria, on the other hand, require air or oxygen for their existence, and produce changes which are generally of a less complex character, but result in the complete oxidation and conversion of the organic matter to simple compounds, such as nitrates and carbonic acid, which are perfectly harmless and inoffensive. The two classes therefore are to a large extent complementary to each other, the anaerobic bacteria converting the animal or vegetable substances into more soluble and simple compounds which are adapted to the needs of the aerobic, which complete the destruction of the organic matter.

In harmony with what has just been said, bacterial treatment of sewage is of two kinds, each of which may be used alone, or in conjunction with a preliminary precipitation-process, but which are generally best used successively. The oldest form of bacterial purification depends mainly on the action of anaerobic bacteria, and is known as the "septic tank." This originally consisted of a tank sometimes filled with small pieces of coke, but generally containing the liquid only, and which was tightly closed to prevent access of air and escape of foul gases. It has, however, been found that if deep tanks (6 to 10 feet) are employed, they soon become in continuous use so covered with scum and floating matter as effectually to prevent access of air and light, or any serious escape of smell. The liquid to be purified is allowed to flow very slowly through a tank or series of tanks of this description, entering about a foot below the surface through a distributing trough at one end, and flowing out similarly at the other, at such a rate as to change the contents of the tank about once in twenty-four hours; and when the tank is in working order, the liquid is much purified by the process, and most of the solid organic matter has become liquefied and disappears. It not unfrequently happens, especially where the septic tank treatment is not very prolonged, that the liquid which escapes has a stronger and more offensive odour than it had on entering the tank. It is nevertheless really purer than before, the increased smell being due to the volatile products of the partially decomposed organic matter; and, by passing the liquid through an open coke-filter, the smell will be effectually removed. In all cases it must be borne in mind that as septic tanks and bacterial filters depend for their efficiency on the organisms they contain, time must be allowed for these to develop and accumulate before good results are obtained; and for this about six weeks' use is generally necessary, after which they will continue to act for an indefinite period until they become choked by sand and inorganic matter.

It must not be supposed that the action in the septic tank is wholly anaerobic; and with weak sewage, most of the organic matter may under favourable circumstances be converted into nitrates and carbonic acid by this means only; but generally a much more complete purification is effected by the subsequent use of "bacterial filters." These in their simplest form consist of tanks of about 4 feet deep, filled with coke, broken bricks, or clinkers, and fitted with drain pipes at the bottom, by which they can be easily emptied. These tanks, often known as "contact-beds," are filled with the sewage or septic tank effluent, which is allowed to remain on them two hours, and the tank is then emptied, and allowed a rest of six hours for oxidation and aeration. In most cases the sewage requires two such treatments, the last often through a bed with finer coke, in order to be completely freed from putrescible matter. In place of the intermittent process, as applied on the contact-beds, continuous aerobic filtration is often employed, the bed being so constructed as to allow of free admission of air at the bottom and sides, and the liquid to be purified being distributed on the surface by a sprinkler, or some similar device, and allowed to trickle through the bed. The continuous process seems likely to supersede the intermittent one, as the beds are not only capable of treating a much larger quantity of sewage in proportion to their area, but are also less liable to choke. About six weeks is required, with either contact-beds or continuous filters, before the material they contain becomes coated with the necessary bacterial layer and they get into full working order. The results as regards the effluent are perfectly satisfactory, and the great difficulty and cost consists in the slow but inevitable choking of the beds, which involves the replacement of the porous material. This is considerably delayed by the use of a settled or precipitated sewage, and in this respect, beside its bacteriological function, the septic tank serves a useful purpose in settling insoluble matter, which is much more cheaply removed from it than from the filter-beds. It will be obvious that ordinary settling-tanks, if deep, fulfil many of the functions of the septic-tank, and both lead to the production of a much more uniform liquid from the different effluents which the tanner produces, which is important in the subsequent bacterial purification. A good deal of interesting information on these subjects will be found in a paper by Mr. W. H. Harrison on the 'Bacteriological Treatment of Sewage.'

Journ. Soc. Chem. Ind., 1900, p. 511.

There are a good many patents in connection with the various methods of sewage purification, and some caution is necessary to avoid their infringement, though of course the general principles of settling and filtration, and the destruction of organic matter by bacterial action, are open to all.

As a general rule the waste-liquors from a tan-yard or leather dye-works are exceedingly impure. They contain the organic matter (in a state of great putrefaction) from the soaks, bates and puers; other organic matter, also more or less putrefied, from the tan-pits; the lime liquors, with their large proportion of lime and of dissolved hide-substance, and in addition the various dyes and other chemicals which may have been used in the conversion of the raw hide into the finished leather; and hence their efficient purification has presented difficulties which do not occur in most other trades.

The different waste liquids are best run into a capacious tank, and, after being thoroughly mixed up together, are allowed to settle for some hours. By this means the greater part of the tanning matter will combine with the lime also present to form a heavy, brown insoluble substance; some of the dye and other organic matter will become entangled in this, and thus be removed from the liquid. The clear liquid is next run off into a bacterial filter (preferably a septic tank, followed by an open coke filter), and then into the nearest stream. If the tannery is near to a town, and the corporation sewers can be utilised, it is probable that a filter made of spent tan may be substituted, as this material will not only remove all excess of lime from the liquid but will also fix much of the colouring matter as well (Koenig). The tan, after being used for this purpose, contains so much lime in its pores that it is said to be useful as manure.

In tanneries where large quantities of disinfectants such as mercuric chloride, carbolic acid, etc., are used, it is necessary that the mixed liquids shall contain so much lime as to make them distinctly alkaline. In this way most of the disinfectants will be either precipitated or rendered inactive. Where arsenic is used in the limes it may be advisable to add a little ferrous sulphate (green vitriol or copperas), in order that the arsenic may form an insoluble compound with the iron, and so be removed along with the sludge. The ink produced by the action of the iron salt on the tan liquors will be completely removed by the bacterial filter.

APPENDICES.

APPENDIX A.
METHOD OF THE INTERNATIONAL ASSOCIATION OF LEATHER TRADES CHEMISTS FOR THE ANALYSIS OF TANNING MATERIALS.
INCLUDING ALTERATIONS ADOPTED AT THE LEEDS CONFERENCE IN 1902.

SECTION I.—SAMPLING FROM BULK.

See London Report, pp. 22-29 and 124.

1. *Liquid Extracts.*—In drawing samples, at least 5 per cent. of the casks must be taken, the numbers being selected as far apart as possible. The heads must be removed, and the contents mixed thoroughly by means of a suitable plunger, care being taken that any sediment adhering to sides or bottom shall be thoroughly stirred in. All samples must be drawn in the presence of a responsible person.

2. *Gambier and Pasty Extracts.*—Gambier and pasty extracts should be sampled from not less than 5 per cent. of blocks, by a tubular sampling tool, which shall be passed completely through the block in seven places. Solid extracts shall be broken, and a sufficient number of portions drawn both from the inner and outer parts of the blocks to fairly represent the bulk. In both cases samples shall be rapidly mixed and enclosed at once in an air-tight bottle or box, sealed and labelled.

3. *Valonia, Algarobilla, Divi-divi, and General Tanning Materials.* Valonia, algarobilla, and all other tanning materials containing dust or fibre, shall be sampled, if possible, by spreading at least 5 per cent. of the bags in layers one above another on a smooth floor, and taking several samples vertically down to the floor. Where this cannot be done, the samples must be drawn from the centre of a sufficient number of bags. While valonia and most materials may be sent to the chemist ground, it is preferable that divi-divi, algarobilla, and other fibrous materials shall be unground. Bark in long rind, and other materials in bundles, shall be sampled by cutting a small section from the middle of 3 per cent. of the bundles with a saw.

4. *Samples for more than one Chemist.*—Samples to be submitted to more than one chemist must be drawn as one sample, and well mixed; then divided

into the requisite number of portions, not less than three, and at once enclosed in suitable packages, sealed and labelled.

Section II.—Preparation for Analysis.

See London Report, p. 40 *et seq*.

1. *Liquid Extracts.*—Liquid extracts shall be thoroughly stirred and mixed immediately before weighing, which shall be rapidly done to avoid loss of moisture. Thick extracts, which cannot be otherwise mixed, may be heated to 50° C., then stirred and rapidly cooled before weighing, but the fact that this has been done must be noted in the Report.

2. *Solid Extracts.*—Solid extracts shall be coarsely powdered and well mixed. Pasty extracts shall be rapidly mixed in a mortar, and the requisite quantity weighed out with as little exposure as possible, to avoid loss of moisture. Where extracts are partly dry and partly pasty, so that neither of these methods is applicable, the entire sample shall be weighed and allowed to dry at the ordinary temperature sufficiently to be pulverised, and shall then be weighed, and the loss of weight taken into calculation as moisture.

In such cases as gambier, in which it is not possible to grind, or by other mechanical means to thoroughly mix the constituents of the sample, it is permissible to dissolve the whole, or a large portion of the sample, in a small quantity of hot water, and immediately after thorough mixing to weigh out a portion of the strong solution for analysis.

3. *Barks, and other Solid Tanning Materials.*—The whole sample, or not less than 250 grms., shall be ground in a mill until it will pass through a sieve of 5 wires per centimetre. Where materials such as barks and divi-divi contain fibrous materials which cannot be ground to powder, the ground sample shall be sieved, and the respective parts which do and do not pass through the sieve shall be weighed separately, and the sample for analysis shall be weighed so as to contain like proportions.

Section III.—Preparation of Infusion.

1. *Strength of Solution.*—The tannin solution employed shall contain from 0·35 to 0·45 grms. per 100 c.c. of tanning matters absorbed by hide. (Paris 1900.)

2. *Solution of Liquid Extracts.*—A sufficient quantity shall be weighed into a covered basin or beaker, from which it shall be washed into a liter flask with boiling water and well shaken, and the flask shall be filled to the mark with boiling water. The neck being covered with a small beaker, the flask shall be placed under a cold water tap or otherwise rapidly cooled to a temperature between 15° and 20° C., and made up accurately to the mark,

after which it shall be thoroughly mixed, and the filtration at once proceeded with.

Note.—Tannin infusions may be kept from fermenting by the addition of 3 to 5 drops of essential oil of mustard per liter. (F. Kathreiner.)

3. *Filtration.*—The filtration of the solution for analysis may take place through any paper which may be considered most suitable for the particular case, and with or without the use of kaolin, absorption of tanning matter, if any, being corrected for by an amount determined by a similar filtration of a clear solution. Perfectly clear solutions need not be filtered.

To determine the correction, about 500 c.c. of the tanning solution of the strength prescribed for analysis is obtained perfectly clear, preferably by the method of filtration which is to be corrected for. After thorough mixing, 50 c.c. is evaporated to determine "total soluble No. 1." A portion of the remainder is then filtered in the manner for which correction is to be made, and 50 c.c. of the filtrate is evaporated for "total soluble No. 2." Deducting No. 2 from No. 1 the difference is the correction required, which must be added to the total soluble found by analysis. It is generally advisable, both in analysis and in the second filtration for correction, to filter first 150 c.c. (which in analysis may be used for the determination of non-tannins), and then to employ the next 50 c.c. for evaporation, keeping the filter full during the operation; but whatever procedure is adopted must be rigidly adhered to in all analyses to which the correction is applied. Where kaolin is employed, a constant weighed quantity (1 or 2 grm.) must be used, which is first washed with 75 c.c. of the liquor by decantation, and then washed on to the filter with a further quantity of liquor, of which 200 c.c. is filtered as above.

It is obvious that in the first instance it will be necessary to determine the correction for each particular material employed, but it will soon be found that the correction is practically constant for large groups of tanning materials, so long as the same method of filtration is rigidly adhered to.

4. *Solid Extracts.*—Solid extracts shall be dissolved by stirring in a beaker with boiling water, the undissolved portions being allowed to settle, and treated with further quantities of boiling water, and the solution poured into a liter flask. After the whole of the soluble matter is dissolved, the solution is treated similarly to that of a liquid extract.

5. *Extraction of Solid Materials.*—Such quantities shall be weighed as will give an infusion of the strength already prescribed. (*Preparation of Infusion*, Resolution 1.) Not less than 500 c.c. of the infusion shall be extracted at a temperature not exceeding 50° C., after which the temperature shall be gradually raised to 100° C., and the extraction continued till the percolate is

free from tannin and the whole made up to one liter, the weaker portions of the solution being first concentrated if necessary by evaporation in a flask, in the neck of which a funnel is placed.

In substances which, like canaigre, contain a large quantity of starch, the extraction should be completed at a temperature of 50° C.—H. R. P.

SECTION IV.—DETERMINATION OF TANNING MATTERS AND NON-TANNINS; ETC.

1. *Total Soluble Matter.*—100 c.c. of the clear filtered tanning solution, or a smaller quantity if the balance employed is of sufficient delicacy, shall be evaporated in an open weighed basin of platinum, hard glass, porcelain, or nickel, on the water-bath, and the basin shall afterwards be dried till constant in an air-oven, at a temperature of 100° to 105° C., or at a temperature not exceeding 100° C. *in vacuo* till constant, care being taken that no loss occurs by splintering of the residue. The use of the vacuum-oven for drying the residues is recommended when possible.

50 c.c. is sufficient, and is the quantity now generally employed.

2. *Determination of Non-Tannins.*—That the filter method shall remain the official method until the next Conference, but that members be permitted to employ the chromed hide-powder method of the American Association of Official Agricultural Chemists of 1901 (Appendix C) where it is desired, the fact being clearly stated on the report that the A.O.A.C. method has been employed, and not that of the I.A.L.T.C. (Leeds, 1902, see note, p. 480.)

That the "bell form" of filter, as described by Professor Procter, shall be employed; not less than 5 grms. of hide-powder be used; the hide-powder should be so packed in the tube that the detannised liquor shall come over at a rate of about one drop in two seconds; and the filtrate be rejected so long as it gives a turbidity with a clear tanning solution. The filtrate may be used for the determination of non-tannin so long as it gives no reaction with salted gelatine solution. The first 30 to 35 c.c. should be thrown away, and the next 50 c.c. of detannised solution, or an aliquot part of it, evaporated in a weighed basin on a water bath, and then dried till constant in an air-oven at a temperature of 100° to 105° C., or, *in vacuo*, not exceeding 100° C.

It is obvious that the exact form and dimensions of the filter must be adapted to the character of the hide-powder available, as considerable differences exist in the absorptive power of different samples.

8 to 9 grams of good gelatine are dissolved in 500 c.c. of hot water, 100 grams of salt added, and the whole cooled and filtered.

3. *Hide-Powder.*—That the hide-powder must be sufficiently absorbent for use in the filter, and that in a blank experiment conducted with distilled water in the same way as an analysis, the residue from the evaporation of 50 c.c. should not exceed 5 milligrams.

The Freiberg Hide-Powder, made by Mehner and Stransky, containing between 10 and 20 per cent. of cellulose (as suggested by Cerych), is recommended by the Conference (Liège, 1901) and is very suitable for the filter method; but the powder, when analysed by the Kjeldahl method and calculated to 18 per cent. of moisture, must not contain less than 11·5 per cent. of nitrogen (Leeds, 1902).

4. *Determination of Moisture and "Total Dry Matter."*—That the moisture in the sample be determined by drying a small portion at the temperature adopted in the determination of the "total soluble." In extracts yielding turbid solutions which can be thoroughly mixed, it is generally preferable after mixing the solution and before filtration, to measure off and evaporate 50 c.c. for the determination of total dry matter (and moisture) in the same manner as the "total soluble."

5. *Statement of Results.*—It is recommended, when full analysis is given, that the Statement should be made in the following manner:—

>(1) *Tanning Matters Absorbed by Hide.*—Obtained by deducting the "soluble non-tanning matters" found by evaporating the hide-powder filtrate from the "total soluble."
>
>(2) *Soluble Non-Tanning Matters.*—Found by evaporation of filtrate from hide-powder filter.
>
>(3) *Insoluble.*—By deducting "total soluble matter" from the "total dry matter."
>
>(4) *Moisture.*—Determined by drying a portion at the temperature adopted in the determination of "total soluble."

If other determinations are given they shall form a separate additional statement.

Density.—The statement of densities of extracts, etc., should be given as specific gravity in preference to arbitrary degrees, such as Baumé, Twaddell, etc.

SECTION V.—COLOUR MEASUREMENT.

Colour Measurement.—It is recommended that the method used by English chemists, namely, measuring with Lovibond's Tintometer (as described by Professor Procter and Dr. Parker, Journ. Soc. Chem. Ind., 1895, 125), shall be used, and the results stated in units of red, yellow and black. The measurement may be made on the solution used for analysis, but must be calculated to one containing 0·5 per cent. of tanning matter, in a centimetre cell.

ANALYSIS OF USED LIQUORS.

It was decided at Liège, 1901, and Leeds, 1902, that the "Shake Method" with chromed hide-powder, of the American Association of Official Agricultural Chemists, 1901 (A.O.A.C.), should be employed in the detannisation of used tanning liquors, as with these the filter method is apt to give too high results owing to the amount of non-volatile acids which they contain. The method of the A.O.A.C. is given in Appendix C.

Procter and Blockey quoted experiments at the Leeds Conference, proving that gallic acid and some other non-tanning substances were largely absorbed by the hide-powder filter, though probably not permanently retained by leather; while the error, though still considerable, was much less when the chromed hide-power shake method was employed. Where only gallotannic and gallic acids are present, as in the case of sumach and commercial gallotannic acids, the most accurate quantitative estimation is probably that by the Löwenthal method carried out as described L.I.L.B., p. 123, but considerable skill is required in its execution.

ANALYSIS OF SPENT TANS.

It was decided at Leeds, 1902, that spent tans must be analysed like fresh tanning materials; but where the prescribed strength of solution cannot otherwise be obtained it is permissible to concentrate the entire solution by evaporation. It is advisable, where suitable apparatus is available, to concentrate *in vacuo*; but failing this, an ordinary flask may be used, in the neck of which a funnel is placed.

APPENDIX B.—THE DECIMAL SYSTEM.

The metrical system of weights and measures, and the Centigrade thermometer scale have been generally used throughout the book, as more international and scientific than the complicated systems still unfortunately in use in this country. They have been fully explained in the Author's 'Laboratory Book,' p. 2; but as this is not always at hand, a short sketch may be permitted here.

The basis of the metrical system is the "meter," which is approximately $\frac{1}{10,000,000}$ of the distance from the earth's pole to the equator, and is equal to

39·3708 English inches, and for many practical purposes may be roughly reckoned as 40 inches. The meter is divided into 10 parts or "decimeters," 100 parts or "centimeters," and 1000 parts or "millimeters." The standard of capacity is a cube of 1 decimeter, or about 4 inches, and consequently contains 1000 cubic centimeters, and is denominated a "liter." The standard of weight is 1 cubic centimeter of water (at 4° C.), which is called a "gram." Hence 1 liter of water weighs 1 "kilogram," or 1000 grams. 1 cubic meter of water contains 1000 liters, and weighs 1000 kilograms, or 1 metrical ton (2200 lb. English). For purposes of reduction, the following figures may be given:—

1 gram = 15·431 grains.

1 lb. av. = 453·6 grams.

1 liter = 0·22 gallon.

1 gallon = 4·543 litres.

Actual reduction is, however, generally unnecessary if the question be treated as one of proportion. Thus a solution of 1 gram per liter is of the same strength as one of 1 lb. per 100 gallons (1000 lb.), and very approximately, as one of 1 oz. avoirdupois per cubic foot. In the case of pits, it is often simplest to measure them directly with a meter rule; length, breadth and depth, measured in decimeters and multiplied together, giving the contents in liters, and, in the case of water, the weight in kilograms.

The Centigrade or Celsius thermometer divides the difference between the freezing and the boiling points of water into 100°. The following table gives the points at which its scale agrees without fractions with that of Fahrenheit:

COMPARISON OF CENTIGRADE AND FAHRENHEIT DEGREES.

°C.	°F.
-20	-4
-15	+5
-10	14
-5	23
0	32
5	41
10	50

15	59
20	68
25	77
30	86
35	95
40	104
45	113
50	122
55	131
60	140
65	149
70	158
75	167
80	176
85	185
90	194
95	203
100	212
105	221
110	230
115	239

APPENDIX C.
OFFICIAL METHOD FOR ANALYSIS OF TANNING MATERIALS, ADOPTED AT THE EIGHTEENTH CONVENTION OF THE AMERICAN ASSOCIATION OF OFFICIAL AGRICULTURAL CHEMISTS, 1901.

I. Preparation of Sample.

Barks, woods, leaves, dry extracts, and similar tanning materials should be ground to such a degree of fineness that they can be thoroughly extracted. Fluid extracts must be heated to 50° C., well shaken, and allowed to cool to room-temperature.

II. Quantity of Material.

In the case of bark and similar material, use such quantity as will give about 0·35 to 0·45 gram tannins per 100 c.c. of solution, extract in Soxhlet or similar apparatus at steam-heat for non-starchy materials. For canaigre and substances containing like amounts of starch use temperature of 50° to 55° C., until near complete extraction, finishing the operation at steam-heat. In case of extract, weigh such quantity as will give 0·35 to 0·45 gram tannins per 100 c.c. of solution, dissolve in 900 c.c. of water at 80° C., let stand twelve hours, and make up to 1000 c.c.

III. Moisture.

(*a*) Place 2 grams, if it be an extract, in a flat-bottom dish, not less than 6 cm. in diameter, add 25 c.c. of water, warm slowly till dissolved, continue evaporation and dry.

(*b*) All dryings called for, after evaporation to dryness on water-bath, or others, shall be done by one of the following methods, the soluble solids and non-tannins being dried under similar, and so far as possible identical conditions:

1. For eight hours at the temperature of boiling water in a steam bath.

2. For six hours at 100° C., in an air bath.

3. To constant weight *in vacuo* at 70° C.

IV. Total Solids.

Shake the solution, and without filtering immediately measure out 100 c.c. with a pipette, evaporate in a weighed dish, and dry to constant weight, at the temperature of boiling water. Dishes should be flat-bottomed, and not less than 6 cm. in diameter.

V. Soluble Solids.

Double-pleated filter paper (S. and S., No. 590, 15 cm.) shall be used. To 2 grams of kaolin add 75 c.c. of the tanning solution, stir, let stand fifteen minutes, and decant as much as possible. Add 75 c.c. more of the solution, pour on filter, keep filter full, reject the first 150 c.c. of filtrate, evaporate the next 100 c.c. and dry. Evaporation during filtration must be guarded against.

VI. Non-Tannins.

Prepare 20 grams of hide-powder by digesting twenty-four hours with 500 c.c. of water, and adding 0·6 gram chrome alum in solution, this solution to be added as follows. One-half at the beginning and the other half at least six hours before the end of the digestion. Wash by squeezing through linen, continue the washing until the wash-water does not give a precipitate with barium chloride. Squeeze thoroughly by hand, and remove as much water as possible by means of a press, weigh the pressed hide, and take approximately one-fourth of it for moisture determination. Weigh this fourth carefully and dry to constant weight. Weigh the remaining three-fourths carefully and add them to 200 c.c. of the original solution; shake ten minutes, throw on funnel with cotton plug in stem, return until clear, evaporate 100 c.c. and dry. The weight of this residue must be corrected for the dilution caused by the water contained in the pressed hide-powder. The shaking must be done in some form of mechanical shaker. The simple machine used by druggists, and known as the milk-shake, is recommended.

For method of correction, see p. 313.

PROVISIONAL METHOD.—To 14 grams of dry chromed hide-powder in a shaker glass add 200 c.c. of the tannin solution, let stand two hours, stirring frequently, shake fifteen minutes, throw on funnel with a cotton plug in the stem, let drain, tamp down the hide-powder in the funnel, return the filtrate until clear and evaporate 100 c.c.

VII. Tannins.

The amount of these is shown by the difference between the soluble solids and the corrected non-tannins.

VIII. Testing Hide-Powder.

(*a*) Shake 10 grms. of hide-powder with 250 c.c. of water for five minutes, strain through linen, squeeze the magma thoroughly by hand; repeat this operation three times, pass the last filtrate through paper (S. and S. No.

590, 15 cm.) till clear, evaporate 100 c.c. and dry. If this residue amounts to more than 10 mg. the hide must be rejected.

(*b*) Prepare a solution of pure gallo-tannin by dissolving 6 grams in 1000 c.c. of water. Determine the total solids by evaporating 100 c.c. of this solution and drying to constant weight. Treat 200 c.c. of the solution with hide-powder exactly as described in paragraph 6. The hide-powder must absorb at least 95 per cent. of the total solids present. The gallo-tannin used must be completely soluble in water, alcohol, acetone and acetic ether, and should not contain more than 1 per cent. of substances not removed by digesting with excess of yellow mercuric oxide on steam-bath for two hours.

IX. TESTING NON-TANNIN FILTRATE.

(*a*) *For Tannin.*—Test a small portion of the clear non-tannin filtrate with a few drops of a 1 per cent. solution of Nelson's gelatin. A cloudiness indicates the presence of tannin, in which case repeat the process described under VI., using 35 instead of 20 grams of hide-powder.

(*b*) *For Soluble Hide.*—To a small portion of the clear non-tannin filtrate add a few drops of the filtered tannin solution. A cloudiness indicates the presence of soluble hide, in which case repeat the process described under VI., giving the hide-powder a more thorough washing.

The temperature of solutions shall be between 16° and 20° when measured or filtered. All dryings should be made in flat-bottomed dishes of at least 6 cm. diameter, S. and S. No. 590, 15 cm. filter paper should be used in all filtrations.

APPENDIX D.

The following Lists of Colours have been furnished by Mr. M. C. Lamb, Director of the Leather Dyeing Department of Herold's Institute, London, who has devoted much time to testing the various dyes with regard to their permanence and suitability for leather. Many of the colours have also been tested and found satisfactory in the Leather Department of the Yorkshire College. The following abbreviations of makers' names are used in the lists:—

B.	BASLER CHEMISCHE FABRIK, A. G. Basle, Switzerland.
B.A.S.F.	BADISCHE ANILIN UND SODA FABRIK. Ludwigshafen

	a. Rhine, Germany.
Ber.	BERLIN ANILINE CO. Berlin S.O., Germany.
B.S. Spl.	BROOKE, SIMPSON & SPILLER. Atlas Dye Works, Hackney Wick, London, N.E.
By.	FARBEN-FABRIKEN, late BAYER & CO. Elberfeld, Germany.
C.	L. CASSELLA & CO. Frankfort a. Main, Germany.
C.A.	FRENCH ANILINE COLOUR WORKS. Vieux-Conde (Norde), France.
C. & R.	CLAUS & RÉE. Clayton, near Manchester.
D.	DAHL & CO. Barmen, Germany.
D. & H.	DURAND, HUGUENIN & CO. Basle, Switzerland.
G.	R. GEIGY & CO. Basle, Switzerland.
Ger.	GERBER & CO. Basle, Switzerland.
K.	KALLE & CO. Bierbrich a. Rhine, Germany.
Leon.	A. LEONHARDT & CO. Muhlheim a. Main, Germany.
Leitch	J. W. LEITCH. Milnsbridge Chemical Works, Huddersfield.
Lev.	LEVINSTEIN LTD. 21 Minshull Street, Manchester.
M.L.B.	MEISTER, LUCIUS & BRUNING. Hoechst a. Main, Germany.
Mo.	GILLIARD, P. MONNET & GARTIER. Lyons, France.
N.	NOETZEL, ISTEL & CO. Griesheim a. Main, Germany.
O.	K. OEHLER & CO. Offenbach a. Main, Germany.
P.	ST. DENIS DYESTUFF CO., late POURIER. St. Denis, near Paris.
R.	SOCIÉTE CHIMIQUE DES USINES DU RHONE. Lyons, France.
R. H. & S.	READ, HOLLIDAY & SONS. Huddersfield.

S.C.Ind.	SOCIETY OF CHEMICAL INDUSTRY. Basle, Switzerland.
Uer.	CHEMISCHE FABRIKEN. Uerdingen a. Rhein, Germany.
W. Bros.	WILLIAMS BROS. & CO. Hounslow, Middlesex.

STAINING.

SINGLE ACID DYES SUITABLE FOR STAINING VEGETABLE TANNED LEATHER.

Browns.

- Solid brown. (M.L.B.)
- Acid brown. (W. Bros.)
- Brown A2. (B.S. Spl.)
- Brown A1. (B.S. Spl.)
- Mikado brown B. (Leon.)
- New acid brown. (B.S. Spl.)
- Bronze acid brown. (By.)
- Golden brown Y. (C.), (By.)
- Acid anthracene brown R. (By.)
- Fast brown N. (B.A.S.F.)
- Nut brown A. (C.)
- Fast brown. (By.)
- Fast brown G. (Ber.)
- Resorcin brown. (Ber.)
- Resorcin brown. (D.)
- Acid brown. (Ber.)
- Dark nut brown. (W. Bros.)
- Acid brown R. (C.)
- Acid brown R. (Uer.)
- Acid brown R. (R. H. & S.)

- New golden brown A1. (C.)
- Dark brown. (C.)
- Acid brown L. (B.A.S.F.)
- Acid brown D. (C.)

Yellows.

- Azo yellow. (Uer.)
- Phosphine subst. (B.S. Spl.)
- Chrysoine. (W. Bros.)
- Azo-acid-yellow. (Ber.)
- New phosphine G. (C.)
- Cuba yellow 2072. (S.C. Ind.)
- Cuba yellow (W. Bros.)
- Azo-flavine RS. (C.) and (B.A.S.F.)
- Azo-flavine 3R. (B.A.S.F.)
- Indian yellow R. (By.)
- Turmeric yellow. (G.)
- Solid yellow G. (Leon.)
- Solid yellow B. (Leon.)
- Indian yellow R. (C.)
- Cuba yellow. (C.)
- Napthol yellow S. (By.), (C.), (B.A.S.F.)
- Turmeric yellow. (C.), (G.)
- Fast acid yellow. (C.A.)

Reds and Oranges.

- Scarlet R. (By.)
- Crocein scarlet 3BN. (By.)
- Orange 2. (M.L.B.), (S.C. Ind.), (C.) and (B.A.S.F.)
- Orange 2B. (By.)

- Mandarin G extra. (Ber.)
- Brill. crocein M.O.O. (C.)
- Bordeaux G. (By.)
- Atlas orange. (B.S. Spl.)
- Bordeaux cov. (Ber.)
- Fast red 21528. (By.)
- Fast red A. (Leon.), (By.), (Ber.), and (B.A.S.F.)
- Bordeaux B. (M.L.B.)

Greens.

- Acid green extra conc. (C.)
- Guinea green B. (Ber.)
- Guinea green G. (Ber.)
- Acid green GG. (By.)
- Acid green BB. (By.)
- Acid green B. (By.)
- Acid green G. (By.)
- Acid green 000. (Leon.)
- Acid green extra. (By.)
- Acid green (Uer.)
- Acid green (R. H. & S.)
- Light green SF. (B.A.S.F.)
- Erioglaucine. (G.)
-

Violets.

- Acid violet 4RS. (Ber.)
- Acid violet 7B. (Ber.)
- Acid violet 6B. (By.)
- Formyl violet S4B. (C.)

Blues.

- Bavarian blue D.B. (Ber.)
- Marine blue o. (K.)
- Solid blue. (M.L.B.)
- Blue 1. (Lev.)
- Blue 2. (Lev.)
- Blue 3. (Lev.)

Single Basic Dyes
suitable for Staining Vegetable Tanned Leather.

Browns.

- Bismark brown GG. (C.)
- Chrysoidine AG. (O.)
- Bismark brown 2B. (K.)
- Bismark brown (By.)
- Bismark brown R.C.E. (Lev.)
- Bismark brown M. (By.)
- Vesuvine conc. (M.L.B.)
- Vesuvine conc. (B.A.S.F.)
- Bismark brown C extra. (Leon.)
- Bismark brown RS. (B.S. Spl.)
- Bismark brown 3762. (W. Bros.)
- Rheonine A. (B.A.S.F.)
- Rheonine N. (B.A.S.F.)
- Brown R. (G.)
- Brown G. (G.)
- Manchester brown. (C.)

Yellows.

- Acridine yellow NC. (Leon.)
- Phosphine N. (Ber.)

- Patent phosphine R. (S.C. Ind.)
- Leather yellow 6730. (C.A.)
- Auramine 2. (By.)
- Chrysoidine cryst. (B.S. Spl.) and (By.)
- Chrysoidine diamond cryst. (W. Bros.)
- Leather yellow o. (M.L.B.)
- Chrysoidine. (R. H. & S.)
- Leather yellow G. (M.L.B.)
- Leather yellow 6730. (C.A.)
- Patent phosphine G. (S.C. Ind.)
- Leather yellow DRR. (Ber.)
- Xanthine. (O.)
- Cannella G. (W. Bros.)
- Pure phosphine. (C.)
- New phosphine G. (C.)
- Cori-phosphine o. (By.)
- Para-phosphine R. (C.)
- Para-phosphine G. (C.)
- Leather yellow 374. (D.)
- Leather yellow 375. (D.)
- Homo-phosphine G. (Leon.)
- Phosphine ABN. (Leon.)
- Auramine 2 patent. (S.C. Ind.)

Greens.

- Methyl green cryst. (Ber.)
- Methylene green. (M.L.B.)
- Solid green. (Leon.)
- Malachite green. (Ber.), (M.L.B.), (P.), (C.A.), (S.C. Ind.), (R. H. & S.), (Lev.), (C.), (B.S. Spl.) and (K.)

Reds.

- Safranine. (M.L.B.), (B.A.S.F.), (S.C. Ind.) and (K.), (Ber.), (By.), (C.A.), (Leon.), (Uer.)
- Russian Red. (By.) and (Ber.)

Violets.

- Methyl violets. (Ber.), (By.), (M.L.B.), (R. H. & S.), (B.S. Spl.), (C.) (S.C. Ind.), (P.) and (D.).

Blacks.

- Corvoline B. (B.A.S.F.)
- Corvoline G. (B.A.S.F.)

DYEING.

SINGLE ACID COLOURS SUITABLE FOR DYEING VEGETABLE TANNED LEATHERS.

For explanation of Roman numerals see end of Appendix D.

Yellows.

II.	Napthol yellow S. (Ber.), (B.A.S.F.), (By.) and (C.).
VII.	Quinoline yellow. (Ber.), (By.) and (B.A.S.F.).
II.	Citronine. (Leon.)
IV.	Solid yellow G. (Leon.)
IV.	Solid yellow B. (Leon.)
V.	Indian yellow S.
V.	Azo-acid yellow.
IV.	Indian yellow T. (C.)
VII.	Indian yellow R. (By.) and (C.).
IV.	Indian yellow G. (By.) and (C.).
IV.	Cuba yellow. (C.), (W. Bros.) and (S.C.Ind.).
V.	Azo-flavine RS. (B.A.S.F.) and (C.).
V.	Azo-flavine 3R. (B.A.S.F.) and (C.).

| VI. | Circumein extra. (Ber.) |
| VII. | Tartrazine. (B.A.S.F.) |

Oranges.

V.	Orange 2. (B.A.S.F.), (C.), (M.L.B.), (S.C. Ind.), (P.) (W. Bros.) and (By.).
V.	Mandarin G extra. (Ber.)
V.	Crocein orange. (K.) and (By.).
VI.	Ponceaux 10RB, 4R, Bo, 4RB, 6RB. (Ber.), (By.) and (D.).

Bordeaux.

VII.	Azo bordeaux. (By.)
IV.	Bordeaux B extra. (By.)
VI.	Bordeaux G. (By.)
V.	Bordeaux Y. (W. Bros.)
V.	Acid maroon. (M.L.B.) and (B.S. Spl.).
VIII.	Chromatrop 6B. (M.L.B.)

Reds.

V.	Fast red A. (Ber.), (By.), (B.A.S.F.), (B.S. Spl.) and (Leon.)
VIII.	Fast red S. (M.L.B.)
VI.	Fast red 21528. (By.)

Scarlets.

V.	Crocein scarlet R. (By.) and (K.).
V.	Crocein scarlet 2R. (By.)
VII.	Fast scarlet B. (B.A.S.F.), (W. Bros.) and (K.)

Browns.

IV.	Acid brown R. (C.)
V.	Acid brown L. (B.A.S.F.)
V.	Acid brown Y. (S.C. Ind.)

IV.	Acid brown D. (C.), (B.A.S.F.)
VI.	Acid brown (R.H. & S.)
IV.	Acid brown 4601. (B.S. Spl.)
V.	Acid brown D. (C.)
VII.	Resorcin brown. (Ber.)
V.	Acid brown. (Uer.)
IV.	Acid brown R. (Ber.)
VIII.	Acid brown Y. (M.L.B.).
VI.	Solid brown o. (M.L.B.)
V.	Fast brown. (By.)
V.	Fast brown. G. (Ber.)
V.	Fast brown. N. (B.A.S.F.)
IV.	Fast brown. 3B. (Ber.)
V.	Bronze acid brown. (By.)
VIII.	Acid anthracine brown R. (By.)
V.	New acid brown. (B.S. Spl.)
VI.	Dark nut brown. (Uer.)
IV.	New golden brown A1. (C.)

Blacks.

IV.	Napthol blue black. (C.)
V.	Napthylamine black 4B. (C.)
V.	Napthylamine black 6B. (C.)
VII.	Phenol black S. (By.)
IV.	Phenylamine black 4B. (By.)
VII.	Victoria black B. (By.)

Blues.

| VIII. | Fast blue R. (Ber.) |

VIII.	Bavarian blue DB. (Ber.)
V.	Erioglaucine. (G.)
IV.	Cyanole ext. (C.)
IV.	Marine blue. (K.)
VII.	Water blue N. (B.A.S.F.)
VIII.	Water blue 4 B. (Ber.)
VII.	Cotton blue II. (By.).
VII.	Toluidine blue. (B.A.S.F.) and (By.).
VII.	Water blue R. (Leon.)
VII.	Water blue 3R. (Leon.)
VII.	Water blue BTR. (B.A.S.F.)

Violets.

	Acid violets (Lev.), (B.A.S.F.) and (By.)
IX.	Acid violets 4R. (B.A.S.F.)
V.	Acid violets R. (C.)
V.	Acid violets R. (B.A.S.F.)
VI.	Acid violets 3BA. (M.L.B.)
IV.	Acid violets 3BN. (Lev.)
II.	Acid violets 6B. (By.) and (C.).
III.	Formyl violet S4B. (C.)

Greens.

IV.	Acid green extra conc. (C.)
IV.	Guinea green B and G. (Ber.)
IV.	Acid green ext. (By.)
IV.	Acid green GG ext. (By.)
IV.	Acid green 225. (By.)
IV.	Acid green BB. ext. (By.)

IV.	Acid green o. (M.L.B.)
IV.	Acid green 5677. (B.S. Spl.)
V.	Capri green 2G. (Lev.)

SINGLE BASIC DYES SUITABLE FOR DYEING VEGETABLE TANNED LEATHERS.

Browns.

IV.	Vesuvine ooo ext. (B.A.S.F.)
II.	Vesuvine B. (B.A.S.F.)
II.	Vesuvine (C.)
III.	Vesuvine conc. (M.L.B.)
III.	Bismark brown ext. (Ber.) and (B.S. Spl.).
III.	Bismark brown ext. M. (By.)
III.	Bismark brown F. (By.)
IV.	Bismark brown YS. (B.S. Spl.)
III.	Bismark brown PS. (C.)
III.	Bismark brown GG. (C.)
III.	Bismark brown O. (L.)
III.	Bismark brown G. (O.)
III.	Bismark brown (S.C. Ind.)
III.	Bismark brown NYY. (W. Bros.)
III.	Bismark brown o. (M.L.B.)
II.	Cannella. (B.S. Spl.)
II.	Cannella. (B.A.S.F.)
II.	Cannella. (C.)
V.	Cannella. (S.C. Ind.)
II.	Cannella S. (Ber.)

III.	Cannella P. (W.)
IV.	Nanking. (B.A.S.F.)
IV.	Nanking. (R.H. & S.)
IV.	Nanking. (S.C. Ind.)
III.	Lavilliere's 122. (By.)
II.	Rheonine. (B.A.S.F.)
IV.	Xanthine. (O.)

Yellowish Oranges.

III.	Chrysoidines, (Leitch); R, (R.H. & S.)
IV.	Chrysoidines ext. (W.).
II.	Chrysoidines (S.C.Ind.); GG,(C.)
III.	Chrysoidines G. (Leon.)
II.	Chrysoidines RE. (Lev.)
III.	Chrysoidines YY. (C.)
III.	Chrysoidines cryst. (B.S. Spl.)
III.	Chrysoidines G. (By.)
V.	Chrysoidines cryst. (C.A.)

Yellows.

III.	Auramine 2. (B.A.S.F.)
III.	Auramine. (S.C. Ind.)
III.	Auramine. (G.)
III.	Auramine. (Ber.)
III.	Auramine. (By.)
III.	Auramine. (L.)
III.	Auramine. (W.)
III.	Auramine. (C.)
III.	Auramine. (W.)

V.	Auramine conc. (M.L.B.).
IV.	Phosphine E. (B.A.S.F.)
IV.	Phosphine L. (B.A.S.F.)
IV.	Phosphine G. (Ber.)
IV.	Phosphine. (O.)
IV.	Phosphine. (C.)
IV.	Phosphine Ext. (M.L.B.)
IV.	Phosphine B ext. (S.C. Ind.)
III.	Phosphine III., II., I. (Leon.)
III.	Phosphine N. (Ber.).
V.	Cori-phosphine. (By.)
V.	Homo-phosphine. (Leon.)
V.	Para-phosphine. (C.)

Greens.

III.	Methyl green cryst. (By.) D.
V.	Methylene green o. (M.L.B.)
II.	Diamond green B and G. (B.A.S.F.)
II.	Benzal green. (O.)
II.	Brillt. green cryst. (M.L.B.)
II.	Brillt. green cryst. (By.)
II.	Brillt. green cryst. (O.)
II.	Brillt. green cryst. (L.)
II.	Brillt. green cryst. (Lev.)
II.	Brillt. green cryst. (Uer.)
II.	Brillt. green cryst. (S.C. Ind.)
II.	Malachite green. (B.S. Spl.)
II.	Malachite green. (Ber.)

II.	Malachite green. (C.A.)
II.	Malachite green. (K.)
II.	Malachite green. (M.L.B.)
II.	Malachite green. (Lev.)
II.	Malachite green. (G.)
II.	Malachite green. (O.)

Blues.

VII.	Methylene blue B, 2B and R. (Ber.)
VII.	Methylene blue. (B.A.S.F.)
VII.	Methylene blue. (M.L.B.)
VII.	Methylene blue. (Lev.)
VII.	Methylene blue. (C.)
VII.	Methylene blue. (C. & R.)
VIII.	New methylene blue. GG. (C.)
VIII.	New methylene blue. BB. (C.)
IV.	New blue R. (Ber.)
V.	New blue R. (By.)
VI.	New patent blue 4B. (By.)

Violets.

IV.	Methyl Violet 4B. (B.A.S.F.)
IV.	Methyl Violet 4R. (K.)
IV.	Methyl Violet 4R. (C.)
IV.	Methyl Violet 3B. (By.)
IV.	Methyl Violet 3B. (Ber.)
IV.	Methyl Violet 2B. (M.L.B.)
IV.	Methyl Violet (D.)

IV.	Methyl Violet 6B. (Leon.)
IV.	Neutral violet ext. (C.)

Bordeaux.

IV.	Magenta WB. (Leon.)
IV.	Magenta 3B. (Ber.)
IV.	Magenta RE. (Leon.)
IV.	Magenta WBG. (Leon.)
IV.	Magenta. (M.L.B.)
IV.	Magenta. (K.)
IV.	Magenta. (B.A.S.F.)
IV.	Magenta 4128. (B.S. Spl.)

Reds.

VIII.	Rhodamine B extra. (Ber.)
VIII.	Rhodamine B. (B.A.S.F.)
VIII.	Rhodamine B. (By.)
VIII.	Rhodamine (S.C. Ind.)
VIII.	Rhodamine (M.L.B.)
VII.	Safranine. (B.A.S.F.)
IV.	Russian red G. (B.A.S.F.).
IV.	Russian red B. (C.)
IV.	Russian red (Ber.)
IV.	Russian red (Uer.)
IV.	Russian red B. (B.A.S.F.)
IV.	Russian red G. (C.)
IV.	Russian red (Ber.)
IV.	Russian red R. (By.)
IV.	Cardinal 4B. (By.)

VIII.	Rhoduline red. (By.)
V.	Safranine G ext. (C.)
VII.	Safranine BS. (By.)
	Safranine G ext. (Ber.)

ACID MIXTURES SUITABLE FOR DYEING AND STAINING VEGETABLE TANNED LEATHERS.

- Orange 2. (M.L.B.)
- Azo-yellow o. (M.L.B.)
- Patent blue V. (M.L.B.)
- Resorcin brown. (Ber.)
- Circumein ext. (Ber.)
- Nigrosine 105. (Ber.)
- Acid brown R. (C.)
- Indian yellow G. (C.)
- Pure soluble blue. (C.)
- New acid brown. (B.S. Spl.)
- Phosphine subst. (B.S. Spl.)
- Induline. (B.S. Spl.)
- Acid brown R. (C.)
- Azo-flavine R.S. (C.)
- Naphtol blue black. (C.)
- Resorcin brown, (Ber.)
- Fast brown G. (Ber.)
- Napthylamine black D. (C.)
- Fast brown G. (Ber.)
- Circumine ext. (Ber.)
- Nigrosine 105. (Ber.)
- Fast brown. (By.)

- Indian yellow R. (By.)
- Fast green blue shade. (By.)
- Acid anthracene brown. (By.)
- Indian yellow R. (By.)
- Fast green blue shade. (By.)
- Fast brown N. (B.A.S.F.)
- Azo-flavine RS. (B.A.S.F.)
- Light green S.F. (B.A.S.F.)
- Dark nut brown. (Uer.)
- Azo-yellow. (Uer.)
- Acid green. (Uer.)
- Acid brown. (D.)
- Crocein orange. (D.)
- Cotton blue 3R. (D.)
- Resorcin brown. (D.)
- Cotton blue 3R. (D.)
- Acid brown B. (S.C. Ind.)
- Cuba yellow 2072. (S.C. Ind.)
- Acid green. (S.C. Ind.)
- Resorcin brown. (W. Bros.)
- Cuba yellow. (W. Bros.)
- Acid green. (W. Bros.)
- Napthol brown. (Leon.)
- Citronine A. (Leon.)
- Acid green 000. (Leon.)
- Acid brown R. (R.H. & S.)
- Acid yellow. (R.H. & S.)
- Nigrosine cryst. (R.H. & S.)

- Orange 2. (P.)
- Yellow oS. (P.)
- Acid green J3E. (P.)
- Acid brown. (C.A.)
- Acid yellow S. (C.A.)
- Pure blue cryst. (C.A.)
- Resorcin brown. (Ber.)
- Azo-acid-yellow or Circumine ext. (Ber.)
- Bavarian blue DB, or Guinea green G. (Ber.)
- Indian yellow R. (C.)
- Acid brown R. (C.)
- Pure soluble blue. (C.)
- Azo-acid-yellow conc. (M.L.B.)
- Solid brown o. (M.L.B.)
- Fast blue o sol. (M.L.B.)
- Bronze acid brown. (By.)
- Indian yellow R. (By.)
- Fast green blue shade. (By.)
- Acid anthracene brown. (By.)
- Indian yellow R. (By.)
- Fast green blue shade. (By.)
- Orange 11. (B.A.S.F.)
- Scarlet GL. (B.A.S.F.)
- Light green SFYS. (B.A.S.F.)
- Azo-flavine RS. (B.A.S.F.)
- Acid brown L. (B.A.S.F.)
- Light green SFYS. (B.A.S.F.)
- Chocolate. (Uer.)

- Tartrazine, (B.A.S.F.); or Azo-yellow, (Uer.)

BASIC MIXTURES SUITABLE FOR DYEING AND STAINING VEGETABLE TANNED LEATHERS.

- Bismark brown M. (By.)
- Auramine 2. (By.)
- Methylene blue BB. (By.)
- Rheonine A. (B.A.S.F.)
- Vesuvine B2. (B.A.S.F.)
- Diamond green G. (B.A.S.F.)
- Bismark brown O. (Leon.)
- Auramine 2. (Leon.)
- Solid green P. (Leon)
- Bismarck Brown ext. (Ber.)
- Philadelphia yellow R. (Ber.)
- Malachite green cryst. (Ber.)
- New phosphine G. (C.)
- Chrysoidine. (C.)
- New blue B. (C.)
- Phosphine ext. (F.)
- Chrysoidine diamond cryst. (F.)
- Bright green cryst. ext. (F.)
- Bismark brown GG. (O.)
- Aniline yellow ext. (O.)
- Neutral violet ext. (O.)
- Dark brown B. (By.)
- Auramine 2. (By.)
- Emerald green cryst. (By.)
- Phosphine 3RB. (Ber.)
- Philadelphia yellow R. (Ber.)

- Russian green 36784. (Ber.)
- Bismark Brown RS. (B.S. Spl.)
- Cannella. (B.S. Spl.)
- Malachite green. (B.S. Spl.)
- Vesuvine conc. (M.L.B.)
- Auramine conc. (M.L.B.)
- Methylene green. (M.L.B.)
- Cutch brown. (Leitch.)
- Lemon yellow G. (Leitch.)
- Russian green 3 B. (Leitch.)
- Bismark brown 2 B. (K.)
- Yellow for leather ext. (K.)
- Malachite green cryst. (K.)
- Auramine. (G.)
- Brown R. (G.)
- Malachite green. (G.)
- Auramine o. (Lev.)
- Bismark brown R.C.E. (Lev.)
- Brill. green. (Lev.)
- Bismark brown Y40. (R.H. & S.)
- Canary 2. (R.H. & S.)
- Green cryst. Y. (R.H. & S.).
- Leather brown A. (S.C. Ind.)
- Auramine 2. (S.C. Ind.)
- Leather black 1. (S.C. Ind.)
- Leather black R. (Uer.).
- Yellow 4803. (Uer.)
- Blue black S. (Uer.)

- Bismark brown NYY. (W. Bros.)
- Cannella G. (W. Bros.)
- Brown for leather 375. (D.)
- Fast yellow 168. (D.)
- Methyl green G ext. fine. (D.)
- Brown N. (D.)
- Leather brown P. (D.)
- Paris violet o. (D.)

CHROME LEATHER.

The following dye-stuffs are suitable for dyeing chrome leather. The leather after tanning, is boraxed in the usual manner and then mordanted by drumming or paddling in a tannin solution; for dark shades 3 per cent. gambier and 3 per cent. fustic extract (the weight being calculated on the leather struck out after boraxing) is suitable; for light shades 1½ per cent. gambier is to be recommended. The leather, after mordanting, is fat-liquored and dyed, adding a weight of sodium or potassium bisulphate equal to that of the dye-stuff, to the dye-bath. The following is not by any means a complete list of the dyes which will dye chrome leather well, but merely representative.

After the goods are dyed, they should be well washed in tepid water to which has been added a little common salt; one pound to every three dozen skins being a suitable amount to use. When the goods have been washed, they are struck out by machine and are then ready for shaving, if the operation has not been performed previous to dyeing. The skins are afterwards nailed out flat, grain-side up, on boards, and a mixture of glycerine and water—3 lb. of glycerine dissolved in one gallon of water being a suitable strength—is well sponged on the grain-side; the goods are now lightly oiled (using a good sperm, neat's-foot or mineral oil), before being taken to the drying room. When thoroughly dry they are taken off the boards, and placed with layers of damp sawdust between each skin, for a few hours in order to allow the goods to become suitably damp for staking. The skins should now be well staked by machine, the Haley (England), Slocomb or Vaughn (America) being good machines for this purpose (p. 192).

After staking, the goods are "soft-boarded," and a thin coat of a weak linseed mucilage is applied to the skins, which are afterwards dried out and seasoned with the following mixture:—

"Soak 10 to 15 oz. of dry egg albumen for four hours in 1 gallon of cold water, with occasional stirring, strain off any insoluble matter and add 1 gallon of milk. A little carbolic acid (phenol) may be added to the above if it is desired to keep the finish for more than two or three days—1 oz. of phenol previously dissolved in a little water, added to each gallon of the finish, being a suitable amount." A little dye should be added to the mixture.

After seasoning, the skins are dried out in the stove, glazed twice round and re-seasoned with the above mixture diluted with its own volume of water. The goods are dried out and again glazed, perched lightly, and finally boarded up from neck to tail in order to raise the popular straight-grain. Should the glaze be too bright the albumen solution may be reduced to half-strength.

When the goods have been glazed they are rubbed over on the grain side with a flannel cloth which is slightly damp with linseed oil, trimmed up, and are ready for sale.

DYES SUITABLE FOR DYEING CHROME-TANNED LEATHER.

Browns.

- Resorcin brown. (Ber.)
- Chocolate. (Uer.)
- Fast brown. (BY.)
- Fast brown. (Ber.)
- New golden brown A.1. (C.)
- Fast brown. (B.A.S.F.)
- Acid brown Y. (S.C. Ind.)
- Acid brown B. (S.C. Ind.)
- Golden brown. (Leitch.)
- Bronze acid brown. (By.)
- Light nut brown. (Uer.)
- Resorcin brown. (W. Bros.)
- Acid brown 5210. (W. Bros.)
- New acid brown. (B.S. Spl.)
- Light nut brown. (R.)

- Brown 2Y. (R.)
- Azo-phosphine. (Uer.)
- Golden brown Y. (W. Bros.)

Yellowish Browns and Yellows.

- Citronine. (Leon.)
- Azo-flavine RS. (B.A.S.F.)
- Cuba yellow 2072. (S.C. Ind.)
- Phosphine substitute. (B.S. Spl.)
- Azo-yellow conc. (M.L.B.)
- Azo-flavine. (R.)
- Golden orange R. (Leitch.)
- Circumein ext. (Ber.)
- Indian yellow G. (By.)
- Turmeric substitute (W. Bros.).
- Azo-yellow R. (M.L.B.).
- Chrysophenin G. (Leon.)
- Indian yellow T. (C.)
- Quinoline yellow. (Ber.)
- Cuba yellow. (C.) and (W. Bros.)
- Indian yellow. G. (C.)
- Chrysoine ext. (W. Bros.)
- Azo-flavine. (B.S. Spl.)
- Turmeric yellow B. (Leitch.)
- Azo-yellow FY. (R.H. & S.)
- Orange 4. (R.H. & S.)
- Naphtol yellow S. (B.A.S.F.)
- Turmeric yellow Y. (Leitch.)
- Azo-flavine 7032. (S.C. Ind.)

- Turmeric yellow. (G.)
- Solid yellow Y. (Leon.)
- Solid yellow B. (Leon.)
- Milling brown G. (Leon.)
- Napthamine yellow 3 G. (K.)
- Orange GG. (C.)
- Resorcin yellow. (Ber.)

Greens.

- Acid green conc. (M.L.B.)
- Acid green ooo. (Leon.)
- Guinea greens G and B. (Ber.)
- Acid green ext. conc. (C.)
- Fast acid green BN. (C.).
- Erioglaucine. (G.)
- Acid green 5677. (W. Bros.)
- Acid green (Uer.)
- Light green SF. (B.A.S.F.)
- Acid green ext. GG. (By.)

Violets and Blues.

- Bavarian blue DB. (Ber.)
- Blue R. (Lev.)
- Water blue TR. (B.A.S.F.)
- Fast blue O. (M.L.B.)
- Water blue 4B. (Leon.)
- Cyanole extra. (C.)
- Acid blue. (C.A.)
- Acid violets 3BN and 6BN. (Lev.)

Oranges.

- Orange 2, (S.C. Ind.); C, (M.L.B.); B, (By.) and (B.A.S.F.).
- Orange A. (Leon.)
- Orange G. (R.H. & S.)
- Ponceaus. (Ber.) and (By.)
- Crocein oranges. (K.) and (By.)
- Mandarine G ext. (Ber.)
- Atlas oranges. (B.S. Spl.)

Scarlets and Reds.

Most acid scarlets and reds dye chrome leather well on the mordant, particulars of which are given above.

Blacks.

These are dyed direct without any mordanting.

- Leather black V. (By.)
- Leather black 1. (S.C.Ind.)
- Naphthylamine blacks 4B and 6B. (C.)
- French black. (Uer.)
- Chrome leather black. (C. & R.)
- Coomassie black 4BS. (Lev.)
- Phenylamine black 4B. (By.)

Titanium salts (potassium titanium oxalate and tanno-titanium oxalate) may be employed in conjunction with the coal-tar colours for dyeing chrome leather, with many advantages over the ordinary mordants, the colour produced being faster to light, rubbing, fuller in shade, and with much less tendency to "grinning." When employing titanium mordants, the leather should be first lightly mordanted with some tannin solution and afterwards dyed with the titanium and dye-stuff in the same bath, in which case only "acid" dyestuffs may be employed. If desired the goods may be mordanted with the tannin mordant, afterwards treated with the titanium salts, washed and dyed; in this case the dyeing and application of the titanium mordant being carried out separately, the leather may be dyed with either the acid or basic dye stuffs. The titanium and tannin mordants may also be applied in the same bath.

Dyeing Chamois Leather.

The following colours dye chamois leather well, after washing the leather in a weak soda solution, mordanting with 3 per cent. basic chrome alum solution, and transferring to the dye-bath without washing. Equal weight of bisulphate of soda to that of the dyestuff is added to the dye-bath.

Basic Coal-Tar Colours.

- Bismark brown extra. (Ber.)
- Philadelphia yellow R. (Ber.)
- Pure phosphine. (C.)
- Leather blue V. (G.)
- Leather brown Y. (S.C. Ind.)
- Leather brown A. (S.C. Ind.)
- Philadelphia brown. (Ber.)

Acid Coal-tar Colours.

- Circumine extra. (Ber.)
- Resorcin brown. (Ber.)
- Induline NN. (B.A.S.F.)
- Orange 2. (M.L.B.)
- Golden brown. (Leitch.)
- Fast brown. (By.)
- Azo-yellow R. (M.L.B.)
- Napthylamine black 4B. (C.)
- Chocolate. (Uer.)
- Azo-flavine RS. (C.)
- Azo-phosphine. (Uer.)
- Acid anthracene brown R. (By.)
- Acid green conc. (M.L.B.)
- Acid brown Y. (S.C. Ind.)
- Acid brown B. (S.C. Ind.)

- Napthylamine black 4B. (O.)
- Jet black cryst. (C.)
- Anthracene brown R. (By.)
- Anthracene brown GG. (By.)
- Anthracene brown W. (By.)
- Dark nut brown. (Uer.)
- Orange 2. (M.L.B.)

NATURAL DYESTUFFS.

- Peachwood extract.
- Sapan ext.
- Logwood ext.
- Fustic ext.
- Turmeric ext.

A variety of shades may be obtained on chamois leather by mordanting in a 1 per cent. solution of the titanium salts above mentioned and then transferring without washing to the dye-liquor, which is best used in the drum. The colours which are most suitable are the Alizarin colours, Janus colours and the natural dyestuffs.

Alizarin Colours.

Alizarin black	produces	light slate.
Alizarin orange	,,	bright orange.
Alizarin blue	,,	blue.
Azo-alizarin black	,,	brownish maroon.
Azo-alizarin brown	,,	reddish violet.
Alizarin red	,,	bright scarlet red.
Azo-alizarin blue	,,	slate blue.
Coerulein	,,	yellowish green.
Azo-alizarin yellow	,,	bright yellow.

Anthracene brown	,,	fawn brown.
Acid anthracene brown G	,,	brownish orange.
Acid anthracene brown R	,,	dull chocolate brown.
Anthracene blue	,,	pale blue.
Mordant yellow	,,	lemon yellow.

Janus Colours.

Janus yellow G. produces		bright orange.
Janus yellow R.	,,	reddish orange.
Janus red	,,	dark maroon.
Janus claret red	,,	bluish maroon.
Janus brown R.	,,	dark reddish chocolate.
Janus blue B.	,,	bluish black.

Natural Dyestuffs.

Barwood	produces	salmon pink.
Logwood	,,	dull reddish brown.
Fustic	,,	bright yellow.
Turmeric	,,	yellow.
Brazil wood	,,	reddish brown.
Sapan wood	,,	light nut brown.
Sumach	,,	buff yellow.
Persian berries	,,	light orange yellow.
Madder	,,	red.
Quercitron bark	,,	light orange yellow.
Cutch	,,	fawn brown.
Campeche	,,	canary yellow.
Peach wood	,,	pale reddish tint.
Divi-Divi	,,	buff yellow.

The leather is run in the dyestuff solution at a temperature of about 45° to 50° C. for about half an hour, and then lightly fat-liquored, if desired, and afterwards dried.

In addition to the dyestuffs mentioned above many basic colours may be employed after the treatment with titanium, some of these producing a colour lake with the titanium mordants.

As regards the permanency of the various colours to light, the reader is referred to an important paper by Mr. Lamb, but in many cases the probable permanency is indicated by a number prefixed to the name of the colour in Roman figures, I. corresponding to the lowest, and X. to the highest permanency. In the research referred to, about 1500 samples of leathers dyed with coal-tar dyes were exposed to light for a series of "periods," each equal in actinic power to nine days of the brightest summer sunshine. The most fugitive colours faded completely, even in the first "period," and the most permanent before the end of the tenth. The prefixed numerals indicate to which of these "periods" the colour survived.

Journal of Society of Chemical Industry, 1902, p. 156.

<hr size=2 width="26%" noshade style='color:black' align=center>

Milton Keynes UK
Ingram Content Group UK Ltd.
UKHW030717041024
449263UK00004B/423